Questions

Quiz 1   question 6 – isn't it A?

Quiz 2   question 1 – why B?

Quiz 2   question 12 – why D? Page

Page 156 – only 802.1Q tagged ports can have service policies?
How about L3 ports?

Quiz 3 – P 136 – Question 4 – why B?

Page 215 – traffic shaping

Page 319 – Q5 – RP – multicast

Q8 ──(*,G)── → only on RP

Q7   ?

CCIE Routing and Switching v5.0 Official Cert Guide, Volume 2

Fifth Edition

Narbik Kocharians, CCIE No. 12410
Terry Vinson, CCIE No. 35347

Cisco Press

800 East 96th Street

Indianapolis, Indiana 46240 USA

CCIE Routing and Switching v5.0 Official Cert Guide, Volume 2, Fifth Edition

Narbik Kocharians, CCIE No. 12410
Terry Vinson, CCIE No. 35347

Copyright© 2015 Pearson Education, Inc.

Published by:
Cisco Press
800 East 96th Street
Indianapolis, IN 46240 USA

All rights reserved. No part of this book may be reproduced or transmitted in any form or by any means, electronic or mechanical, including photocopying, recording, or by any information storage and retrieval system, without written permission from the publisher, except for the inclusion of brief quotations in a review.

Printed in the United States of America

First Printing November 2014

Library of Congress Control Number: 2014950779

ISBN-13: 978-1-58714-491-2

ISBN-10: 1-58714-491-3

Warning and Disclaimer

This book is designed to provide information about the Cisco CCIE Routing and Switching Written Exam. Every effort has been made to make this book as complete and as accurate as possible, but no warranty or fitness is implied.

The information is provided on an "as is" basis. The authors, Cisco Press, and Cisco Systems, Inc. shall have neither liability nor responsibility to any person or entity with respect to any loss or damages arising from the information contained in this book or from the use of the discs or programs that may accompany it.

The opinions expressed in this book belong to the author and are not necessarily those of Cisco Systems, Inc.

Trademark Acknowledgments

All terms mentioned in this book that are known to be trademarks or service marks have been appropriately capitalized. Cisco Press or Cisco Systems, Inc., cannot attest to the accuracy of this information. Use of a term in this book should not be regarded as affecting the validity of any trademark or service mark.

Special Sales

For information about buying this title in bulk quantities, or for special sales opportunities (which may include electronic versions; custom cover designs; and content particular to your business, training goals, marketing focus, or branding interests), please contact our corporate sales department at corpsales@pearsoned.com or (800) 382-3419.

For government sales inquiries, please contact governmentsales@pearsoned.com.

For questions about sales outside the U.S., please contact international@pearsoned.com.

Feedback Information

At Cisco Press, our goal is to create in-depth technical books of the highest quality and value. Each book is crafted with care and precision, undergoing rigorous development that involves the unique expertise of members from the professional technical community.

Readers' feedback is a natural continuation of this process. If you have any comments regarding how we could improve the quality of this book, or otherwise alter it to better suit your needs, you can contact us through email at feedback@ciscopress.com. Please make sure to include the book title and ISBN in your message.

We greatly appreciate your assistance.

Publisher: Paul Boger

Associate Publisher: Dave Dusthimer

Business Operation Manager, Cisco Press: Jan Cornelssen

Executive Editor: Brett Bartow

Managing Editor: Sandra Schroeder

Senior Development Editor: Christopher Cleveland

Senior Project Editor: Tonya Simpson

Copy Editor: John Edwards

Technical Editor(s): Dave Burns, Sean Wilkins

Editorial Assistant: Vanessa Evans

Cover Designer: Mark Shirar

Composition: Tricia Bronkella

Indexer: Tim Wright

Proofreader: Chuck Hutchinson

Americas Headquarters
Cisco Systems, Inc.
170 West Tasman Drive
San Jose, CA 95134-1706
USA
www.cisco.com
Tel: 408 526-4000
800 553-NETS (6387)
Fax: 408 527-0883

Asia Pacific Headquarters
Cisco Systems, Inc.
168 Robinson Road
#28-01 Capital Tower
Singapore 068912
www.cisco.com
Tel: +65 6317 7777
Fax: +65 6317 7799

Europe Headquarters
Cisco Systems International BV
Haarlerbergpark
Haarlerbergweg 13-19
1101 CH Amsterdam
The Netherlands
www-europe.cisco.com
Tel: +31 0 800 020 0791
Fax: +31 0 20 357 1100

Cisco has more than 200 offices worldwide. Addresses, phone numbers, and fax numbers are listed on the Cisco Website at www.cisco.com/go/offices.

©2007 Cisco Systems, Inc. All rights reserved. CCVP, the Cisco logo, and the Cisco Square Bridge logo are trademarks of Cisco Systems, Inc.; Changing the Way We Work, Live, Play, and Learn is a service mark of Cisco Systems, Inc.; and Access Registrar, Aironet, BPX, Catalyst, CCDA, CCDP, CCIE, CCIP, CCNA, CCNP, CCSP, Cisco, the Cisco Certified Internetwork Expert logo, Cisco IOS, Cisco Press, Cisco Systems, Cisco Systems Capital, the Cisco Systems logo, Cisco Unity, Enterprise/Solver, EtherChannel, EtherFast, EtherSwitch, Fast Step, Follow Me Browsing, FormShare, GigaDrive, GigaStack, HomeLink, Internet Quotient, IOS, IP/TV, iQ Expertise, the iQ logo, iQ Net Readiness Scorecard, iQuick Study, LightStream, Linksys, MeetingPlace, MGX, Networking Academy, Network Registrar, Packet, PIX, ProConnect, RateMUX, ScriptShare, SlideCast, SMARTnet, StackWise, The Fastest Way to Increase Your Internet Quotient, and TransPath are registered trademarks of Cisco Systems, Inc. and/or its affiliates in the United States and certain other countries.

All other trademarks mentioned in this document or Website are the property of their respective owners. The use of the word partner does not imply a partnership relationship between Cisco and any other company. (0609R)

About the Authors

Narbik Kocharians, CCIE No. 12410 (Routing and Switching, Security, SP), is a Triple CCIE with more than 32 years of experience in the IT industry. He has designed, implemented, and supported numerous enterprise networks. Narbik is the president of Micronics Training, Inc. (www.Micronicstraining.com), where he teaches CCIE R&S and SP boot camps.

Terry Vinson, CCIE No. 35347 (Routing and Switching, Data Center), is a seasoned instructor with nearly 25 years of experience teaching and writing technical courses and training materials. Terry has taught and developed training content, as well as provided technical consulting for high-end firms in the north Virginia/Washington, D.C. area. His technical expertise lies in the Cisco arena with a focus on all routing and switching technologies as well as the latest data center technologies, including Nexus switching, unified computing, and storage-area networking (SAN) technologies. Terry currently teaches for CCIE R&S and Data Center Bootcamps for Micronics Training, Inc. and enjoys sailing and game design in his "free time."

About the Technical Reviewers

David Burns has in-depth knowledge of routing and switching technologies, network security, and mobility. He is currently a senior systems engineering manager for Cisco, leading the engineering team covering cable/MSO and content service providers in the United States. In July 2008, Dave joined Cisco as a lead systems engineer in several areas, including Femtocell, Datacenter, MTSO, and security architectures, working for a U.S.-based SP Mobility account. He came to Cisco from a large U.S.-based cable company, where he was a senior network and security design engineer. Dave held various roles before joining Cisco during his ten-plus years in the industry, working in SP operations, SP engineering, SP architecture, enterprise IT, and U.S. military intelligence communications engineering. He holds various sales and industry/Cisco technical certifications, including the CISSP, CCSP, CCDP, and two associate-level certifications. Dave recently passed the CCIE Security Written exam and is currently preparing for the CCIE Security Lab. Dave is a big advocate of knowledge transfer and sharing and has a passion for network technologies, especially as they relate to network security. Dave has been a speaker at Cisco Live on topics such as Femtocell (IP mobility) and IPS (security). Dave earned his Bachelor of Science degree in telecommunications engineering technology from Southern Polytechnic State University, Georgia, where he currently serves as a member of the Industry Advisory Board for the Computer & Electrical Engineering Technology School. Dave also earned a Master of Business Administration (MBA) degree from the University of Phoenix.

Sean Wilkins is an accomplished networking consultant for SR-W Consulting and has been in the field of IT since the mid 1990s, working with companies such as Cisco, Lucent, Verizon, and AT&T as well as several other private companies. Sean currently holds certifications with Cisco (CCNP/CCDP), Microsoft (MCSE), and CompTIA (A+ and Network+). He also has a Master of Science degree in information technology with a focus in network architecture and design, a Master of Science in organizational management, a Master's Certificate in network security, a Bachelor of Science in computer networking, and an Associate of Applied Science in computer information systems. In addition to working as a consultant, Sean spends most of his time as a technical writer and editor for various companies. Check out his work at his author website, www.infodispersion.com.

Dedications

From Narbik Kocharians:

I would like to dedicate this book to my wife, Janet, for her love, encouragement, and continuous support, and to my dad, for his words of wisdom.

From Terry Vinson:

I would like to dedicate this book to my father, who has taught me many things in life and include the one thing I've tried to live by: "Never give up on your dreams. Hard work and diligence will see you through so long as you never give up." So it is with all my love, respect, and admiration that I dedicate this to you.

Acknowledgments

From Narbik Kocharians:

First, I would like to thank God for giving me the opportunity and ability to write, teach, and do what I truly enjoy doing. Also, I would like to thank my family, especially my wife of 29 years, Janet, for her constant encouragement and help. She does such an amazing job of interacting with students and handling all the logistics of organizing classes as I focus on teaching. I also would like to thank my children, Chris, Patrick, Alexandra, and my little one Daniel, for their patience.

A special thanks to Mr. Brett Bartow for his patience with our constantly changing deadlines. It goes without saying that the technical editors and reviewers did a phenomenal job; thank you very much. Finally, I would like to thank all my students, who inspire me every day, and you, for reading this book.

From Terry Vinson:

The opportunity to cooperate on the new edition of this book has been an honor and privilege beyond words for me. I have to thank Narbik for approaching me with the opportunity and for all his support and mentoring over the years. If it were not for him, I would not be where I am today. Additionally, I would like to thank all the fine people at Cisco Press for being so cool and understanding over the last few months. Among those people, I want to specifically thank Brett Bartow, whose patience has been almost infinite (yet I managed to tax it), David Burns, and Sean Wilkins for their incredible suggestions and devotion to making sure that I stayed on track. Last but not least among the Cisco Press crew there is Christopher Cleveland, who diligently nudged, kicked, and all-out shoved when necessary to see that things got done.

Personally, I need to thank my wife, Sheila. She has been the difference I was looking for in my life, the impetus to try to do more and to get up each day and try to make myself a better person, a better engineer, and a better instructor. Without her, I would not have the life I have come to love so much.

Finally, I want to thank my students and Micronics Training for giving me the opportunity to do what I enjoy every day. Thanks for all your questions, patience, and unbridled eagerness to learn. You guys are absolutely stellar examples of why this industry is like no other on the planet.

Contents at a Glance

Contents

Icons Used in This Book

Communication Server — PC — PC with Software — Sun Workstation — Macintosh — Branch Office

Headquarters — Terminal — File Server — Web Server — Cisco Works Workstation — House, Regular

Printer — Laptop — IBM Mainframe — Label Switch Router — Cluster Controller

Gateway — Router — Bridge — Hub — ATM router — Cisco MDS 9500

Catalyst Switch — Multilayer Switch — ATM Switch — Route/Switch Processor — LAN2LAN Switch

Cisco MDS 9500 — Optical Services Router — Enterprise Fibre Channel disk — Fibre Channel JBOD — ONS 15540

Network Cloud — Line: Ethernet — Line: Serial — Line: Switched Serial

Command Syntax Conventions

The conventions used to present command syntax in this book are the same conventions used in the IOS Command Reference. The Command Reference describes these conventions as follows:

- **Boldface** indicates commands and keywords that are entered literally as shown. In actual configuration examples and output (not general command syntax), boldface indicates commands that are manually input by the user (such as a **show** command).

- *Italic* indicates arguments for which you supply actual values.

- Vertical bars (|) separate alternative, mutually exclusive elements.

- Square brackets ([ ]) indicate an optional element.

- Braces ({ }) indicate a required choice.

- Braces within brackets ([{ }]) indicate a required choice within an optional element.

Introduction

The Cisco Certified Internetwork Expert (CCIE) certification might be the most challenging and prestigious of all networking certifications. It has received numerous awards and certainly has built a reputation as one of the most difficult certifications to earn in all of the technology world. Having a CCIE certification opens doors professionally, typically results in higher pay, and looks great on a résumé.

Cisco currently offers several CCIE certifications. This book covers the version 5.0 exam blueprint topics of the written exam for the CCIE Routing and Switching certification. The following list details the currently available CCIE certifications at the time of this book's publication; check www.cisco.com/go/ccie for the latest information. The certifications are listed in the order in which they appear on the web page:

- CCDE
- CCIE Collaboration
- CCIE Data Center
- CCIE Routing & Switching
- CCIE Security
- CCIE Service Provider
- CCIE Service Provider Operations
- CCIE Wireless

Each of the CCDE and CCIE certifications requires the candidate to pass both a written exam and a one-day, hands-on lab exam. The written exam is intended to test your knowledge of theory, protocols, and configuration concepts that follow good design practices. The lab exam proves that you can configure and troubleshoot actual gear.

Why Should I Take the CCIE Routing and Switching Written Exam?

The first and most obvious reason to take the CCIE Routing and Switching written exam is that it is the first step toward obtaining the CCIE Routing and Switching certification. Also, you cannot schedule a CCIE lab exam until you pass the corresponding written exam. In short, if you want all the professional benefits of a CCIE Routing and Switching certification, you start by passing the written exam.

The benefits of getting a CCIE certification are varied, among which are the following:

- Better pay
- Career-advancement opportunities
- Applies to certain minimum requirements for Cisco Silver and Gold Channel Partners, as well as those seeking Master Specialization, making you more valuable to Channel Partners

- Better movement through the problem-resolution process when calling the Cisco TAC

- Prestige

- Credibility for consultants and customer engineers, including the use of the Cisco CCIE logo

The other big reason to take the CCIE Routing and Switching written exam is that it recertifies an individual's associate-, professional-, and expert-level Cisco certifications, regardless of his or her technology track. Recertification requirements do change, so please verify the requirements at www.cisco.com/go/certifications.

CCIE Routing and Switching Written Exam 400-101

The CCIE Routing and Switching written exam, at the time of this writing, consists of a two-hour exam administered at a proctored exam facility affiliated with Pearson VUE (www.vue.com/cisco). The exam typically includes approximately 100 multiple-choice questions. No simulation questions are currently part of the written exam.

As with most exams, everyone wants to know what is on the exam. Cisco provides general guidance as to topics on the exam in the CCIE Routing and Switching written exam blueprint, the most recent copy of which can be accessed from www.cisco.com/go/ccie.

Cisco changes both the CCIE written and lab blueprints over time, but Cisco seldom, if ever, changes the exam numbers. However, exactly this change occurred when the CCIE Routing and Switching blueprint was refreshed for v5.0. The previous written exam for v4.0 was numbered as 350-001; the v5.0 written exam is identified by 400-101.

The CCIE Routing and Switching written exam blueprint 5.0, as of the time of publication, is listed in Table I-1. Table I-1 also lists the chapters that cover each topic.

Table I-1 *CCIE Routing and Switching Written Exam Blueprint*

Topics	Book Volume	Book Chapter
1.0 Network Principles		
1.1 Network theory		
1.1.a Describe basic software architecture differences between IOS and IOS XE		
1.1.a (i) Control plane and Forwarding plane	1	1
1.1.a (ii) Impact to troubleshooting and performances	1	1
1.1.a (iii) Excluding specific platform's architecture	1	1
1.1.b Identify Cisco Express Forwarding concepts		
1.1.b (i) RIB, FIB, LFIB, adjacency table	1	6
1.1.b (ii) Load-balancing hash	1	6

Topics	Book Volume	Book Chapter
1.1.b (iii) Polarization concept and avoidance	1	6
1.1.c Explain general network challenges		
1.1.c (i) Unicast flooding	1	4
1.1.c (ii) Out-of-order packets	1	4
1.1.c (iii) Asymmetric routing	1	4
1.1.c (iv) Impact of micro-burst	1	4
1.1.d Explain IP operations		
1.1.d (i) ICMP unreachable, redirect	1	4
1.1.d (ii) IPv4 options, IPv6 extension headers	1	4
1.1.d (iii) IPv4 and IPv6 fragmentation	1	4
1.1.d (iv) TTL	1	4
1.1.d (v) IP MTU	1	4
1.1.e Explain TCP operations		
1.1.e (i) IPv4 and IPv6 PMTU	1	4
1.1.e (ii) MSS	1	4
1.1.e (iii) Latency	1	4
1.1.e (iv) Windowing	1	4
1.1.e (v) Bandwidth delay product	1	4
1.1.e (vi) Global synchronization	1	4
1.1.e (vii) Options	1	4
1.1.f Explain UDP operations		
1.1.f (i) Starvation	1	4
1.1.f (ii) Latency	1	4
1.1.f (iii) RTP/RTCP concepts	1	4
1.2 Network implementation and operation		
1.2.a Evaluate proposed changes to a network		
1.2.a (i) Changes to routing protocol parameters	1	7–10
1.2.a (ii) Migrate parts of a network to IPv6	1	4
1.2.a (iii) Routing protocol migration	1	6
1.2.a (iv) Adding multicast support	2	8
1.2.a (v) Migrate Spanning Tree Protocol	1	3

Topics	Book Volume	Book Chapter
1.2.a (vi) Evaluate impact of new traffic on existing QoS design	2	3, 4, 5
1.3 *Network troubleshooting*		
1.3.a Use IOS troubleshooting tools		
1.3.a (i) debug, conditional debug	1	4
1.3.a (ii) ping, traceroute with extended options	1	4
1.3.a (iii) Embedded packet capture	2	9
1.3.a (iv) Performance monitor	1	5
1.3.b Apply troubleshooting methodologies		
1.3.b (i) Diagnose the root cause of networking issue (analyze symptoms, identify and describe root cause)	1	11
1.3.b (ii) Design and implement valid solutions according to constraints	1	11
1.3.b (iii) Verify and monitor resolution	1	11
1.3.c Interpret packet capture		
1.3.c (i) Using Wireshark trace analyzer	2	9
1.3.c (ii) Using IOS embedded packet capture	2	9
2.0 Layer 2 Technologies		
2.1 *LAN switching technologies*		
2.1.a Implement and troubleshoot switch administration		
2.1.a (i) Managing MAC address table	1	1
2.1.a (ii) errdisable recovery	1	3
2.1.a (iii) L2 MTU	1	1
2.1.b Implement and troubleshoot Layer 2 protocols		
2.1.b (i) CDP, LLDP	1	3
2.1.b (ii) UDLD	1	3
2.1.c Implement and troubleshoot VLAN		
2.1.c (i) Access ports	1	2
2.1.c (ii) VLAN database	1	2
2.1.c (iii) Normal, extended VLAN, voice VLAN	1	2

Topics	Book Volume	Book Chapter
2.1.d Implement and troubleshoot trunking		
2.1.d (i) VTPv1, VTPv2, VTPv3, VTP pruning	1	2
2.1.d (ii) dot1Q	1	2
2.1.d (iii) Native VLAN	1	2
2.1.d (iv) Manual pruning	1	2
2.1.e Implement and troubleshoot EtherChannel		
2.1.e (i) LACP, PAgP, manual	1	3
2.1.e (ii) Layer 2, Layer 3	1	3
2.1.e (iii) Load balancing	1	3
2.1.e (iv) EtherChannel misconfiguration guard	1	3
2.1.f Implement and troubleshoot spanning tree		
2.1.f (i) PVST+/RPVST+/MST	1	3
2.1.f (ii) Switch priority, port priority, path cost, STP timers	1	3
2.1.f (iii) PortFast, BPDU Guard, BPDU Filter	1	3
2.1.f (iv) Loop Guard, Root Guard	1	3
2.1.g Implement and troubleshoot other LAN switching technologies		
2.1.g (i) SPAN, RSPAN, ERSPAN	1	1
2.1.h Describe chassis virtualization and aggregation technologies		
2.1.h (i) Multichassis	1	1
2.1.h (ii) VSS concepts	1	1
2.1.h (iii) Alternative to STP	1	1
2.1.h (iv) Stackwise	1	1
2.1.h (v) Excluding specific platform implementation	1	1
2.1.i Describe spanning-tree concepts		
2.1.i (i) Compatibility between MST and RSTP	1	3
2.1.i (ii) STP dispute, STP Bridge Assurance	1	3
2.2 Layer 2 multicast		
2.2.a Implement and troubleshoot IGMP		
2.2.a (i) IGMPv1, IGMPv2, IGMPv3	2	7
2.2.a (ii) IGMP snooping	2	7

Topics	Book Volume	Book Chapter
2.2.a (iii) IGMP querier	2	7
2.2.a (iv) IGMP filter	2	7
2.2.a (v) IGMP proxy	2	7
2.2.b Explain MLD	2	8
2.2.c Explain PIM snooping	2	8
2.3 Layer 2 WAN circuit technologies		
2.3.a Implement and troubleshoot HDLC	2	6
2.3.b Implement and troubleshoot PPP		
2.3.b (i) Authentication (PAP, CHAP)	2	6
2.3.b (ii) PPPoE	2	6
2.3.b (iii) MLPPP	2	6
2.3.c Describe WAN rate-based Ethernet circuits		
2.3.c (i) Metro and WAN Ethernet topologies	2	6
2.3.c (ii) Use of rate-limited WAN Ethernet services	2	6
3.0 Layer 3 Technologies		
3.1 Addressing technologies		
3.1.a Identify, implement, and troubleshoot IPv4 addressing and subnetting		
3.1.a (i) Address types, VLSM	1	4
3.1.a (ii) ARP	1	4
3.1.b Identify, implement, and troubleshoot IPv6 addressing and subnetting		
3.1.b (i) Unicast, multicast	1	4
3.1.b (ii) EUI-64	1	4
3.1.b (iii) ND, RS/RA	1	4
3.1.b (iv) Autoconfig/SLAAC, temporary addresses (RFC 4941)	1	4
3.1.b (v) Global prefix configuration feature	1	4
3.1.b (vi) DHCP operations	1	4
3.1.b (vii) SLAAC/DHCPv6 interaction	2	10
3.1.b (viii) Stateful, stateless DHCPv6	1	4
3.1.b (ix) DHCPv6 prefix delegation	1	4

Topics	Book Volume	Book Chapter
3.2 Layer 3 multicast		
3.2.a Troubleshoot reverse path forwarding		
3.2.a (i) RPF failure	2	8
3.2.a (ii) RPF failure with tunnel interface	2	8
3.2.b Implement and troubleshoot IPv4 protocol-independent multicast		
3.2.b (i) PIM dense mode, sparse mode, sparse-dense mode	2	8
3.2.b (ii) Static RP, auto-RP, BSR	2	8
3.2.b (iii) Bidirectional PIM	2	8
3.2.b (iv) Source-specific multicast	2	8
3.2.b (v) Group-to-RP mapping	2	8
3.2.b (vi) Multicast boundary	2	8
3.2.c Implement and troubleshoot multicast source discovery protocol		
3.2.c (i) Intra-domain MSDP (anycast RP)	2	8
3.2.c (ii) SA filter	2	8
3.2.d Describe IPv6 multicast		
3.2.d (i) IPv6 multicast addresses	2	7
3.2.d (ii) PIMv6	2	8
3.3 Fundamental routing concepts		
3.3.a Implement and troubleshoot static routing	1	6
3.3.b Implement and troubleshoot default routing	1	7–11
3.3.c Compare routing protocol types		
3.3.c (i) Distance vector	1	7
3.3.c (ii) Link state	1	7
3.3.c (iii) Path vector	1	7
3.3.d Implement, optimize, and troubleshoot administrative distance	1	11
3.3.e Implement and troubleshoot passive interface	1	7–10
3.3.f Implement and troubleshoot VRF Lite	2	11
3.3.g Implement, optimize, and troubleshoot filtering with any routing protocol	1	11

Topics	Book Volume	Book Chapter
3.3.h Implement, optimize, and troubleshoot redistribution between any routing protocol	1	11
3.3.i Implement, optimize, and troubleshoot manual and autosummarization with any routing protocol	1	7–10
3.3.j Implement, optimize, and troubleshoot Policy-Based Routing	1	6
3.3.k Identify and troubleshoot suboptimal routing	1	11
3.3.l Implement and troubleshoot bidirectional forwarding detection	1	11
3.3.m Implement and troubleshoot loop-prevention mechanisms		
3.3.m (i) Route tagging, filtering	1	11
3.3.m (ii) Split Horizon	1	7
3.3.m (iii) Route Poisoning	1	7
3.3.n Implement and troubleshoot routing protocol authentication		
3.3.n (i) MD5	1	7–10
3.3.n (ii) Key-chain	1	7–10
3.3.n (iii) EIGRP HMAC SHA2-256bit	1	8
3.3.n (iv) OSPFv2 SHA1-196bit	1	9
3.3.n (v) OSPFv3 IPsec authentication	1	9
3.4 RIP (v2 and v6)		
3.4.a Implement and troubleshoot RIPv2	1	7
3.4.b Describe RIPv6 (RIPng)	1	7
3.5 EIGRP (for IPv4 and IPv6)		
3.5.a Describe packet types		
3.5.a (i) Packet types (hello, query, update, and so on)	1	8
3.5.a (ii) Route types (internal, external)	1	8
3.5.b Implement and troubleshoot neighbor relationship		
3.5.b (i) Multicast, unicast EIGRP peering	1	8
3.5.b (ii) OTP point-to-point peering	1	8

Topics	Book Volume	Book Chapter
3.5.b (iii) OTP route-reflector peering	1	8
3.5.b (iv) OTP multiple service providers scenario	1	8
3.5.c Implement and troubleshoot loop-free path selection		
3.5.c (i) RD, FD, FC, successor, feasible successor	1	8
3.5.c (ii) Classic metric	1	8
3.5.c (iii) Wide metric	1	8
3.5.d Implement and troubleshoot operations		
3.5.d (i) General operations	1	8
3.5.d (ii) Topology table, update, query, active, passive	1	8
3.5.d (iii) Stuck in active	1	8
3.5.d (iv) Graceful shutdown	1	8
3.5.e Implement and troubleshoot EIGRP stub		
3.5.e (i) Stub	1	8
3.5.e (ii) Leak-map	1	8
3.5.f Implement and troubleshoot load balancing		
3.5.f (i) equal-cost	1	8
3.5.f (ii) unequal-cost	1	8
3.5.f (iii) add-path	1	8
3.5.g Implement EIGRP (multi-address) named mode		
3.5.g (i) Types of families	1	8
3.5.g (ii) IPv4 address-family	1	8
3.5.g (iii) IPv6 address-family	1	8
3.5.h Implement, troubleshoot, and optimize EIGRP convergence and scalability		
3.5.h (i) Describe fast convergence requirements	1	8
3.5.h (ii) Control query boundaries	1	8
3.5.h (iii) IP FRR/fast reroute (single hop)	1	8
3.5.h (iv) Summary leak-map	1	8
3.5.h (v) Summary metric	1	8
3.6 OSPF (v2 and v3)		

Topics	Book Volume	Book Chapter
3.6.a Describe packet types		
3.6.a (i) LSA types (1, 2, 3, 4, 5, 7, 9)	1	9
3.6.a (ii) Route types (N1, N2, E1, E2)	1	9
3.6.b Implement and troubleshoot neighbor relationship	1	9
3.6.c Implement and troubleshoot OSPFv3 address-family support		
3.6.c (i) IPv4 address-family	1	9
3.6.c (ii) IPv6 address-family	1	9
3.6.d Implement and troubleshoot network types, area types, and router types		
3.6.d (i) Point-to-point, multipoint, broadcast, nonbroadcast	1	9
3.6.d (ii) LSA types, area type: backbone, normal, transit, stub, NSSA, totally stub	1	9
3.6.d (iii) Internal router, ABR, ASBR	1	9
3.6.d (iv) Virtual link	1	9
3.6.e Implement and troubleshoot path preference	1	9
3.6.f Implement and troubleshoot operations		
3.6.f (i) General operations	1	9
3.6.f (ii) Graceful shutdown	1	9
3.6.f (iii) GTSM (Generic TTL Security Mechanism)	1	9
3.6.g Implement, troubleshoot, and optimize OSPF convergence and scalability		
3.6.g (i) Metrics	1	9
3.6.g (ii) LSA throttling, SPF tuning, fast hello	1	9
3.6.g (iii) LSA propagation control (area types, ISPF)	1	9
3.6.g (iv) IP FRR/fast reroute (single hop)	1	9
3.6.g (v) LFA/loop-free alternative (multihop)	1	9
3.6.g (vi) OSPFv3 prefix suppression	1	9
3.7 BGP		
3.7.a Describe, implement, and troubleshoot peer relationships		
3.7.a (i) Peer-group, template	2	1

Topics	Book Volume	Book Chapter
3.7.a (ii) Active, passive	2	1
3.7.a (iii) States, timers	2	1
3.7.a (iv) Dynamic neighbors	2	1
3.7.b Implement and troubleshoot iBGP and iBGP		
3.7.b (i) eBGP, iBGP	2	1
3.7.b (ii) 4-byte AS number	2	1
3.7.b (iii) Private AS	2	1
3.7.c Explain attributes and best-path selection	2	1
3.7.d Implement, optimize, and troubleshoot routing policies		
3.7.d (i) Attribute manipulation	2	2
3.7.d (ii) Conditional advertisement	2	2
3.7.d (iii) Outbound route filtering	2	2
3.7.d (iv) Communities, extended communities	2	2
3.7.d (v) Multihoming	2	2
3.7.e Implement and troubleshoot scalability		
3.7.e (i) Route-reflector, cluster	2	2
3.7.e (ii) Confederations	2	2
3.7.e (iii) Aggregation, AS set	2	2
3.7.f Implement and troubleshoot multiprotocol BGP		
3.7.f (i) IPv4, IPv6, VPN address-family	2	2
3.7.g Implement and troubleshoot AS path manipulations		
3.7.g (i) Local AS, allow AS in, remove private AS	2	2
3.7.g (ii) Prepend	2	2
3.7.g (iii) Regexp	2	2
3.7.h Implement and troubleshoot other features		
3.7.h (i) Multipath	2	2
3.7.h (ii) BGP synchronization	2	2
3.7.h (iii) Soft reconfiguration, route refresh	2	2

Topics	Book Volume	Book Chapter
3.7.i Describe BGP fast convergence features		
3.7.i (i) Prefix-independent convergence	2	2
3.7.i (ii) Add-path	2	2
3.7.i (iii) Next-hop address tracking	2	2
3.8 IS-IS (for IPv4 and IPv6)		
3.8.a Describe basic IS-IS network		
3.8.a (i) Single area, single topology	1	10
3.8.b Describe neighbor relationship	1	10
3.8.c Describe network types, levels, and router types		
3.8.c (i) NSAP addressing	1	10
3.8.c (ii) Point-to-point, broadcast	1	10
3.8.d Describe operations	1	10
3.8.e Describe optimization features		
3.8.e (i) Metrics, wide metric	1	10
4.0 VPN Technologies		
4.1 Tunneling		
4.1.a Implement and troubleshoot MPLS operations		
4.1.a (i) Label stack, LSR, LSP	2	11
4.1.a (ii) LDP	2	11
4.1.a (iii) MPLS ping, MPLS traceroute	2	11
4.1.b Implement and troubleshoot basic MPLS L3VPN		
4.1.b (i) L3VPN, CE, PE, P	2	11
4.1.b (ii) Extranet (route leaking)	2	11
4.1.c Implement and troubleshoot encapsulation		
4.1.c (i) GRE	2	10
4.1.c (ii) Dynamic GRE	2	10
4.1.c (iii) LISP encapsulation principles supporting EIGRP OTP	1	8
4.1.d Implement and troubleshoot DMVPN (single hub)		
4.1.d (i) NHRP	2	10
4.1.d (ii) DMVPN with IPsec using preshared key	2	10

Topics	Book Volume	Book Chapter
4.1.d (iii) QoS profile	2	10
4.1.d (iv) Pre-classify	2	10
4.1.e Describe IPv6 tunneling techniques		
4.1.e (i) 6in4, 6to4	2	8
4.1.e (ii) ISATAP	2	8
4.1.e (iii) 6RD	2	8
4.1.e (iv) 6PE/6VPE	2	8
4.1.g Describe basic Layer 2 VPN: wireline		
4.1.g (i) L2TPv3 general principles	2	10
4.1.g (ii) AToM general principles	2	11
4.1.h Describe basic L2VPN—LAN services		
4.1.h (i) MPLS-VPLS general principles	2	10
4.1.h (ii) OTV general principles	2	10
4.2 Encryption		
4.2.a Implement and troubleshoot IPsec with preshared key		
4.2.a (i) IPv4 site to IPv4 site	2	10
4.2.a (ii) IPv6 in IPv4 tunnels	2	10
4.2.a (iii) Virtual Tunneling Interface (VTI)	2	10
4.2.b Describe GET VPN	2	10
5.0 Infrastructure Security		
5.1 Device security		
5.1.a Implement and troubleshoot IOS AAA using local database	2	9
5.1.b Implement and troubleshoot device access control		
5.1.b (i) Lines (VTY, AUX, console)	1	5
5.1.b (ii) SNMP	1	5
5.1.b (iii) Management plane protection	2	9
5.1.b (iv) Password encryption	1	5
5.1.c Implement and troubleshoot control plane policing	2	9

Topics	Book Volume	Book Chapter
6.1 System management		
6.1.a Implement and troubleshoot device management		
6.1.a (i) Console and VTY	1	5
6.1.a (ii) Telnet, HTTP, HTTPS, SSH, SCP	1	5
6.1.a (iii) (T)FTP	1	5
6.1.b Implement and troubleshoot SNMP		
6.1.b (i) v2c, v3	1	5
6.1.c Implement and troubleshoot logging		
6.1.c (i) Local logging, syslog, debug, conditional debug	1	5
6.1.c (ii) Timestamp	2	6
6.2 Quality of service		
6.2.a Implement and troubleshoot end-to-end QoS		
6.2.a (i) CoS and DSCP mapping	2	3
6.2.b Implement, optimize, and troubleshoot QoS using MQC		
6.2.b (i) Classification	2	3
6.2.b (ii) Network-Based Application Recognition (NBAR)	2	3
6.2.b (iii) Marking using IP precedence, DSCP, CoS, ECN	2	3
6.2.b (iv) Policing, shaping	2	5
6.2.b (v) Congestion management (queuing)	2	4
6.2.b (vi) HQoS, subrate Ethernet link	2	3, 4, 5
6.2.b (vii) Congestion avoidance (WRED)	2	4
6.2.c Describe layer 2 QoS		
6.2.c (i) Queuing, scheduling	2	4
6.2.c (ii) Classification, marking	2	2
6.3 Network services		
6.3.a Implement and troubleshoot first-hop redundancy protocols		
6.3.a (i) HSRP, GLBP, VRRP	1	5
6.3.a (ii) Redundancy using IPv6 RS/RA	1	5

Topics	Book Volume	Book Chapter
6.3.b Implement and troubleshoot Network Time Protocol		
6.3.b (i) NTP master, client, version 3, version 4	1	5
6.3.b (ii) NTP Authentication	1	5
6.3.c Implement and troubleshoot IPv4 and IPv6 DHCP		
6.3.c (i) DHCP client, IOS DHCP server, DHCP relay	1	5
6.3.c (ii) DHCP options	1	5
6.3.c (iii) DHCP protocol operations	1	5
6.3.c (iv) SLAAC/DHCPv6 interaction	1	4
6.3.c (v) Stateful, stateless DHCPv6	1	4
6.3.c (vi) DHCPv6 prefix delegation	1	4
6.3.d Implement and troubleshoot IPv4 Network Address Translation		
6.3.d (i) Static NAT, dynamic NAT, policy-based NAT, PAT	1	5
6.3.d (ii) NAT ALG	2	10
6.3.e Describe IPv6 Network Address Translation		
6.3.e (i) NAT64	2	10
6.3.e (ii) NPTv6	2	10
6.4 Network optimization		
6.4.a Implement and troubleshoot IP SLA		
6.4.a (i) ICMP, UDP, jitter, VoIP	1	5
6.4.b Implement and troubleshoot tracking object		
6.4.b (i) Tracking object, tracking list	1	5
6.4.b (ii) Tracking different entities (for example, interfaces, routes, IP SLA, and so on)	1	5
6.4.c Implement and troubleshoot NetFlow		
6.4.c (i) NetFlow v5, v9	1	5
6.4.c (ii) Local retrieval	1	5
6.4.c (iii) Export (configuration only)	1	5
6.4.d Implement and troubleshoot embedded event manager		
6.4.d (i) EEM policy using applet	1	5

Topics	Book Volume	Book Chapter
6.4.e Identify performance routing (PfR)		
6.4.e (i) Basic load balancing	1	11
6.4.e (ii) Voice optimization	1	11

To give you practice on these topics, and pull the topics together, Edition 5 of the *CCIE Routing and Switching v5.0 Official Cert Guide, Volume 2* includes a large set of CD questions that mirror the types of questions expected for the Version 5.0 blueprint. By their very nature, these topics require the application of the knowledge listed throughout the book. This special section of questions provides a means to learn and practice these skills with a proportionally larger set of questions added specifically for this purpose.

These questions will be available to you in the practice test engine database, whether you take full exams or choose questions by category.

About the *CCIE Routing and Switching v5.0 Official Cert Exam Guide, Volume 2*, Fifth Edition

This section provides a brief insight into the contents of the book, the major goals, and some of the book features that you will encounter when using this book.

Book Organization

This volume contains six major parts. Beyond the chapters in these parts of the book, you will find several useful appendixes gathered in Part VIII.

Following is a description of each part's coverage:

- **Part I, "IP BGP Routing" (Chapters 1 and 2):** This part focuses on the details of BGP (Chapter 1), with Chapter 2 looking at BGP path attributes and how to influence BGP's choice of best path.

- **Part II, "QoS" (Chapters 3–5):** This part covers the more popular QoS tools, including some MQC-based tools, as well as several older tools, particularly FRTS. The chapters include coverage of classification and marking (Chapter 3), queuing and congestion avoidance (Chapter 4), plus shaping, policing, and link efficiency (Chapter 5).

- **Part III, "Wide-Area Networks" (Chapter 6):** The WAN coverage has been shrinking over the last few revisions to the CCIE R&S written exam. Chapter 6 includes some brief coverage of PPP and Frame Relay. Note that the previous version (V4.0) and current version (V5.0) of the blueprint include another WAN topic, MPLS, which is covered in Part VI, Chapter 11.

- **Part IV, "IP Multicast" (Chapters 7 and 8):** Chapter 7 covers multicast on LANs, including IGMP and how hosts join multicast groups. Chapter 8 covers multicast WAN topics.

- **Part V, "Security" (Chapters 9 and 10):** Given the CCIE tracks for both Security and Voice, Cisco has a small dilemma regarding whether to cover those topics on CCIE Routing and Switching, and if so, in how much detail. This part covers a variety of security topics appropriate for CCIE Routing and Switching. This chapter focuses on switch and router security.

- **Part VI, "Multiprotocol Label Switching (MPLS)" (Chapter 11):** As mentioned in the WAN section, the CCIE R&S exam's coverage of MPLS has been growing over the last two versions of the blueprint. This chapter focuses on enterprise-related topics such as core MPLS concepts and MPLS VPNs, including basic configuration.

- **Part VII, "Final Preparation" (Chapter 12):** This part provides a set of tools and a study plan to help you complete your preparation for the exams.

- **Part VIII, "Appendixes":**

  Appendix A, "Answers to the 'Do I Know This Already?' Quizzes": This appendix lists answers and explanations for the questions at the beginning of each chapter.

  Appendix B, "CCIE Exam Updates": As of the first printing of the book, this appendix contains only a few words that reference the web page for this book at www.ciscopress.com/title/9781587144912. As the blueprint evolves over time, the authors will post new materials at the website. Any future printings of the book will include the latest newly added materials in printed form inside Appendix B. If Cisco releases a major exam update, changes to the book will be available only in a new edition of the book and not on this site.

NOTE   Appendixes C through F and the Glossary are in printable, PDF format on the CD.

  (CD-only) Appendix C, "Decimal-to-Binary Conversion Table": This appendix lists the decimal values 0 through 255, with their binary equivalents.

  (CD-only) Appendix D, "IP Addressing Practice": This appendix lists several practice problems for IP subnetting and finding summary routes. The explanations to the answers use the shortcuts described in the book.

  (CD-only) Appendix E, "Key Tables for CCIE Study": This appendix lists the most important tables from the core chapters of the book. The tables have much of the content removed so that you can use them as an exercise. You can print the PDF and then fill in the table from memory, checking your answers against the completed tables in Appendix F.

  (CD-only) Appendix F, "Solutions for Key Tables for CCIE Study"

  (CD-only) Glossary: The Glossary contains the key terms listed in the book.

Book Features

The core chapters of this book have several features that help you make the best use of your time:

- **"Do I Know This Already?" Quizzes:** Each chapter begins with a quiz that helps you to determine the amount of time you need to spend studying that chapter. If you score yourself strictly, and you miss only one question, you might want to skip the core of the chapter and move on to the "Foundation Summary" section at the end of the chapter, which lets you review facts and spend time on other topics. If you miss more than one, you might want to spend some time reading the chapter or at least reading sections that cover topics about which you know you are weaker.

- **Foundation Topics:** These are the core sections of each chapter. They explain the protocols, concepts, and configurations for the topics in that chapter.

- **Foundation Summary:** The "Foundation Summary" section of this book departs from the typical features of the "Foundation Summary" section of other Cisco Press Exam Certification Guides. This section does not repeat any details from the "Foundation Topics" section; instead, it simply summarizes and lists facts related to the chapter but for which a longer or more detailed explanation is not warranted.

- **Key topics:** Throughout the "Foundation Topics" section, a Key Topic icon has been placed beside the most important areas for review. After reading a chapter, when doing your final preparation for the exam, take the time to flip through the chapters, looking for the Key Topic icons, and review those paragraphs, tables, figures, and lists.

- **Fill In Key Tables from Memory:** The more important tables from the chapters have been copied to PDF files available on the CD as Appendix E. The tables have most of the information removed. After printing these mostly empty tables, you can use them to improve your memory of the facts in the table by trying to fill them out. This tool should be useful for memorizing key facts. The CD-only Appendix F contains the completed tables so that you can check your work.

- **CD-based practice exam:** The companion CD contains multiple-choice questions and a testing engine. The CD includes 200 questions unique to the CD. As part of your final preparation, you should practice with these questions to help you get used to the exam-taking process, as well as to help refine and prove your knowledge of the exam topics.

- **Special question section for the "Implement Proposed Changes to a Network" section of the Blueprint:** To provide practice and perspectives on these exam topics, a special section of questions has been developed to help you prepare for these new types of questions.

- **Key terms and Glossary:** The more important terms mentioned in each chapter are listed at the end of each chapter under the heading "Definitions." The Glossary, found on the CD that comes with this book, lists all the terms from the chapters. When studying each chapter, you should review the key terms, and for those terms about which you are unsure of the definition, you can review the short definitions from the Glossary.

- **Further Reading:** Most chapters include a suggested set of books and websites for additional study on the same topics covered in that chapter. Often, these references will be useful tools for preparation for the CCIE Routing and Switching lab exam.

Blueprint topics covered in this chapter:

This chapter covers the following subtopics from the Cisco CCIE Routing and Switching written exam blueprint. Refer to the full blueprint in Table I-1 in the Introduction for more details on the topics covered in each chapter and their context within the blueprint.

- Next Hop

- Peering

- Troubleshooting a BGP Route That Will Not Install in the Routing Table

- MP-BGP

CHAPTER 1

Fundamentals of BGP Operations

This chapter covers what might be the single most important topic on both the CCIE Routing and Switching written and lab exams—Border Gateway Protocol (BGP) Version 4. This chapter focuses on how BGP accomplishes its fundamental tasks:

1. Forming neighbor relationships

2. Injecting routes into BGP from some other source

3. Exchanging those routes with other routers

4. Placing routes into IP routing tables

All of these BGP topics have close analogies with those of BGP's IGP cousins, but of course there are many differences in the details.

This chapter focuses on how BGP performs its central role as a routing protocol.

"Do I Know This Already?" Quiz

Table 1-1 outlines the major headings in this chapter and the corresponding "Do I Know This Already?" quiz questions.

Table 1-1   *"Do I Know This Already?" Foundation Topics Section-to-Question Mapping*

Foundation Topics Section	Questions Covered in This Section	Score
Building BGP Neighbor Relationships	1–3	
Building the BGP Table	4–8	
Building the IP Routing Table	9–12	
Total Score		

To best use this pre-chapter assessment, remember to score yourself strictly. You can find the answers in Appendix A, "Answers to the 'Do I Know This Already?' Quizzes."

1. Into which of the following neighbor states must a neighbor stabilize before BGP Update messages can be sent?

   a. Active

   b. Idle

   c. Connected

   d. Established

2. BGP neighbors check several parameters before the neighbor relationship can be completed. Which of the following is not checked?

   a. That the neighbor's router ID is not duplicated with other routers

   b. That the **neighbor** command on one router matches the update source IP address on the other router

   c. If eBGP, that the **neighbor** command points to an IP address in a connected network

   d. That a router's **neighbor remote-as** command refers to the same autonomous system number (ASN) as in the other router's **router bgp** command (assuming that confederations are not used)

3. A group of BGP routers, some with iBGP and some with eBGP connections, all use loopback IP addresses to refer to each other in their **neighbor** commands. Which of the following statements are false regarding the configuration of these peers?

   a. IBGP peers require a **neighbor** *ip-address* **ibgp-multihop** command for the peer to become established.

   b. eBGP peers require a **neighbor** *ip-address* **ebgp-multihop** command for the peer to become established.

   c. eBGP and iBGP peers cannot be placed into the same peer group.

   d. For eBGP peers, a router's BGP router ID must be equal to the IP address listed in the eBGP neighbor's **neighbor** command.

4. A router has routes in the IP routing table for 20.0.0.0/8, 20.1.0.0/16, and 20.1.2.0/24. BGP on this router is configured with the **no auto-summary** command. Which of the following is true when using the BGP **network** command to cause these routes to be injected into the BGP table?

   a. The **network 20.0.0.0** command would cause all three routes to be added to the BGP table.

   b. The **network 20.0.0.0 mask 255.0.0.0** command would cause all three routes to be added to the BGP table.

   c. The **network 20.1.0.0 mask 255.255.0.0** command would cause 20.1.0.0/16 and 20.1.2.0/24 to be added to the BGP table.

   d. The **network 20.0.0.0** command would cause only 20.0.0.0/8 to be added to the BGP table.

5. A router has configured redistribution of EIGRP routes into BGP using the command **redistribute eigrp 1 route-map fred**. This router's BGP configuration includes the **no auto-summary** command. Which of the following are true?

   a. **route-map fred** can consider for redistribution routes listed in the IP routing table as EIGRP-learned routes.

   b. **route-map fred** can consider for redistribution routes in the IP routing table listed as connected routes, but only if those interfaces are matched by EIGRP 1's **network** commands.

   c. **route-map fred** can consider for redistribution routes that are listed in the EIGRP topology table as successor routes but that are not in the IP routing table because a lower administrative distance (AD) route from a competing routing protocol exists.

   d. **route-map fred** can consider for redistribution routes listed in the IP routing table as EIGRP-learned routes, but only if those routes also have at least one feasible successor route.

6. Using BGP, R1 has learned its best route to 9.1.0.0/16 from R3. R1 has a neighbor connection to R2, over a point-to-point serial link using subnet 8.1.1.4/30. R1 has **auto-summary** configured. Which of the following is true regarding what R1 advertises to R2?

   a. R1 advertises only 9.0.0.0/8 to R2, and not 9.1.0.0/16.

   b. If the **aggregate-address 9.0.0.0 255.0.0.0** BGP subcommand is configured, R1 advertises only 9.0.0.0/8 to R2, and not 9.1.0.0/16.

   c. If the **network 9.0.0.0 mask 255.0.0.0** BGP subcommand is configured, R1 advertises only 9.0.0.0/8 to R2, and not 9.1.0.0/16.

   d. None of the other answers is correct.

✓ **7.** Which of the following statements are false regarding what routes a BGP router can advertise to a neighbor? (Assume that no confederations or route reflectors are in use.)

   a. To advertise a route to an eBGP peer, the route cannot have been learned from an iBGP peer.

   b. To advertise a route to an iBGP peer, the route must have been learned from an eBGP peer.

   c. The NEXT_HOP IP address must respond to a **ping** command.

   d. Do not advertise routes if the neighboring router's AS is in the AS_PATH.

   e. The route must be listed as **valid** in the output of the **show ip bgp** command.

✓ **8.** Several different routes were injected into BGP through various methods on R1. Those routes were then advertised through iBGP to R2. R2 summarized the routes using the **aggregate-address summary-only** command, and then advertised through eBGP to R3. Which of the following are true about the ORIGIN path attribute of these routes?

   a. The routes injected using the **network** command on R1 have an ORIGIN value of IGP.

   b. The routes injected using the **redistribute ospf** command on R1 have an ORIGIN value of IGP.

   c. The routes injected using the **redistribute** command on R1 have an ORIGIN value of EGP.

   d. The routes injected using the **redistribute static** command on R1 have an ORIGIN value of incomplete.

   e. If the **as-set** option was not used, the summary route created on R2 has an ORIGIN code of IGP.

/ **9.** Which of the following statements is true regarding the use of BGP synchronization?

   a. With BGP synchronization enabled, a router can add an iBGP-learned route to its IP routing table only if that same prefix is also learned through eBGP.

   b. With BGP synchronization enabled, a router cannot consider an iBGP-learned route as a "best" route to that prefix unless the NEXT_HOP IP address matches an IGP route in the IP routing table.

   c. BGP synchronization can be safely disabled when the routers inside a single AS either create a full mesh of BGP peers or create a hub-and-spoke to the router that learns the prefix through eBGP.

   d. None of the other answers is correct.

10. Which of the following statements are true regarding the operation of BGP confederations?

    a. Confederation eBGP connections act like normal (nonconfederation) eBGP connections with regard to the need for the **neighbor ebgp-multihop** command for nonadjacent neighbor IP addresses.

    b. iBGP-learned routes are advertised over confederation eBGP connections.

    c. A full mesh of iBGP peers inside a confederation sub-AS is not required.

    d. None of the other answers is correct.

11. R1 is BGP peered to R2, R3, R4, and R5 inside ASN 1, with no other peer connections inside the AS. R1 is a route reflector, serving R2 and R3 only. Each router also has an eBGP connection, through which it learns the following routes: 1.0.0.0/8 by R1, 2.0.0.0/8 by R2, 3.0.0.0/8 by R3, 4.0.0.0/8 by R4, and 5.0.0.0/8 by R5. Which of the following are true regarding the propagation of these routes?

    a. NLRI 1.0.0.0/8 is forwarded by R1 to each of the other routers.

    b. NLRI 2.0.0.0/8 is sent by R2 to R1, with R1 forwarding only to R3.

    c. NLRI 3.0.0.0/8 is sent by R3 to R1, with R1 forwarding to R2, R4, and R5.

    d. NLRI 4.0.0.0/8 is sent by R4 to R1, but R1 does not forward the information to R2 or R3.

    e. NLRI 5.0.0.0/8 is sent by R5 to R1; R1 reflects the route to R2 and R3, but not to R4.

12. R1 is in confederation ASN 65001; R2 and R3 are in confederation ASN 65023. R1 is peered to R2, and R2 is peered to R3. These three routers are perceived to be in AS 1 by eBGP peers. Which of the following is true regarding the configuration of these routers?

    a. Each of the three routers has a **router bgp 1** command.

    b. Both R2 and R3 need a **bgp confederation peers 65001** BGP subcommand.

    c. R1 needs a **bgp confederation identifier 1** BGP subcommand.

    d. Both R2 and R3 need a **bgp confederation identifier 65023** BGP subcommand.

Foundation Topics

Like Interior Gateway Protocols (IGP), BGP exchanges topology information for routers to eventually learn the best routes to a set of IP prefixes. Unlike IGPs, BGP does not use a metric to select the best route among alternate routes to the same destination. Instead, BGP uses several BGP *path attributes (PA)* and an involved decision process when choosing between multiple possible routes to the same subnet.

BGP uses the BGP *autonomous system path (AS_PATH)* PA as its default metric mechanism when none of the other PAs has been overly set and configured. Generally speaking, BGP uses PAs to describe the characteristics of a route; this introduces and explains a wide variety of BGP PAs. The AS_PATH attribute lists the path, as defined by a sequence of *autonomous system numbers (ASN)* through which a packet must pass to reach a prefix. Figure 1-1 shows an example.

[handwritten margin notes: ø no metric ↓ path attributes]

[handwritten margin notes: AS_PATH-def metric]

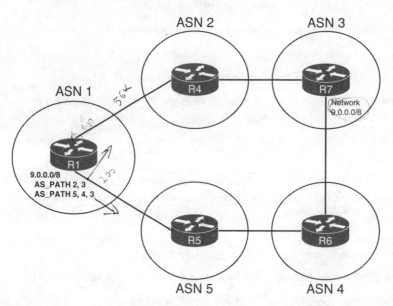

Figure 1-1 *BGP AS_PATHs and Path Vector Logic*

Figure 1-1 shows a classic case of how BGP uses *path vector* logic to choose routes. In the figure, R1 learns of two AS_PATHs by which to reach 9.0.0.0/8—through ASNs 2-3 and through ASNs 5-4-3. If none of the routers has used routing policies to influence other PAs that influence BGP's choice of which route is best, R1 will choose the shortest AS_PATH—in this case, AS_PATH 2-3. In effect, BGP treats the AS_PATH as a vector, and the length of the vector (the number of ASNs in the path) determines the best route. With BGP, the term *route* still refers to traditional hop-by-hop IP routes, but the term *path* refers to the sequence of autonomous systems used to reach a particular destination.

[handwritten margin note: bgp def shortest path]

This chapter follows a similar sequence as several of the IGP chapters. First, the text focuses on neighbor relationships, followed by how BGP exchanges routing information with its neighbors. The chapter ends with a section covering how BGP adds IP routes to a router's IP routing table based on the BGP topology table.

Building BGP Neighbor Relationships

BGP neighbors form a TCP connection with each neighbor, sending BGP messages over the connections—culminating in *BGP Update* messages that contain the routing information. Each router explicitly configures its neighbors' IP addresses, using these definitions to tell a router with which IP addresses to attempt a TCP connection. Also, if a router receives a TCP connection request (to BGP port 179) from a source IP address that is not configured as a BGP neighbor, the router rejects the request.

After the TCP connection is established, BGP begins with BGP *Open* messages. After a pair of BGP Open messages has been exchanged, the neighbors have reached the *established* state, which is the stable state of two working BGP peers. At this point, BGP Update messages can be exchanged.

This section examines many of the details about protocols and configuration for BGP neighbor formation. If you are already familiar with BGP, Table 1-2 summarizes some of the key facts found in this section.

Table 1-2 *BGP Neighbor Summary Table*

BGP Feature	Description and Values
TCP port	179
Setting the keepalive interval and hold time (using the **bgp timers** *keepalive holdtime* router subcommand or **neighbor timers** command, per neighbor)	Default to 60 and 180 seconds; define time between keepalives and time for which silence means that the neighbor has failed
What makes a neighbor internal BGP (iBGP)?	Neighbor is in the same AS
What makes a neighbor external BGP (eBGP)?	Neighbor is in another AS
How is the BGP router ID (RID) determined?	In order: 1. The **bgp router-id** command 2. The highest IP of an up/up loopback at the time that the BGP process starts 3. The highest IP of another up/up interface at the time that the BGP process starts
How is the source IP address used to reach a neighbor determined?	Defined with the **neighbor update-source** command; or, by default, uses the outgoing interface IP address for the route used to reach the neighbor

(handwritten margin notes:) BGP update messages → routing info • explicit config needed for neighbor rel.

(handwritten: "Key Topic")

BGP Feature	Description and Values
How is the destination IP address used to reach a neighbor determined?	Explicitly defined in the **neighbor** command
Auto-summary*	Off by default, enabled with the **auto-summary** router subcommand
Neighbor authentication	MD5 only, using the **neighbor password** command

* Cisco changed the IOS default for BGP **auto-summary** to be disabled as of Cisco IOS Software Release 12.3.

Internal BGP Neighbors

A BGP router considers each neighbor to be either an *internal BGP (iBGP)* peer or an *external BGP (eBGP)* peer. Each BGP router resides in a single AS, so neighbor relationships are either with other routers in the same AS (iBGP neighbors) or with routers in other autonomous systems (eBGP neighbors). The two types of neighbors differ only slightly in regard to forming neighbor relationships, with more significant differences in how the type of neighbor (iBGP or eBGP) impacts the BGP update process and the addition of routes to the routing tables.

iBGP peers often use loopback interface IP addresses for BGP peering to achieve higher availability. Inside a single AS, the physical topology often has at least two routes between each pair of routers. If BGP peers use an interface IP address for their TCP connections, and that interface fails, there still might be a route between the two routers, but the underlying BGP TCP connection will fail. Anytime two BGP peers have more than one route through which they can reach the other router, peering using loopbacks makes the most sense.

Several examples that follow demonstrate BGP neighbor configuration and protocols, beginning with Example 1-1. The example shows some basic BGP configuration for iBGP peers R1, R2, and R3 in AS 123, with the following features, based on Figure 1-2.

- The three routers in ASN 123 will form iBGP neighbor relationships with each other (full mesh).

- R1 will use the **bgp router-id** command to configure its RID, rather than use a loopback.

- R3 uses a **peer-group** configuration for neighbors R1 and R2. This allows fewer configuration commands, and improves processing efficiency by having to prepare only one set of outbound Update packets for the peer group. (Identical Updates are sent to all peers in the peer group.)

- The R1-R3 relationship uses BGP MD5 authentication, which is the only type of BGP authentication supported in Cisco IOS.

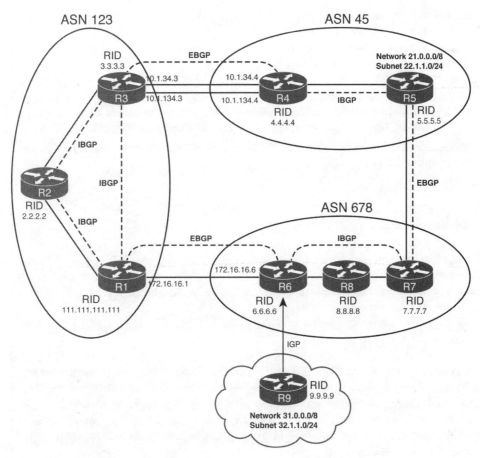

Figure 1-2 *Sample Network for BGP Neighbor Configuration*

Example 1-1 *Basic iBGP Configuration of Neighbors*

```
! R1 Config—R1 correctly sets its update-source to 1.1.1.1 for both R2 and R3,
! in order to match the R2 and R3 neighbor commands. The first three highlighted
! commands below were not typed, but added automatically as defaults by IOS 12.3
! in fact, IOS 12.3 docs imply that the defaults of sync and auto-summary at
! IOS 12.2 has changed to no sync and no auto-summary as of IOS 12.3. Also, R1
! knows that neighbors 2.2.2.2 and 3.3.3.3 are iBGP because their remote-as values
! match R1's router BGP command.
interface Loopback1
 ip address 1.1.1.1 255.255.255.255
!
router bgp 123
 no synchronization
 bgp router-id 111.111.111.111
 bgp log-neighbor-changes
 neighbor 2.2.2.2 remote-as 123
```

```
 neighbor 2.2.2.2 update-source Loopback1
 neighbor 3.3.3.3 remote-as 123
 neighbor 3.3.3.3 password secret-pw
 neighbor 3.3.3.3 update-source Loopback1
 no auto-summary
! R3 Config—R3 uses a peer group called "my-as" for combining commands related
! to R1 and R2. Note that not all parameters must be in the peer group: R3-R2 does
! not use authentication, but R3-R1 does, so the neighbor password command was
! not placed inside the peer group, but instead on a neighbor 1.1.1.1 command.
interface Loopback1
 ip address 3.3.3.3 255.255.255.255
!
router bgp 123
 no synchronization
 bgp log-neighbor-changes
 neighbor my-as peer-group
 neighbor my-as remote-as 123
 neighbor my-as update-source Loopback1
 neighbor 1.1.1.1 peer-group my-as
 neighbor 1.1.1.1 password secret-pw
 neighbor 2.2.2.2 peer-group my-as
 no auto-summary
! Next, R1 has two established peers, but the fact that the status is "established"
! is implied by not having the state listed on the right side of the output, under
! the heading State/PfxRcd. Once established, that column lists the number of
! prefixes learned via BGP Updates received from each peer. Note also R1's
! configured RID, and the fact that it is not used as the update source.
R1# show ip bgp summary
BGP router identifier 111.111.111.111, local AS number 123
BGP table version is 1, main routing table version 1
```

Neighbor	V	AS	MsgRcvd	MsgSent	TblVer	InQ	OutQ	Up/Down	State/PfxRcd
2.2.2.2	4	123	59	59	0	0	0	00:56:52	0
3.3.3.3	4	123	64	64	0	0	0	00:11:14	0

A few features in Example 1-1 are particularly important. First, note that the configuration does not overtly define peers as iBGP or eBGP. Instead, each router examines its own ASN as defined in the **router bgp** command, and compares that value to the neighbor's ASN listed in the **neighbor remote-as** command. If they match, the peer is iBGP; if not, the peer is eBGP.

R3 in Example 1-1 shows how to use the **peer-group** construct to reduce the number of configuration commands. BGP peer groups do not allow any new BGP configuration settings; they simply allow you to group BGP neighbor configuration settings into a group, and then apply that set of settings to a neighbor using the **neighbor peer-group** command. Additionally, BGP builds one set of Update messages for the peer group, applying routing policies for the entire group—rather than one router at a time—thereby reducing some BGP processing and memory overhead.

External BGP Neighbors

The physical topology between eBGP peers is often a single link, mainly because the connection is between different companies in different autonomous systems. As a result, eBGP peering can simply use the interface IP addresses for redundancy, because if the link fails, the TCP connection will fail because there is no longer an IP route between the peers. For example, in Figure 1-2, the R1-R6 eBGP peering uses interface IP addresses defined in the **neighbor** commands.

When IP redundancy exists between two eBGP peers, the eBGP **neighbor** commands should use loopback IP addresses to take advantage of that redundancy. For example, two parallel links exist between R3 and R4. With **neighbor** commands that reference loopback addresses, either of these links could fail, but the TCP connection would remain. Example 1-2 shows additional configuration for the network in Figure 1-2, showing the use of loopbacks between R3 and R4, and interface addresses between R1 and R6.

Example 1-2 *Basic eBGP Configuration of Neighbors*

```
! R1 Config -This example shows only commands added since Example 1-1.
router bgp 123
 neighbor 172.16.16.6 remote-as 678
! R1 does not have a neighbor 172.16.16.6 update-source command configured. R1
! uses its s0/0/0.6 IP address, 172.16.16.1, because R1's route to 172.16.16.6
! uses s0/0/0.6 as the outgoing interface, as seen below.
R1# show ip route 172.16.16.6
Routing entry for 172.16.16.0/24
  Known via "connected", distance 0, metric 0 (connected, via interface)
  Routing Descriptor Blocks:
  * directly connected, via Serial0/0/0.6
      Route metric is 0, traffic share count is 1
R1# show ip int brief | include 0/0/0.6
Serial0/0/0.6               172.16.16.1        YES manual up              up
! R3 Config—Because R3 refers to R4's loopback (4.4.4.4), and R4 is an eBGP
! peer, R3 and R4 have added the neighbor ebgp-multihop command to set TTL to 2.
! R3's update source must be identified as its loopback in order to match
! R4's neighbor 3.3.3.3 commands.
router bgp 123
 neighbor 4.4.4.4 remote-as 45
 neighbor 4.4.4.4 update-source loopback1
 neighbor 4.4.4.4 ebgp-multihop 2
! R3 now has three working neighbors. Also note the three TCP connections, one for
! each BGP peer. Note that because R3 is listed using a dynamic port number, and
! R4 as using port 179, R3 actually initiated the TCP connection to R4.
R3# show ip bgp summary
BGP router identifier 3.3.3.3, local AS number 123
BGP table version is 1, main routing table version 1
```

[handwritten margin note: EBGP- MULTIHOP]

```
Neighbor        V   AS MsgRcvd MsgSent   TblVer  InQ OutQ Up/Down  State/PfxRcd
1.1.1.1         4  123     247     247        0    0    0 03:14:49           0
2.2.2.2         4  123     263     263        0    0    0 03:15:07           0
4.4.4.4         4   45      17      17        0    0    0 00:00:11           0
R3# show tcp brief
TCB        Local Address         Foreign Address        (state)
649DD08C   3.3.3.3.179           2.2.2.2.43521          ESTAB
649DD550   3.3.3.3.179           1.1.1.1.27222          * ESTAB
647D928C   3.3.3.3.21449         4.4.4.4.179            ESTAB
```

EBGP-MULTIHOP ONLY WITH "EBGP!"

The eBGP configurations differ from iBGP configuration in a couple of small ways. First, the **neighbor remote-as** commands refer to a different AS than does the **router bgp** command, which implies that the peer is an eBGP peer. Second, R3 had to configure the **neighbor 4.4.4.4 ebgp-multihop 2** command (and R4 with a similar command) or the peer connection would not have formed. For eBGP connections, Cisco IOS defaults the IP packet's TTL field to a value of 1, based on the assumption that the interface IP addresses will be used for peering (like R1-R6 in Example 1-2). In this example, if R3 had not used multihop, it would have sent packets to R4 with TTL 1. R4 would have received the packet (TTL 1 at that point) and then attempted to route the packet to its loopback interface—a process that would decrement the TTL to 0, causing R4 to drop the packet. So, even though the router is only one hop away, think of the loopback as being on the other side of the router, requiring that extra hop.

Checks Before Becoming BGP Neighbors

Similar to IGPs, BGP checks certain requirements before another router can become a neighbor, reaching the BGP established state. Most of the settings are straightforward; the only tricky part relates to the use of IP addresses. The following list describes the checks that BGP performs when forming neighbor relationships:

Key Topic

1. The router must receive a TCP connection request with a source address that the router finds in a BGP **neighbor** command.

2. A router's ASN (on the **router bgp** *asn* command) must match the neighboring router's reference to that ASN with its **neighbor remote-as** *asn* command. (This requirement is not true of confederation configurations.)

3. The BGP RIDs of the two routers must not be the same.

4. If configured, MD5 authentication must pass.

Figure 1-3 shows the first three items in the list graphically, with R3 initiating a BGP TCP connection to R1. The circled numbers 1, 2, and 3 in the figure correspond to the item numbers in the previous list. Note that R1's check at Step 2 uses the **neighbor** command R1 identified as part of Step 1.

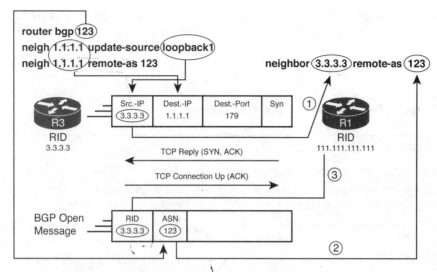

Note: R3's Loopback IP Address is 3.3.3.3

Figure 1-3 *BGP Neighbor Parameter Checking*

In Figure 1-3, R3 initiates a TCP connection with its update source IP address (3.3.3.3) as the source address of the packet. The first check occurs when R1 receives the first packet, looks at the source IP address of the packet (3.3.3.3), and finds that address in a **neighbor** command. The second check has R1 comparing R3's stated ASN (in R3's BGP Open message) to R1's **neighbor** command it identified at Step 1. Step 3 checks to ensure that the BGP RIDs are unique, with the BGP Open message stating the sender's BGP RID.

While the check at Step 1 might seem intuitive, interestingly, the reverse bit of logic does not have to be true for the neighbors to come up. For example, if R1 did not have a **neighbor 3.3.3.3 update-source 1.1.1.1** command, the process shown in Figure 1-3 would still work. Succinctly put, only one of the two routers' update source IP addresses needs to be in the other router's **neighbor** command for the neighbor to come up. Examples 1-1 and 1-2 showed the correct update source on both routers, and that makes good sense, but it works with only one of the two.

BGP uses a *keepalive timer* to define how often that router sends BGP keepalive messages, and a *Hold timer* to define how long a router will wait without receiving a keepalive message before resetting a neighbor connection. The Open message includes each router's stated keepalive timer. If they do not match, each router uses the lower of the values for each of the two timers, respectively. *Mismatched settings do not prevent the routers from becoming neighbors.*

BGP Messages and Neighbor States

The desired state for BGP neighbors is the established state. In that state, the routers have formed a TCP connection, and they have exchanged Open messages, with the parameter checks having passed. At this point, topology information can be exchanged using Update messages. Table 1-3 lists the BGP neighbor states, along with some of their characteristics. Note that if the IP addresses mismatch, the neighbors settle into an active state.

Key Topic

Table 1-3 *BGP Neighbor States*

State	Listen for TCP?	Initiate TCP?	TCP Up?	Open Sent?	Open Received?	Neighbor Up?
Idle	No					
Connect	Yes					
Active	Yes	Yes				
Open sent	Yes	Yes	Yes	Yes		
Open confirm	Yes	Yes	Yes	Yes	Yes	
Established	Yes	Yes	Yes	Yes	Yes	Yes

BGP Message Types

BGP uses four basic messages. Table 1-4 lists the message types and provides a brief description of each.

Key Topic

Table 1-4 *BGP Message Types*

Message	Purpose
Open	Used to establish a neighbor relationship and exchange basic parameters.
Keepalive	Used to maintain the neighbor relationship, with nonreceipt of a keepalive message within the negotiated Hold timer causing BGP to bring down the neighbor connection. (The timers can be configured with the **bgp timers** *keepalive holdtime* subcommand or the **neighbor** [*ip-address* | *peer-group-name*] **timers** *keepalive holdtime* BGP subcommand.)
Update	Used to exchange routing information, as covered more fully in the next section.
Notification	Used when BGP errors occur; causes a reset to the neighbor relationship when sent.

Purposefully Resetting BGP Peer Connections

Example 1-3 shows how to reset neighbor connections by using the **neighbor shutdown** command and, along the way, shows the various BGP neighbor states. The example uses Routers R1 and R6 from Figure 1-2, as configured in Example 1-2.

Example 1-3   *Examples of Neighbor States (Continued)*

```
! R1 shuts down R6's peer connection. debug ip bgp shows moving to a down state,
! which shows as "Idle (Admin)" under show ip bgp summary.
R1# debug ip bgp
BGP debugging is on for address family: BGP IPv4
R1# conf t
Enter configuration commands, one per line.  End with CNTL/Z.
R1(config)# router bgp 123
R1(config-router)# neigh 172.16.16.6 shutdown
R1#
*Mar  4 21:01:45.946: BGP: 172.16.16.6 went from Established to Idle
*Mar  4 21:01:45.946: %BGP-5-ADJCHANGE: neighbor 172.16.16.6 Down Admin. shutdown
*Mar  4 21:01:45.946: BGP: 172.16.16.6 closing
R1# show ip bgp summary | include 172.16.16.6
172.16.16.6      4     678    353     353       0    0    0 00:00:06 Idle (Admin)
! Next, the no neighbor shutdown command reverses the admin state. The various
! debug messages (with some omitted) list the various states. Also note that the
! final message is the one log message in this example that occurs due to the
! default configuration of bgp log-neighbor-changes. The rest are the result of
! a debug ip bgp command.
R1# conf t
Enter configuration commands, one per line.  End with CNTL/Z.
R1(config)# router bgp 123
R1(config-router)# no neigh 172.16.16.6 shutdown
*Mar  4 21:02:16.958: BGP: 172.16.16.6 went from Idle to Active
*Mar  4 21:02:16.958: BGP: 172.16.16.6 open active, delay 15571ms
*Mar  4 21:02:29.378: BGP: 172.16.16.6 went from Idle to Connect
*Mar  4 21:02:29.382: BGP: 172.16.16.6 rcv message type 1, length (excl. header) 26
*Mar  4 21:02:29.382: BGP: 172.16.16.6 rcv OPEN, version 4, holdtime 180 seconds
*Mar  4 21:02:29.382: BGP: 172.16.16.6 went from Connect to OpenSent
*Mar  4 21:02:29.382: BGP: 172.16.16.6 sending OPEN, version 4, my as: 123,
  holdtime 180   seconds
*Mar  4 21:02:29.382: BGP: 172.16.16.6 rcv OPEN w/ OPTION parameter len: 16
BGP: 172.16.16.6 rcvd OPEN w/ remote AS 678
*Mar  4 21:02:29.382: BGP: 172.16.16.6 went from OpenSent to OpenConfirm
*Mar  4 21:02:29.382: BGP: 172.16.16.6 send message type 1, length (incl. header)
  45
*Mar  4 21:02:29.394: BGP: 172.16.16.6 went from OpenConfirm to Established
*Mar  4 21:02:29.398: %BGP-5-ADJCHANGE: neighbor 10.16.16.6 Up
```

All BGP neighbors can be reset with the **clear ip bgp *** EXEC command, which, like the **neighbor shutdown** command, resets the neighbor connection, closes the TCP connection to that neighbor, and removes all entries from the BGP table learned from that neighbor. The **clear** command will be shown in the rest of the chapter as needed, including in coverage of how to clear just some neighbors.

Note The **clear** command can also be used to implement routing policy changes without resetting the neighbor completely, using a feature called *soft reconfiguration*, as covered in the Chapter 2 section, "Soft Reconfiguration."

SOFT RECONFIG (handwritten)

Building the BGP Table

The BGP *topology table*, also called the BGP *Routing Information Base (RIB)*, holds the *network layer reachability information (NLRI)* learned by BGP, as well as the associated PAs. An NLRI is simply an IP prefix and prefix length. This section focuses on the process of how BGP injects NLRI into a router's BGP table, followed by how routers advertise their associated PAs and NLRI to neighbors.

path attribute (handwritten)

Note Technically, BGP does not advertise routes; rather, it advertises PAs plus a set of NLRI that shares the same PA values. However, most people simply refer to NLRI as *BGP prefixes* or *BGP routes*. This book uses all three terms. However, because there is a distinction between a BGP route in the BGP table and an IP route in the IP routing table, the text takes care to refer to the BGP table or IP routing table to distinguish the two tables.

Injecting Routes/Prefixes into the BGP Table

Unsurprisingly, an individual BGP router adds entries to its local BGP table by using the same general methods used by IGPs: by using the **network** command, by hearing the topology information through an Update message from a neighbor, or by redistributing from another routing protocol. The next few sections show examples of how a local BGP router adds routes to the BGP table by methods other than learning them from a BGP neighbor.

BGP network Command

This section, and the next section, assumes that the BGP **no auto-summary** command has been configured. Note that as of the Cisco IOS Software Release 12.3 Mainline, **no auto-summary** is the default; earlier releases defaulted to use **auto-summary**. Following that, the section "Impact of Auto-Summary on Redistributed Routes and the network Command," later in this chapter, discusses the impact of the **auto-summary** command on both the **network** command and the **redistribute** command.

The BGP **network** router subcommand differs significantly from the **network** command used by IGPs. The BGP **network** command instructs that router's BGP process to do the following:

Key Topic

Look for a route in the router's current IP routing table that exactly matches the parameters of the **network** command; if the IP route exists, put the equivalent NLRI into the local BGP table.

With this logic, connected routes, static routes, or IGP routes could be taken from the IP routing table and placed into the BGP table for later advertisement. When the router removes that route from its IP routing table, BGP then removes the NLRI from the BGP table, and notifies neighbors that the route has been withdrawn.

Note that the IP route must be matched exactly when the **no auto-summary** command is configured or used by default.

Table 1-5 lists a few of the key features of the BGP **network** command, whose generic syntax is

```
network {network-number [mask network-mask]} [route-map map-tag]
```

Table 1-5 *Key Features of the BGP* network *Command*

Feature	Implication
No mask is configured	Assumes the default classful mask.
Matching logic with **no auto-summary** configured	An IP route must match both the prefix and prefix length (mask).
Matching logic with **auto-summary** configured	If the **network** command lists a classful network, it matches if any subnets of the classful network exist.
NEXT_HOP of BGP route added to the BGP table*	Uses next hop of IP route.
Maximum number injected by the **network** command into one BGP process	Limited by NVRAM and RAM.
Purpose of the **route-map** option on the **network** command	Can be used to filter routes and manipulate PAs, including NEXT_HOP*.

*NEXT_HOP is a BGP PA that denotes the next-hop IP address that should be used to reach the NLRI.

Example 1-4 shows a sample **network** command as implemented on R5 of Figure 1-4 (R5's BGP neighbors have been shut down so that the BGP table shows only BGP table entries created by the **network** commands on R5). In Example 1-4, R5 uses two **network** commands to add 21.0.0.0/8 and 22.1.1.0/24 to its BGP table.

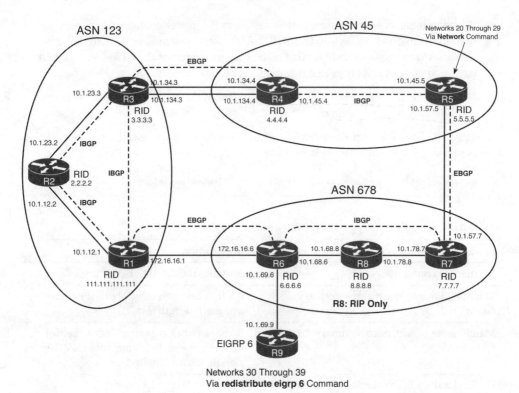

Figure 1-4   *Sample BGP Network, with IP Addresses*

Example 1-4   *Examples of Populating the BGP Table Through the* **network** *Command*

```
! On R5, the network commands specifically match prefixes 21.0.0.0/8 and
! 22.1.1.0/24. The omission of the mask on the first command implies the associated
! classful mask of 255.0.0.0, as the IP address listed (21.0.0.0) is a class A
! address.
router bgp 45
 no synchronization
 bgp log-neighbor-changes
 network 21.0.0.0
 network 22.1.1.0 mask 255.255.255.0
! The neighbor commands are not shown, as they are not pertinent to the topics
! covered in this example.
! Next, the two routes matched by the network commands are indeed in the IP
! routing table. Note that the route to 21.0.0.0/8 is a connected route, and the
! route to 22.1.1.0/24 is a static route.
R5# show ip route | incl 21 | 22
C    21.0.0.0/8 is directly connected, Loopback20
     22.0.0.0/24 is subnetted, 1 subnets
S       22.1.1.0 [1/0] via 10.1.5.9
! Below, the prefixes have been added to the BGP table. Note that the NEXT_HOP
```

```
! PA has been set to 0.0.0.0 for the route (21.0.0.0/8) that was taken from a
! connected route, with the NEXT_HOP for 22.1.1.0/24 matching the IP route.
R5# show ip bgp
BGP table version is 38, local router ID is 5.5.5.5
Status codes: s suppressed, d damped, h history, * valid, > best, i - internal,
              r RIB-failure, S Stale
Origin codes: i - IGP, e - EGP, ? - incomplete

   Network          Next Hop            Metric LocPrf Weight Path
*> 21.0.0.0         0.0.0.0                  0           32768 i
*> 22.1.1.0/24      10.1.5.9                 0           32768 i
```

Connected (handwritten annotation with arrow pointing to 0.0.0.0)

Redistributing from an IGP, Static, or Connected Route

The BGP **redistribute** subcommand can redistribute static, connected, and IGP-learned routes. This section covers a few nuances that are unique to BGP.

BGP does not use the concept of calculating a metric for each alternate route to reach a particular prefix. Instead, BGP uses a stepwise decision process that examines various PAs to determine the best route. As a result, redistribution into BGP does not require any consideration of setting metrics. However, a router might need to apply a route map to the redistribution function to manipulate PAs, which in turn affects the BGP decision process. If a metric is assigned to a route injected into BGP, BGP assigns that metric value to the BGP *Multi-Exit Discriminator (MED)* PA, which is commonly referred to as *metric*.

Note Although this point is not unique to BGP, keep in mind that redistribution from an IGP causes two types of routes to be taken from the routing table—those learned by the routing protocol and those connected routes for which that routing protocol matches with a **network** command.

Example 1-5 shows R6 (from Figure 1-4) filling its BGP table through route redistribution from Enhanced IGRP (EIGRP) process 6 (as configured in Example 1-5 with the **router eigrp 6** command) and redistributing a single static route. EIGRP on R6 learns routes only for networks 30 through 39. The goals of this example are as follows:

■ Redistribute EIGRP routes for networks 31 and 32.

■ Redistribute the static route to network 34, and set the MED (metric) to 9.

■ Do not accidentally redistribute the connected routes that are matched by EIGRP's **network** commands.

■ Use the Cisco IOS Release 12.3 default setting of **no auto-summary**.

Example 1-5 shows the mistake of accidentally redistributing additional routes—the connected subnets of network 10.0.0.0 matched by EIGRP **network** commands. Later in the example, a route map is added to prevent the problem.

Example 1-5   *Example of Populating the BGP Table Through Redistribution*

```
! R6 redistributes EIGRP 6 routes and static routes below, setting the metric on
! redistributed static routes to 9. Note that EIGRP 6 matches subnets 10.1.68.0/24
! and 10.1.69.0/24 with its network command.
router bgp 678
 redistribute static metric 9
 redistribute eigrp 6
!
router eigrp 6
 network 10.0.0.0
!
ip route 34.0.0.0 255.255.255.0 null0
! Commands unrelated to populating the local BGP table are omitted.
! R6 has met the goal of injecting 31 and 32 from EIGRP, and 34 from static.
! It also accidentally picked up two subnets of 10.0.0.0/8 because EIGRP's network
! 10.0.0.0 command matched these connected subnets.
R6# show ip bgp
BGP table version is 1, local router ID is 6.6.6.6
Status codes: s suppressed, d damped, h history, * valid, > best, i - internal,
              r RIB-failure, S Stale
Origin codes: i - IGP, e - EGP, ? - incomplete
   Network          Next Hop         Metric LocPrf Weight Path
*> 10.1.68.0/24     0.0.0.0               0         32768 ?
*> 10.1.69.0/24     0.0.0.0               0         32768 ?
*> 31.0.0.0         10.1.69.9        156160         32768 ?
*> 32.1.1.0/24      10.1.69.9        156160         32768 ?
*> 34.0.0.0/24      0.0.0.0               9         32768 ?
! Below, note the metrics for the two EIGRP routes. The show ip bgp command output
! above shows how BGP assigned the MED (metric) that same value.
R6# show ip route eigrp
     32.0.0.0/24 is subnetted, 1 subnets
D       32.1.1.0 [90/156160] via 10.1.69.9, 00:12:17, FastEthernet0/0
D    31.0.0.0/8 [90/156160] via 10.1.69.9, 00:12:17, FastEthernet0/0
! Below, the redistribute eigrp command has been changed to the following, using
! a route map to only allow routes in networks in the 30s.
redist eigrp 6 route-map just-30-something
! The route map and ACLs used for the filtering are shown next. As a result, the
! two subnets of 10.0.0.0/8 will not be redistributed into the BGP table.
R6# show route-map
route-map just-30-something, permit, sequence 10
  Match clauses:
    ip address (access-lists): permit-30-39
  Set clauses:
  Policy routing matches: 0 packets, 0 bytes
R6# show access-list
```

```
Standard IP access list permit-30-39
    10 permit 32.0.0.0, wildcard bits 7.255.255.255 (1538 matches)
    20 permit 30.0.0.0, wildcard bits 1.255.255.255 (1130 matches)
```

Also note that the NEXT_HOP PA for each route either matches the next hop of the redistributed route or is 0.0.0.0 for connected routes and routes to null0.

Impact of Auto-Summary on Redistributed Routes and the network Command

As it does with IGPs, the BGP **auto-summary** command causes a classful summary route to be created if any component subnet of that summary exists. However, unlike IGPs, the BGP **auto-summary** router subcommand causes BGP to summarize only those routes *injected because of redistribution on that router*. BGP **auto-summary** does not look for classful network boundaries in the topology, and it does not look at routes already in the BGP table. It simply looks for routes injected into the BGP because of the **redistribute** and **network** commands on that same router.

[handwritten margin note: only auto-sum routes injected because of the redistr on that router]

The logic differs slightly based on whether the route is injected with the **redistribute** command or the **network** command. The logic for the two commands is summarized as follows:

Key Topic

- **redistribute:** If any subnets of a classful network would be redistributed, do not redistribute, but instead redistribute a route for the classful network.

- **network:** If a **network** command lists a classful network number, with the classful default mask or no mask, and any subnets of the classful network exist, inject a route for the classful network.

While the preceding definitions are concise for study purposes, a few points deserve further emphasis and explanation. First, for redistribution, the **auto-summary** command causes the redistribution process to inject only classful networks into the local BGP table, and no subnets. The **network** command, with **auto-summary** configured, still injects subnets based on the same logic already described in this chapter. In addition to that logic, if a **network** command matches the classful network number, BGP injects the classful network, as long as at least any one subnet of that classful network exists in the IP routing table.

Example 1-6 shows an example that points out the impact of the **auto-summary** command. The example follows these steps on Router R5 from Figure 1-2:

1. 10.15.0.0/16 is injected into BGP because of the **redistribute** command.

2. Auto-summary is configured, BGP is cleared, and now only 10.0.0.0/8 is in the BGP table.

3. Auto-summary and redistribution are disabled.

4. The **network 10.0.0.0** command, **network 10.12.0.0 mask 255.254.0.0** command, and **network 10.14.0.0 mask 255.255.0.0** command are configured. Only the last of these three commands exactly matches a current route, so only that route is injected into BGP.

5. Auto-summary is enabled, causing 10.0.0.0/8 to be injected, as well as the original 10.14.0.0/16 route.

Example 1-6 *Auto-Summary Impact on Routing Tables*

```
! R5 has shut down all neighbor connections, so the output of show ip bgp only
! shows routes injected on R5.
! Step 1 is below. Only 10.15.0.0/16 is injected by the current configuration. Note
! that the unrelated lines of output have been removed, and route-map only15 only
! matches 10.15.0.0/16.
R5# show run | be router bgp
router bgp 5
 no synchronization
 redistribute connected route-map only15
 no auto-summary
! Below, note the absence of 10.0.0.0/8 as a route, and the presence of
! 10.15.0.0/16,
! as well as the rest of the routes used in the upcoming steps.
R5# show ip route 10.0.0.0
Routing entry for 10.0.0.0/8, 4 known subnets
  Attached (4 connections)
  Redistributing via eigrp 99, bgp 5
  Advertised by bgp 5 route-map only15
C       10.14.0.0/16 is directly connected, Loopback10
C       10.15.0.0/16 is directly connected, Loopback10
C       10.12.0.0/16 is directly connected, Loopback10
C       10.13.0.0/16 is directly connected, Loopback10
! Only 10.15.0.0/16 is injected into BGP.
R5# show ip bgp
BGP table version is 2, local router ID is 5.5.5.5
Status codes: s suppressed, d damped, h history, * valid, > best, i - internal,
              r RIB-failure, S Stale
Origin codes: i - IGP, e - EGP, ? - incomplete

   Network          Next Hop          Metric LocPrf Weight Path
*> 10.15.0.0/16     0.0.0.0                0         32768 ?
! Next, step 2, where auto-summary is enabled. Now, 10.15.0.0/16 is no longer
! injected into BGP, but classful 10.0.0.0/8 is.
R5# conf t
Enter configuration commands, one per line.  End with CNTL/Z.
R5(config)# router bgp 5
R5(config-router)# auto-summary
R5(config-router)# ^Z
R5# clear ip bgp *
R5# show ip bgp
```

```
BGP table version is 2, local router ID is 5.5.5.5
Status codes: s suppressed, d damped, h history, * valid, > best, i - internal,
              r RIB-failure, S Stale
Origin codes: i - IGP, e - EGP, ? - incomplete

   Network          Next Hop            Metric LocPrf Weight Path
*> 10.0.0.0         0.0.0.0                  0         32768 ?
```

! Now, at step 3, **no auto-summary** disables automatic summarization, redistribution is
! disabled, and at step 4, the **network** commands are added. Note that 10.12.0.0/15 is
! not injected, as there is no exact match, nor is 10.0.0.0/8, as there is no exact
! match. However, 10.14.0.0/16 is injected due to the exact match of the prefix and
! prefix length.

```
R5# conf t
Enter configuration commands, one per line.  End with CNTL/Z.
R5(config)# router bgp 5
R5(config-router)# no auto-summary
R5(config-router)# no redist conn route-map only15
R5(config-router)# no redist connected
R5(config-router)# network 10.0.0.0
R5(config-router)# network 10.12.0.0 mask 255.254.0.0
R5(config-router)# network 10.14.0.0 mask 255.255.0.0
R5(config-router)# ^Z
R5# clear ip bgp *
R5# sh ip bgp | begin network
   Network          Next Hop            Metric LocPrf Weight Path
*> 10.14.0.0/16     0.0.0.0                  0         32768 i
```

(handwritten annotation: ← not exact match to 10.12.0.0/16)

(handwritten annotation: } no auto-sum)

! Finally, **auto-summary** is re-enabled (not shown in the example).
! 10.14.0.0/16 is still an exact match, so it is
! still injected. 10.0.0.0/8 is also injected because of the **network 10.0.0.0**
! command.

```
R5# sh ip bgp | begin network
   Network          Next Hop            Metric LocPrf Weight Path
*  10.0.0.0         0.0.0.0                  0         32768 i
*  10.14.0.0/16     0.0.0.0                  0         32768 i
```

(handwritten annotation: } auto-sum with an exactly matching network command)

Manual Summaries and the AS_PATH Path Attribute

As covered in the last several pages, a router can add entries to its BGP table using the **network** command and route redistribution. Additionally, BGP can use manual route summarization to advertise summary routes to neighboring routers, causing the neighboring routers to learn additional BGP routes. BGP manual summarization with the **aggregate-address** command differs significantly from using the **auto-summary** command. It can summarize based on any routes in the BGP table, creating a summary of any prefix length. It does not always suppress the advertisement of the component subnets, although it can be configured to do so.

The aggregate route must include the AS_PATH PA, just like it is required for every other NLRI in the BGP table. However, to fully understand what this command does, you need to take a closer look at the AS_PATH PA.

The AS_PATH PA consists of up to four different components, called *segments*, as follows:

- AS_SEQ (short for AS Sequence)

- AS_SET

- AS_CONFED_SEQ (short for AS Confederation Sequence)

- AS_CONFED_SET

The most commonly used segment is called AS_SEQ. AS_SEQ is the idea of AS_PATH as shown back in Figure 1-1, with the PA representing all ASNs, in order, through which the route has been advertised.

However, the **aggregate-address** command can create a summary route for which the AS_SEQ must be null. When the component subnets of the summary route have differing AS_SEQ values, the router simply can't create an accurate representation of AS_SEQ, so it uses a null AS_SEQ. However, this action introduces the possibility of creating routing loops, because the contents of AS_PATH, specifically AS_SEQ, are used so that when a router receives an update, it can ignore prefixes for which its own ASN is listed.

The AS_PATH AS_SET segment solves the problem when the summary route has a null AS_SEQ. The AS_SET segment holds an unordered list of all the ASNs in all the component subnets' AS_SEQ segments.

Example 1-7 shows an example in which the router does use a null AS_SEQ for a summary route, and then the same summary with the **as-set** option creating the AS_SET segment.

Example 1-7   *Route Aggregation and the* **as-set** *Option*

```
! Note that R3's routes to network 23 all have the same AS_PATH except one new
! prefix, which has an AS_PATH that includes ASN 678. As a result, R3 will
! create a null AS_SEQ for the summary route.
R3# show ip bgp | include 23
*> 23.3.0.0/20      4.4.4.4                          0 45 i
*> 23.3.16.0/20     4.4.4.4                          0 45 i
*> 23.3.32.0/19     4.4.4.4                          0 45 i
*> 23.3.64.0/18     4.4.4.4                          0 45 i
*> 23.3.128.0/17    4.4.4.4                          0 45 i
*> 23.4.0.0/16      4.4.4.4                          0 45 678 i
! The following command is now added to R3's BGP configuration:
aggregate-address 23.0.0.0 255.0.0.0 summary-only
```

```
! Note: R3 will not have a BGP table entry for 23.0.0.0/8; however, R3 will
! advertise this summary to its peers, because at least one component subnet
! exists.
! R1 has learned the prefix, NEXT_HOP 3.3.3.3 (R3's update source IP address for
! R1), but the AS_PATH is now null because R1 is in the same AS as R3.
! (Had R3-R1 been an eBGP peering, R3 would have prepended its own ASN.)
! Note that the next command is on R1.
```

```
R1# sh ip bgp | begin Network
   Network          Next Hop          Metric LocPrf Weight Path
*>i21.0.0.0         3.3.3.3                0    100      0 45 i
*>i23.0.0.0         3.3.3.3                0    100      0 i
```

← no AS_SET

```
! Next, R1 displays the AGGREGATOR PA, which identifies R3 (3.3.3.3) and its AS
! (123) as the aggregation point at which information is lost. Also, the phrase
! "atomic-aggregate" refers to the fact that the ATOMIC_AGGREGATE PA has also
! been set; this PA simply states that this NLRI is a summary.
```

```
R1# show ip bgp 23.0.0.0
BGP routing table entry for 23.0.0.0/8, version 45
Paths: (1 available, best #1, table Default-IP-Routing-Table)
Flag: 0x800
  Advertised to update-groups:
     2
  Local, (aggregated by 123 3.3.3.3), (received & used)
    3.3.3.3 (metric 2302976) from 3.3.3.3 (3.3.3.3)
      Origin IGP, metric 0, localpref 100, valid, internal, atomic-aggregate, best
! R6, in AS 678, receives the summary route from R1, but the lack of information
! in the current AS_PATH allows R6 to learn of the route, possibly causing
! a routing loop. (Remember, one of the component subnets, 23.4.0.0/16, came from
! ASN 678.)
```

```
R6# sh ip bgp nei 172.16.16.1 received-routes | begin Network
   Network          Next Hop          Metric LocPrf Weight Path
*> 21.0.0.0         172.16.16.1                            0 123 45 i
*> 23.0.0.0         172.16.16.1                            0 123 i
! The R3 configuration is changed as shown next to use the as-set option.
```

```
R3# aggregate-address 23.0.0.0 255.0.0.0 summary-only as-set
! R1 now has the AS_SET component of the AS_PATH PA, which includes an unordered
! list of all autonmous systems from all the component subnets' AS_PATHs on R3.
```

```
R1# sh ip bgp | begin Network
   Network          Next Hop          Metric LocPrf Weight Path
*>i21.0.0.0         3.3.3.3                0    100      0 45 i
*>i23.0.0.0         3.3.3.3                0    100      0 {45,678} i
! R6 does receive the 23.0.0.0 prefix from R1, then checks the AS_SET PA, notices
! its own ASN (678), and ignores the prefix to avoid a loop.
```

← AS-SET enabled

```
R6# sh ip bgp nei 172.16.16.1 received-routes | begin Network
   Network          Next Hop          Metric LocPrf Weight Path
*> 21.0.0.0         172.16.16.1                            0 123 45 i
```

Note AS_PATH includes the AS_CONFED_SEQ and AS_CONFED_SET segments as well, which are covered later, in the section "Confederations."

The following list summarizes the actions taken by the **aggregate-address** command when it creates a summary route:

- It does not create the summary if the BGP table does not currently have any routes for NLRI inside the summary.

- If all the component subnets are withdrawn from the aggregating router's BGP table, it also then withdraws the aggregate. (In other words, the router tells its neighbors that the aggregate route is no longer valid.)

- It sets the NEXT_HOP address of the summary, as listed in the local BGP table, as 0.0.0.0.

- It sets the NEXT_HOP address of the summary route, as advertised to neighbors, to the router's update source IP address for each neighbor, respectively.

- If the component subnets inside the summary all have the same AS_SEQ, it sets the new summary route's AS_SEQ to be exactly like the AS_SEQ of the component subnets.

- If the AS_SEQ of the component subnets differs in any way, it sets the AS_SEQ of the new summary route to null.

- When the **as-set** option has been configured, the router creates an AS_SET segment for the aggregate route, but only if the summary route's AS_SEQ is null.

- As usual, if the summary is advertised to an eBGP peer, the router prepends its own ASN to the AS_SEQ before sending the Update.

- It suppresses the advertisement of all component subnets if the **summary-only** keyword is used, advertises all of them if the **summary-only** keyword is omitted, or advertises a subset if the **suppress-map** option is configured.

Example 1-7 shows R3 from Figure 1-4 summarizing 23.0.0.0/8. R3 advertises the summary with ASN 123 as the only AS in the AS_SEQ, because some component subnets have AS_PATHs of 45, and others have 678 45. As a result, R3 uses a null AS_SEQ for the aggregate. The example goes on to show the impact of the **as-set** option.

Note Summary routes can also be added through another method. First, the router would create a static route, typically with destination of interface null0. Then, the prefix/length can be matched with the **network** command to inject the summary. This method does not filter any of the component subnets.

Table 1-6 summarizes the key topics regarding summarization using the **aggregate-address**, **auto-summary**, and **network** commands.

Table 1-6   *Summary: Injecting Summary Routes in BGP*

Command	Component Subnets Removed	Routes It Can Summarize
auto-summary (with redistribution)	All	Only those injected into BGP on that router using the **redistribute** command
aggregate-address	All, none, or a subset	Any prefixes already in the BGP table
auto-summary (with the **network** command)	None	Only those injected into BGP on that router using the **network** command

Adding Default Routes to BGP

The final method covered in this chapter for adding routes to a BGP table is to inject default routes into BGP. Default routes can be injected into BGP in one of three ways:

- By injecting the default using the **network** command

- By injecting the default using the **redistribute** command

- By injecting a default route into BGP using the **neighbor** *neighbor-id* **default-originate** [**route-map** *route-map-name*] BGP subcommand

When you inject a default route into BGP using the **network** command, a route to 0.0.0.0/0 must exist in the local routing table, and the **network 0.0.0.0** command is required. The default IP route can be learned through any means, but if it is removed from the IP routing table, BGP removes the default route from the BGP table.

Injecting a default route through redistribution requires an additional configuration command—**default-information originate**. The default route must first exist in the IP routing table; for example, a static default route to null0 could be created. Then, the **redistribute static** command could be used to redistribute that static default route. However, in the special case of the default route, Cisco IOS also requires the **default-originate** BGP subcommand.

Injecting a default route into BGP by using the **neighbor** *neighbor-id* **default-originate** [**route-map** *route-map-name*] BGP subcommand does not add a default route to the local BGP table; instead, it causes the advertisement of a default to the specified neighbor. In fact, this method does not even check for the existence of a default route in the IP routing table by default, but it can. With the **route-map** option, the referenced route map examines the entries in the IP routing table (not the BGP table); if a route map **permit** clause is matched, the default route is advertised to the neighbor. Example 1-8 shows just such an example on R1, with **route-map check-default** checking for the existence of a default route before R1 would originate a default route to R3.

Example 1-8 *Originating a Default Route to a Neighbor with the* **neighbor default-originate** *Command*

```
! The pertinent parts of the R1 configuration are listed next, with the route map
! matching an IP route to 0.0.0.0/0 with a permit action, enabling the
! advertisement of a default route to neighbor 3.3.3.3 (R3).
router bgp 123
 neighbor 3.3.3.3 remote-as 123
 neighbor 3.3.3.3 update-source Loopback1
 neighbor 3.3.3.3 default-originate route-map check-default
!
ip route 0.0.0.0 0.0.0.0 Null0
!
ip prefix-list def-route seq 5 permit 0.0.0.0/0
!
route-map check-default permit 10
 match ip address prefix-list def-route
! R1 indeed has a default route, as seen below.
R1# show ip route | include 0.0.0.0/0
S*    0.0.0.0/0 is directly connected, Null0
! R3 now learns a default route from R1, as seen below.
R3# show ip bgp | begin Network
   Network          Next Hop          Metric LocPrf Weight Path
*>i0.0.0.0          1.1.1.1                   100      0 i
```

ORIGIN Path Attribute

Depending on the method used to inject a route into a local BGP table, BGP assigns one of three BGP ORIGIN PA codes: IGP, EGP, or incomplete. The ORIGIN PA provides a general descriptor as to how a particular NLRI was first injected into a router's BGP table. The **show ip bgp** command includes the three possible values in the legend at the top of the command output, listing the actual ORIGIN code for each BGP route at the far right of each output line. Table 1-7 lists the three ORIGIN code names, the single-letter abbreviation used by Cisco IOS, and the reasons why a route is assigned a particular code.

Key Topic

The ORIGIN codes and meanings hide a few concepts that many people find counterintuitive. First, routes redistributed into BGP from an IGP actually have an ORIGIN code of incomplete. Also, do not confuse EGP with eBGP; an ORIGIN of EGP refers to Exterior Gateway Protocol, the very old and deprecated predecessor to BGP. In practice, the EGP ORIGIN code should not be seen today.

Table 1-7 *BGP ORIGIN Codes*

ORIGIN Code	Cisco IOS Notation	Used for Routes Injected Because of the Following Commands
IGP	i	**network**, **aggregate-address** (in some cases), and **neighbor default-originate** commands.
EGP	e	Exterior Gateway Protocol (EGP). No specific commands apply.
Incomplete	?	**redistribute**, **aggregate-address** (in some cases), and **default-information originate** command.

The rules regarding the ORIGIN codes used for summary routes created with the **aggregate-address** command can also be a bit surprising. The rules are summarized as follows:

- If the **as-set** option is not used, the aggregate route uses ORIGIN code i.

- If the **as-set** option is used, and all component subnets being summarized use ORIGIN code i, the aggregate has ORIGIN code i.

- If the **as-set** option is used, and at least one of the component subnets has an ORIGIN code ?, the aggregate has ORIGIN code ?.

Note The BGP ORIGIN PA provides a minor descriptor for the origin of a BGP table entry, which is used as part of the BGP decision process.

Advertising BGP Routes to Neighbors

The previous section focused on the tools that BGP can use to inject routes into a local router's BGP table. BGP routers take routes from the local BGP table and advertise a subset of those routes to their BGP neighbors. This section continues to focus on the BGP table because the BGP route advertisement process takes routes from the BGP table and sends them to neighboring routers, where the routes are added to the neighbors' BGP tables. Later, the final major section in the chapter, "Building the IP Routing Table," focuses on the rules regarding how BGP places routes into the IP routing table.

BGP Update Message

After a BGP table has a list of routes, paths, and prefixes, the router needs to advertise the information to neighboring routers. To do so, a router sends BGP Update messages to its neighbors. Figure 1-5 shows the general format of the BGP Update message.

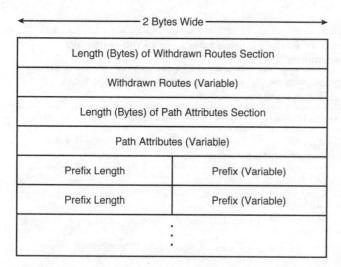

Figure 1-5 *BGP Update Message Format*

Each Update message has three main parts:

■   The Withdrawn Routes field enables BGP to inform its neighbors about failed routes.

■   The Path Attributes field lists the PAs for each route. NEXT_HOP and AS_PATH are sample values for this field.

■   The Prefix and Prefix Length fields define each individual NLRI.

The central concept in an individual Update message is the set of PAs. Then, all the prefixes (NLRIs) that share the exact same set of PAs and PA values are included at the end of the Update message. If a router needs to advertise a set of NLRIs, and each NLRI has a different setting for at least one PA, separate Update messages will be required for each NLRI. However, when many routes share the same PAs—typical of prefixes owned by a particular ISP, for example—multiple NLRIs are included in a single Update. This reduces router CPU load and uses less link bandwidth.

Determining the Contents of Updates

A router builds the contents of its Update messages based on the contents of its BGP table. However, the router must choose which subset of its BGP table entries to advertise to each neighbor, with the set likely varying from neighbor to neighbor. Table 1-8 summarizes the rules about which routes BGP does *not* include in routing updates to each neighbor; each rule is described more fully following the table.

Key Topic

Table 1-8 *Summary of Rules Regarding Which Routes BGP Does Not Include in an Update*

iBGP and/or eBGP	Routes Not Taken from the BGP Table
Both	Routes that are not considered "best"
Both	Routes matched by a **deny** clause in an outbound BGP filter
iBGP	iBGP-learned routes*

*This rule is relaxed or changed as a result of using route reflectors or confederations.

BGP only advertises a route to reach a particular subnet (NLRI) if that route is considered to be the best route. If a BGP router learns of only one route to reach a particular prefix, the decision process is very simple. However, when choosing between multiple paths to reach the same prefix, BGP determines the best route based on a lengthy BGP decision process, as discussed in the Chapter 2 section, "The BGP Decision Process." Assuming that none of the routers has configured any routing policies that impact the decision process, the decision tree reduces to a four-step process that is mainly composed of tie-breakers, as follows:

1. Choose the route with the shortest AS_PATH.

2. If AS_PATH length is a tie, prefer a single eBGP-learned route over one or more iBGP routes.

3. If the best route has not yet been chosen, choose the route with the lowest IGP metric to the NEXT_HOP of the routes.

4. If the IGP metric ties, choose the iBGP-learned route with the lowest BGP RID of the advertising router.

Additionally, BGP rules out some routes from being considered best based on the value of the NEXT_HOP PA. For a route to be a candidate to be considered best, the NEXT_HOP must be either

- 0.0.0.0, as the result of the route being injected on the local router.

- Reachable according to that router's current IP routing table. In other words, the NEXT_HOP IP address must match a route in the routing table.

Because the NEXT_HOP PA is so important with regard to BGP's choice of its best path to reach each NLRI, this section summarizes the logic and provides several examples. The logic is separated into two parts based on whether the route is being advertised to an iBGP or eBGP peer. By default, when sending to an eBGP peer, the NEXT_HOP is changed to an IP address on the advertising router—specifically, to the same IP address the router used as the source IP address of the BGP Update message, for each respective neighbor. When sending to an iBGP peer, the default action is to leave the NEXT_HOP PA unchanged. Both of these default behaviors can be changed through the commands listed in Table 1-9.

Table 1-9 *Conditions for Changing the NEXT_HOP PA*

Type of Neighbor	Default Action for Advertised Routes	Command to Switch to Other Behavior
iBGP	Do not change the NEXT_HOP	Neighbor... next-hop-self
eBGP	Change the NEXT_HOP to the update source IP address	Neighbor... next-hop-unchanged

Note that the NEXT_HOP PA cannot be set through a route map; the only way to change the NEXT_HOP PA is through the methods listed in Table 1-9.

Example: Impact of the Decision Process and NEXT_HOP on BGP Updates

The next several examples together show a sequence of events regarding the propagation of network 31.0.0.0/8 by BGP throughout the network of Figure 1-4. R6 originated the routes in the 30s (as in Example 1-4) by redistributing EIGRP routes learned from R9. The purpose of this series of examples is to explain how BGP chooses which routes to include in Updates under various conditions.

The first example, Example 1-9, focuses on the commands used to examine what R6 sends to R1, what R1 receives, and the resulting entries in R1's BGP table. The second example, Example 1-10, then examines those same routes propagated from R1 to R3, including problems related to R1's default behavior of not changing the NEXT_HOP PA of those routes. Finally, Example 1-11 shows the solution of R1's use of the **neighbor 3.3.3.3 next-hop-self** command, and the impact that has on the contents of the BGP Updates in AS 123.

Example 1-9 *R6 Sending the 30s Networks to R1 Using BGP*

```
! R6 has injected the three routes listed below; they were not learned from
! another BGP neighbor. Note all three show up as >, meaning they are the best
! (and only in this case) routes to the destination NLRIs.
R6# show ip bgp
BGP table version is 5, local router ID is 6.6.6.6
Status codes: s suppressed, d damped, h history, * valid, > best, i - internal,
              r RIB-failure, S Stale
Origin codes: i - IGP, e - EGP, ? - incomplete

   Network          Next Hop          Metric LocPrf Weight Path
*> 31.0.0.0         10.1.69.9         156160         32768 ?
*> 32.0.0.0         0.0.0.0                          32768 i
*> 32.1.1.0/24      10.1.69.9         156160         32768 ?
! R6 now lists the routes it advertises to R1-sort of. This command lists R6's
! BGP table entries that are intended to be sent, but R6 can (and will in this
! case) change the information before advertising to R1. Pay particular attention
```

```
! to the Next Hop column, versus upcoming commands on R1. In effect, this command
! shows R6's current BGP table entries that will be sent to R1, but it shows them
! before R6 makes any changes, including NEXT_HOP.
R6# show ip bgp neighbor 172.16.16.1 advertised-routes
BGP table version is 5, local router ID is 6.6.6.6
Status codes: s suppressed, d damped, h history, * valid, > best, i - internal,
              r RIB-failure, S Stale
Origin codes: i - IGP, e - EGP, ? - incomplete


   Network          Next Hop          Metric LocPrf Weight Path
*> 31.0.0.0         10.1.69.9         156160         32768 ?
*> 32.0.0.0         0.0.0.0                          32768 i
*> 32.1.1.0/24      10.1.69.9         156160         32768 ?
Total number of prefixes 3
! The next command (R1) lists the info in the received BGP update from R6. Note
! that the NEXT_HOP is different; R6 changed the NEXT_HOP before sending the
! update, because it has an eBGP peer connection to R1, and eBGP defaults to set
! NEXT_HOP to itself. As R6 was using 172.16.16.6 as the IP address from which to
! send BGP messages to R1, R6 set NEXT_HOP to that number. Also note that R1 lists
! the neighboring AS (678) in the Path column at the end, signifying the AS_PATH
! for the route.
R1# show ip bgp neighbor 172.16.16.6 received-routes
BGP table version is 7, local router ID is 111.111.111.111
Status codes: s suppressed, d damped, h history, * valid, > best, i - internal,
              r RIB-failure, S Stale
Origin codes: i - IGP, e - EGP, ? - incomplete


   Network          Next Hop          Metric LocPrf Weight Path
*> 31.0.0.0         172.16.16.6       156160          0 678 ?
*> 32.0.0.0         172.16.16.6            0          0 678 i
*> 32.1.1.0/24      172.16.16.6       156160          0 678 ?
Total number of prefixes 3
! The show ip bgp summary command lists the state of the neighbor until the
! neighbor becomes established; at that point, the State/PfxRcd column lists the
! number of NLRIs (prefixes) received (and still valid) from that neighbor.
R1# show ip bgp summary | begin Neighbor
Neighbor        V    AS MsgRcvd MsgSent   TblVer  InQ OutQ Up/Down  State/PfxRcd
2.2.2.2         4   123      55      57        7    0    0 00:52:30            0
3.3.3.3         4   123      57      57        7    0    0 00:52:28            3
172.16.16.6     4   678      53      51        7    0    0 00:48:50            3
! R1 has also learned of these prefixes from R3, as seen below. The routes through
! R6 have one AS in the AS_PATH, and the routes through R3 have two autonomous
! systems, so the routes through R6 are best. Also, the iBGP routes have an "i" for
! "internal" just before the prefix.
```

```
R1# show ip bgp
BGP table version is 7, local router ID is 111.111.111.111
Status codes: s suppressed, d damped, h history, * valid, > best, i - internal,
              r RIB-failure, S Stale
Origin codes: i - IGP, e - EGP, ? - incomplete

   Network          Next Hop         Metric LocPrf Weight Path
*  i31.0.0.0        3.3.3.3               0    100      0 45 678 ?
*>                  172.16.16.6      156160             0 678 ?
*  i32.0.0.0        3.3.3.3               0    100      0 45 678 i
*>                  172.16.16.6           0             0 678 i
*  i32.1.1.0/24     3.3.3.3               0    100      0 45 678 ?
*>                  172.16.16.6      156160             0 678 ?
```

Example 1-9 showed examples of how you can view the contents of the actual Updates sent to neighbors (using the **show ip bgp neighbor advertised-routes** command) and the contents of Updates received from a neighbor (using the **show ip bgp neighbor received-routes** command). RFC 1771 suggests that the BGP RIB can be separated into components for received Updates from each neighbor and sent Updates for each neighbor. Most implementations (including Cisco IOS) keep a single RIB, with notations as to which entries were sent and received to and from each neighbor.

Note   For the received-routes option to work, the router on which the command is used must have the **neighbor** *neighbor-id* **soft-reconfiguration inbound** BGP subcommand configured for the other neighbor.

These **show ip bgp neighbor** commands with the **advertised-routes** option list the BGP table entries that will be advertised to that neighbor. However, note that any changes to the PAs inside each entry are not shown in the command output. For example, the **show ip bgp neighbor 172.16.16.1 advertised-routes** command on R6 listed the NEXT_HOP for 31/8 as 10.1.69.9, which is true of that entry in R6's BGP table. R6 then changes the NEXT_HOP PA before sending the actual Update, with a NEXT_HOP of 172.16.16.6.

By the end of Example 1-9, R1 knows of both paths to each of the three prefixes in the 30s (AS_PATH 678 and 45-678), but has chosen the shortest AS_PATH (through R6) as the best path in each case. Note that the > in the **show ip bgp** output designates the routes as R1's best routes. Next, Example 1-10 shows some possibly surprising results on R3 related to its choices of best routes.

Example 1-10   *Examining the BGP Table on R3*

```
! R1 now updates R3 with R1's "best" routes
R1# show ip bgp neighbor 3.3.3.3 advertised-routes | begin Network
   Network          Next Hop         Metric LocPrf Weight Path
*> 31.0.0.0         172.16.16.6      156160             0 678 ?
*> 32.0.0.0         172.16.16.6           0             0 678 i
```

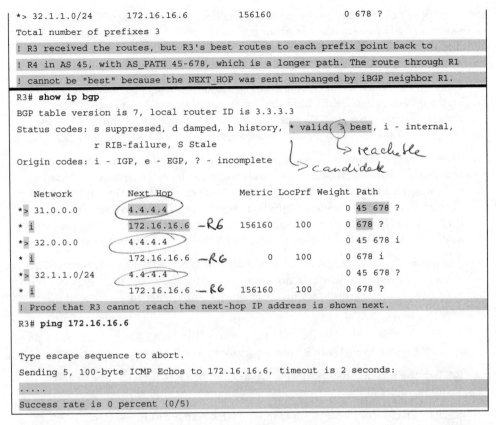

```
*> 32.1.1.0/24        172.16.16.6           156160              0 678 ?
Total number of prefixes 3
! R3 received the routes, but R3's best routes to each prefix point back to
! R4 in AS 45, with AS_PATH 45-678, which is a longer path. The route through R1
! cannot be "best" because the NEXT_HOP was sent unchanged by iBGP neighbor R1.
R3# show ip bgp
BGP table version is 7, local router ID is 3.3.3.3
Status codes: s suppressed, d damped, h history, * valid, > best, i - internal,
              r RIB-failure, S Stale
Origin codes: i - IGP, e - EGP, ? - incomplete

   Network          Next Hop            Metric LocPrf Weight Path
*> 31.0.0.0         4.4.4.4                                0 45 678 ?
*  i                172.16.16.6          156160    100     0 678 ?
*> 32.0.0.0         4.4.4.4                                0 45 678 i
*  i                172.16.16.6               0    100     0 678 i
*> 32.1.1.0/24      4.4.4.4                                0 45 678 ?
*  i                172.16.16.6          156160    100     0 678 ?
! Proof that R3 cannot reach the next-hop IP address is shown next.
R3# ping 172.16.16.6

Type escape sequence to abort.
Sending 5, 100-byte ICMP Echos to 172.16.16.6, timeout is 2 seconds:
.....
Success rate is 0 percent (0/5)
```

Example 1-10 points out a quirk with some terminology in the **show ip bgp** command output, as well as an important design choice with BGP. First, the command output lists * as meaning valid; however, that designation simply means that the route is a candidate for use. Before the route can be actually used and added to the IP routing table, the NEXT_HOP must also be reachable. In some cases, routes that the **show ip bgp** command considers "valid" might not be usable routes, with Example 1-10 showing just such an example.

Each BGP route's NEXT_HOP must be reachable for a route to be truly valid. With all default settings, an iBGP-learned route has a NEXT_HOP IP address of the last eBGP router to advertise the route. For example, R3's route to 31.0.0.0/8 through R1 lists R6's IP address (172.16.16.6) in the NEXT_HOP field. Unfortunately, R3 does not have a route for 172.16.16.6, so that route cannot be considered "best" by BGP.

There are two easy choices to solve the problem:

Key Topic

■ Make the eBGP neighbor's IP address reachable by advertising that subnet into the IGP.

■ Use the **next-hop-self** option on the **neighbor** command that points to iBGP peers.

The first option typically can be easily implemented. Because many eBGP neighbors use interface IP addresses on their **neighbor** commands, the NEXT_HOP exists in a subnet directly connected to the AS. For example, R1 is directly connected to 172.16.16.0/24, so R1 could simply advertise that connected subnet into the IGP inside the AS.

However, this option might be problematic when loopback addresses are used for BGP neighbors. For example, if R1 had been configured to refer to R6's 6.6.6.6 loopback IP address, and it was working, R1 must have a route to reach 6.6.6.6. However, it is less likely that R1 would already be advertising a route to reach 6.6.6.6 into ASN 123.

The second option causes the router to change the NEXT_HOP PA to one of its own IP addresses—an address that is more likely to already be in the neighbor's IP routing table, which works well even if using loopbacks with an eBGP peer. Example 1-11 points out such a case, with R1 using the **neighbor next-hop-self** command, advertising itself (1.1.1.1) as the NEXT_HOP. As a result, R3 changes its choice of best routes, because R3 has a route to reach 1.1.1.1, overcoming the "NEXT_HOP unreachable" problem.

Example 1-11 points out how an iBGP peer can set NEXT_HOP to itself. However, it's also a good example of how BGP decides when to advertise routes to iBGP peers. The example follows this sequence, with the command output showing evidence of these events:

1. The example begins like the end of Example 1-10, with R1 advertising routes with R6 as the next hop, and with R3 not being able to use those routes as best routes.

2. Because R3's best routes are eBGP routes (through R4), R3 is allowed to advertise those routes to R2.

3. R1 then changes its configuration to use NEXT_HOP SELF.

4. R3 is now able to treat the routes learned from R1 as R3's best routes.

5. R3 can no longer advertise its best routes to these networks to R2, because the new best routes are iBGP routes.

Example 1-11   *R3 Advertises the 30s Networks to R2, and Then R3 Withdraws the Routes*

```
! (Step 1): At this point, R3 still believes its best route to all three prefixes
! in the 30s is through R4; as those are eBGP routes, R3 advertises all three
! routes to iBGP peer R2, as seen next.
R3# show ip bgp neighbor 2.2.2.2 advertised-routes
BGP table version is 7, local router ID is 3.3.3.3
Status codes: s suppressed, d damped, h history, * valid, > best, i - internal,
              r RIB-failure, S Stale
Origin codes: i - IGP, e - EGP, ? - incomplete


   Network          Next Hop            Metric LocPrf Weight Path
*> 31.0.0.0         4.4.4.4                          0 45 678 ?
*> 32.0.0.0         4.4.4.4                          0 45 678 i
*> 32.1.1.0/24      4.4.4.4                          0 45 678 ?
```

```
Total number of prefixes 3
```
! (Step 2) R2 lists the number of prefixes learned from R3 next (3).

```
R2# show ip bgp summary | begin Neighbor
Neighbor        V    AS MsgRcvd MsgSent   TblVer  InQ OutQ Up/Down   State/PfxRcd
1.1.1.1         4   123     212     210        7    0    0 03:27:59         3
3.3.3.3         4   123     213     211        7    0    0 03:28:00         3
```
! (Step 3) R1 now changes to use **next-hop-self** to peer R3.

```
R1# conf t
Enter configuration commands, one per line.  End with CNTL/Z.
R1(config)# router bgp 123
R1(config-router)# neigh 3.3.3.3 next-hop-self
```
! (Step 4) R3 now lists the routes through R1 as best, because the new
! NEXT_HOP is R1's update source IP address, 1.1.1.1, which is reachable by R3.

```
R3# show ip bgp
BGP table version is 10, local router ID is 3.3.3.3
Status codes: s suppressed, d damped, h history, * valid, > best, i - internal,
              r RIB-failure, S Stale
Origin codes: i - IGP, e - EGP, ? - incomplete

   Network          Next Hop          Metric LocPrf Weight Path
*  31.0.0.0         4.4.4.4                              0 45 678 ?
*>i                 1.1.1.1           156160    100     0 678 ?
*  32.0.0.0         4.4.4.4                              0 45 678 i
*>i                 1.1.1.1                0    100     0 678 i
*  32.1.1.0/24      4.4.4.4                              0 45 678 ?
*>i                 1.1.1.1           156160    100     0 678 ?
```
! (Step 5) First, note above that all three "best" routes are iBGP routes, as noted
! by the "i" immediately before the prefix. R3 only advertises "best" routes, with
! the added requirement that it must not advertise iBGP routes to other iBGP peers.
! As a result, R3 has withdrawn the routes that had formerly been sent to R2.

```
R3# show ip bgp neighbor 2.2.2.2 advertised-routes


Total number of prefixes 0
```
! The next command confirms on R2 that it no longer has any prefixes learned from
! R3.

```
R2# show ip bgp summary | begin Neighbor
Neighbor        V    AS MsgRcvd MsgSent   TblVer  InQ OutQ Up/Down   State/PfxRcd
1.1.1.1         4   123     213     211        7    0    0 03:28:44         3
3.3.3.3         4   123     214     211        7    0    0 03:28:46         0
```

Summary of Rules for Routes Advertised in BGP Updates

The following list summarizes the rules dictating which routes a BGP router sends in its Update messages:

- Send only the best route listed in the BGP table.

- To iBGP neighbors, do not advertise paths learned from other iBGP neighbors.

- Do not advertise suppressed or dampened routes.

- Do not advertise routes filtered through configuration.

The first two rules have been covered in some depth in this section. The remaining rules are outside the scope of this book.

Building the IP Routing Table

So far, this chapter has explained how to form BGP neighbor relationships, how to inject routes into the BGP table, and how BGP routers choose which routes to propagate to neighboring routers. Part of that logic relates to how the BGP decision process selects a router's best route to each prefix, with the added restriction that the NEXT_HOP must be reachable before the route can be considered as a best route.

This section completes the last step in BGP's ultimate goal—adding the appropriate routes to the IP routing table. In its simplest form, BGP takes the already identified best BGP routes for each prefix and adds those routes to the IP routing table. However, there are some additional restrictions, mainly related to administrative distance (AD) (for eBGP and iBGP routes) and BGP synchronization (iBGP routes only). The sections that follow detail the exceptions.

Adding eBGP Routes to the IP Routing Table

Cisco IOS Software uses simple logic when determining which eBGP routes to add to the IP routing table. The only two requirements are as follows:

- The eBGP route in the BGP table is considered to be a "best" route.

- If the same prefix has been learned through another IGP or through static routes, the AD for BGP external routes must be lower than the ADs for other routing source(s).

By default, Cisco IOS considers eBGP routes to have AD 20, which gives eBGP routes a better (lower) AD than any other dynamic routing protocol's default AD (except for the AD 5 of EIGRP summary routes). The rationale behind the default is that eBGP-learned routes should never be prefixes from within an AS. Under normal conditions, eBGP-learned prefixes should seldom be seen as IGP-learned routes as well, but when they are, the BGP route would win by default.

BGP sets the AD differently for eBGP routes, iBGP routes, and for local (locally injected) routes—with defaults of 20, 200, and 200, respectively. These values can be overridden in two ways, both consistent with the coverage of AD in Chapter 9, "Device and Network Security":

- By using the **distance bgp** *external-distance internal-distance local-distance* BGP subcommand, which allows the simple setting of AD for eBGP-learned prefixes, iBGP-learned prefixes, and prefixes injected locally, respectively

- By changing the AD using the **distance** *distance {ip-address {wildcard-mask}} [ip-standard-list | ip-extended-list]* BGP subcommand

With BGP, the IP address and wildcard mask refer to the IP address used on the **neighbor** command for that particular neighbor, not the BGP RID or NEXT_HOP of the route. The ACL examines the BGP routes received from the neighbor, assigning the specified AD for any routes matching the ACL with a permit action.

EXPLANATION

Key Topic

Finally, a quick note is needed about the actual IP route added to the IP routing table. The route contains the exact same prefix, prefix length, and next-hop IP address as listed in the BGP table—even if the NEXT_HOP PA is an IP address that is not in a connected network. As a result, the IP forwarding process might require a recursive route lookup. Example 1-12 shows such a case on R3, where the three BGP routes each list a next hop of 1.1.1.1, which happens to be a loopback interface on R1. As you can see from Figure 1-4, R3 and R1 have no interfaces in common. The route to 1.1.1.1 lists the actual next-hop IP address to which a packet would be forwarded.

Example 1-12 *R3 Routes with Next Hop 1.1.1.1, Requiring Recursive Route Lookup*

```
! Packets forwarded to 31.0.0.0/8 match the last route, with next-hop 1.1.1.1; R3
! then finds the route that matches destination 1.1.1.1 (the first route), finding
! the appropriate next-hop IP address and outgoing interface.
R3# show ip route | incl 1.1.1.1
D       1.1.1.1 [90/2809856] via 10.1.23.2, 04:01:44, Serial0/0/1
B       32.1.1.0/24 [200/156160] via 1.1.1.1, 00:01:00
B       32.0.0.0/8 [200/0] via 1.1.1.1, 00:01:00
B       31.0.0.0/8 [200/156160] via 1.1.1.1, 00:01:00
```

Backdoor Routes

Having a low default AD (20) for eBGP routes can cause a problem in some topologies. Figure 1-6 shows a typical case, in which Enterprise 1 uses its eBGP route to reach network 99.0.0.0 in Enterprise 2. However, the two enterprises want to use the OSPF-learned route through the leased line between the two companies.

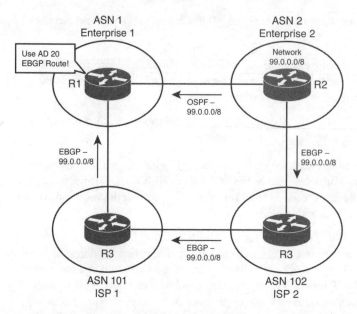

Figure 1-6 *Need for BGP Backdoor Routes*

R1 uses its eBGP route to reach 99.0.0.0 because eBGP has a lower AD (20) than OSPF (110). One solution would be to configure the **distance** command to lower the AD of the OSPF-learned route. However, BGP offers an elegant solution to this particular problem through the use of the **network backdoor** command. In this case, if R1 configures the **network 99.0.0.0 backdoor** router BGP subcommand, the following would occur:

- R1 would use the local AD (default 200) for the eBGP-learned route to network 99.0.0.0.

- R1 does not advertise 99.0.0.0 with BGP.

Given that logic, R1 can use a **network backdoor** command for each prefix for which R1 needs to use the private link to reach Enterprise 2. If the OSPF route to each prefix is up and working, R1 uses the OSPF (AD 110) route over the eBGP-learned (AD 20) route through the Internet. If the OSPF route is lost, the two companies can still communicate through the Internet.

Adding iBGP Routes to the IP Routing Table

Cisco IOS has the same two requirements for adding iBGP routes to the IP routing table as it does for eBGP routes:

- The route must be the best BGP route.

- The route must be the best route (according to the AD) in comparison with other routing sources.

Additionally, for iBGP-learned routes, IOS considers the concept of *BGP synchronization.*

With BGP synchronization (often called *sync*) disabled using the **no synchronization** command, BGP uses the same logic for iBGP routes as it does for eBGP routes regarding which routes to add to the IP routing table. However, enabling BGP sync (with the **synchronization** BGP subcommand) prevents a couple of problems related to IP routing. Figure 1-7 shows the details of just such a problem. In this case, sync was inappropriately disabled in ASN 678, creating a black hole.

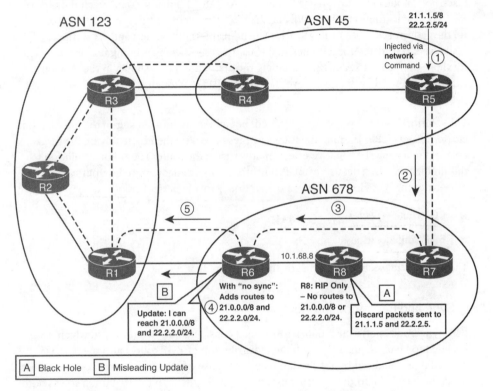

Figure 1-7   *Problem: Routing Black Hole Because of Not Using BGP Sync*

The following list takes a sequential view of what occurs within BGP in Figure 1-7:

1. R5 adds two prefixes (21.0.0.0/8 and 22.2.2.0/24) into its BGP table using two **network** commands.

2. R5 advertises the prefixes to R7, but does not redistribute the routes into its IGP.

3. R7 advertises the prefixes to R6.

4. R6, with synchronization disabled, considers the routes as "best," so R6 adds the routes to its routing table.

5. R6 also advertises the two prefixes to R1.

Two related problems (labeled A and B in the figure) actually occur in this case. The routing *black hole* occurs because R8 does not have a route to either of the prefixes advertised by BGP. R8 is not running BGP—a common occurrence for a router that does not directly connect to an eBGP peer. R7 did not redistribute those two prefixes into the IGP; as a result, R8 cannot route packets for those prefixes. R6, and possibly routers in AS 123, try to forward packets destined to the two prefixes through AS 678, but R8 discards the packets—hence the black hole.

The second related problem, labeled B, occurs at Step 5. R6 exacerbated the routing black-hole problem by advertising to another AS (AS 123) that it could reach the prefixes. R6 considers its routes to 21.0.0.0/8 and 22.2.2.0/24 as "best" routes in its BGP table, so R6 then advertises those routes to R1. Depending on the topology and PA settings, R1 could have considered these routes as its best routes—thereby sending packets destined for those prefixes into AS 678. (Assuming the configuration as shown in the previous examples, R1 would actually believe the one AS_PATH through R3 to AS 45 as the best path.)

The solutions to these problems are varied, but all the solutions result in the internal routers (for example, R8) learning the routes to these prefixes, thereby removing the black hole and removing the negative effect of advertising the route. The original solution to this problem involves the use of BGP synchronization, along with redistributing BGP routes into the IGP. However, two later solutions provide better options today:

- BGP route reflectors
- BGP confederations

The next several sections cover all of these options.

Using Sync and Redistributing Routes

BGP synchronization is best understood when considered in the context in which it was intended to be used—namely, with the redistribution of BGP routes into the IGP. This method is seldom used by ISPs today, mainly because of the large number of routes that would be injected into the IGP. However, using BGP sync with redistribution solves both problems related to the routing black hole.

The key to understanding BGP sync is to know that redistribution solves the routing black-hole problem, and sync solves the problem of advertising a black-hole route to another AS. For example, to solve the routing black-hole problem, R7 redistributes the two prefixes into RIP (from Figure 1-7). R8 then has routes to those prefixes, solving the black-hole problem.

Sync logic on R6 controls the second part of the overall problem, regulating the conditions under which R6 advertises the prefixes to other eBGP peers (like R1). Sync works by controlling whether a BGP table entry can be considered "best"; keep in mind that a route in the BGP table must be considered to be "best" before it can be advertised to another BGP peer. The BGP sync logic controls that decision as follows:

SYNC
LOGIC

> Do not consider an iBGP route in the BGP table as "best" unless the exact prefix was learned through an IGP and is currently in the routing table.

Sync logic essentially gives a router a method to know whether the non-BGP routers inside the AS should have the ability to route packets to the prefix. Note that the route must be IGP-learned because a static route on R6 would not imply anything about what other routers (like R8) might or might not have learned. For example, using Figure 1-7 again, after R6 learns the prefixes through RIP, RIP will place the routes in its IP routing table. At that point, the sync logic on R6 can consider those same BGP-learned prefixes in the BGP table as candidates to be best routes. If chosen as best, R6 can then advertise the BGP routes to R1.

Example 1-13 shows the black hole occurring from R6's perspective, with sync disabled on R6 using the **no synchronization** BGP subcommand. Following that, the example shows R6's behavior after R7 has begun redistributing BGP routes into RIP, with sync enabled on R6.

Example 1-13 *Comparing the Black Hole (No Sync) and Solution (Sync)*

```
! R6 has a "best" BGP route to 21.0.0.0/8 through R7 (7.7.7.7), but a trace
! command shows that the packets are discarded by R8 (10.1.68.8).
R6# show ip bgp | begin Network
   Network          Next Hop         Metric LocPrf Weight Path
*  21.0.0.0         172.16.16.1                       0 123 45 i
*>i                 7.7.7.7               0    100     0 45 i
*  22.2.2.0/24      172.16.16.1                       0 123 45 i
*>i                 7.7.7.7               0    100     0 45 i
R6# trace 21.1.1.5
Type escape sequence to abort.
Tracing the route to 21.1.1.5

  1 10.1.68.8 20 msec 20 msec 20 msec
  2 10.1.68.8 !H  *  !H
! R7 is now configured to redistribute BGP into RIP.
R7# conf t
Enter configuration commands, one per line.  End with CNTL/Z.
R7(config)# router rip
R7(config-router)# redist bgp 678 metric 3
! Next, R6 switches to use sync, and the BGP process is cleared.
R6# conf t
Enter configuration commands, one per line.  End with CNTL/Z.
R6(config)# router bgp 678
R6(config-router)# synchronization
R6(config-router)# ^Z
R6# clear ip bgp *
```

```
! R6's BGP table entries now show "RIB-failure," a status code that can mean
! (as of some 12.2T IOS releases) that the prefix is known via an IGP. 21.0.0.0/8
! is shown to be included as a RIP route in R6's routing table. Note also that R6
! considers the BGP routes through R7 as the "best" routes; these are still
! advertised to R1.
R6# show ip bgp
BGP table version is 5, local router ID is 6.6.6.6
Status codes: s suppressed, d damped, h history, * valid, > best, i - internal,
              r RIB-failure, S Stale
Origin codes: i - IGP, e - EGP, ? - incomplete

   Network          Next Hop          Metric LocPrf Weight Path
r  21.0.0.0         172.16.16.1                       0 123 45 i
r>i                 7.7.7.7                0    100    0 45 i
r  22.2.2.0/24      172.16.16.1                       0 123 45 i
r>i                 7.7.7.7                0    100    0 45 i
R6# show ip route | incl 21.0.0.0
R    21.0.0.0/8 [120/4] via 10.1.68.8, 00:00:15, Serial0/0.8
! R6 considers the routes through R7 as the "best" routes; these are still
! advertised to R1, even though they are in a "RIB-failure" state.
R6# show ip bgp neighbor 172.16.16.1 advertised-routes | begin Network
   Network          Next Hop          Metric LocPrf Weight Path
r>i21.0.0.0         7.7.7.7                0    100    0 45 i
r>i22.2.2.0/24      7.7.7.7                0    100    0 45 i
```

Note   Sync includes an additional odd requirement when OSPF is used as the IGP. If the OSPF RID of the router advertising the prefix is a different number than the BGP router advertising that same prefix, sync still does not allow BGP to consider the route to be the best route. OSPF and BGP use the same priorities and logic to choose their RIDs. However, when using sync, it makes sense to explicitly configure the RID for OSPF and BGP to be the same value on the router that redistributes from BGP into OSPF.

Disabling Sync and Using BGP on All Routers in an AS

A second method to overcome the black-hole issue is to simply use BGP to advertise all the BGP-learned prefixes to all routers in the AS. Because all routers know the prefixes, sync can be disabled safely. The downside is the introduction of BGP onto all routers, and the addition of iBGP neighbor connections between each pair of routers. (In an AS with N routers, $N(N-1)/2$ neighbor connections will be required.) With large autonomous systems, BGP performance and convergence time can degrade as a result of the large number of peers.

BGP needs the full mesh of iBGP peers inside an AS because BGP does not advertise iBGP routes (routes learned from one iBGP peer) to another iBGP peer. This additional restriction helps prevent routing loops, but it then requires a full mesh of iBGP peers—otherwise, only a subset of the iBGP peers would learn each prefix.

BGP offers two tools (confederations and route reflectors) that reduce the number of peer connections inside an AS, prevent loops, and allow all routers to learn about all prefixes. These two tools are covered next.

Confederations

An AS using BGP confederations, as defined in RFC 5065, separates each router in the AS into one of several confederation subautonomous systems. Peers inside the same sub-AS are considered to be *confederation iBGP peers*, and routers in different subautonomous systems are considered to be *confederation eBGP peers*.

Confederations propagate routes to all routers, without a full mesh of peers inside the entire AS. To do so, confederation eBGP peer connections act like true eBGP peers in some respects. In a single sub-AS, the confederation iBGP peers must be fully meshed, because they act exactly like normal iBGP peers—in other words, they do not advertise iBGP routes to each other. However, confederation eBGP peers act like eBGP peers in that they can advertise iBGP routes learned inside their confederation sub-AS into another confederation sub-AS.

Confederations prevent loops inside a confederation AS by using the AS_PATH PA. BGP routers in a confederation add the subautonomous systems into the AS_PATH as part of an AS_PATH segment called the AS_CONFED_SEQ. (The AS_PATH consists of up to four different components, called segments—AS_SEQ, AS_SET, AS_CONFED_SEQ, and AS_CONFED_SET; see the earlier section "Manual Summaries and the AS_PATH Path Attribute" for more information on AS_SEQ and AS_SET.)

Note   The terms *AS* and *sub-AS* refer to the concept of an autonomous system and sub-autonomous system. *ASN* and *sub-ASN* refer to the actual AS numbers used.

Just as the AS_SEQ and AS_SET components help prevent loops between autonomous systems, AS_CONFED_SEQ and AS_CONFED_SET help prevent loops within confederation autonomous systems. Before confederation eBGP peers can advertise an iBGP route into another sub-AS, the router must make sure that the destination sub-AS is not already in the AS_PATH AS_CONFED_SEQ segment. For example, in Figure 1-8, the routers in sub-ASN 65001 learn some routes and then advertise those routes to sub-ASNs 65002 and 65003. Routers in these two sub-ASNs advertise the routes to each other. However, they never re-advertise the routes to routers in sub-ASN 65001 because of AS_CONFED_SEQ, as shown in parentheses inside the figure.

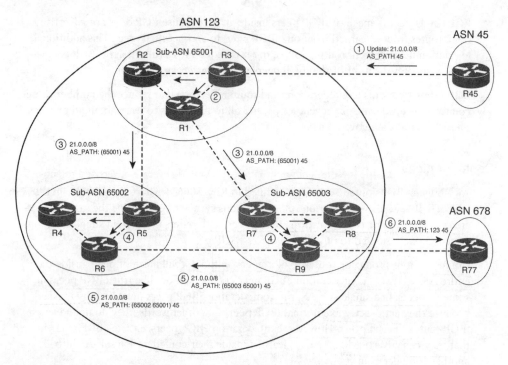

Figure 1-8   *AS_PATH Changes in a Confederation*

Figure 1-8 depicts a detailed example, with the steps in the following list matching the steps outlined in circled numbers in the figure:

1. 21.0.0.0/8 is injected by R45 and advertised through eBGP to AS 123. This route has an AS_PATH of 45.

2. R3 advertises the prefix through its two iBGP connections; however, because of iBGP rules inside the sub-AS, R1 and R2 do not attempt to advertise this prefix to each other.

3. Routers in sub-AS 65001 use eBGP-like logic to advertise 21.0.0.0/8 to their confederation eBGP peers, but first they inject their own sub-AS into the AS_PATH AS_CONFED_SEQ segment. (This part of the AS_PATH is displayed inside parentheses in the output of the **show ip bgp** command, as shown in the figure.)

4. The same process as in Step 2 occurs in the other two subautonomous systems, respectively.

5. R6 and R9 advertise the route to each other after adding their respective ASNs to the AS_CONFED_SEQ.

6. R9 advertises the prefix through a true eBGP connection after removing the sub-AS portion of the AS_PATH.

By the end of these steps, all the routers inside ASN 123 have learned of the 21.0.0.0/8 prefix. Also, ASN 678 (R77 in this case) learned of a route for that same prefix—a route that would work and would not have the black-hole effect. In fact, from ASN 678's perspective, it sees a route that appears to be through ASNs 123 and 45. Also note that routers in sub-AS 65002 and 65003 will not advertise the prefix back into sub-AS 65001 because AS 65001 is already in the confederation AS_PATH.   → split horizone - like

The choice of values for sub-ASNs 65001, 65002, and 65003 is not coincidental in this case. ASNs 64512 through 65535 are *private ASNs*, meant for use in cases where the   Private ASN will not be advertised to the Internet or other autonomous systems. By using private AS #s ASNs, a confederation can hopefully avoid the following type of problem. Imagine that sub-AS 65003 instead used ASN 45. The AS_PATH loop check examines the entire AS_PATH. As a result, the prefixes shown in Figure 1-8 would never be advertised to sub-AS 45, and in turn would not be advertised to ASN 678. Using private ASNs would prevent this problem.

The following list summarizes the key topics regarding confederations:

Key Topic

- Inside a sub-AS, full mesh is required, because full iBGP rules are in effect.

- The confederation eBGP connections act like normal eBGP connections in that iBGP routes are advertised—as long as the AS_PATH implies that such an advertisement would not cause a loop.

- Confederation eBGP connections also act like normal eBGP connections regarding Time to Live (TTL), because all packets use a TTL of 1 by default. (TTL can be changed with the **neighbor ebgp-multihop** command.)

- Confederation eBGP connections act like iBGP connections in every other regard—for example, the NEXT_HOP is not changed by default.

- Confederation ASNs are not considered part of the length of the AS_PATH when a router chooses the best routes based on the shortest AS_PATH.

- Confederation routers remove the confederation ASNs from the AS_PATH in Updates sent outside the confederation; therefore, other routers do not know that a confederation was used.

Configuring Confederations

Configuring confederations requires only a few additional commands beyond those already covered in this chapter. However, migrating to use confederations can be quite painful. The problem is that the true ASN will no longer be configured on the **router bgp** command, but instead on the **bgp confederation identifier** BGP subcommand. So, BGP will simply be out of service on one or more routers while the migration occurs. Table 1-10 lists the key confederation commands and their purpose.

Table 1-10   *BGP Subcommands Used for Confederations*

Purpose	Command
Define a router's sub-AS	router bgp *sub-as*
Define the true AS	bgp confederation identifier *asn*
Identify a neighboring AS as another sub-AS	bgp confederation peers *sub-asn*

Example 1-14 shows a simple configuration for the topology in Figure 1-9.

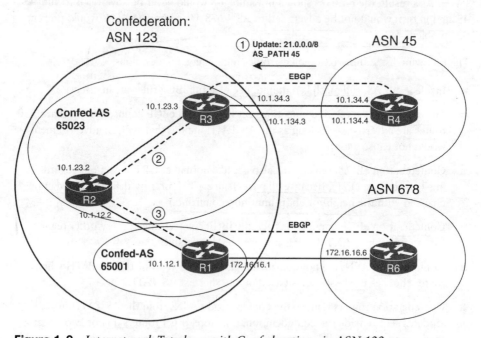

Figure 1-9   *Internetwork Topology with Confederations in ASN 123*

In this internetwork topology, R1 is in sub-AS 65001, with R2 and R3 in sub-AS 65023. In this case, R1 and R3 will not be neighbors. The following list outlines the sequence of events to propagate a prefix:

1. R3 will learn prefix 21.0.0.0/8 through eBGP from AS 45 (R4).

2. R3 will advertise the prefix through iBGP to R2.

3. R2 will advertise the prefix through confederation eBGP to R1.

Example 1-14   *Confederation Inside AS 123 (Continued)*

```
! R1 Configuration. Note the sub-AS in the router bgp command, and the true AS in
! the bgp confederation identifier command. Also note the neighbor ebgp-multihop
! command for confederation eBGP peer R2, as they are using loopbacks. Also, sync
! is not needed now that the confederation has been created.
```

R1

```
router bgp 65001
 no synchronization
 bgp router-id 111.111.111.111
 bgp confederation identifier 123
 bgp confederation peers 65023
 neighbor 2.2.2.2 remote-as 65023
 neighbor 2.2.2.2 ebgp-multihop 2
 neighbor 2.2.2.2 update-source Loopback1
 neighbor 2.2.2.2 next-hop-self
 neighbor 172.16.16.6 remote-as 678
```

→ sub-AS

→ real AS

→ acts like IBGP peers so this line is needed

```
! R2 Configuration. Note the bgp confederation peers 65001 command. Without it,
! R2 would think that neighbor 1.1.1.1 was a true eBGP connection, and remove
! the confederation AS_PATH entries before advertising to R1.
```

 R2

```
router bgp 65023
 no synchronization
 bgp confederation identifier 123
 bgp confederation peers 65001
 neighbor 1.1.1.1 remote-as 65001
 neighbor 1.1.1.1 ebgp-multihop 2
 neighbor 1.1.1.1 update-source Loopback1
 neighbor 3.3.3.3 remote-as 65023
 neighbor 3.3.3.3 update-source Loopback1
```

 R3

```
! R3 Configuration. Note that R3 does not need a bgp confederation peers command,
! as it does not have any confederation eBGP peers.
router bgp 65023
 no synchronization
 bgp log-neighbor-changes
 bgp confederation identifier 123
 neighbor 2.2.2.2 remote-as 65023
 neighbor 2.2.2.2 update-source Loopback1
 neighbor 2.2.2.2 next-hop-self
 neighbor 4.4.4.4 remote-as 45
 neighbor 4.4.4.4 ebgp-multihop 2
 neighbor 4.4.4.4 update-source Loopback1
```

```
! R1 has received the 21.0.0.0/8 prefix, with sub-AS 65023 shown in parentheses,
! and true AS 45 shown outside the parentheses. R1 has also learned the same
! prefix via AS 678 and R6. The route through the sub-AS is best because it is the
! shortest AS_PATH; the shortest AS_PATH logic ignores the confederation sub-
! autonomous systems.
R1# show ip bgp | begin Network
```

important!

Network	Next Hop	Metric	LocPrf	Weight	Path
*> 21.0.0.0	3.3.3.3	0	100	0	(65023) 45 i
*	172.16.16.6			0	678 45 i
*> 22.2.2.0/24	3.3.3.3	0	100	0	(65023) 45 i
*	172.16.16.6			0	678 45 i

```
! R6 shows its received update from R1, showing the removed sub-AS, and the
```

```
! inclusion of the true AS, AS 123.
R6# show ip bgp neighbor 172.16.16.1 received-routes | begin Network
   Network          Next Hop          Metric LocPrf Weight Path
r  21.0.0.0         172.16.16.1                         0 123 45 i
r  22.2.2.0/24      172.16.16.1                         0 123 45 i
```

Route Reflectors

Route reflectors (RR) achieve the same result as confederations: They remove the need for a full mesh of iBGP peers, allow all iBGP routes to be learned by all iBGP routers in the AS, and prevent loops. In an iBGP design using RRs, a partial mesh of iBGP peers is defined. Some routers are configured as RR servers; these servers are allowed to learn iBGP routes from their clients and then advertise them to other iBGP peers. The example in Figure 1-10 shows the key terms and some of the core logic used by an RR; note that only the RR server itself uses different logic, with clients and nonclients acting as normal iBGP peers.

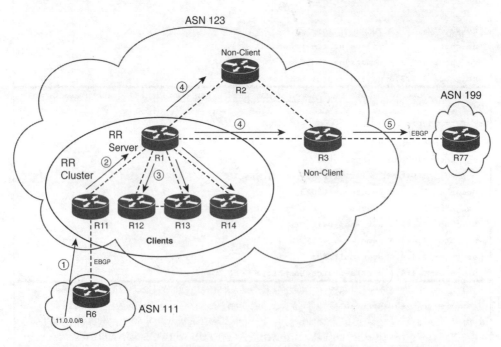

Figure 1-10 *Basic Flow Using a Single RR, Four Clients, and Two Nonclients*

Figure 1-10 shows how prefix 11.0.0.0/8 is propagated through the AS, using the following steps:

1. R11 learns 11.0.0.0/8 using eBGP.

2. R11 uses normal iBGP rules and sends an Update to R1.

3. R1 reflects the routes by sending Updates to all other clients.

4. R1 also reflects the routes to all nonclients.

5. Nonclients use non-RR rules, sending an Update over eBGP to R77.

Only the router acting as the RR uses modified rules; the other routers (clients and non-clients) are not even aware of the RR, nor do they change their operating rules. Table 1-11 summarizes the rules for RR operation, which vary based on from what type of BGP peer the RR receives the prefix. The table lists the sources from which a prefix can be learned, and the types of other routers to which the RR will reflect the prefix information.

Table 1-11   *Types of Neighbors to Which Prefixes Are Reflected*

Location from Which a Prefix Is Learned	Are Routes Advertised to Clients?	Are Routes Advertised to Nonclients?
Client	Yes	Yes
Nonclient	Yes	No
eBGP	Yes	Yes

The one case in which the RR does not reflect routes is when the RR receives a route from a nonclient, with the RR not reflecting that route to other nonclients. The perspective behind that logic is that RRs act like normal iBGP peers with nonclients and with eBGP neighbors—in other words, the RR does not forward iBGP-learned routes to other nonclient iBGP peers. The difference in how the RR behaves relates to when a client sends the RR a prefix or when the RR decides to reflect a prefix to the clients.

One (or more) RR servers, and their clients, create a single RR cluster. A BGP design using RRs can consist of

- Clusters with multiple RRs in a cluster

- Multiple clusters, although using multiple clusters makes sense only when physical redundancy exists as well

With multiple clusters, at least one RR from a cluster must be peered with at least one RR in each of the other clusters. Typically, all RRs are peered directly, creating a full mesh of RR iBGP peers among RRs. Also, if some routers are nonclients, they should be included in the full mesh of RRs. Figure 1-11 shows the concept, with each RR fully meshed with the other RRs in other clusters, as well as with the nonclient.

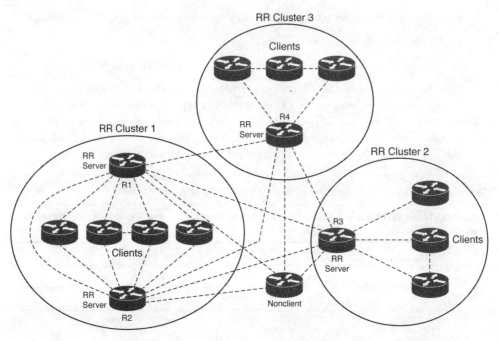

Figure 1-11 *Multiple RR Clusters with Full Mesh Among RRs and Nonclients*

If you consider the logic summary in Table 1-11 compared to Figure 1-11, it appears that routing loops are not only possible but probable with this design. However, the RR feature uses several tools to prevent loops, as follows:

Key
Topic

■ **CLUSTER_LIST:** RRs add their *cluster ID* into a BGP PA called the CLUSTER_LIST before sending an Update. When receiving a BGP Update, RRs discard received prefixes for which their cluster ID already appears. As with AS_PATH for confederations, this prevents RRs from looping advertisements between clusters.

■ **ORIGINATOR_ID:** This PA lists the RID of the first iBGP peer to advertise the route into the AS. If a router sees its own BGP ID as the ORIGINATOR_ID in a received route, it does not use or propagate the route.

■ **Only advertise the best routes:** RRs reflect routes only if the RR considers the route to be a "best" route in its own BGP table. This further limits the routes reflected by the RR. (It also has a positive effect compared with confederations in that an average router sees fewer, typically useless, redundant routes.)

Example 1-15 shows a simple example of using RRs. The design uses two clusters, with two RRs (R9 and R2) and two clients (R1 and R3). The following list outlines the sequence of events to propagate a prefix, as shown in Figure 1-12:

1. R3 learns prefix 21.0.0.0/8 through eBGP from AS 45 (R4).

2. R3 advertises the prefix through iBGP to R2 using normal logic.

3. R2, an RR, receiving a prefix from an RR client, reflects the route through iBGP to R9—a nonclient as far as R2 is concerned.

4. R9, an RR, receiving an iBGP route from a nonclient, reflects the route to R1, its RR client.

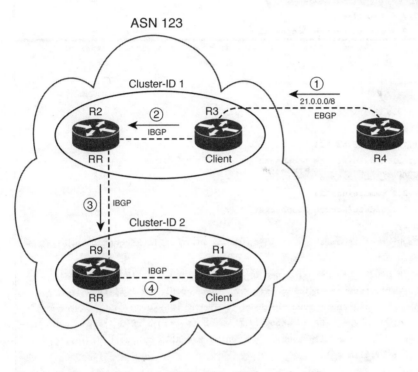

Figure 1-12   *Modified AS 123 Used in RR Example 1-15*

Example 1-15   *RR Configuration for AS 123, Two RRs, and Two Clients*

```
! R3 Configuration. The RR client has no overt signs of being a client; the
! process is completely hidden from all routers except RRs. Also, do not forget
! that one of the main motivations for using RRs is to allow sync to be disabled.
router bgp 123
 no synchronization
 neighbor 2.2.2.2 remote-as 123
 neighbor 2.2.2.2 update-source Loopback1
 neighbor 2.2.2.2 next-hop-self
 neighbor 4.4.4.4 remote-as 45
 neighbor 4.4.4.4 ebgp-multihop 255
 neighbor 4.4.4.4 update-source Loopback1
! R2 Configuration. The cluster ID would default to R2's BGP RID, but it has been
! manually set to "1," which will be listed as "0.0.0.1" in command output. R2
! designates 3.3.3.3 (R3) as a client.
router bgp 123
```

```
  no synchronization
  bgp cluster-id 1
  neighbor 3.3.3.3 remote-as 123
  neighbor 3.3.3.3 update-source Loopback1
  neighbor 3.3.3.3 route-reflector-client
  neighbor 9.9.9.9 remote-as 123
  neighbor 9.9.9.9 update-source Loopback1
```

```
! R9 Configuration. The configuration is similar to R2, but with a different
! cluster ID.
router bgp 123
  no synchronization
  bgp router-id 9.9.9.9
  bgp cluster-id 2
  neighbor 1.1.1.1 remote-as 123
  neighbor 1.1.1.1 update-source Loopback2
  neighbor 1.1.1.1 route-reflector-client
  neighbor 2.2.2.2 remote-as 123
  neighbor 2.2.2.2 update-source Loopback2
 no auto-summary
```

```
! The R1 configuration is omitted, as it contains no specific RR configuration,
! as is the case with all RR clients.
! The 21.0.0.0/8 prefix has been learned by R3, forwarded over iBGP as normal to
! R2. Then, R2 reflected the prefix to its only other peer, R9. The show ip bgp
! 21.0.0.0 command shows the current AS_PATH (45); the iBGP originator of the
! route (3.3.3.3), and the iBGP neighbor from which it was learned ("from
! 2.2.2.2"); and the cluster list, which currently has R2's cluster (0.0.0.1).
! The next output is from R9.
R9# show ip bgp 21.0.0.0
BGP routing table entry for 21.0.0.0/8, version 3
Paths: (1 available, best #1, table Default-IP-Routing-Table)
Flag: 0x820
  Advertised to update-groups:
     2
  45
    3.3.3.3 (metric 2300416) from 2.2.2.2 (2.2.2.2)
      Origin IGP, metric 0, localpref 100, valid, internal, best
      Originator: 3.3.3.3, Cluster list: 0.0.0.1
! RR R9 reflected the prefix to its client (R1), as seen next. Note the changes
! compared to R9's output, with iBGP route being learned from R9 ("from 9.9.9.9"),
! and the cluster list now including cluster 0.0.0.2, as added by R9.
```

```
R1# sho ip bgp 21.0.0.0
BGP routing table entry for 21.0.0.0/8, version 20
Paths: (1 available, best #1, table Default-IP-Routing-Table)
  Not advertised to any peer
  45
```

```
3.3.3.3 (metric 2302976) from 9.9.9.9 (9.9.9.9)
  Origin IGP, metric 0, localpref 100, valid, internal, best
  Originator: 3.3.3.3, Cluster list: 0.0.0.2, 0.0.0.1
```

Multiprotocol BGP

Now we need to discuss the existence of an extension to the BGP-4 protocol. This extension allows the advertisement of customer Virtual Private Network (VPN) routes between provider edge (PE) devices that were injected into customer edge (CE) devices. These prefixes can be learned through a number of dynamic methods to include standard BGP-4, EIGRP, OSPF, or static routes.

We are required to run Multiprotocol BGP (MP-BGP) only within the service provider cloud. As such, each MP-BGP session is an internal BGP session. The session is considered internal because of the fact that the session is formed between two routers that belong to the same autonomous system.

MP-iBGP is required within the MPLS/VPN architecture because the BGP update needs to carry more information than just an IPv4 address. As an example, in the case of the Multiprotocol Label Switching (MPLS) L3 VPNs, the update must communicate the VPN IPv4 address, MPLS label information, and extended or standard BGP communities.

Key Topic

As mentioned, the actual nature of these extensions to the BGP is to provide additional capabilities that allow BGP to carry more information than just the IPv4 address and the typical BGP attributes. As we have discussed thus far, when a BGP session is established between two peers, an OPEN message exchanges initial BGP parameters, such as the ASN. In BGP, the OPEN message is used to communicate other parameters, one of which is Capabilities. This optional parameter is used to define which capabilities the peer can understand and execute; among these capabilities is multiprotocol extensions. It is through the application of multiprotocol extensions that the ability to exchange addresses other than standard IPv4 addresses was introduced into BGP. This process required the creation of some additional Optional attributes needed to provide enhanced functionality in the management and injection of these non-IPv4 addresses.

Specifically, MP-BGP employs two new Optional nontransitive attributes:

- Multiprotocol Reachable NLRI (MP_REACH_NLRI) announces new multiprotocol routes.

- Multiprotocol Unreachable NLRI (MP_UNREACH_NLRI) serves to revoke the routes previously announced by MP_REACH_NLRI.

We need to take a closer look at each of these to better understand the fundamental operation of MP-BGP itself.

MP_REACH_NLRI communicates a set of reachable prefixes together with their next-hop information. The second attribute, MP_UNREACH_NLRI, carries the set of unreachable destinations. For two BGP speakers to exchange multiprotocol data, they must agree on these capabilities during their capabilities exchange.

When a PE router sends an MP-iBGP update to other PE routers, the MP_REACH_NLRI attribute contains one or more triples. Table 1-12 outlines the values defined by these triples.

Table 1-12   *MP-BGP Attributes*

Purpose	Command
Address family information	The address family information identifies the Network layer protocol that is being carried within the Update.
Next-hop information	The next-hop information is the next-hop address of the next router in the path to the destination.
NLRI (network layer reachability information)	The NLRI manages the addition or withdrawal of multiprotocol routes and the next-hop address, and the NLRI prefixes must be in the same address family.

Configuration of Multiprotocol BGP

The configuration of MP-BGP is accomplished by following several steps and various configuration commands in many different configuration contexts. This process is slightly more complicated than the typical BGP configuration processes that we have followed thus far in our discussions. This added complexity and syntax change were created to support the need of the protocol to support multiple PE-to-PE sessions across the service provider cloud as well as to support the possibility that the customer might want to run eBGP as his CE-PE protocol of choice.

In our previous discussion, we covered how the MP-BGP specification defined the concept of an address family and that this was created to allow BGP to carry protocols other than IPv4. Address families come in many forms. As an example, in MPLS/VPN deployments, the address family is called the VPN-IPv4 address and is much longer than a standard IPv4 address. Additionally, we have to also realize that by default, when MP-BGP is activated, it will automatically carry IPv4 unicast routes; this behavior can be problematic in situations where we do not want this to take place. Situations like this can arise in our infrastructure when we only want to communicate applications or protocol-specific addresses like those characteristic to Layer 3 VPNs, to name a few. To alter this behavior, we can disable the automatic advertisement of IPv4 unicast prefixes. Example 1-16 shows the syntax of this command.

Example 1-16   bgp default ipv4-unicast *Command*

```
R1(config)# router bgp 1
R1(config-router)# no bgp default ipv4-unicast
```

The next step in the configuration of MP-iBGP is to define and activate the BGP sessions between PE routers. Just to illustrate the versatility of the command syntax, observe that some of these configurations carry VPN-IPv4 routes, some only IPv4 routes, and others carry VPN-IPv4 and IPv4 routes. The type of BGP session and the specification of which routes the peering sessions will carry are controlled through the use of the address families that we have been discussing. Notice also that each of the BGP configurations manages what routes will be redistributed into and out of BGP. This behavior is best described as context-based routing.

To accomplish this, we must configure a BGP address family for each Virtual Routing and Forwarding (VRF) configured on the PE router and a separate address family to carry no IPv4 routes between PE routers. The initial BGP process, the portion of the configuration that cites no address family specifications, becomes the default address family. This default context becomes the "catch all" where any non-VRF-based or IPv4-specific sessions can be configured. Any prefixes learned or advertised in this default address family will be injected into the global routing table. As such, it must be noted that the configuration of these BGP sessions is exactly the same as the standard BGP configuration we have discussed up to this point, with the exception that the session needs to be activated. The **neighbor** command controls the activation of the session, as shown in Example 1-17.

NEEDS ACTIVATION

Example 1-17   *BGP Standard IPv4 Configuration*

```
R1(config)# router bgp 1
R1(config-router)# neighbor 194.22.15.3 remote-as 1
R1(config-router)# neighbor 194.22.15.3 update-source loopback0
R1(config-router)# neighbor 194.22.15.3 activate
```

The BGP process activates the MP-iBGP session that carries non-IPv4 prefixes through the use of a protocol-specific address family. This configuration creates a routing context for exchanging these non-IPv4 prefixes. Example 1-18 illustrates this command syntax and the relevant commands needed to configure the MP-iBGP session between Routers R1 and R2.

Example 1-18   *Address Family Configuration*

```
R1(config)# router bgp 1
R1(config-router)# address-family ?
  ipv4   Address family
  vpnv4  Address family

R1(config-router)# address-family vpnv4
R1(config-router)# neighbor 194.22.15.3 activate
```

Key Topic

In Example 1-18, notice that the VPNv4 address family configuration requires only one command. This is because the BGP neighbor configuration commands need to be entered under the global BGP process, and therefore need to be activated to carry non-IPv4 prefixes.

The configuration of the VPNv4 address family also adds a further command to the BGP configuration to support the MP-BGP-specific extended community attributes. This command will be added by the IOS by default and is necessary because it instructs BGP to advertise the extended community attributes. Example 1-19 provides the syntax of this command.

Example 1-19 *Enabling Extended Community Support*

```
R1(config-router)# neighbor 194.22.15.3 send-community ?
  both       Send Standard and Extended Community attributes
  extended   Send Extended Community attribute
  standard   Send Standard Community attribute
  <cr>
```

Key Topic

The default behavior is to send only the extended community attribute. If the network design requires the standard community attribute to be attached to these non-IPv4 prefixes, this behavior can be changed through the **neighbor 194.22.15.3 send-community both** command.

We now need to advertise these non-IPv4 routes across the service provider cloud. For the purposes of our discussions, we will explore this syntax using numerous VPNv4 configurations. Note that MP-iBGP communicates these routes across the MP-iBGP sessions running between PE routers. To this end, the routing context must be configured under the BGP process to communicate to BGP which VRF prefixes it needs to advertise.

This is accomplished through the address family configuration under the BGP process, using the IPv4 option of the **address-family** command, as illustrated in Example 1-18. Each VRF needs to be configured under the BGP process using its own address family. Also, these prefixes must be redistributed into BGP if they are to be advertised across the service provider cloud.

Example 1-20 illustrates how this is accomplished using VPNv4 address families to illustrate the syntax used.

Example 1-20 *MP-BGP Redistribution Between VRFs*

```
hostname R1
!
ip vrf VPN_A
 rd 1:100
 route-target export 100:100
 route-target import 100:100
!
ip vrf VPN_B
 rd 1:200
 route-target export 100:200
 route-target import 100:200
!
interface loopback0
 ip address 194.22.15.2 255.255.255.255
!
interface serial0
```

```
 ip vrf forwarding VPN_A
 ip address 10.2.1.5 255.255.255.252
!
interface serial1
ip vrf forwarding VPN_B
 ip address 195.12.2.5 255.255.255.252
!
router rip
 version 2
 !
address-family ipv4 vrf VPN_A
 version 2
 redistribute bgp 1 metric 1
 network 10.0.0.0
 no auto-summary
exit-address-family
 !
address-family ipv4 vrf VPN_B
 version 2
 redistribute bgp 1 metric 1
 network 195.12.2.0
 no auto-summary
exit-address-family
 !
router bgp 1
 no bgp default ipv4-unicast
 neighbor 194.22.15.3 remote-as 1
 neighbor 194.22.15.3 update-source loopback0
 neighbor 194.22.15.3 activate
 neighbor 194.22.15.1 remote-as 1
 neighbor 194.22.15.1 update-source loopback0
 !
address-family ipv4 vrf VPN_A
 redistribute rip metric 1
 no auto-summary
 no synchronization
exit-address-family
 !
address-family ipv4 vrf VPN_B
 redistribute rip metric 1
 no auto-summary
 no synchronization
exit-address-family
 !
address-family vpnv4
```

```
 neighbor 194.22.15.3 activate
 neighbor 194.22.15.3 send-community extended
 neighbor 194.22.15.1 activate
 neighbor 194.22.15.1 send-community extended
exit-address-family
```

Foundation Summary

This section lists additional details and facts to round out the coverage of the topics in this chapter. Unlike most of the Cisco Press Exam Certification Guides, this "Foundation Summary" does not repeat information presented in the "Foundation Topics" section of the chapter. Please take the time to read and study the details in the "Foundation Topics" section of the chapter, as well as review items noted with a Key Topic icon.

Table 1-13 lists some of the key RFCs for BGP.

Table 1-13 *Protocols and Standards for Chapter 1*

Topic	Standard
BGP-4	RFC 4271
BGP Confederations	RFC 5065
BGP Route Reflection	RFC 4456
MD5 Authentication	RFC 2385

Table 1-14 lists the BGP path attributes mentioned in this chapter and describes their purpose.

Table 1-14 *BGP Path Attributes*

Path Attribute	Description	Characteristics
AS_PATH	Lists ASNs through which the route has been advertised	Well-known Mandatory
NEXT_HOP	Lists the next-hop IP address used to reach an NLRI	Well-known Mandatory
AGGREGATOR	Lists the RID and ASN of the router that created a summary NLRI	Optional Transitive
ATOMIC_AGGREGATE	Tags a summary NLRI as being a summary	Well-known Discretionary
ORIGIN	Value implying from where the route was taken for injection into BGP: i(IGP), e(EGP), or ? (incomplete information)	Well-known Mandatory
ORIGINATOR_ID	Used by RRs to denote the RID of the iBGP neighbor that injected the NLRI into the AS	Optional Nontransitive
CLUSTER_LIST	Used by RRs to list the RR cluster IDs to prevent loops	Optional Nontransitive

Table 1-15 lists and describes the methods to introduce entries into the BGP table.

Table 1-15 *Summary: Methods to Introduce Entries into the BGP Table*

Method	Summary Description
network command	Advertises a route into BGP. Depends on the existence of the configured network/subnet in the IP routing table.
Redistribution	Takes IGP, static, or connected routes; metric (MED) assignment is not required.
Manual summarization	Requires at least one component subnet in the BGP table; options for keeping all component subnets, suppressing all from advertisement, or suppressing a subset from being advertised.
default-information originate command	Requires a default route in the IP routing table, plus the **redistribute** command.
neighbor default-originate command	With the optional route map, requires the route map to match the IP routing table with a permit action before advertising a default route. Without the route map, the default is always advertised.

Table 1-16 lists some of the most popular Cisco IOS commands related to the topics in this chapter.

Table 1-16 *Command Reference for Chapter 1*

Command	Command Mode and Description
address-family vpnv4	BGP mode; allows the creation of the MP-BGP session necessary to form the VPNv4 session between PE devices
aggregate-address *address mask* [**as-set**] [**summary-only**] [**suppress-map** *map-name*] [**advertise-map** *map-name*] [**attribute-map** *map-name*]	BGP mode; summarizes BGP routes, suppressing all/none/some of the component subnets
auto-summary	BGP mode; enables automatic summarization to classful boundaries of locally injected routes
bgp client-to-client reflection	BGP mode; on by default, tells an RR server to reflect routes learned from a client to other clients
bgp cluster-id *cluster-id*	BGP mode; defines a nondefault RR cluster ID to an RR server

Command	Command Mode and Description
bgp confederation identifier *as-number*	BGP mode; for confederations, defines the ASN used for the entire AS as seen by other autonomous systems
bgp confederation peers *as-number* [... *as-number*]	BGP mode; for confederations, identifies which neighboring ASNs are in other confederation subautonomous systems
bgp log-neighbor-changes	BGP mode; on by default, it tells BGP to create log messages for significant changes in BGP operation
bgp router-id *ip-address*	BGP mode; defines the BGP router ID
default-information originate	BGP mode; required to allow a static default route to be redistributed into BGP
default-metric *number*	BGP mode; sets the default metric assigned to routes redistributed into BGP; normally defaults to the IGP metric for each route
distance bgp *external-distance internal-distance local-distance*	BGP mode; defines the administrative distance for eBGP, iBGP, and locally injected BGP routes
neighbor {*ip-address*	*peer-group-name*} **default-originate** [**route-map** *map-name*]	BGP mode; tells the router to add a default route to the BGP Update sent to this neighbor, under the conditions set in the optional route map
neighbor {*ip-address*	*peer-group-name*} **description** *text*	BGP mode; adds a descriptive text reference in the BGP configuration
neighbor {*ip-address*	*peer-group-name*} **ebgp-multihop** [*ttl*]	BGP mode; for eBGP peers, sets the TTL in packets sent to this peer to something larger than the default of 1
neighbor *ip-address*	*peer-group-name* **next-hop-self**	BGP mode; causes IOS to reset the NEXT_HOP PA to the IP address used as the source address of Updates sent to this neighbor
neighbor {*ip-address*	*peer-group-name*} **password** *string*	BGP mode; defines the key used in an MD5 hash of all BGP messages to this neighbor
neighbor *ip-address* **peer-group** *peer-group-name*	BGP mode; associates a neighbor's IP address as part of a peer group
neighbor *peer-group-name* **peer-group**	BGP mode; defines the name of a peer group
neighbor {*ip-address*	*peer-group-name*} **remote-as** *as-number*	BGP mode; defines the AS of the neighbor
neighbor {*ip-address*	*peer-group-name*} **shutdown**	BGP mode; administratively shuts down a neighbor, stopping the TCP connection

Command	Command Mode and Description
neighbor [*ip-address*	*peer-group-name*] timers *keepalive holdtime*	BGP mode; sets the two BGP timers, just for this neighbor
neighbor {*ip-address*	*ipv6-address*	*peer-group-name*} update-source *interface-type interface-number*	BGP mode; defines the source IP address used for BGP messages sent to this neighbor
network {*network-number* [mask *network-mask*] [route-map *map-tag*]	BGP mode; causes IOS to add the defined prefix to the BGP table if it exists in the IP routing table
router bgp *as-number*	Global command; defines the ASN and puts the user in BGP mode
synchronization	BGP mode; enables BGP synchronization
timers bgp *keepalive holdtime*	BGP mode; defines BGP timers for all neighbors
show ip bgp [*network*] [*network-mask*] [longer-prefixes] [prefix-list *prefix-list-name*	route-map *route-map-name*] [shorter prefixes mask-length]	Exec mode; lists details of a router's BGP table
show ip bgp injected-paths	Exec mode; lists routes locally injected into BGP
show ip bgp neighbors [*neighbor-address*] [received-routes	routes	advertised-routes	{paths *regexp*}	dampened-routes	*received prefix-filter*]	Exec mode; lists information about routes sent and received to particular neighbors
show ip bgp peer-group [*peer-group-name*] [summary]	Exec mode; lists details about a particular peer group
show ip bgp summary	Exec mode; lists basic statistics for each BGP peer

Memory Builders

The CCIE Routing and Switching written exam, like all Cisco CCIE written exams, covers a fairly broad set of topics. This section provides some basic tools to help you exercise your memory about some of the broader topics covered in this chapter.

Fill In Key Tables from Memory

Appendix E, "Key Tables for CCIE Study," on the CD in the back of this book, contains empty sets of some of the key summary tables in each chapter. Print Appendix E, refer to this chapter's tables in it, and fill in the tables from memory. Refer to Appendix F, "Solutions for Key Tables for CCIE Study," on the CD, to check your answers.

Definitions

Next, take a few moments to write down the definitions for the following terms:

> path attribute, BGP table, BGP Update, established, iBGP, eBGP, EGP, BGP, peer group, eBGP multihop, autonomous system, AS number, AS_PATH, ORIGIN, NLRI, NEXT_HOP, MULTI_EXIT_DISC, LOCAL_PREF, routing black hole, synchronization, confederation, route reflector, confederation identifier, sub-AS, route reflector server, route reflector client, route reflector nonclient, confederation AS, confederation eBGP, weight

Refer to the glossary to check your answers.

Further Reading

Routing TCP/IP, Volume II, by Jeff Doyle and Jennifer DeHaven Carrol

Cisco BGP-4 Command and Configuration Handbook, by William R. Parkhurst

Internet Routing Architectures, by Bassam Halabi

Troubleshooting IP Routing Protocols, by Zaheer Aziz, Johnson Liu, Abe Martey, and Faraz Shamim

Almost every reference can be reached from the Cisco BGP support page at www.cisco.com/en/US/partner/tech/tk365/tk80/tsd_technology_support_sub-protocol_home.html. Requires a Cisco.com username/password.

Blueprint topics covered in this chapter:

This chapter covers the following topics from the Cisco CCIE Routing and Switching written exam blueprint:

- Implement IPv4 BGP synchronization, attributes, and other advanced features

- Fast convergence

CHAPTER 2

BGP Routing Policies

This chapter examines the tools available to define Border Gateway Protocol (BGP) routing policies. A BGP routing policy defines the rules used by one or more routers to impact two main goals: filtering routes and influencing which routes are considered the best routes by BGP.

BGP filtering tools are mostly straightforward, with the exception of AS_PATH filtering. AS_PATH filters use regular expressions to match the AS_PATH path attribute (PA), making the configuration challenging. Beyond that, most of the BGP filtering concepts are directly comparable to IGP filtering concepts.

The other topics in this chapter explain routing policies that focus on impacting the BGP decision process. The decision process itself is first outlined, followed by explanations of how each step in the process can be used to impact which routes are considered best by BGP.

"Do I Know This Already?" Quiz

Table 2-1 outlines the major headings in this chapter and the corresponding "Do I Know This Already?" quiz questions.

Table 2-1 *"Do I Know This Already?" Foundation Topics Section-to-Question Mapping*

Foundation Topics Section	Questions Covered in This Section	Score
Route Filtering and Route Summarization	1–4	
BGP Path Attributes and the BGP Decision Process	5–7	
Configuring BGP Policies	8–12	
BGP Communities	13, 14	
Total Score		

To best use this pre-chapter assessment, remember to score yourself strictly. You can find the answers in Appendix A, "Answers to the 'Do I Know This Already?' Quizzes."

1. A BGP policy needs to be configured to filter all the /20 prefixes whose first two octets are 20.128. Which of the following answers would provide the correct matching logic for the filtering process, matching only the described subnets and no others?

   a. access-list 1 deny 20.128.0.0 0.0.255.255

   b. access-list 101 deny ip 20.128.0.0 0.0.255.255 host 255.255.240.0

   c. ip prefix-list 1 deny 20.128.0.0/16 eq 20

   d. ip prefix-list 2 deny 20.128.0.0/16 ge 20 le 20

2. Router R1 has a working BGP implementation, advertising subnets of 1.0.0.0/8 to neighbor 2.2.2.2 (R2). A route map named fred has been configured on R1 to filter all routes in network 1.0.0.0. R1 has just added the **router bgp** subcommand **neighbor 2.2.2.2 route-map fred out**. No other commands have been used afterward. Which of the following answers, taken as the next step, would allow proper verification of whether the filter indeed filtered the routes?

   a. The **show ip bgp neighbor 2.2.2.2 advertised-routes** command on R1 will no longer list the filtered routes.

   b. The **show ip bgp neighbor 2.2.2.2 advertised-routes** command on R1 will reflect the filtered routes by listing them with a code of **r**, meaning "RIB failure."

   c. The filtering will not occur, and cannot be verified, until R1 issues a **clear ip bgp 2.2.2.2** command.

   d. None of the **show ip bgp** command options on R1 will confirm whether the filtering has occurred.

3. A router needs to match routes with AS_PATHs that include 333, as long as it is not the first ASN in the AS_PATH, while not matching AS_PATHs that include 33333. Which of the following syntactically correct commands could be a part of the complete configuration to match the correct AS_PATHs?

   a. ip filter-list 1 permit ^.*_333_

   b. ip filter-list 2 permit .*333_

   c. ip filter-list 3 permit .*_333.*$

   d. ip filter-list 4 permit _333_$

   e. ip filter-list 5 permit ^.*_333_.*$

4. R1 and R2 are working BGP peers. The following output of the **show ip bgp** command shows the entries learned by R1 from R2. It also shows some configuration that was added later on R1. After the appropriate **clear** command is used to make the new configuration take effect, which of the following entries should R1 have in its BGP table?

```
Network             Next Hop Metric       LocPrf  Weight  Path
*>i11.10.0.0/16     2.2.2.2  4294967294   100     0 4 1   33333 10    200 44 i
*>i11.11.0.0/16     2.2.2.2  4294967294   100     0 4 1   33333 10    200 44 i
*>i11.12.0.0/16     2.2.2.2  4294967294   100     0 4 1   404    303 202   i
! New config shown next
router bgp 1
neighbor 2.2.2.2 distribute-list 1 in
access-list 1 permit 11.8.0.0 0.3.255.255
```

  a. 11.10.0.0/16

  b. 11.11.0.0/16

  c. 11.12.0.0/16

  d. 11.8.0.0/14

  e. None of the listed prefixes

5. Which of the following is true regarding BGP path attribute types?

  a. The BGP features using well-known attributes must be included in every BGP Update.

  b. Optional attributes do not have to be implemented by the programmers that are creating a particular BGP implementation.

  c. Nontransitive attributes cannot be advertised into another AS.

  d. Discretionary attributes contain sensitive information; Updates should be encoded with MD5 for privacy.

6. Which of the following items in the BGP decision tree occur after the check of the AS_PATH length?

  a. Best ORIGIN code

  b. LOCAL_PREF

  c. MED

  d. Whether the next hop is reachable

7. Which of the following steps in the BGP decision process consider a larger value to be the better value?

   a. ORIGIN

   b. LOCAL_PREF

   c. WEIGHT

   d. MED

   e. IGP metric to reach the next hop

8. Which of the following is not advertised to BGP neighbors?

   a. WEIGHT

   b. MED

   c. LOCAL_PREF

   d. ORIGIN

9. The following shows the output of the **show ip bgp** command on R1. Which BGP decision tree step determined which route was best? (Assume that the next-hop IP address is reachable.)

```
Network          Next Hop    Metric       LocPrf Weight Path
*> 11.10.0.0/16  10.1.2.3    4294967294    100      0 4 1  33333 10 200 44 i
*  i             2.2.2.2     4294967294    100      0 4 1  33333 10 200 44 i
*  i             2.2.2.2     4294967294    100      0 4 1  404 505 303 202 i
```

   a. Largest Weight

   b. Best ORIGIN code

   c. Lowest MED

   d. Largest LOCAL_PREF

   e. Better neighbor type

   f. None of the answers is correct.

10. The following shows the output of the **show ip bgp** command on R1. Which BGP decision tree step determined which route was best? (Assume that the NEXT_HOP IP address is reachable.)

```
Network            Next Hop   Metric  LocPrf  Weight  Path
*  11.10.0.0/16   10.1.2.3        3     120      10   4 1  33333 10 200 44 ?
*>i               2.2.2.2         1     130      30   4 33333 10 200 44 i
*  i              2.2.2.2         2     110      20   4 1  404 505 303 202 ?
```

    a. Largest Weight

    b. Best ORIGIN code

    c. Lowest MED

    d. Largest LOCAL_PREF

    e. Better Neighbor Type

    f. None of the answers is correct.

11. The following exhibit lists commands that were typed using a text editor and later pasted into config mode on Router R1. At the time, R1 had a working eBGP connection to several peers, including 3.3.3.3. R1 had learned of several subnets of networks 11.0.0.0/8 and 12.0.0.0/8 through neighbors besides 3.3.3.3. After being pasted, a **clear** command was issued to pick up the changes. Which of the following statements is true regarding the AS_PATH of the routes advertised by R1 to 3.3.3.3?

```
router bgp 1
 neighbor 3.3.3.3 route-map zzz out
ip prefix-list match11 seq 5 permit 11.0.0.0/8 le 32
route-map zzz permit 10
 match ip address prefix-list match11
 set as-path prepend 1 1 1
```

    a. No changes would occur, because the configuration would be rejected because of syntax errors.

    b. Routes to subnets inside network 11.0.0.0/8 would contain three consecutive 1s, but no more, in the AS_PATH.

    c. Routes to subnets inside 11.0.0.0/8 would contain at least four consecutive 1s in the AS_PATH.

    d. Routes to subnets inside 12.0.0.0/8 would have no 1s in the AS_PATH.

    e. Routes to subnets inside 12.0.0.0/8 would have one additional 1 in the AS_PATH.

12. Which of the following must occur or be configured for BGP to mark multiple iBGP routes in the BGP table—entries for the exact same destination prefix/length—as the best routes?

   a. Inclusion of the **maximum-paths** *number* command under router BGP, with a setting larger than 1.

   b. Inclusion of the **maximum-paths ibgp** *number* command under router BGP, with a setting larger than 1.

   c. Multiple routes that tie for all BGP decision process comparisons up through checking a route's ORIGIN code.

   d. BGP cannot consider multiple routes in the BGP table for the exact same prefix as best routes.

13. Which of the following special BGP COMMUNITY values, when set, imply that a route should not be forwarded outside a confederation AS?

   a. LOCAL_AS

   b. NO_ADVERT

   c. NO_EXPORT

   d. NO_EXPORT_SUBCONFED

14. When BGP peers have set and sent COMMUNITY values in BGP Updates, which of the following is true?

   a. The BGP decision process adds a check for the COMMUNITY just before the check for the shortest AS_PATH length.

   b. The lowest COMMUNITY value is considered best by the BGP decision process, unless the COMMUNITY is set to one of the special reserved values.

   c. The COMMUNITY does not impact the BGP decision process directly.

   d. None of the other answers is correct.

Foundation Topics

Route Filtering and Route Summarization

This section focuses on four popular tools used to filter BGP routes:

- Distribution lists
- Prefix lists
- AS_PATH filter lists
- Route maps

Additionally, the **aggregate-address** command can be used to filter component subnets of a summary route. This section covers these five options. (Filtering using special BGP COMMUNITY values will be covered at the end of the chapter in the section "BGP Communities.")

The four main tools have the following features in common:

- All can filter incoming and outgoing Updates, per neighbor or per peer group.
- Peer group configurations require Cisco IOS Software to process the routing policy against the Update only once, rather than once per neighbor.
- The filters cannot be applied to a single neighbor that is configured as part of a peer group; the filter must be applied to the entire peer group, or the neighbor must be reconfigured to be outside the peer group.
- Each tool's matching logic examines the contents of the BGP Update message, which includes the BGP PAs and network layer reachability information (NLRI).
- If a filter's configuration is changed, a **clear** command is required for the changed filter to take effect.
- The **clear** command can use the soft reconfiguration option to implement changes without requiring BGP peers to be brought down and back up.

The tools differ in what they can match in the BGP Update message. Table 2-2 outlines the commands for each tool and the differences in how they can match NLRI entries in an Update.

> **Note** Throughout the book, the *wildcard mask* used in ACLs is abbreviated *WC mask*.

Key
Topic

Table 2-2   *NLRI Filtering Tools*

BGP Subcommand	Commands Referenced by neighbor Command	What Can Be Matched
neighbor distribute-list (standard ACL)	access-list, ip access-list	Prefix, with WC mask
neighbor distribute-list (extended ACL)	access-list, ip access-list	Prefix and prefix length, with WC mask for each
neighbor prefix-list	ip prefix-list	Exact or "first *N*" bits of prefix, plus range of prefix lengths
neighbor filter-list	ip as-path access-list	AS_PATH contents; all NLRIs whose AS_PATHs are matched are considered to be a match
neighbor route-map	route-map	Prefix, prefix length, AS_PATH, and/or any other PA matchable within a BGP route map

This section begins by covering filtering through the use of matching NLRI, distribute lists, prefix lists, and route maps. From there, it moves on to describe how to use BGP filter lists to match AS_PATH information to filter NLRI entries from routing updates.

Filtering BGP Updates Based on NLRI

One difference between BGP distribute lists and IGP distribute lists is that a BGP distribute list can use an extended ACL to match against both the prefix and the prefix length. When used with IGP filtering tools, ACLs called from distribute lists cannot match against the prefix length. Example 2-1 shows how an extended ACL matches the prefix with the source address portion of the ACL commands, and matches the prefix length (mask) using the destination address portion of the ACL commands.

The matching logic used by **prefix-list** and **route-map** commands works just the same for BGP as it does for IGPs. For example, both commands have an implied **deny** action at the end of the list, which can be overridden by matching all routes with the final entry in the **prefix-list** or **route-map** command.

Figure 2-1 shows the important portions of the network used for Example 2-1. The example shows a prefix list, distribute list, and a route map performing the same logic to filter based on NLRI. In this case, the four routers in AS 123 form a full mesh. R3 will learn a set of prefixes from AS 45, and then filter the same two prefixes (22.2.2.0/24 and 23.3.16.0/20) from being sent in Updates to each of R3's three neighbors—in each case using a different tool.

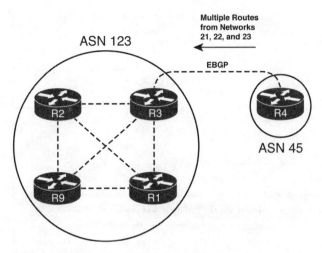

Figure 2-1 *iBGP Full Mesh in AS 123 with Routes Learned from AS 45*

Example 2-1 *Route Filtering on R3 with Route Maps, Distribution Lists, and Prefix Lists*

```
! R3 Configuration. Only the commands related to filtering are shown. Note that
! BGP Updates to R1 and R2 are filtered at this point; filtering to R9 will be
! added later in the example.
router bgp 123
 neighbor 1.1.1.1 route-map rmap-lose-2 out
 neighbor 2.2.2.2 distribute-list lose-2 out
! This ACL matches exactly for a prefix of 23.3.16.0 and 22.2.2.0, as well as
! exactly matching masks 255.255.240.0 and 255.255.255.0, respectively.
ip access-list extended lose-2
 deny    ip host 23.3.16.0 host 255.255.240.0
 deny    ip host 22.2.2.0 host 255.255.255.0
 permit ip any any
! The prefix list matches the exact prefixes and prefix lengths; the omission of
! any ge or le parameter means each line matches only that exact prefix. Also, the
! third line matches all prefixes, changing the default action to permit.
ip prefix-list prefix-lose-2 seq 5 deny 22.2.2.0/24
ip prefix-list prefix-lose-2 seq 10 deny 23.3.16.0/20
ip prefix-list prefix-lose-2 seq 15 permit 0.0.0.0/0 le 32
! The route map refers to ACL lose-2, passing routes that are permitted
! by the ACL, and filtering all others. The two filtered routes are actually
! filtered by the implied deny clause at the end of the route map: Because the ACL
! matches those two prefixes with a deny action, they do not match clause 10 of the
! route map, and are then matched by the implied deny clause.
route-map rmap-lose-2 permit 10
 match ip address lose-2
! Next, R3 has seven prefixes, with the two slated for filtering highlighted.
R3# show ip bgp | begin Network
```

```
     Network          Next Hop          Metric LocPrf Weight Path
*>  21.0.0.0          4.4.4.4                         0 45 i
*>  22.2.2.0/24       4.4.4.4                         0 45 i
*>  23.3.0.0/20       4.4.4.4                         0 45 i
*>  23.3.16.0/20      4.4.4.4                         0 45 i
*>  23.3.32.0/19      4.4.4.4                         0 45 i
*>  23.3.64.0/18      4.4.4.4                         0 45 i
*>  23.3.128.0/17     4.4.4.4                         0 45 i
Total number of prefixes 7
! The next command shows what entries R3 will advertise to R1. Note that the
! correct two prefixes have been removed, with only five prefixes listed. The same
! results could be seen for the Update sent to R2, but it is not shown here.
R3# show ip bgp neighbor 1.1.1.1 advertised-routes | begin Network
     Network          Next Hop          Metric LocPrf Weight Path
*>  21.0.0.0          4.4.4.4                         0 45 i
*>  23.3.0.0/20       4.4.4.4                         0 45 i
*>  23.3.32.0/19      4.4.4.4                         0 45 i
*>  23.3.64.0/18      4.4.4.4                         0 45 i
*>  23.3.128.0/17     4.4.4.4                         0 45 i
Total number of prefixes 5
! Next, R3 adds an outbound prefix list for neighbor R9 (9.9.9.9). However,
! afterwards, R3 still believes it should send all seven prefixes to R9.
R3# conf t
Enter configuration commands, one per line.  End with CNTL/Z.
R3(config)# router bgp 123
R3(config-router)# neigh 9.9.9.9 prefix-list prefix-lose-2 out
R3(config-router)# ^Z
R3# show ip bgp neighbor 9.9.9.9 advertised-routes | begin Network
     Network          Next Hop          Metric LocPrf Weight Path
*>  21.0.0.0          4.4.4.4                         0 45 i
*>  22.2.2.0/24       4.4.4.4                         0 45 i
*>  23.3.0.0/20       4.4.4.4                         0 45 i
*>  23.3.16.0/20      4.4.4.4                         0 45 i
*>  23.3.32.0/19      4.4.4.4                         0 45 i
*>  23.3.64.0/18      4.4.4.4                         0 45 i
*>  23.3.128.0/17     4.4.4.4                         0 45 i
Total number of prefixes 7
! Instead of the clear ip bgp 9.9.9.9 command, which would close the BGP neighbor
! and TCP connection to R9, R3 uses the clear ip bgp 9.9.9.9 out or clear ip bgp *
! soft command to perform a soft reconfiguration. Now R3 filters the correct two
! prefixes.
R3# clear ip bgp 9.9.9.9 out
R3# show ip bgp neighbor 9.9.9.9 advertised-routes | begin Network
     Network          Next Hop          Metric LocPrf Weight Path
*>  21.0.0.0          4.4.4.4                         0 45 i
*>  23.3.0.0/20       4.4.4.4                         0 45 i
```

```
*> 23.3.32.0/19     4.4.4.4                           0 45 i
*> 23.3.64.0/18     4.4.4.4                           0 45 i
*> 23.3.128.0/17    4.4.4.4                           0 45 i
Total number of prefixes 5
```

Route Map Rules for NLRI Filtering

The overall logic used by route maps to filter NLRIs is relatively straightforward: The Update is compared to the route map and the route is filtered (or not) based on the first-matching clause. However, route maps can cause a bit of confusion on a couple of points; the next several pages point out some of the potential confusing points with regard to route maps when they are used to filter BGP routes.

Both the route map and any referenced ACL or prefix list have **deny** and **permit** actions configured, so it is easy to confuse the context in which they are used. The **route-map** command's action—either **deny** or **permit**—defines whether an NLRI is filtered (**deny**) or allowed to pass (**permit**). The **permit** or **deny** action in an ACL or prefix list implies whether an NLRI matches the **route map** clause (**permit** by the ACL/prefix list) or does not match (**deny** in the ACL/prefix list).

For example, **route-map rmap-lose-2 permit 10** from Example 2-1 matched all NLRIs except the two prefixes that needed to be filtered based on named ACL lose-2. The matched routes—all the routes that do not need to be filtered in this case—were then advertised, because clause 10 had a **permit** action configured. The route map then filtered the other two routes by virtue of the implied **deny all** logic at the end of the route map.

Alternatively, the route map could have just as easily used a beginning clause of **route-map rmap-lose-2 deny 10**, with the matching logic only matching the two prefixes that needed to be filtered—in that case, the first clause would have filtered the two routes because of the **deny** keyword in the **route-map** command. Such a route map would then require a second clause that matched all routes, with a **permit** action configured. (To match all NLRIs in a route map, simply omit the **match** command from that **route map** clause. In this case, adding just the command **route-map rmap-lose-2 20**, with no sub-commands, would match all remaining routes and allow them to be advertised.)

Soft Reconfiguration

The end of Example 2-1 shows a BGP feature called *soft reconfiguration*. Soft reconfiguration allows a BGP peer to reapply its routing policies without closing a neighbor connection. To reapply the policies, Cisco IOS uses the **clear** command with either the **soft**, **in**, or **out** options, as shown in the following generic **clear** command syntax:

```
clear ip bgp {* | neighbor-address | peer-group-name} [soft [in | out]]
```

The **soft** option alone reapplies the policy configuration for both inbound and outbound policies, whereas the inclusion of the **in** or **out** keyword limits the reconfiguration to the stated direction.

Cisco IOS supports soft reconfiguration for sent Updates automatically, but BGP must be configured to support soft reconfiguration for inbound Updates. To support soft reconfiguration, BGP must remember the actual sent and received BGP Update information for each neighbor. The **neighbor** *neighbor-id* **soft-reconfiguration inbound** command causes the router to keep a copy of the received Updates from the specified neighbor. (IOS keeps a copy of sent Updates automatically.) With these Updates available, BGP can simply reapply the changed filtering policy to the Update without closing the neighbor connection.

Clearing the neighbor is required to pick up the changes to routing policies that impact Updates sent and received from neighbors. All such changes can be implemented using soft reconfiguration. However, for configuration changes that impact the local injection of routes into the BGP table, soft reconfiguration does not help. The reason is that soft reconfiguration simply reprocesses Updates, and features that inject routes into BGP through the **redistribute** or **network** commands are not injected based on Update messages.

Comparing BGP Prefix Lists, Distribute Lists, and Route Maps

Prefix lists and distribute lists both use their matching logic on the BGP Update's NLRI. However, a prefix list allows more flexible matching of the prefix length because it can match a range of prefixes that extends to a maximum length of less than 32. For example, the command **ip prefix-list test1 permit 10.0.0.0/8 ge 16 le 23** matches a range of prefix lengths, but the same logic using an ACL as a distribute list takes several more lines, or a tricky wildcard mask.

For many BGP filtering tasks, route maps do not provide any benefit over prefix lists, ACLs, and AS_PATH filter lists. If the desired policy is only to filter routes based on matching prefixes/lengths, a route map does not provide any additional function over using a distribute list or prefix list directly. Similarly, if the goal of the policy is to filter routes just based on matching with an AS_PATH filter, the route map does not provide any additional function as compared to calling an AS_PATH filter directly using the **neighbor filter-list** command.

However, only route maps can provide the following two functions for BGP routing policy configurations:

■ Matching logic that combines multiples of the following: prefix/length, AS_PATH, or other BGP PAs

■ The setting of BGP PAs for the purpose of manipulating BGP's choice of which route to use

Many of the features for manipulating the choice of best routes by BGP, as covered later in this chapter, use route maps for that purpose.

Filtering Subnets of a Summary Using the aggregate-address Command

Manual BGP route summarization, using the **aggregate-address** BGP router subcommand, provides the flexibility to allow none, all, or a subset of the summary's component subnets to be advertised out of the BGP table. By allowing some and not others, the **aggregate-address** command can in effect filter some routes. The filtering options on the **aggregate-address** command are as follows:

Key Topic

- Filtering all component subnets of the summary from being advertised, by using the **summary-only** keyword

- Advertising all the component subnets of the summary, by *omitting* the **summary-only** keyword

- Advertising some and filtering other component subnets of the summary, by omitting the **summary-only** keyword and referring to a route map using the **suppress-map** keyword

subset of component routes

The logic behind the **suppress-map** option can be a little tricky. This option requires reference to a route map, with any component subnets matching a route map **permit** clause being *suppressed*—in other words, routes permitted by the route map are filtered and not advertised. The router does not actually remove the suppressed route from its local BGP table; however, it does suppress the advertisement of those routes.

suppress-map
uses a route-map
permit = suppress

Example 2-2 shows how the **suppress-map** option works, with a summary of 23.0.0.0/8 and a goal of allowing all component subnets to be advertised except 23.3.16.0/20.

Example 2-2 *Filtering Routes Using the* **aggregate-address suppress-map** *Command*

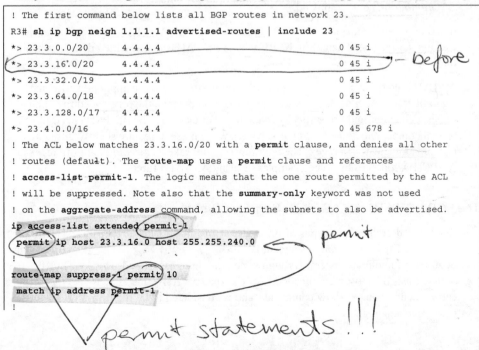

```
! The first command below lists all BGP routes in network 23.
R3# sh ip bgp neigh 1.1.1.1 advertised-routes | include 23
*> 23.3.0.0/20      4.4.4.4                              0 45 i
*> 23.3.16.0/20     4.4.4.4                              0 45 i      - before
*> 23.3.32.0/19     4.4.4.4                              0 45 i
*> 23.3.64.0/18     4.4.4.4                              0 45 i
*> 23.3.128.0/17    4.4.4.4                              0 45 i
*> 23.4.0.0/16      4.4.4.4                              0 45 678 i
! The ACL below matches 23.3.16.0/20 with a permit clause, and denies all other
! routes (default). The route-map uses a permit clause and references
! access-list permit-1. The logic means that the one route permitted by the ACL
! will be suppressed. Note also that the summary-only keyword was not used
! on the aggregate-address command, allowing the subnets to also be advertised.
ip access-list extended permit-1
 permit ip host 23.3.16.0 host 255.255.240.0        <=   permit
!
route-map suppress-1 permit 10
 match ip address permit-1
!
```

permit statements !!!

```
router bgp 123
 aggregate-address 23.0.0.0 255.0.0.0 as-set suppress-map suppress-1
! Below, R3 (after a clear ip bgp * soft command) no longer advertises the route.
R3# sh ip bgp neigh 1.1.1.1 advertised-routes | include 23.3.16.0
R3#
! Note the "s" on the left side of the show ip bgp command output for the
! suppressed route. The route remains in the table; it is simply no longer
! advertised outside the router.
R3# sh ip bgp neigh 1.1.1.1 advertised-routes | include 23
*> 23.3.0.0/20       4.4.4.4                           0 45 i
 s> 23.3.16.0/20     4.4.4.4                           0 45 i
*> 23.3.32.0/19      4.4.4.4                           0 45 i
*> 23.3.64.0/18      4.4.4.4                           0 45 i
*> 23.3.128.0/17     4.4.4.4                           0 45 i
*> 23.4.0.0/16       4.4.4.4                           0 45 678 i
```

[handwritten margin note: not adv. anymore]

[handwritten margin note: deny filtered]

Filtering BGP Updates by Matching the AS_PATH PA

To filter routes by matching the AS_PATH PA, Cisco IOS uses AS_PATH filters. The overall configuration structure is similar to BGP distribute lists and prefix lists, with the matching logic specified in a list and the logic being applied with a **neighbor** command. The main two steps are as follows:

1. Configure the AS_PATH filter using the **ip as-path access-list** *number* {**permit** | **deny**} *regex* command.

2. Enable the AS_PATH filter using the **neighbor** *neighbor-id* **filter-list** *as-path-filter-number* (**in** | **out**) command.

Based on these commands, Cisco IOS examines the AS_PATH PA in the sent or received Updates for the stated neighbor. NLRIs whose AS_PATHs match with a **deny** action are filtered.

AS_PATH filters use *regular expressions* (abbreviated *regex*) to apply powerful matching logic to the AS_PATH. To match the AS_PATH contents, the regex need to match values, delimiters, and other special characters. For example, the AS_PATH itself has several components, called *segments*, which, when present, require slightly different matching logic within a regex. The next few sections take a closer look at both regex and AS_PATHs, followed by some examples of using AS_PATH filters.

The BGP AS_PATH and AS_PATH Segment Types

RFC 1771 describes four types of AS_PATH segments held inside the AS_PATH PA (see Table 2-3). The most common segment is called AS_SEQUENCE, which is an ordered list of all the autonomous systems through which the route has passed. The AS_SEQUENCE segment lists the most recently added ASN as the first ASN; this value is also the leftmost entry when looking at **show** commands, and is considered to be the first ASN for the regex matching logic.

Because the most recently added ASN is the first ASN in the AS_SEQUENCE segment, the process of adding the ASN before advertising routes to external BGP (eBGP) peers is called *AS_PATH prepending*. For example, Figure 2-2 shows a sample network in which a route is injected inside AS 1, advertised to AS 4, and then advertised to AS 123.

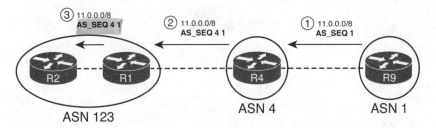

Figure 2-2   *AS_PATH (AS_SEQUENCE) Prepending*

The other three AS_PATH segment types come into play when using confederations and route summarization. Table 2-3 lists and briefly describes all four types.

Table 2-3   *AS_PATH Segment Types*

Component	Description	Delimiters Between ASNs	Character Enclosing the Segment
AS_SEQUENCE	An ordered list of ASNs through which the route has been advertised	Space	None
AS_SET	An unordered list of ASNs through which the route has been advertised	Comma	{}
AS_CONFED_SEQ[1]	Like AS_SEQ, but holds only confederation ASNs	Space	()
AS_CONFED_SET[1]	Like AS_SET, but holds only confederation ASNs	Comma	{}

[1] *Not advertised outside the confederation.*

Figure 2-3 shows an example of AS_SET in which R4 summarizes some routes using the **aggregate-address... as-set** command. As a result of including the **as-set** keyword, R4 creates an AS_SET segment in the AS_PATH of the aggregate route. Note that the AS_SET segment is shown in brackets, and it is listed in no particular order. These facts are all important to the process of AS_PATH filtering.

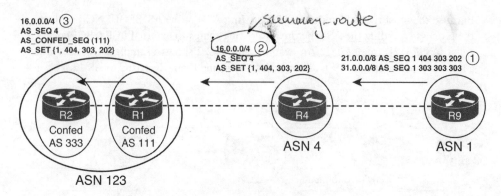

Figure 2-3 *AS_SET and AS_CONFED_SEQ Example*

Also note the addition of the AS_CONFED_SEQ segment by R1 in Figure 2-3. Confederation ASNs are used to prevent loops inside the confederation. Because these ASNs will be removed before advertising the route outside the full AS, the confederation ASNs are kept inside a different segment—the AS_CONFED_SEQ segment. Finally, if a route is aggregated inside a confederation, the AS_CONFED_SET segment holds the confederation ASNs with the same logic as used by the AS_SET segment type, but keeps them separate for easy removal before advertising the routes outside the confederation. Example 2-3 provides sample **show ip bgp** command output showing an AS_SET and AS_CONFED_SEQ. The output shows R2's AS_PATH for the route shown in Figure 2-3.

Example 2-3 *AS_PATH on R2: AS_CONFED_SEQ, AS_SEQUENCE, and AS_SET*

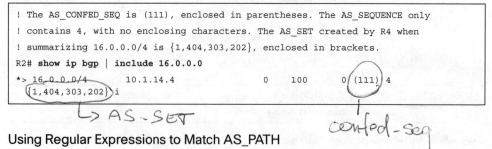

```
! The AS_CONFED_SEQ is (111), enclosed in parentheses. The AS_SEQUENCE only
! contains 4, with no enclosing characters. The AS_SET created by R4 when
! summarizing 16.0.0.0/4 is {1,404,303,202}, enclosed in brackets.
R2# show ip bgp | include 16.0.0.0
*> 16.0.0.0/4        10.1.14.4           0      100      0 (111) 4
   {1,404,303,202} i
```

Using Regular Expressions to Match AS_PATH

A Cisco IOS AS_PATH filter has one or more configured lines, with each line requiring a regex. The logic is then applied as follows:

1. The regex of the first line in the list is applied to the AS_PATH of each route.

2. For matched NLRIs, the NLRI is passed or filtered based on that AS_PATH filter's configured **permit** or **deny** action.

3. For unmatched NLRIs, Steps 1 and 2 are repeated, using the next line in the AS_PATH filter, analyzing all NLRIs yet to be matched by this list.

4. Any NLRI not matched explicitly is filtered.

Regexs contain literal strings as well as metacharacters. The *metacharacters* allow matching using wildcards, matches for different delimiters, and other special operations. Table 2-4 lists the regex metacharacters that are useful for IOS AS_PATH filters.

Table 2-4 *Regex Metacharacters Useful for AS_PATH Matching*

Metacharacter	Meaning
^	Start of line
$	End of line
|	Logical OR applied between the preceding and succeeding characters[1]
_	Any delimiter: blank, comma, start of line, or end of line[2]
.	Any single character
?	Zero or one instance of the preceding character
*	Zero or more instances of the preceding character
+	One or more instances of the preceding character
(*string*)	Parentheses combine enclosed string characters as a single entity when used with ?, *, or +
[*string*]	Creates a wildcard for which any of the single characters in the string can be used to match that position in the AS_PATH

[1] *If preceded by a value in parentheses, the logic applies to the preceding string listed inside the parentheses, and not just to the preceding character.*

[2] *This character is an underscore.*

When the regular expression is applied to a BGP route, Cisco IOS searches the AS_PATH for the first instance of the first item in the regex; from that point forward, it processes the rest of the AS_PATH sequentially. For example, consider two routes, one with an AS_PATH with only an AS_SEQ, set to 12 34 56 and another route with an AS_SEQ of 78 12 34 56. A regular expression of **12_34_56** matches both routes, because IOS looks for the first occurrence of AS 12 and then searches sequentially. However, a regular expression of **^12_34_56** would match only the first route. The second AS_PATH (78 12 34 56) would not match because the regex would immediately match on the ^ (start of line) and then search sequentially—finding AS 78 next, which does not match the regex.

Although Table 2-4 provides a useful reference, Table 2-5 provides a number of examples of using these metacharacters, with explanations of what they match. Take special note of the wording in the explanations. Phrases like "ASN 303" and "ASN beginning with 303" differ in that the first phrase means exactly 303, and not 3031, 30342, and so on, whereas the second phrase would match any of these values.

Table 2-5 *Sample AS_PATH Regex and Their Meanings*

Sample Regex	What Type of AS_PATH It Would Match
.*	All AS_PATHs (useful as a final match to change the default from **deny** to **permit**).
^$	Null (empty)—used for NLRIs originated in the same AS.

Sample Regex	What Type of AS_PATH It Would Match
^123$	An AS_PATH with only one AS, ASN 123.
^123	An AS_PATH whose first ASN begins with or is 123; includes 123, 1232, 12354, and so on.
^123.	An AS_PATH whose first ASN is one of two things: a four-digit number that begins with 123, or a number that begins with ASN 123 and is followed by a delimiter before the next ASN. (It does not match an AS_PATH of only ASN 123, because the period does not match the end-of-line.)
^1234	An AS_PATH whose first ASN begins with 123, with 1233, or is 12333. For example, it includes ASNs 1231 and 12331 because it does not specify what happens after the +.
^123+	An AS_PATH whose first ASN is one of three numbers: 123, 1233, or 12333. It does not match 1231 and 12331, for example, because it requires a delimiter after the last 3.
^123*	An AS_PATH whose first ASN begins with 12, 123, or 1233, or is 12333. Any character can follow these values, because the regex does not specify anything about the next character. For example, 121 would match because the * can represent 0 occurrences of "3". 1231 would match with * representing 1 occurrence of 3.
^123*_	An AS_PATH whose first ASN begins with 12, 123, or 1233, or is 12333. It does not include matches for 121, 1231, and 12331, because the next character must be a delimiter.
^123?	An AS_PATH whose first ASN begins with either 12 or 123.
^123_45$	An AS_PATH with two autonomous systems, beginning with 123 and ending with 45.
^123_.*_45$	An AS_PATH beginning with AS 123 and ending in AS 45, with at least one other AS in between.
^123_.*45	An AS_PATH beginning with AS 123, with zero or more intermediate ASNs and delimiters, and ending with any AS whose last two digits are 45 (including simply AS 45).
(^123_45$)|(^123_.*_45$)	An AS_PATH beginning with 123 and ending with AS 45, with zero or more other ASNs between the two.
^123_45$|^123_.*_45$	(Note: This is the same as the previous example, but without the parentheses.) Represents a common error in attempting to match AS_PATHs that begin with ASN 123 and end with ASN 45. The problem is that the	is applied to the previous character ($) and next character (^), as opposed to everything before and after the |.
^123(_[0..9]+)*_45	Another way to match an AS_PATH beginning with 123 and ending with AS 45.

Sample Regex	What Type of AS_PATH It Would Match
^{123	The AS_PATH begins with an AS_SET or AS_CONFED_SET, with the first three numerals of the first ASN being 123.
[(|303.*[)]	Find the AS_CONFED_SEQ, and match if the first ASN begins with 303.

Example: Matching AS_PATHs Using AS_PATH Filters

NLRI filtering with AS_PATH filters uses two commands:

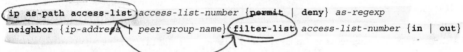

```
ip as-path access-list access-list-number {permit | deny} as-regexp
neighbor {ip-address | peer-group-name} filter-list access-list-number {in | out}
```

Figure 2-4 shows a sample internetwork used in many of the upcoming examples, two of which show the use of AS_PATH filtering.

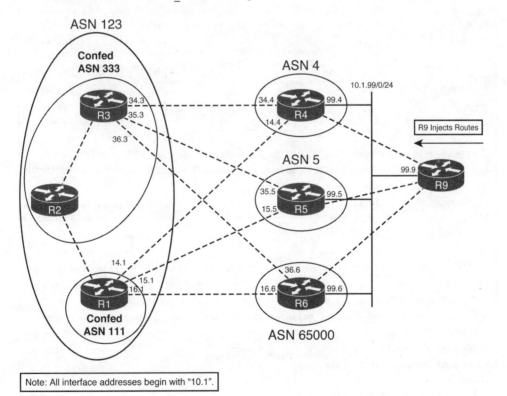

Figure 2-4 *Network Used for AS_PATH Filter Examples*

Example 2-4 shows an AS_PATH filter in which routes are filtered going from R4 to R3. Filtering the outbound Update on R4 will be shown first, followed by filtering of inbound Updates on R3. In both cases, the goal of the filter is as follows:

Filter routes in R4's BGP table whose ASN begins with AS 1, has three additional ASNs of any value, and ends with ASN 44.

The two NLRIs matching these criteria are 11.0.0.0/8 and 12.0.0.0/8.

Example 2-4 *AS_PATH Filtering of Routes Sent from R4 to R3*

```
! R4 learned its best routes to 11.0.0.0/8 and 12.0.0.0/8 from R9 (10.1.99.9), plus
! two other routers. Only the routes learned from R9, with NEXT_HOP 10.1.99.9,
! match the AS_PATH criteria for this example.
R4# show ip bgp
BGP table version is 9, local router ID is 4.4.4.4
Status codes: s suppressed, d damped, h history, * valid, > best, i-internal,
              r RIB-failure, S Stale
Origin codes: i-IGP, e-EGP, ?-incomplete

   Network          Next Hop          Metric LocPrf Weight Path
*  11.0.0.0         10.1.14.1                          0 123 5 1 33333 10 200 44 i
*                   10.1.34.3                          0 123 5 1 33333 10 200 44 i
*>                  10.1.99.9              0            0 1 33333 10 200 44 i
*  12.0.0.0         10.1.14.1                          0 123 5 1 33333 10 200 44 i
*                   10.1.34.3                          0 123 5 1 33333 10 200 44 i
*>                  10.1.99.9              0            0 1 33333 10 200 44 i
! lines omitted for brevity
! R4 currently advertises four routes to R3, as shown next.
R4# show ip bgp neighbor 10.1.34.3 advertised-routes | begin Network
   Network          Next Hop          Metric LocPrf Weight Path
*> 11.0.0.0         10.1.99.9              0            0 1 33333 10 200 44 i
*> 12.0.0.0         10.1.99.9              0            0 1 33333 10 200 44 i
*> 21.0.0.0         10.1.99.9              0            0 1 404 303 202 i
*> 31.0.0.0         10.1.99.9              0            0 1 303 303 303 i
! R4's new AS_PATH filter is shown next. The first line matches AS_PATHs beginning
! with ASN 1, and ending in 44, with three ASNs in between. The second line matches
! all other AS_PATHs, with a permit action-essentially a permit all at the end. The
! list is then enabled with the neighbor filter-list command, for outbound Updates
! sent to R3 (10.1.34.3).
ip as-path access-list 34 deny ^1_.*_.*_.*_44$
ip as-path access-list 34 permit .*
router bgp 4
neighbor 10.1.34.3 filter-list 34 out
! After soft reconfiguration, R4 no longer advertises the routes to networks
! 11 and 12.
R4# clear ip bgp * soft
```

[handwritten annotations: "routes learnt from R9 → starting with AS 1 → matching criteria", "ending with 44", "other matching criteria", "starting with AS 1, ending with AS44 and three ASs in between!!"]

```
R4# show ip bgp neighbor 10.1.34.3 advertised-routes | begin Network
   Network          Next Hop          Metric LocPrf Weight Path
*> 21.0.0.0         10.1.99.9              0               0 1 404 303 202 i
*> 31.0.0.0         10.1.99.9              0               0 1 303 303 303 i
Total number of prefixes 2
```

```
! Not shown: R4's neighbor filter-list command is now removed, and soft
! reconfiguration used to restore the Updates to their unfiltered state.
! R3 lists its unfiltered received Update from R4. Note that R4's ASN was added
! by R4 before sending the Update.
R3# show ip bgp neighbor 10.1.34.4 received-routes | begin Network
   Network          Next Hop          Metric LocPrf Weight Path
*  11.0.0.0         10.1.34.4                              0 4 1 33333 10 200 44 i
*  12.0.0.0         10.1.34.4                              0 4 1 33333 10 200 44 i
*  21.0.0.0         10.1.34.4                              0 4 1 404 303 202 i
*  31.0.0.0         10.1.34.4                              0 4 1 303 303 303 i
! R3 uses practically the same AS_PATH filter, except that it must look for ASN
! 4 as the first ASN.
ip as-path access-list 34 deny ^4_1_.*_.*_.*_44$
ip as-path access-list 34 permit .*
router bgp 333
 neighbor 10.1.34.4 filter-list 34 in
! The show ip as-path-access-list command shows the contents of the list.
R3# show ip as-path-access-list 34
AS path access list 34
    deny ^4_1_.*_.*_.*_44$
    permit .*
! To test the logic of the regex, the show ip bgp command can be used, with the
! pipe (|) and the include option. That parses the command output based on the
! regex at the end of the show command. However, note that some things matchable
! using an AS_PATH filter are not in the show command output-for example, the
! beginning or end of line cannot be matched with a ^ or $, respectively.
! These metacharacters must be omitted for this testing trick to work.
R3# show ip bgp neighbor 10.1.34.4 received-routes | include 4_1_.*_.*_.*_44
*  11.0.0.0         10.1.34.4                              0 4 1 33333 10 200 44 i
*  12.0.0.0         10.1.34.4                              0 4 1 33333 10 200 44 i
! After a clear, it first appears that the routes were not filtered, as they
! still show up in the output below.
R3# clear ip bgp * soft
R3# show ip bgp neighbor 10.1.34.4 received-routes | begin Network
   Network          Next Hop          Metric LocPrf Weight Path
*  11.0.0.0         10.1.34.4                              0 4 1 33333 10 200 44 i
*  12.0.0.0         10.1.34.4                              0 4 1 33333 10 200 44 i
*  21.0.0.0         10.1.34.4                              0 4 1 404 303 202 i
*  31.0.0.0         10.1.34.4                              0 4 1 303 303 303 i
```

```
! However, R3 does not show the routes shown in the received Update from R4 in
! the BGP table; the routes were indeed filtered.
R3# show ip bgp | begin Network
   Network          Next Hop          Metric LocPrf Weight Path
*  11.0.0.0         10.1.36.6                           0 65000 1 33333 10 200 44 i
* i                 10.1.15.5              0    100     0 (111) 5 1 33333 10 200 44 i
*>                  10.1.35.5                           0 5 1 33333 10 200 44 i
*  12.0.0.0         10.1.36.6                           0 65000 1 33333 10 200 44 i
* i                 10.1.15.5              0    100     0 (111) 5 1 33333 10 200 44 i
*>                  10.1.35.5                           0 5 1 33333 10 200 44 i
! lines omitted for brevity
```

The explanations in Example 2-4 cover most of the individual points about using filter lists to filter NLRIs based on the AS_PATH. The example also depicts a couple of broader issues regarding the Cisco IOS BGP **show** commands:

Key Topic

- The **show ip bgp neighbor** *neighbor-id* **advertised-routes** command displays the routes actually sent—in other words, this command reflects the effects of the filtering by omitting the filtered routes from the output.

- The **show ip bgp neighbor** *neighbor-id* **received-routes** command displays the routes actually received from a neighbor, never omitting routes from the output, even if the router locally filters the routes on input.

- Output filter lists are applied before the router adds its own ASN to the AS_PATH. (See Example 2-4's AS_PATH filter on R4 for an example.)

There are also a couple of ways to test regex without changing the routing policy. Example 2-4 showed one example using the following command:

```
show ip bgp neighbor 10.1.34.4 received-routes | include 4_1_.*_.*_.*_44
```

This command parses the entire command output using the regex after the **include** keyword. However, note that this command looks at the ASCII text of the command output, meaning that some special characters (like beginning-of-line and end-of-line characters) do not exist. For example, Example 2-4 left out the caret (^) in the regex, because the text output of the **show** command does not include a ^.

The other method to test a regex is to use the **show ip bgp regexp** *expression* command. This command parses the AS_PATH variables in a router's BGP table, including all special characters, allowing all aspects of the regex to be tested. However, the **regexp** option of the **show ip bgp** command is not allowed with the **received-routes** or **advertised-routes** option.

While Example 2-4 shows BGP using the **neighbor filter-list** command, the AS_PATH ~AS-PATH~
filter list can also be referenced in a route map using the **match as-path** *list-number* com- ~ACC CAN~
mand. In that case, the route map then can be called using the **neighbor route-map** ~BE USED~
command. ~WITH A ROUTE-MAP~

Matching AS_SET and AS_CONFED_SEQ

Example 2-5 shows how to use a BGP filter list to match the AS_SET and AS_CONFED_
SEQ segment types. Figure 2-5 depicts the specifics of the example. In this case, R4
summarizes 16.0.0.0/4, creating an AS_SET entry for the summary and advertising it
to R1 and R3. R1 and R3 in turn advertise the route to R2; R1's route includes an AS_
CONFED_SEQ, because R1 and R2 are confederation eBGP peers.

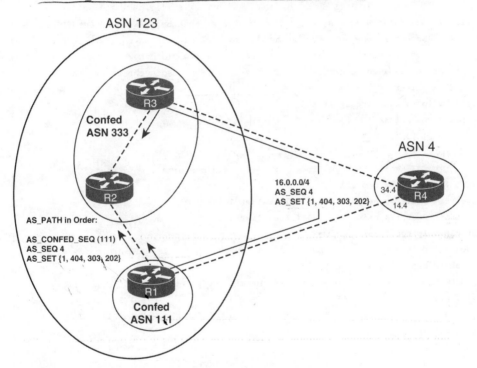

Figure 2-5 *Generating AS_SET and AS_CONFED_SEQ*

Example 2-5 shows two different sample filters, as follows:

■ Filtering routes with ASN 303 anywhere inside the AS_SET

■ Filtering based on the AS_CONFED_SEQ of only ASN 111 to begin the AS_PATH

Example 2-5 *AS_PATH Filtering of Routes Sent from R4 to R3*

```
! The next command shows R2's BGP table before filtering is enabled. R2 has five
! routes with AS_CONFED_SEQ of (111), all learned from R1. R2 also learned the
! same NLRI from R3, with the related AS_PATH not including the beginning
```

```
! AS_CONFED_SEQ of (111), because R3 is in the same confederation sub-AS as R2.
R2# sh ip bgp | begin Network
   Network           Next Hop         Metric LocPrf Weight Path
 * i11.0.0.0         10.1.35.5           0    100      0 5 1 33333 10 200 44 i
 *>                  10.1.15.5           0    100      0 (111) 5 1 33333 10 200 44 i
 * i12.0.0.0         10.1.35.5           0    100      0 5 1 33333 10 200 44 i
 *>                  10.1.15.5           0    100      0 (111) 5 1 33333 10 200 44 i
 * i16.0.0.0/4       10.1.34.4           0    100      0 4 {1,404,303,202} i
 *>                  10.1.14.4           0    100      0 (111) 4 {1,404,303,202} i
 * i21.0.0.0         10.1.34.4           0    100      0 4 1 404 303 202 i
 *>                  10.1.15.5           0    100      0 (111) 5 1 404 303 202 i
 * i31.0.0.0         10.1.34.4           0    100      0 4 1 303 303 303 i
 *>                  10.1.15.5           0    100      0 (111) 5 1 303 303 303 i
! R2 will use AS_PATH access-list 1 to find routes that begin with AS_CONFED_SEQ
! of 111. Note that the "(" must be matched by enclosing it in square brackets, as
! the "(" itself and the ")" are metacharacters, and would otherwise be
! interpreted as a metacharacter. Without the "[(]" to begin the regex, the
! AS_PATH filter would not match.
R2# show ip as-path-access-list 1
AS path access list 1
    deny ^[(]111
    permit .*
! R2 filters incoming routes from both peers, and performs a soft reconfig.
R2(config)# router bgp 333
R2(config-router)# neigh 1.1.1.1 filter-list 1 in
R2(config-router)# neigh 3.3.3.3 filter-list 1 in
R2# clear ip bgp * soft
! Now all routes with AS_CONFED_SEQ of 111 beginning the AS_PATH are gone.
R2# sh ip bgp | begin Network
   Network           Next Hop         Metric LocPrf Weight Path
 *>i11.0.0.0         10.1.35.5           0    100      0 5 1 33333 10 200 44 i
 *>i12.0.0.0         10.1.35.5           0    100      0 5 1 33333 10 200 44 i
 *>i16.0.0.0/4       10.1.34.4           0    100      0 4 {1,404,303,202} i
 *>i21.0.0.0         10.1.34.4           0    100      0 4 1 404 303 202 i
 *>i31.0.0.0         10.1.34.4           0    100      0 4 1 303 303 303 i
! Not shown-R2's switches to using AS_PATH filter-list 2 instead for peer R3
! only, and soft reconfiguration is applied.
! The next command shows the contents
! of the new filter for inbound Updates from R3. Because the "{" and "}" are not
! metacharacters, they can simply be typed directly into the regex. AS_PATH
! access-list 2 matches an AS_SET anywhere in the AS_PATH, as long as 303
! resides anywhere inside the AS_SET.
```

```
R2# show ip as-path-access-list 2
AS path access list 2
    deny {.*303.*}
    permit .*
! The next command is a test to show routes received by R2 from R3 that happen to
! have 303 anywhere in the AS_PATH. Remember, filtered routes are still
! displayed when viewing the BGP table with the received-routes option.
R2# show ip bgp neighbor 3.3.3.3 received-routes | include 303
* i16.0.0.0/4       10.1.34.4                   0    100     0 4 {1,404,303,202} i
* i21.0.0.0         10.1.34.4                   0    100     0 4 1 404 303 202 i
* i31.0.0.0         10.1.34.4                   0    100     0 4 1 303 303 303 i
! R2 has filtered the route with 303 in the AS_SET, but it did not filter the
! routes with 303 in the AS_SEQ.
R2# sh ip bgp | include 10.1.34.4
* i21.0.0.0         10.1.34.4                   0    100     0 4 1 404 303 202 i
* i31.0.0.0         10.1.34.4                   0    100     0 4 1 303 303 303 i
```

Note   While AS_SET and AS_CONFED_SET are both unordered lists, when applying regex logic, Cisco IOS uses the order listed in the output of the **show ip bgp** command.

BGP Path Attributes and the BGP Decision Process

BGP path attributes define different characteristics about the NLRI(s) associated with a PA. For example, the AS_PATH PA lists the ASNs through which the NLRI has been advertised. Some BGP PAs impact the *BGP decision process* by which a router chooses the best path among multiple known routes to the same NLRI. This section explains the BGP decision process and introduces several new PAs and other BGP features that impact that process.

Generic Terms and Characteristics of BGP PAs

Each BGP PA can be described as either a *well-known* or *optional* PA. These terms refer to whether a particular implementation of BGP software must support the PA (well-known) or support for the PA is not required (optional).

Well-known PAs are either one of the following:

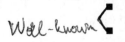

- **Mandatory:** The PA must be in every BGP Update.
- **Discretionary:** The PA is not required in every BGP Update.

These classifications relate not to the capabilities of a BGP implementation, but rather to whether a particular feature has been configured or used by default. For example, the ATOMIC_AGGREGATE PA is a well-known discretionary PA. That means that all implementations of BGP must understand this PA, but a particular router adds this PA only at its discretion, in this case by a router that creates a summary route. Conversely, the AS_PATH PA is a well-known mandatory PA, and as such must be included in every BGP Update.

BGP classifies optional PAs into one of two other categories that relate to a router's behavior when the router's BGP implementation does not understand the PA:

- **Transitive:** The router should silently forward the PA to other routers without needing to consider the meaning of the PA.

- **Nontransitive:** The router should remove the PA so that it is not propagated to any peers.

Table 2-6 summarizes these classification terms and definitions.

Table 2-6 *Definitions of Path Attribute Classification Terms*

Term	All BGP Software Implementations Must Support It	Must Be Sent in Each BGP Update	Silently Forwarded If Not Supported
Well-known mandatory	Yes	Yes	—
Well-known discretionary	Yes	No	—
Optional transitive	No	—	Yes
Optional nontransitive	No	—	No

The BGP PAs that have been mentioned so far in this book provide several good examples of the meanings behind the terms given in Table 2-6. Those PAs are summarized in Table 2-7, along with their characteristics.

Table 2-7 *BGP Path Attributes Covered So Far and Their Characteristics*

Path Attribute	Description	Characteristics
AS_PATH	Lists ASNs through which the route has been advertised	Well-known mandatory
NEXT_HOP	Lists the next-hop IP address used to reach an NLRI	Well-known mandatory
AGGREGATOR	Lists the RID and ASN of the router that created a summary NLRI	Optional transitive
ATOMIC_AGGREGATE	Tags a summary NLRI as being a summary	Well-known discretionary
ORIGIN	Value implying from where the route was taken for injection into BGP; i (IGP), e (EGP), or ? (incomplete information)	Well-known mandatory

Path Attribute	Description	Characteristics
ORIGINATOR_ID	Used by RRs to denote the RID of the iBGP neighbor that injected the NLRI into the AS	Optional nontransitive
CLUSTER_LIST	Used by RRs to list the RR cluster IDs in order to prevent loops	Optional nontransitive

Additions to BGP can be defined through the creation of new optional PAs, without requiring a new baseline RFC and a bump to a new version for BGP. The last two PAs in Table 2-7 list two such examples, both of which were added by RFC 1966 for the route reflectors feature.

The BGP Decision Process

The BGP decision process uses some of the PAs listed in Table 2-7, as well as several others. This section focuses on the decision process as an end to itself, with only brief explanations of new features or PAs. Following that, the text explains the details of some of the PAs that have not yet been covered in the book, as well as some other details that affect the BGP decision process.

When a BGP router learns multiple routes to the same NLRI, it must choose a single best route to reach that NLRI. BGP does not rely on a single concept like an IGP metric, but rather provides a rich set of tools that can be manipulated to affect the choice of routes. The following list defines the core of the BGP decision process to choose routes. Three additional tiebreaker steps are listed later in this section.

Key Topic

1. **Is the NEXT_HOP reachable?** Many texts, as well as RFC 1771, mention the fact that if a router does not have a route to the NEXT_HOP PA for a route, it should be rejected in the decision process.

2. **Highest administrative weight:** This is a Cisco-proprietary feature. The administrative weight can be assigned to each NLRI locally on a router, and the value cannot be communicated to another router. The higher the value, the better the route.

3. **Highest LOCAL_PREF PA:** This well-known discretionary PA can be set on a router inside an AS, and distributed inside the AS only. As a result, this feature can be used by all BGP routers in one AS to choose the same exit point from their AS for a particular NLRI. The higher the value, the better the route.

4. **Locally injected routes:** Pick the route injected into BGP locally (using the **network** command, redistribution, or route summarization). (This step is seldom needed, and is sometimes omitted from other BGP references.)

5. **Shortest AS_PATH length:** The shorter the AS_PATH length, the better the route. The length calculation ignores both AS_CONFED_SET and AS_CONFED_SEQ, and treats an AS_SET as one ASN, regardless of the number of ASNs in the AS_SET.

It counts each ASN in the AS_SEQUENCE as one. (This step is ignored if the **bgp bestpath as-path ignore** command is configured.)

6. **ORIGIN PA:** IGP (I) routes are preferred over EGP (E) routes, which are in turn preferred over incomplete (?) routes.

7. **Smallest Multi-Exit Discriminator (MED) PA:** Traditionally, this PA allows an ISP with multiple peer connections to a customer AS to tell the customer AS which of the peer connections is best for reaching a particular NLRI. The smaller the value, the better the route.

8. **Neighbor Type:** Prefer external BGP (eBGP) routes over internal BGP (iBGP). For this step, treat confederation eBGP as equal to iBGP.

9. **IGP metric for reaching the NEXT_HOP:** IGP metrics for each NLRI's NEXT_HOP are compared. The lower the value, the better the route.

Clarifications of the BGP Decision Process

The goal of this nine-step decision process is to determine the one best route to reach each NLRI. These steps do not attempt to find multiple equal routes, and install equal routes into the IP routing table, until a later step—even if the **maximum-paths** router subcommand has been configured to some number higher than the default of 1. The goal is to find the one best route to each NLRI.

First, you probably noticed that the list starts with NEXT_HOP reachability. I debated whether to include this step at all. Certainly, the statement at Step 1 is true. However, one could argue that this concept is not related to choosing between multiple useful routes, because it is really a restriction as to which routes could be used, thereby being candidates to become the best route. I decided to include it in the list for a couple of reasons: It is prominently mentioned in the corresponding parts of RFC 1771, and it is part of the decision process listed in both *Internet Routing Architectures* (Halabi) and *Routing TCP/IP*, Volume II (Doyle and Carroll). It is an important point, and worth memorizing.

Key Topic

If a step determines the best route for an NLRI, BGP does not bother with the remaining steps. For example, imagine that R1 has five routes to 9.0.0.0/10, two with AS_PATH length 3 and the others with AS_PATH length 5. The decision process did not determine a best route before reaching Step 4 (AS_PATH length). Step 4's logic can determine that two routes are better than the others because they have a shorter AS_PATH length. BGP typically chooses the first-learned valid route as best. For any new alternate routes for the same prefix, BGP applies the BGP decision process to the currently best and new route.

BGP applies this process to each unique NLRI. When overlapping NLRIs exist—for example, 130.1.0.0/16, 130.2.0.0/16, and 130.0.0.0/12—BGP attempts to find the best route for each specific prefix/prefix length.

Three Final Tiebreaker Steps in the BGP Decision Process

It is possible for BGP to fail to determine a best path to an NLRI using Steps 1 through 9, so BGP includes the following tiebreakers. These values would not typically be manipulated in a routing policy to impact the decision process.

10. Keep the oldest eBGP route. If the routes being compared are eBGP, and one of the paths is currently the best path, retain the existing best path. This action reduces eBGP route flaps.

11. Choose the smallest neighbor router ID (RID). Use the route whose next-hop router RID is the smallest. Only perform this step if **bgp bestpath compare-routerid** is configured.

12. Smallest neighbor ID. To get to this step, the local router has at least two neighbor relationships with a single other router. For this atypical case, the router now prefers the route advertised by the lowest neighbor ID, as listed in that router's neighbor commands.

> **Note**   The decision for eBGP routes can reach Step 11 if at Step 10 the formerly best route fails and BGP is comparing two other alternate routes.

> **Note**   For those of you more familiar with BGP, hopefully the lists describing the BGP decision process bring to mind the details you have learned in the past. For those of you less familiar with BGP, you might begin to feel a little overwhelmed by the details of the process. The lists are useful for study and memorization after you understand the background and details, which will be forthcoming in just a few pages. However, a few other general details need to be introduced before you get to the details at each step of the decision process. Hang in there!

Adding Multiple BGP Routes to the IP Routing Table

The BGP decision process has an impact on whether BGP adds multiple routes for a single NLRI to the IP routing table. The following statements summarize the logic:

- If the best path for an NLRI is determined in Steps 1 through 9, BGP adds only one BGP route to the IP routing table—the best route, of course.

- If the best path for an NLRI is determined after Step 9, BGP considers placing multiple BGP routes into the IP routing table.

- Even if multiple BGP routes are added to the IP routing table, BGP still chooses only one route per NLRI as the best route; that best route is the only route to that NLRI that BGP will advertise to neighbors.

The section "The maximum-paths Command and BGP Decision Process Tiebreakers," later in this chapter, details the restrictions.

Mnemonics for Memorizing the Decision Process

Many people do not bother to memorize the BGP decision process steps. However, memorizing the list is very useful for both the CCIE Routing and Switching written and lab exams. This section provides a set of mnemonic devices to aid you in memorizing the list. Please feel free to learn the mnemonic or skip to the next heading, at your discretion.

Table 2-8 is part of the practice effort to memorize the BGP decision tree.

Table 2-8   *BGP Decision Process Mnemonic: N WLLA OMNI*

Trigger Letter	Short Phrase	Which Is Better?
N	Next hop: reachable?	—
W	Weight	Bigger
L	LOCAL_PREF	Bigger
L	Locally injected routes	Locally injected is better than iBGP/eBGP learned
A	AS_PATH length	Smaller
O	ORIGIN	Prefer ORIGIN code I over E, and E over ?
M	MED	Smaller
N	Neighbor Type	Prefer eBGP over iBGP
I	IGP metric to NEXT_HOP	Smaller

The first mnemonic step is to memorize the nine trigger letters—single letters that, after being memorized, should hopefully trigger your memory to recall some short phrase that describes the logic of each decision point. Of course, memorizing nine seemingly random letters is not easy. So, memorize them as three groups:

N

WLLA

OMNI

Note   The nine letters are organized as shown here for several reasons. First, the single letter N, for Step 1, is purposefully separated from the other two groups because it can be argued that this step is not really part of the decision process. OMNI was separated because it is a commonly known English language prefix. And WLLA was just left over after designating OMNI.

After memorizing the trigger letter groups, you should exercise correlating the triggers to the short phrases listed in Table 2-8. (The CD contains memory-builder versions of the tables, including Table 2-8, which you can print and use for this practice if you like.)

Simply write down the nine trigger letters, and exercise your memory by writing out the short phrase associated with each letter. I'd recommend practicing as the first thing you do when you pick up the book for your next reading/study session, and do it for 5 minutes, and typically after a few rounds you will have it memorized.

Of these nine steps, I find also that most people have difficulty correlating the I to the phrase "IGP metric to reach the NEXT_HOP"; in case it helps, memorize also that the first and last of the nine items relate to NEXT_HOP. Based on that fact, and the fact that the trigger letter I implies IGP, maybe the two facts together might trigger your memory.

After you can essentially re-create the first two columns of Table 2-8 from memory, memorize the fact that the first two quantitative decision points use bigger-is-better logic and the rest use smaller-is-better logic. By doing so, you do not have to memorize which specific feature uses which type of logic. As long as you can write down the entire list, you can easily find the first two with quantitative comparisons (specifically Steps 2 and 3, WEIGHT and LOCAL_PREF, respectively).

Finally, Steps 10 and 11 are left to you to simply memorize. Remember that **maximum-paths** comes into play only if the first eight points do not determine a best route.

Configuring BGP Policies

BGP policies include route filters as well as tools that modify PAs and other settings that impact the BGP decision process. This section examines the Cisco IOS tools used to implement routing policies that impact the BGP decision process, covering the tools in the same order as the decision process.

Background: BGP PAs and Features Used by Routing Policies

Before getting into each individual step of the decision process, it is important to have a handy reference for the features the process manipulates, and the command output on routers that will reflect the changes made by each step. First, Table 2-9 summarizes the BGP PAs and other features used in the BGP decision process.

Key Topic

Table 2-9 *Proprietary Features and BGP Path Attributes That Affect the BGP Decision Process*

PA/Other	Description	BGP PA Type
NEXT_HOP	Lists the next-hop IP address used to reach an NLRI.	Well-known mandatory
Weight[1]	Local Cisco-proprietary setting, not advertised to any peers. Bigger is better.	—
LOCAL_PREF	Communicated inside a single AS. Bigger is better; range 0 through $2^{32} - 1$.	Well-known discretionary
AS_PATH length	The number of ASNs in the AS_SEQ, plus 1 if an AS_SET exists.	Well-known mandatory

PA/Other	Description	BGP PA Type
ORIGIN	Value implying that the route was injected into BGP; I (IGP), E (EGP), or ? (incomplete information).	Well-known mandatory
MULTI_EXIT_DISC (MED)	Multi-Exit Discriminator. Set and advertised by routers in one AS, impacting the BGP decision of routers in the other AS. Smaller is better.	Optional nontransitive
Neighbor Type[1]	The type of BGP neighbor from which a route was learned. Confederation eBGP is treated as iBGP for the decision process.	—
IGP metric to reach NEXT_HOP[1]	Smaller is better.	—
BGP RID[1]	Defines a unique identifier for a BGP router. Smaller is better.	—

[1] *This value is not a BGP PA.*

Next, Figure 2-6 shows an example of the **show ip bgp** command. Note that the locations of most of the variables used for the BGP decision process are given in the output.

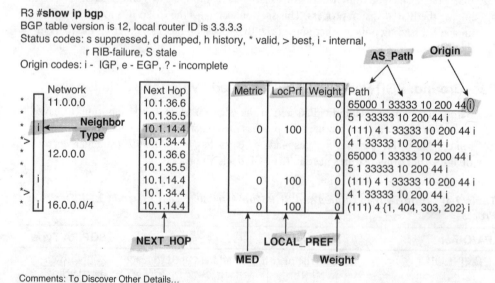

```
R3 #show ip bgp
BGP table version is 12, local router ID is 3.3.3.3
Status codes: s suppressed, d damped, h history, * valid, > best, i - internal,
              r RIB-failure, S stale
Origin codes: i -  IGP, e - EGP, ? - incomplete
```

Comments: To Discover Other Details…
Neighbor Type: No Letter Means "EBGP"
IGP Metric: **show ip route** *next-hop-address*
RID: **show ip bgp** *nlri*

Figure 2-6   *Locating Key BGP Decision Features in the* **show ip bgp** *Command*

The **show ip bgp** command lists most of the settings that impact the decision process, but it does not list the advertising router's RID, the IGP metric to reach the NEXT_HOP, or the neighbor ID that advertised the route. Two other commands do supply these three missing pieces of information. Example 2-6 shows the output of one of those commands, the **show ip bgp 16.0.0.0** command, which lists the advertising router's RID and neighbor ID. The IGP metric, of course, is given by the **show ip route** command.

Example 2-6 *Output of the* **show ip bgp 16.0.0.0** *Command on R3*

```
! Two routes to 16.0.0.0 are listed. The "from z.z.z.z" phrases identify the
! neighbor ID that advertised the route. The "(y.y.y.y)" output that follows lists
! the RID of that same router. Also, note that the
! output first identifies entry #2 as the best one, indicated by that entry (on the
! last line of output) also listing the word "best."
R3# sh ip bgp 16.0.0.0
BGP routing table entry for 16.0.0.0/4, version 8
Paths: (2 available, best #2, table Default-IP-Routing-Table)
  Advertised to update-groups:
                                           ___ AS_SET
      1          2
  (111)  4 (1,404,303,202)  (aggregated by 4 4.4.4.4), (received & used)
      10.1.14.4 (metric 3193856) from 2.2.2.2 (2.2.2.2)  — neighbor id / router-ID
        Origin IGP, metric 0, localpref 100, valid, confed-internal
   4 (1,404,303,202)  (aggregated by 4 4.4.4.4), (received & used)
      10.1.34.4 from 10.1.34.4 (4.4.4.4)
Origin IGP, metric 0, localpref 100, valid, external, best* i11.0.0.0
```

[handwritten annotations: "order" pointing to (111); "AS_SET"; "neighbor id / router-ID"]

Armed with the BGP decision process steps, the definitions for the PAs that impact the process, and a good reference for where you need to look to see the values, the next several sections take a tour of the BGP decision process. Each successive heading examines the decision process steps, in sequence.

Step 1: NEXT_HOP Reachable

This decision step simply prevents BGP from making the poor choice of accepting a BGP route as best, even though that router cannot possibly forward packets to the next-hop router.

Routing policies do not typically attempt to change a NEXT_HOP address to impact a routing choice. However, the NEXT_HOP can be changed by using either the **neighbor** *neighbor-id* **next-hop-self** command (the default for eBGP peers) or the **neighbor** *neighbor-id* **next-hop-unchanged** command (the default for iBGP peers). If **next-hop-self** is used, the NEXT_HOP is set to the IP address used as the source of the BGP Update sent to that neighbor. If **next-hop-unchanged** is used, the NEXT_HOP is not changed.

Step 2: Administrative Weight

The *weight*, more fully titled *administrative weight*, allows a single router to examine inbound BGP Updates and decide which routes to prefer. The weight is not a BGP PA, but simply a Cisco-proprietary setting on a local router. In fact, it cannot be included in a BGP Update sent to another router, because there is no place in the Update message to include the weight. Table 2-10 summarizes the key topics regarding BGP weight.

Table 2-10   *Key Features of Administrative Weight*

Feature	Description
Is it a PA?	No; Cisco-proprietary feature
Purpose	Identifies a single router's best route
Scope	In a single router only
Default	0 for learned routes, 32,768 for locally injected routes
Changing the defaults	Not supported
Range	0 through 65,535 ($2^{16} - 1$)
Which is best?	Bigger values are better
Configuration	Through the **neighbor route-map in** command or the **neighbor weight** command (if a route is matched by both commands, IOS uses the weight specified in the route map)

Figure 2-7 shows an updated version of Figure 2-4 that is used in the next example. Compared to Figure 2-4, Figure 2-7 shows the three routers in AS 123 as a full mesh of iBGP peers, with no confederations.

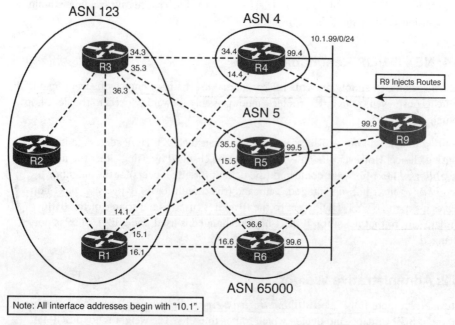

Figure 2-7   *Sample Network: AS 123 Without Confederations*

In Example 2-7, R1 sets the weight for NLRIs learned from R4, R5, and R6. The configuration shows both methods of configuring weight:

- Routes learned from R4 are set to weight 4 by using the **neighbor weight** command.

- Routes learned from R5 are set to weight 200 if ASN 200 is in the AS_PATH, by using a route map.

Example 2-7 *Setting BGP Administrative Weight on R1*

```
! The commands below list only commands that were added to the existing R1
! configuration. All routes from R4 (10.1.14.4) will now be weight 4, and those
! matching clause 10 of the route-map, from R5 (10.1.15.5), will be weight 200.
router bgp 123
 neighbor 10.1.14.4 weight 4        -> all routes learnt from this neighbor
 neighbor 10.1.15.5 route-map set-weight-200 in  =>
! The AS_PATH ACL matches any AS_PATH that includes ASN 200. Note that the
! route-map requires a second permit clause with no match or set, otherwise all
! routes not matched by clause 10 will be filtered.
ip as-path access-list 5 permit _200_
!
route-map set-weight-200 permit 10
 match as-path 5  )  -  if AS 5 is in the AS-path
 set weight 200   =>  set the weight to 200.
!
route-map set-weight-200 permit 20
! The changes are reflected below. Note also that both networks 11 and 12 have
! weights of 200, so those routes were chosen as the best paths.
R1# sh ip bgp | begin Network
   Network          Next Hop        Metric LocPrf Weight Path
 *  11.0.0.0         10.1.14.4       4294967294          4 4 1 33333 10 200 44 i
 * i                 10.1.36.6       4294967294    100   0 65000 1 33333 10 200 44 i
 *                   10.1.16.6       4294967294          0 65000 1 33333 10 200 44 i
 *>                  10.1.15.5       4294967294          200 5 1 33333 10 200 44 i
 *  12.0.0.0         10.1.14.4       4294967294          4 4 1 33333 10 200 44 i
 * i                 10.1.36.6       4294967294    100   0 65000 1 33333 10 200 44 i
 *                   10.1.16.6       4294967294          0 65000 1 33333 10 200 44 i
 *>                  10.1.15.5       4294967294          200 5 1 33333 10 200 44 i
```

Of particular importance in the example is the fact that the route map includes clause 20, with a **permit** action and no **match** or **set** commands. The **neighbor route-map** command creates an implied filtering decision. Any route matched by a **permit** clause in the route map is implied to be allowed through, and routes matched by a **deny** clause will be filtered. Route maps use an implied **deny all** at the end of the route map for any unmatched routes. By including a final clause with just a **permit** keyword, the route map changes to use **permit all** logic, thereby passing all routes.

Step 3: Highest Local Preference (LOCAL_PREF)

The BGP LOCAL_PREF PA allows routers in an AS with multiple exit points to choose which exit point is used to reach a particular NLRI. To do so, the router that is the desired exit point sets the LOCAL_PREF for its eBGP route for that NLRI to a relatively high value and then advertises that route through iBGP. The other routers in the same AS can learn of multiple routes to reach the NLRI, but they will choose the route with the higher LOCAL_PREF as the best route.

Table 2-11 summarizes the key topics regarding LOCAL_PREF.

Table 2-11 *Key Features of LOCAL_PREF*

Feature	Description
PA?	Yes, well-known, discretionary
Purpose	Identifies the best exit point from the AS to reach the NLRI
Scope	Throughout the AS in which it was set, including confederation sub-ASs
Default	100
Changing the default	Using the **bgp default local-preference <0-4294967295>** BGP subcommand
Range	0 through 4,294,967,295 ($2^{32} - 1$)
Which is best?	Higher values are better
Configuration	Through the **neighbor route-map** command; **in** option is required for Updates from an eBGP peer

Figure 2-8 shows a typical example of using LOCAL_PREF. In this case, the engineers for AS 123 want to use R1 to forward packets to 11.0.0.0/8, but use R3 to forward packets to 12.0.0.0/8. If either route fails, the other router should be used instead.

Example 2-8 shows the configuration used on R1 and R3 to implement the following routing policy:

- AS 123 routers should use R1 to reach 11.0.0.0/8.

- AS 123 routers should use R3 to reach 12.0.0.0/8.

- R1 can use any of its three routes to reach 11.0.0.0/8, and R3 can use any of its three routes to reach 12.0.0.0/8.

To meet these design goals, R1 and R3 will set LOCAL_PREF to values higher than the default of 100.

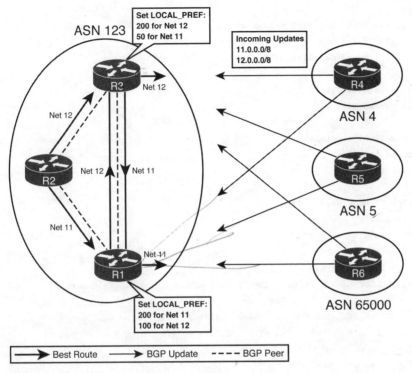

Figure 2-8   *Typical Use of LOCAL_PREF to Influence Exit Point from AS 123*

Example 2-8   *LOCAL_PREF Directing Packets for 11/8 Out R1 and Packets for 12/8 Out R3*

```
! R1 Config-only the relevant configuration is shown. The same route-map is
! called for incoming Updates from R4, R5, and R6. Note that the route-map
! includes a permit clause 20 with no match or set commands to permit
! any routes not specified in clause 10 to pass without changes. The route-map
! allows the LOCAL_PREF for 12.0.0.0/8 to default (100).
router bgp 123
 neighbor 10.1.14.4 route-map 11-high-12-default in
 neighbor 10.1.15.5 route-map 11-high-12-default in
 neighbor 10.1.16.6 route-map 11-high-12-default in
!
access-list 11 permit 11.0.0.0
!
route-map 11-high-12-default permit 10
 match ip address 11
 set local-preference 200
!
route-map 11-high-12-default permit 20
! R3 Config-Same general concept as R1, but the 12.0.0.0/8 route is assigned
! LOCAL_PREF 200, and 11.0.0.0/8 is assigned LOCAL_PREF 50.
```

```
router bgp 123
 neighbor 10.1.34.4 route-map 11-low-12-high in
 neighbor 10.1.35.5 route-map 11-low-12-high in
 neighbor 10.1.36.6 route-map 11-low-12-high in
!
access-list 11 permit 11.0.0.0
access-list 12 permit 12.0.0.0
!
route-map 11-low-12-high permit 10
 match ip address 12
 set local-preference 200
!
route-map 11-low-12-high permit 20
 match ip address 11
 set local-preference 50
!
route-map 11-low-12-high permit 30
! R3 now shows the LOCAL_PREF values. R3's best route to 12.0.0.0 is the one it
! learned from R4 (10.1.34.4). Its best route to 11.0.0.0 is the only one of the
! 4 routes with LOCAL_PREF 200-the one learned from R1. Note also that the
! administrative weights are all tied at 0; otherwise, BGP might have chosen a
! different best route.
R3# show ip bgp | begin Network
   Network          Next Hop         Metric LocPrf Weight Path
*  11.0.0.0         10.1.36.6        4294967294    50       0 65000 1 33333 10 200 44 i
*>i                 10.1.14.4        4294967294   200       0 4 1 33333 10 200 44 i
*                   10.1.35.5        4294967294    50       0 5 1 33333 10 200 44 i
*                   10.1.34.4        4294967294    50       0 4 1 33333 10 200 44 i
*  12.0.0.0         10.1.36.6        4294967294   200       0 65000 1 33333 10 200 44 i
*                   10.1.35.5        4294967294   200       0 5 1 33333 10 200 44 i
*>                  10.1.34.4        4294967294   200       0 4 1 33333 10 200 44 i
R3# show ip bgp 11.0.0.0
! lines omitted for brevity
  4 1 33333 10 200 44, (received & used)
    10.1.14.4 (metric 2681856) from 1.1.1.1 (1.1.1.1)
      Origin IGP, metric 4294967294, localpref 200, valid, internal, best
! lines omitted for brevity
```

```
! Because R3's best route to 11.0.0.0/8 is through R1, R3 does not advertise that
! iBGP route to R2. Similarly, R1's best route to 12.0.0.0/8 is through R3, so R1
! does not advertise its best route to 12.0.0.0/8, again because it is an iBGP
! route. As a result, R2 receives only one route to each of the two networks.
R2# show ip bgp | begin Network
   Network          Next Hop         Metric LocPrf Weight Path
*>i11.0.0.0         10.1.14.4        4294967294   200       0 4 1 33333 10 200 44 i
*>i12.0.0.0         10.1.34.4        4294967294   200       0 4 1 33333 10 200 44 i
```

This example does meet the stated design goals, but note that one design goal states that it does not matter which of the three eBGP routes R1 and R3 use to reach their assigned prefixes. Interestingly, R1 did not choose its best BGP route to network 11.0.0.0/8 based on LOCAL_PREF, nor did R3 choose its best route to 12.0.0.0/8 based on LOCAL_PREF. Note that R1 and R3 had three routes that tied based on LOCAL_PREF. In this case, their decisions happened to fall all the way to Step 10—the lowest advertising BGP RID. As a result, R3 chose the route through R4 (RID 4.4.4.4) instead of R5 (RID 5.5.5.5) or R6 (RID 6.6.6.6).

Had R1 or R3 wanted to impact which of the three eBGP routers to use to reach their respective NLRI, the route map could have been changed to match routes from each neighbor and set the LOCAL_PREF to different high values. For example, the LOCAL_PREF could be set to 204, 205, and 206 for R4, R5, and R6, respectively, thereby making R3 choose to use the route through R6 if 12.0.0.0/8 was learned from each of the three eBGP peers. To match, the **match ip next-hop** or **match ip route-source** command could be used, or a different route map could simply be used per neighbor.

Step 4: Choose Between Locally Injected Routes Based on ORIGIN PA

This logic step is seldom used, but it is a valid part of the BGP decision process. To appreciate why it is so seldom needed, consider the following: BGP assigns a weight of 32,768 to routes locally injected into BGP. As a result, a router would have already picked a locally injected route as best because of its high weight.

Two general cases can occur that cause a router to use the logic for this step. The first case is unlikely. A router must locally inject an NLRI, learn the same NLRI from a neighbor, and use an inbound **route-map** to set the weight of that received NLRI to the same value as the locally injected route. That only occurs in lab experiments.

The second case occurs when a router attempts to inject routes locally through multiple methods, and the same NLRI is injected from two different sources. For example, imagine that R1 injects a route to network 123.0.0.0/8 because of both a **network 123.0.0.0** command and a **redistribute connected** command. Both routes would have default weights of 32,768, and both would default to the same LOCAL_PREF. The two routes would then be compared at this step, with the ORIGIN code determining which route is best.

The logic for the second (and only likely) case to use this step in the decision process can be reduced to the following:

> When the same NLRI is locally injected into BGP from multiple methods, pick the route with the better ORIGIN PA.

The only hard part is memorizing the ORIGIN codes, and that "I" is better than "E" is better than "?".

Step 5: Shortest AS_PATH

Routers can easily determine the shortest AS_PATH length by using a few rules that define how to account for all four parts of the AS_PATH—the AS_SEQ, AS_SET,

AS_CONFED_SEQ, and AS_CONFED_SET. Additionally, routing policies can change the number of ASNs in the AS_PATH. Table 2-12 summarizes the key topics regarding AS_PATH length.

Table 2-12   *Features That Impact the Total Number of ASs in the AS_PATH Length Calculation*

Feature	Description
AS_SET	Regardless of actual length, it counts as a single ASN.
Confederations	AS_CONFED_SEQ and AS_CONFED_SET do not count in the calculation.
aggregate-address command	If the component subnets have different AS PATHs, the summary route has only the local AS in the AS_SEQ; otherwise, the AS_SEQ contains the AS_SEQ from the component subnets. Also, the presence/absence of the **as-set** command option determines whether the AS_SET is included.
neighbor remove-private-as command	Used by a router attached to a private AS (64512–65535), causing the router to remove the private ASN used by the neighboring AS.
neighbor local-as no-prepend command	Allows a router to use a different AS than the one on the **router bgp** command; with the **no-prepend** option, the router does not prepend any ASN when sending eBGP Updates to this neighbor.
AS_PATH prepending	Using a **neighbor route-map** in either direction, the route map can use the **set as-path prepend** command to prepend one or more ASNs into the AS_SEQ.
bgp bestpath as-path ignore command	Removes the AS_PATH length step from the decision tree for the local router.

The typical logic at this step simply requires the router to calculate the number of ASNs in the AS_SEQ, and add 1 if an AS_SET exists. However, the table mentions several other features that impact what ASNs are used and whether an eBGP peer adds an ASN. These additional features are covered next before moving on to Step 5 of the BGP decision process.

Removing Private ASNs

Private ASNs (64,512–65,535) should not be used in AS PATHs advertised into the Internet beyond a single ISP. One purpose of this private range is to conserve the ASN space by assigning private ASNs to customers that only connect to that single ISP. Then, the ISP can simply remove the private ASN before advertising any routes for that customer outside its network.

Figure 2-9 shows the typical case for using a private AS. While the concept is relatively simple, the configuration details can be a bit surprising.

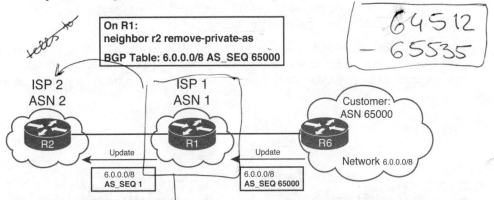

Figure 2-9 *Typical Use of Private ASNs and the* **neighbor remove-private-as** *Command*

Following Figure 2-9 from right to left, here are the key topics:

- R6, inside the private AS, does not require any special commands.

- R1, acting as a router in the sole ISP to which ASN 65000 is connected, lists private AS 65000 in its BGP table for any routes learned from R6.

- R1 needs the command **neighbor R2 remove-private-as** under router BGP, telling R1 to remove any private ASNs from AS_PATHs advertised to Router R2.

Cisco IOS has several restrictions regarding whether a private AS is removed as a protection against causing routing loops:

- Private ASNs can be removed only at the point of sending an eBGP Update.

- If the current AS_SEQ contains both private and public ASNs, the private ASNs will not be removed.

- If the ASN of the eBGP peer is in the current AS_PATH, the private ASNs will not be removed, either.

This feature works with confederations as well, with the same restrictions being applied to the AS_CONFED_SEQ.

AS_PATH Prepending and Route Aggregation

The concept and motivation behind the AS_PATH prepend feature is simple—impact the AS_PATH length decision step by increasing the length of the AS_PATH. To do so, a router simply configures a route map and refers to it with a **neighbor route-map** command, with the route map using the **set as-path prepend** *asn1 asn2...* command. As a result, the route map prepends additional ASNs to the AS_SEQUENCE.

Any ASN can be prepended, but in practice, it makes the most sense to prepend the local router's ASN. The reason is that prepending some other ASN prevents that route from being advertised into that AS—a scenario that might not be intended. Also, if the AS_PATH needs to be lengthened by more than one ASN, the **set** command can repeat the same ASN multiple times, as shown in Example 2-9.

Figure 2-10 shows a design depicting the use of AS_PATH prepending. R6 correctly prepends its own ASN 4 for routes advertised to R1 (in the top part of the figure). R6 also causes problems by prepending ASN 2 for the route sent to R3 (in the lower part of the figure).

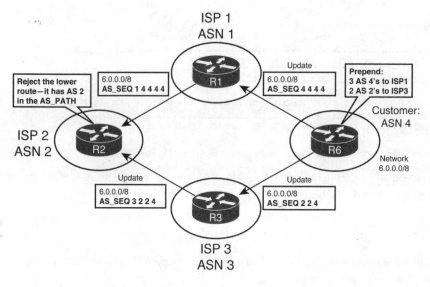

Figure 2-10 *Options for Prepending ASNs*

While AS_PATH prepending lengthens the AS_PATH, route aggregation can actually decrease the AS_PATH length. Route aggregation (summarization) with the BGP **aggregate-address** command impacts the AS_PATH length in a couple of ways:

- The router checks the component subnets' AS_PATH AS_SEQ values. If all the component subnets' AS_SEQ values are identical, the aggregate route uses that same AS_SEQ.

- If the component subnets' AS_SEQ values differ, the aggregating router uses a null AS_SEQ for the aggregate. (When advertised to an eBGP peer, the router does prepend its local ASN, as normal.) Of course, this process shortens the AS_PATH length.

Additionally, the **aggregate-address** command with the **as-set** option can lengthen the AS_PATH length calculation as well. When a router uses this command with the **as-set** option, and the aggregate empties out the AS_SEQ as described in the previous paragraph, the router adds an AS_SET segment to the AS_PATH. (Conversely, if the aggregate does not empty the AS_SEQ, the router does not create the AS_SET, as it is not needed for loop prevention in that case.) The AS_SET includes all ASNs of all component subnets.

The BGP AS_PATH length calculation counts the entire AS_SET as 1, regardless of the actual length.

Example 2-9 shows examples of both AS_PATH prepending and route aggregation on the AS_PATH length. In the example, the familiar network of Figure 2-7 is used. The following features are used in the example:

- R4 prepends route 11.0.0.0/8 with three additional ASN 4s, using an outbound route map, before advertising routes into AS 123.

- R4 and R5 both summarize 16.0.0.0/4, but R4 uses the **as-set** option and R5 does not.

As a result of the second item, R3 learns both summaries, but treats the summary from R5 as better, because the AS_SET in R4's route counts as one ASN in the AS_PATH length calculation.

Example 2-9 *AS_PATH Prepending and an Examination of Route Summarization and AS_PATH Length*

```
! R4's configuration shows the route-map called add3-4s for its neighbor commands
! for R1 (10.1.14.1) and R3 (10.1.34.3). The route-map matches 11.0.0.0/8,
! prepending three additional ASN 4s. The normal process of prepending the local AS
! before advertising over eBGP peer connection adds the 4th instance of ASN 4. As
! usual, the route-map needs a null final clause with a permit so that the rest
! of the routes are not affected.
router bgp 4
 aggregate-address 16.0.0.0 240.0.0.0 as-set
 neighbor 10.1.14.1 route-map add3-4s out
 neighbor 10.1.34.3 route-map add3-4s out
!
ip prefix-list match11 seq 5 permit 11.0.0.0/8
!
route-map add3-4s permit 10
 match ip address prefix-list match11
 set as-path prepend 4 4 4
!
route-map add3-4s permit 20
! Below, first focus on 11.0.0.0/8. The highlighted route with NEXT_HOP 10.1.34.4
! (R4) has four consecutive 4s in the AS_PATH, showing the effects of the prepending
! on R4. The route through 10.1.35.5 ends up being best based on the tiebreaker
! at Step 9.
! Next, look at 16.0.0.0/4. The route through 10.1.34.4 is considered
! to be AS_PATH length 2, but the length through 10.1.35.5 is only 1. The
```

```
! route to 16.0.0.0/4 through NEXT_HOP 10.1.35.5 is chosen over the route through
! 10.1.15.5 because it is eBGP, versus iBGP for the route through 10.1.15.5.
R3# show ip bgp | begin Network
   Network          Next Hop        Metric LocPrf Weight Path
*  11.0.0.0         10.1.36.6    4294967294           0 65000 1 33333 10 200 44 i
* i                 10.1.16.6    4294967294           0 65000 1 33333 10 200 44 i
*                   10.1.34.4    4294967294           0 4 4 4 4 1 33333 10 200 44 i
*>                  10.1.35.5    4294967294           0 5 1 33333 10 200 44 i
*  16.0.0.0/4       10.1.34.4    4294967294           0 4 {1,404,303,202} ?
*>                  10.1.35.5    4294967294           0 5 i
* i                 10.1.15.5    4294967294           0 5 i
```

Step 6: Best ORIGIN PA

The well-known mandatory BGP ORIGIN PA characterizes a route based on how it was injected into BGP. The ORIGIN is either IGP (i), EGP (e), or incomplete (?).

The actual BGP decision process for the ORIGIN code is quite simple. First, an ORIGIN of EGP (e) should not occur today, because EGP is not even supported in current IOS revisions. So, the logic reduces to the following:

> If the set of routes to reach a single NLRI includes only one route of ORIGIN code IGP (i), and all the others as incomplete (?), the route with ORIGIN i is the best route.

BGP routing policies can set the ORIGIN code explicitly by using the **set origin** route map subcommand, although the earlier steps in the BGP decision process are typically better choices for configuring BGP policies. BGP determines the ORIGIN code based on the method used to inject the routes, along with the options used with the **aggregate-address** command.

Chapter 1's section, "ORIGIN Path Attribute," describes more detail about the ORIGIN PA and how NLRIs are assigned an ORIGIN code.

Step 7: Smallest Multi-Exit Discriminator

The purpose of the MED (or MULTI_EXIT_DISC) is to allow routers in one AS to tell routers in a neighboring AS how good a particular route is. In fact, because of how MED works, it is often called the *BGP metric*, even though it is not close to the top of the BGP decision process. Figure 2-11 shows a classic case for the use of MED, where a customer has two links connecting it to a single ISP. The ISP, aware of its best routes for 11.0.0.0/8 and 12.0.0.0/8, can set MED so that the customer routes packets to the eBGP peer that is closest to the destination network.

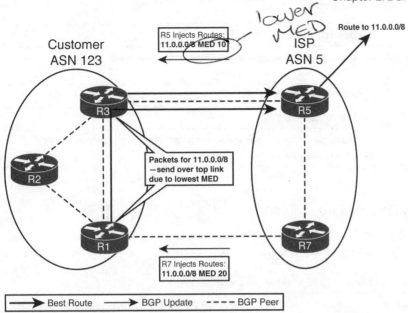

Figure 2-11   *Typical Use of MED*

The ISP, knowing its best route to reach 11.0.0.0/8 is through R5, configures R5 to set a low MED for that prefix and R7 to set a higher MED for the same prefix. As a result, the BGP routers in customer AS 123 choose the route through the top peer connection. The customer could then use the route through the lower link to R7 if the top connection failed.

Figure 2-11 shows the classic topology—a customer using a single ISP but with multiple links to the ISP. Many customers want redundant ISPs as well, or at least connections to multiple autonomous systems controlled by a single, large ISP. MED can also be used in such cases, but it requires the multiple ISPs or multiple ASs in the same ISP to use the same policy when determining the MED values to set. For example, two ISPs might agree that because one ISP has more link bandwidth to a certain range of BGP prefixes, that ISP will set a lower MED for those NLRIs.

Table 2-13 summarizes the key topics regarding MED.

Table 2-13   *Key Features of MED*

Feature	Description
Is it a PA?	Yes, optional nontransitive
Purpose	Allows an AS to tell a neighboring AS the best way to forward packets into the first AS
Scope	Advertised by one AS into another, propagated inside the AS but not sent to any other ASs
Default	0

Feature	Description
Changing the default	Using the **bgp bestpath med missing-as-worst** BGP subcommand; sets it to the maximum value
Range	0 through 4,294,967,295 ($2^{32} - 1$)
Which is best?	Smaller is better
Configuration	Through the **neighbor route-map out** command, using the **set metric** command inside the route map

Configuring MED: Single Adjacent AS

Example 2-10 shows a sample MED configuration that matches Figure 2-11, with R5 and R7 setting the MED for 11.0.0.0/8 to 10 and 20, respectively.

Example 2-10 *Classical MED Example Between Two ASs*

```
! The pertinent R5 configuration follows. R5 simply matches 11.0.0.0/8 and sets
! the metric to 10. The route-map includes a default permit any clause at the end
! to avoid affecting other routes.
router bgp 5
 neighbor 10.1.35.3 route-map set-med out
!
ip prefix-list 11 seq 5 permit 11.0.0.0/8
!
route-map set-med permit 10
 match ip address prefix-list 11
 set metric 10
route-map set-med permit 20
! R7's configuration is not shown, but it is basically the same regarding the
! setting of the MED. However, R7 sets the MED to 20.

! R1 lists routes with R5 (10.1.35.5) and R7 (10.1.17.7) as NEXT_HOP; the route
! through R5 is best due to the lower MED.
R1# show ip bgp | begin Network
   Network          Next Hop        Metric LocPrf Weight Path
*>i11.0.0.0         10.1.35.5           10    100      0 5 1 33333 10 200 44 i
*                   10.1.17.7           20             0 5 1 33333 10 200 44 i
*> 12.0.0.0         10.1.35.5                          0 5 1 33333 10 200 44 i
* i                 10.1.17.7            0    100      0 5 1 33333 10 200 44 i

! R3 sees only the MED 10 route. R1's best route to NEXT_HOP 10.1.35.5 is through
! R3, so R1 did not advertise its best route to 11.0.0.0/8 to iBGP peer R3.
R3# show ip bgp | begin Network
   Network          Next Hop        Metric LocPrf Weight Path
*> 11.0.0.0         10.1.35.5           10             0 5 1 33333 10 200 44 i
*> 12.0.0.0         10.1.35.5                          0 5 1 33333 10 200 44 i
* i                 10.1.17.7            0    100      0 5 1 33333 10 200 44 i
```

Key Topic

It is important that both R5 and R7 set the MED for 11.0.0.0/8. If R5 had set the MED to 10, and R7 had done nothing, the router through R7 would have been the best route. R1 and R3 would have used their assumed default setting of 0 for the MED for the route through R1 and R7, and as with IGP metrics, smaller is better with MED. A better default for MED can be set by using the **bgp bestpath med missing-as-worst** BGP subcommand, which resets a router's default MED to the largest possible MED value, instead of the lowest. Note that it is important that all routers in the same AS either use the default of 0 or configure this command; otherwise, routing choices will be affected.

Configuring MED: Multiple Adjacent Autonomous Systems

By default, a Cisco router ignores MED when the multiple routes to a single NLRI list different neighboring ASNs. This default action makes sense—normally you would not expect two different neighboring ISPs to have chosen to work together to set MEDs. To override this default and consider the MED in all cases, a router needs to configure the **bgp always-compare-med** BGP subcommand. If used on one router, all routers inside the same AS should also use the **bgp always-compare-med** command, or routing loops can result.

Additionally, some Cisco documents imply that the internal BGP decision process for the MED might be different depending on the order of the entries in the BGP table. Interestingly, BGP lists the table entries from newest (most recently learned) to oldest in the output of the **show ip bgp** and **show ip bgp** *prefix* commands. Depending on that order, in some cases in which the competing routes for the same NLRI have different MEDs from different autonomous systems, the order of the entries impacts the final choice of the best route. In part, the difference results from the fact that Cisco IOS (by default) processes the list sequentially—which means that it processes the first pair of routes (newest), picks the best of those two, then compares that one with the next newest, and so on.

Cisco solved this nondeterministic behavior for the MED processing problem by creating an alternative process for analyzing and making the MED decision. With this new process, BGP processes the routes per adjacent AS, picking the best from each neighboring AS and then comparing those routes. This logic provides a deterministic choice based on MED—in other words, it removes the possibility of BGP picking a different route based on the order of the routes in the BGP table. To enable this enhanced logic, add the **bgp deterministic-med** command to the routers in the same AS. In fact, Cisco recommends this setting for all new BGP implementations.

The Scope of MED

The MED PA is not intended to be advertised outside the AS that heard the MED in an incoming BGP Update. Typically, and as shown in the examples in this section, the MED can be set in an outbound route map by a router in one AS to influence the BGP decision process in another AS. So, the MED value is set by routers in one AS and learned by routers in another AS. However, after reaching the other AS, the MED is advertised inside the AS, but not outside the AS. For example, in Figure 2-11, R5 and R7 set the MED and advertise it into AS 123. However, if routers in AS 123 had any other eBGP connections to other ASNs, they would advertise the NLRI, but they would not include the MED value.

MED can also be set through inbound route maps, although that is not the intended design with which to use MED. When you set MED through an inbound route map, the MED is indeed set. The router can advertise the MED to iBGP peers. However, the MED is still not advertised outside the local AS.

Step 8: Prefer Neighbor Type eBGP over iBGP

This step is rather simple and needs very little elucidation. Keeping in mind that the goal is a single best route for each NLRI, this decision point simply looks to see whether a single eBGP route exists. If so, that route is chosen. If multiple eBGP routes exist, this decision point cannot determine the best route.

Interestingly, BGP uses this decision point frequently when two or more enterprise routers connect to the same ISP. Each border BGP router in the enterprise receives the same prefixes with the same AS_PATH lengths from the ISP, and then these border BGP routers advertise these routes to their iBGP peers. So, each enterprise border router knows of one eBGP route to reach each prefix, and one or more iBGP routes to the same prefix learned from that enterprise's other border routers. With no routing policies configured, the routes tie on all decision points up to this one, including AS_PATH length, because all the prefixes were learned from the same neighboring ISP. The decision process reaches this step, at which point the one eBGP route is picked as the best route.

Step 9: Smallest IGP Metric to the NEXT_HOP

This step again requires little explanation. The router looks for the route that would be used to reach the NEXT_HOP listed in each BGP table entry for a particular prefix. It is mentioned here just to complete the list.

The maximum-paths Command and BGP Decision Process Tiebreakers

The goal of the BGP decision tree is to find the one best BGP route to each NLRI, from that router's perspective. That router then considers only its best routes for advertising to other routers, restricting those routes based on AS_PATH loop prevention and routing policy configuration. That router also attempts to add that best route, and that best route only, to its IP routing table. In fact, as long as another routing source has not found a route to the same prefix, with a better administrative distance, the best BGP route is placed into that router's routing table.

If BGP has not chosen a best route for a particular NLRI after Steps 0 through 8, multiple routes tie for being the best route. At this point, BGP needs to make two important decisions:

- **Which route is best?** BGP uses two tiebreakers, discussed next, to determine which route is best.

- **Whether to add multiple BGP routes for that NLRI to the IP routing table:** BGP considers the setting of the **maximum-paths** command to make this decision, as described after the discussion of Steps 10 and 11.

Even if BGP adds to the IP routing table multiple BGP routes to the same prefix, it still picks only one as the best route in the BGP table.

Step 10: Lowest BGP Router ID of Advertising Router (with One Exception)

The first tiebreaker is to pick the route with the lowest RID. The logic is actually two steps, as follows:

1. Examine the eBGP routes only, picking the route advertised by the router with the lowest RID.

2. If only iBGP routes exist, pick the route advertised by the router with the lowest RID.

These straightforward rules are followed in some cases, but not in some others. The exception to this rule occurs when BGP already has a best route to the NLRI, but it has learned new BGP information from other routers, including a new BGP route to reach a previously known prefix. The router then applies its BGP decision process again to decide whether to change its opinion of which route is best for that NLRI. If the decision process does not determine a best route by this step, this step uses the following default logic:

> If the existing best route is an eBGP route, do not replace the existing best route, even if the new route has a smaller RID.

The reasoning is that replacing the route could result in route flaps, so keeping the same route is fine. This behavior can be changed so that the lowest RID is always used, by configuring the **bgp bestpath compare-routerid** BGP subcommand. Note that this exception only applies to eBGP routes. If the currently best route is an iBGP route, the decision is simply based on the lowest advertising router's RID.

Step 11: Lowest Neighbor ID

If Step 10 did not break the tie, the router has at least two **neighbor** commands that point to the same router, and that router happens to have the lowest RID of all current neighbors advertising the NLRI in question. Typically, if redundancy exists between two routers, the configuration uses loopback interfaces, a single **neighbor** command, and the **neighbor ebgp-multihop** command if the neighbor is an eBGP neighbor. However, using a pair (or more) of **neighbor** commands pointing to a single neighboring router is a valid configuration option; this final tiebreaker provides a way to break ties for this case.

At this point, the router looks at the IP addresses on the **neighbor** commands corresponding to all the neighbors from which the route was received, and it picks the lowest neighbor IP address. Note that, as usual, it considers all routes again at this step, so it might not pick the neighboring router with the lowest RID at this point.

The BGP maximum-paths Command

BGP defaults the **maximum-paths** command to a setting of 1; in other words, only the BGP best route in the BGP table could possibly be added to the IP routing table. However, BGP will consider adding multiple entries to the IP routing table, for the same NLRI, under certain conditions—conditions that differ based on whether the best route is an eBGP route or an iBGP route.

First, consider eBGP routes. The following rules determine if and when a router will add multiple eBGP routes to the IP routing table for a single NLRI:

EBGP:

1. BGP must have had to use a tiebreaker (Step 10 or 11) to determine the best route.

2. The **maximum-paths** *number* command must be configured to something larger than the default of 1.

3. Only eBGP routes whose adjacent ASNs are the same ASN as the best route are considered as candidates.

4. If more candidates exist than that called for with the **maximum-paths** command, the tiebreakers of Steps 10 and 11 determine the ones to use.

Although the list is detailed, the general idea is that the router can trust multiple routes, but only if the packets end up in the same adjacent AS. Also, BGP must restrict itself to not use multipath if the best route was found through Steps 1 through 9 of the decision process, because forwarding based on another route could cause loops.

IBGP:

Next, consider iBGP routes. The rules for iBGP have some similarities with eBGP, and a few differences, as follows:

1. Same rule as eBGP rule 1.

2. The **maximum-paths ibgp** *number* command defines the number of possible IP routes, instead of the **maximum-paths** *number* command used for eBGP.

3. Only iBGP routes with differing NEXT_HOP settings are considered as candidates.

4. Same rule as eBGP rule 4.

The rationale is similar to eBGP with regard to most of the logic. Additionally, it does not help to add multiple IP routes if the NEXT_HOP settings are equal, so BGP performs that additional check.

Finally, the **maximum-paths eibgp** *number* command seemingly would apply to both iBGP and eBGP routes. However, this command applies only when MPLS is in use. Table 2-14 summarizes the key commands related to BGP multipath.

Table 2-14 *BGP* **maximum-paths** *Command Options*

Command	Conditions for Use
maximum-paths *number*	eBGP routes only
maximum-paths ibgp *number*	iBGP routes only
maximum-paths eibgp *number*	Both types, but MPLS only

BGP Communities

The BGP COMMUNITY PA provides a mechanism by which to group routes so that routing policies can be applied to all the routes with the same community. By marking a set of routes with the same COMMUNITY string, routers can look for the COMMUNITY string and then make policy decisions—like setting some PA that impacts the BGP decision process or simply filtering the routes. BGP communities are powerful in that they allow routers in one AS to communicate policy information to routers that are one or more autonomous systems distant. In fact, because the COMMUNITY PA is an optional transitive PA, it can pass through autonomous systems that do not even understand the COMMUNITY PA and then still be useful at another downstream AS.

Figure 2-12 shows an example of one way in which communities can be used. The goal with this design is to have the engineers in ASNs 4 and 5 work together to decide which of them has the best route to reach each prefix, and then somehow tell the routers in ASN 123. That might sound familiar—that is exactly the motivation behind using MED, as shown in Figure 2-11. However, MED is relatively far into the BGP decision process, even after the shortest AS_PATH. A better design might be to set the COMMUNITY PA and then let the routers in ASN 123 react to the COMMUNITY string and set LOCAL_PREF based on that value, because LOCAL_PREF is considered early in the BGP decision process.

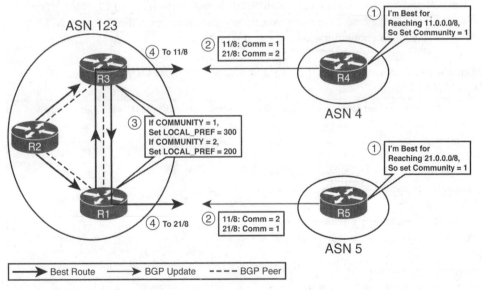

Figure 2-12   *Using COMMUNITY to Augment Routing Policies*

Figure 2-12 depicts the following steps:

1. The engineers at AS 4 and AS 5 agree as to which prefixes are best reached by each AS.

2. They then configure outbound route maps on their respective neighbor connections to AS 123, setting COMMUNITY to 1 for routes for which they are the best path, and setting COMMUNITY to 2 for some other routes.

3. R1 and R3 receive the Updates, match the NLRI based on the COMMUNITY, and set LOCAL_PREF to a large value for routes whose COMMUNITY was set to 1.

4. The LOCAL_PREF settings impact the BGP choice for the best routes.

This design includes several advantages over some of the options covered earlier in the chapter. It includes the best aspects of using LOCAL_PREF, helping AS 123 decide which neighboring AS to use to reach each prefix. However, it puts the choice of which routes should be reached through AS 4 and AS 5 into the hands of the folks running AS 4 and AS 5. If the AS 4 or AS 5 topology changes, link speeds increase, or other changes occur, the route maps that set the COMMUNITY in AS 4 and AS 5 can be changed accordingly. No changes would be required inside AS 123, because it already simply looks at the COMMUNITY string. Assuming that AS 123 is an enterprise, and AS 4 and AS 5 are ISPs, the ISPs can make one set of changes and impact the routing choices of countless customers.

Example 2-11 shows the configuration matching the scenario of Figure 2-12. The configuration follows mostly familiar commands and reasoning, with two additional features:

■ R4 and R5 (AS 4 and AS 5) must use the **neighbor send-community** BGP subcommand, which tells BGP to include the COMMUNITY PA in the Update. Without that command, the Update does not even include the COMMUNITY PA.

■ R1 and R3 (AS 123) need to match NLRIs based on the received COMMUNITY values, so they must configure *community lists* that match the COMMUNITY by using the **ip community-list** command.

Example 2-11   *Setting COMMUNITY and Reacting to COMMUNITY to Set LOCAL_PREF*

```
! R4 must add the neighbor send-community command, otherwise it will not include
! the COMMUNITY PA in Updates sent to R3. The route-map matches 11/8, and sets
! COMMUNITY to 1, and matches 21/8 and sets COMMUNITY to 2.
router bgp 4
 neighbor 10.1.34.3 send-community both
 neighbor 10.1.34.3 route-map comm out
!
ip prefix-list 11 seq 5 permit 11.0.0.0/8
ip prefix-list 21 seq 5 permit 21.0.0.0/8
!
route-map comm permit 10
 match ip address prefix-list 11
 set community 1
!
route-map comm permit 20
 match ip address prefix-list 21
 set community 2
!
route-map comm permit 30
```

```
! R5 has essentially the same configuration, except that R5 sets COMMUNITY to 1
! for 21/8 and to 2 for 11/8-the opposite of R4.
router bgp 5
 neighbor 10.1.15.1 send-community
 neighbor 10.1.15.1 route-map comm out
!
ip prefix-list 11 seq 5 permit 11.0.0.0/8
ip prefix-list 21 seq 5 permit 21.0.0.0/8
!
route-map comm permit 10
 match ip address prefix-list 11
 set community 2
!
route-map comm permit 20
 match ip address prefix-list 21
 set community 1
!
route-map comm permit 30
```

```
! R3 Config: Next, R3 matches on the received COMMUNITY strings and sets
! LOCAL_PREF using a route-map called react-to-comm. The only way to match the
! COMMUNITY is to refer to an ip community-list, which then has the matching
! parameters.
router bgp 123
 neighbor 10.1.34.4 route-map react-to-comm in
!
ip community-list 1 permit 1
ip community-list 2 permit 2
!
route-map react-to-comm permit 10
 match community 1
 set local-preference 300
!
route-map react-to-comm permit 20
 match community 2
 set local-preference 200
!
route-map react-to-comm permit 30
! Not shown-R1 Config. R1's config matches R3's in every way, except for the
! fact that the inbound route-map is applied for the neighbor command pointing
! to R5 (10.1.15.5).
! R3 chooses its best path to 11/8 with NEXT_HOP of R4 (10.1.34.4), as a result
! of R3's assignment of LOCAL_PREF 300, which in turn was a result of the Update
! from R4 listing 11/8 as COMMUNITY 1. R3's best route to 12/8 points to NEXT_HOP
! R5 (10.1.15.1), which happens to point back through R1, because R1 received an
! Update from R5 for 21/8 listing COMMUNITY 1, and then set LOCAL_PREF to 300.
R3# show ip bgp | begin Network
```

```
     Network          Next Hop          Metric LocPrf Weight Path
*> 11.0.0.0          10.1.34.4         4294967294   300        0 4 1 33333 10 200 44 i
*  i12.0.0.0         10.1.15.5         4294967294   100        0 5 1 33333 10 200 44 i
*>                   10.1.34.4         4294967294              0 4 1 33333 10 200 44 i
*>i21.0.0.0          10.1.15.5         4294967294   300        0 5 1 404 303 202 i
*                    10.1.34.4         4294967294   200        0 4 1 404 303 202 i
! R3 now lists its BGP table entries that have COMMUNITY settings that include
! 1 or 2. Note that both commands only list the routes learned directly from R4.
! If R1 had configured a neighbor 3.3.3.3 send-community command, R3 would have
! additional entries using COMMUNITY strings 1 and 2. However, for this design,
! the COMMUNITY strings do not need to be advertised to iBGP peers inside AS 123,
! as R1 and R3 have already reacted to the communities to set the LOCAL_PREF.
R3# show ip bgp community 1
BGP table version is 37, local router ID is 3.3.3.3
Status codes: s suppressed, d damped, h history, * valid, > best, i-internal,
              r RIB-failure, S Stale
Origin codes: i-IGP, e-EGP, ?-incomplete

     Network          Next Hop          Metric LocPrf Weight Path
*> 11.0.0.0          10.1.34.4         4294967294   300        0 4 1 33333 10 200 44 i
R3# show ip bgp community 2 | begin Network
     Network          Next Hop          Metric LocPrf Weight Path
*  21.0.0.0          10.1.34.4         4294967294   200        0 4 1 404 303 202 i
! The COMMUNITY can be seen with the show ip bgp prefix command, as seen below.
! Note that the route learned from R1 (1.1.1.1) does not list a COMMUNITY, as R1
! did not configure a neighbor 3.3.3.3 send-community command.
R3# show ip bgp 21.0.0.0
BGP routing table entry for 21.0.0.0/8, version 35
Paths: (3 available, best #1, table Default-IP-Routing-Table)
Multipath: eBGP
  Advertised to update-groups:
     2
  5 1 404 303 202, (received & used)
    10.1.15.5 (metric 2681856) from 1.1.1.1 (1.1.1.1)
      Origin IGP, metric 4294967294, localpref 300, valid, internal, best
  4 1 404 303 202
    10.1.34.4 from 10.1.34.4 (4.4.4.4)
      Origin IGP, metric 4294967294, localpref 200, valid, external
      Community: 2
  4 1 404 303 202, (received-only)
    10.1.34.4 from 10.1.34.4 (4.4.4.4)
      Origin IGP, metric 4294967294, localpref 100, valid, external
      Community: 2
```

Matching COMMUNITY with Community Lists

Cisco originally created communities as a proprietary feature, treating the 32-bit COMMUNITY as a decimal value (as shown in Example 2-11). When the COMMUNITY PA was added to the BGP standard RFC 1997, the 32-bit COMMUNITY was formatted as AA:NN, where AA is a 16-bit number to potentially represent an ASN and NN represents a value as set by that ASN. However, the COMMUNITY PA remained a 32-bit number.

[handwritten: 32-bit AA:NN]

Cisco routers can use either the original format or the RFC 1997 format for the COMMUNITY PA. By default, **show** commands list the decimal value; to use the AA:NN format, you should configure the global command **ip bgp-community new-format**. Also, the **set** command, as used with route maps, can use either the old decimal format or the newer AA:NN format. However, the absence or presence of the **ip bgp-community new-format** command dictates whether the output of a **show route-map** command lists the values as decimal or as AA:NN, respectively. For this reason, in practice it makes sense to choose and use a single format, typically the newer format, today.

[handwritten: new format]

The COMMUNITY PA also supports multiple entries. For example, the **set community 10 20 30** command, applied within a route map, would actually create a COMMUNITY with all three values. In that case, any existing COMMUNITY value would be replaced with 10, 20, and 30. However, the **set community 10 20 30 additive** command would add the values to the existing COMMUNITY string.

[handwritten: supports multiple entries]

[handwritten: adding vs. replacing com. values]

As a result of the multi-entry COMMUNITY, and as a result of the literal ":" inside the COMMUNITY string when using the new format, Cisco IOS requires some more sophisticated matching capabilities as compared with IP ACLs. For example, community lists can list multiple values on the same **ip community-list** command; to match such a command, the COMMUNITY must include all the values. (The COMMUNITY values are unordered, so the order in which the values are listed in the community list does not matter.) Also, extended community lists (numbered 100–199) allow matching of the COMMUNITY PA with regular expressions. Table 2-15 summarizes some of the key topics related to community lists.

[handwritten: Extended: regular expressions]

Table 2-15 *Comparing Standard and Extended Community Lists*

Feature	Standard	Extended
List numbers	1–99	100–199
Can match multiple communities in a single command?	Yes	Yes
Can match the COMMUNITY PA with regular expressions?	No	Yes
More than 16 lines in a single list?	No	Yes

Example 2-12 shows a few sample community lists just to show the logic. In the example, R4 has set multiple COMMUNITY values for prefixes 11/8 and 12/8. The **show ip bgp community-list** *list-number* command is then used to show whether a match would be made. This command lists the entries of the BGP table that match the associated COMMUNITY PA, much like the **show ip bgp regex** command examines the AS_PATH PA.

Example 2-12 *Matching with IP Community Lists*

```
R3# show ip community-list
Community standard list 2
    permit 0:1234
Community standard list 3
    permit 0:1212 8:9
Community (expanded) access list 111
    permit 0:12.*
! 11/8's COMMUNITY string is listed next, followed by 12/8's COMMUNITY string.
R3# show ip bgp 11.0.0.0 | include Community
      Community: 0:1212 0:1234 8:9 8:12 12:9 12:13
R3# show ip bgp 12.0.0.0 | include Community
      Community: 0:1212 8:12 8:13
! List 2 should match only 11/8, and not 12/8, as only 11/8 has 0:1234 as one of
! the values.
R3# show ip bgp community-list 2 | begin Network
   Network          Next Hop          Metric LocPrf Weight Path
*> 11.0.0.0         10.1.34.4         4294967294        0 4 1 33333 10 200 44 i
! Both 11/8 and 12/8 match the 0:1212 listed in list 3, but list 3 has two
! values configured. The list uses a logical AND between the entries, and only
! 11/8 has matching values for both communities.
R3# show ip bgp community-list 3 | begin Network
   Network          Next Hop          Metric LocPrf Weight Path
*> 11.0.0.0         10.1.34.4         4294967294        0 4 1 33333 10 200 44 i
! List 111 matches any COMMUNITY string with one entry beginning with 0:12,
! followed by any additional characters. 11/8 matches due to the 0:1234, and 12/8
! matches due to the 0:1212. COMMUNITY values 0:12, 0:123, and other would also
! have matched.
R3# show ip bgp community-list 111 | begin Network
   Network          Next Hop          Metric LocPrf Weight Path
*> 11.0.0.0         10.1.34.4         4294967294        0 4 1 33333 10 200 44 i
*> 12.0.0.0         10.1.34.4         4294967294        0 4 1 33333 10 200 44 i
```

[handwritten annotation: → matches 1234 & 1212 → both 11/8 & 12/8]

Removing COMMUNITY Values

[handwritten margin note: To remove all comm. : SET COMMUNITY NONE]

In some cases, a routing policy might need to remove one string from the COMMUNITY PA or even delete the entire COMMUNITY PA. This also can be accomplished with a route map, using the **set** command. Removing the entire COMMUNITY is relatively simple: Include the **set community none** command in a **route-map** clause, and all routes matched by that clause will have their COMMUNITY PA removed. For example, Example 2-11 lists a **route-map react-to-comm** route map on each router. In that design, after the received COMMUNITY string on R1 and R3 was used to match the correct routes and set the LOCAL_PREF values, the COMMUNITY PA was no longer needed. The revised route map in Example 2-13 simply removes the COMMUNITY at that point.

Example 2-13 *Removing the Entire COMMUNITY PA After It Is No Longer Needed*

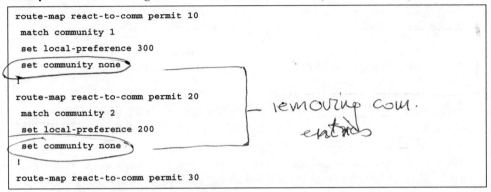

```
route-map react-to-comm permit 10
 match community 1
 set local-preference 300
 set community none
 !
route-map react-to-comm permit 20
 match community 2
 set local-preference 200
 set community none
 !
route-map react-to-comm permit 30
```

removing com. entries

A route map can also remove individual COMMUNITY strings by using the **set comm-list** *community-list-number* **delete** command. This command tells the route map to match routes based on the community list and then delete the COMMUNITY strings listed in the community list. (The referenced community list can contain only one COMMUNITY string per **ip community-list** command in this case.)

To remove indiv. Comm.

Filtering NLRIs Using Special COMMUNITY Values

Routers can use route maps to filter NLRIs from being added to the BGP table or from being sent in Updates to other routers. These route maps can match a BGP route's COMMUNITY by using the **match community** {*standard-list-number* | *expanded-list-number* | *community-list-name* [**exact**]} command, which in turn references a community list.

Additionally, BGP includes several reserved values for the COMMUNITY PA that allow route filtering to occur, but with less effort than is required with community lists and route maps. These special COMMUNITY values, after they are set, affect the logic used by routers when making decisions about to which BGP peers they will advertise the route. The values are listed in Table 2-16.

Table 2-16 *COMMUNITY Values Used Specifically for NLRI Filtering*

Name	Value	Meaning
NO_EXPORT	FFFF:FF01	Do not advertise outside this AS. It can be advertised to other confederation autonomous systems.
NO_ADVERT	FFFF:FF02	Do not advertise to any other peer.
LOCAL_AS[1]	FFFF:FF03	Do not advertise outside the local confederation sub-AS.

[1] *LOCAL_AS is the Cisco term; RFC 1997 defines this value as NO_EXPORT_SUBCONFED.*

→ no transit

A route with COMMUNITY NO_EXPORT is not advertised outside an AS. This value can be used to prevent an AS from being a transit AS for a set of prefixes. For example, a router in AS 1 could advertise an eBGP route into AS 2 with NO_EXPORT set. The routers inside AS 2 would then advertise the route inside AS 2 only. By not advertising the route outside AS 2, AS 2 cannot become a transit AS for that prefix. Note that the routers inside AS 2 do not have to configure a route map to prevent the route from exiting AS 2. However, the iBGP peers inside AS 2 must enable COMMUNITY using the **neighbor send-community** command.

→ sub-AS

The LOCAL_AS COMMUNITY value performs a similar function as NO_EXPORT, put just inside a single confederation sub-AS.

The NO_ADVERT COMMUNITY string might seem a bit unusual at first glance. However, it allows one router to advertise a prefix to a peer, with the intent that the peer will not advertise the route.

Finally, there are a few operational considerations to note regarding these COMMUNITY values. First, a router receiving any of these special communities can match them using an **ip community-list** command with obvious keywords for all three values. Additionally, a router can use a route map to match and then remove these COMMUNITY strings—in effect, ignoring the dictate to limit the scope of advertisement of the routes. Finally, routes with these settings can be seen with commands like **show ip bgp community no-export**, with similar options NO_ADVERT and LOCAL_AS.

Fast Convergence Enhancements

For the purpose of communicating routes and prefixes on the Internet, BGP has been selected for its special characteristics and capabilities, despite many of its inherent drawbacks. BGP is massive in administrative scale and as such it is complex and difficult to master, but above all, it is exceedingly slow to converge. Point in fact: One of the reasons that BGP has been so widely adopted for the Internet is its slowness to converge. However, as the landscapes of networks have changed over the years with the adoption of burgeoning technologies like L3 VPNs, we find ourselves in a unique position. We now have an essential reliance on BGP because of its unparalleled route exchange capacity, but the slowness to converge has become a liability in the network infrastructure. Faced with this dilemma, it was necessary to make modifications to how the BGP code operates in the context of IOS.

To better understand what these modifications are, we will start with an analysis of how the protocol's finite state machine operates. Specifically, we will start by looking at what happens when a BGP peering relationship goes down. In this scenario, we have to point out that even though the IP routing table will represent that the neighbor is not reachable, the underlying BGP process will not reinitiate the convergence process until such time that either the TCP session times out or until the BGP session hold-down timer expires. This process can take up to 3 minutes by default.

Key Topic

The reliance on these session timers is not the only element in the BGP process that translates into slow convergence. We also must recognize that BGP only provides updates to its neighbors periodically using an interval based on the peering type: iBGP peers receive updates every 5 seconds, whereas eBGP peers are updated only every 30 seconds.

Finally, we need to look at BGP's reliance on the underlying interior gateway protocol that is used to resolve next-hop reachability. We know that typically any interior gateway routing protocol will detect changes in the network and reconverge very quickly; in fact they will and can reconverge on a new route far faster than BGP can. This issue is compounded when we consider that BGP will only verify next-hop reachability every 60 seconds.

It does not take long to see that each of these elements quickly combines to create a "perfect storm" of delays that had to be overcome. Now that we understand the nature of the problem, we can better understand the fast convergence optimization made to BGP.

Fast External Neighbor Loss Detection

One of the first modifications to the behavior of BGP in the context of IOS was the advent of fast external fall-over. In this mode of operation, the eBGP session between directly connected eBGP neighbors will be torn down the moment that the connected subnet between the peers is lost. This will result in the immediate flushing of BGP routes, and BGP will immediately begin looking at alternate routes. This feature is not a new advent in the context of IOS, and it is enabled by default in IOS Release 10.0 and later.

Internal Neighbor Loss Detection

Key Topic

This is a new enhancement made to IOS that started in IOS Release 12.0. Whereas fast external fall-over only works for the detection of neighbor loss between eBGP peers and allows IOS to immediately begin reconvergence between those peers, when it comes to internal neighbors, we had no such tools. Until the advent of fast-peering deactivation, an iBGP session could only be optimized through the reduction of keepalive and holdtime values.

Now with the **neighbor fall-over** command, we can alter the behavior between iBGP peers without the added CPU strain of increased keepalive traffic. Now the moment that the IP address of the BGP peer is removed from the routing table, the BGP session with the peer will be torn down, thus resulting in immediate convergence.

Note that we must consider the characteristics of the underlying interior gateway protocol when we use this solution. The IGP protocol must be able to find an alternative route to the BGP peer immediately. If the slightest interruption exists between the moments the original route to the BGP peer is lost and a new route is inserted in the IP routing table, the BGP session would already be disconnected.

Note that hold-down or delay in BGP session deactivation is not used.

EBGP Fast Session Deactivation

BGP fast session deactivation works on all BGP sessions. You can use it to quickly detect failures of eBGP sessions established between loopback interfaces of eBGP peers or to detect eBGP neighbor loss when you disable fast external fall-over.

Fast external fall-over is a global setting, whereas the fast session deactivation is configured per neighbor. You can thus disable fast external fall-over with the **no bgp fast-external-fallover** router configuration command and retain the quick response to interface failures for a selected subset of eBGP.

The eBGP fast session deactivation is identical to the iBGP use case described previously and is implemented through the **neighbor fall-over** command. You can even reflect the rule that the BGP peer has to be directly connected with a **route-map** command that matches only connected subnets.

Foundation Summary

This section lists additional details and facts to round out the coverage of the topics in this chapter. Unlike most Cisco Press Exam Certification Guides, this book does not repeat information listed in the "Foundation Topics" section of the chapter. Please take the time to read and study the details in this section of the chapter, as well as review the items in the "Foundation Topics" section noted with a Key Topic icon.

Table 2-17 lists some of the RFCs for BGP whose concepts were covered in this chapter.

Table 2-17 *Protocols and Standards for Chapter 2*

Topic	Standard
BGP-4	RFC 4271
The NOPEER Community	RFC 3765
BGP Route Reflection	RFC 4456
BGP Communities	RFC 1997

Table 2-18 lists some of the relevant Cisco IOS commands related to the topics in this chapter.

Table 2-18 *Command Reference for Chapter 2*

Command	Command Mode and Description
bgp always-compare-med	BGP mode; tells the router to compare MED even if the neighboring ASNs are different
bgp bestpath med confed	BGP mode; tells the router to consider MED for choosing routes through different confederation sub-ASs
bgp bestpath med missing-as-worst	BGP mode; resets the default MED from 0 to the maximum ($232 - 1$)
bgp default local-preference *number*	BGP mode; sets the default LOCAL_PREF value
bgp deterministic-med	BGP mode; tells IOS to process MED logic based on neighboring AS, rather than on the order in which the routes were learned
bgp maxas-limit *number*	BGP mode; tells the router to discard routes whose AS_PATH length exceeds this setting
clear ip bgp {*	*neighbor-address*	*peer-group-name*} [soft [in	out]]	EXEC mode; clears the BGP process, or neighbors, optionally using soft reconfiguration

Command	Command Mode and Description
distribute-list *acl-number* | **prefix** *list-name* **in** | **out**	BGP mode; defines a BGP distribution list (ACL or prefix list) for filtering routes
ip as-path access-list *access-list-number* {**permit** | **deny**} *as-regexp*	Global config; creates entries in AS_PATH access lists used in matching existing AS_PATH values
ip bgp-community new-format	Global config; tells IOS to display and interpret the COMMUNITY PA in the RFC 1997 format, AA:NN
ip community-list {*standard* | **standard** *list-name* {**deny** | **permit**} [*community-number*] [*AA:NN*] [**internet**] [**local-AS**] [**no-advertise**] [**no-export**]} | {*expanded* | **expanded** *list-name* {**deny** | **permit**} *regexp*}	Global config; creates entries in a community list used in matching existing COMMUNITY values
maximum-paths *number*	BGP mode; sets the number of eBGP routes that can be added to the IP routing table
maximum-paths eibgp *number* [**import** *number*]	BGP mode; sets the number of eBGP and iBGP routes that can be added to the IP routing table when using MPLS
maximum-paths ibgp *number*	BGP mode; sets the number of iBGP routes that can be added to the IP routing table
neighbor {*ip-address* | *peer-group-name*} **distribute-list** {*access-list-number* | *expanded-list-number* | *access-list-name* | *prefix-list-name*} {**in** | **out**}	BGP mode; identifies a distribute list used to filter NLRIs being sent to or received from the neighbor
neighbor {*ip-address* | *peer-group-name*} **filter-list** *access-list-number* {**in** | **out**}	BGP mode; identifies an AS_PATH access list used to filter NLRIs by matching the AS_PATH PA
neighbor {*ip-address* | *peer-group-name*} **local-as** *as-number* [**no-prepend**]	BGP mode; defines an alternate ASN to be prepended in the AS_PATH of sent eBGP Updates, instead of the ASN listed in the **router bgp** command
neighbor {*ip-address* | *peer-group-name*} **prefix-list** {*prefix-list-name* | *clns-filter-expr-name* | *clns-filter-set-name*} {**in** | **out**}	BGP mode; identifies an IP prefix list used to filter NLRIs being sent to or received from the neighbor
neighbor {*ip-address* | *peer-group-name*} **remove-private-as**	BGP mode; used with eBGP peers, removes any private ASNs from the AS_PATH under certain conditions
neighbor {*ip-address* | *peer-group-name*} **route-map** *map-name* {**in** | **out**}	BGP mode; defines a route map and direction for applying routing policies to BGP Updates

Command	Command Mode and Description
neighbor *ip-address* **route-reflector-client**	BGP mode; used on the RR server, identifies a neighbor as an RR client
neighbor {*ip-address* | *peer-group-name*} **send-community** [**both** | **standard** | **extended**]	BGP mode; causes the router to include the COMMUNITY PA in Updates sent to this neighbor
neighbor {*ip-address* | *peer-group-name*} **soft-reconfiguration** [**inbound**]	BGP mode; enables soft reconfiguration of Updates
neighbor {*ip-address* | *peer-group-name*} **unsuppress-map** *route-map-name*	BGP mode; allows a router to identify previously suppressed routes and no longer suppress them
neighbor {*ip-address* | *peer-group-name*} **weight** *number*	BGP mode; sets the BGP weight for all routes learned from the neighbor
network *ip-address* **backdoor**	BGP mode; identifies a network as a backdoor route, considering it to have the same administrative distance as iBGP routes
show ip bgp quote-regexp *regexp*	EXEC mode; displays BGP table entries whose AS_PATH PA is matched by the stated regex
show ip bgp regexp *regexp*	EXEC mode; displays BGP table entries whose AS_PATH PA is matched by the stated regex
show ip community-list [*standard-community-list-number* | *extended-community-list-number* | *community-list-name*] [**exact-match**]	EXEC mode; lists the contents of configured IP community lists
show ip bgp community *community-number* [**exact**]	EXEC mode; lists BGP table entries that include the listed COMMUNITY
show ip bgp filter-list *access-list-number*	EXEC mode; lists the contents of AS_PATH access lists
neighbor *ip-address* **fall-over** [**route-map** *map-name*]	BGP mode; eBGP session between directly connected eBGP neighbors will be torn down the moment the connected subnet between the peers is lost

Table 2-19 lists the route map **match** and **set** commands pertinent to defining BGP routing policies.

Table 2-19   *Route Map* **match** *and* **set** *Commands for BGP*

Command	Function
match as-path *path-list-number*	References an **ip as-path access-list** command to examine the AS_PATH
match community {*standard-list-number* | *expanded-list-number* | *community-list-name* [**exact**]}	References an **ip community-list** command to examine the COMMUNITY PA
match ip address {*access-list-number* [*access-list-number* . . . | *access-list-name* . . .]}	References an IP access list to match based on NLRI
match ip address prefix-list *prefix-list-name* [*prefix-list-name* . . .]}	References an IP prefix list to match based on NLRI
match tag *tag-value* [. . . *tag-value*]	Matches a previously set route tag
set as-path prepend *as-path-string*	Adds the listed ASNs to the beginning of the AS_PATH
set comm-list *community-list-number* | *community-list-name* **delete**	Removes individual strings from the COMMUNITY PA as matched by the referenced community list
set community {*community-number* [**additive**] [*well-known-community*] | **none**}	Sets, replaces, adds to, or deletes the entire COMMUNITY
set ip next-hop *ip-address* [. . . *ip-address*] [**peer-address**]	With the peer address option, resets the NEXT_HOP PA to be the sender's IP address used to send Updates to a neighbor
set local-preference *number-value*	Sets the LOCAL_PREF PA
set metric *metric-value*	Inbound only; sets the MULTI_EXIT_DISC PA
set origin {**igp** | **egp** *as-number* | **incomplete**}	Sets the ORIGIN PA value
set weight *number*	Sets the proprietary administrative weight value

Memory Builders

The CCIE Routing and Switching written exam, like all Cisco CCIE written exams, covers a fairly broad set of topics. This section provides some basic tools to help you exercise your memory about some of the broader topics covered in this chapter.

Fill In Key Tables from Memory

First, take the time to print Appendix E, "Key Tables for CCIE Study," which contains empty sets of some of the key summary tables from the "Foundation Topics" section of this chapter. Then, simply fill in the tables from memory. Refer to Appendix F, "Solutions for Key Tables for CCIE Study," on the CD, to check your answers.

Definitions

Next, take a few moments to write down the definitions for the following terms:

NLRI, soft reconfiguration, AS_PATH access list, AS_PATH prepending, regular expression, AS_SEQUENCE, AS_SET, well-known mandatory, well-known discretionary, optional transitive, optional nontransitive, AS_PATH, NEXT_HOP, AGGREGATOR, ATOMIC AGGREGATE, ORIGINATOR_ID, CLUSTER_LIST, ORIGIN, administrative weight, LOCAL_PREF, AS_PATH length, MULTI_EXIT_DISC (MED), Neighbor Type, BGP decision process, private AS, COMMUNITY, LOCAL_AS, NO_EXPORT, NO_ADVERT, NO_EXPORT_SUBCONFED

Further Reading

Routing TCP/IP, Volume II, by Jeff Doyle and Jennifer DeHaven Carrol

Cisco BGP-4 Command and Configuration Handbook, by William R. Parkhurst

Internet Routing Architectures, by Bassam Halabi

Troubleshooting IP Routing Protocols, by Zaheer Aziz, Johnson Liu, Abe Martey, and Faraz Shamim

Almost every reference can be reached from the Cisco BGP support page at www.cisco.com/en/US/partner/tech/tk365/tk80/tsd_technology_support_sub-protocol_home.html. Requires a Cisco.com username/password.

For the oddities of BGP table sequence impacting the MED-related best-path choice, refer to the following Cisco resource: www.cisco.com/en/US/partner/tech/tk365/technologies_tech_note09186a0080094925.shtml.

Blueprint topics covered in this chapter:

This chapter covers the following subtopics from the Cisco CCIE Routing and Switching written exam blueprint. Refer to the full blueprint in Table I-1 in the Introduction for more details on the topics covered in each chapter and their context within the blueprint.

- Modular QoS CLI (MQC)

- Network-Based Application Recognition (NBAR)

- QoS Classification

- QoS Marking

- Cisco AutoQoS

CHAPTER 3

Classification and Marking

The goal of classification and marking tools is to simplify the classification process of other quality of service (QoS) tools by performing complicated classification steps as few times as possible. For example, a classification and marking tool might examine the source IP address of packets, incoming Class of Service (CoS) settings, and possibly TCP or UDP port numbers. Packets matching all those fields might have their IP Precedence (IPP) or DiffServ Code Points (DSCP) field marked with a particular value. Later, other QoS tools—on the same router/switch or a different one—can simply look for the marked field when making a QoS decision, rather than having to perform the detailed classification again before taking the desired QoS action.

"Do I Know This Already?" Quiz

Table 3-1 outlines the major headings in this chapter and the corresponding "Do I Know This Already?" quiz questions.

Table 3-1 *"Do I Know This Already?" Foundation Topics Section-to-Question Mapping*

Foundation Topics Section	Questions Covered in This Section	Score
Fields That Can Be Marked for QoS Purposes	1–4	
Cisco Modular QoS CLI	5–7	
Classification and Marking Tools	8–10	
AutoQoS	11	
Total Score		

To best use this pre-chapter assessment, remember to score yourself strictly. You can find the answers in Appendix A, "Answers to the 'Do I Know This Already?' Quizzes."

1. According to the DiffServ RFCs, which PHB defines a set of three DSCPs in each service class, with different drop characteristics for each of the three DSCP values?

   a. Expedited Forwarding

   b. Class Selector

   c. Assured Forwarding

   d. Multi-class-multi-drop

2. Which of the following are true about the location of DSCP in the IP header?

   a. High-order 6 bits of ToS byte/DS field.

   b. Low-order 6 bits of ToS byte.

   c. Middle 6 bits of ToS byte.

   d. Its first 3 bits overlap with IP Precedence.

   e. Its last 3 bits overlap with IP Precedence

3. Imagine that a packet is marked with DSCP CS3. Later, a QoS tool classifies the packet. Which of the following classification criteria would match the packet, assuming that the marking had not been changed from the original CS3 marking?

   a. Match on DSCP CS3

   b. Match on precedence 3

   c. Match on DSCP AF32

   d. Match on DSCP AF31

   e. Match on DSCP decimal 24 ·

4. Imagine that a packet is marked with AF31. Later, a QoS tool classifies the packet. Which of the following classification criteria would match the packet, assuming that the marking had not been changed from the original AF31 marking?

   a. Match on DSCP CS3

   b. Match on precedence 3

   c. Match on DSCP 24

   d. Match on DSCP 26

   e. Match on DSCP 28

5. Examine the following output from a router that shows a user adding configuration to a router. Which of the following statements is true about the configuration?

```
Router(config)# class-map fred
Router(config-cmap)# match dscp EF
Router(config-cmap)# match access-group 101
```

   a. Packets that match both DSCP EF and ACL 101 will match the class.

   b. Packets that match either DSCP EF or ACL 101 will match the class.

   c. Packets that match ACL 101 will match the class, because the second **match** command replaces the first.

   d. Packets will only match DSCP EF because the first match exits the class map.

6. Router R1 is configured with the following three class maps. Which class map(s) would match an incoming frame whose CoS field is set to 3, IP Precedence is set to 2, and DSCP is set to AF21?

```
class-map match-all c1
  match cos 3 4
class-map match-any c2  ·
  match cos 2 3
  match cos 1
class-map match-all c3
  match cos 3 4
  match cos 2
```

    a. c1

    b. c2

    c. c3

    d. All of these answers are correct.

7. Examine the following example of commands typed in configuration mode to create a class map. Assuming that the **class fred** command was used inside a policy map, and the policy map was enabled on an interface, which of the following would be true with regard to packets classified by the class map?

```
Router(config)# class-map fred
Router(config-cmap)# match ip dscp ef
Router(config-cmap)# match ip dscp af31
```

    a. Match packets with both DSCP EF and AF31

    b. Match packets with either DSCP EF or AF31

    c. Match all packets that are neither EF nor AF31

    d. Match no packets

    e. Match packets with precedence values of 3 and 5

8. The **service-policy output fred** command is found in Router R1's configuration under Frame Relay subinterface s0/0.1. Which of the following could be true about this CB Marking policy map?

    a. The policy map can classify packets using class maps that match based on the DE bit.

    b. The policy map can refer to class maps that match based on DSCP.

    c. The policy map can set CoS.

    d. The policy map can set CLP.

    e. The policy map can set DE.

9. Which of the following is true regarding the listed configuration steps?

```
Router(config)# class-map barney
Router(config-cmap)# match protocol http url "this-here.jpg"
Router(config-cmap)# policy-map fred
Router(config-pmap)# class barney
Router(config-pmap-c)# set dscp af21
Router(config-pmap-c)# interface fa0/0
Router(config-if)# service-policy output fred
```

   a. If not already configured, the **ip cef** global command is required.

   b. The configuration does not use NBAR because the **match nbar** command was not used.

   c. The **service-policy** command would be rejected because **match protocol** is not allowed as an output function.

   d. None of these answers are correct.

10. In which mode(s) can the **qos pre-classify** command be issued on a router?

   a. In crypto map configuration mode

   b. In GRE tunnel configuration mode

   c. In point-to-point subinterface configuration mode

   d. Only in physical interface configuration mode

   e. In class map configuration mode

   f. In global configuration mode

11. Which of the following statements about Cisco AutoQoS are true?

   a. It can be used only on switches, not routers.

   b. It makes QoS configuration quicker, easier, and cheaper.

   c. AutoQoS can be used to configure quality of service for voice, video, and other types of data.

   d. AutoQoS commands are applied at the interface.

   e. AutoQoS must be disabled before its settings can be modified.

Foundation Topics

This chapter has three major sections. The chapter begins by examining the fields that can be marked by the classification and marking (C&M) tools. Next, the chapter covers the mechanics of the Cisco IOS Modular QoS CLI (MQC), which is used by all the IOS QoS tools that begin with the words "Class-Based." Finally, the C&M tools are covered, with most of the content focused on the most important C&M tool, Class-Based Marking (CB Marking).

[handwritten: Class of Service] L2

Fields That Can Be Marked for QoS Purposes

[handwritten: IPP] *[handwritten: DSCP]* *[handwritten: ToS } L3]*

The IP header, LAN trunking headers, Frame Relay header, and ATM cell header all have at least one field that can be used to perform some form of QoS marking. This section lists and defines those fields, with the most significant coverage focused on the IP header IP Precedence (IPP) and Differentiated Services Code Point (DSCP) fields.

IP Precedence and DSCP Compared

The IP header is defined in RFC 791, including a 1-byte field called the Type of Service *[handwritten: ToS]* (ToS) byte. The ToS byte was intended to be used as a field to mark a packet for treatment with QoS tools. The ToS byte itself was further subdivided, with the high-order 3 bits defined as the *IP Precedence (IPP)* field. The complete list of values from the ToS byte's original IPP 3-bit field, and the corresponding names, is provided in Table 3-2.

Key Topic

Table 3-2   *IP Precedence Values and Names*

[handwritten: first 3 bits → IP Precedence]

Name	Decimal Value	Binary Value	
Routine	Precedence 0	000	
Priority	Precedence 1	001	
Immediate	Precedence 2	010	
Flash	Precedence 3	011	
Flash Override	Precedence 4	100	
Critic/Critical	Precedence 5	101	
Internetwork Control	Precedence 6	110	
Network Control	Precedence 7	111	

Bits 3 through 6 of the ToS byte included flag fields that were toggled on or off to imply a particular QoS service. The final bit (bit 7) was not defined in RFC 791. The flags were not used very often, so in effect, the ToS byte's main purpose was to hold the 3-bit IPP field.

A series of RFCs collectively called *Differentiated Services (DiffServ)* came along later. DiffServ needed more than 3 bits to mark packets, so DiffServ standardized a redefinition of the ToS byte. The ToS byte itself was renamed the *Differentiated Services (DS) field*, and IPP was replaced with a 6-bit field (high-order bits 0–5) called the *Differentiated Services Code Point (DSCP)* field. Later, RFC 3168 defined the low-order 2 bits of the DS field for use with the QoS *Explicit Congestion Notification (ECN)* feature. Figure 3-1 shows the ToS byte's format with the pre-DiffServ and post-DiffServ definition of the field.

[handwritten margin note: 6 bits of the ToS byte is used now]

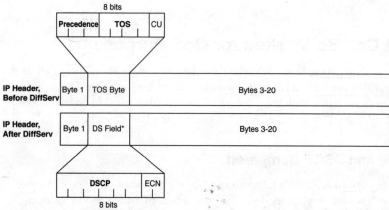

Figure 3-1 *IP ToS Byte and DS Field Compared*

C&M tools often mark DSCP or IPP because the IP packet remains intact as it is forwarded throughout an IP network. The other possible marking fields reside inside Layer 2 headers, which means that the headers are discarded when forwarded by a Layer 3 process. Thus, the latter cannot be used to carry QoS markings beyond the current hop.

DSCP Settings and Terminology

Several DiffServ RFCs suggest a set of values to use in the DSCP field and an implied meaning for those settings. For example, RFC 3246 defines a DSCP of decimal 46, with a name *Expedited Forwarding (EF)*. According to that RFC, packets marked as EF should be given queuing preference so that they experience minimal latency, but the packets should be policed to prevent them from taking over a link and preventing any other types of traffic from exiting an interface during periods when this high-priority traffic reaches or exceeds the interface bandwidth. These suggested settings, and the associated QoS behavior recommended when using each setting, are called *Per-Hop Behaviors (PHB)* by DiffServ. (The particular example listed in this paragraph is called the Expedited Forwarding PHB.)

Class Selector PHB and DSCP Values

IPP overlaps with the first 3 bits of the DSCP field because the DS field is simply a redefinition of the original ToS byte in the IP header. Because of this overlap, RFC 2475 defines a set of DSCP values and PHBs, called *Class Selector (CS)* PHBs that provide backward compatibility with IPP. A C&M feature can set a CS DSCP value, and if another router or switch just looks at the IPP field, the value will make sense from an IPP perspective. Table 3-3 lists the CS DSCP names and values, and the corresponding IPP values and names.

Table 3-3 *Default and Class Selector DSCP Values*

DSCP Class Selector Names	Binary DSCP Values	IPP Binary Values	IPP Names
Default/CS0*	000000	000	Routine
CS1	001000	001	Priority
CS2	010000	010	Immediate
CS3	011000	011	Flash
CS4	100000	100	Flash Override
CS5	101000	101	Critical
CS6	110000	110	Internetwork Control
CS7	111000	111	Network Control

*The terms "CS0" and "Default" both refer to a binary DSCP of 000000, but most Cisco IOS commands allow only the keyword "default" to represent this value.

Besides defining eight DSCP values and their text names, the CS PHB also suggests a simple set of QoS actions that should be taken based on the CS values. The CS PHB simply states that packets with larger CS DSCPs should be given better queuing preference than packets with lower CS DSCPs.

Assured Forwarding PHB and DSCP Values

The *Assured Forwarding (AF) PHB* (RFC 2597) defines four classes for queuing purposes, along with three levels of drop probability inside each queue. To mark packets and distinguish into which of four queues a packet should be placed, along with one of three drop priorities inside each queue, the AF PHB defines 12 DSCP values and their meanings. The names of the AF DSCPs conform to the following format:

AFxy

where x implies one of four queues (values 1 through 4) and y implies one of three drop priorities (values 1 through 3).

The AF PHB suggests that the higher the value of x in the DSCP name AFxy, the better the queuing treatment a packet should get. For example, packets with AF11 DSCPs should get worse queuing treatment than packets with AF23 DSCP values. Additionally, the AF PHB suggests that the higher the value of y in the DSCP name AFxy, the worse the drop treatment for those packets. (Treating a packet worse for drop purposes means that the packet has a higher probability of being dropped.) For example, packets with

AF11 DSCPs should get better drop treatment than packets with AF23 DSCP values. Table 3-4 lists the names of the DSCP values, the queuing classes, and the implied drop likelihood.

dropping pref

Key Topic

Table 3-4 *Assured Forwarding DSCP Values—Names, Binary Values, and Decimal Values*

Queue Class	Low Drop Probability Name/Decimal/Binary	Medium Drop Probability Name/Decimal/Binary	High Drop Probability Name/Decimal/Binary
1	AF11/10/001010	AF12/12/001100	AF13/14/001110
2	AF21/18/010010	AF22/20/010100	AF23/22/010110
3	AF31/26/011010	AF32/28/011100	AF33/30/011110
4	AF41/34/100010	AF42/36/100100	AF43/38/100110

queuing class   *queing class*   *queing class*

The text AF PHB names do not follow the "bigger-is-better" logic in all cases. For example, the name AF11 represents a decimal value of 10, and the name AF13 represents a decimal DSCP of 14. However, AF11 is "better" than AF13, because AF11 and AF13 are in the same queuing class, but AF11 has a lower probability of being dropped than AF13.

The binary version of the AF DSCP values shows the patterns of the values. The first 3 bits of the binary DSCP values designate the queuing class (bits 0 through 2 counting left to right), and the next 2 bits (bits 3 and 4) designate the drop preference. As a result, queuing tools that operate only on IPP can still react to the AF DSCP values, essentially making the AF DSCPs backward compatible with non-DiffServ nodes for queuing purposes.

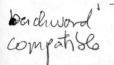
backward compatible

Key Topic

Note   To convert from the AF name to the decimal equivalent, you can use a simple formula. If you think of the AF values as AFxy, the formula is

$$8x + 2y = \text{decimal value}$$

For example, AF41 gives you a formula of $(8 * 4) + (2 * 1) = 34$.

isn't it 8x + y?

Expedited Forwarding PHB and DSCP Values

RFC 2598 defines the *Expedited Forwarding (EF) PHB*, which was described briefly in the introduction to this section. This RFC defines a very simple pair of PHB actions:

■   Queue EF packets so that they get scheduled quickly, to give them low latency.

■   Police the EF packets so that they do not consume all bandwidth on the link or starve other queues.

The DSCP value defined for EF is named EF, with decimal value 46, binary value 101110.

Non-IP Header Marking Fields

As IP packets pass through an internetwork, the packet is encapsulated in a variety of other headers. In several cases, these other headers have QoS fields that can be used for classification and marking.

Ethernet LAN Class of Service

Ethernet supports a 3-bit QoS marking field, but the field only exists when the Ethernet header includes either an 802.1Q or ISL trunking header. IEEE 802.1Q defines its QoS field as the 3 most-significant bits of the 2-byte *Tag Control* field, calling the field the *user-priority bits*. ISL defines the 3 least-significant bits from the 1-byte *User* field, calling this field the *Class of Service (CoS)*. Generally speaking, most people (and most IOS commands) refer to these fields as *CoS*, regardless of the type of trunking. Figure 3-2 shows the general location of the CoS field inside ISL and 802.1P headers.

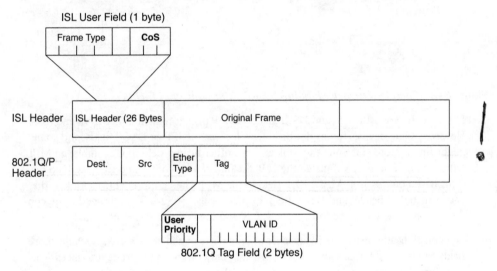

Figure 3-2 *LAN CoS Fields*

WAN Marking Fields

Frame Relay and ATM support a single bit that can be set for QoS purposes, but these single bits are intended for a very strict use related to drop probability. Frames or cells with these bits set to 1 are considered to be better candidates to be dropped than frames or cells without the bit set to 1. Named the Frame Relay *Discard Eligibility (DE)* bit and the ATM *Cell Loss Priority (CLP)* bit, these bits can be set by a router, or by an ATM or Frame Relay switch. Router and switch drop features can then be configured to more aggressively drop frames and cells that have the DE or CLP bit set, respectively.

MPLS defines a 3-bit field called the *MPLS Experimental (EXP)* bit that is intended for general QoS marking. Often, C&M tools are used on the edge of MPLS networks to remap DSCP or IPP values to MPLS Experimental bit values to provide QoS inside the MPLS network.

Locations for Marking and Matching

Figure 3-3 shows a sample network, with notes about the locations of the QoS fields.

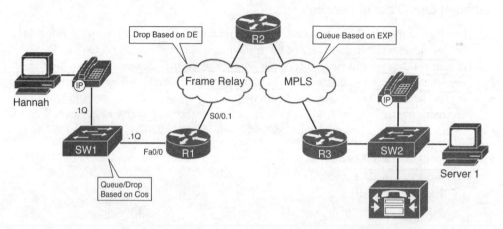

Figure 3-3 *Sample Network Showing Non-IP Markable QoS Fields*

In such a network, the IPP and DSCP inside the IP packet remain intact from end to end. However, some devices might not be able to look at the IPP or DSCP fields, and some might find it more convenient to look at some other header field. For example, an MPLS Label Switch Router (LSR) inside the MPLS cloud can be configured to make QoS decisions based on the 3-bit MPLS EXP field in the MPLS label, but unable to look at the encapsulated IP header and DSCP field. In such cases, QoS tools might need to be configured on edge devices to look at the DSCP and then mark a different field.

The non-IP header markable fields exist in only parts of the network. As a result, those fields can be used for classification or marking only on the appropriate interfaces. The rules for where these fields (CoS, DE, CLP, EXP) can be used are as follows:

Key
Topic

- **For classification:** On ingress only, and only if the interface supports that particular header field

- **For marking:** On egress only, and only if the interface supports that particular header field

For example, if CB Marking were to be configured on R1's fa0/0.1 802.1Q subinterface, it could classify incoming frames based on their CoS values, and mark outgoing frames with a CoS value. However, on ingress, it could not mark CoS, and on egress, it could not classify based on CoS. Similarly, on that same fa0/0.1 subinterface, CB Marking could neither classify nor mark based on a DE bit, CLP bit, or MPLS EXP bits, because these headers never exist on Ethernet interfaces.

Table 3-5 summarizes the QoS marking fields.

Table 3-5 *Marking Field Summary*

Field	Location	Length
IP Precedence (IPP)	IP header	3 bits
IP DSCP	IP header	6 bits
DS field	IP header	1 byte
ToS byte	IP header	1 byte
CoS	ISL and 802.1Q header	3 bits
Discard Eligible (DE)	Frame Relay header	1 bit
Cell Loss Priority (CLP)	ATM cell header	1 bit
MPLS Experimental	MPLS header	3 bits

Cisco Modular QoS CLI

For many years and over many IOS releases, Cisco added QoS features and functions, each of which used its own separate set of configuration and exec commands. Eventually, the number of different QoS tools and different QoS commands got so large that QoS configuration became a big chore. Cisco created the *Modular QoS CLI (MQC)* to help resolve these problems, by defining a common set of configuration commands to configure many QoS features in a router or switch.

MQC is not a totally new CLI, different from IOS configuration mode, for configuring QoS. Rather, it is a method of categorizing IOS classification, marking, and related actions into logical groupings to unify the command-line interface. MQC defines a new set of configuration commands—commands that are typed in using the same IOS CLI, in configuration mode. However, after you understand MQC, you typically need to learn only one new command to know how to configure any additional MQC-based QoS tools. You can identify MQC-based tools by the name of the tool; they all begin with the phrase "Class-Based" (abbreviated CB for this discussion). These tools include CB Marking, CB Weighted Fair Queuing (CBWFQ), CB Policing, CB Shaping, and CB Header Compression.

Mechanics of MQC

MQC separates the classification function of a QoS tool from the action (PHB) that the QoS tool wants to perform. To do so, there are three major commands with MQC, with several subordinate commands:

- The **class-map** command defines the matching parameters for classifying packets into service classes.

- The PHB actions (marking, queuing, and so on) are configured under a **policy-map** command.

- The policy map is enabled on an interface by using a **service-policy** command.

Figure 3-4 shows the general flow of commands.

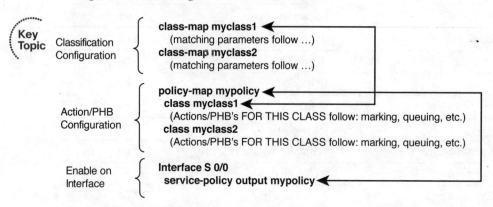

Figure 3-4 *MQC Commands and Their Correlation*

In Figure 3-4, the network's QoS policy calls for treating packets in one of two categories, called *QoS service classes*. (The actual types of packets that are placed into each class are not shown, to keep the focus on the general flow of how the main commands work together.) Classifying packets into two classes calls for the use of two **class-map** commands. Each **class-map** command would be followed by a **match** subcommand, which defines the actual parameters that are compared to the frame/packet header contents to match packets for classification.

For each class, some QoS action (PHB) needs to be performed; this action is configured using the **policy-map** command. Under a single policy map, multiple classes can be referenced; in Figure 3-4, the two classes are myclass1 and myclass2. Inside the single policy called mypolicy, under each of the two classes myclass1 and myclass2, you can configure separate QoS actions. For example, you could apply different markings to packets in myclass1 and myclass2 at this point. Finally, when the **service-policy** command is applied to an interface, the QoS features are enabled either inbound or outbound on that interface.

The next section takes a much closer look at packet classification using class maps. Most of the discussion of policy maps will be included when specifically covering CB Marking configuration later in the chapter.

Classification Using Class Maps

MQC-based tools classify packets using the **match** subcommand inside an MQC class map. The following list details the rules surrounding how class maps work for matching and classifying packets:

- The **match** command has many options for matching packets, including QoS fields, ACLs, and MAC addresses.
- Class-map names are case sensitive.

- The **match protocol** command means that IOS uses Network-Based Application Recognition (NBAR) to perform that match.

- The **match any** command matches any packet—in other words, any and all packets.

Example 3-1 shows a simple CB Marking configuration, with comments focused on the classification configuration. Note that the names and logic match Figure 3-4.

Example 3-1 *Basic CB Marking Example*

```
! CEF is required for CB Marking. Without it, the class map and policy map
! configuration would be allowed, but the service-policy command would be rejected.
ip cef
! The first class map matches all UDP/RTP packets with UDP ports between 16384 and
! 32767 (the 2nd number is added to the first to get the end of the range.) The
! second class map matches any and all packets.
class-map match-all myclass1
  match ip rtp 16384 16383
class-map match-all myclass2
  match any
! The policy map calls each of the two class maps for matching. The set command
! implies that the PHB is marking, meaning that this is a CB Marking config.
policy-map mypolicy
  class myclass1
    set dscp EF
  class myclass2
    set dscp default
! The policy map processes packets leaving interface fa0/0.
interface Fastethernet0/0
 service-policy output mypolicy
```

With Example 3-1, each packet leaving interface fa0/0 will match one of the two classes. Because the policy map uses a **set dscp** command in each class, and all packets happen to match either myclass1 or myclass2, each packet will leave the interface marked either with DSCP EF (decimal 46) or default (decimal 0). (If the matching logic was different and some packets match neither myclass1 nor myclass2, those packets would not be marked, and would retain their existing DSCP values.)

Using Multiple match Commands

In some cases, a class map might need to examine multiple items in a packet to decide whether the packet should be part of that class. Class maps can use multiple **match** commands, and even nest class maps inside other class maps, to achieve the desired combination of logic. The following list summarizes the key points regarding these more complex matching options:

- Up to four (CoS and IPP) or eight (DSCP) values can be listed on a single **match cos**, **match precedence**, or **match dscp** command, respectively. If any of the values are found in the packet, the statement is matched.

- If a class map has multiple **match** commands in it, the **match-any** or **match-all** (default) parameter on the **class-map** command defines whether a logical OR or a logical AND (default) is used between the **match** commands, respectively.

- The **match class** *name* command refers to another class map by name, nesting the named class map's matching logic; the **match class** *name* command is considered to match if the referenced class map also results in a match.

Example 3-2 shows several examples of this more complicated matching logic, with notations inside the example of what must be true for a class map to match a packet.

Example 3-2 *Complex Matching with Class Maps*

```
! class-map example1 uses match-all logic (default), so this class map matches
! packets that are permitted by ACL 102, and that also have an IP precedence of 5.
class-map match-all example1
 match access-group 102
 match precedence 5
! class-map example2 uses match-any logic, so this class map matches packets that
! are permitted by ACL 102, or have DSCP AF21, or both.
class-map match-any example2
  match access-group 102
  match dscp AF21
! class-map example3 matches no packets, due to a common mistake—the two match
! commands use a logical AND between them due to the default match-all argument,
! meaning that a single packet must have DSCP 0 and DSCP 1, which is impossible.
! class-map example4 shows how to correctly match either DSCP 0 or 1.
class-map match-all example3
  match dscp 0
  match dscp 1
 !
class-map match-any example4
  match dscp 0 1
! class-map i-am-nesting refers to class-map i-am-nested through the match class
! i-am-nested command. The logic is explained after the example.
class-map match-all i-am-nested
  match access-group 102
  match precedence 5
 !
class-map match-any i-am-nesting
  match class i-am-nested
  match cos 5
```

The trickiest part of Example 3-2 is how the class maps can be nested, as shown at the end. **class-map i-am-nesting** uses OR logic between its two **match** commands, meaning "I will match if the CoS is 5, or if **class-map i-am-nested** matches the packet, or both."

When combined with the match-all logic of the **i-am-nested** class map, the logic matches the following packets/frames:

Packets that are permitted by ACL 102, AND marked with precedence 5

or

frames with CoS 5

Classification Using NBAR

NBAR classifies packets that are normally difficult to classify. For example, some applications use dynamic port numbers, so a statically configured **match** command, matching a particular UDP or TCP port number, simply could not classify the traffic. NBAR can look past the UDP and TCP header, and refer to the host name, URL, or MIME type in HTTP requests. (This deeper examination of the packet contents is sometimes called *deep packet inspection*.) NBAR can also look past the TCP and UDP headers to recognize application-specific information. For example, NBAR allows recognition of different Citrix application types, and allows searching for a portion of a URL string.

NBAR itself can be used for a couple of different purposes. Independent of QoS features, NBAR can be configured to keep counters of traffic types and traffic volume for each type. For QoS, NBAR can be used by CB Marking to match difficult-to-match packets. Whenever the MQC **match protocol** command is used, IOS is using NBAR to match the packets. Table 3-6 lists some of the more popular uses of the **match protocol** command and NBAR.

Table 3-6 *Popular Fields Matchable by CB Marking Using NBAR*

Field	Comments
RTP audio versus video	RTP uses even-numbered UDP ports from 16,384 to 32,768. The odd-numbered port numbers are used by RTCP for call control traffic. NBAR allows matching the even-numbered ports only, for classification of voice payload into a different service class from that used for voice signaling.
Citrix applications	NBAR can recognize different types of published Citrix applications.
Host name, URL string, MIME type	NBAR can also match URL strings, including the host name and the MIME type, using regular expressions for matching logic.
Peer-to-peer applications	NBAR can find file-sharing applications like KaZaa, Morpheus, Grokster, and Gnutella.

Classification and Marking Tools

The final major section of this chapter covers CB Marking, with a brief mention of a few other, less popular marking tools.

Class-Based Marking (CB Marking) Configuration

As with the other QoS tools whose names begin with the phrase "Class-Based," you will use MQC commands to configure CB Marking. The following list highlights the key points regarding CB Marking configuration and logic:

- CB Marking requires CEF (enabled using the **ip cef** global command).

- Packets are classified based on the logic in MQC class maps.

- An MQC policy map refers to one or more class maps using the **class** *class-map-name* command; packets classified into that class are then marked.

- CB Marking is enabled for packets either entering or exiting an interface using the MQC **service-policy in | out** *policy-map-name* interface subcommand.

- A CB Marking policy map is processed sequentially; after a packet has matched a class, it is marked based on the **set** command(s) defined for that class.

- You can configure multiple **set** commands in one class to set multiple fields, for example, to set both DSCP and CoS.

- Packets that do not explicitly match a defined class are considered to have matched a special class called *class-default*.

- For any class inside the policy map for which there is no **set** command, packets in that class are not marked.

Table 3-7 lists the syntax of the CB Marking **set** command, showing the familiar fields that can be set by CB Marking. Table 3-8 lists the key **show** commands available for CB Marking.

Table 3-7 set *Configuration Command Reference for CB Marking*

Command	Function
set [ip] precedence *ip-precedence-value*	Marks the value for IP Precedence for IPv4 and IPv6 packets if the **ip** parameter is omitted; sets only IPv4 packets if the **ip** parameter is included
set [ip] dscp *ip-dscp-value*	Marks the value for IP DSCP for IPv4 and IPv6 packets if the **ip** parameter is omitted; sets only IPv4 packets if the **ip** parameter is included
set cos *cos-value*	Marks the value for CoS
set qos-group *group-id*	Marks the group identifier for the QoS group
set atm-clp	Sets the ATM CLP bit
set fr-de	Sets the Frame Relay DE bit

Table 3-8 *EXEC Command Reference for CB Marking*

Command	Function
show policy-map *policy-map-name*	Lists configuration information about a policy map
show policy-map *interface-spec* [input | output] [**class** *class-name*]	Lists statistical information about the behavior of a policy map when enabled on an interface

CB Marking Example

The first CB Marking example uses the network shown in Figure 3-5. Traffic was generated in the network to make the **show** commands more meaningful. Two G.711 voice calls were completed between R4 and R1 using *Foreign Exchange Station (FXS)* cards on these two routers, with *Voice Activity Detection (VAD)* disabled. Client1 performed an FTP get of a large file from Server1, and downloaded two large HTTP objects, named important.jpg and not-so.jpg. Finally, Client1 and Server1 held a Microsoft NetMeeting conference, using G.723 for the audio and H.263 for the video.

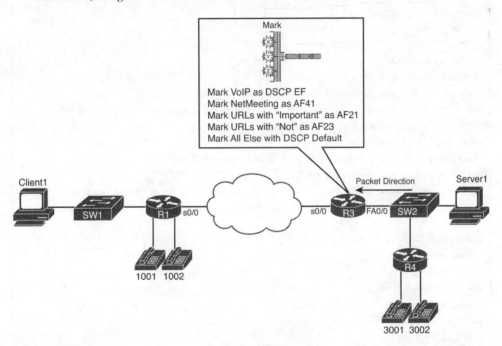

Figure 3-5 *Sample Network for CB Marking Examples*

The following criteria define the requirements for marking the various types of traffic for Example 3-3:

■ VoIP payload is marked with DSCP EF.

■ NetMeeting video traffic is marked with DSCP AF41.

- Any HTTP traffic whose URL contains the string "important" anywhere in the URL is marked with AF21.

- Any HTTP traffic whose URL contains the string "not-so" anywhere in the URL is marked with AF23.

- All other traffic is marked with DSCP Default (0).

Example 3-3 lists the annotated configuration, including the appropriate **show** commands.

Example 3-3   *CB Marking Example 1, with* **show** *Command Output*

```
ip cef
! Class map voip-rtp uses NBAR to match all RTP audio payload, but not the video
! or the signaling.
class-map voip-rtp
 match protocol rtp audio
! Class map http-impo matches all packets related to downloading objects whose
! name contains the string "important," with any text around it. Similar logic
! is used for class-map http-not.
class-map http-impo
 match protocol http url "*important*"
!
class-map http-not
 match protocol http url "*not-so*"
! Class map NetMeet matches two RTP subtypes—one for G.723 audio (type 4) and
! one for H.263 video (type 34). Note the match-any logic so that if either is
! true, a match occurs for this class map.
class-map match-any NetMeet
 match protocol rtp payload-type 4
 match protocol rtp payload-type 34
! policy-map laundry-list calls each of the class maps. Note that the order
! listed here is the order in which the class commands were added to the policy
! map.
policy-map laundry-list
 class voip-rtp
  set ip dscp EF
 class NetMeet
  set ip dscp AF41
 class http-impo
  set ip dscp AF21
 class http-not
  set ip dscp AF23
 class class-default
  set ip DSCP default
! Above, the command class class-default is only required if some nondefault action
! needs to be taken for packets that are not explicitly matched by another class.
```

```
! In this case, packets not matched by any other class fall into the class-default
! class, and are marked with DSCP Default (decimal 0). Without these two commands,
! packets in this class would remain unchanged.
!!!!!!!!!!!!!!!!!!!!!!!!!!!!!!!!!!!!!!!!!!!!!!!!!!!!!!!!!!!!!!!!!!!!!!!!!!!!!!!!!!!!!!!!
!!!
! Below, the policy map is enabled for input packets on fa0/0.
 interface Fastethernet 0/0
 service-policy input laundry-list
! The command show policy-map laundry-list simply restates the configuration.
R3# show policy-map laundry-list
  Policy Map laundry-list
    Class voip-rtp
      set ip dscp 46
    Class NetMeet
      set ip dscp 34
    Class http-impo
      set ip dscp 18
    Class http-not
      set ip dscp 22
    Class class-default
      set ip dscp 0
! The command show policy-map interface lists statistics related to MQC features.
! Several stanzas of output were omitted for brevity.
R3# show policy-map interface fastethernet 0/0 input
Fastethernet0/0

  Service-policy input:      laundry-list

    Class-map: voip-rtp (match-all)
      35268 packets, 2609832 bytes
      5 minute offered rate      59000 bps, drop rate 0 bps
      Match: protocol rtp audio
      QoS Set
        ip dscp 46
            Packets marked 35268

    Class-map: NetMeet (match-any)
      817 packets, 328768 bytes
      5 minute offered rate      19000 bps, drop rate 0 bps
      Match: protocol rtp payload-type 4
             protocol rtp payload-type 34
      QoS Set
        ip dscp 34
            Packets marked 817

! omitting stanza of output for class http-impo
```

```
! omitting stanza of output for class http-not


   Class-map: class-default (match-all)
      33216 packets, 43649458 bytes
      5 minute offered rate     747000 bps, drop rate 0 bps
      Match: any
      QoS Set
        ip dscp 0
Packets marked 33301
```

Example 3-3 includes several different classification options using the **match** command, including the matching of Microsoft NetMeeting traffic. NetMeeting uses RTP for the video flows, and by default uses G.723 for audio and H.323 for video. To match both the audio and video for NetMeeting, a class map that matches either of the two RTP payload subtypes for G.723 and H.263 is needed. So, class map **NetMeet** uses match-any logic, and matches on RTP payload types 4 (G.723) and 34 (H.263). (For more background information on RTP payload types, refer to www.cisco.com/en/US/products/ps6616/products_white_paper09186a0080110040.shtml.)

The **show policy-map interface** command provides statistical information about the number of packets and bytes that have matched each class in the policy maps. The generic syntax is as follows:

```
show policy-map interface interface-name [vc [vpi/] vci] [dlci dlci]
   [input | output] [class class-name]
```

The end of Example 3-3 shows a sample of the command, which lists statistics for marking. If other MQC-based QoS features were configured, statistics for those features would also be displayed. As you can see from the generic command, the **show policy-map interface** command allows you to select just one interface, either input or output, and even select a single class inside a single policy map for display.

The **load-interval** interface subcommand can also be useful when looking at any QoS tool's statistics. The **load-interval** command defines the time interval over which IOS measures packet and bit rates on an interface. With a lower load interval, the statistics change more quickly; with a larger load interval, the statistics change more slowly. The default setting is 5 minutes, and it can be lowered to 30 seconds.

Example 3-3 also shows a common oversight with QoS configuration. Note that the first class in **policy-map laundry-list** is **class voip-rtp**. Because that class map matches all RTP audio, it matches the Microsoft NetMeeting audio stream as well, so the NetMeeting audio is not matched by class **NetMeet** that follows. If the first two classes (**voip-rtp** and **NetMeet**) called in the policy map had been reversed, the NetMeeting audio would have been correctly matched in the **NetMeet** class, and all other audio would have been marked as part of the **voip-rtp** class.

Key Topic

MQC marking is sequential!

CB Marking of CoS and DSCP

Example 3-4 shows how a router might be configured for CB Marking when an attached LAN switch is performing QoS based on CoS. In this case, R3 looks at frames coming in its fa0/0 interface, marking the DSCP values based on the incoming CoS settings. Additionally, R3 looks at the DSCP settings for packets exiting its fa0/0 interface toward the switch, setting the CoS values in the 802.1Q header. The actual values used on R3's fa0/0 interface for classification and marking are as follows:

- Frames entering with CoS 5 will be marked with DSCP EF.

- Frames entering with CoS 1 will be marked with DSCP AF11. $\rightarrow 8 \times 2 + 2 \times 1 = 10$

- Frames entering with any other CoS will be marked DSCP 0.

- Packets exiting with DSCP EF will be marked with CoS 5.

- Packets exiting with DSCP AF11 will be marked with CoS 1.

- Packets exiting with any other DSCP will be marked with CoS 0.

Example 3-4   *Marking DSCP Based on Incoming CoS, and Vice Versa*

```
! The class maps each simply match a single CoS or DSCP value.
class-map cos1
 match cos 1
!
class-map cos5
 match cos 5
!
class-map AF11
 match dscp af11
!
class-map EF
 match dscp EF
! This policy map will map incoming CoS to a DSCP value
policy-map map-cos-to-dscp
 class cos1
  set DSCP af11
 class cos5
  set ip DSCP EF
 class class-default
  set ip dscp default
! This policy map will map incoming DSCP to outgoing CoS. Note that the DSCP
! value is not changed.
policy-map map-dscp-to-cos
 class AF11
  set cos 1
 class EF
  set cos 5
```

```
    class class-default
      set cos 0
!!!!!!!!!!!!!!!!!!!!!!!!!!!!!!!!!!!!!!!!!!!!!!!!!!!!!!!!!!!!!!!!!!!!!!!!!!!!!!!!!!!!!!!!
! The policy maps are applied to an 802.1q subinterface.
interface FastEthernet0/0.1
 encapsulation dot1Q 102
 service-policy input map-cos-to-dscp
 service-policy output map-dscp-to-cos
!
interface FastEthernet0/0.2
 encapsulation dot1Q 2 native
```

no policy-map can be applied as no 802.1Q header [handwritten annotation]

The QoS policy requires two policy maps in this example. Policy map **map-cos-to-dscp** matches CoS values for frames entering R3's fa0/0.1 interface, and marks DSCP values, for packets flowing right to left in Figure 3-5. Therefore, the policy map is enabled on input of R3's fa0/0.1 interface. Policy map **map-dscp-to-cos** matches DSCP values for packets exiting R3's fa0/0.1 interface, and marks the corresponding CoS value. Therefore, the policy map was enabled on the output of R3's fa0/0.1 interface. Neither policy map could be applied on the WAN interface, because only interfaces configured for 802.1Q accept **service-policy** commands that reference policy maps that either classify or mark based on CoS.

Note that you cannot enable a **policy-map** that refers to CoS on interface fa0/0.2 in this example. That subinterface is in the native VLAN, meaning that no 802.1Q header is used.

Network-Based Application Recognition

CB Marking can make use of NBAR's powerful classification capabilities through the **match protocol** subcommand. Example 3-5 shows a configuration for CB Marking and NBAR in which the following requirements are met:

- Any HTTP traffic whose URL contains the string "important" anywhere in the URL is marked with AF21.

- Any HTTP traffic whose URL contains the string "not-so" anywhere in the URL is marked with DSCP default.

- All other traffic is marked with AF11.

Example 3-5 shows the configuration, along with a few NBAR-related **show** commands.

Example 3-5 *CB Marking Based on URLs, Using NBAR for Classification*

```
ip cef
! The "*" in the url string is a wildcard meaning "0 or more characters."
class-map http-impo
     match protocol http url "*important*"
class-map http-not
     match protocol http url "*not-so*"
```

```
! The policy map lists the three classes in order, setting the DSCP values.
policy-map http
 class http-impo
  set dscp AF21
 !
 class http-not
  set dscp default
 !
 class class-default
  set DSCP AF11
! The ip nbar protocol discovery command may or may not be required—see the notes
! following this example.
interface fastethernet 0/0
 ip nbar protocol-discovery
 service-policy input http
! The show ip nbar command only displays statistics if the ip nbar
! protocol-discovery command is applied to an interface. These statistics are
! independent of those created by CB Marking. This example shows several of
! the large number of options on the command.
R3# show ip nbar protocol-discovery interface fastethernet 0/0 stats packet-count
   top-n 5
FastEthernet0/0
                       Input                 Output
                       Packet Count          Packet Count
   Protocol
   ------------------  -------------------   -----------------------

   http                721                   428
   eigrp               635                   0
   netbios             199                   0
   icmp                1                     1
   bgp                 0                     0
   unknown             46058                 63
   Total               47614                 492
```

 Key Topic

Note   Before the 12.2T/12.3 IOS releases, the **ip nbar protocol-discovery** command was required on an interface before using a **service-policy** command that used NBAR matching. With 12.2T/12.3 train releases, this command is no longer required.

The use of the **match protocol** command implies that NBAR will be used to match the packet.

Unlike most other IOS features, NBAR can be upgraded without changing to a later IOS version. Cisco uses a feature called *Packet Description Language Modules (PDLM)* to define new protocols that NBAR should match. When Cisco decides to add one or more new protocols to the list of protocols that NBAR should recognize, it creates and compiles a PDLM. You can then download the PDLM from Cisco, copy it into Flash memory, and add the **ip nbar pdlm** *pdlm-name* command to the configuration, where *pdlm-name* is the name of the PDLM file in Flash memory. NBAR can then classify based on the protocol information from the new PDLM.

CB Marking Design Choices

The intent of CB Marking is to simplify the work required of other QoS tools by marking packets of the same class with the same QoS marking. For other QoS tools to take advantage of those markings, packets should generally be marked as close to the ingress point of the packet as possible. However, the earliest possible point might not be a trusted device. For example, in Figure 3-5 (the figure upon which Examples 3-3 and 3-4 are based), Server1 could set its own DSCP and even CoS if its network interface card (NIC) supported trunking. However, trusting the server administrator might or might not be desirable. So, the following rule summarizes how to choose the best location to perform marking:

Key Topic

- Mark as close to the ingress edge of the network as possible, but not so close to the edge that the marking is made by an untrusted device.

Cisco QoS design guide documents make recommendations not only as to where to perform marking, but also as to which CoS, IPP, and DSCP values to set for certain types of traffic. Table 3-9 summarizes those recommendations.

Key Topic

Table 3-9 *RFC-Recommended Values for Marking*

Type of Traffic	CoS	IPP	DSCP
Voice payload	5	5	EF
Video payload	4	4	AF41
Voice/video signaling	3	3	CS3
Mission-critical data	3	3	AF31, AF32, AF33
Transactional data	2	2	AF21, AF22, AF23
Bulk data	1	1	AF11, AF12, AF13
Best effort	0	0	BE
Scavenger (less than best effort)	0	0	2, 4,6

Also note that Cisco recommends not to use more than four or five different service classes for data traffic. When you use more classes, the difference in behavior between the various classes tends to blur. For the same reason, do not give too many data service classes high-priority service.

Marking Using Policers

Traffic policers measure the traffic rate for data entering or exiting an interface, with the goal of determining whether a configured *traffic contract* has been exceeded. The contract has two components: a *traffic rate*, configured in bits/second, and a *burst size*, configured as a number of bytes. If the traffic is within the contract, all packets are

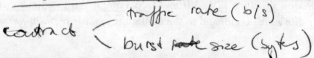

considered to have *conformed* to the contract. However, if the rate or burst exceeds the contract, some packets are considered to have *exceeded* the contract. QoS actions can be taken on both categories of traffic.

The simplest form of policing enforces the traffic contract strictly by forwarding conforming packets and discarding packets that exceed the contract. However, both IOS policers allow a compromise action in which the policer *marks down* packets instead of dropping them. To mark down the packet, the policer re-marks a QoS field, typically IPP or DSCP, with a value that makes the packet more likely to be discarded downstream. For example, a policer could re-mark AF11 packets that exceed a contract with a new DSCP value of AF13, but not discard the packet. By doing so, the packet still passes through the router, but if the packet experiences congestion later in its travels, it is more likely to be discarded than it would have otherwise been. (Remember, DiffServ suggests that AF13 is more likely to be discarded than AF11 traffic.)

When marking requirements can be performed by using CB Marking, CB Marking should be used instead of either policer. However, if a requirement exists to mark packets based on whether they conform to a traffic contract, marking with policers must be used. Chapter 5, "Shaping, Policing, and Link Fragmentation," covers CB policing, with an example of the syntax it uses for marking packets.

QoS Pre-Classification

With unencrypted, unencapsulated traffic, routers can match and mark QoS values, and perform ingress and egress actions based on markings, by inspecting the IP headers. However, what happens if the traffic is encrypted? If we encapsulate traffic inside a VPN tunnel, the original headers and packet contents are unavailable for inspection. The only thing we have to work with is the ToS byte of the original packet, which is automatically copied to the tunnel header (in IPsec transport mode, in tunnel mode, and in GRE tunnels) when the packet is encapsulated. But features like NBAR are broken when we are dealing with encapsulated traffic.

The issue that arises from this inherent behavior of tunnel encapsulation is the inability of a router to take egress QoS actions based on encrypted traffic. To mitigate this limitation, Cisco IOS includes a feature called QoS pre-classification. This feature can be enabled on VPN endpoint routers to permit the router to make egress QoS decisions based on the original traffic, before encapsulation, rather than just the encapsulating tunnel header. QoS pre-classification works by keeping the original, unencrypted traffic in memory until the egress QoS actions are taken.

You can enable QoS pre-classification in tunnel interface configuration mode, virtual-template configuration mode, or crypto map configuration mode by issuing the **qos pre-classify** command. You can view the effects of pre-classification using several **show** commands, which include **show interface** and **show crypto-map**.

Table 3-10 lists the modes in which you apply the **qos pre-classify** command.

Table 3-10 *Where to Use the* qos pre-classify *Command*

Configuration Command Under Which qos pre-classify Is Configured	VPN Type
interface tunnel	GRE and IPIP
interface virtual-template	L2F and L2TP
crypto map	IPsec

Policy Routing for Marking

Policy routing provides the capability to route a packet based on information in the packet besides the destination IP address. The policy routing configuration uses route maps to classify packets. The **route-map** clauses include **set** commands that define the route (based on setting a next-hop IP address or outgoing interface).

Policy routing can also mark the IPP field, or the entire ToS byte, using the **set** command in a route map. When you use policy routing for marking purposes, the following logic sequence is used:

1. Packets are examined as they enter an interface.

2. A route map is used to match subsets of the packets.

3. Mark either the IPP or entire ToS byte using the **set** command.

4. The traditional policy routing function of using the **set** command to define the route might also be configured, but it is not required.

Policy routing should be used to mark packets only in cases where CB Marking is not available, or when a router needs to both use policy routing and mark packets entering the same interface.

AutoQoS

AutoQoS is a macro that helps automate class-based quality of service (QoS) configuration. It creates and applies QoS configurations based on Cisco best-practice recommendations. Using AutoQoS provides the following benefits:

- Simpler QoS deployment.

- Less operator error, because most steps are automated.

- Cheaper QoS deployment because less staff time is involved in analyzing network traffic and determining QoS configuration.

- Faster QoS deployment because there are dramatically fewer commands to issue.

- Companies can implement QoS without needing an in-depth knowledge of QoS concepts.

There are two flavors—AutoQoS for VoIP and AutoQoS for the Enterprise—as discussed in the following sections.

AutoQoS for VoIP

[handwritten: AutoCos — VOIP / Enterprise]

AutoQoS for VoIP is supported on most Cisco switches and routers, and provides QoS configuration for voice and video applications. It is enabled on individual interfaces, but creates both global and interface configurations. When enabled on access ports, AutoQoS uses Cisco Discovery Protocol (CDP) to detect the presence or absence of a Cisco phone or softphone, and configures the interface QoS appropriately. When enabled on uplink or trunk ports, it trusts the COS or DSCP values received and sets up the interface QoS.

AutoQoS VoIP on Switches

AutoQoS assumes that switches will have two types of interfaces: user access and uplink. It also assumes that a user access interface might or might not have an IP phone connected to it. There is no need to enable QoS globally. After it is enabled for any interface, the command starts a macro that globally enables QoS, configures interface ingress and egress queues, configures class maps and policy maps, and applies the policy map to the interface.

AutoQoS is enabled for an access interface by the interface-level command **auto qos voip** {**cisco-phone** | **cisco-softphone**}. When you do this, the switch uses CDP to determine whether a Cisco phone or softphone is connected to the interface. If one is not found, the switch marks all traffic down to DSCP 0 and treats it as best effort. This is the default behavior for a normal trunk port. If a phone is found, the switch then trusts the QoS markings it receives. On the ingress interface, the following traffic is put into the priority, or expedite, queue:

- Voice and video control traffic

- Real-time video traffic

- Voice traffic   *[handwritten: priority queue traffic]*

- Routing protocol traffic

- Spanning-tree BPDU traffic

All other traffic is placed in the normal ingress queue. On the egress side, voice is placed in the priority queue. The remaining traffic is distributed among the other queues, depending on the number and type of egress queues supported by that particular switch or switch module.

AutoQoS is enabled for an uplink port by the interface-level command **auto qos voip trust**. When this command is given, the switch trusts the COS values received on a Layer 2 port and the DSCP values received on a Layer 3 port.

The AutoQoS macro also creates quite a bit of global configuration in the switch. It generates too much to reproduce here, but the following list summarizes the configuration created:

- Globally enables QoS.

- Creates COS-to-DCSP mappings and DSCP-to-COS mappings. As the traffic enters the switch, the frame header containing the COS value is removed. The switch uses the COS value in the frame header to assign a DSCP value to the packet. If the packet exits a trunk port, the internal DSCP value is mapped back to a COS value.

- Enables priority or expedite ingress and egress queues.

- Creates mappings of COS values to ingress and egress queues and thresholds.

- Creates mappings of DSCP values to ingress and egress queues and thresholds.

- Creates class maps and policy maps to identify, prioritize, and police voice traffic. Applies those policy maps to the interface.

For best results, enable AutoQoS before configuring any other QoS on the switch. You can then go back and modify the default configuration if needed to fit your specific requirements.

AutoQoS VoIP on Routers

The designers of AutoQoS assumed that routers would be connecting to downstream switches or the WAN, rather than user access ports. Therefore, the VoIP QoS configuration is simpler. The command to enable it is **auto qos voip [trust]**. Make sure that the interface bandwidth is configured before giving this command. If you change it later, the QoS configuration will not change. When you issue the **auto qos voip** command on an individual data circuit, the configuration it creates differs depending on the bandwidth of the circuit itself. Compression and fragmentation are enabled on links of 768 kbps bandwidth and lower. They are not enabled on links faster than 768 kbps. The router additionally configures traffic shaping and applies an AutoQoS service policy regardless of the bandwidth.

When you issue the command on a serial interface with a bandwidth of 768 kbps or less, the router changes the interface encapsulation to PPP. It creates a PPP Multilink interface and enables Link Fragmentation and Interleave (LFI) on the interface. Serial interfaces with a configured bandwidth greater than 768 kbps keep their configured encapsulation, and the router merely applies an AutoQoS service policy to the interface.

If you use the **trust** keyword in the command, the router creates class maps that group traffic based on its DSCP values. It associates those class maps with a created policy map and assigns it to the interface. You would use this keyword when QoS markings are assigned by a trusted device.

If you do not use the **trust** keyword, the router creates access lists that match voice and video data and call control ports. It associates those access lists with class maps with a created policy map that marks the traffic appropriately. Any traffic not matching those access lists is marked with DSCP 0. You would use this command if the traffic either arrives at the router unmarked or arrives marked by an untrusted device.

Verifying AutoQoS VoIP

Displaying the running configuration shows all the mappings, class and policy maps, and interface configurations created by the AutoQoS VoIP macro. Use the following commands to get more specific information:

- **show auto qos:** Displays the interface AutoQoS commands

- **show mls qos:** Has several modifiers that display queuing and COS/DSCP mappings

- **show policy-map interface:** Verifies the actions of the policy map on each interface specified

AutoQoS for the Enterprise

AutoQoS for the Enterprise is supported on Cisco routers. The main difference between it and AutoQoS VoIP is that it automates the QoS configuration for VoIP plus other network applications, and is meant to be used for WAN links. It can be used for Frame Relay and ATM subinterfaces only if they are point-to-point links. It detects the types and amounts of network traffic and then creates policies based on that. As with AutoQoS for VoIP, you can modify those policies if you desire. There are two steps to configuring Enterprise AutoQoS. The first step discovers the traffic, and the second step provides the recommended QoS configuration.

Discovering Traffic for AutoQoS Enterprise

The command to enable traffic discovery is **auto discovery qos [trust]** and is issued at the interface, DLCI, or PVC configuration level. Make sure that Cisco Express Forwarding (CEF) is enabled, that the interface bandwidth is configured, and that no QoS configuration is on the interface before giving the command. Use the **trust** keyword if the traffic arrives at the router already marked, and if you trust those markings, because the AutoQoS policies will use those markings during the configuration stage.

Traffic discovery uses NBAR to learn the types and amounts of traffic on each interface where it is enabled. You should run it long enough for it to gather a representative sample of your traffic. The router will classify the traffic collected into one of ten classes. Table 3-11 shows the classes, the DSCP values that will be mapped to each if you use the **trust** option in the command, and sample types of traffic that NBAR will map to each. Note that the traffic type is not a complete list, but is meant to give you a good feel for each class.

Table 3-11 *AutoQoS for the Enterprise Classes and DSCP Values*

Class	DSCP/PHB Value	Traffic Types
Routing	CS6	EIGRP, OSPF
VoIP	EF (46)	RTP Voice Media
Interactive video	AF41	RTP Video Media
Streaming video	CS4	Real Audio, Netshow
Control	CS3	RTCP, H323, SIP
Transactional	AF21	SAP, Citrix, Telnet, SSH
Bulk	AF11	FTP, SMTP, POP3, Exchange
Scavenger	CS1	Peer-to-peer applications
Management	CS2	SNMP, Syslog, DHCP, DNS
Best effort	All others	All others

Generating the AutoQoS Configuration

When the traffic discovery has collected enough information, the next step is to issue the **auto qos** command on the interface. This runs a macro that creates templates based on the traffic collected, creates class maps to classify that traffic, and creates a policy map to allocate bandwidth and mark the traffic. The router then automatically applies the policy map to the interface. In the case of a Frame Relay DLCI, the router applies the policy map to a Frame Relay map class, and then applies that class to the DLCI. You can optionally turn off NBAR traffic collection with the **no auto discovery qos** command.

Verifying AutoQoS for the Enterprise

As with AutoQoS VoIP, displaying the running configuration will show all the mappings, class and policy maps, and interface configurations created by the AutoQoS macro. Use the following commands to get more specific information:

- **show auto discovery qos:** Lists the types and amounts of traffic collected by NBAR
- **show auto qos:** Displays the class maps, policy maps, and interface configuration generated by the AutoQoS macro
- **show policy-map interface:** Displays each policy map and the actual effect it had on the interface traffic

Foundation Summary

This section lists additional details and facts to round out the coverage of the topics in this chapter. Unlike most of the Cisco Press Exam Certification Guides, this "Foundation Summary" does not repeat information presented in the "Foundation Topics" section of the chapter. Please take the time to read and study the details in the "Foundation Topics" section of the chapter, as well as review items noted with a Key Topic icon.

Table 3-12 lists the various **match** commands that can be used for MQC tools like CB Marking.

Table 3-12 match *Configuration Command Reference for MQC Tools*

Command	Function
match [ip] precedence *precedence-value* [*precedence-value precedence-value precedence-value*]	Matches precedence in IPv4 packets when the **ip** parameter is included; matches IPv4 and IPv6 packets when the **ip** parameter is missing.
match access-group {*access-group* | **name** *access-group-name*}	Matches an ACL by number or name.
match any	Matches all packets.
match class-map *class-map-name*	Matches based on another class map.
match cos *cos-value* [*cos-value cos-value cos-value*]	Matches a CoS value.
match destination-address mac *address*	Matches a destination MAC address.
match fr-dlci *dlci-number*	Matches a particular Frame Relay DLCI.
match input-interface *interface-name*	Matches an ingress interface.
match ip dscp [*ip-dscp-value ip-dscp-value ip-dscp-value ip-dscp-value ip-dscp-value ip-dscp-value ip-dscp-value*]	Matches DSCP in IPv4 packets when the **ip** parameter is included; matches IPv4 and IPv6 packets when the **ip** parameter is missing.
match ip rtp *starting-port-number port-range*	Matches the RTP's UDP port-number range, even values only.
match mpls experimental *number*	Matches an MPLS Experimental value.
match mpls experimental topmost *value*	When multiple labels are in use, matches the MPLS EXP field in the topmost label.
match not *match-criteria*	Reverses the matching logic. In other words, things matched by the matching criteria do *not* match the class map.

Command	Function
match packet length {**max** *maximum-length-value* [**min** *minimum-length-value*] | **min** *minimum-length-value* [**max** *maximum-length-value*]}	Matches packets based on the minimum length, maximum length, or both.
match protocol citrix app *application-name-string*	Matches NBAR Citrix applications.
match protocol http [**url** *url-string* | **host** *hostname- string* | **mime** *MIME-type*]	Matches a host name, URL string, or MIME type.
match protocol *protocol-name*	Matches NBAR protocol types.
match protocol rtp [**audio** | **video** | **payload-type** *payload-string*]	Matches RTP audio or video payload, based on the payload type. Also allows explicitly specifying payload types.
match qos-group *qos-group-value*	Matches a QoS group.
match source-address mac *address-destination*	Matches a source MAC address.

Table 3-13 lists AutoQoS and QoS verification commands.

Table 3-13 *AutoQoS and QoS Verification Commands*

Command	Function
auto qos voip {**cisco-phone** | **cisco-softphone**}	Enables AutoQoS VoIP on a switch access interface
auto qos voip trust	Enables AutoQoS VoIP on a switch uplink interface
auto qos voip [**trust**]	Enables AutoQoS VoIP on a router interface
auto discovery qos [**trust**]	Enables NBAR traffic discovery for AutoQoS Enterprise
auto qos	Enables AutoQoS Enterprise on an interface
show auto qos	Displays the interface AutoQoS commands
show mls qos	Displays queueing and COS/DSCP mappings
show policy-map interface	Displays the interface queuing actions caused by the policy map
show auto discovery qos	Displays the traffic collected by NBAR
show auto qos	Displays the configuration generated by the AutoQoS macro

Table 3-14 lists the RFCs related to DiffServ.

Table 3-14   *DiffServ RFCs*

RFC	Title	Comments
2474	Definition of the Differentiated Services Field (DS Field) in the IPv4 and IPv6 Headers	Contains the details of the 6-bit DSCP field in an IP header
2475	An Architecture for Differentiated Service	The core DiffServ conceptual document
2597	Assured Forwarding PHB Group	Defines a set of 12 DSCP values and a convention for their use
3246	An Expedited Forwarding PHB	Defines a single DSCP value as a convention for use as a low-latency class
3260	New Terminology and Clarifications for DiffServ	Clarifies, but does not supersede, existing DiffServ RFCs

Memory Builders

The CCIE Routing and Switching written exam, like all Cisco CCIE written exams, covers a fairly broad set of topics. This section provides some basic tools to help you exercise your memory about some of the broader topics covered in this chapter.

Fill In Key Tables from Memory

Appendix E, "Key Tables for CCIE Study," on the CD in the back of this book, contains empty sets of some of the key summary tables in each chapter. Print Appendix E, refer to this chapter's tables in it, and fill in the tables from memory. Refer to Appendix F, "Solutions for Key Tables for CCIE Study," on the CD, to check your answers.

Definitions

Next, take a few moments to write down the definitions for the following terms:

IP Precedence, ToS byte, Differentiated Services, DS field, Per-Hop Behavior, Assured Forwarding, Expedited Forwarding, Class Selector, Class of Service, Differentiated Services Code Point, User Priority, Discard Eligible, Cell Loss Priority, MPLS Experimental bits, class map, policy map, service policy, Modular QoS CLI, Class-Based Marking, Network-Based Application Recognition, QoS preclassification, AutoQoS

Refer to the glossary to check your answers.

Further Reading

Cisco QoS Exam Certification Guide, by Wendell Odom and Michael Cavanaugh

End-to-End QoS Network Design, by Tim Szigeti and Christina Hattingh

"The Enterprise QoS SRND Guide," posted at www.cisco.com/en/US/docs/solutions/ Enterprise/WAN_and_MAN/QoS_SRND/QoS-SRND-Book.html, provides great background and details for real-life QoS deployments.

Blueprint topics covered in this chapter:

This chapter covers the following subtopics from the Cisco CCIE Routing and Switching written exam blueprint. Refer to the full blueprint in Table I-1 in the Introduction for more details on the topics covered in each chapter and their context within the blueprint.

- Class-Based Weighted Fair Queuing (CBWFQ)

- Low-Latency Queuing (LLQ)

- Modified Deficit Round-Robin (MDRR)

- Weighted Random Early Detection (WRED)

- Random Early Detection (RED)

- Weighted Round-Robin (WRR)

- Shaped Round-Robin (SRR)

- Resource Reservation Protocol (RSVP)

CHAPTER 4

Congestion Management and Avoidance

Congestion management, commonly called *queuing*, refers to how a router or switch manages packets or frames while they wait to exit a device. With routers, the waiting occurs when IP forwarding has been completed, so the queuing is always considered to be output queuing. LAN switches often support both output queuing and input queuing, where input queuing is used for received frames that are waiting to be switched to the switch's output interfaces.

Congestion avoidance refers to the logic used when deciding if and when packets should be dropped as a queuing system becomes more congested. This chapter covers a wide variety of Cisco IOS queuing tools, along with the most pervasive congestion avoidance tool, namely weighted random early detection (WRED).

"Do I Know This Already?" Quiz

Table 4-1 outlines the major headings in this chapter and the corresponding "Do I Know This Already?" quiz questions.

Table 4-1 *"Do I Know This Already?" Foundation Topics Section-to-Question Mapping*

Foundation Topics Section	Questions Covered in This Section	Score
Cisco Router Queuing Concepts	1	
Queuing Tools: CBWFQ and LLQ	2–3	
Weighted Random Early Detection	4–5	
Modified Deficit Round-Robin	6	
LAN Switch Congestion Management and Avoidance	7–8	
RSVP	9	
Total Score		

To best use this pre-chapter assessment, remember to score yourself strictly. You can find the answers in Appendix A, "Answers to the 'Do I Know This Already?' Quizzes."

1. What is the main benefit of the hardware queue on a Cisco router interface?

   a. Prioritizes latency-sensitive packets so that they are always scheduled next

   b. Reserves a minimum amount of bandwidth for particular classes of traffic

   c. Provides a queue in which to hold a packet so that, as soon as the interface is available to send another packet, the packet can be sent without requiring an interrupt to the router CPU

   d. Allows configuration of a percentage of the remaining link bandwidth, after allocating bandwidth to the LLQ and the class-default queue

2. Examine the following configuration snippet. If a new class, called class3, is added to the policy map, which of the following commands could be used to reserve 25 kbps of bandwidth for the class?

   ```
   policy-map fred
    class class1
     priority 20
    class class2
     bandwidth 30
   !
   interface serial 0/0
    bandwidth 100
    service-policy output fred
   ```

   a. priority 25

   b. bandwidth 25

   c. bandwidth percent 25

   d. bandwidth remaining-percent 25

   [handwritten: only one type of bw command is allowed in a pol map]

3. Examine the following configuration snippet. How much bandwidth does Cisco IOS assign to class2?

   ```
   policy-map fred
    class class1
     priority percent 20
    class class2
     bandwidth remaining percent 20
   interface serial 0/0
    bandwidth 100
    service-policy output fred
   ```

   [handwritten: not aware of unreservable bw]

   a. 10 kbps

   b. 11 kbps

   c. 20 kbps

   d. 21 kbps

   e. Not enough information to tell

4. Which of the following impacts the percentage of packet discards when using WRED, when the current average queue depth is between the minimum and maximum thresholds?

   a. The **bandwidth** command setting on the interface

   b. The mark probability denominator (MPD)

   c. The exponential weighting constant

   d. The congestive discard threshold

5. Which of the following commands, under an interface like s0/0, would enable WRED and tell it to use IP Precedence (IPP) when choosing its default traffic profiles?

   a. **random-detect**

   b. **random-detect precedence-based**

   c. **random-detect dscp-based**

   d. **random-detect precedence 1 20 30 40**

6. On a Catalyst 3560 switch, interface fa0/1 has been configured for SRR scheduling, and fa0/2 has been configured for SRR scheduling with a priority queue. Which of the following is true regarding interface fa0/2?

   a. It must be configured with the **priority-queue out** command.

   b. The last parameter (*w4*) of the **srr-queue bandwidth share** *w1 w2 w3 w4* command must be 0.

   c. Only CoS 5 frames can be placed into queue 1, the expedite queue.

   d. Only DSCP EF frames can be placed into queue 1, the expedite queue.

7. In modified deficit round-robin, what is the function of QV?

   a. Sets the ratio of bandwidth to be sent from each queue on each pass through the queues

   b. Sets the absolute bandwidth for each queue on each pass through the queues

   c. Sets the number of bytes removed from each queue on each pass through the queues

   d. Identifies the MDRR priority queue

8. The Cisco 3560 switch uses SRR and WTD for its queuing and congestion management methods. How many ingress queues and egress queues can be configured on each port of a 3560 switch, and how many priority queues are configurable on ingress and egress?

    a. One ingress queue, four egress queues; one priority queue on each side

    b. One ingress queue, four egress queues; one priority queue on the egress side

    c. Two ingress queues, four egress queues; one priority queue on the egress side

    d. Two ingress queues, four egress queues; one priority queue on each side

9. What interface command would configure RSVP to reserve up to one-quarter of a 100-Mbps link, but only allow each individual flow to use 1 Mbps?

    a. ip rsvp bandwidth 25000 1000

    b. ip rsvp-bandwidth 25 1

    c. rsvp bandwidth 100 2500

    d. ip rsvp bandwidth 25 1

Foundation Topics

Cisco Router Queuing Concepts

Cisco routers can be configured to perform *fancy queuing* for packets that are waiting to exit an interface. For example, if a router receives 5 Mbps of traffic every second for the next several seconds, and all that traffic needs to exit a T1 serial link, the router can't forward all the traffic. So, the router places the packets into one or more *software queues*, which can then be managed—thus impacting which packets get to leave next and which packets might be discarded.

Software Queues and Hardware Queues

Although many network engineers already understand queuing, many overlook some of the details behind the concepts of a hardware queue and a software queue associated with each physical interface. The queues created on an interface by the popularly known queuing tools are called *software queues*, as these queues are implemented in software. However, when the queuing scheduler picks the next packet to take from the software queues, the packet does not move directly out the interface. Instead, the router moves the packet from the interface software queue to a small hardware FIFO (first-in, first-out) queue on each interface. Cisco calls this separate, final queue either the *transmit queue* (Tx queue) or *transmit ring* (Tx ring), depending on the model of the router; generically, these queues are called *hardware queues*.

Hardware queues provide the following features: 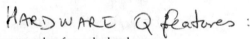 HARDWARE Q features :

**Key
Topic**

- When an interface finishes sending a packet, the next packet from the hardware queue can be encoded and sent out the interface, without requiring a software interrupt to the CPU—ensuring full use of interface bandwidth.

- Always use FIFO logic.

- Cannot be affected by IOS queuing tools.

- IOS automatically shrinks the length of the hardware queue to a smaller length than the default when a queuing tool is present.

- Short hardware queue lengths mean packets are more likely to be in the controllable software queues, giving the software queuing more control of the traffic leaving the interface.

The only function of a hardware queue that can be manipulated is the length of the queue. Example 4-1 shows how to see the current length of the queue and how to change the length.

Example 4-1   *Tx Queue Length: Finding and Changing the Length*

```
! The example begins with only FIFO queuing on the interface. For this
! router, it defaults to a TX queue length 16.
R3# show controllers serial 0/0
Interface Serial0/0
! about 30 lines omitted for brevity
tx_limited=0(16)
! lines omitted for brevity
! Next, the TX ring is set to length 1.
! (The smallest recommended value is 2.)
R3# conf t
Enter configuration commands, one per line.  End with CNTL/Z.
R3(config)# int s 0/0
R3(config-if)# tx-ring-limit 1
R3(config-if)# ^Z
```

Queuing on Interfaces Versus Subinterfaces and Virtual Circuits

IOS queuing tools can create and manage software queues associated with a physical interface, and then the packets drain into the hardware queue associated with the interface. Additionally, queuing tools can be used in conjunction with traffic shaping. Traffic-shaping tools delay packets to ensure that a class of packets does not exceed a defined traffic rate. While delaying the packets, the shaping function queues the packets—by default in a FIFO queue. Depending on the type of shaping tool in use, various queuing tools can be configured to manage the packets delayed by the shaping tool.

Chapter 5, "Shaping, Policing, and Link Fragmentation," covers traffic shaping, including how to use queuing tools with shapers. The queuing coverage in this chapter focuses on the implementation of software queuing tools directly on the physical interface.

Comparing Queuing Tools

Cisco IOS provides a wide variety of queuing tools. The upcoming sections of this chapter describe several different IOS queuing tools, with a brief summary ending the section on queuing. Table 4-2 summarizes the main characteristics of different queuing tools that you will want to keep in mind while comparing each successive queuing tool.

Key Topic

Table 4-2   *Key Comparison Points for Queuing Tools*

Feature	Definition
Classification	The ability to look at packet headers to choose the right queue for each packet
Drop policy	The rules used to choose which packets to drop as queues begin to fill

Feature	Definition
Scheduling	The logic used to determine which packet should be dequeued next
Maximum number of queues	The number of unique classes of packets for a queuing tool
Maximum queue length	The maximum number of packets in a single queue

Queuing Tools: CBWFQ and LLQ

This section hits the highlights of the modern queuing tools in Cisco IOS and covers detailed configuration for the more popular tools—specifically, class-based weighted fair queuing (CBWFQ) and low-latency queuing (LLQ). Because the CCIE Routing and Switching exam blueprint no longer includes the priority queuing (PQ) and custom queuing (CQ) legacy queuing methods, they are not covered in this book. Furthermore, WFQ is covered only in the context of CBWFQ and not as a standalone feature.

Cisco created CBWFQ and LLQ using some of the best concepts from the legacy queuing methods PQ and CQ, as well as WFQ, while adding several additional features. CBWFQ reserves bandwidth for each queue, and provides the ability to use WFQ concepts for packets in the default (class-default) queue. LLQ adds to CBWFQ the concept of a priority queue, but unlike legacy PQ, LLQ prevents the high-priority queue from starving other queues. Additionally, both CBWFQ and LLQ use Modular QoS CLI (MQC) for configuration, which means that they have robust classification options, including Network-Based Application Recognition (NBAR).

CBWFQ and LLQ use almost identical configuration; the one major difference is whether the **bandwidth** command (CBWFQ) or the **priority** command (LLQ) is used to configure the tool. Because both tools use MQC, both use class maps for classification and policy maps to create a set of classes to be used on an interface. The classes defined in the policy map each define a single queue; as a result, the terms *queue* and *class* are often used interchangeably when working with LLQ and CBWFQ.

CBWFQ and LLQ support 64 queues/classes. The maximum queue length can be changed, with the maximum possible value and the default length varying based on the model of router and the amount of memory installed. They both also have one special queue called the *class-default queue*. This queue exists even if it is not configured. If a packet does not match any of the explicitly configured classes in a policy map, IOS places the packet into the class-default class/queue. CBWFQ settings can be configured for the class-default queue.

The sections that follow cover the details of CBWFQ and then LLQ.

CBWFQ Basic Features and Configuration

The CBWFQ scheduler guarantees a minimum percentage of a link's bandwidth to each class/queue. If all queues have a large number of packets, each queue gets the percentage bandwidth implied by the configuration. However, if some queues are empty and do not need their bandwidth for a short period, the bandwidth is proportionally allocated across the other classes. (Cisco does not publish the details of how CBWFQ achieves these functions.)

Table 4-3 summarizes some of the key features of CBWFQ.

Table 4-3   *CBWFQ Functions and Features*

CBWFQ Feature	Description
Classification	Classifies based on anything that MQC commands can match
Drop policy	Tail drop or WRED, configurable per queue
Number of queues	64
Maximum queue length	Varies based on router model and memory
Scheduling inside a single queue	FIFO on 63 queues; FIFO or WFQ on class-default queue[1]
Scheduling among all queues	Result of the scheduler provides a percentage of guaranteed bandwidth to each queue

[1] Cisco 7500 series routers support FIFO or WFQ in all the CBWFQ queues.

Table 4-4 lists the key CBWFQ commands that were not covered in Chapter 3, "Classification and Marking."

Table 4-4   *Command Reference for CBWFQ*

Command	Mode and Function
bandwidth {*bandwidth-kbps*	**percent** *percent*}	Class subcommand; sets literal or percentage bandwidth for the class
bandwidth {remaining percent *percent*}	Class subcommand; sets percentage of remaining bandwidth for the class
queue-limit *queue-limit*	Class subcommand; sets the maximum length of a CBWFQ queue
fair-queue [queue-limit *queue-value*]	Class subcommand; enables WFQ in the class (class-default only)

Example 4-2 shows a simple CBWFQ configuration that uses the class-default queue. The configuration was created on R3 in Figure 4-1, using the following requirements:

- All VoIP payload traffic is placed in a queue.

- All other traffic is placed in another queue.

- Give the VoIP traffic 50 percent of the bandwidth.

- WFQ should be used on the non-VoIP traffic.

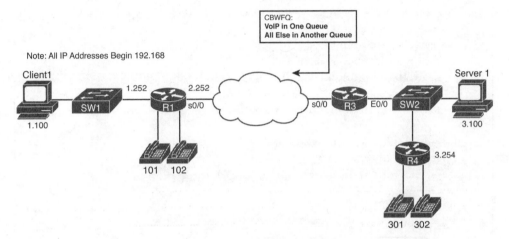

Figure 4-1 *Network Used with CBWFQ and LLQ Configuration Examples*

Example 4-2 *CBWFQ with VoIP in One Queue, Everything Else in Class-Default*

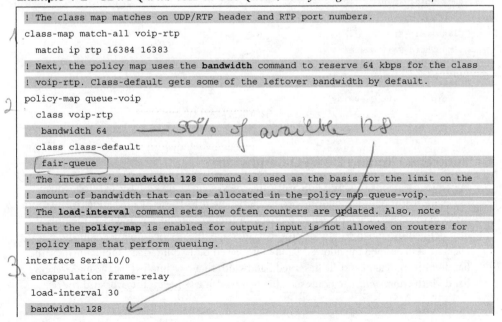

```
   service-policy output queue-voip
! This command lists counters, reserved bandwidth, maximum queue length (listed
! as max threshold), and a reminder that WFQ is used in the class-default queue.
R3# show policy-map int s 0/0
 Serial0/0
  Service-policy output:    queue-voip

    Class-map: voip-rtp (match-all)
      136435 packets, 8731840 bytes
      30 second offered rate 51000 bps, drop rate 0 bps
      Match:    ip rtp 16384 16383
      Weighted Fair Queueing
        Output Queue: Conversation 265
        Bandwidth 64 (kbps) Max Threshold 64 (packets)
        (pkts matched/bytes matched) 48550/3107200
        (depth/total drops/no-buffer drops) 14/0/0


    Class-map: class-default (match-any)
      1958 packets, 1122560 bytes
      30 second offered rate 59000 bps, drop rate 0 bps
      Match: any
      Weighted Fair Queueing
        Flow Based Fair Queueing
        Maximum Number of Hashed Queues 256
        (total queued/total drops/no-buffer drops) 15/0/0
! This command just lists the configuration in a concise manner.
R3# show policy-map
  Policy Map queue-voip
    Class voip-rtp
      Weighted Fair Queueing
              Bandwidth 64 (kbps) Max Threshold 64 (packets)
    Class class-default
      Weighted Fair Queueing
Flow based Fair Queueing Max Threshold 64 (packets)
```

Defining and Limiting CBWFQ Bandwidth

In previous versions of Cisco IOS Software, the system checks a CBWFQ policy map to ensure that it does not allocate too much bandwidth. These older versions of IOS perform the check when the **service-policy output** command was added; if the policy map defined too much bandwidth for that interface, the **service-policy** command was rejected. IOS defined the allowed bandwidth based on two interface subcommands: the **bandwidth** command and the reserved bandwidth that was implied by the **max-reserved-bandwidth** command. The nonreservable bandwidth was meant for overhead traffic.

In the IOS 15 code releases, the **max-reserved-bandwidth** command does not have any effect on the queuing system. IOS does not even check a policy map's total reservation parameters against the **max-reserved-bandwidth** settings. What's more, these versions of IOS even notify you of this fact. IOS allows a policy map to allocate bandwidth based on the **int-bw**. In other words, on an interface with **int-bw** of 256 (256 kbps), the policy map could allocate the entire 256 kbps of bandwidth.

The bandwidth can also be defined as percentages using either the **bandwidth percent** or **bandwidth remaining percent** command. When you use percentages, it is easier to ensure that a policy map does not attempt to allocate too much bandwidth.

percentages vs kb/s

The two percentage-based **bandwidth** command options work in slightly different ways. Figure 4-2 shows the concept for each.

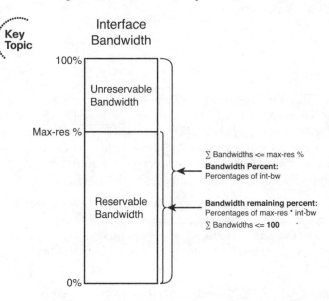

Figure 4-2   *Bandwidth Percent and Bandwidth Remaining Percent Concepts*

The **bandwidth percent** *bw-percent* command sets a class's reserved bandwidth as a percentage of **int-bw**. For example, in Example 4-2, if the **bandwidth percent 50** command had been used instead of **bandwidth 64**, the voip-rtp class would have used 50% × 128 kbps, or 64 kbps.

The **bandwidth remaining percent** *bw-percent* command sets a class's reserved bandwidth as a percentage of remaining bandwidth.

Note   Using the **bandwidth remaining percent** command is particularly useful with LLQ and will be explained in that context later in the chapter. The reason is that the remaining bandwidth calculation is changed by the addition of LLQ.

only one of them can be used within a single pol-map!

Note that in a single policy map, only one of the three variations of the **bandwidth** command can be used. Table 4-5 summarizes the three methods for reserving bandwidth with CBWFQ.

Key Topic

Table 4-5 *Reference for CBWFQ Bandwidth Reservation*

Method	Amount of Bandwidth Reserved by the bandwidth Command	The Sum of Values in a Single Policy Map Must Be <= ...
Explicit bandwidth	As listed in commands	max-res × int-bw
Percent	A percentage of the **int-bw**	max-res setting
Remaining percent	A percentage of the reservable bandwidth (**int-bw** × **max-res**)	100

Low-Latency Queuing

Low-latency queuing sounds like the best queuing tool possible, just based on the name. What packet wouldn't want to experience low latency? As it turns out, for delay (latency) sensitive traffic, LLQ is indeed the queuing tool of choice. LLQ looks and acts just like CBWFQ in most regards, except it adds the capability for some queues to be configured as low-latency queues. LLQ schedules these specific queues as strict-priority queues. In other words, LLQ always services packets in these priority queues first.

LLQ lingo can sometimes be used in a couple of different ways. With a single policy map that has at least one low-latency queue, the policy map might be considered to be implementing LLQ, while at the same time, that one low-latency queue is often called "the LLQ." Sometimes, a single low-latency queue is even called "the PQ" as a reference to the legacy PQ-like behavior, or even a "priority queue."

While LLQ adds a low-latency queue to CBWFQ, it also prevents the queue starvation that occurs with legacy PQ. LLQ actually *polices* the PQ based on the configured bandwidth. In effect, the bandwidth given to an LLQ priority queue is both the guaranteed minimum and policed maximum. (You might recall from Chapter 3 that the DiffServ Expedited Forwarding PHB formally defines the priority queuing and policing PHBs.) As a result, the packets that make it out of the queue experience low latency, but some might be discarded to prevent starving the other queues.

Figure 4-3 depicts the scheduler logic for LLQ. Note that the PQ logic is shown, but with the policer check as well.

LLQ configuration requires one more command in addition to the commands used for CBWFQ configuration. Instead of using the **bandwidth** command on a class, use the **priority** command:

```
priority {bandwidth-kbps | percent percentage} [burst]
```

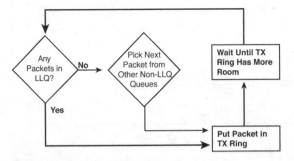

Figure 4-3 *LLQ Scheduler Logic*

This **class** subcommand enables LLQ in the class, reserves bandwidth, and enables the policing function. You can also configure the burst size for the policer with this command, but the default setting of 20 percent of the configured bandwidth is typically a reasonable choice.

Example 4-3 shows a sample LLQ configuration, using the following criteria. Like Example 4-2, the LLQ policy is applied to R3's s0/0 interface from Figure 4-1:

■ R3's s0/0 bandwidth is 128 kbps.

■ Packets will already have been marked with good Differentiated Services Code Point (DSCP) values.

■ VoIP payload is already marked DSCP EF and should be LLQed with 58 kbps of bandwidth.

■ AF41, AF21, and AF23 traffic should get 22, 20, and 8 kbps, respectively.

■ All other traffic should be placed into class class-default, which should use WRED and WFQ.

Example 4-3 *LLQ for EF; CBWFQ for AF41, AF21, AF23; and All Else*

```
! The class maps used by the queue-on-dscp are not shown, but the names imply what
! each class map has been configured to match. Note the priority 58 command makes
! class dscp-ef an LLQ.
policy-map queue-on-dscp
  class dscp-ef
    priority 58
  class dscp-af41
   bandwidth 22
  class dscp-af21
   bandwidth 20
   random-detect dscp-based
  class dscp-af23
   bandwidth 8
   random-detect dscp-based
```

```
      class class-default
       fair-queue
       random-detect dscp-based
    ! max-res has to be raised or the policy map would be rejected.
    interface Serial0/0
     bandwidth 128
     encapsulation frame-relay
     load-interval 30
     max-reserved-bandwidth 85
     service-policy output queue-on-dscp
    ! Below, for class dscp-ef, note the phrase "strict priority," as well as the
    ! computed policing burst of 1450 bytes (20% of 58 kbps and divided by 8 to convert
    ! the value to a number of bytes.)
    R3# show policy-map queue-on-dscp
       Policy Map queue-on-dscp
        Class dscp-ef
         Weighted Fair Queueing
           Strict Priority
            Bandwidth 58 (kbps) Burst 1450 (Bytes)
    ! lines omitted for brevity
    ! Note the statistics below. Any packets dropped due to the policer would show
    ! up in the last line below.
    R3# show policy-map interface s 0/0 output class dscp-ef
     Serial0/0
      Service-policy output: queue-on-dscp
        Class-map: dscp-ef (match-all)
          227428 packets, 14555392 bytes
          30 second offered rate 52000 bps, drop rate 0 bps
          Match: ip dscp ef
          Weighted Fair Queueing
            Strict Priority
            Output Queue: Conversation 40
            Bandwidth 58 (kbps) Burst 1450 (Bytes)
            (pkts matched/bytes matched) 12194/780416
     (total drops/bytes drops) 0/0
```

Defining and Limiting LLQ Bandwidth

The LLQ **priority** command provides two syntax options for defining the bandwidth of an LLQ—a simple explicit amount or bandwidth as a percentage of interface bandwidth. (There is no remaining bandwidth equivalent for the **priority** command.) However, unlike the **bandwidth** command, both the explicit and percentage versions of the **priority** command can be used inside the same policy map.

IOS still limits the amount of bandwidth in an LLQ policy map, with the actual bandwidth from both LLQ classes (with **priority** commands) and non-LLQ classes (with **bandwidth** commands) not being allowed to exceed **max-res × int-bw**. Although the math is easy, the details can get confusing, especially because a single policy map could have one queue configured with **priority** *bw*, another with **priority percent** *bw*, and others with one of the three versions of the **bandwidth** command. Figure 4-4 shows an example with three versions of the commands.

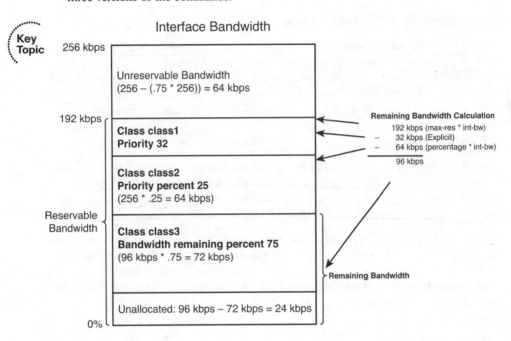

Figure 4-4 *Priority, Priority Percent, and Bandwidth Remaining Percent*

The figure shows both versions of the **priority** command. Class1 has an explicit **priority 32** command, which reserves 32 kbps. Class2 has a **priority percent 25** command, which, when applied to the interface bandwidth (256 kbps), gives class2 64 kbps.

The most interesting part of Figure 4-4 is how IOS views the remaining-bandwidth concept when **priority** queues are configured. IOS subtracts the bandwidth reserved by the priority commands as well. As a result, a policy map can essentially allocate nonpriority classes based on percentages of the leftover (remaining) bandwidth, with those values totaling 100 (100 percent).

LLQ with More Than One Priority Queue

LLQ allows multiple queues/classes to be configured as priority queues. This begs the question, "Which queue gets scheduled first?" As it turns out, LLQ actually places the packets from multiple LLQs into a single internal LLQ. So, packets in the different configured priority queues still get scheduled ahead of nonpriority queues, but they are serviced based on their arrival time for all packets in any of the priority queues.

So why use multiple priority queues? The answer is *policing*. By policing traffic in one class at one speed, and traffic in another class at another speed, you get more granularity for the policing function of LLQ. For example, if you are planning for video and voice, you can place each into a separate LLQ and get low-latency performance for both types of traffic, but at the same time prevent video traffic from consuming the bandwidth engineered for voice and vice versa.

Miscellaneous CBWFQ/LLQ Topics

CBWFQ and LLQ allow a policy map to either allocate bandwidth to the class-default class, or not. When a **bandwidth** command is configured under **class class-default**, the class is indeed reserved that minimum bandwidth. (IOS will not allow the **priority** command in **class-default**.) When **class class-default** does not have a **bandwidth** command, IOS internally allocates any unassigned bandwidth among all classes. As a result, **class class-default** might not get much bandwidth unless the class is configured a minimum amount of bandwidth using the **bandwidth** command.

This chapter's coverage of guaranteed bandwidth allocation is based on the configuration commands. In practice, a policy map might not have packets in all queues at the same time. In that case, the queues get more than their reserved bandwidth. IOS allocates the extra bandwidth proportionally to each active class's bandwidth reservation.

Finally, IOS uses queuing only when congestion occurs. IOS considers congestion to be occurring when the hardware queue is full; that generally happens when the offered load of traffic is far less than the clock rate of the link. So, a router could have a **service-policy out** command on an interface, with LLQ configured, but the LLQ logic would be used only when the hardware queue is full.

Queuing Summary

Table 4-6 summarizes some of the key points regarding the IOS queuing tools covered in this chapter.

Table 4-6 *Queuing Protocol Comparison*

Feature	CBWFQ	LLQ
Includes a strict-priority queue	No	Yes
Polices priority queues to prevent starvation	No	Yes
Reserves bandwidth per queue	Yes	Yes
Includes robust set of classification fields	Yes	Yes
Classifies based on flows	Yes[1]	Yes[1]
Supports RSVP	Yes	Yes
Maximum number of queues	64	64

[1] WFQ can be used in the class-default queue or in all CBWFQ queues in 2900 Series routers running 15.3 code.

Weighted Random Early Detection

When a queue is full, IOS has no place to put newly arriving packets, so it discards them. This phenomenon is called *tail drop*. Often, when a queue fills, several packets are tail dropped at a time, given the bursty nature of data packets.

Tail drop can have an overall negative effect on network traffic, particularly TCP traffic. When packets are lost, for whatever reason, TCP senders slow their rate of sending data. When tail drops occur and multiple packets are lost, the TCP connections slow even more. Also, most networks send a much higher percentage of TCP traffic than UDP traffic, meaning that the overall network load tends to drop after multiple packets are tail dropped.

Interestingly, overall throughput can be improved by discarding a few packets as a queue begins to fill, rather than waiting for the larger impact of tail drops. Cisco created *weighted random early detection (WRED)* specifically for the purpose of monitoring queue length and discarding a percentage of the packets in the queue to improve overall network performance. As a queue gets longer and longer, WRED begins to discard more packets, hoping that a small reduction in offered load that follows might be just enough to prevent the queue from filling.

WRED uses several numeric settings when making its decisions. First, WRED uses the measured *average queue depth* when deciding whether a queue has filled enough to begin discarding packets. WRED then compares the average depth to a minimum and maximum queue threshold, performing different discard actions depending on the outcome. Table 4-7 lists the actions.

When the average queue depth is very low or very high, the actions are somewhat obvious, although the term *full drop* in Table 4-7 might be a bit of a surprise. When the average depth rises above the maximum threshold, WRED discards all new packets. Although this action might seem like tail drop, technically it is not, because the actual queue might not be full. So, to make this fine distinction, WRED calls this action category *full drop*.

Table 4-7   *WRED Discard Categories*

Average Queue Depth Versus Thresholds	Action	WRED Name for Action
Average < minimum threshold	No packets dropped.	No drop
Minimum threshold < average depth < maximum threshold	A percentage of packets dropped. Drop percentage increases from 0 to a maximum percent as the average depth moves from the minimum threshold to the maximum.	Random drop
Average depth > maximum threshold	All new packets discarded; similar to tail drop.	Full drop

When the average queue depth is between the two thresholds, WRED discards a percentage of packets. The percentage grows linearly as the average queue depth grows from the minimum threshold to the maximum, as depicted in Figure 4-5 (which shows WRED's default settings for IPP 0 traffic).

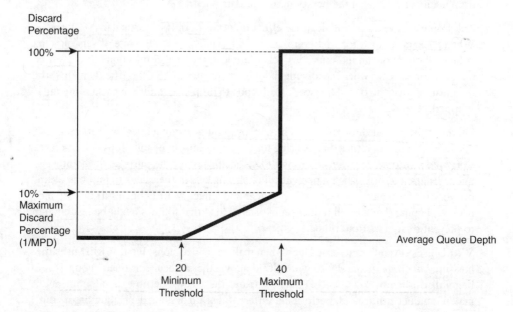

Figure 4-5   *WRED Discard Logic with Defaults for IPP 0*

The last of the WRED numeric settings that affect its logic is the *mark probability denominator (MPD)*, from which the maximum percentage of 10 percent is derived in Figure 4-5. IOS calculates the discard percentage used at the maximum threshold based on the simple formula 1/MPD. In the figure, an MPD of 10 yields a calculated value of 1/10, meaning that the discard rate grows from 0 percent to 10 percent as the average queue depth grows from the minimum threshold to the maximum. Also, when WRED discards packets, it randomly chooses the packets to discard.

How WRED Weights Packets

WRED gives preference to packets with certain IP Precedence (IPP) or DSCP values. To do so, WRED uses different traffic profiles for packets with different IPP and DSCP values. A WRED *traffic profile* consists of a setting for three key WRED variables: the minimum threshold, the maximum threshold, and the MPD. Figure 4-6 shows just such a case, with two WRED traffic profiles (for IPP 0 and IPP 3).

As Figure 4-6 illustrates, IPP 3's minimum threshold was higher than for IPP 0. As a result, IPP 0 traffic will be discarded earlier than IPP 3 packets. Also, the MPD is higher for IPP 3, resulting in a lower discard percentage (based on the formula discard percentage = 1/MPD).

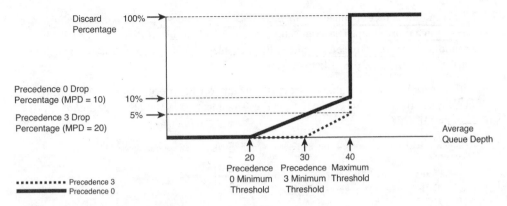

Figure 4-6 *Example WRED Profiles for Precedences 0 and 3*

Table 4-8 lists the IOS default WRED profile settings for various DSCP values. You might recall from Chapter 3 that Assured Forwarding DSCPs whose names end in 1 (for example, AF21) should get better WRED treatment than those settings that end in 2 (for example, AF32). The IOS defaults listed in Table 4-8 achieve that goal by setting lower minimum thresholds for the appropriate AF DSCPs.

Table 4-8 *Cisco IOS Software Default WRED Profiles for DSCP-Based WRED*

DSCP	Minimum Threshold	Maximum Threshold	MPD	1/MPD
AFx1	33	40	10	10%
AFx2	28	40	10	10%
AFx3	24	40	10	10%
EF	37	40	10	10%

WRED Configuration

Because WRED manages drops based on queue depth, WRED must be configured alongside a particular queue. However, most queuing mechanisms do not support WRED; as a result, WRED can be configured only in the following locations:

- On a physical interface (with FIFO queuing)

- For a non-LLQ class inside a CBWFQ policy map

- For an ATM VC

To use WRED directly on a physical interface, IOS actually disables all other queuing mechanisms and creates a single FIFO queue. WRED then manages the queue with regard to drops. For CBWFQ, WRED is configured in a class inside a policy map, in the same location as the **bandwidth** and **priority** commands discussed earlier in this chapter.

The **random-detect** command enables WRED, either under a physical interface or under a class in a policy map. This command enables WRED to use IPP, and not DSCP. The **random-detect dscp-based** command both enables WRED and tells it to use DSCP for determining the traffic profile for a packet.

To change WRED configuration from the default WRED profile for a particular IPP or DSCP, use the following commands, in the same location as the other **random-detect** command:

```
random-detect precedence precedence min-threshold max-threshold
    [mark-prob-denominator]
random-detect dscp dscpvalue min-threshold max-threshold
    [mark-probability-denominator]
```

Finally, calculation of the rolling average queue depth can be affected through configuring a parameter called the *exponential weighting constant*. A low exponential weighting constant means that the old average is a small part of the calculation, resulting in a more quickly changing average. The setting can be changed with the following command, although changing it is not recommended:

```
random-detect exponential-weighting-constant exponent
```

Note that earlier, Example 4-4 showed basic WRED configuration inside some classes of a CBWFQ configuration.

Modified Deficit Round-Robin

Modified deficit round-robin (MDRR) is a queuing feature implemented only in the Cisco 12000 Series router family. Because the 12000 Series does not support CBWFQ and LLQ, MDRR serves in place of these features. Its main claims to fame are better fairness than legacy queuing methods such as priority queuing and custom queuing, and that it supports a priority queue (like LLQ). For the CCIE Routing and Switching qualifying exam, you must understand how MDRR works at the conceptual level, but you don't need to know how to configure it.

MDRR allows classifying traffic into seven round-robin queues (0–6), with one additional priority queue. When no packets are placed into the priority queue, MDRR normally services its queues in a round-robin approach, cycling through each queue once per cycle. With packets in the priority queue, MDRR has two options for how to include the priority queue in the queue service algorithm:

- Strict priority mode

- Alternate mode

Strict priority mode serves the priority queue whenever traffic is present in that queue. The benefit is, of course, that this traffic gets the first service regardless of what is going on in the other queues. The downside is that it can lead to queue starvation in other queues if there is always traffic in the priority queue. In this mode, the priority queue also can get more than the configured bandwidth percentage, because this queue is served more than once per cycle.

In contrast, alternate mode serves the priority queue in between serving each of the other queues. Let's say that five queues are configured: 0, 1, 2, 3, and the priority queue (P). Assuming that there is always traffic in each queue, here is how it would be processed: 0, P, 1, P, 2, P, 3, P, and so on. The result is that queue starvation in nonpriority queues does not occur, because each queue is being served. The drawback of this mode is that it can cause jitter and additional latency for the traffic in the priority queue, compared to strict priority mode.

Two terms in MDRR, unique to this queuing method, help to differentiate MDRR from other queuing tools:

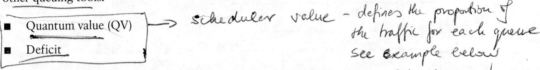

- Quantum value (QV)

- Deficit

scheduler value – defines the proportion of the traffic for each queue
See example below

Key Topic

MDRR supports two types of scheduling, one of which uses the same general algorithm as the legacy CQ feature in Cisco IOS routers (other than the 12000 Series). MDRR removes packets from a queue until the quantum value (QV) for that queue has been removed. The QV quantifies a number of bytes and is used much like the byte count is used by the CQ scheduler. MDRR repeats the process for every queue, in order from 0 through 7, and then repeats this round-robin process. The end result is that each queue gets some percentage bandwidth of the link.

MDRR deals with the CQ scheduler's problem by treating any "extra" bytes sent during a cycle as a "deficit." If too many bytes were taken from a queue, next time around through the queues, the number of extra bytes sent by MDRR is subtracted from the QV. In effect, if more than the QV is sent from a queue in one pass, that many fewer bytes are taken in the next pass. As a result, averaged over many passes through the cycle, the MDRR scheduler provides an exact bandwidth reservation.

Figure 4-7 shows an example of how MDRR works. In this case, MDRR is using only two queues, with QVs of 1500 and 3000, respectively, and with all packets at 1000 bytes in length.

Some discussion of how to interpret Figure 4-7 can help you digest what is going on. The figure shows the action during the first round-robin pass in the top half of the figure, and the action during the second pass in the lower half of the figure. The example begins with six packets (labeled P1 through P6) in queue 1, and six packets (labeled P7 through P12) in queue 2. Each arrowed line to the right sides of the queues, pointing to the right, represents the choice by MDRR to send a single packet.

When a queue first fills, the queue's deficit counter (DC) is set to the QV for that queue, which is 1500 for queue 1 and 3000 for queue 2. In Figure 4-7, MDRR begins by taking one packet from queue 1, decrementing the DC to 500, and deciding that the DC is still greater than 0. Therefore, MDRR takes a second packet from queue 1, decrementing the DC to –500. MDRR then moves on to queue 2, taking three packets, after which the deficit counter (DC) for queue 2 has decremented to 0.

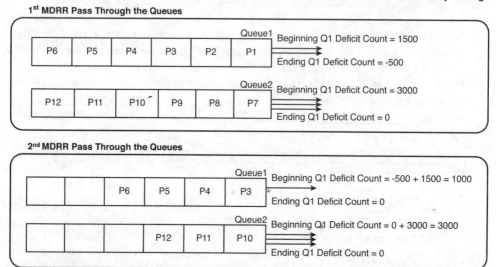

Figure 4-7 *MDRR: Making Up Deficits*

That concludes the first round-robin pass through the queues. MDRR has taken 2000 bytes from queue 1 and 3000 bytes from queue 2, giving the queues 40 percent and 60 percent of link bandwidth, respectively.

In the second round-robin pass, shown in the lower half of Figure 4-7, the process begins by MDRR adding the QV for each queue to the DC for each queue. Queue 1's DC becomes 1500 + (–500), or 1000, to begin the second pass. During this pass, MDRR takes P3 from queue 1, decrements DC to 0, and then moves on to queue 2. After taking three more packets from queue 3, decrementing queue 2's DC to 0, MDRR completes the second pass. Over these two round-robin passes, MDRR has taken 3000 bytes from queue 1 and 6000 bytes from queue 2—which is the same ratio as the ratio between the QVs. In other words, MDRR has exactly achieved the configured bandwidth ratio between the two queues.

The deficit feature of MDRR provides a means that, over time, gives each queue a guaranteed bandwidth based on the following formula:

$$\frac{\text{QV for Queue X}}{\text{Sum of All QVs}}$$

For additional examples of the operation of the MDRR deficit feature, refer to www.cisco.com/warp/public/63/toc_18841.html. Alternatively, you can go to Cisco.com and search for "Understanding and Configuring MDRR and WRED on the Cisco 12000 Series Internet Router."

LAN Switch Congestion Management and Avoidance

This section looks at the ingress and egress queuing features on Cisco 3560 switches.

Cisco Switch Ingress Queuing

Cisco 3560 switches perform both ingress and egress queuing. They have two ingress queues, one of which can be configured as a priority queue. The ingress queues in the Cisco 3560 use a method called *weighted tail drop*, or WTD, to set discard thresholds for each queue.

This section addresses the details of ingress queuing features.

The 3560 packet scheduler uses a method called *shared round-robin (SRR)* to control the rates at which packets are sent from the ingress queues to the internal switch fabric. In shared mode, SRR shares the bandwidth between the two queues according to the weights that you configure. Bandwidth for each queue is guaranteed, but it is not limited. If one queue is empty and the other has packets, that queue is allowed to use all the bandwidth. SRR uses weights that are relative rather than absolute—only the ratios affect the frequency of dequeuing. SRR's shared operation is much like CBWFQ configured for percentages rather than bandwidth.

If you plan to configure ingress queuing on your switches, you must determine the following:

- Which traffic to put in each queue. By default, COS 5 traffic is placed in queue 2, and all other traffic is in queue 1. Traffic can also be mapped to queues based on DSCP value.

- Whether some traffic needs priority treatment. If so, you will need to configure one of the queues as a priority queue.

- How much bandwidth and buffer space to allocate to each queue to achieve the traffic split you need.

- Whether the default WTD thresholds are appropriate for your traffic. The default treatment is to drop packets when the queue is 100 percent full. Each queue can have three different points, or thresholds, at which it drops traffic.

Creating a Priority Queue

Either of the two ingress queues can be configured as a priority queue. You would usually use a priority queue for voice traffic to ensure that it is forwarded ahead of other traffic to reduce latency. To enable ingress priority queuing, use the **mls qos srr-queue input priority-queue** *queue-id* **bandwidth** *weight* command. The *weight* parameter defines the percentage of the link's bandwidth that can be consumed by the priority queue when there is competing traffic in the nonpriority queue.

Key Topic

For example, consider a case with queue 2 as the priority queue, with a configured bandwidth of 20 percent. If frames have been coming in only queue 1 for a while and then some frames arrive in queue 2, the scheduler would finish servicing the current frame from queue 1 but then immediately start servicing queue 2. It would take frames from queue 2 up to the bandwidth configured with the *weight* command. It would then share the remaining bandwidth between the two queues.

Example 4-4 begins by showing the default CoS-to-input-queue and DSCP-to-input-queue assignments. The defaults include the mapping of CoS 5 to queue 2 and drop threshold 1, and CoS 6 to queue 1, threshold 1. The example then shows the configuration of queue 2 as a priority queue, and the mapping of CoS 6 to input queue 2.

Example 4-4   *Mapping Traffic to Input Queues and Creating a Priority Queue*

```
sw2# show mls qos maps cos-input-q
   Cos-inputq-threshold map:
               cos:  0   1   2   3   4   5   6   7
            ------------------------------------
   queue-threshold:  1-1 1-1 1-1 1-1 1-1 2-1 1-1 1-1
!
sw2# show mls qos maps dscp-input-q
   Dscp-inputq-threshold map:
      d1 :d2   0    1    2    3    4    5    6    7    8    9

      ------------------------------------------------------------
       0 :    01-01 01-01 01-01 01-01 01-01 01-01 01-01 01-01 01-01 01-01
       1 :    01-01 01-01 01-01 01-01 01-01 01-01 01-01 01-01 01-01 01-01
       2 :    01-01 01-01 01-01 01-01 01-01 01-01 01-01 01-01 01-01 01-01
       3 :    01-01 01-01 01-01 01-01 01-01 01-01 01-01 01-01 01-01 01-01
       4 :    02-01 02-01 02-01 02-01 02-01 02-01 02-01 02-01 01-01 01-01
       5 :    01-01 01-01 01-01 01-01 01-01 01-01 01-01 01-01 01-01 01-01
       6 :    01-01 01-01 01-01 01-01
!
sw2# conf t
sw2(config)# mls qos srr-queue input cos-map queue 2 6
!
sw2(config)# mls qos srr-queue input priority-queue 2 bandwidth 20
!
sw2# show mls qos maps cos-input-q
Cos-inputq-threshold map:
               cos:  0   1   2   3   4   5   6   7
            ------------------------------------
   queue-threshold:  1-1 1-1 1-1 1-1 1-1 2-1 2-1 1-1
```

Next, you will allocate the ratio by which to divide the ingress buffers to the two queues using the **mls qos srr-queue input buffers** *percentage1 percentage2* command. By default, 90 percent of the buffers are assigned to queue 1 and 10 percent to queue 2. In addition, you need to configure the bandwidth percentage for each queue. This sets the frequency at which the scheduler takes packets from the two buffers, using the **mls qos srr-queue input bandwidth** *weight1 weight2* command. The default bandwidth values are 4 and 4, which divides traffic evenly between the two queues. (Although the command uses the **bandwidth** keyword, the parameters are just relative weightings and do not represent any particular bit rate.) These two commands, together, determine how much data the switch can buffer and send before it begins dropping packets.

SUMMARY

When QoS is enabled on a Cisco 3560 switch, the default ingress queue settings are as follows:

- Queue 2 is the priority queue.

- Queue 2 is allocated 10 percent of the interface bandwidth.

- CoS 5 traffic is placed in queue 2.

3 things to config:
1.) CoS/DSCP to queue mapping
2.) buffer size for each queue
3.) bw for each queue

Cisco 3560 Congestion Avoidance

The Cisco 3560 uses a congestion avoidance method known as *weighted tail drop*, or WTD. WTD is turned on by default when QoS is enabled on the switch. It creates three thresholds per queue, based on CoS value, for tail drop when the associated queue reaches a particular percentage.

Because traffic in the priority queue is usually UDP traffic, you will probably leave that at the default of dropping at 100 percent. But in the other queue, you might want to drop less business-critical traffic more aggressively than others. For example, you can configure threshold 1 so that it drops traffic with CoS values of 0–3 when the queue reaches 40 percent full, threshold 2 so that it drops traffic with CoS 4 and 5 at 60 percent full, and finally threshold 3 drops CoS 6 and 7 traffic only when the queue is 100 percent full. The behavior of threshold 3 cannot be changed; it always drops traffic when the queue is 100 percent full. Figure 4-8 shows this behavior.

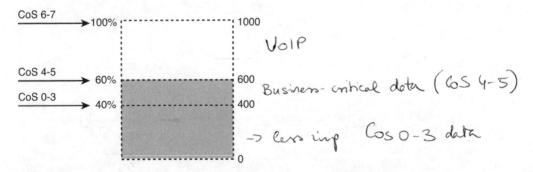

VoIP
Business-critical data (CoS 4-5)
→ less imp CoS 0-3 data

Figure 4-8 *WTD Configuration in Graphical Form*

Because WTD is configurable separately for all six queues in the 3560 (two ingress, four egress), a great deal of granularity is possible in 3560 configuration (maybe even *too* much!).

Notice in Example 4-4 that each CoS and DSCP is mapped by default to drop threshold 1. If you are trusting CoS, and thus queue traffic based on the received CoS value, use the command **mls qos srr-queue input cos-map threshold** *threshold-id cos1 . . . cos8* to assign specific CoS values to a specific threshold. If you trust DSCP, use the command **mls qos srr-queue input dscp-map threshold** *threshold-id dscp1 . . . dscp8* to assign up to eight DSCP values to a threshold. To configure the tail drop percentages for each threshold, use the command **mls qos srr-queue input threshold** *queue-id threshold-percentage1 threshold-percentage2*. Example 4-5 builds on the configuration in Example 4-4, adding configuration of the buffers, bandwidth, and drop thresholds.

Example 4-5 *Configuring Ingress Queue Buffers, Bandwidth, and Drop Thresholds*

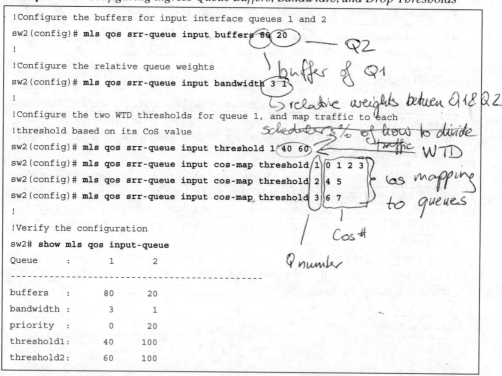

```
!Configure the buffers for input interface queues 1 and 2
sw2(config)# mls qos srr-queue input buffers 80 20
!
!Configure the relative queue weights
sw2(config)# mls qos srr-queue input bandwidth 3 1
!
!Configure the two WTD thresholds for queue 1, and map traffic to each
!threshold based on its CoS value
sw2(config)# mls qos srr-queue input threshold 1 40 60
sw2(config)# mls qos srr-queue input cos-map threshold 1 0 1 2 3
sw2(config)# mls qos srr-queue input cos-map threshold 2 4 5
sw2(config)# mls qos srr-queue input cos-map threshold 3 6 7
!
!Verify the configuration
sw2# show mls qos input-queue
Queue      :      1       2
-----------------------------------------------
buffers    :     80      20
bandwidth  :      3       1
priority   :      0      20
threshold1:      40     100
threshold2:      60     100
```

With the configuration in Examples 4-4 and 4-5, the switch will place traffic with CoS values of 5 and 6 into queue 2, which is a priority queue. It will take traffic from the priority queue based on its weight configured in the **priority-queue bandwidth** statement. It will then divide traffic between queues 1 and 2 based on the relative weights configured in the **input bandwidth** statement. Traffic in queue 1 has WTD thresholds of 40, 60, and 100 percent. Traffic with CoS values 0–3 are in threshold 1, with a WTD drop percent of 40. Traffic with CoS values 4 and 5 are in threshold 2, with a WTD drop percent of 60. CoS values 6 and 7 are in threshold 3, which has a nonconfigurable drop percent of 100.

Note   The ingress QoS commands are given at the global configuration mode, so they apply to all interfaces.

Cisco 3560 Switch Egress Queuing

The concepts of egress queuing are similar to ingress. There are four queues per interface rather than two, but you can configure which CoS and DCSP values are mapped to those queues, the relative weight of each queue, and the drop thresholds of each. You can configure a priority queue, but it must be queue 1. WTD is used for the queues, and thresholds can be configured as with ingress queuing. One difference between the two is that many of the egress commands are given at the interface, whereas the ingress commands were global.

A key difference between the ingress and egress queues is that the 3560 has a shaping feature that slows egress traffic. This can help prevent some types of denial of service (DoS) attacks and provides the means to implement subrate speed for Metro Ethernet implementations.

The Cisco 3560 uses a relatively simple classification scheme, assuming that you consider only what happens when the forwarding decision has been made. These switches make most internal QoS decisions based on an *internal DSCP* setting. The internal DSCP is determined when the frame is forwarded. So, when a frame has been assigned an internal DSCP and an egress interface, the following logic determines into which of the four interface output queues the frame is placed:

1. The frame's internal DSCP is compared to a global DSCP-to-CoS map to determine a CoS value.

2. The per-interface CoS-to-queue map determines the queue for a frame based on the assigned CoS.

This section focuses on the scheduler, assuming that frames have been classified and placed into the four output queues. In particular, the 3560 has two options for the scheduler, both using the acronym SRR: shared round-robin and shaped round-robin. The key differences between the two schedulers is that while both help to prevent queue starvation when a priority queue exists, the shaped option also rate-limits (shapes) the queues so that they do not exceed the configured percentage of the link's bandwidth.

To see the similarities and differences, it is helpful to think about both options without a PQ and with two scenarios: first, with all four queues holding plenty of frames, and second, with only one queue holding frames.

In the first case, with all four output queues holding several frames, both shared and shaped modes work the same. Both use the configuration of weights for each queue, with the queues serviced proportionally based on the weights. The following two commands configure the weights, depending on which type of scheduling is desired on the interface:

```
srr-queue bandwidth share weight1 weight2 weight3 weight4
srr-queue bandwidth shape weight1 weight2 weight3 weight4
```

For example, with the default weights of 25 for each queue in shared mode, still assuming that all four queues contain frames, the switch would service each queue equally.

The two schedulers' operations differ, however, when the queues are not all full. Consider a second scenario, with frames only in one queue with a weight of 25 (default) in that queue. With shared scheduling, the switch would keep servicing this single queue with that queue getting all the link's bandwidth. However, with shaped scheduling, the switch would purposefully wait to service the queue, not sending any data out the interface so that the queue would receive only its configured percentage of link bandwidth—25 percent in this scenario.

Next, consider the inclusion of queue 1 as the priority queue. First, consider a case where queues 2, 3, and 4 all have frames, queue 1 has no frames, and then some frames arrive in the egress PQ. The switch completes its servicing of the current frame but then transitions over to serve the PQ. However, instead of starving the other queues, while all the queues have frames waiting to exit the queues, the scheduler limits the bandwidth used for the PQ to the configured bandwidth. However, this limiting queues the excess rather than discarding the excess. (In this scenario, the behavior is the same in both shaped and shared mode.)

Finally, to see the differences between shared and shaped modes, imagine that the PQ still has many frames to send, but queues 2, 3, and 4 are now empty. In shared mode, the PQ would send at full line rate. In shaped mode, the switch would simply not service the PQ part of the time so that its overall rate would be the bandwidth configured for that queue.

Hopefully, these examples help demonstrate some of the similarities and differences between the SRR scheduler in shaped and shared modes. The following list summarizes the key points:

- Both shared and shaped mode scheduling attempt to service the queues in proportion to their configured bandwidths when more than one queue holds frames.

- Both shared and shaped mode schedulers service the PQ as soon as possible if at first the PQ is empty but then frames arrive in the PQ.

- Both shared and shaped mode schedulers prevent the PQ from exceeding its configured bandwidth when all the other queues have frames waiting to be sent.

- The shaped scheduler never allows any queue, PQ or non-PQ, to exceed its configured percentage of link bandwidth, even if that means that link sits idle.

Note The 3560 supports the ability to configure shared mode scheduling on some queues, and shaped mode on others, on a single interface. The difference in operation is that the queues in shaped mode never exceed their configured bandwidth setting.

Mapping DSCP or CoS values to queues is done in global configuration mode, as with ingress queuing. Each interface belongs to one of two egress *queue-sets*. Buffer and

WTD threshold configurations are done in global configuration mode for each queue-set. Bandwidth weights, shaped or shared mode, and priority queuing are configured per interface.

Example 4-6 shows an egress queue configuration. Buffers and the WTD thresholds for one of the queues are changed for queue-set 2. Queue-set 1 is assigned to an interface, which then has sharing configured for queue 2 with a new command: **srr-queue bandwidth share** *weight1 weight2 weight3 weight4*. Shaping is configured for queues 3 and 4 with the similar command **srr-queue bandwidth shape** *weight1 weight2 weight3 weight4*. Queue 1 is configured as a priority queue. When you configure the priority queue, the switch ignores any bandwidth values assigned to the priority queue in the **share** or **shape** commands. The 3560 also gives the ability to rate-limit the interface bandwidth with the command **srr-queue bandwidth limit** *percent*. In this example, the interface is limited by default to using 75 percent of its bandwidth.

Example 4-6   *Egress Queue Configuration*

```
sw2(config)# mls qos queue-set output 1 buffers 40 20 30 10
!
sw2(config)# mls qos queue-set output 1 threshold 2 40 60 100 100
!
sw2(config)# int fa 0/2
sw2(config-if)# queue-set 1
sw2(config-if)# srr-queue bandwidth share 10 10 1 1
sw2(config-if)# srr-queue bandwidth shape 10 0 20 20
sw2(config-if)# priority-queue out
!
sw2# show mls qos int fa 0/2 queueing
FastEthernet0/2
Egress Priority Queue : enabled
Shaped queue weights (absolute) :   10 0 20 20
Shared queue weights   :   10 10 1 1
The port bandwidth limit : 75  (Operational Bandwidth:75.0)
The port is mapped to qset : 1
```

Key
Topic

Resource Reservation Protocol (RSVP)

RSVP is an IETF protocol that is unique among the quality of service (QoS) methods in that it can reserve end-to-end resources for the length of the data flow. The QoS techniques covered so far allocate bandwidth or prioritize traffic at an individual router or switch interface. The actual treatment of a packet can vary from router to router based on the interface congestion when the packet arrives and on each router's configuration. Previous techniques are concerned with providing quality of service to individual frames or packets, rather than traffic flows.

When RSVP is used, each RSVP-enabled router along the path reserves bandwidth and the requested QoS for the duration of that flow. Reservations are made on a flow-by-flow basis, so each has its own reservation. In addition, reservations are unidirectional; one is made from source to destination, and another must be made from destination back to the source. RSVP is typically used in networks that have limited bandwidth and frequent congestion. It is most appropriate for traffic that cannot tolerate much delay or packet loss, such as voice and video.

RSVP Process Overview

Some applications and devices are RSVP aware and initiate their own reservations. More typically, the gateways act in proxy for the devices, creating a reserved path between them. Figure 4-9 shows how a reservation is created. Reservations are made per direction per flow; a flow is identified in RSVP by a destination IP address, protocol ID, and destination port. One reservation is made from terminating to originating gateway, and another reservation is made from originating to terminating gateway.

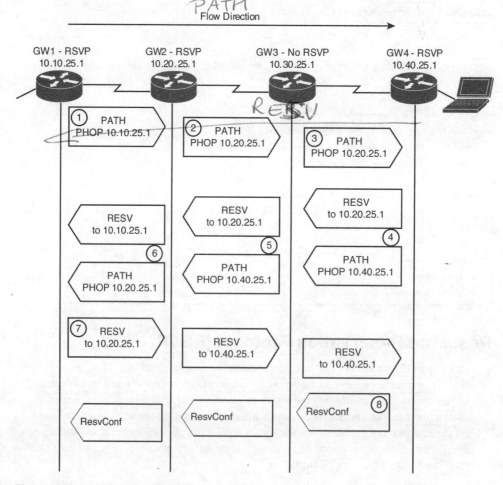

Figure 4-9   *RSVP Reservation Process*

In Figure 4-9, neither endpoint application is RSVP aware. The RSVP reservation setup proceeds as follows:

1. Router GW1 receives the first packet in a flow that needs a reservation made for it. GW1 sends an RSVP PATH message toward the destination IP address. PATH messages contain the IP address of the previous hop (PHOP) so that return messages can follow the same path back. They also describe the bandwidth and QoS needs of the traffic.

2. The next-hop router, GW2, is configured with RSVP. It records the previous-hop information and forwards the PATH message on. Notice that it inserts its IP address as the previous hop. The destination address is unchanged.

3. The third router, GW3, does not have RSVP configured. The PATH message looks just like an IP packet to this router, and it will route the message untouched toward the destination, just as it would any IP packet.

4. When the fourth router, GW4, receives the PATH message, it replies with a reservation (RESV) message to the previous-hop address listed in the PATH message. This RESV message requests the needed QoS. If any router along the way does not have sufficient resources, it returns an error message and discards the RSVP message. GW4 also initiates a PATH message toward GW1, to reserve resources in the other direction.

5. The RESV and PATH messages again look like normal IP packets to GW3, the non-RSVP router, so it just routes the packets toward GW2. No resources are reserved on this gateway.

6. GW2 receives the RESV message and checks to see whether it can supply the requested resources. If the check succeeds, it creates a reservation for that flow, and then forwards the RESV message to the previous-hop IP address listed in the PATH message it received earlier. When the other PATH message arrives, GW2 processes it and sends it on to GW1.

7. When GW1 receives the RESV message, it knows that its reservation has succeeded. However, a reservation must be made in each direction for QoS to be provided to traffic flowing in both directions.

8. GW1 responds to the second PATH message with an RESV message, which proceeds through the network as before. When GW4 receives the RESV message, resources have been reserved in both directions. GW4 responds with a ResvConf message, confirming the reservation.

Data transmission has been delayed during the exchange of messages. When GW1 receives the ResvConf message, it knows that reservations have been made in both directions. Traffic can now proceed. RSVP will send periodic refresh messages along the call path, enabling it to dynamically adjust to network changes.

Configuring RSVP

Before configuring RSVP, decide how much bandwidth to allocate per flow and how much total bandwidth to allow RSVP to use, per interface. Remember to allow bandwidth for all other applications that will use that interface.

RSVP must be configured on each router that will create reservations, and at each interface the traffic will traverse. It is enabled at the interface configuration mode with the **ip rsvp bandwidth** *total-kbps single-flow-kbps* command. If you do not specify the total bandwidth to reserve, the router reserves 75 percent of the interface bandwidth. If no flow value is specified, any flow can reserve the entire bandwidth.

To set the DSCP value for RSVP control messages, use the interface command **ip rsvp signalling dscp** *dscp-value*.

It is not necessary to configure RSVP on every single router within the enterprise. Because RSVP messages are passed through non-RSVP-enabled routers, it can be used selectively. You might enable it in sections of the network prone to congestion, such as areas with low bandwidth. In the core of the network, where bandwidth is higher, you might rely on LLQ/CBWFQ to handle the traffic. This helps in scaling RSVP, cutting down on the number of routers that must track each session and be involved in RSVP messaging.

Figure 4-10 shows a network with remote sites connecting to a core IP WAN. The core might be enterprise owned or it might be a service provider's multiprotocol packet label switched (MPLS) network, for example. The remote site links are all T1 and carry both voice and data. WAN interfaces of the remote site routers are all configured for RSVP. Bandwidth will be reserved when they send data between each other. When traffic goes across the core IP WAN, reservations will be made on the WAN interfaces of the edge routers based on resources available on the remote site routers. The core will not participate in RSVP, so other means of QoS must be done there.

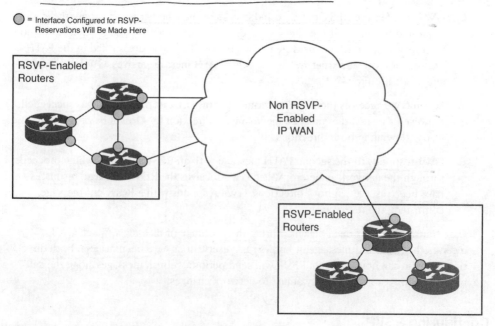

Figure 4-10 *Using RSVP in a Larger Network*

Using RSVP for Voice Calls

RSVP reserves resources, but it is up to each router to implement the appropriate QoS techniques to deliver those resources. Low-latency queuing (LLQ) is the QoS mechanism typically used for voice, putting voice in a priority queue with guaranteed but policed bandwidth. This is part of the DiffServ model of QoS. However, RSVP has its own set of queues that it puts reserved traffic into by default. These queues have a low weight, but they are not prioritized. What is needed is a way to put reserved voice traffic into the low-latency queue.

By default, RSVP uses weighted fair queuing (WFQ) to provide its QoS. When using LLQ with class-based weighted fair queuing (CBWFQ), disable RSVP's use of WFQ with the interface command **ip rsvp resource-provider none**. Also, by default, RSVP will attempt to process every packet (not just voice traffic). Turn this off with the interface command **ip rsvp data-packet classification none**. LLQ and CBWFQ should be configured as usual. RSVP will then reserve bandwidth for voice calls, and the gateway's QoS processes will place voice traffic into the priority queue.

Note   When you are using LLQ, the priority queue size includes Layer 2 overhead. RSVP's bandwidth statement does not take Layer 2 overhead into consideration. Therefore, when using both LLQ and RSVP, be sure to set the RSVP bandwidth equal to the Priority Queue minus the Layer 2 overhead.

Example 4-7 shows RSVP configured on an interface. This interface uses CBWFQ with an LLQ, so RSVP is configured appropriately.

Example 4-7   *Configuring RSVP*

```
R4(config)# int s0/1/0
R4(config-if)# ip rsvp bandwidth 128 64          → allocate max 128, per flow 64K   max
R4(config-if)# ip rsvp signalling dscp 40        → use a DCSP of 40
R4(config-if)# ip rsvp resource-provider none    → only disable WFQ
R4(config-if)# ip rsvp data-packet classification none  → only VoIP
R4(config-if)# service-policy output LLQ
!
!The next two commands verify the interface RSVP
!configuration.
R4# show ip rsvp interface
interface    allocated  i/f max  flow max sub max
Se0/1/0       0          128K     64K       0
!
R4# show ip rsvp interface detail
 Se0/1/0:
   Interface State: Down
   Bandwidth:
     Curr allocated: 0 bits/sec
```

```
  Max. allowed (total): 128K bits/sec
  Max. allowed (per flow): 64K bits/sec
  Max. allowed for LSP tunnels using sub-pools: 0 bits/sec
  Set aside by policy (total): 0 bits/sec
Admission Control:
  Header Compression methods supported:
    rtp (36 bytes-saved), udp (20 bytes-saved)
Traffic Control:
  RSVP Data Packet Classification is OFF
  RSVP resource provider is: none
Signalling:
  DSCP value used in RSVP msgs: 0x28
  Number of refresh intervals to enforce blockade state: 4
  Number of missed refresh messages: 4
  Refresh interval: 30
Authentication: disabled
```

Foundation Summary

Please take the time to read and study the details in the "Foundation Topics" section of the chapter, as well as review the items in the "Foundation Topics" section noted with a Key Topic icon.

Memory Builders

The CCIE Routing and Switching written exam, like all Cisco CCIE written exams, covers a fairly broad set of topics. This section provides some basic tools to help you exercise your memory about some of the broader topics covered in this chapter.

Fill In Key Tables from Memory

Appendix E, "Key Tables for CCIE Study," on the CD in the back of this book, contains empty sets of some of the key summary tables in each chapter. Print Appendix E, refer to this chapter's tables in it, and fill in the tables from memory. Refer to Appendix F, "Solutions for Key Tables for CCIE Study," on the CD, to check your answers.

Definitions

Next, take a few moments to write down the definitions for the following terms:

class-based weighted fair queuing, low-latency queuing, weighted round-robin, modified deficit round-robin, shared round-robin, shared mode, shaped mode, WTD, WRR, quantum value, alternate mode, tail drop, full drop, priority queue, sequence number, finish time, modified tail drop, scheduler, queue starvation, strict priority, software queue, hardware queue, remaining bandwidth, maximum reserved bandwidth, actual queue depth, average queue depth, minimum threshold, maximum threshold, mark probability denominator, exponential weighting constant, expedite queue, DSCP-to-CoS map, DSCP-to-threshold map, internal DSCP, differentiated tail drop, AutoQoS, RSVP

Refer to the glossary to check your answers.

Further Reading

Cisco QoS Exam Certification Guide, Second Edition, by Wendell Odom and Michael Cavanaugh.

Cisco Catalyst QoS: Quality of Service in Campus Networks, by Mike Flanagan, Richard Froom, and Kevin Turek.

Cisco.com includes a great deal more information on the very detailed aspects of 3560 QoS configuration, including SRR and WTD, at www.cisco.com/en/US/partner/docs/switches/lan/catalyst3560/software/release/12.2_52_se/configuration/guide/swqos.html.

Blueprint topics covered in this chapter:

This chapter covers the following subtopics from the Cisco CCIE Routing and Switching written exam blueprint. Refer to the full blueprint in Table I-1 in the Introduction for more details on the topics covered in each chapter and their context within the blueprint.

- Marking
- Shaping
- Policing
- Hierarchical QoS
- Troubleshooting Quality of Service (QoS)

Shaping, Policing, and Link Fragmentation

Traffic-shaping tools delay packets exiting a router so that the overall bit rate does not exceed a defined shaping rate. This chapter covers the concepts behind IOS traffic shaping mechanisms like Class-Based Shaping (CB Shaping).

Traffic policers measure bit rates for packets either entering or exiting an interface. If the defined rate is exceeded, the policer either discards enough packets so that the rate is not exceeded or marks some packets such that the packets are more likely to be discarded later. This chapter covers the concepts and configuration behind Class-Based Policing (CB Policing), with a brief mention of committed access rate (CAR).

"Do I Know This Already?" Quiz

Table 5-1 outlines the major headings in this chapter and the corresponding "Do I Know This Already?" quiz questions.

Table 5-1   *"Do I Know This Already?" Foundation Topics Section-to-Question Mapping*

Foundation Topics Section	Questions Covered in This Section	Score
Traffic-Shaping Concepts	1–2	
Generic Traffic Shaping	3	
Class-Based Shaping Configuration	4–5	
Policing Concepts and Configuration	6–7	
QoS Troubleshooting and Commands	8	
Total Score		

To best use this pre-chapter assessment, remember to score yourself strictly. You can find the answers in Appendix A, "Answers to the 'Do I Know This Already?' Quizzes."

1. When does Class-Based Shaping add tokens to its token bucket, and how many tokens does it add when Bc and Be are both set to something larger than 0?

   a. Upon the arrival of each packet, a pro-rated portion of Bc is added to the token bucket.

   b. Upon the arrival of each packet, a pro-rated portion of Bc + Be is added to the token bucket.

   c. At the beginning of each time interval, Bc worth of tokens are added to the token bucket.

   d. At the beginning of each time interval, Bc + Be worth of tokens are added to the token bucket.

   e. None of the answers is correct.

2. If shaping was configured with a rate of 128 kbps and a Bc of 3200 bits, what value would be calculated for Tc?

   a. 125 ms

   b. 125 sec

   c. 25 ms

   d. 25 sec

   e. Shaping doesn't use a Tc.

   f. Not enough information is provided to tell.

3. Which of the following statements about Generic Traffic Shaping are true?

   a. The configuration can be created once and then used for multiple interfaces.

   b. It is not supported on ATM interfaces.

   c. It must be configured under each individual interface or subinterface where shaping is required.

   d. You can specify which traffic will be shaped and which will not.

   e. It supports adaptive traffic shaping.

4. Which of the following commands, when typed in the correct configuration mode, enables CB Shaping to be 128 kbps?

a. shape average 128000 8000 0

b. shape average 128 8000 0

c. shape average 128000

d. shape peak 128000 8000 0

e. shape peak 128 8000 0

f. shape peak 128000

5. Examine the following configuration, noting the locations of the comment lines labeled point 1, point 2, and so on. Assume that a correctly configured policy map that implements CBWFQ, called **queue-it**, is also configured but not shown. To enable CBWFQ for the packets queued by CB Shaping, what command is required, and at what point in the configuration is the command required?

```
policy-map shape-question
! point 1
 class class-default
! point 2
   shape average 256000 5120
! point 3
interface serial 0/0
! point 4
   service-policy output shape-question
! point 5
interface s0/0.1 point-to-point
! point 6
  ip address 1.1.1.1
! point 7
```

a. service-policy queue-it, at point 1

b. service-policy queue-it, at point 3

c. service-policy queue-it, at point 5

d. shape queue service-policy queue-it, at point 1

e. shape queue service-policy queue-it, at point 3

f. shape queue service-policy queue-it, at point 6

6. Which of the following commands, when typed in the correct configuration mode, enables CB Policing at 128 kbps, with no excess burst?

    a. police 128000 conform-action transmit exceed-action transmit violate-action drop

    b. police 128 conform-action transmit exceed-action transmit violate-action drop

    c. police 128000 conform-action transmit exceed-action drop

    d. police 128 conform-action transmit exceed-action drop

    e. police 128k conform-action transmit exceed-action drop

7. Which of the following features of CB Policing are not supported by CAR?

    a. The capability to categorize packets as conforming, exceeding, and violating a traffic contract

    b. The capability to police all traffic at one rate, and subsets of that same traffic at other rates

    c. The capability to configure policing using MQC commands

    d. The capability to police input or output packets on an interface

8. To troubleshoot a suspected QoS issue, you need to see the QoS policy configured on an interface along with which queues are filling up and dropping packets. Which of the following commands will display that information?

    a. show policy-map interface *interface*

    b. show queue *interface*

    c. show queue-list interface *interface*

    d. show ip policy interface *interface*

Foundation Topics

Traffic-Shaping Concepts

Traffic shaping prevents the bit rate of the packets exiting an interface from exceeding a configured shaping rate. To do so, the shaper monitors the bit rate at which data is being sent. If the configured rate is exceeded, the shaper delays packets, holding the packets in a *shaping queue.* The shaper then releases packets from the queue such that, over time, the overall bit rate does not exceed the shaping rate.

Traffic shaping solves two general types of problems that can occur in multiaccess networks. First, if a service provider purposefully discards any traffic on a VC when the traffic rate exceeds the committed information rate (CIR), it makes sense for the router to not send traffic faster than the CIR.

Egress blocking is the second type of problem for which shaping provides some relief. *Egress blocking* occurs when a router sends data into an ATM service, and the egress switch has to queue the data before it can be sent out to the router on the other end of the VC. For example, when a T1-connected router sends data, it must be sent at T1 speed. If the router on the other end of the VC has a link clocked at 256 kbps, the frames/cells will start to back up in the output queue of the egress switch. Likewise, if that same T1 site has VCs to 20 remote sites, and each remote site uses a 256-kbps link, when all 20 remote sites send at about the same time, frames/cells will be queued, waiting to exit the WAN egress switch to the T1 router. In this case, shaping can be used to essentially prevent egress queuing, moving the packets back into a queue in the router, where they can then be manipulated with fancy queuing tools.

Shaping Terminology

Routers can send bits out an interface only at the physical clock rate. To average sending at a lower rate, the router has to alternate between sending packets and being silent. For example, to average sending at a packet rate of half the physical link speed, the router should send packets half of the time and not send packets the other half of the time. Over time, it looks like a staccato series of sending and silence. Figure 5-1 shows a graph of what happens when a router has a link with a clock rate of 128 kbps and a shaper configured to shape traffic to 64 kbps.

Figure 5-1 shows the sending rate and implies quite a bit about how Cisco IOS implements shaping. A shaper sets a static time interval, called *Tc*. Then, it calculates the number of bits that can be sent in the Tc interval such that, over time, the number of bits/second sent matches the shaping rate.

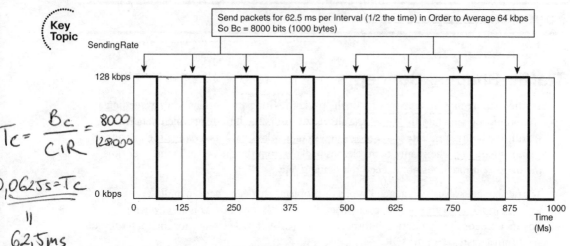

$$Tc = \frac{Bc}{CIR} = \frac{8000}{128000}$$

$$\underline{0,0625 = Tc}$$
$$||$$
$$62,5 ms$$

Figure 5-1 *Mechanics of Traffic Shaping—128-kbps Access Rate, 64-kbps Shaped Rate*

The number of bits that can be sent in each Tc is called the *committed burst (Bc)*. In Figure 5-1, an 8000-bit Bc can be sent in every 125-ms Tc to achieve a 64-kbps average rate. In other words, with a Tc of 125 ms, there will be eight Tc intervals per second. If Bc bits (8000) are sent each Tc, eight sets of 8000 bits will be sent each second, resulting in a rate of 64,000 bps.

Because the bits must be encoded on the link at the clock rate, the 8000 bits in each interval require only 62.5 ms (8000/128,000) to exit the interface onto the link. The graph shows the results: The interface sends at the line rate (access rate) for 62.5 ms, and then waits for 62.5 ms, while packets sit in the shaping queue.

Table 5-2 lists the terminology related to this shaping model. Note in particular that the term *CIR* refers to the traffic rate for a VC based on a business contract, and *shaping rate* refers to the rate configured for a shaper on a router.

Table 5-2 *Shaping Terminology*

Term	Definition
Tc	Time interval, measured in milliseconds, over which the committed burst (Bc) can be sent. With many shaping tools, Tc = Bc/CIR.
Bc	Committed burst size, measured in bits. This is the amount of traffic that can be sent during the Tc interval. Typically defined in the traffic contract.
CIR	Committed information rate, in bits per second, which defines the rate of a VC according to the business contract.
Shaped rate	The rate, in bits per second, to which a particular configuration wants to shape the traffic. It might or might not be set to the CIR.
Be	Excess burst size, in bits. This is the number of bits beyond Bc that can be sent after a period of inactivity.

Shaping with an Excess Burst

To accommodate bursty data traffic, shapers implement a concept by which, after a period in which an interface sends relatively little data compared to its CIR, more than Bc bits can be sent in one or more time intervals. This concept is called *excess burst (Be)*. When using a Be, the shaper can allow, in addition to the Bc bits per Tc, Be extra bits to be sent. Depending on the settings, it might take one time interval to send the extra bits, or it might require multiple time intervals. Figure 5-2 shows a graph of the same example in Figure 5-1, but with a Be also equal to 8000 bits. In this case, the Be extra bits are all sent in the first time interval after the relative inactivity.

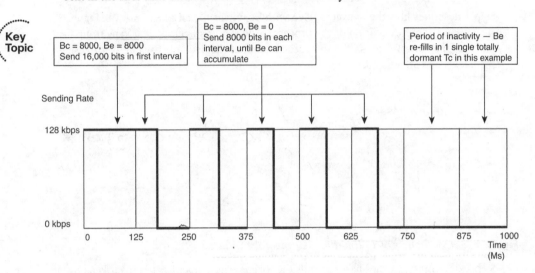

Figure 5-2 *Bc and Be, After a Period of Inactivity*

In the first interval, traffic shaping can send a total of 16,000 bits (Bc + Be bits). On a 128-kbps link, assuming a 125-ms Tc, all 125 ms is required to send 16,000 bits. In this particular case, after a period of inactivity, R1 sends continuously for the entire first interval. In the second interval, the shaper allows the usual Bc bits to be sent. In effect, with these settings, the shaper allows 187.5 ms of consecutive sending after a period of low activity.

Underlying Mechanics of Shaping

Shapers apply a simple formula to the Tc, Bc, and shaping rate parameters:

Tc = Bc/shaping rate

For example, in Figures 5-1 and 5-2, if the shaping rate (64 kbps) and the Bc (8000 bits) were both configured, the shaper would then calculate the Tc as 8000/64,000 = 0.125 seconds. Alternatively, if the rate and Tc had been configured, the shaper would have calculated Bc as Bc = rate * Tc (a simple derivation of the formula listed earlier), or 64 kbps * 0.125 s = 8000 bits. (CB Shaping uses default values in some cases, as described in the configuration sections of this chapter.)

Traffic shaping uses a *token bucket* model to manage the shaping process. First, consider the case in which the shaper is not using Be. Imagine a bucket of size Bc, with the bucket filled with tokens at the beginning of each Tc. Each token lets the shaper buy the right to send 1 bit. So, at the beginning of each Tc, the shaper has the ability to release Bc worth of bits.

Shapers perform two main actions related to the bucket:

1. Refill the bucket with new tokens at the beginning of each Tc.

2. Spend tokens to gain the right to forward packets.

Step 1 describes how the bucket is filled with Bc tokens to start each interval. Figure 5-3 shows a visual representation of the process. Note that if some of the tokens from the previous time interval are still in the bucket, some of the new tokens spill over the side of the bucket and are wasted.

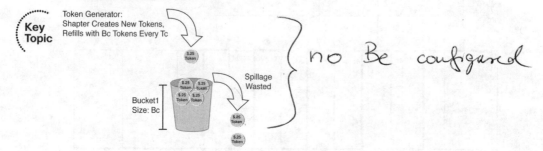

no Be configured

Figure 5-3 *Mechanics of Filling the Shaping Token Bucket*

Step 2 describes how the shaper spends the tokens. The shaper has to take tokens from the bucket equal to the number of bits in a packet to release that packet for transmission. For example, if the packet is 1000 bits long, the shaper must remove 1000 tokens from the bucket to send that packet. When traffic shaping tries to send a packet, and the bucket does not have enough tokens in it to buy the right to send the packet, traffic shaping must wait until the next interval, when the token bucket is refilled.

Traffic shaping implements Be by making the single token bucket bigger, with no other changes to the token-bucket model. In other words, only Bc tokens are added each Tc, and tokens must still be consumed to send packets. The key difference using Be (versus not using Be) is that when some of the tokens are left in the bucket at the end of the time interval, and Bc tokens are added at the beginning of the next interval, more than Bc tokens are in the bucket—therefore allowing a larger burst of bits in this new interval.

Be Configed explained

Generic Traffic Shaping

In older versions of IOS, there was a concept of Generic Traffic Shaping (GTS) that functioned as a simple form of traffic shaping that was supported on most router interfaces but could not be used with flow switching. GTS was configured and applied to an interface or subinterface. In its basic configuration, it shaped all traffic leaving the interface. You could modify that behavior with an access list, permitting the traffic to be shaped and denying any traffic that should be passed through unshaped. We will entertain how this feature functioned in the IOS Release 12 train, to better understand how IOS Release 15 code's implementation of QoS mechanisms has changed.

GTS was enabled for all interface traffic with this interface-level command:

```
traffic-shape rate shaped-rate [Bc] [Be] [buffer-limit]
```

In this command, the shaped rate was specified in bps, the Bc was in bits, and the Be was in bits. The buffer limit set the maximum size of the queue buffer and was specified in bps. Only the shaped rate was required. If you did not specify the Bc or the Be, both would have been set to one-quarter of the shaped rate by default.

To limit the types of traffic that would be shaped, you could configure an access list that permitted that traffic and denied all other traffic. Then you would apply it to the GTS with the following command:

```
traffic-shape group access-list-number shaped-rate {Bc} {Be}
```

Example 5-1 shows a GTS example where Internet Control Message Protocol (ICMP) traffic would have been shaped to only 500 kbps. An access list was first created and then GTS was configured on the interface. The example also shows the output verification for this legacy command set.

Example 5-1 *Generic Traffic Shaping*

```
! Access list 101 permits ICMP.  All other traffic is denied by default.
access-list 101 permit icmp any any
!
! Generic Traffic Shaping is configured on the interface. The access list
! is associated with the shaping.  A CIR of 500 kbps is specified, but no
! Bc or Be.
interface fa 0/0
 traffic-shape group 101 500000
!
! The shaping configuration is verified. Note that the router has added a
! Bc and Be of 12 kb each. It has also calculated a Tc of 24 ms. This
! command also shows that shaping is not currently active.
R3# show traffic-shape fa 0/0

Interface   Fa0/0
   Access  Target Byte  Sustain   Excess  Interval Increment Adapt
VC List     Rate   Limit bits/int bits/int (ms)     (bytes)   Active
-   101     500000 3000  12000     12000    24       1500      -
!
! Once shaping is active, the statistics and queue information is shown in
!  the following two commands.
```

[Handwritten annotations: "500 Kb/s" next to traffic-shape group line; "?" over Interval/Increment columns; "12000 is not 1/4 of the shaped rate 500.000kb/s"]

```
Router# show traffic-shape statistics

          Acc.   Queue  Packets  Bytes     Packets   Bytes      Shaping
I/F       List   Depth  Delayed  Delayed                        Active
Fa0/0     101    24     10542    14753352  10252     14523964   yes


Router# show traffic-shape queue
Traffic queued in shaping queue on FastEthernet0/0
 Traffic shape group: 101
  Queueing strategy: weighted fair
  Queueing Stats: 10/1000/64/0 (size/max total/threshold/drops)
     Conversations  2/3/32 (active/max active/max total)
     Reserved Conversations 0/0 (allocated/max allocated)
     Available Bandwidth 500 kilobits/sec

 (depth/weight/total drops/no-buffer drops/interleaves) 4/32384/0/0/0
 Conversation 16, linktype: ip, length: 1514
 source: 10.2.2.2, destination: 10.1.1.4, id: 0x014D, ttl: 255, prot: 1

 (depth/weight/total drops/no-buffer drops/interleaves) 6/32384/0/0/0
 Conversation 15, linktype: ip, length: 1514
 source: 10.2.2.2, destination: 10.1.1.3, id: 0x0204, ttl: 255, prot: 1
```

Class-Based Shaping

Class-Based Shaping (CB Shaping) is the Cisco-recommended way to configure traffic shaping. It allows you to create class maps and policy maps once and then reuse them for multiple interfaces, rather than redoing the entire configuration under each individual interface. This lessens the likelihood of operator error or typos. CB Shaping also provides more granular control over the QoS operation.

Class-Based Shaping implements all the core concepts described so far in this chapter, plus several other important features. First, it allows several Cisco IOS queuing tools to be applied to the packets delayed by the shaping process. At the same time, it allows fancy queuing tools to be used on the interface software queues. It also allows classification of packets, so that some types of packets can be shaped at one rate, a second type of packet can be shaped at another rate, while allowing a third class of packets to not be shaped at all.

The only new MQC command required to configure CB Shaping is the **shape** command. The "Foundation Summary" section, later in this chapter, provides a CB Shaping command reference, in Table 5-10:

shape [**average** | **peak**] *mean-rate* [[*burst-size*] [*excess-burst-size*]]

CB Shaping can be implemented for output packets only, and it can be associated with either a physical interface or a subinterface.

To enable CB Shaping, the **service-policy output** command is configured under either the interface or the subinterface, with the referenced policy map including the **shape** command.

Example 5-2 shows a simple CB Shaping configuration that uses the following criteria:

- Interface clock rate is 128 kbps.

- Shape all traffic at a 64-kbps rate.

- Use the default setting for Tc.

- Shape traffic exiting subinterface s0/0.1.

- The software queuing on s0/0 will use WFQ (the default).

- The shaping queue will use FIFO (the default).

Example 5-2 *CB Shaping of All Traffic Exiting S0/0.1 at 64 kbps*

```
! Policy map shape-all places all traffic into the class-default class, matching
! all packets. All packets will be shaped to an average of 64 kbps. Note the
! units are in bits/second, so 64000 means 64 kbps.
policy-map shape-all
  class class-default
    shape average 64000
! The physical interface will not show the fair-queue command, but it is
! configured by default, implementing WFQ for interface s0/0/0 software queuing.
interface serial0/0/0
 bandwidth 128
! Below, CB Shaping has been enabled for all packets forwarded out s0/0/0.1.
interface serial0/0/0.1
 service-policy output shape-all
! Refer to the text after this example for more explanations of this next command.
R3# show policy-map interface s0/0/0.1
 Serial0/0/0.1

  Service-policy output: shape-all

    Class-map: class-default (match-any)
      1 packets, 328 bytes
      5 minute offered rate 0000 bps, drop rate 0000 bps
      Match: any
      Queueing
      queue limit 64 packets
      (queue depth/total drops/no-buffer drops) 0/0/0
      (pkts output/bytes output) 1/328
      shape (average) cir 64000, bc 256, be 256
      target shape rate 64000
```

(Handwritten annotations on the page)

- kb/s
- WFQ
- shaping enabled on the sf.
- 96000 / 24000 / 4
- $T_c = \dfrac{8000}{64000} = 9.125$
- $\dfrac{64000 \text{ bits}}{8} = 8000$
- $\dfrac{8000}{4} = 2000\text{b/k}$
- why?
- $\rightarrow T_c = 32\text{ms}$

The configuration itself is relatively straightforward. The **shape-all** policy map matches all packets in a single class (class-default) and is enabled on s0/0.1. So, all packets exiting s0/0.1 will be shaped to the defined rate of 64 kbps.

The output of the **show policy-map interface s0/0/0.1** command shows the settings for all the familiar shaping concepts, but it uses slightly different terminology. CB Shaping defaults to a Bc and Be of 256 bits each.

The CB Shaping **shape** command requires the shaping rate to be set. However, Bc and Be can be omitted, and Tc cannot be set directly. As a result, CB Shaping calculates some or all of these settings. CB Shaping calculates the values differently based on whether the shaping rate exceeds 320 kbps. Table 5-3 summarizes the rules.

Key Topic

Table 5-3 *CB Shaping Calculation of Default Variable Settings*

Variable	Rate <= 320 kbps	Rate > 320 kbps
Bc	8000 bits	Bc = shaping rate * Tc
Be	Be = Bc = 8000	Be = Bc
Tc	Tc = Bc/shaping rate	25 ms

Tuning Shaping for Voice Using LLQ and a Small Tc

Example 5-2 in the previous section shows default settings for queuing for the interface software queues (WFQ) and for the shaping queue (FIFO). Example 5-3 shows an alternative configuration that works better for voice traffic by using low-latency queuing (LLQ) for the shaped traffic. Also, the configuration forces the Tc down to 10 ms, which means that each packet will experience only a short delay waiting for the beginning of the next Tc. By keeping Tc to a small value, the LLQ logic applied to the shaped packets does not have to wait nearly as long to release packets from the PQ, as compared with the default Tc settings.

The revised requirements, as compared with Example 5-2, are as follows:

- Enable LLQ to support a single G.729 voice call.

- Shape to 96 kbps—less than the clock rate (128 kbps), but more than the CIR of the VC.

- Tune Tc to 10 ms.

Example 5-3 *CB Shaping on R3, 96-kbps Shape Rate, with LLQ for Shaping Queues*

```
class-map match-all voip-rtp
 match ip rtp 16384 16383
! queue-voip implements a PQ for VoIP traffic, and uses WFQ in the default class.
policy-map queue-voip
 class voip-rtp
```

```
    priority 32
  class class-default
    fair-queue
! shape-all shapes all traffic to 96 kbps, with Bc of 960. Tc is calculated as
! 960/96000 or 10 ms. Also note the service-policy queue-voip command. This applies
! policy map queue-voip to all packets shaped by the shape command.
policy-map shape-all
  class class-default
    shape average 96000 960
    service-policy queue-voip
!
interface serial0/0.1
  service-policy output shape-all
! Note the Interval is now listed as 10 ms. Also, note the detailed stats for LLQ
! are also listed at the end of the command.
R3# show policy-map interface serial 0/0.1
 Serial0/0.1

  Service-policy output: shape-all

    Class-map: class-default (match-any)
      5189 packets, 927835 bytes
      30 second offered rate 91000 bps, drop rate 0 bps
      Match: any
      Traffic Shaping
           Target/Average   Byte   Sustain   Excess   Interval  Increment
              Rate          Limit  bits/int  bits/int  (ms)      (bytes)
           96000/96000      1200    960        960      10        120


      Adapt  Queue    Packets   Bytes    Packets   Bytes     Shaping
      Active Depth                       Delayed   Delayed   Active
       —      17       5172     910975    4002     831630    yes


    Service-policy : queue-voip
      Class-map: voip-rtp (match-all)
        4623 packets, 295872 bytes
        30 second offered rate 25000 bps, drop rate 0 bps
        Match: ip rtp 16384 16383
        Weighted Fair Queueing
          Strict Priority
          Output Queue: Conversation 24
          Bandwidth 32 (kbps) Burst 800 (Bytes)
          (pkts matched/bytes matched) 3528/225792
          (total drops/bytes drops) 0/0

      Class-map: class-default (match-any)
        566 packets, 631963 bytes
```

Handwritten annotations:

nested policy-map

$$T_c = \frac{960(B_c)}{CIR\ 96000} = 0.010s$$

↳ LLQ & shaping together

```
           30 second offered rate 65000 bps, drop rate 0 bps
           Match: any
           Weighted Fair Queueing
             Flow Based Fair Queueing
             Maximum Number of Hashed Queues 16
 (total queued/total drops/no-buffer drops) 17/0/0
```

Example 5-3 shows how to use LLQ against the packets shaped by CB Shaping by calling an LLQ policy map with the **service-policy** command. Note that the command syntax (**service-policy queue-voip**) does not include the **output** keyword; the output direction is implied. Figure 5-4 shows the general idea behind what is happening in the configuration.

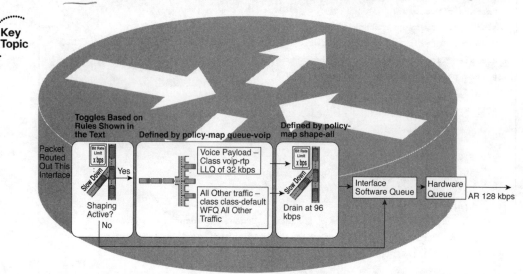

Figure 5-4 *Interaction Between Shaping Policy Map* **shape-all** *and Queuing Policy Map* **queue-voip**

Scanning Figure 5-4 from left to right, CB Shaping must make the first decision after a packet has been routed out the subinterface. CB Shaping first needs to decide whether shaping is active; if it is, CB Shaping should put the packet into a shaping queue. If it is not active, the packet can move right on to the appropriate interface software queue. Shaping becomes active only when a single packet exceeds the traffic contract; it becomes inactive again when all the shaping queues are drained.

Assuming that a packet needs to be delayed by CB Shaping, the LLQ logic of **policy-map queue-voip** determines into which of the two shaping queues the packet should be placed. Later, when CB Shaping decides to release the next packet (typically when the next Tc begins), LLQ determines which packets are taken next. This example has only two queues, one of which is an LLQ, so packets are always taken from the LLQ if any are present in that queue.

When a packet leaves one of the two shaping queues, it drains into the interface software queues. For routers with many VCs on the same physical interface, the VCs compete for the available interface bandwidth. Examples 5-1 and 5-2 both defaulted to use WFQ on the interface. However, LLQ or class-based weighted fair queuing (CBWFQ) could have been used on the interface in addition to its use on the shaping function, simply by adding a **service-policy output policy-map-name** command under s0/0.

> **Note**   When one policy map refers to another, as in Example 5-3, the configurations are sometimes called "hierarchical" policy maps. Other times, they are called "nested" policy maps. Or, you can just think of it as how CBWFQ and LLQ can be configured for the shaping queues.

Configuring Shaping by Bandwidth Percent

The **shape** command allows the shaping rate to be stated as a percentage of the setting of the interface or subinterface **bandwidth** setting. Configuring based on a simple percentage of the bandwidth command setting seems obvious at first. However, you should keep in mind the following facts when configuring the **shape** command based on percentage of interface bandwidth:

Key Topic

- The **shape percent** command uses the bandwidth of the interface or subinterface under which it is enabled.

- Subinterfaces do not inherit the bandwidth setting of the physical interface, so if it is not set through the **bandwidth** command, it defaults to 1544.

- The Bc and Be values are configured as a number of milliseconds; the values are calculated as the number of bits that can be sent at the configured shaping rate, in the configured time period.

- Tc is set to configure the Bc value, which is in milliseconds.

Example 5-4 shows a brief example of CB Shaping configuration using percentages, including explanations of the points from the preceding list.

Example 5-4   *Shaping Based on Percent*

```
! With s0/0.1 bandwidth of 128, the rate is 50% * 128, or 64 kbps. At 64 kbps, 8000
! bits can be sent in the configured 125-ms time interval (64000 * 0.125 = 8000).
! Note that the ms parameter in the shape command is required after the Bc
! (shown) or Be (not shown), otherwise the command is rejected. Not shown: The
! Tc was set to 125 ms, the exact value configured for Bc.
policy-map percent-test
  class class-default
    shape average percent 50 125 ms
interface Serial0/1
 bandwidth 128
 service-policy output percent-test
```

CB Shaping to a Peak Rate

The **shape average** command has been used in all the examples so far. However, the command **shape peak** *mean-rate* is also allowed, which implements slightly different behavior as compared with **shape average** for the same configured rate. The key actions of the **shape peak** *mean-rate* command are summarized as follows:

Key
Topic

■   It calculates (or defaults) Bc, Be, and Tc the same way as the **shape average** command.

■   It refills Bc + Be tokens (instead of just Bc tokens) into the token bucket for each time interval.

This logic means that CB Shaping gets the right to send the committed burst, and the excess burst, every time period. As a result, the actual shaping rate is as follows:

Key
Topic

$$\text{Shaping\_rate} = \text{configured\_rate} \ (1 + Be/Bc)$$

For example, the **shape peak 64000** command, with Bc and Be defaulted to 8000 bits each, results in an actual shaping rate of 128 kbps, based on the following formula:

64 (1 + 8000/8000) = 128

$64 \times (1 + 1) = 128$

Adaptive Shaping

Adaptive shaping configuration requires only a minor amount of effort compared to the topics covered so far. To configure it, just add the **shape adaptive** *min-rate* command under the **shape** command. Example 5-5 shows a short example.

Example 5-5   *Adaptive CB Shaping Configuration*

```
policy-map shape-all
  class class-default
    shape average 96000 9600
    shape adaptive 32000
```

Policing Concepts and Configuration

Class-Based Policing (CB Policing) performs different internal processing than the older, alternative policer in Cisco router IOS, namely committed access rate (CAR). This section focuses on CB Policing, starting with concepts and then covering configuration details.

CB Policing Concepts

CB Policing is enabled for packets either entering or exiting an interface, or those entering or exiting a subinterface. It monitors, or *meters*, the bit rate of the combined packets; when a packet pushes the metered rate past the configured policing rate, the policer takes action against that packet. The most aggressive action is to discard the packet. Alternately, the policer can simply re-mark a field in the packet. This second option allows the packets through, but if congestion occurs at later places during a marked-down packet's journey, it is more likely to be discarded.

Table 5-4 lists the keywords used to imply the policer's actions.

Table 5-4   *Policing Actions Used in CB Policing*

Command Option	Mode and Function
drop	Drops the packet
set-dscp-transmit	Sets the DSCP and transmits the packet
set-prec-transmit	Sets the IP Precedence (0 to 7) and sends the packet
set-qos-transmit	Sets the QoS Group ID (1 to 99) and sends the packet
set-clp-transmit	Sets the ATM CLP bit (ATM interfaces only) and sends the packet
transmit	Sends the packet

CB Policing categorizes packets into two or three categories, depending on the style of policing, and then applies one of these actions to each category of packet. The categories are *conforming* packets, *exceeding* packets, and *violating* packets. The CB Policing logic that dictates when packets are placed into a particular category varies based on the type of policing. The next three sections outline the types of CB Policing logic.

Single-Rate, Two-Color Policing (One Bucket)

Single-rate, two-color policing is the simplest option for CB Policing. This method uses a single policing rate with no excess burst. The policer will then use only two categories (*conform* and *exceed*), defining a different action on packets of each type. (Typically, the conform action is to transmit the packet, with the exceed action either being to drop the packet or mark it down.)

While this type of policing logic is often called *single-rate, two-color* policing, it is sometimes called *single-bucket, two-color* policing because it uses a single token bucket for internal processing. Like shaping's use of token buckets, the policer's main logic relates to filling the bucket with tokens and then spending the tokens. Over time, the policer refills the bucket according to the policing rate. For example, policing at 96 kbps, over the course of 1 second, adds 12,000 tokens to the bucket. (A token represents a byte with policers, so 12,000 tokens is 96,000 bits' worth of tokens.)

CB Policing does not refill the bucket based on a time interval. Instead, CB Policing reacts to the arrival of a packet by replenishing a prorated number of tokens into the bucket. The number of tokens is defined by the following formula:

(Current_packet_arrival_time - Previous_packet_arrival_time) x Police_rate

8

Note   Note that a token represents the right to send 1 byte, so the formula includes the division by 8 to convert the units to bytes instead of bits.

refreshed

The idea behind the formula is simple—essentially, a small number of tokens are replenished before each packet is policed; the end result is that tokens are replenished at the policing rate. For example, for a police rate of 128 kbps, the policer should replenish 16,000 tokens per second. If 1 second has elapsed since the previous packet arrived, CB Policing would replenish the bucket with 16,000 tokens. If 0.1 second has passed since the previous packet had arrived, CB Policing would replenish the bucket with 0.1 second's worth of tokens, or 1600 tokens. If 0.01 second had passed, CB Policing would replenish 160 tokens at that time.

$$\frac{128,000}{8} = 16000$$

The policer then considers whether it should categorize the newly arrived packet as either conforming or exceeding the traffic contract. The policer compares the number of bytes in the packet (represented here as Xp, with "p" meaning "packet") to the number of tokens in the token bucket (represented here as Xb, with "b" meaning "bucket"). Table 5-5 shows the decision logic, along with whether the policer spends/removes tokens from the bucket.

packet < bucket = conform

Key Topic

Table 5-5   *Single-Rate, Two-Color Policing Logic for Categorizing Packets*

Category	Requirements	Tokens Drained from Bucket
Conform	If $Xp <= Xb$	Xp tokens
Exceed	If $Xp > Xb$	None

As long as the overall bit rate does not exceed the policing rate, the packets will all conform. However, if the rate is exceeded, as tokens are removed for each conforming packet, the bucket will eventually empty—causing some packets to exceed the contract. Over time, tokens are added back to the bucket, so some packets will conform. After the bit rate lowers below the policing rate, all packets will again conform to the contract.

Single-Rate, Three-Color Policer (Two Buckets)

When you want the policer to police at a particular rate, but to also support a Be, the policer uses two token buckets. It also uses all three categories for packets—conform, exceed, and violate. Combining those concepts together, such policing is typically called *single-rate, three-color policing.*

As before, CB Policing fills the buckets in reaction to packet arrival. (For lack of a better set of terms, this discussion calls the first bucket the Bc bucket, because it is Bc in size, and the other one the Be bucket, because it is Be in size.) CB Policing fills the Bc bucket just like a single-bucket model. However, if the Bc bucket has any tokens left in it, some will spill; these tokens then fill the Be bucket. Figure 5-5 shows the basic process.

Refill Bytes Upon Arrival of Packet, per Formula:
(New_packet_arrival_time - previous_packet_arrival_time) * Policed_rate / 8

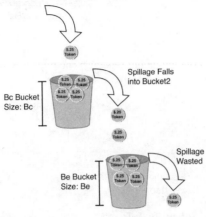

Figure 5-5 *Refilling Dual Token Buckets with CB Policing*

After filling the buckets, the policer then determines the category for the newly arrived packet, as shown in Table 5-6. In this case, X_{bc} is the number of tokens in the Bc bucket, and X_{be} is the number in the Be bucket.

Table 5-6 *Single-Rate, Three-Color Policing Logic for Categorizing Packets*

Category	Requirements	Tokens Drained from Bucket
Conform	$X_p <= X_{bc}$	X_p tokens from the Bc bucket
Exceed	$X_p > X_{bc}$ and $X_p <= X_{be}$	X_p tokens from the Be bucket
Violate	$X_p > X_{bc}$ and $X_p > X_{be}$	None

CIR   PIR

conform < exceed < violate

Two-Rate, Three-Color Policer (Two Buckets)

The third main option for CB Policing uses two separate policing rates. The lower rate is the previously discussed committed information rate (CIR), and the higher, second rate is called the *peak information rate (PIR)*. Packets that fall under the CIR conform to the traffic contract. Packets that exceed the CIR, but fall below PIR, are considered to exceed the contract. Finally, packets beyond the PIR are considered to violate the contract.

The key difference between the single-rate and dual-rate three-color policers is that the dual-rate method essentially allows sustained excess bursting. With a single-rate, three-color policer, an excess burst exists, but the burst is sustained only until the Be bucket empties. A period of relatively low activity has to occur to refill the Be bucket. With the dual-rate method, the Be bucket does not rely on spillage when filling the Bc bucket, as depicted in Figure 5-6. (Note that these buckets are sometimes called the CIR and PIR buckets with dual-rate policing.)

diff btw
single vs dual

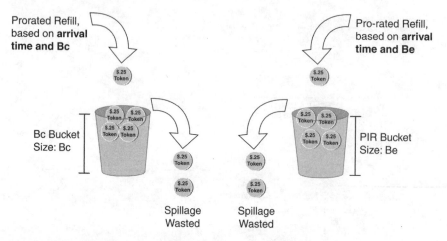

Figure 5-6   *Refilling CIR and PIR Dual Token Buckets*

The refilling of the two buckets based on two different rates is very important. For example, imagine that you set a CIR of 128 kbps (16 kilobytes/second) and a PIR of 256 kbps (32 KBps). If 0.1 second passed before the next packet arrived, the CIR bucket would be replenished with 1600 tokens (1/10 of 1 second's worth of tokens, in bytes), while the PIR bucket would be replenished with 3200 tokens. So, there are more tokens to use in the PIR bucket, as compared to the CIR bucket.

Next, the policer categorizes the packet. The only difference in logic as compared with the single-rate, three-color policer is highlighted in Table 5-7, specifically related to how tokens are consumed for conforming packets.

Table 5-7   *Two-Rate, Three-Color Policing Logic for Categorizing Packets*

Category	Requirements	Tokens Drained from Bucket
Conform	$Xp <= Xbc$	Xp tokens from the Bc bucket
		and
		Xp tokens from the Be bucket
Exceed	$Xp > Xbc$ and $Xp <= Xbe$	Xp tokens from the Be bucket
Violate	$Xp > Xbc$ and $Xp > Xbe$	None

While Table 5-7 does outline each detail, the underlying logic might not be obvious from the table. In effect, by filling the Be bucket based on the higher PIR, but also draining tokens from the Be bucket for packets that conform to the lower CIR, the Be bucket has tokens that represent the difference between the two rates.

Class-Based Policing Configuration

CB Policing uses the familiar Modular QoS CLI (MQC) commands for configuration. As a result, a policy map can police all packets using the convenient class-default class, or it can separate traffic into classes, apply different policing parameters to different classes of traffic, or even simply not police some classes.

The **police** command configures CB Policing inside a policy map. On the **police** command, you define the policing rate in bps, the **Bc** in bytes, and the **Be** in bytes, along with the actions for each category:

```
police bps burst-normal burst-max conform-action action exceed-action action
    [violate-action action]
```

Single-Rate, Three-Color Policing of All Traffic

Example 5-6 shows how to police all traffic, with criteria as follows:

- Create a single-rate, three-color policing configuration.

- All traffic is policed at 96 kbps at ingress. $\approx$ 12000bytes $\approx$ 12

- Bc of 1 second's worth of traffic is allowed.

- Be of 0.5 second's worth of traffic is allowed.

- The conform, exceed, and violate actions should be to forward, mark down to DSCP 0, and discard, respectively.

Example 5-6   *Single-Rate, Three-Color CB Policing at 96 kbps*

```
! The police command sets the rate (in bps), Bc and Be (in bytes), and the three
! actions.
policy-map police-all
   class class-default                               96000
                                                     ───── = 12000
! note: the police command wraps around to a second line.   8
   police cir 96000 bc 12000 be 6000 conform-action transmit exceed-action set-dscp-
      transmit 0 violate-action drop
!
interface Serial1/0
  encapsulation frame-relay
  service-policy input police-all
! The show command below lists statistics for each of the three categories.
ISP-edge# show policy-map interface s 1/0
  Serial1/0
  Service-policy input: police-all

    Class-map: class-default (match-any)
      8375 packets, 1446373 bytes
      30 second offered rate 113000 bps, drop rate 15000 bps
```

```
Match: any
police:
    cir 96000 bps, conform-burst 12000, excess-burst 6000
    conformed 8077 packets, 1224913 bytes; action: transmit
    exceeded 29 packets, 17948 bytes; action: set-dscp-transmit 0
    violated 269 packets, 203512 bytes; action: drop
    conformed 95000 bps, exceed 0 bps violate 20000 bps
```

The **police** command defines a single rate, but the fact that it is a three-color policing configuration, and not a two-color configuration, is not obvious at first glance. To configure a single-rate, three-color policer, you need to configure a violate action or explicitly set Be to something larger than 0.

Policing a Subset of the Traffic

One of the advantages of CB Policing is the ability to perform policing per class. Example 5-7 shows CB Policing with HTTP traffic classified and policed differently than the rest of the traffic, with the following criteria:

- Police web traffic at 80 kbps at ingress to the ISP-edge router. Transmit conforming and exceeding traffic, but discard violating traffic.

- Police all other traffic at 16 kbps at ingress to the ISP-edge router. Mark down exceeding and violating traffic to DSCP 0.

- For both classes, set Bc and Be to 1 second's worth and 0.5 second's worth of traffic, respectively.

Example 5-7 *CB Policing 80 kbps for Web Traffic, 16 kbps for the Rest with Markdown to Be, at ISP-Edge Router*

```
class-map match-all match-web
 match protocol http
! The new policy map uses the new class to match http, and class-default to
! match all other traffic.
policy-map police-web
 class match-web
    police cir 80000 bc 10000 be 5000 conform-action transmit exceed-action
       transmit
violate-action drop
 class class-default
    police cir 16000 bc 2000 be 1000 conform-action transmit exceed-action
set-dscp-transmit 0 violate-action set-dscp-transmit 0
!
interface Serial1/0
 encapsulation frame-relay
 service-policy input police-web
```

Handwritten annotations:
1s => bc = 10000 byts
0.5s => be = 5000 byte

CB Policing Defaults for Bc and Be

If you do not configure a Bc value on the **police** command, CB Policing configures a default value equivalent to the bytes that could be sent in 1/4 second at the defined policing rate. The formula is as follows:

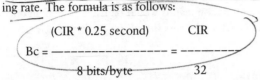

$$Bc = \frac{(CIR * 0.25 \text{ second})}{8 \text{ bits/byte}} = \frac{CIR}{32}$$

The only part that might not be obvious is the division by 8 on the left—that is simply for the conversion from bits to bytes. The math reduces to CIR/32. Also, if the formula yields a number less than 1500, CB Policing uses a Bc of 1500.

If the **police** command does not include a Be value, the default Be setting depends on the type of policing. Table 5-8 summarizes the details.

Key Topic

Table 5-8   *Setting CB Policing Bc and Be Defaults*

Type of Policing Configuration	Telltale Signs in the police Command	Defaults
Single-rate, two-color	No **violate-action** configured	Bc = CIR/32; Be = 0
Single-rate, three-color	**violate-action** is configured	Bc = CIR/32; Be = Bc
Dual-rate, three-color	PIR is configured	Bc = CIR/32; Be = PIR/32

Configuring Dual-Rate Policing

Dual-rate CB Policing requires the same MQC commands, but with slightly different syntax on the **police** command, as shown here:

```
police ({cir} cir} [bc conform-burst] {pir} pir} [be peak-burst]
   [conform-action action [exceed-action action [violate-action action]]]
```

Note that the syntax of this command requires configuration of both the CIR and a PIR because the curly brackets mean that the parameter is required. The command includes a place to set the Bc value and the Be value as well, plus the same set of options for conform, exceed, and violate actions. For example, if you wanted to perform dual-rate policing, with a CIR of 96 kbps and a PIR of 128 kbps, you would simply use a command like **police cir 96000 pir 128000**, with optional settings of Bc and Be, plus the settings for the actions for each of the three categories.

Multi-Action Policing

When CB Policing re-marks packets instead of discarding them, the design might call for marking more than one field in a packet. Marking multiple fields in the same packet with CB Policing is called *multi-action policing*.

The **police** command uses a slightly different syntax to implement multi-action policing. By omitting the actions from the command, the **police** command places the user into a policing subconfiguration mode in which the actions can be added through separate commands (the **conform-action**, **exceed-action**, and **violate-action** commands). To configure multiple actions, one of these three **action** commands would be used more than once, as shown in Example 5-8, which marks DSCP 0 and sets FR DE for packets that violate the traffic contract.

Example 5-8 *Multi-Action Policing*

```
R3# conf t
Enter configuration commands, one per line.  End with CNTL/Z.
R3(config)# policy-map testpoll
R3(config-pmap)# class class-default
! This command implements dual-rate policing as well, but it is not required
R3(config-pmap-c)# police 128000 256000
R3(config-pmap-c-police)# conform-action transmit
R3(config-pmap-c-police)# exceed-action transmit
R3(config-pmap-c-police)# violate-action set-dscp-transmit 0
R3(config-pmap-c-police)# violate-action set-frde-transmit
```

Policing by Percentage

As it does with the **shape** command, Cisco IOS supports configuring policing rates as a percentage of link bandwidth. The Bc and Be values are configured as a number of milliseconds, from which IOS calculates the actual Bc and Be values based on how many bits can be sent in that many milliseconds. Example 5-9 shows an example of a dual-rate policing configuration using the **percentage** option.

Example 5-9 *Configuring Percentage-Based Policing*

```
R3# show running-config
! Portions omitted for Brevity
 policy-map test-pol6
  class class-default
   police cir percent 25 bc 500 ms pir percent 50 be 500 ms conform transmit exceed
      transmit        violate drop
!
interface serial0/0
 bandwidth 256
 service-policy output test-pol6
! The output below shows the configured percentage for the rate and the time for
! Bc and Be, with the calculated values immediately below.
R3# show policy-map interface s0/0
! lines omitted for brevity
      police:
           cir 25 % bc 500 ms
```

$256 \times 0.125 = 64000$ bps

```
    cir 64000 bps, bc 4000 bytes
    pir 50 % be 500 ms
    pir (128000 bps), be 8000 bytes
! lines omitted       L  256×0,5= 128 kbps
```

Committed Access Rate

CAR implements single-rate, two-color policing. As compared with that same option in
CB Policing, CAR and CB Policing have many similarities. They both can police traffic
either entering or exiting an interface or subinterface; they can both police subsets of
that traffic based on classification logic; and they both set the rate in bps, with Bc and Be
configured as a number of bytes.

both egress & ingress

CAR differs from CB Policing regarding four main features, as follows: *Diff. btw CAR& CB policing*

■ CAR uses the **rate-limit** command, which is not part of the MQC set of commands.

■ CAR has a feature called *cascaded* or *nested* **rate-limit** commands, which allows
multiple **rate-limit** commands on an interface to process the same packet.

■ CAR does support Be; however, even in this case, it still supports only conform and
exceed categories, and never supports a third (violate) category.

■ When CAR has a Be configured, the internal logic used to determine which packets
conform and exceed differs as compared with CB Policing.

CAR puts most parameters on the **rate-limit** command, which is added under an interface
or subinterface:

```
rate-limit {input | output} [access-group [rate-limit] acl-index] bps burst-
    normal burst-max conform-action conform-action exceed-action exceed-action
```

Example 5-10 shows an example CAR configuration for perspective. The criteria for the
CAR configuration in Example 5-10 are as follows:

■ All traffic is policed at 96 kbps at ingress to the ISP-edge router.

■ Bc of 1 second's worth of traffic is allowed.

■ Be of 0.5 second's worth of traffic is allowed.

■ Traffic that exceeds the contract is discarded.

■ Traffic that conforms to the contract is forwarded with Precedence reset to 0.

Example 5-10   *CAR at 96 kbps at ISP-Edge Router*

```
! The rate-limit command omits the access-group option, meaning that it has no
! matching parameters, so all packets are considered to match the command. The rest
! of the options simply match the requirements.
interface Serial1/0.1 point-to-point
```

```
ip address 192.168.2.251 255.255.255.0
! note: the rate-limit command wraps around to a second line.
 rate-limit input 96000 12000 18000 conform-action set-prec-transmit 0
   exceed-action drop
 frame-relay interface-dlci 103
! The output below confirms the parameters, including matching all traffic.
ISP-edge# show interfaces s 1/0.1 rate-limit
  Input
    matches: all traffic
      params:  96000 bps, 12000 limit, 18000 extended limit
      conformed 2290 packets, 430018 bytes; action: set-prec-transmit 0
      exceeded 230 packets, 67681 bytes; action: drop
      last packet: 0ms ago, current burst: 13428 bytes
last cleared 00:02:16 ago, conformed 25000 bps, exceeded 3000 bps
```

To classify traffic, CAR requires the use of either a normal access control list (ACL) or a *rate-limit ACL*. A rate-limit ACL can match Multiprotocol Label Switching (MPLS) Experimental bits, IP Precedence, or MAC Address. For other fields, an IP ACL must be used. Example 5-11 shows an example in which CAR polices three different subsets of traffic using ACLs for matching the traffic, as well as limiting the overall traffic rate. The criteria for this example are as follows (note that CAR allows only policing rates that are multiples of 8 kbps):

- Police all traffic on the interface at 496 kbps, but before sending this traffic on its way...

- Police all web traffic at 400 kbps.

- Police all FTP traffic at 160 kbps.

- Police all VoIP traffic at 200 kbps.

- Choose Bc and Be so that Bc has 1 second's worth of traffic and Be provides no additional burst capability over Bc.

Example 5-11 *Cascaded CAR rate-limit Commands, with Subclassifications*

```
! ACL 101 matches all HTTP traffic
! ACL 102 matches all FTP traffic
! ACL 103 matches all VoIP traffic
interface s 0/0
rate-limit input 496000 62000 62000 conform-action continue exceed-action drop
rate-limit input access-group 101 400000 50000 50000 conform-action transmit
   exceed-action drop
rate-limit input access-group 102 160000 20000 20000 conform-action transmit
   exceed-action drop
rate-limit input access-group 103 200000 25000 25000 conform-action transmit
   exceed-action drop
```

The CAR configuration refers to IP ACLs to classify the traffic, using three different IP ACLs in this case. ACL 101 matches all web traffic, ACL 102 matches all FTP traffic, and ACL 103 matches all VoIP traffic.

Under subinterface S0/0.1, four **rate-limit** commands are used. The first sets the rate for all traffic, dropping traffic that exceeds 496 kbps. However, the conform action is "continue." This means that packets conforming to this statement will be compared to the next **rate-limit** statements, and when matching a statement, some other action will be taken. For example, web traffic matches the second **rate-limit** command, with a resulting action of either transmit or drop. VoIP traffic would be compared with the next three **rate-limit** commands before matching the last one. As a result, all traffic is limited to 496 kbps, and three particular subsets of traffic are prevented from taking all the bandwidth.

CB Policing can achieve the same effect of policing subsets of traffic by using nested policy maps.

Hierarchical Queuing Framework (HQF)

Thus far we have discussed the deployment of our quality of service mechanism through the use of the MQC. It is the MQC that provides a means to configure QoS using a generic command-line interface to all types of interfaces and protocols. MQC is important because it is the mechanism of choice used to configure HQF for queuing and shaping.

HQF is a logical engine used to support QoS features. The HQF hierarchy is a tree structure that is built using policy maps. When data passes through an interface using HQF, the data is classified so that it traverses the branches of the tree. Data arrives at the top of the tree and is classified on one of the leaves. Data then traverses down the hierarchy (tree) until it is transmitted out the interface at the root (trunk).

Example 5-12 illustrates how to build a QoS hierarchy.

Example 5-12   *QoS Hierarchy*

```
policy-map class
 class c1
  bandwidth 14
 class c2
  bandwidth 18

policy-map map1
 class class-default
  shape average 64000
  service-policy class

policy-map map2
 class class-default
  shape average 96000
```

Check out the diagram explaining the config on page 284

```
map-class frame-relay fr1
 service-policy output map1

map-class frame fr2
 service-policy output map2

interface serial4/1
 encapsulation frame-relay
 frame-relay interface-dlci 16
  class fr1
 frame-relay interface-dlci 17
  class fr2
```

The command-line entries in Example 5-15 act to create a structured application of QoS mechanisms; the nature of this structure can be seen in Figure 5-7.

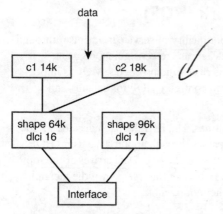

Figure 5-7   *HQF Tree Structure*

Now that we understand what the structure looks like, we need to underline the main benefits of the structure. QoS Hierarchical Queuing Framework allows for faster deployment of QoS queuing and shaping in large-scale networks. Furthermore, it also enables consistent queuing behavior that can be applied with a common MQC across all main Cisco IOS Software releases, making implementation of QoS easier and transparent regardless of the Cisco IOS Software release being used.

HQF has built-in functionality that supports both distributed and nondistributed implementations, providing consistency of QoS feature behavior across all software-forwarding hardware, thus making implementation of QoS easier and transparent, regardless of the platform being used. This consistency of behavior we are describing results in accelerated delivery of feature enhancements and new QoS features in different Cisco IOS Software releases through different hardware deployments. In addition, advantages of HQF include multiple levels of packet scheduling and support for integrated Class-Based Shaping and queuing, as well as the ability to apply fair queuing and drop policies on a per-class basis.

These benefits are all made possible in the context of HQF because of new functionality that has been introduced. These features include the placement of hierarchical policies with queuing features situated at every level of the HQF structure. This translates into the ability to apply Class-Based Queuing to any traffic class in the parent or child level of a hierarchical policy while simultaneously creating discrete service levels for different sessions or subscribers.

In Example 5-13, we see that traffic belonging to class parent-c2 has more scheduling time than class parent-c1.

Example 5-13 *QoS Hierarchy*

```
policy-map class
 class c1
  bandwidth 14
 class c2
  bandwidth 18

policy-map map1
 policy-map child
 class child-c1
  bandwidth 400
 class child-c2
  bandwidth 400

policy-map parent
 class parent-c1
  bandwidth 1000
  service-policy child
 class parent-c2
  bandwidth 2000
  service-policy child
```

There are a number of behavioral changes that are also part of HFQ that sets it apart from traditional MQC. These changes are discussed in the following sections.

Flow-Based Fair-Queuing Support in Class-Default   ⁊ BFQ

The fair-queuing behavior for the class-default class is flow based. This is a change from the weighted fair queuing (WFQ) behavior in previous releases. With flow-based fair queuing, the flow queues in the class-default class are scheduled equally instead of by weight based on the IP Precedence bits.

Default Queuing Implementation for Class-Default

When you do not explicitly configure the class-default class in a policy map, its default queuing behavior is first in, first out (FIFO). You can configure the **bandwidth, fair-queue,** or **service-policy** commands in the class-default class to achieve different queuing behaviors.

Class-Default and Bandwidth

The bandwidth assigned to the class-default class is the unused interface bandwidth not consumed by user-defined classes. By default, the class-default class receives a minimum of 1 percent of the interface bandwidth.

Default Queuing Implementation for Shape Class

When you configure the **shape** command in a class, the default queuing behavior for the shape queue is FIFO instead of weighted fair queuing (WFQ). You can configure the **bandwidth, fair-queue,** or **service-policy** commands in shape class to achieve different queuing behaviors.

Policy Map and Interface Bandwidth

In HQF, a policy map can reserve up to 100 percent of the interface bandwidth. If you do not assign an explicit bandwidth guarantee to the class-default class, you can assign a maximum of 99 percent of the interface bandwidth to user-defined classes and reserve the other 1 percent for the class-default class.

If you are migrating to Cisco IOS Release 12.4(20)T and the configured policy map allocates 100 percent of the bandwidth to the user-defined classes, an error message appears in the console after booting the HQF image. The message indicates that the allocated bandwidth exceeds the allowable amount, and the service policy is rejected. In HQF, you must reconfigure the policy to account for the minimum 1 percent bandwidth guaranteed for the class-default. Then you can apply a service policy to the interface.

Per-Flow Queue Limit in Fair Queue

In HQF, when you enable fair queuing, the default per-flow queue limit is 1/4 of the class queue limit. If you do not enable the queue limit in a class, the default per-flow queue limit is 16 packets (1/4 of 64).

Oversubscription Support for Multiple Policies on Logical Interfaces

When you attach a shaping policy to multiple logical interfaces including a subinterface, and the sum of the shape rate exceeds the physical interface bandwidth, congestion at the physical interface results in back pressure to each logical interface policy. This back pressure causes each policy to reduce the output rate to its fair share of the interface bandwidth.

Shaping on a GRE Tunnel

In HQF, you can apply the shaping to a generic routing encapsulation (GRE) tunnel by using a hierarchical service policy after encapsulation. This means that the shape rate is based on packets with tunnel encapsulation and L2 encapsulation.

When configuring the shape feature in the parent policy applied to the tunnel interface, you can use the class-default class only. You cannot configure a user-defined class in the parent policy.

Some QoS deployments include a service policy with queuing features applied at the tunnel or a virtual interface and a service policy with queuing features applied at the physical interface. You can apply a service policy with queuing features only at one of these interfaces.

Nested Policy and Reference Bandwidth for Child-Policy

In HQF, when you configure a nested policy with a child queuing policy under a parent shaping class, the reference bandwidth for the child queuing policy is taken from the following: minimum (parent shaper rate, parent class's implicit/explicit bandwidth guarantee). When you do not define bandwidth for the parent class, the interface bandwidth divides equally among all parent classes as the implicit bandwidth guarantee.

Handling Traffic Congestion on an Interface Configured with Policy Map

If an interface configured with a policy map is full of heavy traffic, the implicitly defined policer allows the traffic as defined in the **bandwidth** statement of each traffic class. The policer is activated whenever there is traffic congestion on an interface.

QoS Troubleshooting and Commands

QoS problems are almost all administrator related and typically result from one of three causes:

- A lack of proper prior planning for the QoS requirements of your network, resulting in an improper QoS configuration

- Failure to track changes in network applications and network traffic, resulting in an outdated QoS configuration

- A lack of good network documentation (or a failure to check that documentation before adding a device or application to the network)

The focus of this section is to provide you with a set of Cisco IOS–based tools, beyond the more common ones that you already know, as well as some guidance on the troubleshooting process for QoS issues that you might encounter. In the CCIE R&S lab exam, you will encounter an array of troubleshooting situations that require you to have mastered fast, efficient, and thorough troubleshooting skills. In the written exam, you'll need a different set of skills (mainly the knowledge of troubleshooting techniques that are specific to Cisco routers and switches, and the ability to interpret the output of various **show** commands and possibly **debug** output). You can also expect to be given an example along with a problem statement. You will need to quickly narrow the question down to possible solutions and then pinpoint the final solution.

You should expect, as in all CCIE exams, that the easiest or most direct ways to a solution might be unavailable to you. In troubleshooting, perhaps the easiest way to the source of most problems is through the **show run** command or variations on it. Therefore, we'll institute a simple "no **show run**" rule in this section that will force you to use your knowledge of more in-depth troubleshooting commands in the Cisco IOS portion of this section.

In addition, you can expect that the issues that you'll face in this part of the written exam will need more than one command or step to isolate and resolve.

Troubleshooting Slow Application Response

You have a QoS policy enabled in your network, but users have begun complaining about slow response to a particular application. First, examine your policy to ensure that you are allocating enough bandwidth for that application. Check the bandwidth, latency, and drop requirements for the application, and then look at your documentation to see whether your policy supplies these.

If it does, you might want to verify the response time using IP service-level agreements (SLA). IP SLA was explained in Volume 1, Chapter 5, "IP Services." Set it up on the routers or switches closest to the traffic source and destination, using the application's destination port number. Schedule it to run, and then verify the results with the **show ip sla statistics** command. If the response time is indeed slow but your documentation shows that you have properly set up the policy, check that the QoS policy is configured on each hop in the network. In a large network, you should have a management tool that allows you to check QoS configuration and operation. If you are doing it manually, however, the **show policy-map** command displays your configured policy maps, and **show class-map** displays the associated class maps. The **show policy-map interface** command is a great way to see which policies are applied at which interfaces, and what actions they are taking.

For example, suppose that your users are complaining about Citrix response times. Your documentation shows that the network's QoS policy has the following basic settings:

- **Voice queue:** Prioritize and allocate bandwidth

- **Citrix queue:** Allocate bandwidth to typical Citrix ports such as 1494 and 2512

- **Web queue:** Allocate limited bandwidth to ports 80 and 443

- **Default queue:** Allocate bandwidth to all other traffic

The network performed well until a popular new Internet video came out that was streamed over port 80. The administrator who created the QoS policy didn't realize that Citrix also uses ports 80 and 443. The **show policy-map interface** command showed that web queue was filling up, so Citrix traffic was being delayed or dropped along with the normal Internet traffic. You could pinpoint this by turning on Network-Based Application Recognition (NBAR) to learn what types of traffic are traversing the interfaces. Use the **show ip nbar protocol-discovery** command to see the traffic types found.

One solution is to classify Citrix traffic using NBAR rather than port numbers. Classification using NBAR is explained in Chapter 3, "Classification and Marking."

Troubleshooting Voice and Video Problems

Introducing voice/video over IP into the network is the impetus for many companies to institute QoS. Cisco has made this easy with the AutoQoS function for voice. Adding video is trickier because it has the latency constraints of voice, but can handle drops better. Plus, streaming one-way video uses bandwidth differently than interactive video, so your QoS policy must allow for that.

If you are experiencing poor voice or video quality, you can check several QoS-related items on both switches and routers:

- Verify that QoS is enabled and that either AutoQoS or manual policies are configured. The **show mls qos** command will tell you whether QoS is enabled.

- Examine the QoS policy maps and class maps to ensure correct configuration with the **show policy-map** and **show class-map** commands. Verify that voice and video are classified correctly and guaranteed appropriate bandwidth.

- Examine the results of the service policy using the **show policy-map interface** command.

- Possibly use IP SLA between various pairs of devices to narrow down the problem location.

Troubleshooting techniques unique to switches include the following:

- Make sure an expedite (or priority) queue has been enabled both for ingress and egress traffic. Use the **show mls qos input-queue** command for ingress queues and the **show mls qos** *interface* **queueing** command for egress queues.

- Make sure that the correct traffic is being mapped into the correct queues. For input queues, the command is **show mls qos maps cos-input-q**. On a 3560 switch, CoS 5 is mapped to ingress queue 2 by default, so if queue 1 is your priority queue and you have not changed the default mapping, that will be a problem. For egress queues, the command is **show mls qos maps cos-output-q**. On egress queues, CoS 5 is mapped to queue 1 by default.

- Make sure that the CoS values are being mapped to the correct internal Differentiated Services Code Point (DSCP) values, and that the DSCP values are in turn being mapped back to the correct class of service (CoS) values. For CoS-to-DSCP mapping, use the **show mls qos maps cos-dscp** command. For DSCP-to-CoS mapping, use the **show mls qos maps dscp-cos** command. (See Chapter 4, "Congestion Management and Avoidance," for a review of switch queuing and examples of output from these commands.)

Routers have some other troubleshooting spots:

- Viewing the CoS-to-DSCP mapping on a router is easier than on a switch because it uses just one command: **show mls qos maps**.

- If traffic shaping is enabled on a WAN interface, make sure that the time interval (Tc) is tuned down to 10 ms. Otherwise you might induce too much latency, resulting in bad voice and video quality. You can use the **show traffic-shape** command to determine this setting.

- If your WAN service provider has different levels of service, make sure that your voice and video traffic are marked correctly to map to its queue.

Other QoS Troubleshooting Tips

Even networks with properly configured QoS can run into problems that are, at least indirectly, caused by QoS. One issue that especially shows up in networks where people and offices move frequently is because of either a lack of documentation or a network administrator not checking the documentation.

Suppose, for example, that you have a switch that was dedicated to user ports but some of the users have moved to a different location. You now need some ports for printers or servers. All the switch ports are set up with AutoQoS for voice, and with input and egress expedite queues. If the administrator just connects a printer or server to one of those ports, performance will not be optimal. There is only one type of traffic going through those ports, so only one ingress and one egress queue are needed. Also, there is no need to introduce the latency, however minimal, involved in attempting to map the nonexistent input CoS to a queue. The port should be reconfigured as a data port, with just one queue. A quick way to remove all configuration from an interface is to use the global command **default interface** *interface*.

Network applications change, and a network set up for good QoS operation today might need something different tomorrow. Monitor your network traffic and QoS impact. Review the monitoring results periodically. Consider whether any policy changes will be necessary before introducing a new application into the network, or upgrading an existing one.

Approaches to Resolving QoS Issues

In this final section of the chapter, we present a table with several generalized types of issues and ways of approaching them, including the relevant Cisco IOS commands. Table 5-9 summarizes these techniques.

Table 5-9   *Troubleshooting Approach and Commands*

Problem	Approach	Helpful IOS Commands
Troubleshooting possible QoS misconfiguration on either a router or a switch (commands common to both)	Verify that QoS is enabled.	show mls qos
	Verify the class map configuration.	show class-map
	Verify the policy map configuration.	show policy-map
		show policy-map interface *interface*
	Verify the operation of the service policy.	
Possible switch QoS misconfiguration	Use **show** commands to determine how interface input and egress queuing are configured.	show mls qos input-queue
		show mls qos interface *interface* queueing
		show mls qos maps cos-input-q
		show mls qos maps cos-output-q
		show mls qos maps cos-dscp
		show mls qos maps dscp-cos
Possible router QoS misconfiguration	Use **show** commands to determine how queuing is configured.	show mls qos maps
		show traffic-shape

Foundation Summary

This section lists additional details and facts to round out the coverage of the topics in this chapter. Unlike most of the Cisco Press Exam Certification Guides, this "Foundation Summary" does not repeat information presented in the "Foundation Topics" section of the chapter. Please take the time to read and study the details in the "Foundation Topics" section of the chapter, as well as review items noted with a Key Topic icon.

Table 5-10 lists commands related to CB Shaping.

Table 5-10 *Class-Based and Generic Shaping Command Reference*

Command	Mode and Function
traffic-shape rate shaped-rate [*Bc*] [*Be*] [*buffer-limit*]	Interface command to enable Generic Traffic Shaping
shape [**average** | **peak**] mean-rate [[*burst-size*] [*excess-burst-size*]]	Class configuration mode; enables shaping for the class
shape [**average** | **peak**] **percent** *percent* [[*burst- size*] [*excess-burst-size*]]	Enables shaping based on percentage of bandwidth
shape adaptive *min-rate*	Enables the minimum rate for adaptive shaping
shape fecn-adapt	Causes reflection of BECN bits after receipt of an FECN
service-policy {**input** | **output**} *policy-map-name*	Interface or subinterface configuration mode; enables CB Shaping on the interface
shape max-buffers number-of-buffers	Sets the maximum queue length for the default FIFO shaping queue
show policy-map *policy-map-name*	Lists configuration information about all MQC-based QoS tools
show policy-map *interface-spec* [**input** | **output**] [**class** *class-name*]	Lists statistical information about the behavior of all MQC-based QoS tools

Table 5-11 provides a command reference for CB Policing.

Table 5-11 *Class-Based Policing Command Reference*

Command	Mode and Function
police *bps burst-normal burst-max* **conform-action** *action* **exceed-action** *action* [**violate-action** *action*]	**policy-map** class subcommand; enables policing for the class
police cir percent *percent* [**bc** *conform-burst-in-msec*] [**pir percent** *percent*] [**be** *peak-burst-in-msec*] [**conform-action** *action* [**exceed-action** *action* [**violate-action** *action*]]]	**policy-map** class subcommand; enables policing using percentages of bandwidth

Command	Mode and Function
police {**cir** *cir*} [**bc** *conform-burst*] {**pir** *pir*} [**be** *peak-burst*] [**conform-action** *action* [**exceed-action** *action* [**violate-action** *action*]]]	**policy-map** class subcommand; enables dual-rate policing
service-policy {**input** | **output**} *policy-map-name*	Enables CB Policing on an interface or subinterface

Memory Builders

The CCIE Routing and Switching written exam, like all Cisco CCIE written exams, covers a fairly broad set of topics. This section provides some basic tools to help you exercise your memory about some of the broader topics covered in this chapter.

Fill In Key Tables from Memory

Appendix E, "Key Tables for CCIE Study," on the CD in the back of this book, contains empty sets of some of the key summary tables in each chapter. Print Appendix E, refer to this chapter's tables in it, and fill in the tables from memory. Refer to Appendix F, "Solutions for Key Tables for CCIE Study," on the CD, to check your answers.

Definitions

Next, take a few moments to write down the definitions for the following terms:

Tc, Bc, Be, CIR, GTS shaping rate, policing rate, token bucket, Bc bucket, Be bucket, adaptive shaping, BECN, ForeSight, ELMI, mincir, map class, marking down, single-rate two-color policer, single-rate three-color policer, dual-rate three-color policer, conform, exceed, violate, traffic contract, dual token bucket, PIR, nested policy maps, multi-action policing

Refer to the glossary to check your answers.

Further Reading

Cisco QoS Exam Certification Guide, by Wendell Odom and Michael Cavanaugh

Cisco IOS Quality of Service Solutions Configuration Guide, www.cisco.com/en/US/docs/ios/qos/configuration/guide/12_4/qos_12_4_book.html

Blueprint topics covered in this chapter:

This chapter covers the following topics from the Cisco CCIE Routing and Switching written exam blueprint:

- HDLC
- PPP
- Ethernet WAN

CHAPTER 6

Wide-Area Networks

This chapter covers several protocols and details about two of the most commonly used data link layer protocols in wide-area networks (WAN): Point-to-Point Protocol (PPP) and Ethernet WAN.

"Do I Know This Already?" Quiz

Table 6-1 outlines the major headings in this chapter and the corresponding "Do I Know This Already?" quiz questions.

Table 6-1 *"Do I Know This Already?" Foundation Topics Section-to-Question Mapping*

Foundation Topics Section	Questions Covered in This Section	Score
Point-to-Point Protocol	1–3	
PPPoE	4, 5	
Metro-Ethernet	6	
Total Score		

To best use this pre-chapter assessment, remember to score yourself strictly. You can find the answers in Appendix A, "Answers to the 'Do I Know This Already?' Quizzes."

1. Imagine that a PPP link failed and has just recovered. Which of the following features is negotiated last?

   a. CHAP authentication

   b. RTP header compression

   c. Looped link detection

   d. Link Quality Monitoring

2. Interfaces s0/0, s0/1, and s1/0 are up and working as part of a multilink PPP bundle that connects to another router. The multilink interface has a bandwidth setting of 1536. When a 1500-byte packet is routed out the multilink interface, which of the following determines out which link the packet will flow?

   a. The current CEF FIB and CEF load-balancing method.

   b. The current fast-switching cache.

   c. The packet is sent out one interface based on round-robin scheduling.

   d. One fragment is sent over each of the three links.

3. R1 and R2 connect over a leased line, with each interface using its s0/1 interface. When configuring CHAP to use a locally defined name and password, which of the following statements are false about the commands and configuration mode in which they are configured?

   a. The **encapsulation ppp** interface subcommand

   b. The **ppp authentication chap** interface subcommand

   c. The **username** *R1* **password** *samepassword* global command on R1

   d. The **username** *R2* **password** *samepassword* interface subcommand on R2

4. At a minimum, what command must be entered on the PPPoE server to support remote connections from clients?

   a. **ip dhcp**

   b. **ip address**

   c. **no virtual-reassembly**

   d. **ip unnumbered**

   e. **ip peer default ip address**

5. PPP headers add how much additional overhead to each frame?

   a. 4 bytes

   b. 6 bytes

   c. 8 bytes

   d. No overhead is added.

6. Which one of the following architectural requirements is not part of the VPLS forwarding operation?

   a. Autodiscovery of provider edges

   b. Signaling of pseudo-wires used to connect to VSIs

   c. Loop prevention

   d. Static configuration of the provider edge

   e. MAC address withdrawal

Foundation Topics

Layer 2 Protocols

The two most popular Layer 2 protocols used on point-to-point links are *High-Level Data Link Control (HDLC)* and *Point-to-Point Protocol (PPP).* The ISO standard for the much older HDLC does not include a Type field, so the Cisco HDLC implementation adds a Cisco-proprietary 2-byte Type field to support multiple protocols over an HDLC link. It is this Cisco-proprietary version of HDLC that is the default serial interface encapsulation used on Cisco routers.

[handwritten: 1. HDLC 2. PPP]

[handwritten: default encaps. on Cisco serial if.]

Key Topic

HDLC

The default serial encapsulation on Cisco routers is Cisco HDLC, so it does not need to be explicitly configured on the router. As a result, the encapsulation type is not displayed in the configuration.

With a back-to-back serial connection, the router connected to the data communications equipment (DCE) end of the cable provides the clock signal for the serial link. The **clockrate** command in the interface configuration mode enables the router at the DCE end of the cable (R1, in this example) to provide the clock signal for the serial link. Issue the **show controllers** command to determine which end of the cable is connected to the serial interface.

[handwritten: Show CONTROLLER, shows who is DCE]

In Example 6-1, the DCE end of the cable is connected to R1, and the data terminal equipment (DTE) end is connected to R2. The clock rate is now part of the default configuration of our serial interfaces, and will be applied automatically. However, it is still necessary to understand that you can manipulate this value on a case-by-case basis, depending on the environment in which your devices are installed.

Example 6-1   *HDLC Configuration*

```
! First we will apply the ip address to R1
! and "no shut" the interface
R1(config)# interface serial0/0
R1(config-if)# ip address 10.1.12.1 255.255.255.0
R1(config-if)# no shut
R1(config-if)#
! Now we will do the same for R2
R2# conf t
R2(config)# interface serial0/0
R2(config-if)# ip address 10.1.12.2 255.255.255.0
R2(config-if)# no shut
```

There are only a few commands that we need to utilize to verify this configuration:

- show controllers

- ping

- show interface

The output shown in Example 6-2 illustrates the results of these commands used in this sample configuration.

Example 6-2   *HDLC Configuration*

```
! Show controllers on R1:
R1# show controllers serial 0/0
Interface Serial0/0
Hardware is GT96K
DCE 530, clock rate 2000000
! ---- Output Omitted ----
!
! Now for the Ping test from R1 to R2:
!
R1# ping 10.1.12.2

Type escape sequence to abort.
Sending 5, 100-byte ICMP Echos to 10.1.12.2, timeout is 2 seconds:
!!!!!
Success rate is 100 percent (5/5), round-trip min/avg/max = 1/2/4 ms
R1#
!
! Lastly we will look at the output of the show interface serial 0/0 command on R1:
!
R1# show interface serial 0/0
Serial0/0 is up, line protocol is up
  Hardware is GT96K Serial
  Internet address is 10.1.12.1/24
  MTU 1500 bytes, BW 1544 Kbit/sec, DLY 20000 usec,
     reliability 255/255, txload 1/255, rxload 1/255
  Encapsulation HDLC, loopback not set
!
! Notice that the above output indicates that we are running HDLC Encapsulation
!
  Keepalive set (10 sec)
  CRC checking enabled
  Last input 00:00:01, output 00:00:02, output hang never
  Last clearing of "show interface" counters never
  Input queue: 0/75/0/0 (size/max/drops/flushes); Total output drops: 0
  Queueing strategy: weighted fair
```

[handwritten annotation: shows clock rate]

```
Output queue: 0/1000/64/0 (size/max total/threshold/drops)
   Conversations  0/1/256 (active/max active/max total)
   Reserved Conversations 0/0 (allocated/max allocated)
   Available Bandwidth 1158 kilobits/sec
 5 minute input rate 0 bits/sec, 0 packets/sec
 5 minute output rate 0 bits/sec, 0 packets/sec
   129 packets input, 8280 bytes, 0 no buffer
   Received 124 broadcasts, 0 runts, 0 giants, 0 throttles
   0 input errors, 0 CRC, 0 frame, 0 overrun, 0 ignored, 0 abort
   133 packets output, 8665 bytes, 0 underruns
   0 output errors, 0 collisions, 7 interface resets
   0 unknown protocol drops
   0 output buffer failures, 0 output buffers swapped out
   0 carrier transitions
   DCD=up  DSR=up  DTR=up  RTS=up  CTS=up
```

Point-to-Point Protocol

PPP, defined in RFC 1661, includes an architected Protocol field, plus a long list of rich features. Table 6-2 points out some of the key comparison points of these two protocols.

Table 6-2   *HDLC and PPP Comparisons*

Feature	HDLC	PPP
Error detection?	Yes	Yes
Error recovery?	No	Yes*
Standard Protocol Type field?	No	Yes
Defaults on IOS serial links?	Yes	No
Supports synchronous and asynchronous links?	No	Yes

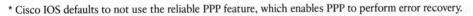

* Cisco IOS defaults to not use the reliable PPP feature, which enables PPP to perform error recovery.

PPP framing (RFC 1662) defines the use of a simple HDLC header and trailer for most parts of the PPP framing, as shown in Figure 6-1. PPP simply adds the Protocol field and optional Padding field to the original HDLC framing. (The Padding field allows PPP to ensure that the frame has an even number of bytes.)

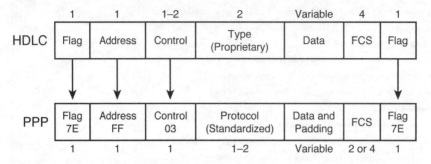

Figure 6-1 *HDLC and PPP Framing Compared*

PPP Link Control Protocol

PPP standards can be separated into two broad categories—those features unrelated to any specific Layer 3 protocol and those specific to a Layer 3 protocol. The PPP *Link Control Protocol (LCP)* controls the features independent of any specific Layer 3 protocol. For each Layer 3 protocol supported by PPP, PPP defines a *Network Control Protocol (NCP)*. For example, the PPP Internet Protocol Control Protocol (IPCP) defines PPP features for IP, such as dynamic address assignment.

When a PPP serial link first comes up—for example, when a router senses the Clear to Send (CTS), Data Send Read (DSR), and Data Carrier Detect (DCD) leads come up at the physical layer—LCP begins parameter negotiation with the other end of the link. For example, LCP controls the negotiation of which authentication methods to attempt, and in what order, and then allows the authentication protocol (for example, Challenge Handshake Authentication Protocol) to complete its work. After all LCP negotiation has completed successfully, LCP is considered to be "up." At that point, PPP begins each Layer 3 Control Protocol.

Table 6-3 lists and briefly describes some of the key features of LCP. Following that, several of the key LCP features are covered in more detail.

Table 6-3 *PPP LCP Features*

Function	Description
Link Quality Monitoring (LQM)	LCP exchanges statistics about the percentage of frames received without any errors; if the percentage falls below a configured value, the link is dropped.
Looped link detection	Each router generates and sends a randomly chosen magic number. If a router receives its own magic number, the link is looped and might be taken down.
Layer 2 load balancing	Multilink PPP (MLP) balances traffic by fragmenting each frame into one fragment per link, and sending one fragment over each link.
Authentication	Supports CHAP and PAP.

Basic LCP/PPP Configuration

PPP can be configured with a minimal number of commands, requiring only an **encapsulation ppp** command on each router on opposite ends of the link. Example 6-3 shows a simple configuration with basic PPP encapsulation, plus the optional LQM and CHAP authentication features. For this configuration, Routers R3 and R4 connect to each other's s0/1/0 interfaces.

Example 6-3   *PPP Configuration with LQM and CHAP*

```
! R3 configuration is first. The username/password could be held in a AAA server,
! but is shown here as a local username/password. The other router (R4) sends
! its name "R4" with R3 being configured with that username and password setting.
username R4 password 0 rom838
!!!!!!!!!!!!!!!!!!!!!!!!!!!!!!!!!!!!!!!!!!!!!!!!!!!!!!!!!!!!!!!!!!!!!!!!!!!!!!!!!!!!!!
! The LQM percentage is set with the ppp quality command. CHAP simply needs to be
! enabled, with this router reacting to the other router's host name as stated in
! the CHAP messages.
interface Serial0/1/0
 ip address 10.1.34.3 255.255.255.0
 encapsulation ppp
 ppp quality 80
 ppp authentication chap
! R4 configuration is next. The configuration is mostly a mirror image of R3.
username R3 password 0 rom838
!
interface Serial0/1/0
 ip address 10.1.34.4 255.255.255.0
 encapsulation ppp
 ppp quality 70
 ppp authentication chap
! Next, on R3, the show command lists the phrase "LCP Open," implying that LCP has
! completed negotiations. On the next line, two NCPs (CDPCP and IPCP) are listed.
R3# show int s 0/1/0
Serial0/1/0 is up, line protocol is up
  Hardware is GT96K Serial
  Internet address is 10.1.34.3/24
  MTU 1500 bytes, BW 1544 Kbit, DLY 20000 usec,
     reliability 255/255, txload 1/255, rxload 1/255
  Encapsulation PPP, LCP Open
  Open: CDPCP, IPCP, loopback not set
  Keepalive set (10 sec)
! (The following debug output has been shortened in several places.) The link was
! shut/no shut after issuing the debug ppp negotiation command. The first messages
! state a configuration request, listing CHAP for authentication, that LQM should
! be used, and with the (default) setting of using magic numbers to detect loops.
```

(Handwritten annotations: "LQM check" pointing at `ppp quality 80`; "auth type" pointing at `ppp authentication chap`.)

```
*Apr 11 14:48:14.795: Se0/1/0 PPP: Phase is ESTABLISHING, Active Open
*Apr 11 14:48:14.795: Se0/1/0 LCP: O CONFREQ [Closed] id 186 len 23
*Apr 11 14:48:14.795: Se0/1/0 LCP:    AuthProto CHAP (0x0305C22305)
*Apr 11 14:48:14.795: Se0/1/0 LCP:    QualityType 0xC025 period 1000
(0x0408C025000003E8)
*Apr 11 14:48:14.795: Se0/1/0 LCP:    MagicNumber 0x13403093 (0x050613403093)
*Apr 11 14:48:14.807: Se0/1/0 LCP: State is Open
! LCP completes, with authentication occurring next. In succession below, the
! challenge is issued in both directions ("O" means "output," "I" means "Input").
! Following that, the response is made, with the hashed value. Finally, the
! confirmation is sent ("success"). Note that by default the process occurs in
! both directions.
*Apr 11 14:48:14.807: Se0/1/0 PPP: Phase is AUTHENTICATING, by both
*Apr 11 14:48:14.807: Se0/1/0 CHAP: O CHALLENGE id 85 len 23 from "R3"
*Apr 11 14:48:14.811: Se0/1/0 CHAP: I CHALLENGE id 41 len 23 from "R4"
*Apr 11 14:48:14.811: Se0/1/0 CHAP: Using hostname from unknown source
*Apr 11 14:48:14.811: Se0/1/0 CHAP: Using password from AAA
*Apr 11 14:48:14.811: Se0/1/0 CHAP: O RESPONSE id 41 len 23 from "R3"
*Apr 11 14:48:14.815: Se0/1/0 CHAP: I RESPONSE id 85 len 23 from "R4"
*Apr 11 14:48:14.819: Se0/1/0 CHAP: O SUCCESS id 85 len 4
*Apr 11 14:48:14.823: Se0/1/0 CHAP: I SUCCESS id 41 len 4
*Apr 11 14:48:14.823: Se0/1/0 PPP: Phase is UP
```

Multilink PPP

Multilink PPP, abbreviated as MLP, MP, or MLPPP, defines a method to combine multiple parallel serial links at Layer 2. The original motivation for MLP was to combine multiple ISDN B-channels without requiring any Layer 3 load balancing; however, MLP can be used to load-balance traffic across any type of point-to-point serial link.

MLP balances traffic by fragmenting each data link layer frame, either based on the number of parallel links or on a configured fragmentation delay. MLP then sends the fragments over different links. For example, with three parallel links, MLP fragments each frame into three fragments and sends one over each link. To allow reassembly on the receiving end, MLP adds a header (either 4 or 2 bytes) to each fragment. The header includes a Sequence Number field as well as Flag bits designating the beginning and ending fragments.

MLP can be configured using either multilink interfaces or virtual templates. Example 6-4 shows an MLP multilink interface with two underlying serial interfaces. Following the configuration, the example shows some interface statistics that result from a ping from one router (R4) to the other router (R3) across the MLP connection.

Example 6-4 *MLP Configuration and Statistics with Multilink Interfaces—R3*

```
! All Layer 3 parameters are configured on the multilink interface. The
! serial links are associated with the multilink interface using the ppp
! multilink group commands.
interface Multilink1
 ip address 10.1.34.3 255.255.255.0
 encapsulation ppp
 ppp multilink
 ppp multilink group 1
!
interface Serial0/1/0
 no ip address
 encapsulation ppp
 ppp multilink group 1
!
interface Serial0/1/1
 no ip address
 encapsulation ppp
 ppp multilink group 1
! Below, the interface statistics reflect that each of the two serial links sends
! the same number of packets, one fragment of each original packet. Note that the
! multilink interface shows roughly the same number of packets, but the bit rate
! matches the sum of the bit rates on the two serial interfaces. These stats
! reflect the fact that the multilink interface shows prefragmentation
! counters, and the serial links show post-fragmentation counters.
R3# sh int s 0/1/0
Serial0/1/0 is up, line protocol is up
! lines omitted for brevity
  5 minute input rate 182000 bits/sec, 38 packets/sec
  5 minute output rate 182000 bits/sec, 38 packets/sec
     8979 packets input, 6804152 bytes, 0 no buffer
     8977 packets output, 6803230 bytes, 0 underruns
R3# sh int s 0/1/1
Serial0/1/1 is up, line protocol is up
! lines omitted for brevity
  5 minute input rate 183000 bits/sec, 38 packets/sec
  5 minute output rate 183000 bits/sec, 38 packets/sec
     9214 packets input, 7000706 bytes, 0 no buffer
     9213 packets output, 7000541 bytes, 0 underruns
R3# sh int multilink1
Multilink1 is up, line protocol is up
! lines omitted for brevity
  Hardware is multilink group interface
  Internet address is 10.1.34.3/24
```

```
MTU 1500 bytes, BW 3088 Kbit, DLY 100000 usec,
    reliability 255/255, txload 31/255, rxload 30/255
Encapsulation PPP, LCP Open, multilink Open
Open: CDPCP, IPCP, loopback not set
5 minute input rate 374000 bits/sec, 40 packets/sec
5 minute output rate 377000 bits/sec, 40 packets/sec
    9385 packets input, 14112662 bytes, 0 no buffer
    9384 packets output, 14243723 bytes, 0 underruns
```

MLP Link Fragmentation and Interleaving

The term *Link Fragmentation and Interleaving (LFI)* refers to a type of Cisco IOS QoS tool that prevents small, delay-sensitive packets from having to wait on longer, delay-insensitive packets to be completely serialized out an interface. To do so, LFI tools fragment larger packets, and then send the delay-sensitive packet after just a portion of the original, longer packet. The key elements include fragmentation, the ability to interleave parts of one packet between fragments of another packet, and a queuing scheduler that interleaves the packets. Figure 6-2 depicts the complete process. A 1500-byte packet is fragmented and a 60-byte packet is interleaved between the fragments by the queuing scheduler after the first two fragments.

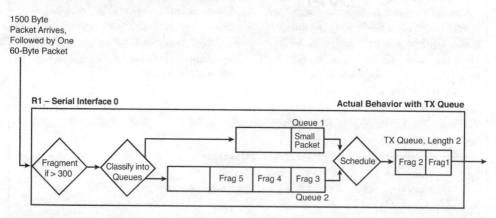

Figure 6-2 *MLP LFI Concept*

MLP supports LFI, the key elements of which are detailed in the following list:

- The **ppp multilink interleave** interface subcommand tells the router to allow interleaving.

- The **ppp multilink fragment-delay** x command defines the fragment size indirectly, based on the following formula. Note that the unit for the delay parameter is milliseconds, so the units for the interface bandwidth must also be converted.

$$size = x * \text{bandwidth}$$

- MLP LFI can be used with only one link or with multiple links.

■ The queuing scheduler on the multilink interface determines the next packet to send; as a result, many implementations use LLQ to always interleave delay-sensitive traffic between fragments.

Example 6-5 shows an updated version of the configuration in Example 6-2, with LFI enabled.

Example 6-5 *MLP LFI with LLQ to Interleave Voice*

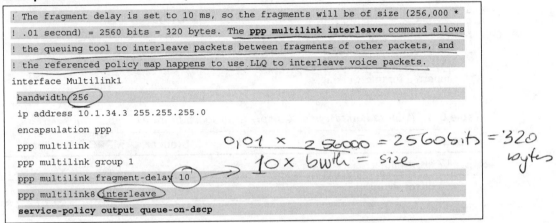

```
! The fragment delay is set to 10 ms, so the fragments will be of size (256,000 *
! .01 second) = 2560 bits = 320 bytes. The ppp multilink interleave command allows
! the queuing tool to interleave packets between fragments of other packets, and
! the referenced policy map happens to use LLQ to interleave voice packets.
interface Multilink1
bandwidth 256
ip address 10.1.34.3 255.255.255.0
encapsulation ppp
ppp multilink
ppp multilink group 1
ppp multilink fragment-delay 10
ppp multilink8 interleave
service-policy output queue-on-dscp
```

PPP Compression

PPP can negotiate to use Layer 2 payload compression, TCP header compression, and/or RTP header compression. Each type of compression has pros and cons, with the most obvious relating to what is compressed, as shown in Figure 6-3.

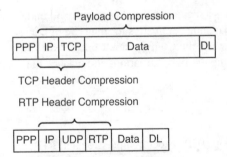

Figure 6-3 *Fields Compressed with Compression Features*

Comparing payload compression and header compression, payload compression works best with longer packet lengths, and header compression with shorter packet lengths. Header compression takes advantage of the predictability of headers, achieving a compression ratio for the header fields around 10:1 to 20:1. However, when the data inside the packet is much larger than the header, saving some bytes with header compression might be only a small reduction in the overall bandwidth required, making payload compression more appealing.

PPP Layer 2 Payload Compression

Cisco IOS Software supplies three different payload compression options for PPP, namely, Lempel-Ziv Stacker (LZS), Microsoft Point-to-Point Compression (MPPC), and Predictor. Stacker and MPPC both use the same underlying Lempel-Ziv (LZ) compression algorithm, with Predictor using an algorithm called Predictor. LZ uses more CPU and less memory in comparison to Predictor, and LZ typically results in a better compression ratio.

Table 6-4 summarizes some of the key topics regarding payload compression. Note that of the three options, only LZS is supported on Frame Relay and HDLC links. Also note that for payload compression when using ATM–to–Frame Relay Service Interworking, MLP must be used; as a result, all payload compression types supported by PPP are also supported for Interworking.

Table 6-4 *Point-to-Point Payload Compression Tools: Feature Comparison*

Feature	Stacker	MPPC	Predictor
Uses LZ algorithm?	Yes	Yes	No
Uses Predictor algorithm?	No	No	Yes
Supported on HDLC?	Yes	No	No
Supported on PPP?	Yes	Yes	Yes
Supported on Frame Relay?	Yes	No	No
Supports ATM and ATM–to–Frame Relay Service Interworking (using MLP)?	Yes	Yes	Yes

Configuring payload compression simply requires a matching **compress** command under each interface on each end of the link(s), with matching parameters for the type of compression. After compression is configured, PPP starts the Compression Control Protocol (CCP), which is another NCP, to perform the compression negotiations and manage the compression process.

Header Compression

PPP supports two styles of IP header compression: TCP header compression and RTP header compression. (Figure 6-3 shows the headers compressed by each.)

Voice and video flows use the RTP encapsulation shown at the bottom of Figure 6-3. Voice flows, particularly for low-bit-rate codecs, have very small data fields. For example, with G.729, the packet is typically 60 bytes, with 40 bytes of the 60 bytes being the IP/UDP/RTP headers. RTP header compression compresses the IP/UDP/RTP headers (40 bytes) into 2 or 4 bytes. With G.729 in use, RTP header compression reduces the required bandwidth by more than 50 percent.

TCP header compression compresses the combined IP and TCP headers, a combined 40 bytes, into 3 or 5 bytes. For TCP packets with small payloads, the saving can be significant; the math is similar to the RTP compression example in the previous paragraph. However, TCP header compression might not be worth the CPU and memory expense for larger packets. For example, for a 1500-byte packet, compressing the 40 bytes of the header into 3 bytes reduces the packet size by only about 2 percent.

Header compression can be configured using a pair of legacy commands, or it can be configured using Modular QoS CLI (MQC) commands. The legacy commands are **ip tcp header-compression [passive]** and **ip rtp header-compression [passive]**, used under the serial (PPP) or multilink (MLP) interfaces on each end of the link. PPP reacts to this command by using IPCP to negotiate to enable each type of compression. (If you use the **passive** keyword, that router waits for the other router to initiate the IPCP negotiation.) With this style of configuration, all TCP flows and/or all RTP flows using the link are compressed.

Example 6-6 shows the alternative method using an MQC policy map to create class-based header compression. In the example, TCP header compression is applied only to the class that holds Telnet traffic. As a result, TCP header compression is applied to the packets that are most likely to benefit from TCP compression, without wasting CPU and memory to compress larger packets. (Recall that Telnet sends one keystroke per TCP segment, unless **service nagle** is configured, making Telnet highly inefficient by default.)

Example 6-6 *MQC Class-Based Header Compression*

```
! RTP compression is enabled in the voice class, TCP header compression in the
! critical data class, and no compression in the class-default class.
policy-map cb-compression
 class voice
 bandwidth 82
 compress header ip rtp
 class critical
 bandwidth 110
 compress header ip tcp
!
interface Multilink1
 bandwidth 256
 service-policy output cb-compression
```

PPPoE

PPP over Ethernet (PPPoE) provides the capability to connect hosts on a network over a simple bridging device to a remote aggregation concentrator. PPPoE is the predominant access protocol in broadband networks worldwide. PPPoE typically is deployed with a software stack housed on the end-customer's (subscriber's) PC. This software allows the network service provider to "own" the customer as the PPP session runs from the customer PC to the service provider network.

PPPoE provides an emulated (and optionally authenticated) point-to-point link across a shared medium, typically a broadband aggregation network such as those found in DSL service providers. In fact, a very common scenario is to run a PPPoE client on the customer side, which connects to and obtains its configuration from the PPPoE server (head-end router) at the ISP side.

Server Configuration

Example 6-7 demonstrates the very first step that must be taken at the ISP end. It is here that we will create a Broadband Aggregation (BBA) group that will handle incoming PPPoE connections. For the purposes of our discussion, we will name the bba-group **BBA-Group** and bind it to a virtual template that we will create later.

Example 6-7   *Virtual Template Configuration*

```
ISP(config)# bba-group pppoe BBA-GROUP
ISP(config-bba-group)# virtual-template 1
```

Another useful option would be to apply PPPoE session limits just as a protective measure. To limit the number of sessions established based on the associated MAC addresses, you would enter the following, for example:

```
ISP(config-bba-group)# sessions per-mac limit 2
```

In this scenario, we will specify a limit of 2. This will allow a new session to be established immediately if the prior session has been dropped or is waiting to expire.

The next important step will be to create the virtual template, the one we mentioned previously, that will service the client-facing interface:

```
ISP(config)# interface virtual-template 1
```

When a PPPoE client initiates a session with this router, the router will dynamically create a virtual interface. This interface will act as the placeholder for the point-to-point connection spawned by this process.

To operate properly, the virtual template will need two components: an IP address and a pool of IP addresses that will be used to issue negotiated addresses to clients. This process, illustrated in Example 6-8, would have to be considered the absolute basic elements needed to create an operational process.

Example 6-8   *PPPoE Basic Configuration*

```
ISP(config-if)# ip address 10.0.0.1 255.255.255.0
ISP(config-if)# peer default ip address pool PPOE_POOL
```

Now we will need to define the range of addresses that will be issued as part of the pool. To configure the local IP pool named **PPPOE-POOL** with the starting and ending addresses of an IP range, you would enter the following in global configuration mode:

```
ISP(config)# ip local pool PPPOE_POOL 10.0.0.2 10.0.0.254
```

The final step is to enable the PPPoE group on the interface facing the client, as shown in Example 6-9.

Example 6-9 *PPPoE Enabling the PPPoE Group*

```
ISP(config)# interface f0/0
ISP(config-if)# no ip address
ISP(config-if)# pppoe enable group MyGroup
ISP(config-if)# no shutdown
```

Note that this interface is not configured with an IP address; in this case, the addressing will be issued by the virtual template that we configured previously.

Client Configuration

Compared to the server configuration, creating a client is far less complicated. First, we will create a dialer interface to handle the PPPoE connection and then associate it with the physical interface that will be used to provide transport.

Creating the PPPoE dialer interface configuration can be seen in Example 6-10.

Example 6-10 *PPPoE Dialer Interface*

```
CPE(config)# interface dialer1
CPE(config-if)# dialer pool 1
CPE(config-if)# encapsulation ppp
CPE(config-if)# ip address negotiated
```

The **ip address negotiated** command tells the client to use an IP address provided by the PPPoE server.

As part of this process, the PPP header adds 8 bytes of overhead to each frame. This could be problematic in situations where we might have packets close to the default Ethernet MTU of 1500 bytes, and to manage this eventuality, we will need to lower the MTU of the specific dialer interface to 1492 to avoid fragmentation. Example 6-11 demonstrates this as well as shows how to assign the ISP interface to our newly created PPPoE dial group.

Example 6-11 *PPPoE Session Limits*

```
CPE(config-if)# mtu 1492
CPE(config-if)# exit
CPE(config)# interface f0/0
CPE(config-if)# no ip address
CPE(config-if)# pppoe-client dial-pool-number 1
CPE(config-if)# no shutdown
!!!!!!!!!!!!!!!!!!!!!!!!!!!!!!!!!!!!!!!!!!!!!!!!!!!!!!!!!!!!!!!!!!!!!!!!!!!!!!!!!
!!!If all is well, you should see a notification indicating the PPPoE session has
!!!successfully formed:
```

```
!!!!!!!!!!!!!!!!!!!!!!!!!!!!!!!!!!!!!!!!!!!!!!!!!!!!!!!!!!!!!!!!!!!!!!!!!!!!!!!!!!!!!!
%DIALER-6-BIND: Interface Vi1 bound to profile Di1
%LINK-3-UPDOWN: Interface Virtual-Access1, changed state to up
%LINEPROTO-5-UPDOWN: Line protocol on Interface Virtual-Access1, changed
state to up
```

We can verify that interface Dialer1 has negotiated an IP address from the ISP router through the commands found in Example 6-12.

Example 6-12 *PPPoE Verification*

```
CPE# show ip interface brief
Interface               IP-Address      OK? Method Status            Protocol
FastEthernet0/0         unassigned      YES manual up                up
[...]
Virtual-Access1         unassigned      YES unset  up                up
Dialer1                 10.0.0.2        YES IPCP   up                up
!!!!!!!!!!!!!!!!!!!!!!!!!!!!!!!!!!!!!!!!!!!!!!!!!!!!!!!!!!!!!!!!!!!!!!!!!!!!!!!!!!!!!
!!!!
!!! show pppoe session shows our PPPoE session with the ISP router terminated on
!!! Dialer0, via FastEthernet0/0:
!!!!!!!!!!!!!!!!!!!!!!!!!!!!!!!!!!!!!!!!!!!!!!!!!!!!!!!!!!!!!!!!!!!!!!!!!!!!!!!!!!!!!
!!!
CPE# show pppoe session
 1 client session

Uniq ID  PPPoE  RemMAC         Port                 Source  VA         State
         SID    LocMAC                                      VA-st
N/A      16     ca00.4843.0008 Fa0/0                Di1     Vi1        UP
                ca01.4843.0008                              UP
```

Authentication

Now we need to consider the fact that at this point, anyone can connect through PPPoE. This is a less-than-satisfactory situation because we will need to restrict access to trusted clients. To accomplish this, we will configure authentication. This is probably the most prudent course of action available. As we discussed previously, PPP can use PAP or CHAP to authenticate clients, with the latter heavily preferred. To explore the authentication option in the context of PPPoE, we will configure our ISP router with a local user account named **PPP** and the password **PPPpassword**. This process can be seen in the output of Example 6-13.

Example 6-13 *PPPoE Authentication*

```
ISP(config)# username PPP password PPPpassword
!!!!!!!!!!!!!!!!!!!!!!!!!!!!!!!!!!!!!!!!!!!!!!!!!!!!!!!!!!!!!!!!!!!!!!!!!!!!!!!!
!!! Next we enforce CHAP authentication on our virtual template
!!!!!!!!!!!!!!!!!!!!!!!!!!!!!!!!!!!!!!!!!!!!!!!!!!!!!!!!!!!!!!!!!!!!!!!!!!!!!!!!
ISP(config)# interface virtual-template 1
ISP(config-if)# ppp authentication chap callin
!!!!!!!!!!!!!!!!!!!!!!!!!!!!!!!!!!!!!!!!!!!!!!!!!!!!!!!!!!!!!!!!!!!!!!!!!!!!!!!!
!!! This will terminate our client session, as we can see from the logs on CPE:
!!!!!!!!!!!!!!!!!!!!!!!!!!!!!!!!!!!!!!!!!!!!!!!!!!!!!!!!!!!!!!!!!!!!!!!!!!!!!!!!
%DIALER-6-UNBIND: Interface Vi1 unbound from profile Di1
%LINK-3-UPDOWN: Interface Virtual-Access1, changed state to down
%LINEPROTO-5-UPDOWN: Line protocol on Interface Virtual-Access1, changed state to
  down
!!!!!!!!!!!!!!!!!!!!!!!!!!!!!!!!!!!!!!!!!!!!!!!!!!!!!!!!!!!!!!!!!!!!!!!!!!!!!!!!
!!! To reestablish the connection from CPE, we'll need to enter the proper
!!! credentials:
!!!!!!!!!!!!!!!!!!!!!!!!!!!!!!!!!!!!!!!!!!!!!!!!!!!!!!!!!!!!!!!!!!!!!!!!!!!!!!!!
CPE(config)# interface dialer 1
CPE(config-if)# ppp chap password MyPassword
!!!!!!!!!!!!!!!!!!!!!!!!!!!!!!!!!!!!!!!!!!!!!!!!!!!!!!!!!!!!!!!!!!!!!!!!!!!!!!!!
!!! We should see the PPPoE session come back up a few seconds later after
!!! successfully authenticating. debug ppp authentication can be used on the ISP
!!! router to monitor the CHAP exchange:
!!!!!!!!!!!!!!!!!!!!!!!!!!!!!!!!!!!!!!!!!!!!!!!!!!!!!!!!!!!!!!!!!!!!!!!!!!!!!!!!
ppp50 PPP: Using vpn set call direction
ppp50 PPP: Treating connection as a callin
ppp50 PPP: Session handle[E800003A] Session id[50]
ppp50 PPP: Authorization required
ppp50 CHAP: O CHALLENGE id 1 len 24 from "ISP"
ppp50 CHAP: I RESPONSE id 1 len 24 from "CPE"
ppp50 PPP: Sent CHAP LOGIN Request
ppp50 PPP: Received LOGIN Response PASS
Vi1.1 PPP: Sent LCP AUTHOR Request
Vi1.1 PPP: Sent IPCP AUTHOR Request
Vi1.1 LCP: Received AAA AUTHOR Response PASS
Vi1.1 IPCP: Received AAA AUTHOR Response PASS
Vi1.1 CHAP: O SUCCESS id 1 len 4
```

Ethernet WAN

After you've spent so much time learning about the various capabilities and features of Ethernet technologies, it should come as no surprise that industry trends have pushed this technology from the typical local-area deployment and into the arena of wide-area networks. As early as ten years ago, WAN technologies included a short list of protocols and features that included Frame Relay, ATM, and Synchronous Optical Network (SONET). Today the ever-increasing demand for bandwidth between geographically isolated environments has created a new breed of interconnectivity solutions that utilize Ethernet and Ethernet features at their core. This list includes but is not limited to technologies like Virtual Private LAN Services (VPLS), Multi-Protocol Label Switching (MPLS), Any-Transport Over MPLS (ATOM), Dot1Q-in-Dot1Q Tunnels (QnQ Tunnels), and Metro-Ethernet.

These technologies create "borderless networks"; that is, networks where a service can be turned up anywhere and at any time. Furthermore, these technologies provide LAN-like user performance normally only found in headquarter offices. All this is accomplished through the primary technology: Ethernet Wide-Area Networks (EWAN).

Ethernet has evolved from just a LAN technology to a scalable, cost-effective, and manageable WAN solution for businesses of all sizes. Ethernet offers numerous cost and operational advantages over conventional WAN solutions. Ethernet Wide-Area Networks maintain the high bandwidth and simplicity of Layer 2 Ethernet, and the flat network design makes the connected sites appear as a single logical network and simplifies connectivity back to the headquarters and between remote sites.

For the purposes of our discussions, we will first look at Virtual Private LAN Services (VPLS), which is designed to deliver Layer 2 connectivity to all endpoints in the EWAN configuration and then move to another service type called Metro-Ethernet. Both of these technologies are often simply referred to as Layer 2 VPNs and, more often than not, will use MPLS as an enabling technology.

VPLS

VPLS enables the carriers to bring the various WAN connections (over either IP or MPLS networks) together as a single logical Ethernet network where quality of service (QoS) levels can be defined to ensure that audio or video applications get their required bandwidth.

Very simply, VPLS is an architecture that allows MPLS networks to provide multipoint Ethernet LAN services, often referred to as Transparent LAN Service (TLS). A multipoint network service is one that allows a customer edge (CE) endpoint or node to communicate directly with all other CE nodes associated with the multipoint service. By contrast, using a point-to-point network service such as ATM, the end customer typically designates one CE node to be the hub to which all spoke sites are connected. In this scenario, if a spoke site needs to communicate with another spoke site, it must communicate through the hub, and this requirement can introduce transmission delay.

To provide multipoint Ethernet capability, the IETF VPLS drafts describe the concept of linking virtual Ethernet bridges using MPLS Pseudo-Wires (PW). As a VPLS forwards Ethernet frames at Layer 2, the operation of VPLS is exactly the same as that found within IEEE 802.1 bridges in that VPLS will self-learn the source MAC address to port associations, and frames are forwarded based upon the destination MAC address. If the destination address is unknown, or is a broadcast or multicast address, the frame is flooded to all ports associated with the virtual bridge. Although the forwarding operation of VPLS is relatively simple, the VPLS architecture needs to be able to perform other operational functions, such as

- Autodiscover other provider edges (PE) associated with a particular VPLS instance

- Signaling of PWs to interconnect VPLS virtual switch instances (VSI)

- Loop avoidance

- MAC address withdrawal

Metro-Ethernet

Ethernet on the metropolitan-area network (MAN) can be used as pure Ethernet, Ethernet over MPLS, or Ethernet over Dark Fiber, but regardless of the transport medium, we have to recognize that in network deployments requiring medium-distance backhaul or metropolitan (in the same city) connectivity, this Ethernet WAN technology is king. Why do we have so many different types of Metro-E solutions? The answer is that each has advantages and disadvantages. As an example, pure Ethernet-based deployments are cheaper but less reliable and scalable, and are usually limited to small-scale or experimental deployments. Dark Fiber–based deployments are useful when there is an existing infrastructure already in place, whereas solutions that are MPLS based are costly but highly reliable and scalable, and as such are used typically by large corporations.

We will focus briefly on the idea of employing Metro-Ethernet by using MPLS because of the fact that MPLS figures so prominently in our CCIE R&S written studies. An MPLS-based Metro-Ethernet network uses MPLS in the service provider's network. The subscriber will get an Ethernet interface on copper (for example, 100BASE-TX) or fiber (such as 100BASE-FX). The customer's Ethernet packet is transported over MPLS, and the service provider network uses Ethernet again as the underlying technology to transport MPLS. So MPLS-based Metro-E is effectively Ethernet over MPLS over Ethernet.

Label Distribution Protocol (LDP) signaling can be used to provide site-to-site signaling for the inner label (VC label) and Resource Reservation Protocol-Traffic Engineering (RSVP-TE), or LDP can be used to provide the network signaling for the outer label.

It should also be noted that a typical Metro-Ethernet system has a star network or mesh network topology, with individual routers or servers interconnected through cable or fiber-optic media. This is important when it becomes necessary to troubleshoot Metro-Ethernet solutions.

Foundation Summary

This section lists additional details and facts to round out the coverage of the topics in this chapter. Unlike most Cisco Press Exam Certification Guides, this book does not repeat information listed in the "Foundation Topics" section of the chapter. Please take the time to read and study the details in this section of the chapter, as well as review the items in the "Foundation Topics" section noted with a Key Topic icon.

Table 6-5 lists the key protocols covered in this chapter.

Table 6-5   *Protocols and Standards for Chapter 6*

Topic	Standard
Point-to-Point Protocol (PPP)	RFC 1661
PPP in HDLC-like Framing	RFC 1662
PPP Internet Protocol Control Protocol (IPCP)	RFC 1332
IP Header Compression over PPP	RFC 3544
PPP Multilink Protocol (MLP)	RFC 1990
PPPoE	RFC 2684
Virtual Private LAN Service (VPLS)	RFC 4762
Metro-Ethernet (GMPLS)	RFC 6004

Table 6-6 lists the Cisco IOS commands related to serial links, as covered in this chapter.

Table 6-6   *Command Reference for Chapter 6*

Command	Mode and Function
interface virtual-template *number*	Global mode; creates a virtual template interface for MLP and moves the user into virtual template configuration mode
ppp authentication {*protocol1* [*protocol2...*]} [if-needed] [*list-name* | default] [callin] [one-time] [optional]	Interface mode; defines the authentication protocol (PAP, CHAP, EAP) and other parameters
ppp multilink [bap]	Interface mode; enables MLP on an interface
ppp multilink fragment-delay *delay-max*	Interface mode; defines the fragment size based on the delay and interface bandwidth
ppp multilink group *group-number*	Interface mode; associates a physical interface to a multilink interface
ppp multilink interleave	Interface mode; allows the queuing scheduled to interleave packets between fragments of another packet

Command	Mode and Function
compress [predictor | stac | mppc [ignore-pfc]]	Interface mode; configures payload compression
ip rtp header-compression [passive]	Interface mode; enables RTP header compression
ip tcp header-compression [passive]	Interface mode; enables TCP header compression
compression header ip [rtp | tcp]	Class configuration mode; enables RTP or TCP header compression inside an MQC class
ppp quality *percentage*	Interface mode; enables LQM monitoring at the stated percentage
debug ppp negotiation	Enables debugging that shows the various stages of PPP negotiation

See Chapter 5, "Shaping, Policing, and Link Fragmentation," for more information about the **class-map**, **policy-map**, and **service-policy** commands.

Memory Builders

The CCIE Routing and Switching written exam, like all Cisco CCIE written exams, covers a fairly broad set of topics. This section provides some basic tools to help you exercise your memory about some of the broader topics covered in this chapter.

Fill In Key Tables from Memory

First, take the time to print Appendix E, "Key Tables for CCIE Study," on the CD, which contains empty sets of some of the key summary tables from the "Foundation Topics" section of this chapter. Then, simply fill in the tables from memory. Refer to Appendix F, "Solutions for Key Tables for CCIE Study," also on the CD, to check your answers.

Definitions

Next, take a few moments to write down the definitions for the following terms:

PPP, MLP, LCP, NCP, IPCP, CDPCP, MLP, PPPoE LFI, CHAP, PAP, LFI, Layer 2 payload compression, TCP header compression, RTP header compression, VC, PVC, SVC, DTE, DCE, access rate, access link, Service Interworking, Using Multilink PPP (MLP)

Refer to the glossary to check your answers.

Further Reading

www.cisco.com/c/en/us/td/docs/ios-xml/ios/bbdsl/configuration/15-mt/bba-15-mt-book.html

http://tools.ietf.org/html/draft-ietf-l2vpn-vpls-ldp-09

Blueprint topics covered in this chapter:

This chapter covers the following subtopics from the Cisco CCIE Routing and Switching written exam blueprint. Refer to the full blueprint in Table I-1 in the Introduction for more details on the topics covered in each chapter and their context within the blueprint.

- IP Multicast

CHAPTER 7

Introduction to IP Multicasting

IP multicast concepts and protocols are an important part of the CCIE Routing and Switching written exam. Demand for IP multicast applications has increased dramatically over the last several years. Almost all major campus networks today use some form of multicasting. This chapter covers why multicasting is needed, the fundamentals of multicast addressing, and how multicast traffic is distributed and controlled over a LAN.

"Do I Know This Already?" Quiz

Table 7-1 outlines the major headings in this chapter and the corresponding "Do I Know This Already?" quiz questions.

Table 7-1 *"Do I Know This Already?" Foundation Topics Section-to-Question Mapping*

Foundation Topics Section	Questions Covered in This Section	Score
Why Do You Need Multicasting?	1	
Multicast IP Addresses	2–4	
Managing Distribution of Multicast Traffic with IGMP	5–6	
LAN Multicast Optimizations	7	
Total Score		

To best use this pre-chapter assessment, remember to score yourself strictly. You can find the answers in Appendix A, "Answers to the 'Do I Know This Already?' Quizzes."

1. Which of the following reasons for using IP multicasting are valid for one-to-many applications?

    a. Multicast applications use connection-oriented service.

    b. Multicast uses less bandwidth than unicast.

    c. A multicast packet can be sent from one source to many destinations.

    d. Multicast eliminates traffic redundancy.

2. Which of the following statements is true of a multicast address?

   a. Uses a Class D address that can range from 223.0.0.0 to 239.255.255.255

   b. Uses a subnet mask ranging from 8 bits to 24 bits

   c. Can be permanent or transient

   d. Can be entered as an IP address on an interface of a router only if the router is configured for multicasting

3. Which of the following multicast addresses are reserved and not forwarded by multicast routers?

   a. 224.0.0.1 and 224.0.0.13

   b. 224.0.0.9 and 224.0.1.39

   c. 224.0.0.10 and 224.0.1.40

   d. 224.0.0.5 and 224.0.0.6

4. From the following pairs of Layer 3 multicast addresses, select a pair that will use the same Ethernet multicast MAC address of 0x0100.5e4d.2643.

   a. 224.67.26.43 and 234.67.26.43

   b. 225.77.67.38 and 235.77.67.38

   c. 229.87.26.43 and 239.87.26.43

   d. 227.77.38.67 and 238.205.38.67

5. From the following statements, select the true statement(s) regarding IGMP Query messages and IGMP Report messages.

   a. Hosts, switches, and routers originate IGMP Membership Report messages.

   b. Hosts, switches, and routers originate IGMP Query messages.

   c. Hosts originate IGMP Query messages and routers originate IGMP Membership messages.

   d. Hosts originate IGMP Membership messages and routers originate IGMP Query messages.

   e. Hosts and switches originate IGMP Membership messages and routers originate IGMP Query messages.

6. Seven hosts and a router on a multicast LAN network are using IGMPv2. Hosts 5, 6, and 7 are members of group 226.5.6.7, and the other four hosts are not. Which of the following answers is/are true about how the router will respond when Host 7 sends an IGMPv2 Leave message for the group 226.5.6.7?

   a. Sends an IGMPv2 General Query to multicast destination address 224.0.0.1

   b. Sends an IGMPv2 Group-Specific Query to multicast destination address 224.0.0.1

   c. Sends an IGMPv2 General Query to multicast destination address 226.5.6.7

   d. Sends an IGMPv2 Group-Specific Query to multicast destination address 226.5.6.7

   e. First sends an IGMPv2 Group-Specific Query to multicast destination address 226.5.6.7, and then sends an IGMPv2 General Query to multicast destination address 224.0.0.1

7. Which of the following statements is/are true regarding CGMP and IGMP snooping?

   a. CGMP and IGMP snooping are used to constrain the flooding of multicast traffic in LAN switches.

   b. CGMP is a Cisco-proprietary protocol and uses the well-known Layer 2 multicast MAC address 0x0100.0cdd.dddd.

   c. IGMP snooping is preferable in a mixed-vendor environment; however, if implemented using Layer 2–only LAN switches, it can cause a dramatic reduction in switch performance.

   d. CGMP is simple to implement, and in CGMP only routers send CGMP messages, while switches only listen for CGMP messages.

   e. All of these answers are correct.

Foundation Topics

Why Do You Need Multicasting?

"Necessity is the mother of all invention," a saying derived from Plato's *Republic*, holds very true in the world of technology. In the late 1980s, Dr. Steve Deering was working on a project that required him to send a message from one computer to a group of computers across a Layer 3 network. After studying several routing protocols, Dr. Deering concluded that the functionality of the routing protocols could be extended to support "Layer 3 multicasting." This concept led to more research, and in 1991, Dr. Deering published his doctoral thesis, "Multicast Routing in a Datagram Network," in which he defined the components required for IP multicasting, their functions, and their relationships with each other.

The most basic definition of IP multicasting is as follows:

> Sending a message from a single source to selected multiple destinations across a Layer 3 network in one data stream.

If you want to send a message from one source to one destination, you could send a unicast message. If you want to send a message from one source to all the destinations on a local network, you could send a broadcast message. However, if you want to send a message from one source to selected multiple destinations spread across a routed network in one data stream, the most efficient method is IP multicasting.

Demand for multicast applications is increasing with the advent of such applications as audio and video web content; broadcasting TV programs, radio programs, and concerts over the Internet; communicating stock quotes to brokers; transmitting a corporate message to employees; and transmitting data from a centralized warehouse to a chain of retail stores. Success of one-to-many multicast applications has created a demand for the second generation of multicast applications that are referred to as "many-to-many" and "many-to-few," in which there are many sources of multicast traffic. Examples of these types of applications include playing games on an intranet or the Internet and conducting interactive audio and video meetings. The primary focus of this chapter and the next chapter is to help you understand concepts and technologies required for implementing one-to-many multicast applications.

Problems with Unicast and Broadcast Methods

Why not use unicast or broadcast methods to send a message from one source to many destinations? Figure 7-1 shows a video server as a source of a video application and the video data that needs to be delivered to a group of receivers—H2, H3, and H4—two hops away across a WAN link.

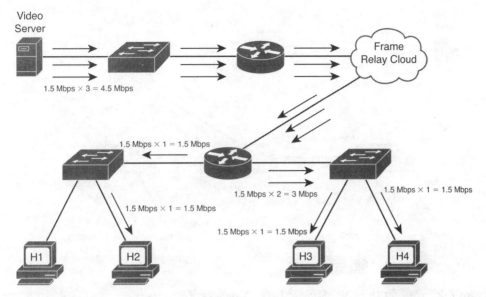

Figure 7-1   *Unicast*

The unicast method requires that the video application send one copy of each packet to every group member's unicast address. To support full-motion, full-screen viewing, the video stream requires approximately 1.5 Mbps of bandwidth for each receiver. If only a few receivers exist, as shown in Figure 7-1, this method works fine but still requires $n \times$ 1.5 Mbps of bandwidth, where n is the number of receiving hosts.

Figure 7-2 shows that as the number of receivers grows into the hundreds or thousands, the load on the server to create and send copies of the same data also increases, and replicated unicast transmissions consume a lot of bandwidth within the network. For 100 users, as indicated in the upper-left corner of Figure 7-2, the bandwidth required to send the unicast transmission increases to 150 Mbps. For 1000 users, the bandwidth required would increase to 1.5 Gbps.

You can see from Figure 7-2 that the unicast method is not scalable. Figure 7-3 shows that the broadcast method requires transmission of data only once, but it has some serious issues. First, as shown in Figure 7-3, if the receivers are in a different broadcast domain from the sender, routers need to forward broadcasts. However, forwarding broadcasts might be the worst possible solution, because broadcasting a packet to all hosts in a network can waste bandwidth and increase processing load on all the network devices if only a small group of hosts in the network actually needs to receive the packet.

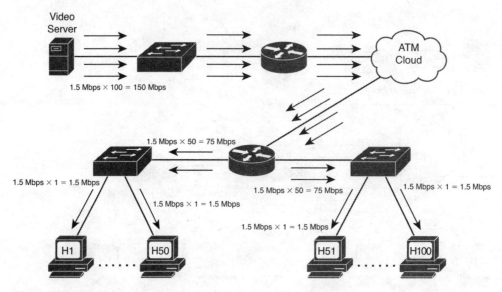

Figure 7-2 *Unicast Does Not Scale to Large Numbers of Receivers*

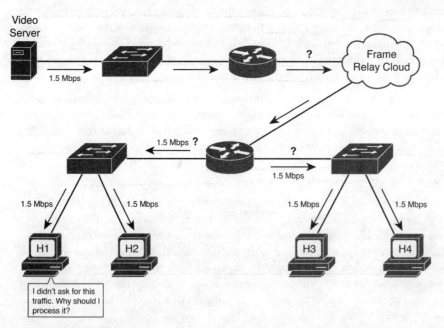

Figure 7-3 *Broadcast Wastes Bandwidth and Increases Processing Load on the CPU*

How Multicasting Provides a Scalable and Manageable Solution

The six basic requirements for supporting multicast across a routed network are as follows:

- A designated range of Layer 3 addresses that can only be used by multicast applications must exist. A network administrator needs to install a multicast application on a multicast server using a Layer 3 multicast address from the designated range.

- A multicast address must be used only as a destination IP address and specifically not as a source IP address. Unlike a unicast IP packet, a destination IP address in a multicast packet does not specify a recipient's address but rather signifies that the packet is carrying multicast traffic for a specific multicast application.

- The multicast application must be installed on all the hosts in the network that need to receive the multicast traffic for the application. The application must be installed using the same Layer 3 multicast address that was used on the multicast server. This is referred to as *launching an application* or *joining a group*.

- All hosts that are connected to a LAN must use a standard method to calculate a Layer 2 multicast address from the Layer 3 multicast address and assign it to their network interface cards (NIC). For example, if multiple routers are connected to an Ethernet segment and all of them are using the Open Shortest Path First (OSPF) routing protocol, all the routers on their Ethernet interfaces will also be listening to the Layer 2 multicast address 0x0100.5e00.0005 in addition to their Burned-In Addresses (BIA). This Layer 2 multicast address 0x0100.5e00.0005 is calculated from the multicast Layer 3 address 224.0.0.5, which is reserved for the OSPF routing protocol.

- There must be a mechanism by which a host can dynamically indicate to the connected router whether it would like to receive the traffic for the installed multicast application. The Internet Group Management Protocol (IGMP) provides communication between hosts and a router connected to the same subnet. The Cisco Group Management Protocol (CGMP) or IGMP snooping helps switches learn which hosts have requested to receive the traffic for a specific multicast application and to which switch ports these hosts are connected.

- There must be a multicast routing protocol that allows routers to forward multicast traffic from multicast servers to hosts without overtaxing network resources. Some of the multicast routing protocols are Distance Vector Multicast Routing Protocol (DVMRP), Multicast Open Shortest Path First (MOSPF), and Protocol Independent Multicast dense mode (PIM-DM) and sparse mode (PIM-SM).

This chapter discusses the first five bulleted items, and Chapter 8, "IP Multicast Routing," covers the multicast routing protocols.

Figure 7-4 shows how multicast traffic is forwarded in a Layer 3 network. The purpose of this illustration is to give you an overview of how multicast traffic is forwarded and received by selected hosts.

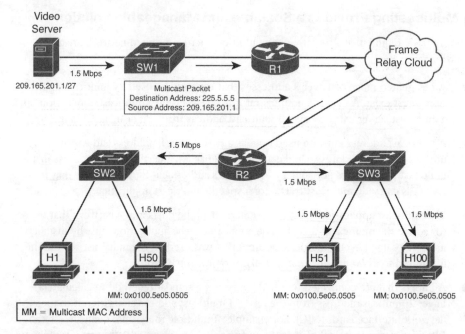

Figure 7-4 *How Multicast Delivers Traffic to Selected Users*

Assume that a video multicast application was installed on the video server using the special Layer 3 multicast address 225.5.5.5. Hosts 1 to 50, located across a WAN link, are not interested at this time in receiving traffic for this application. Hosts 51 to 100 are interested in receiving traffic for this application and launch this application on their PCs. When the host launches the application, the host *joins the group*, which means that the host now wants to receive multicast packets sent to 225.5.5.5. Hosts 51 to 100 join group 225.5.5.5 and indicate to R2 their desire to receive traffic for this multicast application by using IGMP. The multicast application calculates the Layer 2 multicast address 0x0100.5e05.0505 from the Layer 3 multicast address 225.5.5.5, and NICs of hosts 51 to 100 are listening to this address in addition to their BIAs.

A multicast routing protocol is configured on R1 and R2 so that they can forward the multicast traffic. R2 has one WAN link connected to the Frame Relay cloud and two Ethernet links connected to two switches, SW2 and SW3. R2 knows that it has hosts on both Ethernet links that would like to receive multicast traffic for the group 225.5.5.5 because these hosts have indicated their desire to receive traffic for the group using IGMP. Both switches have also learned on which ports they have hosts that would like to receive the multicast traffic for this application by using either CGMP or IGMP snooping.

A multicast packet travels from the video server over the Ethernet link to R1, and R1 forwards a single copy of the multicast packet over the WAN link to R2. When R2 receives a multicast packet on the WAN link with the destination address 225.5.5.5, it makes a copy of the packet and forwards a copy on each Ethernet link. Because it is a multicast packet for the group (application) 225.5.5.5, R2 calculates the Layer 2 destination multicast address of 0x0100.5e05.0505 and uses it as the destination MAC address on each packet it forwards to both switches. When the switches receive these packets, they forward them on appropriate ports to hosts. When the hosts receive the packets, their NICs compare the destination MAC address with the multicast MAC address they are listening to, and because they match, inform the higher layers to process the packet.

You can see from Figure 7-4 that the multicast traffic is sent once over the WAN links and is received by the hosts that have requested it. Should additional hosts request to receive the same multicast traffic, neither the multicast server nor the network resources would incur any additional burden, as shown in Figure 7-5.

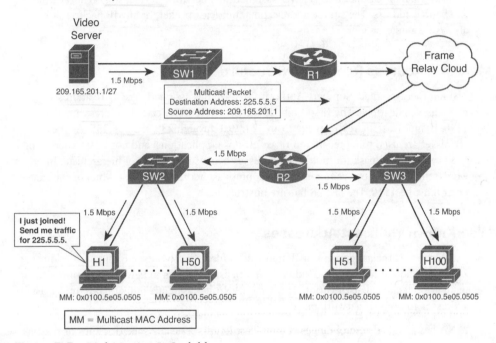

Figure 7-5 *Multicasting Is Scalable*

Assume that hosts 1 to 50 have also indicated their desire to receive traffic for the multicast group 225.5.5.5 using IGMP. R2 is already forwarding the traffic to both switches. Either CGMP or IGMP snooping can help SW2 (shown in Figure 7-5) learn that hosts 1 to 50 have also requested the multicast traffic for the group so that it can start forwarding the multicast traffic on ports connected to hosts 1 to 50. The additional 50 users are now receiving multicast traffic, and the load on the multicast server, load on other network devices, and demand for bandwidth on the WAN links remain the same. The load on SW2 shown in Figure 7-5 increases because it has to make 50 more copies of the multicast traffic and forward it on 50 more ports; however, it is now operating at the same level as the other switch. You can see that IP multicast is scalable.

Although multicast offers many advantages, it also has some disadvantages. Multicast is UDP based and hence unreliable. Lack of TCP windowing and "slow start" mechanisms can result in network congestion. Some multicast protocol mechanisms occasionally generate duplicate packets and deliver packets out of order.

DISADVAN-TAGE OF MULTICAST

Multicast IP Addresses

Multicast applications always use a multicast IP address. This multicast address represents the multicast application and is referred to as a multicast *group*. Unlike a unicast IP address, which uniquely identifies a single IP host, a multicast address used as a destination address on an IP packet signifies that the packet is carrying traffic for a specific multicast application. For example, if a multicast packet is traveling over a network with a destination address 225.5.5.5, it is proclaiming to the network devices that, "I am carrying traffic for the multicast application that uses multicast group address 225.5.5.5; do you want it?" A multicast address is never assigned to a network device, so it is never used as a source address. The source address on a multicast packet, or any IP packet, should always be a unicast address.

Multicast Address Range and Structure

Key Topic

The Internet Assigned Numbers Authority (IANA) has assigned class D IP addresses to multicast applications. The first 4 bits of the first octet for a class D address are always 1110. IP multicast addresses range from 224.0.0.0 through 239.255.255.255. As these addresses are used to represent multicast groups (applications) and not hosts, there is no need for a subnet mask for multicast addresses because they are not hierarchical. In other words, there is only one requirement for a multicast address: The first 4 bits of the first octet must be 1110. The last 28 bits are unstructured.

first 4 bits must be 1110
11
224.0...

Well-Known Multicast Addresses

IANA controls the assignment of IP multicast addresses. To preserve multicast addresses, IANA is reluctant to assign individual IP multicast addresses to new applications without a good technical justification. However, IANA has assigned individual IP multicast addresses to popular network protocols.

IANA has assigned several ranges of multicast IP addresses for specific types of reasons. Those types are as follows:

Key Topic

- Permanent multicast groups, in the range 224.0.0.0–224.0.1.255

- Addresses used with Source-Specific Multicast (SSM), in the range 232.0.0.0–232.255.255.255

- GLOP addressing, in the range 233.0.0.0–233.255.255.255

- Private multicast addresses, in the range 239.0.0.0–239.255.255.255

This section provides some insights into each of these four types of reserved IP multicast addresses. The rest of the multicast addresses are referred to as *transient* groups, which are covered later in this chapter in the section "Multicast Addresses for Transient Groups."

Multicast Addresses for Permanent Groups

IANA has reserved two ranges of permanent multicast IP addresses. The main distinction between these two ranges of addresses is that the first range is used for packets that should not be forwarded by routers, and the second group is used when packets should be forwarded by routers.

[handwritten: 2 range of perm. multicast IP addr.]

The range of addresses used for local (not routed) purposes is 224.0.0.0 through 224.0.0.255. These addresses should be somewhat familiar from the routing protocol discussions earlier in the book. For example, the 224.0.0.5 and 224.0.0.6 IP addresses used by OSPF fit into this first range of permanent addresses. Other examples include the IP multicast destination address of 224.0.0.1, which specifies that all multicast-capable hosts on a local network segment should examine this packet. Similarly, the IP multicast destination address of 224.0.0.2 on a packet specifies that all multicast-capable routers on a local network segment should examine this packet.

The range of permanent group addresses used when the packets should be routed is 224.0.1.0 through 224.0.1.255. This range includes 224.0.1.39 and 224.0.1.40, which are used by Cisco-proprietary Auto-Rendezvous Point (Auto-RP) protocols (covered in Chapter 8). Table 7-2 shows some of the well-known addresses from the permanent address range.

Table 7-2   *Some Well-Known Reserved Multicast Addresses*

Address	Usage
224.0.0.1	All multicast hosts
224.0.0.2	All multicast routers
224.0.0.4	DVMRP routers
224.0.0.5	All OSPF routers
224.0.0.6	OSPF designated routers
224.0.0.9	RIPv2 routers
224.0.0.10	EIGRP routers
224.0.0.13	PIM routers
224.0.0.22	IGMPv3
224.0.0.25	RGMP
224.0.1.39	Cisco-RP-Announce
224.0.1.40	Cisco-RP-Discovery

[handwritten annotations: "On the local (LAN) subnets only" bracketing the first group; "needs routing" bracketing the last two entries]

Multicast Addresses for Source-Specific Multicast Applications and Protocols

IANA has allocated the range 232.0.0.0 through 232.255.255.255 for SSM applications and protocols. The purpose of these applications is to allow a host to select a source for the multicast group. SSM makes multicast routing efficient, allows a host to select a better-quality source, and helps network administrators minimize multicast denial of service (DoS) attacks.

Multicast Addresses for GLOP Addressing

IANA has reserved the range 233.0.0.0 through 233.255.255.255 (RFC 3180), called GLOP addressing, on an experimental basis. It can be used by anyone who owns a registered autonomous system number (ASN) to create 256 global multicast addresses that can be owned and used by the entity. IANA reserves addresses to ensure global uniqueness of addresses; for similar reasons, each autonomous system should be using an assigned unique ASN.

By using a value of 233 for the first octet, and by using the ASN for the second and third octets, a single autonomous system can create globally unique multicast addresses as defined in the GLOP addressing RFC. For example, the autonomous system using registered ASN 5663 could convert ASN 5663 to binary (00010110 00011111). The first 8 bits, 00010110, equals 22 in decimal notation, and the last 8 bits, 00011111, equals 31 in decimal notation. Mapping the first 8 bits to the second octet and the last 8 bits to the third octet in the 233 range addresses, the entity that owns the ASN 5663 is automatically allocated the address range 233.22.31.0 through 233.22.31.255.

Note   GLOP is not an acronym and does not stand for anything. One of the authors of RFC 2770, David Meyer, started referring to this range of addresses as "GLOP" addressing, and since then the range has been identified by the name GLOP addressing.

Multicast Addresses for Private Multicast Domains

The last of the reserved multicast address ranges mentioned here is the range of *administratively scoped* addresses. IANA has assigned the range 239.0.0.0 through 239.255.255.255 (RFC 2365) for use in private multicast domains, much like the IP unicast ranges defined in RFC 1918, namely, 10.0.0.0/8, 172.16.0.0/12, and 192.168.0.0/16. IANA will not assign these administratively scoped multicast addresses to any other protocol or application. Network administrators are free to use multicast addresses in this range; however, they must configure their multicast routers to ensure that multicast traffic in this address range does not leave their multicast domain boundaries.

Multicast Addresses for Transient Groups

When an enterprise wants to use globally unique unicast addresses, it needs to get a block of addresses from its ISP or from IANA. However, when an enterprise wants to use a multicast address for a global multicast application, it can use any multicast address that is not part of the well-known permanent multicast address space covered in the previous sections. These remaining multicast addresses are called *transient groups* or *transient multicast addresses*. This means that the entire Internet must share the transient multicast addresses; they must be dynamically allocated when needed and must be released when no longer in use.

TRANSIENT
MULTICAST

Because these addresses are not permanently assigned to any application, they are called transient. Any enterprise can use these multicast addresses without requiring any registration or permission from IANA, but the enterprise is expected to release these multicast addresses after their use. At the time of this writing, there is no standard method available for using the transient multicast addresses. However, a great deal of work is being done by IETF to define and implement a standard method for dynamically allocating multicast addresses.

Summary of Multicast Address Ranges

Table 7-3 summarizes various multicast address ranges and their use.

Key
Topic

Table 7-3 *Multicast Address Ranges and Their Use*

Multicast Address Range	Usage
224.0.0.0 to 239.255.255.255	This range represents the entire IPv4 multicast address space. It is reserved for multicast applications.
224.0.0.0 to 224.0.0.255	This range is part of the permanent groups. Addresses from this range are assigned by IANA for network protocols on a local segment. Routers do not forward packets with destination addresses used from this range.
224.0.1.0 to 224.0.1.255	This range is also part of the permanent groups. Addresses from this range are assigned by IANA for the network protocols that are forwarded in the entire network. Routers forward packets with destination addresses used from this range.
232.0.0.0 to 232.255.255.255	This range is used for SSM applications.
233.0.0.0 to 233.255.255.255	This range is called the GLOP addressing. It is used for automatically allocating 256 multicast addresses to any enterprise that owns a registered ASN.
239.0.0.0 to 239.255.255.255	This range is used for private multicast domains. These addresses are called administratively scoped addresses.
Remaining ranges of addresses in the multicast address space	Addresses from these ranges are called transient groups. Any enterprise can allocate a multicast address from the transient groups for a global multicast application and should release it when the application is no longer in use.

Mapping IP Multicast Addresses to MAC Addresses

Assigning a Layer 3 multicast address to a multicast group (application) automatically generates a Layer 2 multicast address. Figure 7-6 shows how a multicast MAC address is calculated from a Layer 3 multicast address. The MAC address is formed using an IEEE-registered OUI of 01005E, then a binary 0, and then the last 23 bits of the multicast IP address. The method is identical for Ethernet and Fiber Distributed Data Interface (FDDI).

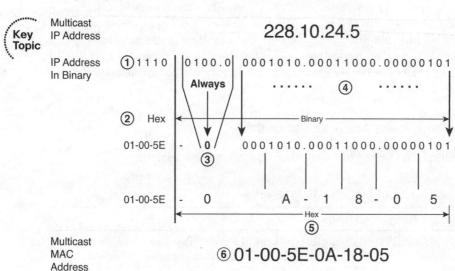

Figure 7-6 *Calculating a Multicast Destination MAC Address from a Multicast Destination IP Address*

To understand the mechanics of this process, use the following six steps, which are referenced by number in Figure 7-6:

Step 1. Convert the IP address to binary. Notice the first 4 bits; they are always 1110 for any multicast IP address.

Step 2. Replace the first 4 bits 1110 of the IP address with the 6 hexadecimal digits (or 24 bits) 01-00-5E as multicast OUI, in the total space of 12 hexadecimal digits (or 48 bits) for a multicast MAC address.

Step 3. Replace the next 5 bits of the binary IP address with one binary 0 in the multicast MAC address space.

Step 4. Copy the last 23 bits of the binary IP address in the last 23-bit space of the multicast MAC address.

Step 5. Convert the last 24 bits of the multicast MAC address from binary to 6 hexadecimal digits.

Step 6. Combine the first 6 hexadecimal digits 01-00-5E with the last 6 hexadecimal digits, calculated in Step 5, to form a complete multicast MAC address of 12 hexadecimal digits.

Unfortunately, this method does not provide a unique multicast MAC address for each multicast IP address, because only the last 23 bits of the IP address are mapped to the MAC address. For example, the IP address 238.10.24.5 produces exactly the same MAC address, 0x01-00-5E-0A-18-05, as 228.10.24.5. In fact, because 5 bits from the IP address are always mapped to 0, 25 (32) different class D IP addresses produce exactly the same MAC address. IETF points out that the chances of two multicast applications on the same LAN producing the same MAC address are very low. If it happens accidentally, a packet from a different IP multicast application can be identified at Layer 3 and discarded; however, network administrators should be careful when they implement multicast applications so that they can avoid using IP addresses that produce identical MAC addresses.

Managing Distribution of Multicast Traffic with IGMP

Refer to Figure 7-4. Assume that R2 has started receiving multicast traffic from the server. R2 has to make a decision about forwarding this traffic on the Ethernet links. R2 needs to know the answers to the following questions:

- Is there any host connected to any of my Ethernet links that has shown interest in receiving this traffic?

- If none of the hosts has shown any interest in receiving this traffic, why should I forward it on the Ethernet links and waste bandwidth?

- If any host has shown interest in receiving this traffic, where is it located? Is it connected to one of my Ethernet links or to both?

As you can see, a mechanism is required for hosts and a local router to communicate with each other. The IGMP was designed to enable communication between a router and connected hosts.

Not only do routers need to know out which LAN interface to forward multicast packets, but switches also need to know on which ports they should forward the traffic. By default, if a switch receives a multicast frame on a port, it will flood the frame through-out the VLAN, just like it would do for a broadcast or unknown unicast frame. The reason is that switches will never find a multicast MAC address in their Content Addressable Memory (CAM) table, because a multicast MAC address is never used as a source address.

A switch's decision to flood multicast frames means that if any host or hosts in a VLAN request to receive the traffic for a multicast group, all the remaining hosts in the same VLAN, whether or not they have requested to receive the traffic for the multicast group, will receive the multicast traffic. This behavior is contrary to one of the major goals of multicast design, which is to deliver multicast traffic to only those hosts that have requested it, while maximizing bandwidth efficiency. To forward traffic more efficiently in Figure 7-4, SW2 and SW3 need to know the answers to the following questions:

- Should I forward this multicast traffic on all the ports in this VLAN or only on specific ports?

- If I should forward this multicast traffic on specific ports of a VLAN, how will I find those port numbers?

Three different tools, namely CGMP, IGMP snooping, and RGMP, allow switches to optimize their multicast forwarding logic by answering these kinds of questions. These topics are covered in more depth later in the chapter. For now, this section focuses on how routers and hosts use IGMP to make sure that the router knows whether it should forward multicasts out the router's LAN interfaces.

Joining a Group

Before a host can receive any multicast traffic, a multicast application must be installed and running on that host. The process of installing and running a multicast application is referred to as *launching an application* or *joining a multicast group*. After a host joins a group, the host software calculates the multicast MAC address, and its NIC then starts listening to the multicast MAC address, in addition to its BIA.

Before a host (or a user) can join a group, the user needs to know what groups are available and how to join them. For enterprise-scale multicast applications, the user can simply find a link on a web page and click it, prompting the user's multicast client application to start working with the correct multicast address—totally hiding the multicast address details. Alternately, for an internally developed multicast application, the multicast address can be preconfigured on the client application. For example, a user might be required to log on to a server and authenticate with a name and a password; if the user is authenticated, the multicast application automatically installs on the user's PC, which means that the user has joined the multicast group. When the user no longer wants to use the multicast application, the user must leave the group. For example, the user can simply close the multicast application to leave the group.

The process by which a human discovers which multicast IP address to listen for and join can be a challenge, particularly for multicast traffic on the Internet. The problem is similar to when you have a satellite or digital cable TV system at home: You might have literally thousands of channels, but finding the channel that has the show you want to watch might require a lot of surfing through the list of channels and time slots. For IP multicast, a user needs to discover what applications he might want to use, and the multicast IP addresses used by the applications. A lot of work remains to be done in this area, but some options are available. For example, online TV program guides and web-based schedules advertise events that will use multicast groups and specify who to contact if you want to see the event, lecture, or concert. Tools like Session Description Protocol (SDP) and Service Advertising Protocol (SAP) also describe multicast events and advertise them. However, a detailed discussion of the different methods, their limitations, and procedures for using them is beyond the scope of this book. The rest of the discussion in this section assumes that hosts have somehow learned about a multicast group.

Internet Group Management Protocol

IGMP has evolved from the Host Membership Protocol, described in Dr. Steve Deering's doctoral thesis, to IGMPv1 (RFC 1112), to IGMPv2 (RFC 2236), to the latest, IGMPv3 (RFC 3376). IGMP messages are sent in IP datagrams with IP protocol number 2, with the IP Time-to-Live (TTL) field set to 1. IGMP packets pass only over a LAN and are not forwarded by routers, because of their TTL field values.

The two most important goals of IGMP are as follows:

Key
Topic

- To inform a local multicast router that a host wants to receive multicast traffic for a specific group

- To inform local multicast routers that a host wants to leave a multicast group (in other words, the host is no longer interested in receiving the multicast group traffic)

Multicast routers use IGMP to maintain information for each router interface about which multicast group traffic they should forward and which hosts want to receive it.

The following section examines IGMPv2 in detail and introduces important features of IGMPv3. In the figures that show the operation of IGMP, Layer 2 switches are not shown because IGMP is used for communication between hosts and routers. Later in the chapter, the sections "Cisco Group Management Protocol," "IGMP Snooping," and "Router-Port Group Management Protocol" discuss the operation of multicasting at Layer 2.

IGMP is automatically enabled when multicast routing and PIM are configured on a router. The version can be changed on an interface-by-interface basis. Version 2 is the current default version.

IGMP Version 2

Figure 7-7 shows the 8-octet format of an IGMPv2 message.

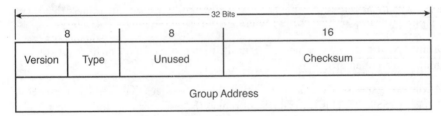

Figure 7-7 *IGMPv2 Message Format*

IGMPv2 has four fields, which are defined as follows:

Key
Topic

- **Type:** 8-bit field that is one of four message types defined by IGMPv2:

    - **Membership Query (Type code = 0x11):** Used by multicast routers to discover the presence of group members on a subnet. A General Membership Query message sets the Group Address field to 0.0.0.0. A Group-Specific Query sets the Group Address field to the address of the group being queried. It is sent by a router after it receives the IGMPv2 Leave Group message from a host.

    - **Version 1 Membership Report (Type code = 0x12):** Used by IGMPv2 hosts for backward compatibility with IGMPv1.

- **Version 2 Membership Report (Type Code = 0x16):** Sent by a group member to inform the router that at least one group member is present on the subnet.

- **Leave Group (Type code = 0x17):** Sent by a group member if it was the last member to send a Membership Report to inform the router that it is leaving the group.

- **Maximum Response Time:** 8-bit field included only in Query messages. The units are 1/10 of a second, with 100 (10 seconds) being the default. The values range from 1 to 255 (0.1 to 25.5 seconds).

- **Checksum:** Carries the 16-bit checksum computed by the source. The IGMP checksum is computed over the entire IP payload, not just over the first 8 octets, even though IGMPv2 messages are only 8 bytes in length.

- **Group Address:** Set to 0.0.0.0 in General Query messages and to the group address in Group-Specific messages. Membership Report messages carry the address of the group being reported in this field; Leave Group messages carry the address of the group being left in this field.

IGMPv2 supports complete backward compatibility with IGMPv1. The IGMPv2 Type codes 0x11 and 0x12 match the type codes for IGMPv1 for the Membership Query and Membership Report messages. This enables IGMPv2 hosts and routers to recognize IGMPv1 messages when IGMPv1 hosts or routers are on the network.

One of the primary reasons for developing IGMPv2 was to provide a better Leave mechanism to shorten the leave latency compared to IGMPv1. IGMPv2 has the following features:

- **Leave Group messages:** Provide hosts with a method for notifying routers that they want to leave the group.

- **Group-Specific Query messages:** Permit the router to send a query for a specific group instead of all groups.

- **Maximum Response Time field:** A field in Query messages that permits the router to specify the MRT. This field allows for tuning the response time for the Host Membership Report. This feature can be useful when a large number of groups are active on a subnet and you want to decrease the burstiness of the responses by spreading the responses over a longer period of time.

- **Querier election process:** Provides the method for selecting the preferred router for sending Query messages when multiple routers are connected to the same subnet.

IGMPv2 helps reduce surges in IGMPv2 Solicited Report messages sent by hosts in response to IGMPv2 Query messages by allowing the network administrator to change the Query Response Interval. Setting the MRT, which ranges from 0.1 to 25.5 seconds, to a value slightly longer than 10 seconds spreads the hosts' collective IGMPv2 Solicited Report messages over a longer time period, resulting in more uniform consumption of subnet bandwidth and router resources. The unit of measurement for the MRT is 0.1 second. For example, a 3-second MRT is expressed as 30.

A multicast host can send an IGMP Report in response to a Query or simply send a Report when the host's application first comes up. The IGMPv2 router acting as the IGMPv2 querier sends general IGMP Query messages every 60 seconds. The operations of IGMPv2 General Query messages and Report messages are covered next.

IGMPv2 Host Membership Query Functions

As illustrated in Figure 7-8, multicast routers send IGMPv2 Host Membership Query messages out LAN interfaces to determine whether a multicast group member is on any interface. Routers send these messages every Query Interval, which is 60 seconds by default. Host Membership Queries use a destination IP address and MAC address of 224.0.0.1 and 01-00-5e-00-00-01, with the source IP address and MAC address of the router's interface IP address and BIA, respectively. IGMPv2 Queries use a TTL of 1 to prevent the packet from being routed.

60 s
by def.

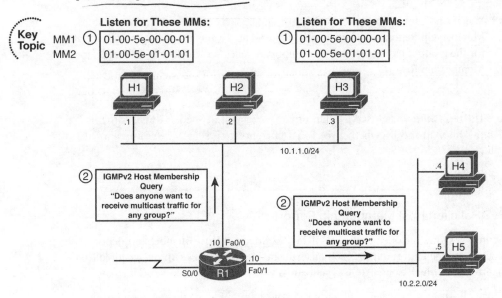

Figure 7-8 *IGMPv2 Host Membership Query Process*

The details of the two steps are as follows:

1. Hosts H1 and H3 join multicast group 226.1.1.1. The hosts prepare to receive messages sent to both 226.1.1.1 (the joined group) and 224.0.0.1 (the address to which IGMPv2 Queries will be sent). The Join causes these hosts to calculate the two multicast MAC (MM) addresses, 01-00-5e-01-01-01 (from 226.1.1.1) and 01-00-5e-00-00-01 (from 224.0.0.1), and then listen for frames sent to these two MMs.

2. R1 periodically sends an IGMPv2 Host Membership Query out each LAN interface, looking for any host interested in receiving packets for any multicast group. After sending IGMPv2 Queries, R1 expects any host that has joined any group to reply with an IGMPv2 Report.

At this point, Router R1 still does not know whether any hosts need to receive any multicast traffic. The next section covers how the hosts respond with IGMP Report messages to inform R1 of their interest in receiving multicast packets.

IGMPv2 Host Membership Report Functions

Key Topic

Hosts use IGMPv2 Host Membership Report messages to reply to IGMP Queries and communicate to a local router for which multicast groups they want to receive traffic.

In IGMPv2, a host sends a Host Membership Report under the following two conditions:

- When a host receives an IGMPv2 Query from a local router, it is supposed to send an IGMPv2 Host Membership Report for all the multicast groups for which it wants to receive multicast traffic. This Report is called an IGMPv2 Solicited Host Membership Report.

- When a host joins a new group, the host immediately sends an IGMPv2 Host Membership Report to inform a local router that it wants to receive multicast traffic for the group it has just joined. This Report is called an IGMPv2 Unsolicited Host Membership Report.

Note   The term *Solicited Host Membership Report* is not defined in RFC 2236. It is used in this book to specify whether the IGMPv2 Report was sent in response to a Query (solicited).

IGMPv2 Solicited Host Membership Report

Figure 7-9 shows the operation of the IGMPv2 Solicited Host Membership Report process and the Report Suppression mechanism. Figure 7-9 picks up the example from Figure 7-8, in which Router R1 had sent an IGMPv2 Query.

If many hosts have launched multicast applications and if all of them respond to the Host Membership Query, unnecessary bandwidth and router resources would be used to process all the redundant reports. A multicast router needs to receive only one report for each application on each of its LAN interfaces. It forwards multicast traffic on an interface whether 1 user or 200 users belong to a given multicast group.

The Report Suppression mechanism helps to solve these problems. It uses the IGMPv2 Maximum Response Time (MRT) timer to suppress many of the unnecessary IGMP Reports. This timer is called the *Query Response Interval.* In other words, when any host receives an IGMPv2 Query, it has a maximum of the configured MRT to send the IGMP Report if it wants to receive multicast traffic for that application. Each host picks a random time between 0 and the MRT and starts a timer. When this timer expires, the host will send a Host Membership report—but only if it has not already heard another host send a report for its group. This is called *Report Suppression* and is designed to reduce redundant reports.

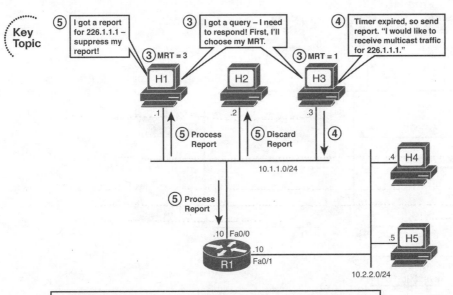

Figure 7-9 *IGMPv2 Solicited Host Membership Report and Report Suppression Processes*

The following three steps describe the sequence of events for the IGMPv2 Solicited Host Membership Report and Report Suppression mechanism shown in Figure 7.9:

3. Assume that H1 and H3 have received an IGMPv2 Query (as shown in Step 2 of Figure 7-8). Because both H1 and H3 have joined the group 226.1.1.1, they need to send an IGMPv2 Solicited Host Membership Report. Furthermore, assume that H1 and H3 have randomly picked an MRT of 3 seconds and 1 second, respectively.

4. H3's timer expires in 1 second; it prepares and sends the IGMPv2 Solicited Host Membership Report with the TTL value of 1. H3 uses the destination IP address 226.1.1.1 and its source IP address 10.1.1.3, the destination MAC address 01-00-5e-01-01-01 calculated from the Layer 3 address 226.1.1.1, and its BIA as the source address. By using the group address of 226.1.1.1, H3 is telling the multicast router, "I would like to receive multicast traffic for group 226.1.1.1."

5. Hosts H1, H2, and R1 see the IGMPv2 Solicited Host Membership Report, but only H1 and R1 process the Report. H2 discards the frame sent because it is not listening to that multicast MAC address. H1 realizes that H3's Report is for the same multicast group as 226.1.1.1. Therefore, H1, suppresses its own Report and does not send it.

R1 has now received the IGMPv2 Solicited Host Membership Report on its fa0/0 interface requesting traffic for multicast group 226.1.1.1, but it has not received a Host Membership Report on its fa0/1 interface. Figure 7-10 shows that R1 has started forwarding multicast traffic for group 226.1.1.1 on its fa0/0 interface.

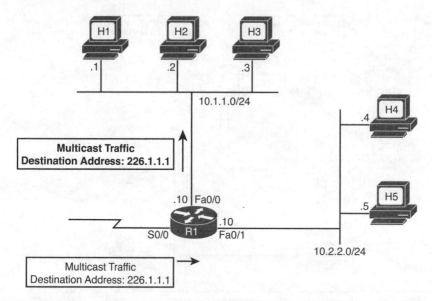

Figure 7-10 *R1 Forwarding Traffic for Group 226.1.1.1 on Its Fa0/0 Interface*

IGMPv2 Unsolicited Host Membership Report

In IGMPv2, a host does not have to wait for a Host Membership Query message from the router. Hosts can send an IGMPv2 Unsolicited Host Membership Report anytime a user launches a multicast application. This feature reduces the waiting time for a host to receive traffic for a multicast group. For example, Figure 7-11 shows that a user has launched a multicast application that uses 226.1.1.1 on H4. H4 sends an IGMPv2 Unsolicited Host Membership Report, and R1 then starts forwarding traffic for 226.1.1.1 on its fa0/1 interface.

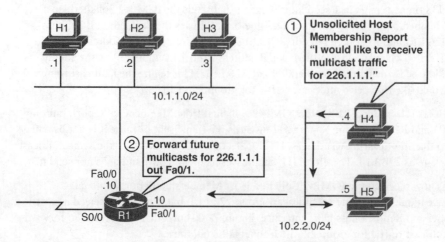

Figure 7-11 *H4 Sends IGMPv2 Unsolicited Host Membership Report*

IGMPv2 Leave Group and Group-Specific Query Messages

The IGMPv2 Leave Group message is used to significantly reduce the leave latency, while the IGMPv2 Group-Specific Query message prevents a router from incorrectly stopping the forwarding of packets on a LAN when a host leaves a group. In IGMPv2, when a host leaves a group, it sends an IGMPv2 Leave message. When an IGMPv2 router receives a Leave message, it immediately sends a Group-Specific Query for that group. The Group-Specific Query asks only whether any remaining hosts still want to receive packets for that single multicast group. As a result, the router quickly knows whether to continue to forward traffic for that multicast group.

The main advantage of IGMPv2 over IGMPv1 is IGMPv2's shorter leave latency. An IGMPv1 router takes, by default, 3 minutes to conclude that the last host on the subnet has left a group and no host on the subnet wants to receive traffic for the group. Meanwhile, the IGMPv1 router continues forwarding the group traffic on the subnet and wastes bandwidth. On the other hand, an IGMPv2 router concludes in 3 seconds that no host on the subnet wants to receive traffic for a group and stops forwarding it on the subnet.

Note   IGMPv2 RFC 2236 recommends that a host sends a Leave Group message only if the leaving member was the last host to send a Membership Report in response to a Query. However, most IGMPv2 vendor operating systems have implemented the Leave Group processing by always sending a Leave Group message when any host leaves the group.

Figure 7-12 shows the operation of the IGMPv2 Leave process and the IGMP Group-Specific Query. In Figure 7-12, hosts H1 and H3 are currently members of group 226.1.1.1; H1 wants to leave the group.

The following three steps, referenced in Figure 7-12, describe the sequence of events for the IGMPv2 Leave mechanism when H1 leaves:

1. H1 sends an IGMPv2 Leave Group message. The destination address is 224.0.0.2, the well-known address for All Multicast Routers to inform all routers on the subnet that "I don't want to receive multicast traffic for 226.1.1.1 anymore."

2. R1 sends a Group-Specific Query. Routers do not keep track of hosts that are members of the group, only the group memberships that are active. Because H1 has decided to leave 226.1.1.1, R1 needs to make sure that no other hosts off this interface still need to receive packets for group 226.1.1.1. Therefore, R1 sends a Group-Specific Query using 226.1.1.1 as the destination address on the packet so that only hosts that are members of this group will receive the message and respond. Through this message, R1 is asking any remaining hosts on the subnet, "Does anyone want to receive multicast traffic for 226.1.1.1?"

3. H3 sends a Membership Report. H3 hears the Group-Specific Query and responds with an IGMPv2 Membership Report to inform the routers on the subnet that it is still a member of group 226.1.1.1 and would like to keep receiving traffic for group 226.1.1.1.

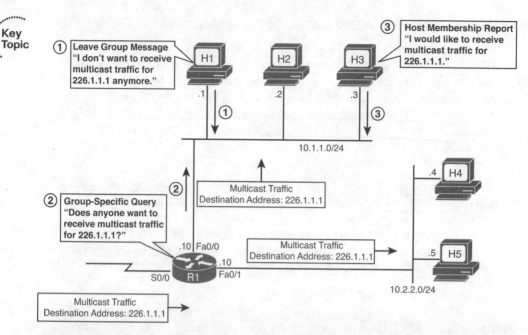

Figure 7-12   *How Group-Specific Queries Work with the IGMPv2 Leave Process*

> **Note**   The Report Suppression mechanism explained earlier for the General Group Query is also used for the Group-Specific Query.

IGMPv2 routers repeat the process of Step 2 in this example each time they receive a Leave message. In the next example, H3 is the only remaining member of group 226.1.1.1 on the subnet. Figure 7-13 shows what happens when H3 also wants to leave the group.

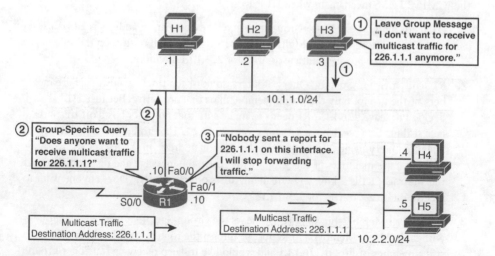

Figure 7-13   *IGMPv2 Leave Process—No Response to the Group-Specific Query*

The following three steps, referenced in Figure 7-13, describe the sequence of events for the IGMPv2 Leave mechanism when H3 leaves:

1. H3 sends an IGMPv2 Leave Group message. The destination address on the packet is 224.0.0.2 to inform all routers on the subnet that "I don't want to receive multicast traffic for 226.1.1.1 anymore."

2. When R1 receives the Leave Group message from H3, it sends a Group-Specific Query to determine whether any hosts are still members of group 226.1.1.1. R1 uses 226.1.1.1 as the destination address on the packet.

3. Because there are now no remaining members of 226.1.1.1 on the subnet, R1 does not receive a response to the Group-Specific Query. As a result, R1 stops forwarding multicasts for 226.1.1.1 out its fa0/0 interface.

Step 3 of this example provides a nice backdrop from which to describe the concepts of a *Last Member Query Interval* and a *Last Member Query Count*. These values determine how long it takes a router to believe that all hosts on a LAN have left a particular group. By default, routers use an MRT of 10 (1 second) for Group-Specific Queries. Because a router should receive a response to a Group-Specific Query in that amount of time, the router uses the MRT value as the value of the Last Member Query Interval. So, the router uses the following process:

Key
Topic

1. Send a Group-Specific Query in response to an IGMP Leave.

2. If no Report is received within the Last Member Query Interval, repeat Step 1.

3. Repeat Step 1 the number of times defined by the value of the Last Member Query Count.

The Last Member Query Count is the number of consecutive Group-Specific Queries a router will send before it concludes that there are no active members of the group on a subnet. The default value for the Last Member Query Count is 2. So the leave latency is typically less than 3 seconds, compared to up to 3 minutes with IGMPv1.

3 sec vs 3 min
IGMPv2 vs IGMPv1

IGMPv2 Querier

IGMPv2 defines a querier election process that is used when multiple routers are connected to a subnet. When IGMPv2 routers start, they each send an IGMPv2 General Query message to the well-known All Hosts group 224.0.0.1. When an IGMPv2 router receives a General Query message, it compares the source IP address of the General Query message with its own interface address. The router with the lowest IP address on the subnet is elected as the IGMP querier. The nonquerier routers do not send queries but monitor how frequently the querier is sending general IGMPv2 Queries. When the elected querier does not send a query for two consecutive Query Intervals plus one half of one Query Response Interval, it is considered to be dead, and a new querier is elected. RFC 2236 refers to this time interval as the *Other Querier Present Interval*. The default value for the Other Querier Present Interval is 255 seconds, because the default General IGMPv2 Query Interval is 125 seconds and the default Query Response Interval is 10 seconds.

Lowest IP on the segment will be the Querier

$(2 \times 125) + 2 \times (10 : 2) = 255$

IGMPv2 Timers

Table 7-4 summarizes important timers used in IGMPv2, their usage, and default values.

Table 7-4   *Important IGMPv2 Timers*

Timer	Usage	Default Value
Query Interval	A time period between General Queries sent by a router.	60 seconds
Query Response Interval	The maximum response time for hosts to respond to the periodic general Queries.	10 seconds; can be between 0.1 and 25.5 seconds
Group Membership Interval	A time period during which, if a router does not receive an IGMP Report, the router concludes that there are no more members of the group on the subnet.	260 seconds
Other Querier Present Interval	A time period during which, if the IGMPv2 nonquerier routers do not receive an IGMP Query from the querier router, the nonquerier routers conclude that the querier is dead.	255 seconds
Last Member Query Interval	The maximum response time inserted by IGMPv2 routers into the Group-Specific Queries and the time period between two consecutive Group-Specific Queries sent for the same group.	1 second
Version 1 Router Present Timeout	A time period during which, if an IGMPv2 host does not receive an IGMPv1 Query, the IGMPv2 host concludes that there are no IGMPv1 routers present and starts sending IGMPv2 messages.	400 seconds

IGMP Version 3

In October 2002, RFC 3376 defined specifications for IGMPv3, which is a major revision of the protocol. To use the new features of IGMPv3, last-hop routers have to be updated, host operating systems have to be modified, and applications have to be specially designed and written. This section does not examine IGMPv3 in detail; instead, it summarizes IGMPv3's major features.

In IGMPv2, when a host makes a request to join a group, a multicast router forwards the traffic for the group to the subnet regardless of the source IP address of the packets. In very large networks, such as an Internet broadcast, this can cause problems. For example, assume that a multimedia conference is in session. A group member decides to maliciously disturb the session by sending talking or music to the same group. Although multimedia applications allow a user to mute any of the other members, it does not stop the unwanted traffic from being delivered to the host. In addition, if a group of hackers decides to flood a company's network with bogus high-bandwidth data using the same multicast group address that the company's employees have joined, it can create a DoS attack for the company by overwhelming low-speed links. Neither IGMPv1 nor IGMPv2 has a mechanism to prevent such an attack.

IGMPv3 allows a host to filter incoming traffic based on the source IP addresses from which it is willing to receive packets, through a feature called *Source-Specific Multicast (SSM)*. SSM allows a host to indicate interest in receiving packets only from specific source addresses, or from all but specific source addresses, sent to a particular multicast address. Figure 7-14 shows the basic operation of the IGMPv3 Membership Report process.

SSH

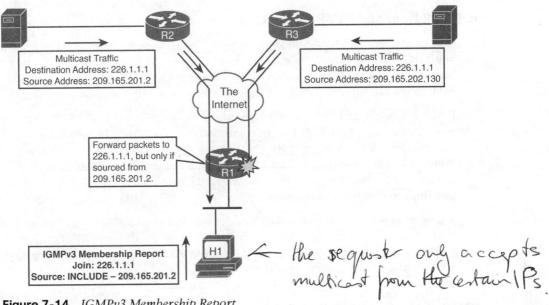

Figure 7-14 *IGMPv3 Membership Report*

In Figure 7-14, the multicast traffic for the group 226.1.1.1 is available from two sources. R1 receives traffic from both the sources. H1 prepares an IGMPv3 Membership Report using the destination address 224.0.0.22, specially assigned by IANA for the IGMPv3 Membership Report. The message type is 0x22 (defined in RFC 3376), with a note "Source–INCLUDE—209.165.201.2," which means, "I would like to join multicast group 226.1.1.1, but only if the group traffic is coming from the source 209.165.201.2."

224.0.0.22 — *IGMPv3 membership report*

Cisco has designed URL Rendezvous Directory (URD) and IGMP v3lite to use the new features of IGMPv3 until IGMPv3 applications are available and operating systems are updated. A detailed discussion of URD and IGMP v3lite is beyond the scope of this book. IGMPv3 is compatible with IGMPv1 and IGMPv2. ⟳ *backward comp.*

Note The following URL provides more information on IGMPv3, URD, and IGMP v3lite: www.cisco.com/en/US/docs/ios/ipmulti/configuration/guide/12_4/imc_12_4_book.html.

IGMPv1 and IGMPv2 Interoperability

IGMPv2 is designed to be backward compatible with IGMPv1. RFC 2236 defines some special interoperability rules. The next two sections explore the following interoperability scenarios:

■ **"IGMPv2 Host and IGMPv1 Routers"**: Defines how an IGMPv2 host should behave in the presence of an IGMPv1 router on the same subnet.

■ **"IGMPv1 Host and IGMPv2 Routers"**: Defines how an IGMPv2 router should behave in the presence of an IGMPv1 host on the same subnet.

IGMPv2 Host and IGMPv1 Routers

When a host sends the IGMPv2 Report with the message type 0x16, which is not defined in IGMPv1, a version 1 router would consider 0x16 an invalid message type and ignore it. Therefore, a version 2 host must send IGMPv1 Reports when a version 1 router is active. But how does an IGMPv2 host detect the presence of an IGMPv1 router on the subnet?

IGMPv2 hosts determine whether the querying router is an IGMPv1 or IGMPv2 host based on the value of the MRT field of the periodic general IGMP Query. In IGMPv1 Queries, this field is 0, whereas in IGMPv2, it is nonzero and represents the MRT value. When an IGMPv2 host receives an IGMPv1 Query, it knows that the IGMPv1 router is present on the subnet and marks the interface as an IGMPv1 interface. The IGMPv2 host then stops sending IGMPv2 messages.

Whenever an IGMPv2 host receives an IGMPv1 Query, it starts a 400-second Version 1 Router Present Timeout timer. This timer is reset whenever it receives an IGMPv1 Query. If the timer expires, which indicates that there are no IGMPv1 routers present on the subnet, the IGMPv2 host starts sending IGMPv2 messages.

IGMPv1 Host and IGMPv2 Routers

IGMPv2 routers can easily determine whether any IGMPv1 hosts are present on a LAN based on whether any hosts send an IGMPv1 Report message (type 0x12) or IGMPv2 Report message (type 0x16). Like IGMPv1 routers, IGMPv2 routers send periodic IGMPv2 General Queries. An IGMPv1 host responds normally because IGMPv2 General Queries are very similar in format to IGMPv1 Queries—except for the second octet, which is ignored by IGMPv1 hosts. So, an IGMPv2 router will examine all Reports to find out whether any IGMPv1 hosts exist on a LAN.

> **Note** If IGMPv2 hosts are also present on the same subnet, they would send IGMPv2 Membership Reports. However, IGMPv1 hosts do not understand IGMPv2 Reports and ignore them; they do not trigger Report Suppression in IGMPv1 hosts. Therefore, sometimes an IGMPv2 router receives both an IGMPv1 Report and an IGMPv2 Report in response to a General Query.

While an IGMPv2 router knows that an IGMPv1 host is present on a LAN, the router ignores Leave messages and the Group-Specific Queries triggered by receipt of the Leave messages. This is necessary because if an IGMPv2 router responds to a Leave Group message with a Group-Specific Query, IGMPv1 hosts will not understand it and thus ignore the message. When an IGMPv2 router does not receive a response to its Group-Specific Query, it might erroneously conclude that nobody wants to receive traffic for the group and thus stop forwarding it on the subnet. So with one or more IGMPv1 hosts listening for a particular group, the router essentially suspends the optimizations that reduce leave latency.

IGMPv2 routers continue to ignore Leave messages until the IGMPv1-Host-Present Countdown timer expires. RFC 2236 defines that when IGMPv2 routers receive an IGMPv1 Report, they must set an IGMPv1-host-present countdown timer. The timer value should be equal to the Group Membership Interval, which defaults to 180 seconds in IGMPv1 and 260 seconds in IGMPv2. (Group Membership Interval is a time period during which, if a router does not receive an IGMP Report, the router concludes that there are no more members of the group on a subnet.)

Comparison of IGMPv1, IGMPv2, and IGMPv3

Table 7-5 compares the important features of IGMPv1, IGMPv2, and IGMPv3.

Table 7-5 *Comparison of IGMPv1, IGMPv2, and IGMPv3*

Feature	IGMPv1	IGMPv2	IGMPv3
First Octet Value for the Query Message	0x11	0x11	0x11
Group Address for the General Query	0.0.0.0	0.0.0.0	0.0.0.0
Destination Address for the General Query	224.0.0.1	224.0.0.1	224.0.0.1
Default Query Interval	60 seconds	125 seconds	125 seconds
First Octet Value for the Report	0x12	0x16	0x22
Group Address for the Report	Joining multicast group address	Joining multicast group address	Joining multicast group address and source address
Destination Address for the Report	Joining multicast group address	Joining multicast group address	224.0.0.22
Is Report Suppression Mechanism Available?	Yes	Yes	No

Feature	IGMPv1	IGMPv2	IGMPv3
Can Maximum Response Time Be Configured?	No, fixed at 10 seconds	Yes, 0 to 25.5 seconds	Yes, 0 to 53 minutes
Can a Host Send a Leave Group Message?	No	Yes	Yes
Destination Address for the Leave Group Message	—	224.0.0.2	224.0.0.22
Can a Router Send a Group-Specific Query?	No	Yes	Yes
Can a Host Send Source- and Group-Specific Reports?	No	No	Yes
Can a Router Send Source- and Group-Specific Queries?	No	No	Yes
Rule for Electing a Querier	None (depends on multicast routing protocol)	Router with the lowest IP address on the subnet	Router with the lowest IP address on the subnet
Compatible with Other Versions of IGMP?	No	Yes, only with IGMPv1	Yes, with both IGMPv1 and IGMPv2

LAN Multicast Optimizations

This final major section of this chapter introduces the basics of three tools that optimize the flow of multicast over a LAN. Specifically, this section covers the following topics:

- Cisco Group Management Protocol (CGMP)

- IGMP snooping

- Router-Port Group Management Protocol (RGMP)

Cisco Group Management Protocol

IGMP helps routers to determine how to distribute multicast traffic. However, IGMP works at Layer 3, and switches do not understand IGMP messages. Switches, by default, flood multicast traffic to all the hosts in a broadcast domain, which wastes bandwidth. Figure 7-15 illustrates the problem.

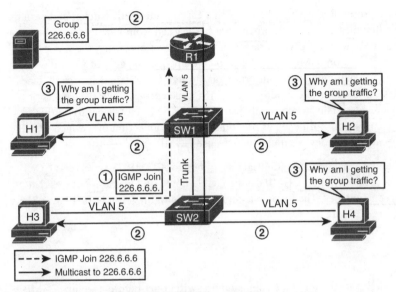

Figure 7-15 *Switches Flood Multicast Traffic*

Hosts H1, H2, H3, H4, and R1 are all in the same broadcast domain of VLAN 5. The following three steps, referenced in Figure 7-15, describe the sequence of events when H3 sends an IGMP Join message:

1. H3 sends an IGMP Join message for group 226.6.6.6.

2. R1 forwards the group traffic to SW1. The destination MAC address on the frame is 0x0100.5e06.0606. SW1 cannot find this address in its CAM table because it is never used by any device as a source address. Therefore, SW1 starts forwarding the group traffic to H1, H2, and SW2 because the group traffic is for VLAN 5. Similarly, SW2 starts forwarding the group traffic to H3 and H4.

3. All the hosts, H1 to H4, receive the group traffic, but only H3 requested it. H3 requested the group traffic and has started receiving it. However, H1, H2, and H4 did not ask for the group traffic, and they are flooded by switches with the group traffic.

In this illustration, only four hosts are shown in the broadcast domain of VLAN 5. What happens if a broadcast domain is flat and has hundreds of users? If a single host joins a multicast group, all the hosts would be flooded with the group traffic whether or not they have requested the group traffic. The goal of multicasting is to deliver the group traffic to only those hosts that have requested it and maximize the use of bandwidth.

There are two popular methods for helping Layer 2 switches determine how to distribute the multicast traffic to hosts:

■ CGMP, which is Cisco proprietary and discussed throughout the rest of this section.

■ IGMP snooping, discussed in the next section.

CGMP, a Layer 2 protocol, is configured on both a Cisco router and switches and permits the router to communicate Layer 2 information it has learned from IGMP to switches. A multicast router knows the MAC addresses of the multicast hosts, and the groups to which they listen, based on IGMP communication with hosts. The goal of CGMP is to enable the router to communicate this information through CGMP messages to switches so that switches can dynamically modify their CAM table entries. Only the routers produce CGMP messages, while switches only listen to the CGMP messages. To do this, CGMP must be enabled at both ends of the router-switch connection over which CGMP is operating, because both devices must know to use CGMP.

Layer 3 switches, such as the Cisco 3560, act as routers for CGMP. They serve as CGMP servers only. On these switches, CGMP can be enabled only on Layer 3 interfaces that connect to Layer 2 switches. The following commands configure a router or a Layer 3 switch interface for CGMP:

```
int fa 0/1
  ip cgmp
```

On a Layer 3 switch, use the interface command **no switchport** before enabling CGMP.

The destination address on the CGMP messages is always the well-known CGMP multicast MAC address 0x0100.0cdd.dddd. The use of the multicast destination MAC address on the CGMP messages forces switches to flood the message through all the ports so that all the switches in a network receive the CGMP messages. The important information in the CGMP messages is one or more pairs of MAC addresses:

- Group Destination Address (GDA)

- Unicast Source Address (USA)

The following five steps describe the general process of CGMP. Later, these steps are explained using a detailed example.

1. When a CGMP-capable router gets connected to the switch, it sends a CGMP Join message with the GDA set to 0 and the USA set to its own MAC address. The CGMP-capable switch now knows that a multicast router is connected to the port on which it received the router's CGMP message. The router repeats the message every 60 seconds. A router can also tell the switch that it no longer participates in CGMP by sending a CGMP Leave message with the GDA set to 0 and the USA set to its own MAC address.

2. When a host joins a group, it sends an IGMP Join message. Normally, a multicast router examines only Layer 3 information in the IGMP Join message, and the router does not have to process any Layer 2 information. However, when CGMP is configured on a router, the router also examines the Layer 2 destination and source MAC addresses of the IGMP Join message. The source address is the unicast MAC address of the host that sent the IGMP Join message. The router then generates a CGMP Join message that includes the multicast MAC address associated with the multicast IP address (to the GDA field of the CGMP join) and the unicast MAC address of the

host (to the USA field of the CGMP message). The router sends the CGMP Join message using the well-known CGMP multicast MAC address 0x0100.0cdd.dddd as the destination address.

3. When switches receive a CGMP Join message, they search in their CAM tables for the port number associated with the host MAC address listed in the USA field. Switches create a new CAM table entry (or use an existing entry if it was already created before) for the multicast MAC address listed in the GDA field of the CGMP Join message, add the port number associated with the host MAC address listed in the USA field to the entry, and forward the group traffic on the port.

4. When a host leaves a group, it sends an IGMP Leave message. The router learns the host's unicast MAC address (USA) and the IP multicast group it has just left. Because the Leave messages are sent to the All Multicast Routers MAC address 0x0100.5e00.0002 and not to the multicast group address the host has just left, the router calculates the multicast MAC address (GDA) from the IP multicast group the host has just left. The router then generates a CGMP Leave message, copies the multicast MAC address it has just calculated in the GDA field and unicast MAC address in the USA field of the CGMP Leave message, and sends it to the well-known CGMP multicast MAC address.

5. When switches receive a CGMP Leave message, they again search for the port number associated with the host MAC address listed in the USA field. Switches remove this port from the CAM table entry for the multicast MAC address listed in the GDA field of the CGMP Leave message and stop forwarding the group traffic on the port.

Thus, CGMP helps switches send group traffic to only those hosts that want it, which helps to avoid wasted bandwidth.

Figures 7-16, 7-17, and 7-18 show a complete example of how routers and switches use CGMP in response to a host joining and then leaving a group. Figure 7-16 begins the example by showing a router's reaction to an IGMP Report, which is to send a CGMP Join to the switches on a LAN. The following two steps, referenced in Figure 7-16, describe the sequence of events when H3 sends an IGMP Join message:

1. H3 sends an IGMP Join message for 226.6.6.6. At Layer 2, H3 uses 0x0100.5e06.0606 (the multicast MAC address associated with 226.6.6.6) as the destination address of a frame and its own BIA 0x0006.7c11.1103 as the source MAC address.

2. R1 generates a CGMP Join message. When a CGMP-capable router receives an IGMP Join message, it generates a Layer 2 CGMP Join message. The destination address on the frame is the well-known multicast MAC address 0x0100.0cdd.dddd, which is understood only by Cisco switches but is forwarded by all switches. R1 sets the GDA to the group MAC address 0x0100.5e06.0606 and sets the USA to H3's MAC address 0x0006.7c11.1103, which communicates to switches that "A host with the USA 0x0006.7c11.1103 has requested multicast traffic for the GDA 0x0100.5e06.0606, so map your CAM tables accordingly." This message is received by both switches.

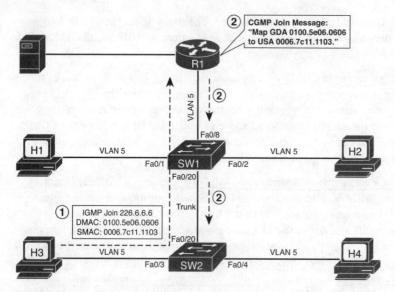

Figure 7-16 *CGMP Join Message Process*

SW1 and SW2 search their CAM table entries and find that a host with the USA 0x0006.7c11.1103 is located on their port number fa0/20 and fa0/3, respectively. Figure 7-17 shows that SW1 and SW2 have mapped the GDA 0x0100.5e06.0606 to their port numbers fa0/20 and fa0/3, respectively.

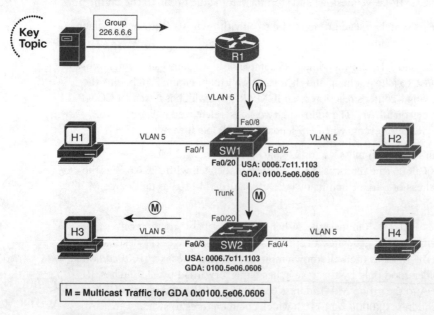

Figure 7-17 *Switches Map GDA to Port Numbers and Don't Flood All the Hosts in a Broadcast Domain*

When R1 forwards multicast traffic with GDA 0x0100.5e06.0606 to SW1, as shown in Figure 7-17, SW1 searches its CAM table and notices that this traffic should be forwarded only on port fa0/20. Therefore, only SW2 receives the group traffic. Similarly, SW2 searches its CAM table and forwards the group traffic only on its port fa0/3, and only H3 receives the group traffic.

CGMP optimizes the forwarding of IGMP traffic as well. Although not shown in the figures, assume that H1 sends an IGMP Join message for 226.6.6.6. R1 will send another CGMP Join message, and SW1 will add the GDA 0x0100.5e06.0606 to its port fa0/1 also. When a router sends IGMP General Queries, switches forward them to host members who have joined any group, for example, H1 and H3. When hosts send IGMP Reports, switches forward them to the members of the group and the router.

[handwritten margin note: further optimization through CGMP]

The final step of the example, shown in Figure 7-18, demonstrates what happens when H3 leaves the group. Note that for this example, H1 has also joined the same multicast group.

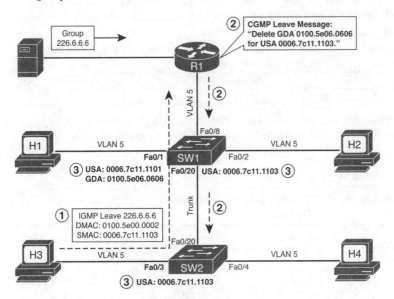

Figure 7-18 *CGMP Leave Message Process*

The following three steps, referenced in Figure 7-18, describe the sequence of events when H3 sends an IGMP Leave message:

1. H3 sends an IGMP Leave message for 226.6.6.6. At Layer 2, H3 uses the All Multicast Routers MAC address 0x0100.5e00.0002 as the destination address and its own BIA 0x0006.7c11.1103 as the source address.

2. R1 generates a CGMP Leave message. When a CGMP-capable router receives an IGMP Leave message, it generates a Layer 2 CGMP Leave message. The destination address on the frame is the well-known multicast MAC address 0x0100.0cdd.dddd. R1 calculates the group MAC address 0x0100.5e06.0606 from the Layer 3 address 226.6.6.6 and sets the GDA to that value. It sets the USA to H3's MAC unicast MAC

address of 0x0006.7c11.1103. This Leave message communicates to switches that "A host with the USA 0x0006.7c11.1103 does not want to receive multicast traffic for GDA 0x0100.5e06.0606, so update your CAM tables accordingly." This message is received by both switches.

3. Switches update their CAM table entries. SW1 and SW2 search their CAM table entries and find that a host with the USA 0x0006.7c11.1103 is located on their port numbers fa0/20 and fa0/3, respectively. Figure 7-18 shows that SW1 and SW2 have removed the GDA 0x0100.5e06.0606 from their port numbers fa0/20 and fa0/3, respectively.

H1 is still a member of the group 226.6.6.6, so R1 keeps forwarding the traffic with GDA 0x0100.5e06.0606 to SW1, as shown in Figure 7-18. SW1 searches its CAM table and finds that this traffic should be forwarded only on port fa0/1. Therefore, only H1 receives the group traffic.

H1: last member leaves the group

Continuing the example further, now assume that H1 sends an IGMP Leave message for 226.6.6.6. R1 will send a Group-Specific Query for 226.6.6.6. Because no host is currently a member of this group, R1 does not receive any IGMP Membership Reports for the group. R1 sends the CGMP Leave message with the GDA set to the group MAC address and the USA set to 0. This message communicates to switches that "No hosts are interested in receiving the multicast group traffic for the MAC address 0x0100.5e06.0606, so remove all the CAM table entries for this group."

Table 7-6 summarizes the possible combinations of the GDA and the USA in CGMP messages and the meanings of each. The first five messages have been discussed.

Key Topic

Table 7-6   *CGMP Messages*

Type	Group Destination Address	Unicast Source Address	Meaning
Join	Group MAC	Host MAC	Add USA port to group
Leave	Group MAC	Host MAC	Delete USA port from group
Join	Zero	Router MAC	Learn which port connects to the CGMP router
Leave	Zero	Router MAC	Release CGMP router port
Leave	Group MAC	Zero	Delete the group from the CAM
Leave	Zero	Zero	Delete all groups from the CAM

no more members

The last Leave message in Table 7-6, Delete All Groups, is used by the router for special maintenance functions. For example, when the **clear ip cgmp** command is entered at the router for clearing all the CGMP entries on the switches, the router sends the CGMP Leave message with GDA set to 0 and USA set to 0. When switches receive this message, they delete all group entries from the CAM tables.

IGMP Snooping → *intercepts IGMP messages*

What happens if your network has non-Cisco switches? You cannot use CGMP because it is Cisco proprietary. IGMP snooping can be used for a multivendor switched network to control distribution of multicast traffic at Layer 2. IGMP snooping requires the switch software to eavesdrop on the IGMP conversation between multicast hosts and the router. The switch examines IGMP messages and learns the location of multicast routers and group members.

> **Note** Many Cisco switches support IGMP snooping, including the 3560 switches used in the CCIE Routing and Switching lab exam.

The following three steps describe the general process of IGMP snooping. Later, these steps are explained in detail.

1. To detect whether multiple routers are connected to the same subnet, Cisco switches listen to the following routing protocol messages to determine on which ports routers are connected:

   - IGMP General Query message with GDA 01-00-5e-00-00-01
   - OSPF messages with GDA 01-00-5e-00-00-05 or 01-00-5e-00-00-06
   - Protocol Independent Multicast (PIM) version 1 and Hot Standby Routing Protocol (HSRP) Hello messages with GDA 01-00-5e-00-00-02
   - PIMv2 Hello messages with GDA 01-00-5e-00-00-0d
   - Distance Vector Multicast Routing Protocol (DVMRP) Probe messages with GDA 01-00-5e-00-00-04

   As soon as the switch detects router ports in a VLAN, they are added to the port list of all GDAs in that VLAN.

2. When the switch receives an IGMP Report on a port, its CPU looks at the GDA, creates an entry in the CAM table for the GDA, and adds the port to the entry. The router port is also added to the entry. The group traffic is now forwarded on this port and the router port. If other hosts send their IGMP Reports, the switch adds their ports to the group entry in the CAM table and forwards the group traffic on these ports.

3. Similarly, when the switch receives an IGMP Leave message on a port, its CPU looks at the GDA, removes the port from the group entry in the CAM table, and does not forward the group traffic on the port. The switch checks whether this is the last nonrouter port for the GDA. If it is not the last nonrouter port for the GDA, which means that there is at least one host in the VLAN that wants the group traffic, the switch discards the Leave message; otherwise, it sends the Leave message to the router. *if not the last one discards the leave message*

Thus, IGMP snooping helps switches send group traffic to only those hosts that want it and helps to avoid wasted bandwidth.

For efficient operations, IGMP snooping requires hardware filtering support in a switch so that it can differentiate between IGMP Reports and actual multicast traffic. The switch CPU needs to see IGMP Report messages (and Multicast Routing Protocol messages) because the IGMP snooping process requires the CPU. However, the forwarding of multicast frames does not require the CPU, instead requiring only a switch's forwarding ASICs. Older switches, particularly those that have no Layer 3 awareness, could not identify a packet as IGMP; these switches would have overburdened their CPUs by having to send all multicasts to the CPU. Most of today's more modern switches support enough Layer 3 awareness to recognize IGMP so that IGMP snooping does not overburden the CPU.

IGMP snooping is enabled by default on the Cisco 3560 switches used in the lab, and most other Layer 3 switches. The exact VLANs it snoops on can be controlled, as well as timers. The following configuration assumes that IGMP snooping has been disabled. It reenables snooping, disables it for VLAN 20, and reduces the last-member query interval from the default of 1000 seconds to 500 seconds. In addition, because VLAN 22 is connected only to hosts, it enables the switch to immediately remove a port when an IGMP Leave is received. Notice that commands are given globally.

```
sw2(config)# ip igmp snooping
sw2(config)# no ip igmp snooping vlan 20
sw2(config)# ip igmp snooping last-member-query-interval 500
sw2(config)# ip igmp snooping vlan 22 immediate-leave
```

> **Note**   CGMP was a popular Cisco switch feature in years past because IGMP implementations on some switches would have required too much work. Today, many of the Cisco current switch product offerings do not even support CGMP, in deference to IGMP snooping, or support it only for connecting to lower-end Layer 2 switches.

Figure 7-19 shows an example of the IGMP snooping process.

The following three steps, referenced in Figure 7-19, describe the sequence of events when H1 and H2 send IGMP Join messages:

1. H1 sends an IGMP Join message for 226.6.6.6. At Layer 2, H1 uses the multicast MAC address 0x0100.5e06.0606 (the MAC for group 226.6.6.6) as the destination address and uses its own BIA 0x0006.7c11.1101 as the source address. SW1 receives the packet on its fa0/1 port and, noticing that it is an IGMP packet, forwards the packet to the switch CPU. The CPU uses the information to set up a multicast forwarding table entry, as shown in the CAM table that includes the port numbers 0 for CPU, 1 for H1, and 8 for R1. Notice that the CAM table lists two entries for the same destination MAC address 0x0100.5e06.0606—one for the IGMP frames for port 0 and the other for the non-IGMP frames for ports 1 and 8. The CPU of the switch instructs the switching engine to not forward any non-IGMP frames to port 0, which is connected to the CPU.

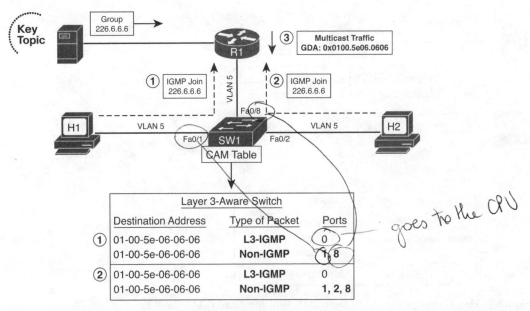

Figure 7-19   *Joining a Group Using IGMP Snooping and CAM Table Entries*

2. H2 sends an IGMP Join message for 226.6.6.6. At Layer 2, H2 uses the multicast
   MAC address 0x0100.5e06.0606 as the destination address and uses its own BIA
   0x0006.7c11.1102 as the source address. SW1 receives the packet on its fa0/2 port,
   and its switching engine examines the packet. The process of analyzing the packet,
   as described in Step 1, is repeated and the CAM table entries are updated as shown.

3. Router R1 forwards the group traffic. R1 is receiving multicast traffic for group
   226.6.6.6 and starts forwarding the traffic to SW1. SW1 starts receiving the multicast
   traffic on its port fa0/8. The switching engine would examine the packet and determine that this is a non-IGMP packet, search its CAM table, and determine that it
   should forward the packet on ports fa0/1 and fa0/2.

Compared to CGMP, IGMP snooping is less efficient in maintaining group information.
In Figure 7-20, when R1 periodically sends IGMP General Queries to the All Hosts group,
224.0.0.1 (GDA 0x0100.5e00.0001), SW1 intercepts the General Queries and forwards
them through all ports in VLAN 5. In CGMP, because of communication from the router
through CGMP messages, the switch knows exactly on which ports multicast hosts are
connected and, therefore, forwards IGMP General Queries only on those ports. Also, in
IGMP snooping, when hosts send IGMP Reports, the switch must intercept them to maintain GDA information in the CAM table. As a result, the hosts do not receive each other's
IGMP Report, which breaks the Report Suppression mechanism and forces each host to
send an IGMP Report. However, the switch sends only one IGMP Report per group to
the router. In CGMP, the switch does not have to intercept IGMP Reports, because maintaining group information in the switch is not dependent on examining IGMP packets
from hosts; instead, the switch uses CGMP messages from the router.

Figure 7-20 shows the Leave process for IGMP snooping.

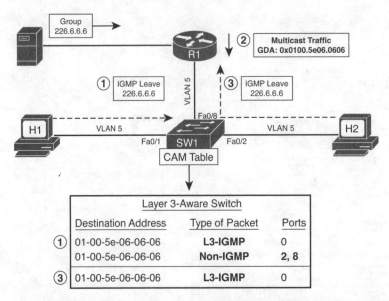

Figure 7-20   *Leaving a Group Using IGMP Snooping and CAM Table Entries*

The following three steps, referenced in Figure 7-20, describe the sequence of events when H1 and H2 send IGMP Leave messages:

1.   H1 sends an IGMP Leave message for 226.6.6.6, but SW1 does not forward it to Router R1 in this case. At Layer 2, H1 uses the All Multicast Routers MAC address 0x0100.5e00.0002 as the destination address and uses its own BIA 0x0006.7c11.1101 as the source address. SW1 captures the IGMP Leave message on its fa0/1 port, and its switching engine examines the packet. The switch sends an IGMP General Query on port fa0/1 to determine whether there are any other hosts that are members of this group on the port. (This feature was designed to protect other hosts if they are connected to the same switch port using a hub.) If an IGMP Report is received on port fa0/1, the switch discards the Leave message received from H1. Because, in this example, there is only one host connected to port fa0/1, the switch does not receive any IGMP Report and deletes the port fa0/1 from the CAM table entry, as shown in Figure 7-20. H2 connected with port fa0/2 is still a member of the group, and its port number is in the CAM table entry. Hence, SW1 does not forward the IGMP Leave message to the router.

2.   Router R1 continues forwarding the group traffic. R1 continues forwarding multicast traffic for group 226.6.6.6 to SW1 because R1 did not even know that H1 left the group. Based on the updated CAM table entry for the group shown in Figure 7-20, SW1 now forwards this traffic only on port fa0/2.

3.   H2 sends an IGMP Leave message for 226.6.6.6, and SW1 does forward it to Router R1 in this case. At Layer 2, H2 uses the All Multicast Routers MAC address 0x0100.5e00.0002 as the destination address and uses its own BIA 0x0006.7c11.1102 as the source address. Again, SW1 captures the IGMP Leave message on its fa0/2 port, and its switching engine examines the packet. The switch sends an IGMP

General Query on port fa0/2 to determine whether there are any other hosts that are members of this group on the port. Because, in this example, there is only one host connected to port fa0/2, the switch does not receive any IGMP Report and deletes the port fa0/2 from the CAM table entry. After SW1 deletes the port, it realizes that this was the last nonrouter port for the CAM table entry for 0x0100.5e06.0606. Therefore, SW1 deletes the CAM table entry for this group, as shown in Figure 7-20, and forwards the IGMP Leave message to R1, which sends an IGMP Group-Specific Query and, when no hosts respond, stops forwarding traffic for 226.6.6.6 toward SW1.

IGMP snooping becomes more complicated when multiple multicast routers are used and many LAN switches are interconnected through high-speed trunks. Also, CGMP and IGMP snooping control distribution of multicast traffic only on ports where hosts are connected. They do not provide any control mechanism for ports where routers are connected. The next section briefly examines how Router-Port Group Management Protocol (RGMP) helps switches control distribution of multicast traffic on ports where routers are connected.

Router-Port Group Management Protocol

RGMP is a Layer 2 protocol that enables a router to communicate to a switch which multicast group traffic the router does and does not want to receive from the switch. By being able to restrict the multicast destinations that a switch forwards to a router, a router can reduce its overhead. In fact, RGMP was designed to help routers reduce overhead when they are attached to high-speed LAN backbones. It is enabled at the interface configuration mode using the simple command **ip rgmp**.

Although RGMP is Cisco proprietary, oddly enough it cannot work concurrently with Cisco-proprietary CGMP. When RGMP is enabled on a router or a switch, CGMP is silently disabled; if CGMP is enabled on a router or a switch, RGMP is silently disabled. Note also that while it is proprietary, RGMP is published as informational RFC 3488.

RGMP works well in conjunction with IGMP snooping. In fact, IGMP snooping would typically learn the ports of all multicast routers by listening for IGMP and multicast routing protocol traffic. In some cases, some routers might not want all multicast traffic, so RGMP provides a means to reduce the unwanted traffic. The subtle key to the need for RGMP when using IGMP snooping is to realize this important fact about IGMP snooping:

> IGMP snooping helps switches control distribution of multicast traffic on ports where multicast hosts are connected, but it does not help switches control distribution of multicast traffic on ports where multicast routers are connected.

For example, consider the simple network shown in Figure 7-21. SW2 has learned of Routers R3 and R4 with IGMP snooping, so it forwards multicasts sent to all multicast groups out to both R3 and R4.

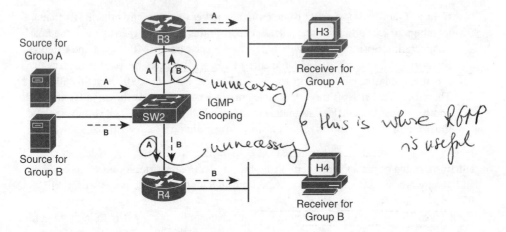

handwritten annotations: "unnecessary" (×2), "This is where RGMP is useful"

Figure 7-21 *IGMP Snooping Without RGMP*

As you can see from Figure 7-21, R3 needs to receive traffic only for group A, and R4 needs to receive traffic only for group B. However, IGMP snooping causes the switch to forward all multicast packets to each router. To combat that problem, RGMP can be used by a router to tell the switch to only forward packets for particular multicast groups. For example, Figure 7-22 shows the same network as Figure 7-21, but with RGMP snooping. In this case, RGMP Join messages are enabled in both the routers and the switch, with the results shown in Figure 7-22.

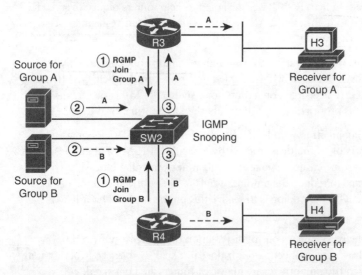

Figure 7-22 *More Efficient Forwarding with RGMP Added to IGMP Snooping*

Figure 7-22 shows the following three main steps, with the first step showing the RGMP function with the RGMP Join message. The Join message allows a router to identify the groups for which the router wants to receive traffic:

1. R3 sends an RGMP Join for group A, and R4 sends an RGMP Join for group B. As a result, SW2 knows to forward multicasts for group A only to R3, and for group B only to R4.

2. The sources send a packet to groups A and B, respectively.

3. SW2 forwards the traffic for group A only to R3 and the packets for group B only to R4.

While Figure 7-22 shows just one example and one type of RGMP message, RGMP includes four different messages. All the RGMP messages are generated by a router and are sent to the multicast IP address 224.0.0.25. The following list describes the four RGMP messages:

Key Topic

- When RGMP is enabled on a router, the router sends RGMP Hello messages by default every 30 seconds. When the switch receives an RGMP Hello message, it stops forwarding all multicast traffic on the port on which it received the Hello message.

- When the router wants to receive traffic for a specific multicast group, the router sends an RGMP Join G message, where G is the multicast group address, to the switch. When the switch receives an RGMP Join message, it starts forwarding the requested group traffic on the port on which it received the Hello message.

  Join G message

- When the router does not want to receive traffic for a formerly RGMP-joined specific multicast group, the router sends an RGMP Leave G message, where G is the multicast group address, to the switch. When the switch receives an RGMP Leave message, it stops forwarding the group traffic on the port on which it received the Hello message.

  Leave G message

- When RGMP is disabled on the router, the router sends an RGMP Bye message to the switch. When the switch receives an RGMP Bye message, it starts forwarding all IP multicast traffic on the port on which it received the Hello message.

IGMP Filtering

As we have discussed earlier in this chapter, IGMP snooping is a protocol that learns and maintains multicast group membership at the Layer 2 level. IGMP snooping looks at IGMP traffic to decide which ports should be allowed to receive multicast traffic from certain sources and for certain groups. This information is used to forward multicast traffic to only interested ports. The main benefit of IGMP snooping is to reduce flooding of packets.

Another enhancement that works in unison with IGMP Snooping is IGMP filtering. IGMP filtering allows users to configure filters on a switch virtual interface (SVI), a per-port, or a per-port per-VLAN basis to control the propagation of IGMP traffic through the network. By managing the IGMP traffic, IGMP filtering provides the capability to manage IGMP snooping, which in turn optimizes the forwarding of multicast traffic.

When an IGMP packet is received, IGMP filtering uses the filters configured by the user to determine whether the IGMP packet should be discarded or allowed to be processed by the existing IGMP snooping code. With an IGMP version 1 or version 2 packet, the entire packet is discarded. With an IGMPv3 packet, the packet will be rewritten to remove message elements that were denied by the filters.

IGMP traffic filters control the access of a port to multicast traffic. Access can be restricted based on the following:

■ Which multicast groups or channels can be joined on a given port. Keep in mind that channels are joined by IGMPv3 hosts that specify both the group and the source of the multicast traffic.

■ Maximum number of groups or channels allowed on a specific port or interface (regardless of the number of hosts requesting service).

■ IGMP protocol versions (for example, disallow all IGMPv1 messages).

When an IGMP filtering command is configured, a user policy is applied to a Layer 3 SVI interface, a Layer 2 port, or a particular VLAN on a Layer 2 trunk port. The Layer 2 port can be an access port or a trunk port. The IGMP filtering features will work only if IGMP snooping is enabled (either on the interface or globally). Thus it is important to keep in mind that this is a supplementary feature to IGMP snooping and not a standalone option.

Typically, IGMP filters are applied on access switches that are connected to end-user devices. Additionally, there are three different types of IGMP filters: IGMP group and channel access control, several IGMP groups and channels limit, and an IGMP minimum version. These filters are configurable and operate differently on different types of ports:

■ Per SVI

■ Per port

■ Per VLAN basis on a trunk port

You can configure filters separately for each VLAN passing through a trunk port.

IGMP Proxy

An IGMP proxy enables hosts in a unidirectional link routing (UDLR) environment that are not directly connected to a downstream router to join a multicast group sourced from an upstream network.

Figure 7-23 illustrates a sample topology that shows a UDLR scenario.

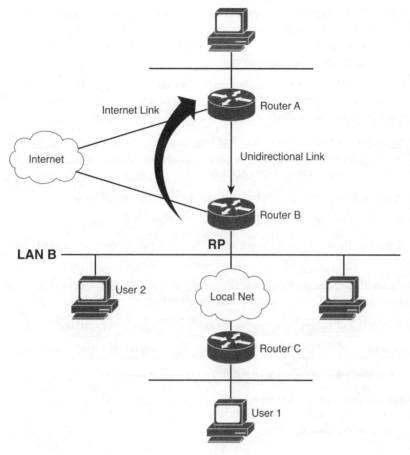

Figure 7-23   *UDLR Scenario*

Before you can see how this optimization improves multicast performance, you need to explore what a UDL routing scenario actually is. UDL creates a scenario that would normally be an issue for standard multicast and unicast routing protocols because of the fact that these routing protocols forward data on interfaces from which they have received routing control information. This model works only on bidirectional links for most existing routing protocols like those that we have discussed thus far; however, some networks use broadcast satellite links, which are by their very nature unidirectional. For networks that use broadcast satellite links, accomplishing two-way communication over broadcast satellite links presents a problem in terms of discovering and sharing knowledge of a network topology through traditional protocols like OSPF or Enhanced Interior Gateway Routing Protocol (EIGRP). This impacts Protocol Independent Multicast (PIM) operation because of PIM reliance on these protocols.

Specifically, in unicast routing, when a router receives an update message on an interface for a prefix, it forwards data for destinations that match that prefix out that same interface. This is the case in distance vector routing protocols like EIGRP. Similarly, in multicast routing, when a router receives a Join message for a multicast group on an interface, it forwards copies of data destined for that group out that same interface. Based on these principles, existing unicast and multicast routing protocols cannot be supported over UDLs. UDLR was designed to enable the operation of routing protocols over UDLs without changing the routing protocols themselves.

[handwritten left margin: unidirectional links]

The topology illustrated in Figure 7-23 represents a topology involving a UDL that you need to use to work with multicast and IGMP. To do this, we will need to use another multicast optimization known as IGMP Proxy.

[handwritten left margin: To resolve this problem:]

The IGMP proxy mechanism is needed to enable hosts that are not directly connected to a downstream device to join a multicast group sourced from an upstream network. In this scenario, the following sequence of events occurs:

1. User 1 sends an IGMP membership report requesting interest in group G.

2. Router C sends a PIM Join message hop by hop to the RP (Router B).

3. Router B receives the PIM Join message and adds a forwarding entry for group G on LAN B.

4. Router B periodically checks its mroute table and proxies the IGMP membership report to its upstream UDL device across the Internet link.

5. Router A creates and maintains a forwarding entry on the unidirectional link (UDL).

To make this feature work, you will need to apply configuration on each end of the UDL.

You will start with the upstream device as follows:

```
sw2(config)# interface gigabitethernet 0/0/0
sw2(config)# ip address 10.1.1.1 255.255.255.0
sw2(config)# ip pim dense-mode
sw2(config)#!
sw2(config)# interface gigabitethernet 1/0/0
sw2(config)# ip address 10.2.1.1 255.255.255.0
sw2(config)# ip pim dense-mode
sw2(config)# ip igmp unidirectional-link
sw2(config)#!
sw2(config)# interface gigabitethernet 2/0/0
sw2(config)# ip address 10.3.1.1 255.255.255.0
```

The remaining configuration would need to be applied on the downstream device:

```
sw3(config)# ip pim rp-address 10.5.1.1 5
sw3(config)# access-list 5 permit 239.0.0.0 0.255.255.255
sw3(config)#!
sw3(config)# interface loopback 0
sw3(config)# ip address 10.7.1.1 255.255.255.0
sw3(config)# ip pim dense-mode
sw3(config)# ip igmp helper-address udl ethernet 0
sw3(config)# ip igmp proxy-service
```

```
sw3(config)#!
sw3(config)# interface gigabitethernet 0/0/0
sw3(config)# ip address 10.2.1.2 255.255.255.0
sw3(config)# ip pim dense-mode
sw3(config)# ip igmp unidirectional-link
sw3(config)#!
sw3(config)# interface gigabitethernet 1/0/0
sw3(config)# ip address 10.5.1.1 255.255.255.0
sw3(config)# ip pim sparse-mode
sw3(config)# ip igmp mroute-proxy loopback 0
sw3(config)#!
sw3(config)# interface gigabitethernet 2/0/0
sw3(config)# ip address 10.6.1.1 255.255.255.0
```

Note   For more information on UDLR, see the "Configuring Unidirectional Link Routing" documentation at Cisco.com or visit the following URL: http://tinyurl.com/CiscoUDLR.

Foundation Summary

This section lists additional details and facts to round out the coverage of the topics in this chapter. Unlike most of the Cisco Press Exam Certification Guides, this "Foundation Summary" does not repeat information presented in the "Foundation Topics" section of the chapter. Please take the time to read and study the details in the "Foundation Topics" section of the chapter, as well as review items noted with a Key Topic icon.

Table 7-7 lists some of the key protocols and facts regarding IGMP.

Table 7-7 *Protocols and Standards for Chapter 7*

Name	Standard
GLOP Addressing in 233/8	RFC 3180
Administratively Scoped IP Multicast	RFC 2365
IGMP version 0	RFC 988
Host Extensions for IP Multicasting [IGMPv1]	RFC 1112
Internet Group Management Protocol, Version 2	RFC 2236
Internet Group Management Protocol, Version 3	RFC 3376
Multicast Listener Discovery (MLD) for IPv6	RFC 2710
Cisco Systems Router-Port Group Management Protocol (RGMP)	RFC 3488

Configuring multicasting on a Cisco router is relatively easy. You must first configure a multicast routing protocol on a Cisco router. The multicast routing protocols are covered in the next chapter, which also presents all the important configuration commands in the "Foundation Summary" section.

Memory Builders

The CCIE Routing and Switching written exam, like all Cisco CCIE written exams, covers a fairly broad set of topics. This section provides some basic tools to help you exercise your memory about some of the broader topics covered in this chapter.

Fill In Key Tables from Memory

Appendix E, "Key Tables for CCIE Study," on the CD in the back of this book, contains empty sets of some of the key summary tables in each chapter. Print Appendix E, refer to this chapter's tables in it, and fill in the tables from memory. Refer to Appendix F, "Solutions for Key Tables for CCIE Study," on the CD, to check your answers.

Definitions

Next, take a few moments to write down the definitions for the following terms:

> multicasting, multicast address range, multicast address structure, permanent multicast group, source-specific addresses, GLOP addressing, administratively scoped addresses, transient multicast group, multicast MAC address, joining a group, IGMP, MRT, Report Suppression mechanism, IGMPv2 Host Membership Query, IGMPv2 Leave, IGMPv2 Group-Specific Query, IGMPv2 Host Membership Report, SSM, querier election, CGMP, IGMP snooping, RGMP

Refer to the glossary to check your answers.

Further Reading

Beau Williamson, *Developing IP Multicast Networks*, Volume I, Cisco Press, 2000.

References in This Chapter

"Multicast in a Campus Network: CGMP and IGMP Snooping (Document ID 10559)," www.cisco.com/en/US/products/hw/switches/ps708/products_tech_note-09186a00800b0871.shtml

Router-Port Group Management Protocol, www.cisco.com/en/US/docs/ios/12_1t/12_1t5/feature/guide/dtrgmp.html

"Configuring Unidirectional Link Routing," www.cisco.com/c/en/us/td/docs/ios/12_2/ip/configuration/guide/fipr_c/1cfudlr.html

Blueprint topics covered in this chapter:

This chapter covers the following subtopics from the Cisco CCIE Routing and Switching written exam blueprint. Refer to the full blueprint in Table I-1 in the Introduction for more details on the topics covered in each chapter and their context within the blueprint.

- Protocol Independent Multicast (PIM) sparse mode

- Multicast Source Discovery Protocol (MSDP)

- Interdomain multicast routing

- PIM Auto-Rendezvous Point (Auto-RP), unicast rendezvous point (RP), and BootStrap Router (BSR)

- Implement multicast tools, features, and source-specific multicast (SSM)

- IPv6 Multicast Operation

CHAPTER 8

IP Multicast Routing

In Chapter 7, "Introduction to IP Multicasting," you learned how a multicast router communicates with hosts and then decides whether to forward or stop the multicast traffic on a subnet. But how does a multicast router receive the group traffic? How is the multicast traffic forwarded from a source so that all the group users receive it? This chapter provides answers to those questions.

This chapter first defines the multicast routing problem by identifying the difference between unicast and multicast routing. It then provides an overview of the basic design concepts of multicast routing protocols, and shows how they solve multicast routing problems. Next, the chapter covers the operations of the Protocol Independent Multicast routing protocol in dense mode (PIM-DM) and sparse mode (PIM-SM). The chapter also covers the basic functions of Distance Vector Multicast Routing Protocol (DVMRP) and Multicast OSPF (MOSPF) as well as IPv6 Multicast Operation.

"Do I Know This Already?" Quiz

Table 8-1 outlines the major headings in this chapter and the corresponding "Do I Know This Already?" quiz questions.

Table 8-1 *"Do I Know This Already?" Foundation Topics Section-to-Question Mapping*

Foundation Topics Section	Questions Covered in This Section	Score
Multicast Routing Basics	1	
Dense-Mode Routing Protocols	2–4	
Sparse-Mode Routing Protocols	5–8	
IPv6 Multicast PIM	9–10	
Total Score		

To best use this pre-chapter assessment, remember to score yourself strictly. You can find the answers in Appendix A, "Answers to the 'Do I Know This Already?' Quizzes."

1. When a multicast router receives a multicast packet, which one of the following tasks will it perform first?

    a. Examine the IP multicast destination address on the packet, consult the multicast routing table to determine the next-hop address, and forward the packet through appropriate interface(s).

    b. Depending on the multicast routing protocol configured, either forward the packet on all the interfaces or forward the packet on selected interfaces except the one on which the packet was received.

    c. Determine the interface this router would use to send packets to the source of the packet, and decide whether the packet arrived in that interface or not.

    d. Send a Prune message to its upstream neighbor if it does not have any directly connected group members or active downstream routers.

2. A PIM router receives a PIM Assert message on a LAN interface. Which of the following statements is (are) true about the response of the router?

    a. The router does not have to take any action.

    b. If the router is configured with the PIM-DM routing protocol, it will process the Assert message; otherwise, it will ignore it.

    c. If the router is configured with the PIM-SM routing protocol, it will process the Assert message; otherwise, it will ignore it.

    d. The router will send a PIM Assert message.

3. When a PIM-DM router receives a Graft message from a downstream router after it has sent a Prune message to its upstream router for the same group, which of the following statements is (are) true about its response?

    a. It will send a Graft message to the downstream router and a Prune message to the upstream router.

    b. It will send a Prune message to the downstream router and a Graft message to the upstream router.

    c. It will reestablish adjacency with the upstream router.

    d. It will send a Graft message to the upstream router.

4. On Router R1, the **show ip mroute 239.5.130.24** command displays **Serial2, Prune/Dense, 00:01:34/00:01:26** for the (S,G) entry under the outgoing interface list. Which of the following statements provide correct interpretation of this information?

    a. Router R1 has sent a Prune message on its Serial2 interface to its upstream router 1 minute and 34 seconds ago.

    b. Router R1 will send a Graft message on its Serial2 interface to its upstream router after 1 minute and 26 seconds.

    c. Router R1 received a Prune message on its Serial2 interface from its downstream router 1 minute and 34 seconds ago.

    d. Router R1 will send a Prune message on its Serial2 interface to its upstream router after 1 minute and 26 seconds.

    e. Router R1 will forward the traffic for the group on its Serial2 interface after 1 minute and 26 seconds.

5. From the following statements, select the true statement(s) regarding when a PIM-SM RP router will send the unicast PIM Register-Stop messages to the first-hop DR.

    a. If the RP has no need for the traffic

    b. If the RP is already receiving traffic on the shared tree

    c. When the RP begins receiving multicast traffic through SPT from the source

    d. When the RP sends multicast traffic through SPT to the downstream router

6. R1, a PIM-SM router, sends an (S,G) RP-bit Prune to its upstream neighbor. Assume that all the PIM-SM routers in the network are using the Cisco default **spt-threshold** value. Which of the following statements is (are) true about the status of different routers in the PIM-SM network at this time?

    a. At R1, the root-path tree and shortest-path tree diverge.

    b. R1 is switching over from shortest-path tree to root-path tree.

    c. R1 is switching over from root-path tree to shortest-path tree.

    d. At R1, the RPF neighbor for the (S,G) entry is different from the RPF neighbor of the (*,G) entry.

7. In a PIM-SM LAN network using Auto-RP, one of the routers is configured to send Cisco-RP-Announce and Cisco-RP-Discovery messages. All the routers show all the interfaces with correct PIM neighbors in sparse mode. However, the network administrator is puzzled by inconsistent RP mapping information shown on many routers. Some routers show correct RP mappings, but many leaf routers do not show any RP mappings. Which of the following statements represent(s) the most likely cause(s) for the above problem?

    a. The links between the leaf routers and the mapping agent are congested.

    b. All the interfaces of all the routers are configured with the command **ip pim sparse-mode**.

    c. The leaf routers are configured with a static RP address using an **override** option.

    d. The RPF check on the leaf routers is failing.

8. PIM-SM Router R1 has two interfaces listed, s0/0 and fa0/0, in its (*,G) entry for group 227.7.7.7 in its multicast routing table. Assuming that nothing changes in that (*,G) entry in the next 10 minutes, which of the following could be true?

    a. R1 is sending PIM Join messages toward the RP.

    b. R1 does not need to send Join messages toward the RP as long as the RP is continuing to forward multicasts for group 227.7.7.7 to R1.

    c. R1 is receiving PIM Join messages periodically on one or both of interfaces s0/0 and fa0/0.

    d. R1 is receiving IGMP Report messages periodically on interface fa0/0.

    e. The RP has been sending PIM Prune messages to R1 periodically, but R1 has been replying with PIM Reject messages because it still needs to receive the packets.

9. MLD uses what three types of messages?

    a. Query

    b. Null

    c. Report

    d. Done

10. Which of the following list of IPv6 addresses is used to represent an embedded RP address in IPv6?

    a. FE7E:0240:2001:2:2:2:0:1

    b. F17E:0240:2001:2:2:2:0:1

    c. FF7E:0240:2001:2:2:2:0:1

    d. F07E:0240:2001:2:2:2:0:1

Foundation Topics

Multicast Routing Basics

The main function of any routing protocol is to help routers forward a packet in the right direction, causing the packet to keep moving closer to its desired destination and ultimately reaching its destination. To forward a unicast packet, a router examines the packet's destination address, finds the next-hop address from the unicast routing table, and forwards the packet through the appropriate interface. A unicast packet is forwarded along a single path from the source to the destination.

The top part of Figure 8-1 shows how a router can easily make a decision about forwarding a unicast packet by consulting its unicast routing table. However, when a router receives a multicast packet, as shown at the bottom of Figure 8-1, it cannot forward the packet because multicast IP addresses are not listed in the unicast routing table. Also, routers often have to forward multicast packets out multiple interfaces to reach all receivers. These requirements make the multicast forwarding process more complex than unicast forwarding.

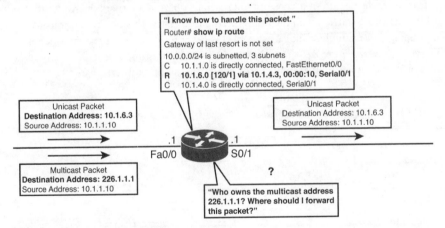

Figure 8-1   *Multicast Routing Problem*

Figure 8-1 shows that the router has received a multicast packet with the destination address 226.1.1.1. The destination address represents a dynamically changing group of recipients, not any one recipient's address. How can the router find out where these users are? Where should the router forward this packet?

An analogy can help you to better understand the difficulty of multicast routing. Assume that you want to send party invitations through the mail, but instead of creating dozens of invitations, you create only one. Before mailing the invitation, you put a destination address on it, "This envelope contains my party invitation," and then drop it in a mailbox. When the postal system examines the destination address on your envelope, where should it deliver your envelope? And because it is only one invitation, does the postal system need to make copies? Also, how can the postal system figure out to which addresses to deliver the copies? By contrast, if IP multicast were the post office, it would know who you want to invite to the party, know where they are located, and make copies of the invitation and deliver them all to the correct addresses.

The next few sections discuss solutions for forwarding multicast traffic and controlling the distribution of multicast traffic in a routed network.

Overview of Multicast Routing Protocols

DENSE
VS
SPARSE

Routers can forward a multicast packet by using either a *dense-mode multicast routing protocol* or a *sparse-mode multicast routing protocol*. This section examines the basic concepts of multicast forwarding using dense mode, the Reverse Path Forwarding (RPF) check, and multicast forwarding using sparse mode, all of which help to solve the multicast routing problem.

Multicast Forwarding Using Dense Mode

Dense-mode routing protocols assume that the multicast group application is so popular that every subnet in the network has at least one receiver wanting to receive the group traffic. Therefore, the design of a dense-mode routing protocol instructs the router to forward the multicast traffic on all the configured interfaces, with some exceptions to prevent looping. For example, a multicast packet is never forwarded out the interface on which it was received. Figure 8-2 shows how a dense-mode routing protocol receives a multicast on one interface, and then forwards copies out all other interfaces.

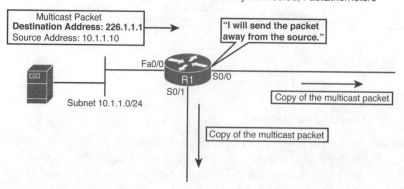

Figure 8-2 *R1 Forwarding a Multicast Packet Using a Dense-Mode Routing Protocol*

Figure 8-2 shows the dense-mode logic on R1, with R1 *flooding* copies of the packet out all interfaces except the one on which the packet was received. Although Figure 8-2 shows only one router, other routers can receive these multicasts and repeat the same process. All subnets will receive a copy of the original multicast packet.

Dense-mode protocols assume that all subnets need to receive a copy of the packets; however, dense-mode protocols do allow routers to ask to not receive traffic sent to a particular multicast group. Dense-mode routers typically do not want to receive multicast packets for a particular group if both of the following are true:

Key Topic

- The router does not have any active downstream routers that need packets for that group.

- The router does not know of any hosts on directly connected subnets that have joined that group.

no downstream router

no local host

Prune message

When both of these conditions are true, the router needs to inform its upstream router not to send traffic for the group, which it does by using a special message called a Prune message. The mechanics of how dense-mode routers communicate with each other are discussed in detail in the PIM-DM section, later in this chapter.

DVMRP, PIM-DM, and MOSPF are the dense-mode routing protocols discussed in this chapter, with most of the attention being paid to PIM-DM.

Reverse Path Forwarding Check

Routers cannot simply use logic by which they receive a multicast packet and then forward a copy of it out all other interfaces, without causing multicast packets to loop around the internetwork. To prevent such loops, routers do not forward multicasts out the same interface on which they were received. Multicast routers use a *Reverse Path Forwarding (RPF) check* to prevent loops. The RPF check adds this additional step to a dense-mode router's forwarding logic:

Key Topic

Look at the source IP address of the multicast packet. If my route that matches the source lists an outgoing interface that is the actual interface on which the packet was received, the packet passes the RPF check. If not, do not replicate and forward the packet.

Figure 8-3 shows an example in which R3 uses the RPF check on two separate copies of the same original multicast packet. Host S1 sends a multicast packet, with R1 flooding it to R2 and R3. R2 receives its copy, and floods it as well. As a result, R3 receives the same packet from two routers: on its s0/0 interface from R2 and on its s0/1 interface from R1. Without the RPF check, R3 would forward the packet it got from R1 to R2, and vice versa, and begin the process of looping packets. With this same logic, R1 and R2 also keep repeating the process. This duplication creates multicast routing loops and generates multicast storms that waste bandwidth and router resources.

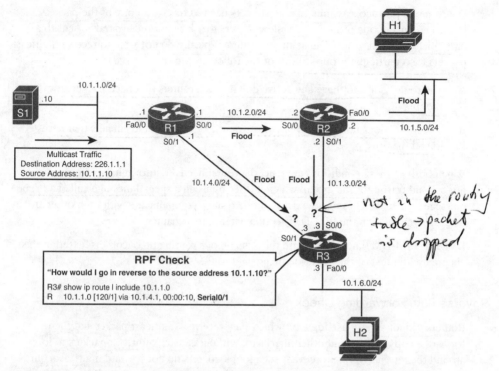

Figure 8-3 *R3 Performs the RPF Check*

A multicast router does not forward any multicast packet unless the packet passes the RPF check. In Figure 8-3, R3 has to decide whether it should accept the multicast packets coming from R1 and R2. R3 makes this decision by performing the RPF check, described in detail as follows:

1. R3 examines the source address of each incoming multicast packet, which is 10.1.1.10. The source address is used in the RPF check of Step 2.

2. R3 determines the reverse path interface based on its route used to forward packets to 10.1.1.10. In this case, R3's route to 10.1.1.0/24 is matched, and it lists an outgoing interface of s0/1, making s0/1 R3's RPF interface for IP address 10.1.1.10.

3. R3 compares the reverse path interface determined in Step 2 with the interface on which the multicast packet arrived. If they match, it accepts the packet and forwards it; otherwise, it drops the packet. In this case, R3 floods the packet received on s0/1 from R1, but it ignores the packet received on s0/0 from R2.

The RPF check implements a strategy by which routers accept packets that arrive over the shortest path, and discard those that arrive over longer routes. Multicast routing protocols cannot use the destination address to help routers forward a packet, because that address represents the group traffic. So, multicast routing protocols use the RPF check to determine whether the packet arrived at the router using the shortest-path route from the source to the router. If it did, multicast routing protocols accept the packet and forward it; otherwise, they drop the packet and thereby avoid routing loops and duplication.

Different multicast routing protocols determine their RPF interfaces in different ways, as follows:

- Distance Vector Multicast Routing Protocol (DVMRP) maintains a separate multicast routing table and uses it for the RPF check.

- Protocol Independent Multicast (PIM) and Core-Based Tree (CBT) generally use the unicast routing table for the RPF check, as shown in Figure 8-3.

- PIM and CBT can also use the DVMRP route table, the Multiprotocol Border Gateway Protocol (MP-BGP) route table, or statically configured multicast route(s) for the RPF check.

- Multicast OSPF does not use the RPF check, because it computes both forward and reverse shortest-path source-rooted trees by using the Dijkstra algorithm.

Multicast Forwarding Using Sparse Mode

A dense-mode routing protocol is useful when a multicast application is so popular that you need to deliver the group traffic to almost all the subnets of a network. However, if the group users are located on a few subnets, a dense-mode routing protocol will still flood the traffic in the entire internetwork, wasting bandwidth and resources of routers. In those cases, a sparse-mode routing protocol, such as PIM-SM, could be used to help reduce the waste of network resources.

The fundamental difference between dense-mode and sparse-mode routing protocols relates to their default behavior. By default, dense-mode protocols keep forwarding the group traffic unless a downstream router sends a message stating that it does not want that traffic. Sparse-mode protocols do not forward the group traffic to any other router unless it receives a message from that router requesting copies of packets sent to a particular multicast group. A downstream router requests to receive the packets only for one of two reasons:

- The router has received a request to receive the packets from some downstream router.

- A host on a directly connected subnet has sent an Internet Group Management Protocol (IGMP) Join message for that group.

Figure 8-4 shows an example of what must happen with PIM-SM before a host (H2 in this case) can receive packets sent by host S1 to multicast group address 226.1.1.1. The PIM sparse-mode operation begins with the packet being forwarded to a special router called the *rendezvous point (RP)*. When the group traffic arrives at an RP, unlike the dense-mode design, the RP does not automatically forward the group traffic to any router; the group traffic must be specifically requested by a router.

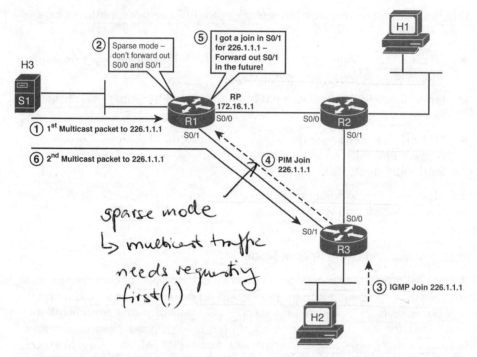

Figure 8-4   *R1 Forwarding a Multicast Packet Using a Sparse-Mode Routing Protocol*

> **Note**   Throughout this chapter, the solid arrowed lines in the figures represent multicast packets, with dashed arrowed lines representing PIM and IGMP messages.

Before you look at the numbered steps in Figure 8-4, consider the state of this internetwork. PIM-SM is configured on all the routers, R1 is selected as an RP, and in all three routers, the IP address 172.16.1.1 of R1 is configured statically as the RP address. Usually, a loopback interface address is used as an RP address and the loopback network is advertised in the unicast routing protocol so that all the routers learn how to locate an RP. At this point, R1, as the RP, can receive multicast packets sent to 226.1.1.1, but it will not forward them.

The following list describes the steps shown in Figure 8-4:

1. Host S1 sends a multicast to the RP, with destination address 226.1.1.1.

2. R1 chooses to ignore the packet, because no routers or local hosts have told the RP (R1) that they want to receive copies of multicast packets.

3. Host H2 sends an IGMP Join message for group 226.1.1.1.

4. R3 sends a PIM Join message to the RP (R1) for address 226.1.1.1.

5. R1's logic now changes, so future packets sent to 226.1.1.1 will be forwarded by R1 out s0/1 to R3.

6. Host S1 sends a multicast packet to 226.1.1.1, and R1 forwards it out s0/1 to R3.

In a PIM-SM network, it is critical for all the routers to somehow learn the IP address of an RP. One option in a small network is to statically configure the IP address of an RP in every router. Later in the chapter, the section "Dynamically Finding RPs and Using Redundant RPs" covers how routers can dynamically discover the IP address of the RP.

The example in Figure 8-4 shows some of the savings in using a sparse-mode protocol like PIM-SM. R2 has not received any IGMP Join messages on its LAN interface, so it does not send any request to the RP to forward the group traffic. As a result, R1 does not waste link bandwidth on the link from R1 to R2. R3 will not forward multicasts to R2 either in this case.

> **Note**   In Figure 8-4, R3 first performs its RPF check by using the IP address of the RP rather than the IP address of the source of the packet, because it is receiving the group traffic from the RP. If the RPF check succeeds, R3 forwards the traffic on its LAN.

Multicast Scoping

Multicast scoping confines the forwarding of multicast traffic to a group of routers, for administrative, security, or policy reasons. In other words, multicast scoping is the practice of defining boundaries that determine how far multicast traffic will travel in your network. The following sections discuss two methods of multicast scoping:

■   TTL scoping

■   Administrative scoping

TTL Scoping

With TTL scoping, routers compare the time to live (TTL) value on a multicast packet with a configured TTL value on each outgoing interface. A router forwards the multicast packet only on those interfaces whose configured TTL value is less than or equal to the TTL value of the multicast packet. In effect, TTL scoping resets the TTL value at which the router discards multicasts from the usual value of 0 to some higher number. Figure 8-5 shows an example of a multicast router with various TTL threshold values configured on its interfaces.

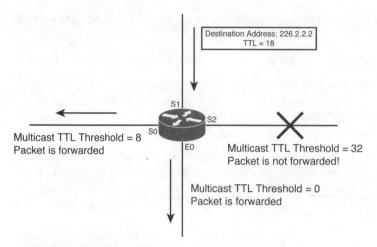

Figure 8-5 *Multicast Scoping Using TTL Thresholds*

In Figure 8-5, a multicast packet arrives on the s1 interface with a TTL of 18. The router decreases the packet's TTL by 1 to 17. Assume that the router is configured with a dense-mode routing protocol on all four interfaces and the RPF check succeeds—in other words, the router will want to forward a copy of the packet on each interface. The router compares the remaining TTL of the packet, which is now 17, with the TTL threshold of each outgoing interface. If the packet's TTL is higher than or equal to the interface TTL, it forwards a copy of the packet on that interface; otherwise, it does not forward it. On a Cisco router, the default TTL value on all the interfaces is 0.

On the s0 and s2 interfaces in Figure 8-5, the network administrator has configured the TTL as 8 and 32, respectively. A copy of the packet is forwarded on the s0 and e0 interfaces because their TTL thresholds are less than 17. However, the packet is not forwarded on the s2 interface because its TTL threshold is 32, which is higher than 17.

TTL scoping has some weaknesses. First, it is difficult to implement in a large and complex network, because estimating correct TTL thresholds on many routers and many interfaces so that the network correctly confines only the intended sessions becomes an extremely demanding task. Another problem with TTL scoping is that a configured TTL threshold value on an interface applies to all multicast packets. If you want flexibility for some multicast sessions, you have to manipulate the applications to alter the TTL values when packets leave the servers.

Administrative Scoping

Recall from Chapter 7 that administratively scoped multicast addresses are private addresses in the range 239.0.0.0 to 239.255.255.255. They can be used to set administrative boundaries to limit the forwarding of multicast traffic outside of a domain. It requires manual configuration. You can configure and apply a filter on a router's interface so that multicast traffic with group addresses in the private address range is not allowed to enter or exit the interface.

> **Note**   This chapter assumes that you have read Chapter 7 or are thoroughly familiar with the operation of IGMP; if neither is true, read Chapter 7 before continuing with this chapter.

Dense-Mode Routing Protocols

There are three dense-mode routing protocols:

- Protocol Independent Multicast Dense Mode (PIM-DM)

- Distance Vector Multicast Routing Protocol (DVMRP)

- Multicast Open Shortest Path First (MOSPF)

This section covers the operation of PIM-DM in detail and provides an overview of DVMRP and MOSPF.

Operation of Protocol Independent Multicast Dense Mode

Protocol Independent Multicast (PIM) defines a series of protocol messages and rules by which routers can provide efficient forwarding of multicast IP packets. PIM previously existed as a Cisco-proprietary protocol, although it has been offered as an experimental protocol through RFCs 2362, 3446, and 3973. The PIM specifications spell out the rules mentioned in the earlier examples in this chapter—things like the RPF check, the PIM dense-mode logic of flooding multicasts until routers send Prune messages, and the PIM sparse-mode logic of not forwarding multicasts anywhere until a router sends a Join message. This section describes the PIM-DM protocols in more detail.

PIM gets its name from its ability to use the unicast IP routing table for its RPF check—independent of whatever unicast IP routing protocol(s) was used to build the unicast routing table entries. In fact, the name "PIM" really says as much about the two other dense-mode protocols—DVMRP and MOSPF—as it does about PIM. These other two protocols do not use the unicast IP routing table for their RPF checks, instead building their own independent tables. PIM simply relies on the unicast IP routing table, independent of which unicast IP routing protocol built a particular entry in the routing table.

Forming PIM Adjacencies Using PIM Hello Messages

PIM routers form adjacencies with neighboring PIM routers for the same general reasons, and with the same general mechanisms, as many other routing protocols. PIMv2, the current version of PIM, sends Hello messages every 30 seconds (default) on every interface on which PIM is configured. By receiving Hellos on the same interface, routers discover neighbors, establish adjacency, and maintain adjacency. PIMv2 Hellos use IP protocol number 103 and reserved multicast destination address 224.0.0.13, called the All-PIM-Routers multicast address. The Hello messages contain a Holdtime value, typically three times the sender's PIM hello interval. If the receiver does not receive a Hello message from the sender during the Holdtime period, it considers the sending neighbor to be dead.

> **Note** The older version, PIMv1, does not use Hellos, instead using a PIM Query message. PIMv1 messages are encapsulated in IP packets with protocol number 2 and use the multicast destination address 224.0.0.2.

As you will see in the following sections, establishing and maintaining adjacencies with directly connected neighbors are very important for the operation of PIM. A PIM router sends other PIM messages only on interfaces on which it has known active PIM neighbors.

Source-Based Distribution Trees

Dense-mode routing protocols are suitable for dense topology in which there are many multicast group members relative to the total number of hosts in a network. When a PIM-DM router receives a multicast packet, it first performs the RPF check. If the RPF check succeeds, the router forwards a copy of the packet to all the PIM neighbors except the one on which it received the packet. Each PIM-DM router repeats the process and floods the entire network with the group traffic. Ultimately, the packets are flooded to all leaf routers that have no downstream PIM neighbors.

The logic described in the previous paragraph actually describes the concepts behind what PIM calls a *source-based distribution tree*. It is also sometimes called a *shortest-path tree (SPT)* or simply a *source tree*. The tree defines a path between the source host that originates the multicast packets and all subnets that need to receive a copy of the multicasts sent by that host. The tree uses the source as the root, the routers as the nodes in the tree, and the subnets connected to the routers as the branches and leaves of the tree. Figure 8-3, earlier in the chapter, shows the concept behind an SPT.

The configuration required on the three routers in Figure 8-3 is easy: Just add the global command **ip multicast-routing** on each router and the interface command **ip pim dense-mode** on all the interfaces of all the routers.

PIM-DM might have a different source-based distribution tree for each combination of source and multicast group, because the SPT will differ based on the location of the source and the locations of the hosts listening for each multicast group address. The notation (S,G) refers to a particular SPT, or to an individual router's part of a particular SPT, where S is the source's IP address and G is the multicast group address. For example, the (S,G) notation for the example in Figure 8-3 would be written as (10.1.1.10, 226.1.1.1).

Example 8-1 shows part of the (S,G) SPT entry on R3, from Figure 8-3, for the (10.1.1.0, 226.1.1.1) SPT. Host S1 is sending packets to 226.1.1.1, and host H2 sends an IGMP Join message for the group 226.1.1.1. Example 8-1 shows R3's multicast configuration and a part of its multicast routing table, as displayed using the **show ip mroute** command.

Example 8-1 *Multicast Configuration and Route Table Entry*

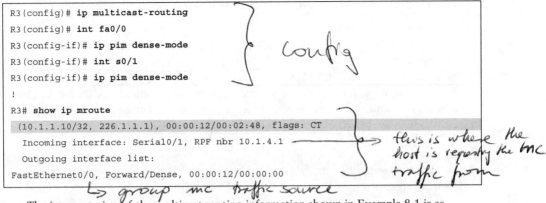

```
R3(config)# ip multicast-routing
R3(config)# int fa0/0
R3(config-if)# ip pim dense-mode
R3(config-if)# int s0/1
R3(config-if)# ip pim dense-mode
!
R3# show ip mroute
 (10.1.1.10/32, 226.1.1.1), 00:00:12/00:02:48, flags: CT
  Incoming interface: Serial0/1, RPF nbr 10.1.4.1
  Outgoing interface list:
FastEthernet0/0, Forward/Dense, 00:00:12/00:00:00
```

[handwritten annotations: "Config", "this is where the host is requesting the mc traffic from", "group mc traffic source"]

The interpretation of the multicast routing information shown in Example 8-1 is as follows:

- The shaded line shows that the (S,G) entry for (10.1.1.10/32, 226.1.1.1) has been up for 12 seconds, and that if R3 does not forward an (S,G) packet in 2 minutes and 48 seconds, it will expire. Every time R3 forwards a packet using this entry, the timer is reset to 3 minutes. *[handwritten: → 3 min reset timer]*

- The C flag indicates that R3 has a directly connected group member for 226.1.1.1. The T flag indicates that the (S,G) traffic is forwarded on the shortest-path tree.

- The incoming interface for the group 226.1.1.1 is s0/1, and the RPF neighbor (the next-hop IP address to go in the reverse direction toward the source address 10.1.1.10) is 10.1.4.1.

- The group traffic is forwarded out on the fa0/0 interface. This interface has been in the forwarding state for 12 seconds. The second timer is listed as 00:00:00, because it cannot expire with PIM-DM, as this interface will continue to forward traffic until pruned.

> **Note** The multicast routing table flags mentioned in this list, as well as others, are summarized in Table 8-7 in the "Foundation Summary" section of this chapter. *[handwritten: → P396 !]*

The next two sections show how PIM-DM routers use information learned from IGMP to dynamically expand and contract the source-based distribution trees to satisfy the needs of the group users.

Prune Message

PIM-DM creates a new SPT when a source first sends multicast packets to a new multicast group address. The SPT includes all interfaces except RPF interfaces, because PIM-DM assumes that all hosts need to receive a copy of each multicast packet. However, some subnets might not need a copy of the multicasts, so PIM-DM defines a process by which routers can remove interfaces from an SPT by using PIM Prune messages.

For example, in Figure 8-3, hosts H1 and H2 need a copy of the multicast packets sent to 226.1.1.1. However, as shown, when R2 gets the multicast from R1, R2 then forwards the multicasts to R3. As it turns out, R3 is dropping the packets for the group traffic from 10.1.1.10, sent to 226.1.1.1, because those packets fail R3's RPF check. In this case, R3 can cause R2 to remove its s0/1 interface from its outgoing interface list for (10.1.1.10, 226.1.1.1) by sending a Prune message to R2. As a result, R2 will not forward the multicasts to R3, thereby reducing the amount of wasted bandwidth.

Note The term *outgoing interface list* refers to the list of interfaces in a forwarding state, listed for an entry in a router's multicast routing table.

The following is a more formal definition of a PIM Prune message:

Key Topic

The PIM Prune message is sent by one router to a second router to cause the second router to remove the link on which the Prune is received from a particular (S,G) SPT.

Figure 8-6 shows the same internetwork and example as Figure 8-3, but with R3's Prune messages sent to R2.

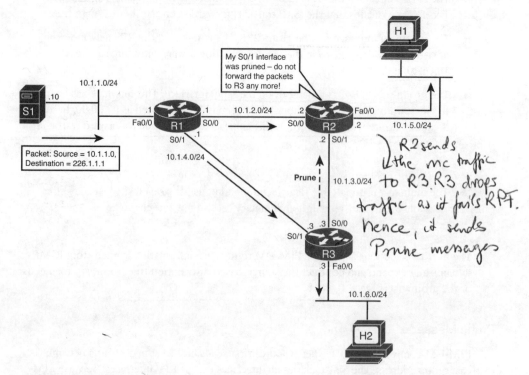

Figure 8-6 *R3 Sends a Prune Message to R2*

As a result of the Prune message from R3 to R2, R2 will prune its s0/1 interface from the SPT for (10.1.1.10, 226.1.1.1). Example 8-2 shows the multicast route table entry for R2 in Figure 8-6, with the line that shows the pruned state highlighted.

Example 8-2 *Multicast Route Table Entry for the Group 226.1.1.1 for R2*

```
(10.1.1.10/32, 226.1.1.1), 00:00:14/00:02:46, flags: CT
 Incoming interface: Serial0/0, RPF nbr 10.1.2.1
 Outgoing interface list:
   FastEthernet0/0, Forward/Dense, 00:00:14/00:00:00
   Serial0/1, Prune/Dense, 00:00:08/00:02:52
```
3 min PRONE TIMER

Most of the information shown in Example 8-2 is similar to the information shown in Example 8-1. Notice the Serial0/1 information shown under the outgoing interface list. It shows that this interface was pruned 8 seconds ago because R3 sent a Prune message to R2. This means that, at this time, R2 is not forwarding traffic for 226.1.1.1 on its s0/1 interface.

Because PIM-DM's inherent tendency is to flood traffic through an internetwork, the pruned s0/1 interface listed in Example 8-2 will be changed back to a forwarding state after 2 minutes and 52 seconds. In PIM-DM, when a router receives a Prune message on an interface, it starts a (default) 3-minute Prune timer, counting down to 0. When the Prune timer expires, the router changes the interface to a forwarding state again. If the downstream router does not want the traffic, it can again send a Prune message. This feature keeps a downstream router aware that the group traffic is available on a particular interface from the upstream neighbor.

Note   PIMv2 offers a better solution to maintaining the pruned state of an interface, using State Refresh messages. These messages are covered later in the chapter, in the section "Steady-State Operation and the State Refresh Message."

Note that a multicast router can have more than one interface in the outgoing interface list, but it can have only one interface in the incoming interface list. The only interface in which a router will receive and process multicasts from a particular source is the RPF interface. Routers still perform an RPF check, with the incoming interface information in the beginning of the **show ip mroute** output stating the RPF interface and neighbor.

PIM-DM: Reacting to a Failed Link

When links fail, or any other changes affect the unicast IP routing table, PIM-DM needs to update the RPF interfaces based on the new unicast IP routing table. Because the RPF interface can change, (S,G) entries might also need to list different interfaces in the outgoing interface list. This section describes an example of how PIM-DM reacts.

Figure 8-7 shows an example in which the link between R1 and R3, originally illustrated in Figure 8-6, has failed. After the unicast routing protocol converges, R3 needs to update its RPF neighbor IP address from 10.1.4.1 (R1) to 10.1.3.2 (R2). Also in this case, H1 has issued an IGMP Leave message.

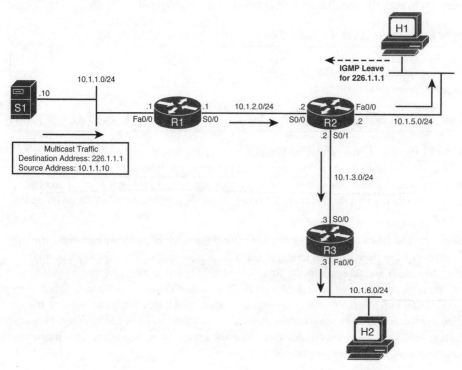

Figure 8-7 *Direct Link Between R1 and R3 Is Down, and Host H1 Sends an IGMP Leave Message*

Example 8-3 shows the resulting multicast route table entry for R3 in Figure 8-7. Note that the RPF interface and neighbor IP address have changed to point to R2.

Example 8-3 *Multicast Route Table Entry for the Group 226.1.1.1 for R3*

```
(10.1.1.10/32, 226.1.1.1), 00:02:16/00:01:36, flags: CT
  Incoming interface: Serial0/0, RPF nbr 10.1.3.2
  Outgoing interface list:
    FastEthernet0/0, Forward/Dense, 00:02:16/00:00:00
```

Example 8-3 shows how R3's view of the (10.1.1.10, 226.1.1.1) SPT has changed. However, R2 had pruned its s0/1 interface from that SPT, as shown in Figure 8-6. So, R2 needs to change its s0/1 interface back to a forwarding state for SPT (10.1.1.10, 226.1.1.1). Example 8-4 shows the resulting multicast route table entry for (10.1.1.10, 226.1.1.1) in R2.

Example 8-4   *Multicast Route Table Entry for the Group 226.1.1.1 for R2*

```
(10.1.1.10/32, 226.1.1.1), 00:03:14/00:02:38, flags: T         ← C missing
  Incoming interface: Serial0/0, RPF nbr 10.1.2.1
  Outgoing interface list:
  Serial0/1, Forward/Dense, 00:02:28/00:00:00
```

[handwritten: PIM graft.]

Note   R2 changed its s0/1 to a forwarding state because of a PIM Graft message sent by R3. The upcoming section "Graft Message" explains the details.

In Example 8-4, notice the outgoing interface list for R2. R2 has now removed interface fa0/0 from the outgoing interface list and stopped forwarding traffic on the interface because it received no response to the IGMP Group-Specific query for group 226.1.1.1. As a result, R2 has also removed the C flag (C meaning "connected") from its multicast routing table entry for (10.1.1.10, 226.1.1.1). Additionally, R2 forwards the traffic on its s0/1 interface toward R3 because R3 is still forwarding traffic on its fa0/0 interface and has not sent a Prune message to R2.

Rules for Pruning

Key Topic

This section explains two key rules that a PIM-DM router must follow to decide when it can request a prune. Before you learn another example of how PIM-DM reacts to changes in an internetwork, a couple of new multicast terms must be defined. To simplify the wording, the following statements define *upstream router* and *downstream router* from the perspective of a router named R1.   *[handwritten: ADDITIONAL TERMINOLOGY.]*

- R1's upstream router is the router from which R1 receives multicast packets for a particular SPT.

- R1's downstream router is a router to which R1 forwards some multicast packets for a particular SPT.

Key Topic

For example, R1 is R2's upstream router for the packets that S1 is sending to 226.1.1.1 in Figure 8-7. R3 is R2's downstream router for those same packets, because R2 sends those packets to R3.

PIM-DM routers can choose to send a Prune message for many reasons, one of which was covered earlier with regard to Figure 8-6. The main reasons are summarized here: *[handwritten: → WHY WOULD A ROUTER SEND A PRUNE MESSAGE?]*

- When receiving packets on a non-RPF interface.

- When a router realizes that both of the following are true:

  - No locally connected hosts in a particular group are listening for packets.

  - No downstream routers are listening for the group.

This section shows the logic behind the second reason for sending prunes. At this point in the explanation of Figure 8-6 and Figure 8-7, the only host that needs to receive packets sent to 226.1.1.1 is H2. What would the PIM-DM routers in this network do if H2 leaves group 226.1.1.1? Figure 8-8 shows just such an example, with H2 sending an IGMP Leave message for group 226.1.1.1. Figure 8-8 shows how PIM-DM uses this information to dynamically update the SPT.

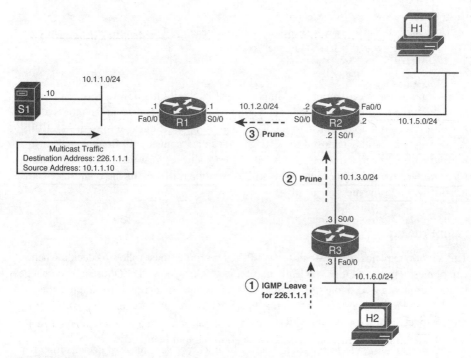

Figure 8-8 *R3 and R2 Sending Prune Messages*

Figure 8-8 shows three steps, with the logic in Steps 2 and 3 being similar but very im-- portant:

1. H2 leaves the multicast group by using an IGMP Leave message.

2. R3 uses an IGMP Query to confirm that no other hosts on the LAN want to receive traffic for group 226.1.1.1. So, R3 sends a Prune, referencing the (10.1.1.10, 226.1.1.1) SPT, out its RPF interface R2.

3. R2 does not have any locally connected hosts listening for group 226.1.1.1. Now, its only downstream router has sent a Prune for the SPT with source 10.1.1.10, group 226.1.1.1. Therefore, R2 has no reason to need packets sent to 226.1.1.1 anymore. So, R2 sends a Prune, referencing the (10.1.1.10, 226.1.1.1) SPT, out its RPF interface R1.

After the pruning is complete, both R3 and R2 will not be forwarding traffic sent to 226.1.1.1 from source 10.1.1.10. In the routers, the **show ip mroute** command shows that fact using the P (prune) flag, which means that the router has completely pruned itself from that particular (S,G) SPT.

Example 8-5 shows R3's command output with a null outgoing interface list.

Example 8-5 *Multicast Route Table Entry for the Group 226.1.1.1 for R3*

```
(10.1.1.10/32, 226.1.1.1), 00:03:16/00:01:36, flags: PT
  Incoming interface: Serial0/0, RPF nbr 10.1.3.2
    Outgoing interface list: Null
```
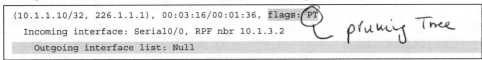 *(handwritten: ← pruning Tree)*

After all the steps in Figure 8-8 have been completed, R1 also does not need to send packets sent by 10.1.1.10 to 226.1.1.1 out any interfaces. After receiving a Prune message from R2, R1 has also updated its outgoing interface list, which shows that there is only one outgoing interface and that it is in the pruned state at this time. Example 8-6 shows the details.

Example 8-6 *Multicast Route Table Entry for the Group 226.1.1.1 for R1*

```
(10.1.1.10/32, 226.1.1.1), 00:08:35/00:02:42, flags: CT
  Incoming interface: FastEthernet0/0, RPF nbr 0.0.0.0
  Outgoing interface list:
    Serial0/0, Prune/Dense, 00:00:12/00:02:48
```

Of particular interest in the output, R1 has also set the C flag, but for R1 the C flag does not indicate that it has directly connected group members. In this case, the combination of a C flag and an RPF neighbor of 0.0.0.0 indicates that the connected device is the source for the group.

In reality, there is no separate Prune message and Join message; instead, PIM-DM and PIM-SM use a single message called a Join/Prune message. A Prune message is actually a Join/Prune message with a group address listed in the Prune field, and a Join message is a Join/Prune message with a group address listed in the Join field.

Steady-State Operation and the State Refresh Message

As mentioned briefly earlier in the chapter, with PIM-DM, an interface stays pruned only for 3 minutes by default. Prune messages list a particular source and group [in other words, a particular (S,G) SPT]. Whenever a router receives a Prune message, it finds the matching (S,G) SPT entry and marks the interface on which the Prune message was received as "pruned." However, it also sets a Prune timer, default 3 minutes, so that after 3 minutes, the interface is placed into a forwarding state again.

So, what happens with PIM-DM and pruned links? Well, the necessary links are pruned, and 3 minutes later they are added back. More multicasts flow, and the links are pruned. Then they are added back. And so on. So, when Cisco created PIM V2 (published as experimental RFC 3973), it included a feature called *state refresh*. State Refresh messages can prevent this rather inefficient behavior in PIM-DM version 1 of pruning and automatically unpruning interfaces.

Figure 8-9 shows an example that begins with the same state as the network described at the end of the preceding section, where the link between R1 and R2 and the link between

R2 and R3 have been pruned. Almost 3 minutes have passed, and the links are about to be added to the SPT again because of the expiration of the Prune timers.

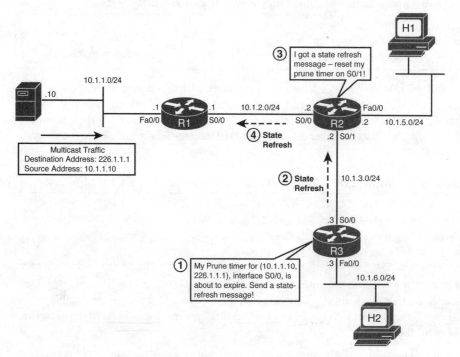

Figure 8-9   *How PIM-DM Version 2 Uses State Refresh Messages*

The PIM State Refresh message can be sent, just before a neighbor's Prune timer expires, to keep the interface in a pruned state. In Figure 8-9, the following steps do just that:

1. R3 monitors the time since it sent the last Prune to R2. Just before the Prune timer expires, R3 decides to send a State Refresh message to R2.

2. R3 sends the State Refresh message to R2, referencing SPT (10.1.1.10, 226.1.1.1).

3. R2 reacts by resetting its Prune timer for the interface on which it received the State Refresh message.

4. Because R2 had also pruned itself by sending a Prune message to R1, R2 also uses State Refresh messages to tell R1 to leave its s0/0 interface in a pruned state.

As long as R3 keeps sending a State Refresh message before the Prune timer on the upstream router (R2) expires, the SPT will remain stable, and there will not be the periodic times of flooding of more multicasts for that (S,G) tree. Note that the State Refresh timer has a default value of 60 seconds. Sending of a State Refresh message is not tied to the expiration of the Prune timer as the text implies.

60s def timer for STATE REFRESH!

Graft Message

When new hosts join a group, routers might need to change the current SPT for a particular (S,G) entry. With PIM-DM, one option could be to wait on the pruned links to expire. For example, in Figure 8-9, R3 could simply quit sending State Refresh messages, and within 3 minutes at most, R3 would be receiving the multicast packets for some (S,G) SPT again. However, waiting on the (default) 3-minute Prune timer to expire is not very efficient. To allow routers to "unprune" a previously pruned interface from an SPT, PIM-DM includes the *Graft* message, which is defined as follows:

> A router sends a Graft message to an upstream neighbor—a neighbor to which it had formerly sent a Prune message—causing the upstream router to put the link back into a forwarding state [for a particular (S,G) SPT].

Key Topic

Figure 8-10 shows an example that uses the same ongoing example network. The process shown in Figure 8-10 begins in the same state as described at the end of the preceding section. Neither host H1 nor H2 has joined group 226.1.1.1, and R2 and R3 have been totally pruned from the (10.1.1.10, 226.1.1.1) SPT. Referring to Figure 8-10, R1's s0/0 interface has been pruned from the (S,G) SPT, so R2 and R3 are not receiving the multicasts sent by server S1 to 226.1.1.1. The example then begins with host H2 joining group 226.1.1.1 again.

GRAFT M.
DEFINITION

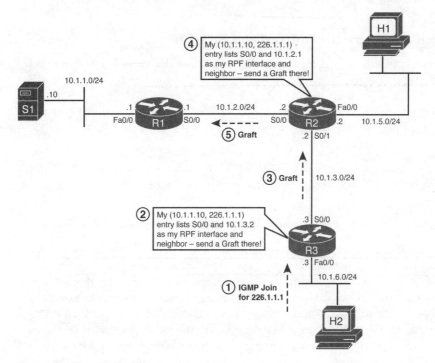

Figure 8-10 *R3 and R2 Send Graft Messages*

Without the Graft message, host H2 would have to wait for as much as 3 minutes before it would receive the group traffic. However, with the following steps, as listed in Figure 8-10, H2 will receive the packets in just a few seconds:

1. Host H2 sends an IGMP Join message.

2. R3 looks for the RPF interface for its (S,G) state information for the group 226.1.1.1 (see earlier Example 8-5), which shows the incoming interface as s0/0 and RPF neighbor as 10.1.3.2 for the group.

3. R3 sends the Graft message out s0/0 to R2.

4. R2 now knows it needs to be receiving messages from 10.1.1.10, sent to 226.1.1.1. However, R2's (S,G) entry also shows a P flag, meaning that R2 has pruned itself from the SPT. So, R2 finds its RPF interface and RPF neighbor IP address in its (S,G) entry, which references interface s0/0 and Router R1.

5. R2 sends a graft to R1.

At this point, R1 immediately puts its s0/0 back into the outgoing interface list, as does R2, and now H2 receives the multicast packets. Note that R1 also sends a Graft Ack message to R2 in response to the Graft message, and R2 sends a Graft Ack in response to R3's Graft message as well.

LAN-Specific Issues with PIM-DM and PIM-SM

This section covers three small topics related to operations that only matter when PIM is used on LANs:

■ Prune Override

■ Assert messages

■ Designated routers

Both PIM-DM and PIM-SM use these features in the same way.

Prune Override

In both PIM-DM and PIM-SM, the Prune process on multiaccess networks operates differently from how it operates on point-to-point links. The reason for this difference is that when one router sends a Prune message on a multiaccess network, other routers might not want the link pruned by the upstream router. Figure 8-11 shows an example of this problem, along with the solution through a PIM Join message that is called a *Prune Override*. In this figure, R1 is forwarding the group traffic for 239.9.9.9 on its fa0/0 interface, with R2 and R3 receiving the group traffic on their e0 interfaces. R2 does not have any connected group members, and its outgoing interface list would show null. The following list outlines the steps in logic shown in Figure 8-11, in which R3 needs to send a Prune Override:

1. R2 sends a Prune for group 239.9.9.9 because R2 has a null outgoing interface list for the group.

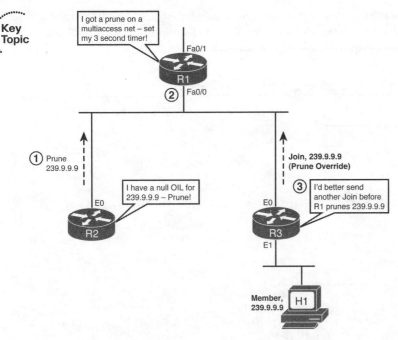

Figure 8-11 *Prune Override*

2. R1, realizing that it received the Prune on a multiaccess network, knows that other routers might still want to get the messages. So, instead of immediately pruning the interface, R1 sets a 3-second timer that must expire before R1 will prune the interface.

3. R3 also receives the Prune message sent by R2, because Prune messages are multicast to the All-PIM-Routers group address 224.0.0.13. R3 still needs to get traffic for 239.9.9.9, so R3 sends a Join message on its e0 interface.

4. (Not shown in Figure 8-11) R1 receives the Join message from R3 before removing its LAN interface from the outgoing interface list. As a result, R1 does not prune its Fa0/0 interface.

This process is called *Prune Override* because R3 overrides the Prune sent by R2. The Prune Override is actually a Join message, sent by R3 in this case. The message itself is no different from a normal Join. As long as R1 receives a Join message from R3 before its 3-second timer expires, R3 continues to receive traffic without interruption.

Assert Message — enables routers to negotiate

The final PIM-DM message covered in this chapter is the PIM Assert message. The Assert message is used to prevent wasted effort when more than one router attaches to the same LAN. Rather than sending multiple copies of each multicast packet onto the LAN, the PIM Assert message allows the routers to negotiate. The winner gets the right to be responsible for forwarding multicasts onto the LAN.

Figure 8-12 shows an example of the need for the Assert message. R2 and R3 both attach to the same LAN, with H1 being an active member of the group 227.7.7.7. Both R2 and R3 are receiving the group traffic for 227.7.7.7 from the source 10.1.1.10.

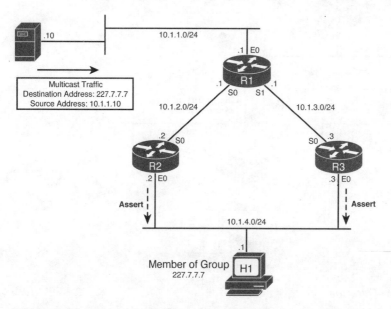

Figure 8-12   *R2 and R3 Sending Assert Messages*

The goal of the Assert message is to assign the responsibility of forwarding group traffic on the LAN to the router that is closest to the source. When R2 and R3 receive group traffic from the source on their s0 interfaces, they forward it on their e0 interfaces. Both of them have their s0 interfaces in the incoming interface list and e0 interfaces in the outgoing interface list. Now, R2 and R3 receive a multicast packet for the group on their e0 interfaces, which will cause them to send an Assert message to resolve who should be the forwarder.

The Assert process picks a winner based on the routing protocol and metric used to find the route to reach the unicast address of the source. In this example, that means that R2 or R3 will win based on the routes they each use to reach 10.1.1.10. R2 and R3 send and receive Assert messages that include their respective administrative distances of the routing protocols used to learn the route that matches 10.1.1.10, as well as the metric for those routes. The routers on the LAN compare their own routing protocol administrative distance and metrics to those learned in the Assert messages. The winner of the Assert process is determined as follows:

1. The router advertising the lowest administrative distance of the routing protocol used to learn the route wins.

2. If a tie occurs, the router with the lowest advertised routing protocol metric for that route wins.

3. If a tie occurs, the router with the highest IP address on that LAN wins.

Designated Router

PIM Hello messages are also used to elect a designated router (DR) on a multiaccess network. A PIM-DM or PIM-SM router with the highest IP address becomes the DR for the link. This behavior should be easy to remember because it is very much like the operation of how an OSPF DR router is elected using the highest router-id or RID.

The PIM DR concept applies mainly when IGMPv1 is used. IGMPv1 does not have a mechanism to elect a querier. That is to say that IGMPv1 has no way to decide which of the many routers on a LAN should send IGMP Queries. When IGMPv1 is used, the PIM DR is used as the IGMP Querier. IGMPv2 can directly elect a querier (the router with the lowest IP address), so the PIM DR is not used as the IGMP Querier when IGMPv2 is used.

Note that on a LAN, one router might win the Assert process for a particular (S,G) SPT, while another might become the IGMP Querier (PIM DR for IGMPv1, IGMP Querier for IGMPv2). The winner of the Assert process is responsible for forwarding multicasts onto the LAN, whereas the IGMP Querier is responsible for managing the IGMP process by being responsible for sending IGMP Query messages on the LAN. Note also that the IGMPv2 Querier election chooses the lowest IP address, and the Assert process uses the highest IP address as a tiebreaker, making it slightly more likely that different routers are chosen for each function.

IGMP querier & the router that wins the Assert negotiation do not need to be the same

Summary of PIM-DM Messages

This section concludes the coverage of PIM-DM. Table 8-2 lists the key PIM-DM messages covered in this chapter, along with a brief definition of their use.

Table 8-2   *Summary of PIM-DM Messages*

PIM Message	Definition
Hello	Used to form neighbor adjacencies with other PIM routers, and to maintain adjacencies by monitoring for received Hellos from each neighbor. Also used to elect a PIM DR on multiaccess networks.
Prune	Used to ask a neighboring router to remove the link over which the Prune flows from that neighboring router's outgoing interface list for a particular (S,G) SPT.
State Refresh	Used by a downstream router, sent to an upstream router on an RPF interface, to cause the upstream router to reset its Prune timer. This allows the downstream router to maintain the pruned state of a link, for a particular (S,G) SPT.
Assert	Used on multiaccess networks to determine which router wins the right to forward multicasts onto the LAN, for a particular (S,G) SPT.

PIM Message	Definition
Prune Override (Join)	On a LAN, a router can multicast a Prune message to its upstream routers. Other routers on the same LAN, wanting to prevent the upstream router from pruning the LAN, immediately send another Join message for the (S,G) SPT. (The Prune Override is not actually a Prune Override message— it is a Join. This is the only purpose of a Join message in PIM-DM, per RFC 3973.)
Graft/Graft-Ack	When a pruned link needs to be added back to an (S,G) SPT, a router sends a Graft message to its RPF neighbor. The RPF neighbor acknowledges with a Graft-Ack.

The next two short sections introduce two other dense-mode protocols, DVMRP and MOSPF.

Distance Vector Multicast Routing Protocol

RFC 1075 describes Version 1 of DVMRP. DVMRP has many versions. The operation of DVMRP is similar to PIM-DM. The major differences between PIM-DM and DVMRP are defined as follows:

- Cisco IOS does not support a full implementation of DVMRP; however, it does support connectivity to a DVMRP network.

- DVMRP uses its own distance vector routing protocol that is similar to RIPv2. It sends route updates every 60 seconds and considers 32 hops as infinity. Use of its own routing protocol adds more overhead to DVMRP operation compared to PIM-DM.

- DVMRP uses Probe messages to find neighbors using the All DVMRP Routers group address 224.0.0.4.

- DVMRP uses a truncated broadcast tree, which is similar to an SPT with some links pruned.

Multicast Open Shortest Path First

MOSPF is defined in RFC 1584, "Multicast Extensions to OSPF," which is an extension to the OSPFv2 unicast routing protocol. The MOSPF RFC, 1584, has been changed to historic status, so MOSPF implementations are unlikely today. For perspective, the basic operation of MOSPF is described here:

- MOSPF uses the group membership link-state advertisement (LSA), Type 6, which it floods throughout the originating router's area. As with unicast OSPF, all MOSPF routers in an area must have identical link-state databases so that every MOSPF router in an area can calculate the same SPT.

- The SPT is calculated "on demand," when the first multicast packet for the group arrives.

- Through the SPF calculation, all the routers know where the attached group members are, based on the group membership LSAs.

- After the SPF calculation is completed, entries are made into each router's multicast forwarding table.

- Just like unicast OSPF, the SPT is loop free, and every router knows the upstream interface and downstream interfaces. As a result, an RPF check is not required.

- Obviously, MOSPF can only work with the OSPF unicast routing protocol. MOSPF is suitable for small networks. As more hosts begin to source multicast traffic, routers must perform a higher number of Dijkstra algorithm computations, which demands an increasing level of router CPU resources.

Note   Cisco IOS does not support MOSPF.

Sparse-Mode Routing Protocols

There are two sparse-mode routing protocols:

- Protocol Independent Multicast Sparse Mode (PIM-SM)

- Core-Based Tree (CBT)

This section covers the operation of PIM-SM.

Operation of Protocol Independent Multicast Sparse Mode

PIM-SM works with a completely opposite strategy from that of PIM-DM, although the mechanics of the protocol are not exactly opposite. PIM-SM assumes that no hosts want to receive multicast packets until they specifically ask to receive them. As a result, until a host in a subnet asks to receive multicasts for a particular group, multicasts are never delivered to that subnet. With PIM-SM, downstream routers must request to receive multicasts using PIM Join messages. Also, after they are receiving those messages, the downstream router must continually send Join messages to the upstream router; otherwise, the upstream router stops forwarding, putting the link in a pruned state. This process is opposite to that used by PIM-DM, in which the default is to flood multicasts, with downstream routers needing to continually send Prunes or State Refresh messages to keep a link in a pruned state.

PIM-SM makes the most sense with a small percentage of subnets that need to receive packets sent to any multicast group.

Similarities Between PIM-DM and PIM-SM

PIM-SM has many similarities to PIM-DM. Like PIM-DM, PIM-SM uses the unicast routing table to perform RPF checks—regardless of what unicast routing protocol populated the table. (Like PIM-DM, the "protocol independent" part of the PIM acronym comes from the fact that PIM-SM is not dependent on any particular unicast IP routing protocol.) In addition, PIM-SM also uses the following mechanisms that are used by PIM-DM:

- PIM Neighbor discovery through exchange of Hello messages.

- Recalculation of the RPF interface when the unicast routing table changes.

- Election of a DR on a multiaccess network. The DR performs all IGMP processes when IGMPv1 is in use on the network.

- The use of Prune Overrides on multiaccess networks.

- Use of Assert messages to elect a designated forwarder on a multiaccess network. The winner of the Assert process is responsible for forwarding unicasts onto that subnet.

Note   The preceding list was derived, with permission, from *Routing TCP/IP*, Volume II, by Jeff Doyle and Jennifer DeHaven Carroll.

These mechanisms are described in the section "Operation of Protocol Independent Multicast Dense Mode," earlier in this chapter, and thus are not repeated in this section.

Sources Sending Packets to the Rendezvous Point

PIM-SM uses a two-step process to initially deliver multicast packets from a particular source to the hosts wanting to receive packets. Later, the process is improved beyond these initial steps. The steps for the initial forwarding of multicasts with PIM-SM are as follows:

1. Sources send the packets to a router called the rendezvous point (RP).

2. The RP sends the multicast packets to all routers/hosts that have registered to receive packets for that group. This process uses a shared tree.

Note   In addition to these two initial steps, routers with local hosts that have sent an IGMP Join message for a group can go a step further, joining the source-specific tree for a particular (S,G) SPT.

This section describes the first of these two steps, in which the source sends packets to the RP. To make that happen, the router connected to the same subnet as the source host must register with the RP. The RP accepts the registration only if the RP knows of any routers or hosts that need to receive a copy of those multicasts.

Figure 8-13 shows an example of the registration process in which the RP knows that no hosts currently want the IP multicasts sent to group 228.8.8.8—no matter which source is sending them. All routers are configured identically with the global command ip multicast-routing and the interface command ip pim sparse-mode on all their physical interfaces. Also, all routers have statically configured R3 as the RP by using the global command ip pim rp-address 10.1.10.3. This includes R3; a router knows that it is an RP when it sees its interface address listed as an RP address. Usually, a loopback interface address is used as an RP address. The loopback network 10.1.10.3/32 of R3 is advertised in the unicast routing protocol so that all the routers know how to reach the RP. The configuration for R3 is shown in Example 8-7. The other routers have the same multicast configuration, without the loopback interface.

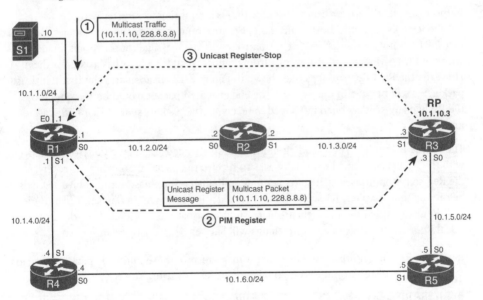

Figure 8-13 *Source Registration Process When RP Has Not Received a Request for the Group from Any PIM-SM Router*

Example 8-7 *Multicast Sparse-Mode and RP Configuration on R3*

```
ip multicast-routing
ip pim rp-address 10.1.10.3
!
interface Loopback2
 ip address 10.1.10.3 255.255.255.255
 ip pim sparse-mode
!
interface Serial0
```

```
 ip pim sparse-mode
!
interface Serial1
 ip pim sparse-mode
```

The following three steps, referenced in Figure 8-13, describe the sequence of events for the Source Registration process when the RP has not received a request for the group from any PIM-SM router because no host has yet joined the group.

[handwritten left margin: RP has not received a request for the group from any PIM-SM router]

1. Host S1 begins sending multicasts to 228.8.8.8, and R1 receives those multicasts because it connects to the same LAN.

2. R1 reacts by sending unicast PIM Register messages to the RP. The Register messages are unicasts sent to the RP IP address, 10.1.10.3 in this case.

3. R3 sends unicast Register-Stop messages back to R1 because R3 knows that it does not have any need to forward packets sent to 228.8.8.8.

In this example, the router near the source (R1) is attempting to register with the RP, but the RP tells R1 not to bother anymore, because no one wants those multicast messages. R1 has not forwarded any of the native multicast messages at this point, in keeping with the PIM-SM strategy of not forwarding multicasts until a host has asked for them. However, the PIM Register message shown in Figure 8-13 encapsulates the first multicast packet. As will be seen in Figure 8-14, the encapsulated packet would be forwarded by the RP had any senders been interested in receiving the packets sent to that multicast group.

The source host might keep sending multicasts, so R1 needs to keep trying to register with the RP in case some host finally asks to receive the packets. So, when R1 receives the Register-Stop messages, it starts a 1-minute Register-Suppression timer. Five seconds before the timer expires, R1 sends another Register message with a flag set, called the Null-Register bit, without any encapsulated multicast packets. As a result of this additional Register message, one of two things will happen:

- If the RP still knows of no hosts that want to receive these multicast packets, it sends another Register-Stop message to R1, and R1 resets its Register-Suppression timer.

- If the RP now knows of at least one router/host that needs to receive these multicast packets, it does not reply to this briefer Register message. As a result, R1, when its timer expires, again sends its multicast packets to R3 (RP) encapsulated in PIM Register messages.

Joining the Shared Tree

[handwritten left margin: RPT]

So far, this section on PIM-SM has explained the beginnings of the registration process, by which a router near the source of multicast packets registers with the RP. Before completing that discussion, however, the concept of the shared tree for a multicast group, also called the *root-path tree (RPT)*, must be explained. As mentioned earlier, PIM-SM initially causes multicasts to be delivered in a two-step process: First, packets are sent from the source to the RP, and then the RP forwards the packets to the subnets that have hosts that need a copy of those multicasts. PIM-SM uses this shared tree in the second part of the process.

The RPT is a tree, with the RP at the root that defines over which links multicasts should be forwarded to reach all required routers. One such tree exists for each multicast group that is currently active in the internetwork. So, after the multicast packets sent by each source are forwarded to the RP, the RP uses the RPT for that multicast group to determine where to forward these packets.

PIM-SM routers collectively create the RPT by sending PIM Join messages toward the RP. PIM-SM routers choose to send a Join under two conditions:

- When a PIM-SM router receives a PIM Join message on any interface other than the interface used to route packets toward the RP

- When a PIM-SM router receives an IGMP Membership Report message from a host on a directly connected subnet

Figure 8-14 shows an example of the PIM-SM join process, using the same network as Figure 8-12 but with H1 joining group 228.8.8.8. The routers react to the IGMP Join by sending a Join toward the RP, to become part of the shared SPT (*,228.8.8.8).

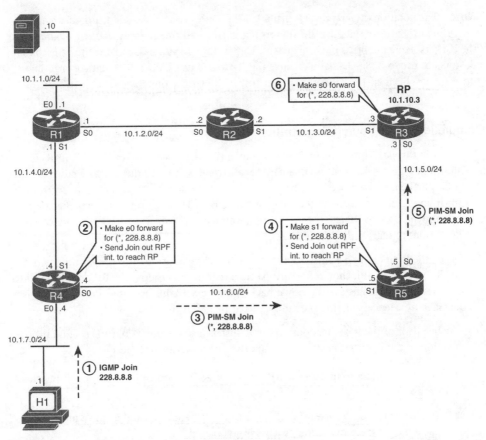

Figure 8-14 *Creating a Shared Tree for (*,228.8.8.8)*

Figure 8-14 shows how H1 causes a shared tree (*,228.8.8.8) to be created, as described in the following steps:

[handwritten: PIM register messages]

1. H1 sends an IGMP Join message for the group 228.8.8.8.

2. R4 realizes that it needs to ask the RP for help, specifically asking the RP to forward packets destined to 228.8.8.8. So, R4 sends a PIM Join for the shared tree for group 228.8.8.8 toward the RP. R4 also puts its e0 interface into a forwarding state for the RPT for group 228.8.8.8.

3. R5 receives the Join on its s1 interface, so R5 puts its s1 interface in a forwarding state for the shared tree [represented by (*,228.8.8.8)]. R5 also knows it needs to forward the Join toward the RP.

4. R5 sends the Join toward the RP.

5. R3, the RP, puts its s0 interface in a forwarding state for the (*,288.8.8.8) shared tree.

[handwritten left margin: Host requesting a mc group]

By the end of this process, the RP knows that at least one host wants packets sent to 228.8.8.8. The RPT for group 228.8.8.8 is formed with R3's s0 interface, R5's s1 interface, and R4's e0 interface.

> **Note** The notation (*,G) represents a single RPT. The * represents a wildcard, meaning "any source," because the PIM-SM routers use this shared tree regardless of the source of the packets. For example, a packet sent from any source IP address, arriving at the RP and destined to group 228.8.8.8, would cause the RP to use its (*,228.8.8.8) multicast routing table entries, because these entries are part of the RPT for group 228.8.8.8.

Completion of the Source Registration Process

So far in this description of PIM-SM, a source (10.1.1.10) sent packets to 228.8.8.8, as shown in Figure 8-13—but no one cared at the time, so the RP did not forward the packets. Next, you learned what happens when a host does want to receive packets, with the routers reacting to create the RPT for that group. This section completes the story by showing how an RP reacts to a PIM Register message when the RP knows that some hosts want to receive those multicasts.

When the RP receives a Register message for an active multicast group—in other words, the RP believes that it should forward packets sent to the group—the RP does not send a Register-Stop message, as was shown back in Figure 8-13. Instead, it reacts to the Register message by deencapsulating the multicast packet and forwarding it.

The behavior of the RP in reaction to the Register message points out the second major function of the Register message. Its main two functions are as follows:

[Key Topic icon]

■ To allow a router to inform the RP that it has a local source for a particular multicast group

■ To allow a router to forward multicasts to the RP, encapsulated inside a unicast packet, until the registration process is completed

To show the complete process, Figure 8-15 shows an example. In the example, host H1 has already joined group 228.8.8.8, as shown in Figure 8-14. The following steps match those identified in Figure 8-15. Note that Step 3 represents the forwarding of the multicasts that were encapsulated inside Register messages at Step 2.

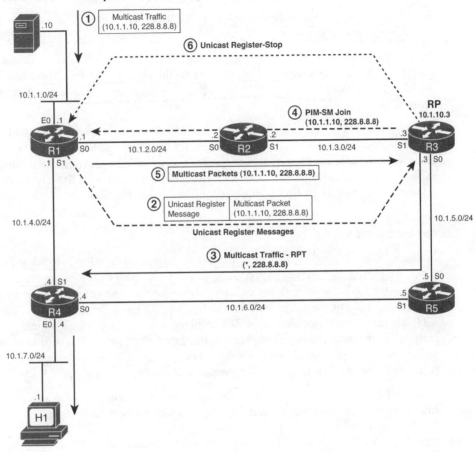

Figure 8-15 *Source Registration When the RP Needs to Receive Packets Sent to That Group*

1. Host S1 sends multicasts to 228.8.8.8.

2. Router R1 encapsulates the multicasts, sending them inside Register messages to the RP, R3.

3. R3, knowing that it needs to forward the multicast packets, deencapsulates the packets and sends them toward H1. (This action allows R1 and R3 to distribute the multicasts while the registration process completes.) R5 forwards the group traffic to R4 and R4 forwards it on its LAN.

4. R3 joins the SPT for source 10.1.1.10, group 228.8.8.8, by sending a PIM-SM Join message for group (10.1.1.10, 228.8.8.8) toward the source 10.1.1.10.

5. When R1 and R2 receive the PIM-SM Join message from R3 requesting the group traffic from the source, they start forwarding group traffic toward the RP. At this point, R3 (the RP) now receives this traffic on the SPT from the source. However, R1 is also still sending the Register messages with encapsulated multicast packets to R3.

6. R3 sends unicast Register-Stop messages to R1. When R1 receives the Register-Stop messages from R3, it stops sending the encapsulated unicast Register messages to R3.

The process might seem like a lot of trouble, but at the end of the process, multicasts are delivered to the correct locations. The process uses the efficient SPT from the source to the RP and the shared tree (*,228.8.8.8) from the RP to the subnets that need to receive the traffic.

Note that the PIM protocols could have just let a router near the source, such as R1 in this example, continue to encapsulate multicasts inside the unicast Register messages. However, it is inefficient to make R1 encapsulate every multicast packet, make R3 deencapsulate every packet, and then make R3 forward the traffic. So, PIM-SM has the RP, R3 in this case, join the group-specific tree for that (S,G) combination.

Shared Distribution Tree

In Figure 8-15, the group traffic that flows over the path from the RP (R3) to R5 to R4 is called a *shared distribution tree*. It is also called a *root-path tree (RPT)* because it is rooted at the RP. If the network has multiple sources for the same group, traffic from all the sources would first travel to the RP (as shown with the traffic from host S1 in Figure 8-14) and then travel down this shared RPT to all the receivers. Because all sources in the multicast group use a common shared tree, a wildcard notation of (*,G) is used to identify an RPT, where * represents all sources and G represents the multicast group address. The RPT for the group 228.8.8.8 shown in Figure 8-14 would be written as (*,228.8.8.8).

Example 8-8 shows the multicast route table entry for R4 in Figure 8-15. On a Cisco router, the **show ip mroute** command displays the multicast route table entries.

Example 8-8   *Multicast Route Table Entry for the Group 228.8.8.8 for R4*

```
(*, 228.8.8.8), 00:00:08/00:02:58, RP 10.1.10.3, flags: SC
  Incoming interface: Serial0, RPF nbr 10.1.6.5
  Outgoing interface list:
    Ethernet0, Forward/Sparse, 00:00:08/00:02:52
```

The interpretation of the information shown in Example 8-8 is as follows:

- The first line shows that the (*,G) entry for the group 228.8.8.8 was created 8 seconds ago, and if R4 does not forward group packets using this entry in 2 minutes and 58 seconds, it will expire. Every time R4 forwards a packet, the timer is reset to 3 minutes. This entry was created because R4 received an IGMP Join message from H1.

- The RP for this group is 10.1.10.3 (R3). The S flag indicates that this group is using the sparse-mode (PIM-SM) routing protocol. The C flag indicates that R4 has a directly connected group member for 228.8.8.8.

- The incoming interface for this (*,228.8.8.8) entry is s0 and the RPF neighbor is 10.1.6.5. Note that for the SPT, the RPF interface is chosen based on the route to reach the RP, not the route used to reach a particular source.

- Group traffic is forwarded out on the Ethernet0 interface. In this example, Ethernet0 was added to the outgoing interface list because an IGMP Report message was received on this interface from H1. This interface has been in the forwarding state for 8 seconds. The Prune timer indicates that if an IGMP Join is not received again on this interface within the next 2 minutes and 52 seconds, it will be removed from the outgoing interface list.

Steady-State Operation by Continuing to Send Joins

To maintain the forwarding state of interfaces, PIM-SM routers must send PIM Join messages periodically. If a router fails to send Joins periodically, PIM-SM moves interfaces back to a pruned state.

PIM-SM routers choose to maintain the forwarding state on links based on two general criteria:

Key Topic

- A downstream router continues to send PIM Joins for the group.

- A locally connected host still responds to IGMP Query messages with IGMP Report messages for the group.

Figure 8-16 shows an example in which R5 maintains the forwarding state of its link to R3 based on both of these reasons. H2 has also joined the shared tree for 228.8.8.8. H1 had joined earlier, as shown in Figures 8-14 and 8-15.

Example 8-9 shows the multicast route table entry for R5 in Figure 8-16, with these two interfaces in a forwarding state.

Example 8-9 *Multicast Route Table Entry for the Group 228.8.8.8 for R5*

```
(*,228.8.8.8), 00:00:05/00:02:59, RP 10.1.10.3, flags: SC
  Incoming interface: Serial0, RPF nbr 10.1.5.3
  Outgoing interface list:
    Serial1, Forward/Sparse, 00:01:15/00:02:20
    Ethernet0, Forward/Sparse, 00:00:05/00:02:55
```

In Example 8-9, two interfaces are listed in the outgoing interface list. The s1 interface is listed because R5 has received a PIM-SM Join message from R4. In PIM-SM, the downstream routers need to keep sending PIM-SM Join messages every 60 seconds to the upstream router. When R5 receives another PIM-SM Join from R4 on its s1 interface, it resets the Prune timer to the default value of 3 minutes. If R5 does not receive a PIM-SM Join from R4 before R5's Prune timer on that interface expires, R5 places its s1 interface in a pruned state and stops forwarding the traffic on the interface.

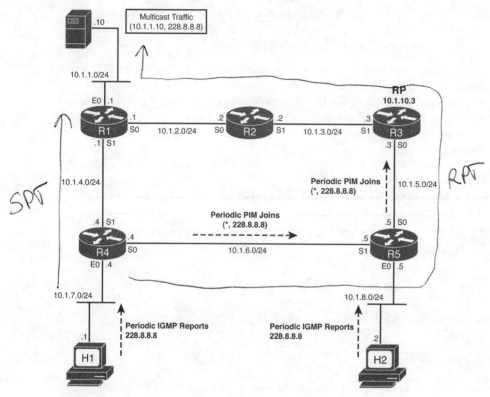

Figure 8-16   *Host H2 Sends an IGMP Join Message*

By contrast, R5's e0 interface is listed as forwarding in R5's outgoing interface list because R5 has received an IGMP Join message from H2. Recall from Chapter 7 that a multicast router sends an IGMP general query every 60 seconds on its LAN interfaces. It must receive at least one IGMP Report/Join message as a response for a group; otherwise, it stops forwarding the group traffic on the interface. When R5 receives another IGMP Report message on its e0 interface, it resets the Prune timer for the entry to the default value of 3 minutes.

Note also that on R5, the receipt of the PIM Join from R4, or the IGMP Report on e0, triggers R5's need to send the PIM Join toward the RP.

Examining the RP's Multicast Routing Table

In the current state of the ongoing example, as last shown in Figure 8-16, the RP (R3) has joined the SPT for source 10.1.1.10, group 228.8.8.8. The RP also is the root of the shared tree for group 228.8.8.8. Example 8-10 shows both entries in R3's multicast route table.

I'am RP! (handwritten)

Example 8-10 *Multicast Route Table Entry for the Group 228.8.8.8 for R3*

```
(*,228.8.8.8), 00:02:27/00:02:59, RP 10.1.10.3, flags: S
  Incoming interface: Null, RPF nbr 0.0.0.0
  Outgoing interface list:
    Serial0, Forward/Sparse, 00:02:27/00:02:33
(10.1.1.10/32, 228.8.8.8), 00:02:27/00:02:33, flags: T
  Incoming interface: Serial1, RPF nbr 10.1.3.2,
  Outgoing interface list:
  Outgoing interface list: Null
```

SHARED TREE TOWARDS THE SOURCE (handwritten)

The first entry shows the shared tree, as indicated by the S flag. Notice the incoming interface is Null because R3, as RP, is the root of the tree. Also, the RPF neighbor is listed as 0.0.0.0 for the same reason. In other words, it shows that the shared-tree traffic for the group 228.8.8.8 has originated at this router and it does not depend on any other router for the shared-tree traffic.

The second entry shows the SPT entry on R3 for multicast group 228.8.8.8, source 10.1.1.10. The T flag indicates that this entry is for an SPT, and the source is listed at the beginning of that same line (10.1.1.10). The incoming interface is s1 and the RPF neighbor for the source address 10.1.1.10 is 10.1.3.2. *(R2)* (handwritten)

As you can see, an RP uses the SPT to pull the traffic from the source to itself and uses the shared tree to push the traffic down to the PIM-SM routers that have requested it.

Shortest-Path Tree Switchover

PIM-SM routers could continue forwarding packets through the PIM-SM two-step process, whereby sources send packets to the RP, and the RP sends them to all other routers using the RPT. However, one of the most fascinating aspects of PIM-SM operations is that each PIM-SM router can build the SPT between itself and the source of a multicast group and take advantage of the most efficient path available from the source to the router. In Figure 8-16, R4 is receiving the group traffic from the source through the path R1-R2-R3-R5-R4. However, it is obvious that it would be more efficient for R4 to receive the group traffic directly from R1 on R4's s1 interface.

In the section "Completion of the Source Registration Process," earlier in this chapter, you saw that the PIM-SM design allows an RP to build an SPT between itself and the router that is directly connected with the source (also called the source DR) to pull the group traffic. Similarly, the PIM-SM design also allows any other PIM-SM router to build *(R4 → R4)* (handwritten) an SPT between the router and the source DR. This feature allows a PIM-SM router to avoid using the inefficient path, such as the one used by R4 in Figure 8-16. Also, after the router starts receiving the group traffic over the SPT, it can send a Prune message to the upstream router of the shared tree to stop forwarding the traffic for the group.

The question is, when should a router switch over from RPT to SPT? RFC 2362 for PIM-SM specifies that "The recommended policy is to initiate the switch to the SP-tree after receiving a significant number of data packets during a specified time interval from a particular source." What number should be considered as a significant number? The RFC does not specify that. Cisco routers, by default, switch over from the RPT to the source-specific SPT after they receive the first packet from the shared tree.

> **Note**   You can change this behavior by configuring the global command **ip pim spt-threshold** *rate* on any router for any group. After the traffic rate exceeds the stated rate (in kbps), the router joins the SPT. The command impacts the behavior only on the router(s) on which it is configured.

If a router is going to switch to SPT, why join the RPT first? In PIM-SM, a router does not know the IP address of a source until it receives at least one packet for the group from the source. After it receives one packet on the RPT, it can learn the IP address of a source, and initialize a switchover to the SPT for that (source,group) combination.

With the default Cisco PIM-SM operation, when multicast packets begin arriving on R4's s0 interface through the shared tree, R4 attempts to switch to the SPT for source 10.1.1.10. Figure 8-17 shows the general steps.

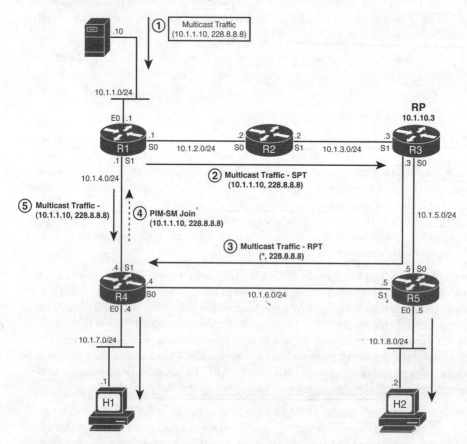

Figure 8-17   *R4 Initializing Switchover from RPT to SPT by Sending a PIM-SM Join to R1*

The first three steps in Figure 8-17 are as follows:

1. The source (S1,10.1.1.10) sends a multicast packet to the first-hop Router R1.

2. R1 forwards the packet to the RP (R3).

3. The RP forwards the packet to R4 through the shared tree.

At Step 3, R4 learned that the source address of the multicast group 228.8.8.8 is 10.1.1.10. So, besides forwarding the packet at Step 3, R4 can use that information to join the SPT for group 228.8.8.8, from source 10.1.1.10, using the following steps from Figure 8-17:

4. R4 consults its unicast routing table, finds the next-hop address and outgoing interface it would use to reach source 10.1.1.10, and sends the PIM-SM Join message out that interface (s1) to R1. This PIM-SM Join message is specifically for the SPT of (10.1.1.10,228.8.8.8). The Join travels hop by hop until it reaches the source DR.

5. As a result of the Join, R1 places its s1 interface in a forwarding state for SPT (10.1.1.10,228.8.8.8). So, R1 starts forwarding multicasts from 10.1.1.10 to 228.8.8.8 out its s1 interface as well.

R4 now has a multicast routing table entry for the SPT, as shown in Example 8-11.

Example 8-11 *Multicast Route Table Entry for the Group 228.8.8.8 for R4*

```
(*,228.8.8.8), 00:02:36/00:02:57, RP 10.1.10.3, flags: SCJ
  Incoming interface: Serial0, RPF nbr 10.1.6.5
  Outgoing interface list:
    Ethernet0, Forward/Sparse, 00:02:36/00:02:13
(10.1.1.10/32, 228.8.8.8), 00:00:23/00:02:33, flags: CJT
  Incoming interface: Serial1, RPF nbr 10.1.4.1,
  Outgoing interface list:
Ethernet0, Forward/Sparse, 00:00:23/00:02:37
```

[handwritten annotation: traffic was switched from RPT to SPT]

In Example 8-11, you see two entries for the group. The J flag (for join) on both the entries indicates that the traffic was switched from RPT to SPT, and now the (S,G) entry will be used for forwarding multicast packets for the group. Notice that the incoming interfaces for the (*,G) entry and (S,G) entry are different.

Pruning from the Shared Tree

When a PIM-SM router has joined a more efficient SPT, it might not need to receive multicast packets over the RPT anymore. For example, when R4 in Figure 8-17 notices that it is receiving the group traffic over RPT and SPT, it can and should ask the RP to stop sending the traffic.

To stop the RP from forwarding traffic to a downstream router on the shared tree, the downstream router sends a PIM-SM Prune message to the RP. The Prune message references the (S,G) SPT, which identifies the IP address of the source. Essentially, this prune means the following to the RP:

> Stop forwarding packets from the listed source IP address, to the listed group address, down the RPT.

For example, in Figure 8-18, which continues the example shown in Figure 8-17, R4 sends a Prune out its s0 interface toward R5. The Prune lists (S,G) entry (10.1.1.10,228.8.8.8), and it sets a bit called the RP-tree bit (RPT-bit). By setting the RPT-bit in the Prune message, R4 informs R5 (the upstream router) that it has switched to SPT and the Prune message is for the redundant traffic for the group 228.8.8.8, from 10.1.1.10, that R4 is receiving on the shared tree.

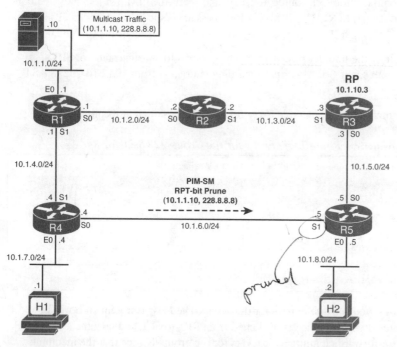

Figure 8-18 *R4 Sends a PIM-SM Prune with RP Bit Set to R5*

To stop the packets from being sent over the RPT to R4, R5 must prune its interface s1 in the RPT (*, 228.8.8.8). R5 can go on to join the SPT for (10.1.1.10,228.8.8.8) as well.

This concludes the coverage of the operations of PIM-SM. The next section covers some details about how routers can learn the IP address of the PIM RP.

Dynamically Finding RPs and Using Redundant RPs

In a PIM-SM network, every router must somehow learn the IP address of an RP. A PIM-SM router can use one of the following three methods to learn the IP address of an RP:

■   With Unicast RP, the RP address is statically configured on all the PIM-SM routers (including the RP) with the Cisco IOS global command **ip pim rp-address** *address*. This is the method used for the five-router topology shown in Figure 8-18.

- The Cisco-proprietary Auto-RP protocol can be used to designate the RP and advertise its IP address so that all PIM-SM routers can learn its IP address automatically.

- A standard BootStrap Router (BSR) protocol can be used to designate the RP and advertise its IP address so that all the PIM-SM routers can learn its IP address automatically.

Additionally, because PIM-SM relies so heavily on the RP, it makes sense to have redundant RPs. Cisco IOS offers two methods of providing redundant RPs, which are also covered in this section:

- Anycast RP using the Multicast Source Discovery Protocol (MSDP)
- BootStrap Router (BSR)

Dynamically Finding the RP Using Auto-RP

Static RP configuration is suboptimal under the following conditions:

- When an enterprise has a large number of PIM-SM routers and the enterprise wants to use many different RPs for different groups, it becomes time consuming and cumbersome to statically configure the IP addresses of many RPs for different groups on all the routers.

- When an RP fails or needs to be changed because a new RP is being installed, it becomes extremely difficult in a statically configured PIM-SM domain to switch over to an alternative RP without considerable downtime.

Auto-RP provides an alternative in which routers dynamically learn the unicast IP address used by each RP. Auto-RP uses a two-step process, which is shown in Figure 8-19 and Figure 8-20. In the first step, the RP sends RP-Announce messages to the reserved multicast address 224.0.1.39, stating that the router is an RP. The RP-Announce message also allows the router to advertise the multicast groups for which it is the RP, thereby allowing some load balancing of the RP workload among different routers. The RP continues to send these RP-Announce messages every minute.

For example, Figure 8-19 shows R3 as an RP that uses Auto-RP. R3 supports all multicast groups in this case. The RP-Announce message is shown as Step 1, to link it with Step 2 in Figure 8-20.

The second step for Auto-RP requires that one router be configured as a mapping agent. The mapping agent is usually the same router that was selected as an RP, but can be a different PIM-SM router. The mapping agent learns all the RPs and the multicast groups they each support. Then, the mapping agent multicasts another message, called RP-Discovery, that identifies the RP for each range of multicast group addresses. This message goes to reserved multicast address 224.0.1.40. It is this RP-Discovery message that actually informs the general router population as to which routers they should use as RPs.

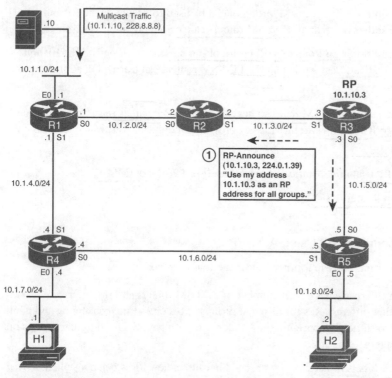

Figure 8-19 *R3 Sends RP-Announce Messages*

For example, in Figure 8-20, R2 is configured as a mapping agent. To receive all RP-Announce messages, R2 locally joins the well-known Cisco-RP-Announce multicast group 224.0.1.39. In other words, the mapping agent has become a group member for 224.0.1.39 and is listening for the group traffic. When R2 receives the RP-Announce packets shown in Figure 8-19, it examines the packet, creates group-to-RP mappings, and maintains this information in its cache, as shown in Figure 8-20.

At first glance, the need for the mapping agent might not be obvious. Why not just let the RPs announce themselves to all the other routers? Well, if Auto-RP supported only one RP, or even only one RP to support each multicast group, the mapping agent would be a waste of effort. However, to support RP redundancy—in other words, to support multiple RPs that can act as RP for the same multicast group—the Auto-RP mapping agent decides which RP should be used to support each group at the moment. To do so, the mapping agent selects the router with the highest IP address as an RP for the group. (Note that you can also configure multiple mapping agents, for redundancy.)

As soon as Cisco routers are configured with PIM-SM and Auto-RP, they automatically join the well-known Cisco-RP-Discovery multicast group 224.0.1.40. That means that they are listening to the group address 224.0.1.40, and when they receive a 224.0.1.40 packet, they learn group-to-RP mapping information and maintain it in their cache. When a PIM-SM router receives an IGMP Join message for a group or PIM-SM Join message from a downstream router, it checks the group-to-RP mapping information in its cache. Then it can proceed as described throughout the PIM-SM explanations in this chapter, using that RP as the RP for that multicast group.

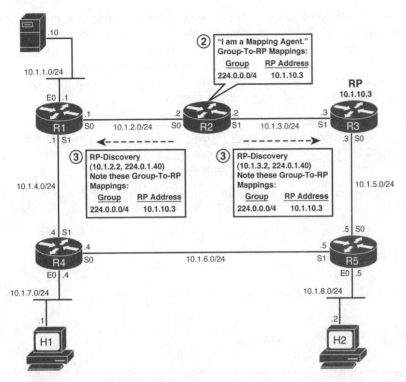

Figure 8-20 *R2 Creates Group-to-RP Mappings and Sends Them in RP-Discovery Messages*

The following list summarizes the steps used by Auto-RP:

Key
Topic

1. Each RP is configured to use Auto-RP and to announce itself and its supported multicast groups through RP-Announce messages (224.0.1.39).

2. The Auto-RP mapping agent, which might or might not also be an RP router, gathers information about all RPs by listening to the RP-Announce messages.

3. The mapping agent builds a mapping table that lists the currently best RP for each range of multicast groups, with the mapping agent picking the RP with the highest IP address if multiple RPs support the same multicast groups.

4. The mapping agent sends RP-Discover messages to 224.0.1.40 advertising the mappings.

5. All routers listen for packets sent to 224.0.1.40 to learn the mapping information and find the correct RP to use for each multicast group.

Key
Topic

Auto-RP creates a small chicken-and-egg problem in that the purpose of Auto-RP is to find the RPs, but to get the RP-Announce and RP-Discovery messages, PIM-SM routers would need to send a Join toward the RP, which they do not know yet. To overcome this problem, one option is to use a variation of PIM called *sparse-dense mode*. In PIM sparse-dense mode, a router uses PIM-DM rules when it does not know the location of the RP and PIM-SM rules when it does know the location of the RP. So, under normal conditions with Auto-RP, the routers would use dense mode long enough to learn the group-to-RP mappings from the mapping agent, and then switch over to sparse mode. However, if any other multicast traffic occurred before the routers learned of the RPs using Auto-RP, the multicast packets would be forwarded using dense-mode rules. This can result in extra network traffic. PIM sparse-dense mode is configured per interface using the **ip pim sparse-dense-mode** interface subcommand.

To avoid unnecessary dense-mode flooding, configure each router as an *Auto-RP Listener* and use sparse-mode on the interface. When you enable this feature, only Auto-RP traffic (groups 224.0.1.39 and 224.0.1.40) is flooded out all sparse-mode interfaces. You configure this feature with the global command **ip pim autorp listener**.

Example 8-12 shows the configuration for Routers R1, R2, and R3 from Figure 8-20. R1 is a normal multicast router using Auto-RP Listener, R2 is an Auto-RP mapping agent, and R3 is an RP.

Example 8-12   *Configuring Auto-RP*

```
!R1 Configuration (Normal MC Router)
ip multicast-routing
!
interface Serial0
 ip pim sparse-mode ! Repeat this command on each MC interface
!
ip pim autorp listener


!R2 Configuration (Auto-RP Mapping Agent)
ip multicast-routing
!
!The following command designates this router an Auto-RP Mapping Agent
!Optionally a source interface could be added
ip pim send-rp-discovery scope 10
!
interface Serial0
 ip pim sparse-mode ! Repeat this command on each MC interface


!R3 Configuration (Auto-RP Rendezvous Point)
ip multicast-routing
!
interface Loopback0
 ip address 10.1.10.3 255.255.255.255
 ip pim sparse-mode !Must be configured on source interface
!
interface Serial0
 ip pim sparse-mode ! Repeat this command on each MC interface
```

```
!
!The following command designates this router an Auto-RP RP
ip pim send-rp-announce loopback0 scope 10
```

Dynamically Finding the RP Using BSR (Boot-strap Router)

Cisco provided the proprietary Auto-RP feature to solve a couple of specific problems. PIM Version 2, which came later, provided a different solution to the same problem, namely the BootStrap Router (BSR) feature. From a very general perspective, BSR works similarly to Auto-RP. Each RP sends a message to another router, which collects the group-to-RP mapping information. That router then distributes the mapping information to the PIM routers. However, any examination of BSR beyond that level of detail shows that these two tools do differ in many ways.

It is helpful to first understand the concept of the bootstrap router, or BSR router, before thinking about the RPs. One router acts as BSR, which is similar to the mapping agent in Auto-RP. The BSR receives mapping information from the RPs, and then it advertises the information to other routers. However, there are some specific differences between the actions of the BSR, and their implications, and the actions of the Auto-RP mapping agent:

- The BSR router does not pick the best RP for each multicast group; instead, the BSR router sends all group-to-RP mapping information to the other PIM routers inside bootstrap messages.

- PIM routers each independently pick the currently best RP for each multicast group by running the same hash algorithm on the information in the bootstrap message.

- The BSR floods the mapping information in a bootstrap message sent to the all-PIM-routers multicast address (224.0.0.13).

- The flooding of the bootstrap message does not require the routers to have a known RP or to support dense mode. (This will be described in more detail in the next few pages.)

Figure 8-21 shows an example, described next, of how the BSR floods the bootstrap message. PIMv2 creates specific rules for BSR bootstrap messages, stating that PIM routers should flood these messages. PIM-SM routers flood bootstrap messages out all non-RPF interfaces, which in effect guarantees that at least one copy of the message makes it to every router. Note that this logic is not dependent on a working dense- or sparse-mode implementation. As a result, BSR overcomes the chicken-and-egg problem of Auto-RP.

For example, in Figure 8-21, imagine that R4's s1 interface is its RPF interface to reach R2, and R5's RPF interface to reach R2 is its s0 interface. So, they each forward the bootstrap messages at Step 3 of Figure 8-21. However, because R4 receives the bootstrap message from R5 on one of R4's non-RPF interfaces, R4 discards the packet, thereby preventing loops. R5 also does not forward the bootstrap message any farther for the same basic reasons.

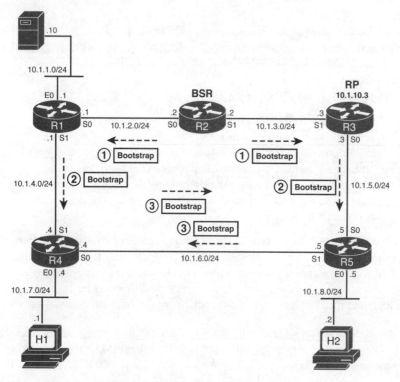

Figure 8-21   *BSR Flooding Bootstrap Messages*

The other important part of BSR operation is for each candidate RP (c-RP) to inform the BSR router that it is an RP and to identify the multicast groups it supports. This part of the process with BSR is simple if you keep in mind the following point:

All PIM routers already know the unicast IP address of the BSR based on the earlier receipt of bootstrap messages.

So, the c-RPs simply send unicast messages, called c-RP advertisements, to the BSR. These c-RP advertisements include the IP address used by the c-RP, and the groups it supports.

The BSR feature supports redundant RPs and redundant BSRs. As mentioned earlier, the bootstrap message sent by the BSR router includes all candidate RPs, with each router using the same hash algorithm to pick the currently best RP for each multicast group. The mapping information can list multiple RPs that support the same group addresses.

Additionally, multiple BSR routers can be configured. In that case, each candidate BSR (c-BSR) router sends bootstrap messages that include the priority of the BSR router and its IP address. The highest-priority BSR wins, or if a tie occurs, the highest BSR IP address wins. Then, the winning BSR, called the preferred BSR, continues to send bootstrap messages, while the other BSRs monitor those messages. If the preferred BSR's bootstrap messages cease, the redundant BSRs can attempt to take over.

Configuring BSR is similar to configuring Auto-RP. At a minimum, you need to tell a router that it is a candidate RP or candidate BSR, and which interface to use for the source of its messages. You can optionally tie an access list with the command to limit the groups for which the router will be the RP, or specify a preference to control the election among multiple BSRs.

Example 8-13 shows the configuration of a BSR and an RP.

Example 8-13   *Configuring a BSR and an RP*

```
!On the BSR (R2 in Figure 8-21)
ip multicast-routing
!
interface Loopback0
 ip pim sparse-mode !Must be configured on source interface
!
interface Serial0
 ip pim sparse-mode ! Repeat this command on each MC interface
!
!The following command configures the router as a candidate BSR with source
!interface of Lo0 and a priority of 0 (default)
ip pim bsr-candidate Loopback0 0
```

```
!On the RP (R3 in Figure 8-21)
ip multicast-routing
!
interface Loopback2
ip address 10.1.10.3 255.25.255.255
 ip pim sparse-mode !Must be configured on source interface
!
interface Serial0
 ip pim sparse-mode ! Repeat this command on each MC interface
!
!The following command configures the router as a candidate RP with source
!interface Lo2
ip pim rp-candidate Loopback2
```

Anycast RP with MSDP

The final tool covered here for finding a router's RP is called Anycast RP with Multicast Source Discovery Protocol (MSDP). Anycast RP is actually an implementation feature more than a new feature with new configuration commands. As will be explained in the upcoming pages, Anycast RP can actually use static RP configuration, Auto-RP, and BSR.

The key differences between using Anycast RP and using either Auto-RP or BSR relate to how the redundant RPs are used. The differences are as follows:

Key Topic

■ **Without Anycast RP:** RP redundancy allows only one router to be the active RP for each multicast group. Load sharing of the collective work of the RPs is accomplished by using one RP for some groups and another RP for other groups.

■ **With Anycast RP:** RP redundancy and load sharing can be achieved with multiple RPs concurrently acting as the RP for the same group.

The way Anycast RP works is to have each RP use the same IP address. The RPs must advertise this address, typically as a /32 prefix, with its IGP. Then, the other methods of learning an RP—static configuration, Auto-RP, and BSR—all view the multiple RPs as a single RP. At the end of the process, any packets sent to "the" RP are routed per IGP routes to the closest RP. Figure 8-22 shows an example of the process.

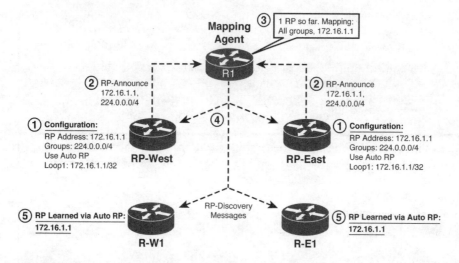

Figure 8-22   *Learning the RP Address with Anycast RP*

Figure 8-22 shows a design using two RPs (RP-East and RP-West) along with Auto-RP. The steps shown in the figure are as follows:

1. Both RPs are configured with 172.16.1.1/32, and configured to use that IP address for RP functions. In this case, both are configured to be the RP for all multicast groups.

2. Both RPs act as normal for Auto-RP by sending RP-Announce messages to 224.0.1.39.

3. The Auto-RP mapping agent builds its mapping table with a single entry, because it cannot tell the difference between the two RPs, because both use IP address 172.16.1.1.

4. The Auto-RP mapping agent acts as normal, sending an RP-Discovery message to 224.0.1.40. It includes (in this case) a single mapping entry: All groups map to 172.16.1.1.

5. All the routers, including Routers R-W1 and R-E1, learn through Auto-RP that the single RP for all groups is 172.16.1.1.

The last step described in the list brings the discussion to the main benefit of Anycast RP. At this point, the core Auto-RP function of advertising the IP address of the RP is complete. Of course, the IP address exists on two routers in Figure 8-22, but it could be more than that in other designs. Because of the IGP routes, when routers in the western part of the network (like R-W1) send packets to the RP at 172.16.1.1, they are actually sending the packets to RP-West. Likewise, when routers in the eastern part of the network (like R-E1) send packets to the RP (172.16.1.1), they are actually sending the packets to RP-East. This behavior is only achieved by using the Anycast RP implementation option beyond simply using Auto-RP.

The two biggest benefits of this design with Anycast RP are as follows: *Benefits of this solution*

(Key Topic)

■ Multiple RPs share the load for a single multicast group.

■ Recovery after a failed RP happens quickly. If an RP fails, multicast traffic is only interrupted for the amount of time it takes the IGP to converge to point to the other RP sharing the same IP address.

Interdomain Multicast Routing with MSDP

The design of Anycast RP can create a problem because each individual RP builds its own shared tree, but any multicast source sends packets to only one of the RPs. For example, Figure 8-23 shows the same network as Figure 8-22, but now with a multicast source in the western part of the network. The routers in the west side of the figure receive the packets as distributed by RP-West through its shared tree. However, the routers in RP-East's shared tree do not get the packets because RP-East never gets the packet sent by the server in the west side.

In Figure 8-23, East and West are two *multicast domains*. In this case, they are part of the same company, but multicast domains might also belong to different companies, or different ISPs. The solution to this problem is for the RPs to tell each other about all known sources by using MSDP. When a PIM router registers a multicast source with its RP, the RP uses MSDP to send messages to peer RPs. These *Source Active (SA)* messages list the IP addresses of each source for each multicast group, and are sent as unicasts over a TCP connection maintained between peer RPs. MSDP peers must be statically configured, and RPs must have routes to each of their peers and to the sources. Typically, Border Gateway Protocol (BGP) or Multicast BGP (MBGP) is used for this routing.

In Figure 8-23, RP-West could use MSDP to tell RP-East about the multicast source for 226.1.1.1 at unicast IP address 172.16.5.5. Then, RP-East would flood that information to any other MSDP peers. The receiver in its domain can then join the SPT of source 172.16.5.5, group 226.1.1.1, just as it would have done if it had received the multicast traffic directly from 172.16.5.5. If an RP has no receivers for a multicast group, it caches the information for possible later use. MSDP RPs continue to send SA messages every 60 seconds, listing all of its groups and sources. An RP can also request an updated list by using an SA request message. The peer responds with an SA response message.

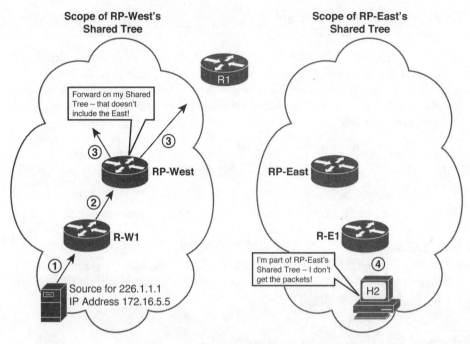

Figure 8-23 *Anycast RP Problem (Later Solved with MSDP)*

To use MSDP, first configure either Auto-RP or BSR. If running MSDP between routing domains, make sure that BGP is configured and there are routes to the MSDP peer. Then you can specify the MSDP peers on each router. Example 8-14 builds on Example 8-13. In Example 8-14, BSR is already configured. Routers RP-East and RP-West are then configured as MSDP peers with each other, using the **ip msdp peer** *address* command. BGP has also been configured between the two routers. The configuration is verified with the **show ip msdp peer** command on RP-West and the **show ip pim rp** command on RP-East. Note that RP-East shows RP-West as the RP for multicast group 226.1.1.1 from Figure 8-23.

Verification

Example 8-14 *Configuring Interdomain MC Routing with MSDP*

```
!RP-East Configuration

interface Loopback2
 ip address 10.1.10.3 255.255.255.255
 ip pim sparse-mode
!
ip multicast-routing
ip pim rp-candidate Loopback2
```

```
ip msdp peer 172.16.1.1
```

```
!RP-West Configuration
interface Loopback0
 ip address 172.16.1.1 255.255.255.255
 ip pim sparse-mode
!
ip multicast-routing
ip pim rp-candidate Loopback0
ip msdp peer 10.1.10.3 connect-source Loopback0
!
RP-West# show ip msdp peer
MSDP Peer 10.1.10.3 (?), AS 65001
  Connection status:
    State: Listen, Resets: 0, Connection source: Loopback0 (172.16.1.1)
    Uptime(Downtime): 00:30:18, Messages sent/received: 0/0
    Output messages discarded: 0
    Connection and counters cleared 00:30:18 ago
  SA Filtering:
    Input (S,G) filter: none, route-map: none
    Input RP filter: none, route-map: none
    Output (S,G) filter: none, route-map: none
    Output RP filter: none, route-map: none
  SA-Requests:
    Input filter: none
  Peer ttl threshold: 0
  SAs learned from this peer: 0
  Input queue size: 0, Output queue size: 0
!
```

```
RP-East# show ip pim rp
Group: 226.1.1.1, RP: 172.16.1.1, v2, uptime 00:23:56, expires 00:03:09
```

Summary: Finding the RP

This section covers the concepts behind four separate methods for finding the RP. Three are specific configuration features, namely static configuration, Auto-RP, and BSR. The fourth, Anycast RP, actually uses any of the first three methods, but with the design that includes having the RPs use the same unicast IP address to achieve better redundancy features. Table 8-3 summarizes the methods of finding the RP with PIM-SM.

Key
Topic

Table 8-3 *Comparison of Methods of Finding the RP*

Method	RP Details	Mapping Info	Redundant RP Support?	Load Sharing of One Group?
Static	Simple reference to unicast IP address.	—	No	No
Auto-RP	Sends RP-Announce to 224.0.1.39; relies on sparse-dense mode.	Mapping agent sends through RP-Discovery to 224.0.1.40	Yes	No
BSR	Sends c-RP advertisements as unicasts to BSR IP address; does not need sparse-dense mode.	Sends bootstrap messages flooded over non-RPF path	Yes	No
Anycast RP	Each RP uses identical IP addresses.	Can use Auto-RP or BSR normal processes	Yes	Yes

Bidirectional PIM

PIM-SM works efficiently with a relatively small number of multicast senders. However, in cases with a large number of senders and receivers, PIM-SM becomes less efficient. Bidirectional PIM addresses this relative inefficiency by slightly changing the rules used by PIM-SM.

To appreciate bidirectional PIM, a brief review of PIM-SM's normal operations is useful. While many variations can occur, the following general steps can be used by PIM-SM:

1. The RP builds a shared tree, with itself as the root, for forwarding multicast packets.

2. When a source first sends multicasts, the router nearest the source forwards the multicasts to the RP, encapsulated inside a PIM Register message.

3. The RP joins the source-specific tree for that source by sending a PIM Join toward that source.

4. Later, the routers attached to the same LANs as the receivers can send a PIM Join toward the source to join the SPT for that source.

With bidirectional PIM, the last three steps in this list are not performed. Bidirectional PIM instead follows these steps:

Key
Topic

1. As with normal PIM-SM, the RP builds a shared tree, with itself as the root, for forwarding multicast packets.

2. When a source sends multicasts, the router receiving those multicasts does not use a PIM Register message. Instead, it forwards the packets in the opposite direction of the shared tree, back up the tree toward the RP. This process continues for all multicast packets from the source.

3. The RP forwards the multicasts through the shared tree.

4. All packets are forwarded per Steps 2 and 3. The RP does not join the source tree for the source, and the leaf routers do not join the SPT, either.

The name "bidirectional" comes from Step 2, in which the router near the source forwards packets back up the tree toward the RP. The other direction in the tree is used at Step 3, with the RP forwarding multicasts using the shared tree.

Comparison of PIM-DM and PIM-SM

One of the most confusing parts of the PIM-DM and PIM-SM designs is that it appears that if sources keep sending, and receivers keep listening, there is no difference between the end results of the end-user multicast packet flow using these two options. After PIM-SM completes its more complicated processes, the routers near the receivers have all joined the SPT to the source, and the most efficient forwarding paths are used for each (S,G) tree.

Although its underlying operation is a bit more complicated, PIM-SM tends to be the more popular option today. PIM-SM's inherent strategy of not forwarding multicasts until hosts request them makes it more efficient during times of low usage. When the numbers of senders and receivers increase, PIM-SM quickly moves to use the SPT—the same SPT that would have been derived using PIM-DM. As such, PIM-SM has become a more popular option for most enterprise implementations today. It has also become a popular option for interdomain multicast as well.

Table 8-4 summarizes the important features of PIM-DM and PIM-SM.

Key Topic

Table 8-4 *Comparison of PIM-DM and PIM-SM*

Feature	PIM-DM	PIM-SM
Destination address for Version 1 Query messages, and IP protocol number	224.0.0.2 and 2	224.0.0.2 and 2
Destination address for Version 2 Hello messages, and IP protocol number	224.0.0.13 and 103	224.0.0.13 and 103
Default interval for Query and Hello messages	30 seconds	30 seconds
Default Holdtime for Versions 1 and 2	90 seconds	90 seconds
Rule for electing a designated router on a multiaccess network	Router with the highest IP address on the subnet	Router with the highest IP address on the subnet

Feature	PIM-DM	PIM-SM
Main design principle	A router automatically receives the traffic. If it does not want the traffic, it has to say no (send a Prune message) to its sender.	Unless a router specifically makes a request to an RP, it does not receive multicast traffic.
SPT or RPT?	Uses only SPT	First uses RPT and then switches to SPT
Uses Join/Prune messages?	Yes	Yes
Uses Graft and Graft-Ack messages?	Yes	No
Uses Prune Override mechanism?	Yes	Yes
Uses Assert message?	Yes	Yes
Uses RP?	No	Yes
Uses source registration process?	No	Yes

Source-Specific Multicast

The multicast scenarios we've discussed so far use Internet Standard Multicast (ISM). With ISM, receivers join an MC group without worrying about the source of the multicast. In very large networks, such as television video or the Internet, this can lead to problems such as the following:

- **Overlapping multicast IP addresses:** With a limited number of multicast addresses and a large amount of multicasts, multiple streams might use the same address. Receivers will then get the stream they wanted plus any others using that address. Hopefully, the application will drop the unwanted multicast, but it has used up network resources unnecessarily.

- **Denial of service attacks:** If an attacker acts as a source sending traffic to a known multicast address, that traffic is then forwarded through the network to all receivers in the group. Enough traffic could interrupt the actual stream and overburden network routers and switches.

- **Deployment complexity:** The deployment of RPs, Auto-RP, BSR, and MSDP can get complex in a very large network with many sources and receivers.

Source Specific Multicast (SSM) is a solution to those limitations. SSM receivers know the unicast IP address of their source, and specify it when they join a group. With SSM, receivers subscribe to an (S,G) channel, giving both the source address and the multicast group address. This helps relieve the problems listed previously:

- Because each stream, or channel, is identified by the combination of a unicast source and multicast group address, overlapping group addresses are okay. Hosts only receive traffic from their specified sources.

- Denial of service attacks are more difficult because an attacker has to know both the source and group addresses, and the path to their source has to pass RPF checks through the network.

- RPs are not needed to keep track of which sources are active, because source addresses are already known. In addition, SSM can be deployed in a network already set up for PIM-SM. Only edge routers nearest the hosts need to be configured for SSM.

SSM uses IGMP Version 3, which was briefly described in Chapter 7. To configure basic SSM, you enable it globally with the **ip pim ssm {default | range** *access-list*} command. The multicast address range of 232.0.0.0 through 232.255.255.255 has been designated by IANA as the SSM range. The keyword **default** permits the router to forward all multicasts in that range. You can limit the multicast groups by defining them in an access list and using the **range** keyword.

You must also enable IGMPv3 under each interface with the **ip igmp version 3** command. Example 8-15 shows a router configured for SSM. Notice that PIM—either sparse mode or sparse-dense mode—must also be enabled under each interface.

Example 8-15   *Configuring SSM and IGMPv3*

```
ip multicast-routing
!
interface FastEthernet0/0
 ip pim sparse-mode
 ip igmp version 3
!
ip pim ssm default
```

Implementing IPv6 Multicast PIM

It is necessary to explicitly enable multicast routing for any IPv6 environment through the global configuration command **ipv6 multicast-routing**. The results of this command can be observed on all IPv6-enabled interfaces on a given device, which are then automatically enabled for all IPv6-enabled interfaces. This default configuration of each IPv6 interface assumes the IPv6 PIM, and it does not appear in the interface configuration. When PIMv6 is enabled on an interface, that interface always operates in sparse mode. PIM-SM uses unicast routing to provide reverse-path information for multicast tree building, but it is not dependent on any particular unicast routing protocol.

It is possible to disable PIM on a given interface through the **no ipv6 pim** command under the interface configuration context.

We will run OSPFv3 in our lab to create a functional IPv6 multicast environment. We will then observe the possible behaviors associated with IPv6 and multicast packet delivery in the topology illustrated in Figure 8-24.

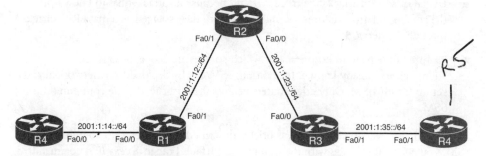

Figure 8-24 *IPv6 Multicast Topology*

To enable IPv6 multicast routing on all the devices outlined in Figure 8-24, use the commands found in Example 8-16.

Example 8-16 *Basic IPv6 Multicast Configuration*

```
R4# conf t
Enter configuration commands, one per line.  End with CNTL/Z.
R4(config)# ipv6 multicast-routing
!
R1# conf t
Enter configuration commands, one per line.  End with CNTL/Z.
R1(config)# ipv6 multicast-routing
!
R2# conf t
Enter configuration commands, one per line.  End with CNTL/Z.
R2(config)# ipv6 multicast-routing
!
R3# conf t
Enter configuration commands, one per line.  End with CNTL/Z.
R3(config)# ipv6 multicast-routing
!
R5# conf t
Enter configuration commands, one per line.  End with CNTL/Z.
R5(config)# ipv6 multicast-routing
```

This is the first stage where the multicast behavior of IPv6 shows its differences from IPv4 multicast routing. Notice immediately the formation of tunnels on each of these devices through the console messages. Example 8-17 illustrates this situation and shows how to verify the situation by looking specifically at the tunnels that are formed dynamically.

It forms dynamically tunnels

[handwritten margin note: enabling IPv6 multicast brogh ← this tunnel up.]

Example 8-17   *IPv6 Multicast Tunnel Verification*

```
R1(config)#
*Mar  9 17:22:57.754: %LINEPROTO-5-UPDOWN: Line protocol on Interface Tunnel0,
  changed state to up
R1(config)#
!!!!!!!!!!!!!!!!!!!!!!!!!!!!!!!!!!!!!!!!!!!!!!!!!!!!!!!!!!!!!!!!!!!!!!!!!!!!!!!!!!!!!
!!We can look at the statistics for these tunnels by:
!!!!!!!!!!!!!!!!!!!!!!!!!!!!!!!!!!!!!!!!!!!!!!!!!!!!!!!!!!!!!!!!!!!!!!!!!!!!!!!!!!!!!
R1# show int tunnel 0
Tunnel0 is up, line protocol is up
  Hardware is Tunnel
  MTU 1514 bytes, BW 9 Kbit/sec, DLY 500000 usec,
     reliability 255/255, txload 1/255, rxload 1/255
  Encapsulation TUNNEL, loopback not set
  Keepalive not set
  Tunnel source 2001:1:1:1::1 (Loopback0), destination UNKNOWN
  Tunnel protocol/transport PIM/IPv6
  Tunnel TTL 255
  Tunnel is transmit only
  Tunnel transmit bandwidth 8000 (kbps)
  Tunnel receive bandwidth 8000 (kbps)
  Last input never, output never, output hang never
  Last clearing of "show interface" counters never
  Input queue: 0/75/0/0 (size/max/drops/flushes); Total output drops: 0
  Queueing strategy: fifo
  Output queue: 0/0 (size/max)
  5 minute input rate 0 bits/sec, 0 packets/sec
  5 minute output rate 0 bits/sec, 0 packets/sec
     0 packets input, 0 bytes, 0 no buffer
     Received 0 broadcasts, 0 runts, 0 giants, 0 throttles
     0 input errors, 0 CRC, 0 frame, 0 overrun, 0 ignored, 0 abort
     0 packets output, 0 bytes, 0 underruns
     0 output errors, 0 collisions, 0 interface resets
     0 unknown protocol drops
     0 output buffer failures, 0 output buffers swapped out
R1#
```

Note that the tunnel is up, and that it is using the Tunnel Mode of PIM and IPv6 protocol for transit. Additionally, to observe these neighbor relationships, we can use the **show ipv6 pim neighbors** command, as demonstrated in Example 8-18.

Example 8-18 *PIM Neighbor Verification*

[handwritten margin note: PIM neighbor between link local address]

```
R4# show ipv6 pim neighbor
Neighbor Address              Interface        Uptime     Expires DR pri Bidir

FE80::1                       FastEthernet0/1  00:06:46   00:01:27 1      B
!!!!!!!!!!!!!!!!!!!!!!!!!!!!!!!!!!!!!!!!!!!!!!!!!!!!!!!!!!!!!!!!!!!!!!!!!!!!!!!!!
R1# show ipv6 pim neighbor
Neighbor Address              Interface        Uptime     Expires DR pri Bidir

FE80::2                       FastEthernet0/0  00:06:53   00:01:20 1 (DR) B
FE80::4                       FastEthernet0/1  00:07:23   00:01:19 1 (DR) B
!!!!!!!!!!!!!!!!!!!!!!!!!!!!!!!!!!!!!!!!!!!!!!!!!!!!!!!!!!!!!!!!!!!!!!!!!!!!!!!!!
R2# show ipv6 pim neighbor
Neighbor Address              Interface        Uptime     Expires DR pri Bidir

FE80::1                       FastEthernet0/0  00:07:24   00:01:16 1      B
FE80::3                       FastEthernet0/1  00:06:53   00:01:20 1 (DR) B
!!!!!!!!!!!!!!!!!!!!!!!!!!!!!!!!!!!!!!!!!!!!!!!!!!!!!!!!!!!!!!!!!!!!!!!!!!!!!!!!!
R3# show ipv6 pim neighbor
Neighbor Address              Interface        Uptime     Expires DR pri Bidir

FE80::5                       FastEthernet0/0  00:07:05   00:01:36 1 (DR) B
FE80::2                       FastEthernet0/1  00:07:32   00:01:39 1      B
!!!!!!!!!!!!!!!!!!!!!!!!!!!!!!!!!!!!!!!!!!!!!!!!!!!!!!!!!!!!!!!!!!!!!!!!!!!!!!!!!
R5# show ipv6 pim neighbor
Neighbor Address              Interface        Uptime     Expires DR pri Bidir

FE80::3                       FastEthernet0/0  00:08:06   00:01:33 1      B
```

[handwritten margin note: on the link]

Observe that the neighbor relationships form using the "link-local" addresses and that we still elect DRs. These values can be manipulated in similar fashion to those in IPv4.

Designated Priority Manipulation

By directly manipulating the **dr-priority** value, you can manually designate what router on a given link will assume the role of the designated router. In topology shown in Figure 8-24, you will change the value of the **dr-priority** on R5 to ensure that it becomes the designated router, using the highest possible value to accomplish this, as shown in Example 8-19.

Example 8-19 *Designated Priority Manipulation*

```
R3# conf t
Enter configuration commands, one per line.  End with CNTL/Z.
R5(config)# int f0/0
R5(config-if)# ipv6 pim dr-priority ?                    — Changing DR priority
  <0-4294967295>  Hello DR priority, preference given to larger value

R5(config-if)# ipv6 pim dr-priority 4294967295
R5(config-if)# exit
!!!!!!!!!!!!!!!!!!!!!!!!!!!!!!!!!!!!!!!!!!!!!!!!!!!!!!!!!!!!!!!!!!!!!!!!!!!!!!!!!!!
!!Upon completion of this task we can observe the fact that R3 is now the DR for
!!the segment in question via the show ipv6 pim neighbor command:
!!!!!!!!!!!!!!!!!!!!!!!!!!!!!!!!!!!!!!!!!!!!!!!!!!!!!!!!!!!!!!!!!!!!!!!!!!!!!!!!!!!
!!!!!
R3# show ipv6 pim neighbor
Neighbor Address           Interface        Uptime    Expires DR pri Bidir

FE80::5                    FastEthernet0/0  00:20:53  00:01:36 1      B
FE80::2                    FastEthernet0/1  00:21:19  00:01:16 1      B
!!!!!!!!!!!!!!!!!!!!!!!!!!!!!!!!!!!!!!!!!!!!!!!!!!!!!!!!!!!!!!!!!!!!!!!!!!!!!!!!!!!
!!In this instance we do not see a value of (DR) which would indicate that this
!!device is serving as the DR. We can see this on R5.
!!!!!!!!!!!!!!!!!!!!!!!!!!!!!!!!!!!!!!!!!!!!!!!!!!!!!!!!!!!!!!!!!!!!!!!!!!!!!!!!!!!
R5# show ipv6 pim neighbor
Neighbor Address           Interface        Uptime    Expires DR pri Bidir

FE80::3                    FastEthernet0/0  00:23:25  00:01:20 4294967295 (DR) B
!!!!!!!!!!!!!!!!!!!!!!!!!!!!!!!!!!!!!!!!!!!!!!!!!!!!!!!!!!!!!!!!!!!!!!!!!!!!!!!!!!!
!!As expected we see that R3 is the DR for the segment connected to Fa0/0.
!!!!!!!!!!!!!!!!!!!!!!!!!!!!!!!!!!!!!!!!!!!!!!!!!!!!!!!!!!!!!!!!!!!!!!!!!!!!!!!!!!!
```

(handwritten note: R5 on fa0/0 became DR)

PIM6 Hello Interval

As covered in the discussion of PIM for IPv4, the PIM process begins when the router
establishes a PIM neighbor adjacency by sending PIM hello messages. Hello messages are
sent periodically at the interval of 30 seconds. When all neighbors have replied, the PIM
software chooses the router with the highest priority on each LAN segment as the designated router (DR). The DR priority is based on a DR priority value as we saw previously,
but that information is contained in the PIM hello message. Additionally, if the DR priority value is not supplied by all routers, or if the priorities match, the highest IP address is
used to elect the DR.

The hello message also contains a holdtime value, which is typically 3.5 times the hello interval. If this holdtime expires without a subsequent hello message from its neighbor, the device detects a PIM failure on that link.

For added security, you can configure an MD5 hash value that the PIM software uses to authenticate PIM hello messages with PIM neighbors. Example 8-20 observes this behavior by manipulating the hello-interval period and exploring the affects this has in our environment.

Example 8-20 *PIMv6 Hello Interval*

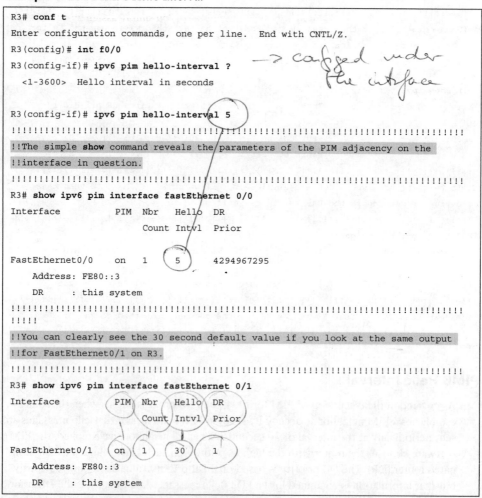

```
R3# conf t
Enter configuration commands, one per line.  End with CNTL/Z.
R3(config)# int f0/0
R3(config-if)# ipv6 pim hello-interval ?
  <1-3600>  Hello interval in seconds

R3(config-if)# ipv6 pim hello-interval 5
!!!!!!!!!!!!!!!!!!!!!!!!!!!!!!!!!!!!!!!!!!!!!!!!!!!!!!!!!!!!!!!!!!!!!!!!!!!!!!!!!!!!
!!The simple show command reveals the parameters of the PIM adjacency on the
!!interface in question.
!!!!!!!!!!!!!!!!!!!!!!!!!!!!!!!!!!!!!!!!!!!!!!!!!!!!!!!!!!!!!!!!!!!!!!!!!!!!!!!!!!!!
R3# show ipv6 pim interface fastEthernet 0/0
Interface          PIM  Nbr   Hello  DR
                        Count Intvl  Prior

FastEthernet0/0    on   1     5      4294967295
    Address: FE80::3
    DR      : this system
!!!!!!!!!!!!!!!!!!!!!!!!!!!!!!!!!!!!!!!!!!!!!!!!!!!!!!!!!!!!!!!!!!!!!!!!!!!!!!!!!!!!
!!!!!
!!You can clearly see the 30 second default value if you look at the same output
!!for FastEthernet0/1 on R3.
!!!!!!!!!!!!!!!!!!!!!!!!!!!!!!!!!!!!!!!!!!!!!!!!!!!!!!!!!!!!!!!!!!!!!!!!!!!!!!!!!!!!
R3# show ipv6 pim interface fastEthernet 0/1
Interface          PIM  Nbr   Hello  DR
                        Count Intvl  Prior

FastEthernet0/1    on   1     30     1
    Address: FE80::3
    DR      : this system
```

Note that you can also clearly see the DR status.

IPv6 Sparse-Mode Multicast

When it comes to multicast operation, IPv6 supports a few options when it comes to designating an RP. These options included static assignment, IPv6 BSR, and the Embedded RP approach. We will observe each of these in our multicast lab environment starting with static assignment. Note that IPv6 multicast does not support Auto-RP or dense mode operation.

no dense mode / Auto-RP

IPv6 Static RP

This operation is no different that its IPv4 counterpart. You simply assign an RP, but you do it through an IPv6 address. You will assign R2 to be the RP in the topology presented in Figure 8-25. Example 8-21 shows the command syntax.

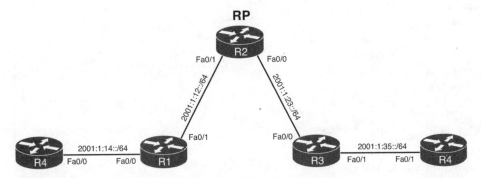

Figure 8-25 *IPv6 Static RP Multicast Topology*

Example 8-21 *IPv6 Static RP Configuration and Verification*

```
R4# conf t
Enter configuration commands, one per line.  End with CNTL/Z.
R4(config)# ipv6 pim rp-address 2001:2:2:2::2
!!!!!!!!!!!!!!!!!!!!!!!!!!!!!!!!!!!!!!!!!!!!!!!!!!!!!!!!!!!!!!!!!!!!!!!!!!!!!!!!!!
R1# conf t
Enter configuration commands, one per line.  End with CNTL/Z.
R1(config)# ipv6 pim rp-address 2001:2:2:2::2
!!!!!!!!!!!!!!!!!!!!!!!!!!!!!!!!!!!!!!!!!!!!!!!!!!!!!!!!!!!!!!!!!!!!!!!!!!!!!!!!!!
R2# conf t
Enter configuration commands, one per line.  End with CNTL/Z.
R2(config)# ipv6 pim rp-address 2001:2:2:2::2
!!!!!!!!!!!!!!!!!!!!!!!!!!!!!!!!!!!!!!!!!!!!!!!!!!!!!!!!!!!!!!!!!!!!!!!!!!!!!!!!!!
R3# conf t
Enter configuration commands, one per line.  End with CNTL/Z.
R3(config)# ipv6 pim rp-address 2001:2:2:2::2
!!!!!!!!!!!!!!!!!!!!!!!!!!!!!!!!!!!!!!!!!!!!!!!!!!!!!!!!!!!!!!!!!!!!!!!!!!!!!!!!!!
```

Static config

```
R5# conf t
Enter configuration commands, one per line.  End with CNTL/Z.
R5(config)# ipv6 pim rp-address 2001:2:2:2::2
```

In this task, you are statically assigning R2 to act as the IPv6 RP for the multicast topology. This configuration is most simply confirmed by checking the status of the **show ipv6 pim range-list** command on all devices in the network, as shown in Example 8-22.

Example 8-22 *IPv6 Range-List Verification*

```
R4# show ipv6 pim range-list
Static SSM Exp: never Learnt from : ::
  FF33::/32 Up: 01:19:06
  FF34::/32 Up: 01:19:06
  FF35::/32 Up: 01:19:06
  FF36::/32 Up: 01:19:06
  FF37::/32 Up: 01:19:06
  FF38::/32 Up: 01:19:06
  FF39::/32 Up: 01:19:06
  FF3A::/32 Up: 01:19:06
  FF3B::/32 Up: 01:19:06
  FF3C::/32 Up: 01:19:06
  FF3D::/32 Up: 01:19:06
  FF3E::/32 Up: 01:19:06
  FF3F::/32 Up: 01:19:06
Static SM RP: 2001:2:2:2::2 Exp: never Learnt from : ::
  FF00::/8 Up: 00:04:28
```

Example 8-23 shows that an additional verification step for this configuration would be to generate multicast traffic from a device in the topology, and verify that it registers with R2.

Example 8-23 *IPv6 Multicast Ping Test*   PING TEST

```
R4# ping FF08::1 r 10
Output Interface: FastEthernet0/1
Type escape sequence to abort.
Sending 10, 100-byte ICMP Echos to FF08::1, timeout is 2 seconds:
Packet sent with a source address of 2001:1:14::4

Request 0 timed out
Request 1 timed out
Request 2 timed out
Request 3 timed out
Request 4 timed out
Request 5 timed out
Request 6 timed out
```

```
Request 7 timed out
Request 8 timed out
Request 9 timed out
Success rate is 0 percent (0/10)
0 multicast replies and 0 errors.
```

You see that you are not getting any successful responses, but that is to be expected because you have no devices interested in being receivers for this group. You can look at R2 to see whether there is an (S,G) pair for the group FF08::1 in its routing table, as illustrated in Example 8-24.

Example 8-24 *IPv6 Multicast Routing Table Verification*

```
R2# sh ipv6 mroute
Multicast Routing Table
Flags: D - Dense, S - Sparse, B - Bidir Group, s - SSM Group,
       C - Connected, L - Local, I - Received Source Specific Host Report,
       P - Pruned, R - RP-bit set, F - Register flag, T - SPT-bit set,
       J - Join SPT
Timers: Uptime/Expires
Interface state: Interface, State

(2001:1:14::4, FF08::1), 00:00:22/00:03:07, flags: SP       pruned
  Incoming interface: FastEthernet0/0
  RPF nbr: FE80::1
  Outgoing interface list: Null
```

Note that we see the (S,G) pair and that it is sparse-mode and pruned (for lack of interested receivers).

IPv6 BSR

We will start again in the current topology by removing our static IPv6 RP address configurations. Now we will look to create an environment where the RP is elected dynamically. This will be accomplished by making R1 and R3 candidate RPs, and R2 the bootstrap router. We will not walk through the removal of the static RP mappings, but suffice it to say that we will simply use the **no** form of the **ipv6 pim rp-address** command on each device, as is done in Example 8-25. With that completed, we will now make R2 the BSR.

Example 8-25 *Remove Static IPv6 RP Assignment and Apply BSR*

```
R2(config)#
R2(config)# no ipv6 pim rp-address 2001:2:2:2::2
R2(config)#!
R2(config)# ipv6 pim bsr candidate bsr 2001:2:2:2::2
!!!!!!!!!!!!!!!!!!!!!!!!!!!!!!!!!!!!!!!!!!!!!!!!!!!!!!!!!!!!!!!!!!!!!!!!!!!!!!!!!!!
```

```
!!Now that R2 has been configured to act as the BSR we will make R1 and R3
!!candidate RPs
!!!!!!!!!!!!!!!!!!!!!!!!!!!!!!!!!!!!!!!!!!!!!!!!!!!!!!!!!!!!!!!!!!!!!!!!!!!!!!!!!!!!
R1# conf t
Enter configuration commands, one per line.  End with CNTL/Z.
R1(config)# ipv6 pim bsr candidate rp 2001:1:1:1::1

R3# conf t
Enter configuration commands, one per line.  End with CNTL/Z.
R3(config)# ipv6 pim bsr candidate rp 2001:3:3:3::3
```

You will first confirm that all devices agree on the group-to-RP mappings through the
show ipv6 pim range-list command, as demonstrated in Example 8-26.

Example 8-26   *BSR Verification Procedures*

```
R4# show ipv6 pim range-list | be BSR
BSR SM RP: 2001:1:1:1::1 Exp: 00:01:44 Learnt from : 2001:2:2:2::2
  FF00::/8 Up: 00:02:38
BSR SM RP: 2001:3:3:3::3 Exp: 00:01:44 Learnt from : 2001:2:2:2::2
  FF00::/8 Up: 00:01:45
!!!!!!!!!!!!!!!!!!!!!!!!!!!!!!!!!!!!!!!!!!!!!!!!!!!!!!!!!!!!!!!!!!!!!!!!!!!!!!!!!
R1# show ipv6 pim range-list | be BSR
BSR SM RP: 2001:1:1:1::1 Exp: 00:01:49 Learnt from : 2001:2:2:2::2
  FF00::/8 Up: 00:04:33
BSR SM RP: 2001:3:3:3::3 Exp: 00:01:49 Learnt from : 2001:2:2:2::2
  FF00::/8 Up: 00:03:40
!!!!!!!!!!!!!!!!!!!!!!!!!!!!!!!!!!!!!!!!!!!!!!!!!!!!!!!!!!!!!!!!!!!!!!!!!!!!!!!!!
R2# show ipv6 pim range-list | be BSR
BSR SM RP: 2001:1:1:1::1 Exp: 00:02:26 Learnt from : 2001:2:2:2::2
  FF00::/8 Up: 00:04:56
BSR SM RP: 2001:3:3:3::3 Exp: 00:02:26 Learnt from : 2001:2:2:2::2
  FF00::/8 Up: 00:04:04
!!!!!!!!!!!!!!!!!!!!!!!!!!!!!!!!!!!!!!!!!!!!!!!!!!!!!!!!!!!!!!!!!!!!!!!!!!!!!!!!!
R3# show ipv6 pim range-list | be BSR
BSR SM RP: 2001:1:1:1::1 Exp: 00:01:58 Learnt from : 2001:2:2:2::2
  FF00::/8 Up: 00:05:25
BSR SM RP: 2001:3:3:3::3 Exp: 00:01:58 Learnt from : 2001:2:2:2::2
  FF00::/8 Up: 00:04:32
!!!!!!!!!!!!!!!!!!!!!!!!!!!!!!!!!!!!!!!!!!!!!!!!!!!!!!!!!!!!!!!!!!!!!!!!!!!!!!!!!
R5# show ipv6 pim range-list | be BSR
```

RP's
as per the
information
gathered &
sent out by
the BSR

```
BSR SM RP: 2001:1:1:1::1 Exp: 00:01:33 Learnt from : 2001:2:2:2::2
  FF00::/8 Up: 00:05:50
BSR SM RP: 2001:3:3:3::3 Exp: 00:01:33 Learnt from : 2001:2:2:2::2
  FF00::/8 Up: 00:04:57
```

You see that the devices agree on the possible RPs in the topology, and that they have been "learned" from the BSR (2002:2:2:2::2). To check the topology, you will generate IPv6 multicast traffic on R4, the results of which can be seen in Example 8-27.

Example 8-27 *IPv6 Ping Verification*

```
R4# ping FF08::1 repeat 10
Output Interface: FastEthernet0/1
Type escape sequence to abort.
Sending 10, 100-byte ICMP Echos to FF08::1, timeout is 2 seconds:
Packet sent with a source address of 2001:1:14::4


Request 0 timed out
Request 1 timed out
Request 2 timed out
Request 3 timed out
Request 4 timed out
Request 5 timed out
Request 6 timed out
Request 7 timed out
Request 8 timed out
Request 9 timed out
Success rate is 0 percent (0/10)
0 multicast replies and 0 errors.
!!!!!!!!!!!!!!!!!!!!!!!!!!!!!!!!!!!!!!!!!!!!!!!!!!!!!!!!!!!!!!!!!!!!!!!!!!!!!!!!
!!Now you will look to see if we can find the S,G entry in the multicast routing
!!table of R1 and R3.
!!!!!!!!!!!!!!!!!!!!!!!!!!!!!!!!!!!!!!!!!!!!!!!!!!!!!!!!!!!!!!!!!!!!!!!!!!!!!!!!
R1# show ipv6 mroute
Multicast Routing Table
Flags: D - Dense, S - Sparse, B - Bidir Group, s - SSM Group,
       C - Connected, L - Local, I - Received Source Specific Host Report,
       P - Pruned, R - RP-bit set, F - Register flag, T - SPT-bit set,
       J - Join SPT
Timers: Uptime/Expires
Interface state: Interface, State

(2001:1:14::4, FF08::1), 00:02:28/00:01:01, flags: SPFT
  Incoming interface: FastEthernet0/1
  RPF nbr: FE80::4
  Outgoing interface list: Null
```

```
!!!!!!!!!!!!!!!!!!!!!!!!!!!!!!!!!!!!!!!!!!!!!!!!!!!!!!!!!!!!!!!!!!!!!!!!!!!!!!!!!!!!!!!!
R3# show ipv6 mroute
Multicast Routing Table
Flags: D - Dense, S - Sparse, B - Bidir Group, s - SSM Group,
       C - Connected, L - Local, I - Received Source Specific Host Report,
       P - Pruned, R - RP-bit set, F - Register flag, T - SPT-bit set,
       J - Join SPT
Timers: Uptime/Expires
Interface state: Interface, State

(2001:1:14::4, FF08::1), 00:04:05/00:03:05, flags: SP
  Incoming interface: FastEthernet0/1
  RPF nbr: FE80::2
  Outgoing interface list: Null
```

You see the (S,G) pair as you would expect. Now you will look closer at the different components of the topology. Starting with the BSR, you will look to see what RP candidates are announcing their presence to the R2. You expect to see R1 and R3 appearing in this list, the results of which are shown in Example 8-28.

Example 8-28   *Observing the IPv6 BSR RP-Cache*

```
R2# show ipv6 pim bsr rp-cache
PIMv2 BSR C-RP Cache

BSR Candidate RP Cache

Group(s) FF00::/8, RP count 2
  RP 2001:1:1:1::1 SM
    Priority 192, Holdtime 150
    Uptime: 00:14:28, expires: 00:02:03
  RP 2001:3:3:3::3 SM
    Priority 192, Holdtime 150
    Uptime: 00:13:36, expires: 00:01:56
!!!!!!!!!!!!!!!!!!!!!!!!!!!!!!!!!!!!!!!!!!!!!!!!!!!!!!!!!!!!!!!!!!!!!!!!!!!!!!!!!!!!!!!!
!!On R3, one of our C-RPs, we clearly see the parameters being announced to the
!!Boot Strap Router.
!!!!!!!!!!!!!!!!!!!!!!!!!!!!!!!!!!!!!!!!!!!!!!!!!!!!!!!!!!!!!!!!!!!!!!!!!!!!!!!!!!!!!!!!
R3# show ipv6 pim bsr candidate-rp
PIMv2 C-RP information
  Candidate RP: 2001:3:3:3::3 SM
    All Learnt Scoped Zones, Priority 192, Holdtime 150
    Advertisement interval 60 seconds
    Next advertisement in 00:00:25
```

The next section covers the concept of the "embedded RP."

Multicast Listener Discovery (MLD)

Thus far in the discussions regarding IPv6 multicast routing, you have not seen a single successful multicast ping. This is because you have not assigned any host for any of the tested groups. You will correct this issue now, by making R5's FastEthernet0/0 interface join the multicast group FF08::1, as shown in Example 8-29.

Example 8-29 *Enable MLD Joins to IPv6 Multicast Groups*

```
R5# conf t
Enter configuration commands, one per line.  End with CNTL/Z.
R5(config)# int f0/0
R5(config-if)# ipv6 mld join-group FF08::1
```

In a nutshell, IPv6 multicast replaces IGMP with Multicast Listener Discovery Protocol. For the best comparison of features, you can consider that MLDv1 is similar to IGMP Version 2, while MLDv2 is similar to IGMP Version 3. That means that MLDv2 will support Source Specific Multicast in IPv6 networks.

$MLD_{v1} = IGMP_{v2}$

$v2 = IGMP_{v3}$

Using MLD, hosts can indicate they want to receive multicast transmissions for select groups. Just like in IGMP, it is the elected queriers that are responsible for managing the flow of multicast traffic in the network through the use of MLD. These messages are carried inside Internet Control Message Protocol (ICMP); however, it must be noted that these messages are link-local in scope, and each has the router alert option set.

MLD uses three types of messages: Query, Report, and Done. The Done message is like the Leave message in IGMP Version 2. It indicates that a host no longer wants to receive the multicast transmission. This triggers a Query to check for any more receivers on the segment.

Configuration options for MLD will be very similar to configuration tasks we needed to master for IGMP. You can limit the number of receivers with the **ipv6 mld limit** command. If you want the interface to "permanently" subscribe, you can use the **ipv6 mld join-group** command. Also, as in IGMP, there are several timers you can manipulate for the protocol's mechanics.

Configuring IPv6 multicast routing with the **ipv6 multicast-routing** global configuration command automatically configures Protocol Independent Multicast on all active interfaces. This also includes the automatic configuration of MLD. Example 8-30 demonstrates what this would look like in our environment.

Example 8-30 *IPv6 PIM Join Verification*

```
R3# show ipv6 pim interface
Interface          PIM  Nbr   Hello  DR
                        Count Intvl  Prior

Tunnel2            off  0     30     1
    Address: FE80::211:21FF:FEDF:8360
    DR    : not elected
```

```
Loopback0            on   0    30      1
   Address: FE80::211:21FF:FEDF:8360
   DR    : this system
VoIP-Null0           off  0    30      1
   Address: ::
   DR    : not elected
FastEthernet0/0    on   1    5       4294967295
   Address: FE80::3
   DR    : this system
FastEthernet0/1    on   1    30      1
   Address: FE80::3
   DR    : this system
Serial0/0            off  0    30      1
   Address: ::
   DR    : not elected
Serial0/1            off  0    30      1
   Address: ::
   DR    : not elected
Tunnel0              off  0    30      1
   Address: FE80::211:21FF:FEDF:8360
   DR    : not elected
Tunnel1              off  0    30      1
   Address: FE80::211:21FF:FEDF:8360
   DR    : not elected
Tunnel3              off  0    30      1
   Address: FE80::211:21FF:FEDF:8360
   DR    : not elected
```

Notice that PIM is enabled on all interfaces that you have manually configured in this scenario. With this complete, you need to take a closer look at MLD. This is done by using the **show ipv6 mld interface fa0/0** command, as shown in Example 8-31.

Example 8-31 *Enabling PIM for IPv6 at the Interface Level*

```
R3# show ipv6 mld interface fa0/0
FastEthernet0/0 is up, line protocol is up
  Internet address is FE80::3/10
  MLD is enabled on interface
  Current MLD version is 2
  MLD query interval is 125 seconds
  MLD querier timeout is 255 seconds
  MLD max query response time is 10 seconds
  Last member query response interval is 1 seconds
  MLD activity: 8 joins, 0 leaves
  MLD querying router is FE80::3 (this system)
```

Note how similar MLD is to IGMP. Now that you have an interested host in the environment, you need to see what candidate RP registered the MLD Join message coming from
R5. Based on what you know about RP election and BSR, the candidate with the highest
IP address should have registered the (*,G) for FF08::1. You will first look at R1, however,
just to verify that the Join is not in the multicast routing table there:

```
R1# show ipv6 mroute
No mroute entries found
```

Now look at R3, where you would expect to see the (*,G) entry, as verified in Example
8-32.

Example 8-32   *Verifying the IPv6 Routing Table with BSR Enabled*

```
R3# show ipv6 mroute
Multicast Routing Table
Flags: D - Dense, S - Sparse, B - Bidir Group, s - SSM Group,
       C - Connected, L - Local, I - Received Source Specific Host Report,
       P - Pruned, R - RP-bit set, F - Register flag, T - SPT-bit set,
       J - Join SPT
Timers: Uptime/Expires
Interface state: Interface, State

(*, FF08::1), 00:24:13/never, RP 2001:3:3:3::3, flags: SCJ
  Incoming interface: Tunnel3
  RPF nbr: 2001:3:3:3::3
  Immediate Outgoing interface list:
    FastEthernet0/0, Forward, 00:24:13/never
!!!!!!!!!!!!!!!!!!!!!!!!!!!!!!!!!!!!!!!!!!!!!!!!!!!!!!!!!!!!!!!!!!!!!!!!!!!!!!!!!!!!
!!Now that there is an interested host in the topology for FF08::1 we should be
!!able to successfully ping the group from R4.
!!!!!!!!!!!!!!!!!!!!!!!!!!!!!!!!!!!!!!!!!!!!!!!!!!!!!!!!!!!!!!!!!!!!!!!!!!!!!!!!!!!!
R4# ping FF08::1 repeat 10
Output Interface: FastEthernet0/1
Type escape sequence to abort.
Sending 10, 100-byte ICMP Echos to FF08::1, timeout is 2 seconds:
Packet sent with a source address of 2001:1:14::4

Reply to request 0 received from 2001:1:35::5, 24 ms
Reply to request 1 received from 2001:1:35::5, 0 ms
Reply to request 1 received from 2001:1:35::5, 4 ms
Reply to request 2 received from 2001:1:35::5, 0 ms
Reply to request 3 received from 2001:1:35::5, 0 ms
Reply to request 4 received from 2001:1:35::5, 0 ms
Reply to request 5 received from 2001:1:35::5, 0 ms
Reply to request 6 received from 2001:1:35::5, 0 ms
```

```
Reply to request 7 received from 2001:1:35::5, 0 ms
Reply to request 8 received from 2001:1:35::5, 0 ms
Reply to request 9 received from 2001:1:35::5, 0 ms
Success rate is 100 percent (10/10), round-trip min/avg/max = 0/2/24 ms
11 multicast replies and 0 errors.
```

Before moving on, you want to look at what traffic is traversing R2. The **show ipv6 pim traffic** command, illustrated in Example 8-33, will show the packets and messages that we have been discussing.

Example 8-33 *Verification of IPv6 Traffic Counters*

```
R3# show ipv6 pim traffic
PIM Traffic Counters
Elapsed time since counters cleared: 02:59:09


                                Received        Sent
Valid PIM Packets               830             2054
Hello                           725             2212
Join-Prune                      0               20
Data Register                   7               -
Null Register                   12              0
Register Stop                   0               15
Assert                          0               0
Bidir DF Election               0               0


Errors:
Malformed Packets                               0
Bad Checksums                                   0
Send Errors                                     0
Packet Sent on Loopback Errors                  362
Packets Received on PIM-disabled Interface      0
Packets Received with Unknown PIM Version       0


Lastly we will look at the nature of the tunnels we have seen and discussed:
R3# show ipv6 pim tunnel
Tunnel0*
  Type  : PIM Encap
  RP    : Embedded RP Tunnel
  Source: 2001:3:3:3::3
Tunnel1*
  Type  : PIM Encap
  RP    : 2001:1:1:1::1
  Source: 2001:3:3:3::3
```

```
Tunnel2*
  Type  : PIM Encap
  RP    : 2001:3:3:3::3*
  Source: 2001:3:3:3::3
Tunnel3*
  Type  : PIM Decap
  RP    : 2001:3:3:3::3*
  Source:  -
```

Embedded RP

Embedded RP is a handy feature that enables the identity of the RP to be embedded as part of the multicast group address. Any multicast router that sees this specific group address can extract the RP's identity and begin to use it for the shared tree immediately. This requires the identity of the RP to be explicitly configured on the device that will be used as the actual RP. No other configuration is required because all other routers in the domain will dynamically learn the RP address from the group address itself. However, an issue surfaces when you try to embed a 128-bit RP address into a 128-bit group address while leaving space for the group identity.

To accomplish the embedding of the RP address in the 128-bit multicast group address, you need to follow a few rules:

- **Rule 1:** You must indicate that the multicast group contains an embedded RP by setting the first 8 bits to all 1s. As such, we are saying that an embedded RP multicast address would always begin with FF70::/12 or 1111 1111 0111.

- **Rule 2:** You need numeric designations to specify a scope associated with the given address range, where the selected scope appears like so: FF7x. The value of "x" indicates the nature of the address in question. The following list shows your options:

  - **1:** Interface-Local scope
  - **2:** Link-Local scope
  - **4:** Admin-Local scope
  - **5:** Site-Local scope
  - **8:** Organization-Local scope
  - **E:** Global scope

- **Rule 3:** Isolate the three values from the RP address itself. These three values are

  - RP interface ID
  - Prefix length in hex
  - RP prefix

When we create the embedded RP address, the individual components mentioned in the preceding list are organized in the following pattern:

FF7*<Scope>*:0*<RP interface ID><Hex prefix length>*:*<64-bit RP prefix>*:*<32-bit group ID>*:*<1–F>*

We will execute this feature in the topology shown in Figure 8-26.

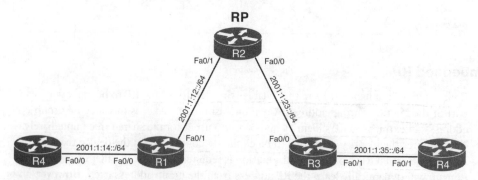

Figure 8-26 *IPv6 RP Advertisement Through Embedded RP Topology*

First, you must isolate the values you need to construct the Embedded RP group. You will use the address 2001:2:2:2::2/64 as the address, which means that

- The RP interface ID is 2 (taken from ::2).

- The prefix length is 64, which converts to 40 in hexadecimal.

- The RP prefix is 2001:2:2:2.

global

Next, you define the scope. You want the scope to be global, so you will use "E." The 32-bit group ID will most commonly be "0" but it could be other values. With these values isolated and defined, we can construct the embedded RP address like so:

FF7*<Scope>*:0*<RP interface ID><Hex prefix length>*:*<64-bit RP prefix>*:*<32-bit group ID>*:*<1–F>*
FF7E:0240:2001:2:2:2:0:1

You will arbitrarily select the value of 1 as the last digit. So in this topology, you would have R5 or any of the routers join this group: FF7E:240:2001:2:2:2:0:1. This is accomplished by following the configuration and verification procedures shown in Example 8-34.

Example 8-34 *Embedded RP Configuration*

```
R5(config)# int f0/0
R5(config-if)# ipv6 mld join-group FF7E:240:2001:2:2:2:0:1
!!!!!!!!!!!!!!!!!!!!!!!!!!!!!!!!!!!!!!!!!!!!!!!!!!!!!!!!!!!!!!!!!!!!!!!!!!!!!!!!!!!!!!!!!!
!!Remember, you need to notify R2 that it is the RP. You will do that via the
!!static RP method
```

```
!!!!!!!!!!!!!!!!!!!!!!!!!!!!!!!!!!!!!!!!!!!!!!!!!!!!!!!!!!!!!!!!!!!!!!!!!!!!!!!!!!!!!!!!
R2# conf t
R2(config)# ipv6 pim rp-address 2001:2:2:2::2
!!!!!!!!!!!!!!!!!!!!!!!!!!!!!!!!!!!!!!!!!!!!!!!!!!!!!!!!!!!!!!!!!!!!!!!!!!!!!!!!!!!!!!!!
!!Next, you will go to R4 and test by pinging the group FF7E:240:2001:2:2:2:0:1
!!!!!!!!!!!!!!!!!!!!!!!!!!!!!!!!!!!!!!!!!!!!!!!!!!!!!!!!!!!!!!!!!!!!!!!!!!!!!!!!!!!!!!!!
R4# ping FF7E:240:2001:2:2:2:0:1 repeat 10
Output Interface: FastEthernet0/1
Type escape sequence to abort.
Sending 10, 100-byte ICMP Echos to FF7E:240:2001:2:2:2:0:1, timeout is 2 seconds:
Packet sent with a source address of 2001:1:14::4

Reply to request 0 received from 2001:1:35::5, 20 ms
Reply to request 1 received from 2001:1:35::5, 0 ms
Reply to request 1 received from 2001:1:35::5, 16 ms
Reply to request 2 received from 2001:1:35::5, 0 ms
Reply to request 3 received from 2001:1:35::5, 0 ms
Reply to request 4 received from 2001:1:35::5, 0 ms
Reply to request 5 received from 2001:1:35::5, 0 ms
Reply to request 6 received from 2001:1:35::5, 0 ms
Reply to request 7 received from 2001:1:35::5, 0 ms
Reply to request 8 received from 2001:1:35::5, 0 ms
Reply to request 9 received from 2001:1:35::5, 0 ms
Success rate is 100 percent (10/10), round-trip min/avg/max = 0/3/20 ms
11 multicast replies and 0 errors.
```

You can see that the configuration is working, and you can also verify that R2 is the RP being used by executing the command illustrated in Example 8-35.

Example 8-35   *Verification of the Multicast Routing Table with Embedded RP Enabled*

```
R2# show ipv6 mroute
Multicast Routing Table
Flags: D - Dense, S - Sparse, B - Bidir Group, s - SSM Group,
       C - Connected, L - Local, I - Received Source Specific Host Report,
       P - Pruned, R - RP-bit set, F - Register flag, T - SPT-bit set,
       J - Join SPT
Timers: Uptime/Expires
Interface state: Interface, State

(*, FF7E:240:2001:2:2:2:0:1), 00:02:29/00:03:00, RP 2001:2:2:2::2, flags: S
  Incoming interface: Tunnel2
  RPF nbr: 2001:2:2:2::2
```

```
   Immediate Outgoing interface list:
     FastEthernet0/1, Forward, 00:02:29/00:03:00


(2001:1:14::4, FF7E:240:2001:2:2:2:0:1), 00:01:25/00:03:03, flags: ST
  Incoming interface: FastEthernet0/0
  RPF nbr: FE80::1
  Immediate Outgoing interface list:
     FastEthernet0/1, Forward, 00:01:25/00:03:00
```

You can see that the identity of the RP is being communicated by embedding it into the group address itself. You can verify this directly by using the command illustrated in Example 8-36.

Example 8-36 *Identifying the RP Through the Embedded RP on a Router*

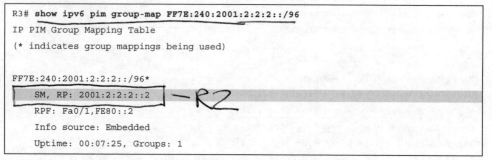

```
R3# show ipv6 pim group-map FF7E:240:2001:2:2:2::/96
IP PIM Group Mapping Table
(* indicates group mappings being used)


FF7E:240:2001:2:2:2::/96*
    SM, RP: 2001:2:2:2::2           - R2
    RPF: Fa0/1,FE80::2
    Info source: Embedded
    Uptime: 00:07:25, Groups: 1
```

This represents the local Multicast Listener Discovery information used to discriminate the embedded RP information.

Foundation Summary

This section lists additional details and facts to round out the coverage of the topics in this chapter. Unlike most of the Cisco Press Exam Certification Guides, this "Foundation Summary" does not repeat information presented in the "Foundation Topics" section of the chapter. Please take the time to read and study the details in the "Foundation Topics" section of the chapter, as well as review items noted with a Key Topic icon.

Table 8-5 lists the protocol standards referenced in this chapter.

Table 8-5   *RFC Reference for Chapter 8*

RFC	What It Defines
3973	PIM-DM
3618	MSDP
3446	Anycast RP
4601	PIM-SM
1584	Multicast Extensions to OSPF
4604, 4607, 4608	Source Specific Multicast
3810	Multicast Listener Discovery Version 2 (MLDv2)
2710	Multicast Listener Discovery for IPv6

Table 8-6 lists some of the most common Cisco IOS commands related to the topics in this chapter and Chapter 7.

Table 8-6   *Command Reference for Chapters 7 and 8*

Command	Command Mode and Description
ip multicast-routing	Global mode; required first command on Cisco routers to use multicasting.
ip msdp peer *address*	Interface config mode; configures the router as an MSDP peer.
ip pim dense-mode*	Interface config mode; configures the interface to use PIM-DM routing protocol.
ip pim sparse-mode*	Interface config mode; configures the interface to use PIM-SM routing protocol.
ip pim sparse-dense-mode*	Interface config mode; configures the interface to use PIM-SM routing protocol for a group if the RP address is known; otherwise, uses PIM-DM routing protocol.

Command	Command Mode and Description
ip pim ssm {default | range *access-list*}	Global config mode; enables Source Specific Multicast and specifies the multicast groups that the router will forward traffic for.
ip igmp version {1 | 2 | 3}	Interface config mode; sets the IGMP version on an interface. The default is 2.
ip igmp query-interval *seconds*	Interface config mode; changes the interval for IGMP queries sent by the router from the default 60 seconds.
ip igmp query-max-response-time *seconds*	Interface config mode; changes the Max Response Time advertised in IGMP Queries from the default of 10 seconds for IGMPv2 and IGMPv3.
ip igmp join-group *group-address*	Interface config mode; configures a router to join a multicast group. The group-address is a multicast IP address in four-part dotted-decimal notation.
ip multicast boundary *access-list* [*filter-autorp*]	Interface config mode; configures an interface as a multicast boundary for administrative scoping. A numbered or named access list controls the range of group addresses affected by the boundary. (Optional) **filter-autorp** filters Auto-RP messages denied by the boundary ACL.
ip multicast ttl-threshold *ttl-value*	Interface config mode; configures an interface as a multicast boundary for TTL scoping. Time-to-Live value represents number of hops, ranging from 0 to 255. The default value is 0, which means that all multicast packets are forwarded out the interface.
ip cgmp	Interface config mode; enables support for CGMP on an interface.
ip pim version {1 | 2}	Interface config mode; sets the PIM version on an interface. The default is 2.
ip pim query-interval *seconds*	Interface config mode; changes the interval for PIMv2 Hello or PIMv1 Router Query messages from the default 30 seconds.
ip pim spt-threshold {kbps | infinity} [group-list *access-list-number*]	Global mode; specifies the incoming rate for the multicast traffic for a PIM-SM router to switch from RPT to SPT. The default is to switch after the first multicast packet is received. If the **group-list** option is used, the command parameters are applied only to the groups permitted by the access list; otherwise, they are applied to all groups.

Command	Command Mode and Description
ip pim rp-address [*access-list*] [override]	Global mode; statically configures the IP address of an RP, where *rp-address* is a unicast IP address in four-part, dotted notation. (Optional) *access-list* represents a number or name of an access list that defines for which multicast groups the RP should be used. (Optional) **override** indicates that if there is a conflict, the RP configured with this command prevails over the RP learned dynamically by Auto-RP or any other method.
ip pim send-rp-announce *interface-type interface-number* **scope** *ttl-value* [**group-list** *access-list*] [**interval** *seconds*]	Global mode; configures the router to be an RP, and the router sends RP-Announce messages using the Auto-RP method for the interface address selected. Scope represents the TTL. (Optional) **group-list** defines the multicast groups for which this router is RP. (Optional) **interval** changes the announcement frequency from the default 60 seconds.
ip pim send-rp-discovery [*interface-type interface-number*] **scope** *ttl-value*	Global mode; configures the router to be a mapping agent, and the router sends RP-Discovery messages using the Auto-RP method. **scope** represents the TTL. (Optional) The IP address of the interface specified is used as the source address for the messages. The default is to use the IP address of the interface on which the message is sent as the source address.
ip pim rp-announce-filter rp-list *access-list* **group-list** *access-list*	Global mode; configures a mapping agent to filter RP-Announce messages coming from specific RPs. **rp-list** *access-list* specifies a number or name of a standard access list that specifies that this filter is only for the RP addresses permitted in this ACL. **group-list** *access-list* specifies a number or name of a standard access list that describes permitted group addresses. The filter defines that only the group range permitted in the **group-list** *access-list* should be accepted from the RP-Announcements received from the RP addresses permitted by the **rp-list** *access-list*.
show ip igmp groups [*group-name* | *group-address* | *interface-type interface-number*] [**detail**]	User mode; displays the list of multicast groups for which the router has directly connected group members, learned through IGMP.
show ip mroute [*group-address* | *group-name*] [*source-address* | *source-name*] [*interface-type interface-number*] [**summary**] [**count**] [**active** kbps]	User mode; displays the contents of the IP multicast routing table.

Command	Command Mode and Description
show ip pim neighbor [*interface-type interface-number*]	User mode; displays the list of neighbors discovered by PIM.
show ip pim rp [mapping [elected | in-use] | metric] [*rp-address*]	User mode; displays the active RPs associated with multicast groups.
show ip rpf {*source-address* | *source-name*} [metric]	User mode; displays the information IP multicasting routing uses to perform the RPF check.
clear ip cgmp [*interface-type interface-number*]	Enable mode; the router sends a CGMP Leave message and instructs the switches to clear all group entries they have cached.
debug ip igmp	Enable mode; displays IGMP messages received and sent, and IGMP-host-related events.
debug ip pim	Enable mode; displays PIM messages received and sent, and PIM-related events.

[*] When you configure any one of these commands on a LAN interface, IGMPv2 is automatically enabled on the interface.

Table 8-7 summarizes important flags displayed in an mroute entry when you use the **show ip mroute** command.

Table 8-7   mroute *Flags*

Flag	Description
D (dense)	Entry is operating in dense mode.
S (sparse)	Entry is operating in sparse mode.
C (connected)	A member of the multicast group is present on the directly connected interface.
L (local)	The router itself is a member of the multicast group.
P (pruned)	Route has been pruned.
R (RP-bit set)	Indicates that the (S,G) entry is pointing toward the RP. The RP is typically in a pruned state along the shared tree after a downstream router has switched to SPT for a particular source.
F (register flag)	Indicates that the software is registering for a multicast source.
T (SPT-bit set)	Indicates that packets have been received on the shortest-path source tree.

Flag	Description
J (join SPT)	This flag has meaning only for sparse-mode groups. For (*,G) entries, the J flag indicates that the rate of traffic flowing down the shared tree has exceeded the SPT-Threshold set for the group. This calculation is done once a second. On Cisco routers, the default SPT-Threshold value is 0 kbps. When the J flag is set on the (*,G) entry and the router has a directly connected group member denoted by the C flag, the next (S,G) packet received down the shared tree will trigger a switchover from RPT to SPT for source S and group G. For (S,G) entries, the J flag indicates that the entry was created because the router has switched over from RPT to SPT for the group. When the J flag is set for the (S,G) entries, the router monitors the traffic rate on SPT and switches back to RPT for this source if the traffic rate on the source tree falls below the group's SPT-Threshold for more than 1 minute.

Memory Builders

The CCIE Routing and Switching written exam, like all Cisco CCIE written exams, covers a fairly broad set of topics. This section provides some basic tools to help you exercise your memory about some of the broader topics covered in this chapter.

Fill In Key Tables from Memory

Appendix E, "Key Tables for CCIE Study," on the CD in the back of this book, contains empty sets of some of the key summary tables in each chapter. Print Appendix E, refer to this chapter's tables in it, and fill in the tables from memory. Refer to Appendix F, "Solutions for Key Tables for CCIE Study," on the CD, to check your answers.

Definitions

Next, take a few moments to write down the definitions for the following terms:

> dense-mode protocol, RPF check, sparse-mode protocol, RP, multicast scoping, TTL scoping, administrative scoping, PIM-DM, PIM Hello message, designated router, source-based distribution tree, multicast state information, Join/Prune message, upstream router, downstream router, Graft message, Graft Ack message, Prune Override, Assert message, DVMRP, MOSPF, PIM-SM, source DR, source registration, shared distribution tree, shortest-path tree switchover, PIM-SM (S,G), RP-bit Prune, Auto-RP, BSR, SSM, MSDP, MLD, IPv6 mroute, embedded RP, IPv6 BSR, MLD Limiting

Refer to the glossary to check your answers.

Further Reading

Developing IP Multicast Networks, Volume I, by Beau Williamson (Cisco Press, 2000).

Interdomain Multicast Solutions Guide, by Cisco Systems, Inc. (Cisco Press, 2003).

Blueprint topics covered in this chapter:

This chapter covers the following subtopics from the Cisco CCIE Routing and Switching written exam blueprint. Refer to the full blueprint in Table I-1 in the Introduction for more details on the topics covered in each chapter and their context within the blueprint.

- Access Lists

- Zone-Based Firewall and Classic IOS Firewall

- Unicast Reverse Path Forwarding

- IP Source Guard

- Authentication, Authorization, and Accounting (router configuration)

- Control-Plane Policing (CoPP)

- Secure Shell (SSH)

- 802.1X

- Device Access Control

- IPv6 First Hop Security

- RA Guard

- DHCP Guard

- Binding Table

- Device Tracking

- ND Inspection

- Source Guard

- PACL

CHAPTER 9

Device and Network Security

Over the years, the CCIE program has expanded to add several CCIE certifications besides the Routing and Switching track. As a result, some topics previously covered in the Routing and Switching exam have been removed, or shortened, because they are more appropriate for another CCIE track. For example, the CCIE Routing and Switching track formerly covered voice to some degree, but the CCIE Voice track now covers voice to a much deeper level.

The topics in this chapter are certainly covered in more detail in the CCIE Security written and lab exams. However, because security has such an important role in networks, and because many security features relate specifically to router and switch operations, some security details remain within the CCIE Routing and Switching track. This chapter covers many of the core security features related to routers and switches.

"Do I Know This Already?" Quiz

Table 9-1 outlines the major headings in this chapter and the corresponding "Do I Know This Already?" quiz questions.

Table 9-1 *"Do I Know This Already?" Foundation Topics Section-to-Question Mapping*

Foundation Topics Section	Questions Covered in This Section	Score
Router and Switch Device Security	1–3	
Layer 2 Security	4–7	
Layer 3 Security	8, 9	
Total Score		

To best use this pre-chapter assessment, remember to score yourself strictly. You can find the answers in Appendix A, "Answers to the 'Do I Know This Already?' Quizzes."

1. Consider the following configuration commands, which will be pasted into a router's configuration. Assuming that no other AAA configuration or other security-related configuration exists before pasting in this configuration, which of the following is true regarding the process and sequences for authentication of a user attempting to enter privileged mode?

```
enable secret fred
enable authentication wilma
username barney password betty
aaa new-model
aaa authentication enable default group radius enable
aaa authentication enable wilma group fred local
aaa authentication login default group radius local
aaa authentication login fred line group radius none
radius-server host 10.1.1.1 auth-port 1812 acct-port 1646
radius-server host 10.1.1.2 auth-port 1645 acct-port 1646
radius-server key cisco
aaa group server radius fred
server 10.1.1.3 auth-port 1645 acct-port 1646
server 10.1.1.4 auth-port 1645 acct-port 1646
line con 0
 password cisco
 login authentication fred
line vty 0 4
 password cisco
```

(handwritten annotations: "cannot follow", "not imp as we are looking into privilidged mode")

a. The user will only need to supply a password of fred without a username.

b. The RADIUS server at either 10.1.1.1 or 10.1.1.2 must approve the username/password supplied by the user.

c. The RADIUS server at 10.1.1.3 is checked first; if no response, the server at 10.1.1.4 is checked.

d. None of these answers is correct.

2. Using the same exhibit and conditions as Question 1, which of the following is true regarding the process and sequences for authentication of a user attempting to log in through the console?

a. A simple password of cisco will be required.

b. The user will supply a username/password, which will be authenticated if either server 10.1.1.1 or 10.1.1.2 returns a RADIUS message approving the user.

c. The username/password is presented to the RADIUS server at 10.1.1.3 first; if no response, the server at 10.1.1.4 is checked next.

d. None of these answers is correct.

3. Using the same exhibit and conditions as Question 1, which of the following is true regarding the process and sequences for authentication of a user attempting to log in through Telnet?

   a. A simple password of cisco will be required.

   b. The router will attempt authentication with RADIUS server 10.1.1.1 first. If no response, then 10.1.1.2; if no response, it will require password cisco.

   c. The router will attempt authentication with RADIUS server 10.1.1.1 first. If no response, then 10.1.1.2; if no response, it will require a username/password of barney/betty.

   d. The username/password is presented to the RADIUS server at 10.1.1.3 first; if no response, the server at 10.1.1.4 is checked next.

   e. If neither 10.1.1.1 nor 10.1.1.2 responds, the user cannot be authenticated and is rejected.

   f. None of the other answers is correct.

4. Which of the following are considered best practices for Layer 2 security?

   a. Inspect ARP messages to prevent hackers from causing hosts to create incorrect ARP table entries.

   b. Enable port security.

   c. Put all management traffic in VLAN 1, but no user traffic.

   d. Configure DTP to use the auto setting.

   e. Shut down unused ports.

5. Assuming a Cisco 3560 switch, which of the following is true regarding the port security feature?

   a. The default maximum number of MACs allowed to be reached on an interface is three.

   b. Sticky-learned MAC addresses are automatically added to the startup configuration after they are learned the first time.

   c. Dynamic (nonsticky)–learned MAC addresses are added to the running configuration, but they can be saved using the **copy run start** command.

   d. A port must be set to be a static access or trunking port for port security to be allowed on the interface.

   e. None of the other answers is correct.

6. Which of the following is true regarding the use of IEEE 802.1X for LAN user authentication?

   a. The EAPoL protocol is used between the authenticator and authentication server.

   b. The supplicant is client software on the user's device.

   c. A switch acts in the role of 802.1X authentication server.

   d. The only traffic allowed to exit a currently unauthenticated 802.1X port is 802.1X-related messages.

7. The following ACE is typed into configuration mode on a router: **access-list 1 permit 10.44.38.0 0.0.3.255**. If this statement had instead used a different mask, with nothing else changed, which of the following choices for mask would result in a match for source IP address 10.44.40.18?

   a. 0.0.1.255

   b. 0.0.5.255

   c. 0.0.7.255

   d. 0.0.15.255

8. An enterprise uses a registered class A network. A smurf attack occurs from the Internet, with the enterprise receiving lots of ICMP Echoes, destined to subnet broadcast address 9.1.1.255, which is the broadcast address of an actual deployed subnet (9.1.1.0/24) in the enterprise. The packets all have a source address of 9.1.1.1. Which of the following tools might help mitigate the effects of the attack?

   a. Ensure that the **no ip directed-broadcast** command is configured on the router interfaces connected to the 9.1.1.0/24 subnet.

   b. Configure an RPF check so that the packets would be rejected based on the invalid source IP address.

   c. Routers will not forward packets to subnet broadcast addresses, so there is no need for concern in this case.

   d. Filter all packets sent to addresses in subnet 9.1.1.0/24.

9. Which of the following statements is true regarding the router Cisco IOS Software TCP intercept feature?

   a. Always acts as a proxy for incoming TCP connections, completing the client-side connection, and only then creating a server-side TCP connection.

   b. Can monitor TCP connections for volume and for incomplete connections, as well as serve as a TCP proxy.

   c. If enabled, must operate on all TCP connection requests entering a particular interface.

   d. None of the other answers is correct.

Foundation Topics

Router and Switch Device Security

Securing access to a router or switch command-line interface (CLI) is one of the first steps in securing a routed/switched network. Cisco includes several basic mechanisms appropriate for protecting devices in a lab, as well as more robust security features appropriate for devices deployed in production environments. Additionally, these same base authentication features can be used to authenticate dial Point-to-Point Protocol (PPP) users. The first section of this chapter examines each of these topics.

Simple Password Protection for the CLI

Figure 9-1 provides a visual reminder of some hopefully familiar details about how users can reach a router's CLI user mode, and move into enable (privileged) mode using the **enable** command.

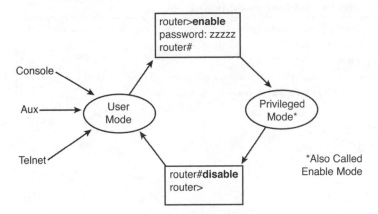

Figure 9-1 *Router User and Enable Modes*

Figure 9-1 shows three methods to reach user mode on a router. The figure also applies to Cisco IOS–based switches, except that Cisco switches do not have auxiliary ports.

Cisco IOS can be configured to require simple password protection for each of the three methods to access user mode. To do so, the **login** line subcommand is used to tell Cisco IOS to prompt the user for a password, and the **password** command defines the password. The configuration mode implies for which of the three access methods the password should be required. Example 9-1 shows a simple example.

Example 9-1   *Simple User Mode CLI Password Protection*

```
! The login and password commands under line con 0 tell the router to supply a
! password prompt, and define the password required at the console port,
! respectively.
line con 0
 login
 password fred
!
! The login and password commands under line vty 0 15 tell the router to supply a
! password prompt, and define the password required at the vty lines, respectively.
line vty 0 15
 login
 password barney
```

These passwords are stored as clear text in the configuration, but they can be encrypted by including the **service password-encryption** global command. Example 9-2 shows the results of adding this command.

Example 9-2   *Using the* service password-encryption *Command*

```
! The service password-encryption global command causes all existing clear-text
! passwords in the running config to be encrypted.
service password-encryption
! The "7" in the password commands means that the following value is the
! encrypted password per the service password-encryption command.
line con 0
 password 7 05080F1C2243
 login
line vty 0 4
 password 7 00071A150754
 login
```

Note that when the **service password-encryption** command is added to the configuration, all clear-text passwords in the running configuration are changed to an encrypted value. The passwords in the startup configuration are not changed until the **copy running-config startup-config** (or **write memory** for all you fellow old-timers out there) command has been used to save the configuration. Also, after you disable password encryption (**no service password-encryption**), passwords are not automatically decrypted. Instead, Cisco IOS waits for a password to be changed before listing the password in its unencrypted form.

Note that the encryption used by the **service password-encryption** command is weak. Publicly available tools can decrypt the password. The encryption is useful to prevent the curious from logging in to a router or switch, but it provides no real protection against a hacker with even modest ability.

Better Protection of Enable and Username Passwords

The password required by the **enable** command can be defined by either the **enable password** *pw* command or the **enable secret** *pw* command. If both are configured, the **enable exec** command only accepts the password defined in the **enable secret** command.

The password in the **enable password** command follows the same encryption rules as login passwords, only being encrypted if the **service password-encryption** command is configured. However, the **enable secret** password is not affected by **service password-encryption**. Example 9-3 shows how Cisco IOS represents this subtle difference in how the password values are stored.

Example 9-3   *Differences in Hashed/Encrypted Enable Passwords*

```
! The enable password lists a 7 in the output to signify an encrypted value
! per the service password-encryption command; the
! enable secret command lists a 5, signifying an MD5-hashed value.
service password-encryption
!
enable secret 5 $1$GvDM$ux/PhTwSscDNOyNIyr5Be/
enable password 7 070C285F4D064B
```

(handwritten annotations: "enable secret", "service password enc!")

Using Secure Shell Protocol

Example 9-1 showed how to require a password for Telnet access through the vty lines. Telnet has long been used to manage network devices; however, Telnet traffic is sent in clear text. Anyone able to sniff that traffic would see your password and any other information sent during the Telnet session. Secure Shell (SSH) is a much more secure way to manage your routers and switches. It is a client/server protocol that encrypts the traffic in and out through the vty ports.

Cisco routers and switches can act as SSH clients by default, but must be configured to be SSH servers. That is, they can use SSH when connecting *to* another device, but require configuration before allowing devices to connect through SSH to them. They also require some method of authenticating the client. This can be either a local username and password, or authentication with a AAA server (AAA is detailed in the next section).

There are two versions of SSH. SSH version 2 is an IETF standard that is more secure than version 1. Version 1 is more vulnerable to man-in-the-middle attacks, for example. Cisco devices support both types of connections, but you can specify which version to use.

Telnet is enabled by default, but configuring even a basic SSH server requires several steps: *(handwritten: "→ to support SSH")*

Step 1.   Ensure that your IOS supports SSH. You need a K9 image for this.

Step 2.   Configure a host name, unless this was done previously.   *(handwritten: "⊕ Username")*

Step 3.   Configure a domain name, unless this was done previously.   *(handwritten: "⊕ domain name")*

Step 4.   Configure a client authentication method.   *(handwritten: "⊕ auth. method")*

generate RSA key

Step 5. Tell the router or switch to generate the Rivest, Shamir, and Adelman (RSA) keys that will be used to encrypt the session.

Step 6. Specify the SSH version, if you want to use version 2.

Step 7. Disable Telnet on the VTY lines.

Step 8. Enable SSH on the VTY lines.

Example 9-4 shows a router being configured to act as an SSH server.

Example 9-4 *SSH Configuration*

```
router(config)# hostname R3
R3(config)# ip domain-name CCIE2B
R3(config)# username cisco password Cisco
R3(config)# crypto key generate rsa
The name for the keys will be: R3.CCIE2B
Choose the size of the key modulus in the range of 360 to 2048 for your
  General Purpose Keys. Choosing a key modulus greater than 512 may take
  a few minutes.
How many bits in the modulus [512]: 1024
% Generating 1024 bit RSA keys ...[OK]

R3(config)#
*May 22 02:06:51.923: %SSH-5-ENABLED: SSH 1.99 has been enabled
R3(config)# ip ssh version 2
!
R3(config)# line vty 0 4
R3(config-line)# transport input none
R3(config-line)# transport input ssh
R3(config-line)#^Z
!
R3# show ip ssh
SSH Enabled - version 2.0
Authentication timeout: 120 secs; Authentication retries: 3
```

User Mode and Privileged Mode AAA Authentication

The term *authentication, authorization, and accounting (AAA)* refers to a variety of common security features. This section focuses on the first "A" in AAA—authentication—and how it is used to manage access to a router or IOS switch's user mode and privileged mode.

The strongest authentication method to protect the CLI is to use a TACACS+ or RADIUS server. The *Cisco Secure Access Control Server (ACS)* is a Cisco Systems software product that can be installed on UNIX, Linux, and several Windows platforms, holding the set of usernames and passwords used for authentication. The routers and switches then need to receive the username and password from the user, send it as encrypted traffic to the server, and receive a reply—either accepting or rejecting the user. Table 9-2 summarizes some of the key facts about RADIUS and TACACS+.

Table 9-2 *Comparing RADIUS and TACACS+ for Authentication*

	RADIUS	**TACACS+**
Scope of Encryption: packet payload or just the password	Password only	Entire payload
Layer 4 Protocol	UDP	TCP
Well-Known Port/IOS Default Port Used for Authentication	1812/1645[1]	49/49
Standard or Cisco-Proprietary	RFC 2865	Proprietary

[1] RADIUS originally defined port 1645 as the well-known port, which was later changed to port 1812.

Using a Default Set of Authentication Methods

AAA authentication configuration includes commands by which a set of authentication methods is defined. A single *authentication method* is exactly what it sounds like—a way to authenticate a user. For example, one method is to ask a RADIUS server to authenticate a login user; another is to let a router look at a set of locally defined **username** commands. A set of configuration methods represents an ordered list of authentication methods, each of which is tried in order until one of the methods returns an authentication response, either accepting or rejecting the user.

The simplest AAA configuration defines a default set of authentication methods used for all router or switch logins, plus a second set of default authentication methods used by the **enable** command. The defined default login authentication methods apply to all login access—console, Telnet, and aux (routers only). The default authentication methods used by the **enable** command simply dictate what Cisco IOS does when a user types the **enable** command. The overall configuration uses the following general steps:

Step 1.   Enable AAA authentication with the **aaa new-model** global command.

Step 2.   If using RADIUS or TACACS+, define the IP address(es) and encryption keys used by the server(s) by using the **radius-server host, radius-server key, tacacs-server host,** and **tacacs-server key** commands.

Step 3.   Define the default set of authentication methods used for all CLI access by using the **aaa authentication login default** command.

Step 4.   Define the default set of authentication methods used for enable-mode access by using the **aaa authentication enable default** command.

Example 9-5 shows a sample router configuration using these commands. In this case, two RADIUS servers are configured. One of the servers uses the Cisco IOS default port of 1645, and the other uses the reserved well-known port 1812. Per the following configuration, this router attempts the following authentication:

- When a login attempt is made, Cisco IOS attempts authentication using the first RADIUS server; if there's no response, IOS tries the second RADIUS server; if there's no response, the user is allowed in (authentication mode **none**).

- When any user issues the **enable** command, the router tries the RADIUS servers, in order; if none of the RADIUS servers replies, the router will accept the single username/password configured on the router of **cisco/cisco**.

Example 9-5 *Example AAA Configuration for Login and Enable*

```
! The next command shows that the enable secret password is still configured,
! but it will not be used. The username command defines a user/password that
! will be used for enable authentication if the RADIUS servers are not reachable.
! Note that the 0 in the username command means the password is not encrypted.
R1# show running-config
! lines omitted for brevity
enable secret 5 $1$GvDM$ux/PhTwSscDNOyNIyr5Be/
username cisco password 0 cisco
! Next, AAA is enabled, and the default enable and login authentication is
! defined.
aaa new-model
aaa authentication enable default group radius local
aaa authentication login default group radius none
! Next, the two RADIUS servers are configured. The port numbers were omitted when
! the radius-server host 10.1.1.2 command was issued, and IOS filled in its
! default. Similarly, radius-server host 10.1.1.1 auth-port 1812 was issued,
! with IOS adding the accounting port number default into the command.
radius-server host 10.1.1.1 auth-port 1812 acct-port 1646
radius-server host 10.1.1.2 auth-port 1645 acct-port 1646
radius-server key cisco
! Before adding AAA configuration, both the console and vtys had both the login
! and password commands as listed in Example 9-1. The act of enabling AAA
! deleted the login command, which now by default uses the settings on global
! command aaa authentication login default. The passwords remaining below would
! be used only if the aaa authentication login command listed a method of "line."
line con 0
 password cisco
line vty 0 4
 password cisco
```

Using Multiple Authentication Methods

AAA authentication allows a reference to multiple servers and to multiple authentication methods so that a user can be authenticated even if one authentication method is not working. The **aaa authentication** command supports up to four methods on a single command. Additionally, there is no practical limit to the number of RADIUS or TACACS+ servers that can be referenced in a RADIUS or TACACS+ server group. The logic used by Cisco IOS when using these methods is as follows:

Key Topic

- Use the first listed method first; if that method does not respond, move on to the next, and then the next, and so on until a method responds. Use the first-responding-method's decision (allow or reject).

- If a method refers to a set of more than one server, try the first server, with "first" being based on the order of the commands in the configuration file. If no response, move on to the next sequential server, and so on, until a server responds. Use the first-responding-server's decision (allow or reject).

- If no response occurs for any method, reject the request.

For example, Example 9-5 listed RADIUS servers 10.1.1.1 and 10.1.1.2, in that order, so those servers would be checked in that same order. If neither replies, the next method would be used—**none** for login sessions (meaning automatically allow the user in) and local (meaning authenticate based on configured **username** commands).

Table 9-3 lists the authentication methods allowed for login and enable (privileged EXEC) mode, along with a brief description.

Key Topic

Table 9-3   *Authentication Methods for Login and Enable*

Method	Meaning
group radius	Use the configured RADIUS servers.
group tacacs+	Use the configured TACACS+ servers.
aaa group server ldap	Defines the AAA server group with a group name and enters LDAP server group configuration mode.
group *name*	Use a defined group of either RADIUS or TACACS+ servers.
enable	Use the enable password, based on **enable secret** or **enable password** commands.
line[1]	Use the password defined by the **password** command in **line** configuration mode.
local	Use **username** commands in the local configuration; treats the username as case insensitive, but the password as case sensitive.
local-case	Use **username** commands in the local configuration; treats both the username and password as case sensitive.
none	No authentication required; user is automatically authenticated.

[1] Cannot be used for enable authentication.

Groups of AAA Servers

By default, Cisco IOS automatically groups RADIUS and TACACS+ servers configured with the **radius-server host** and **tacacs-server host** commands into groups, aptly named *radius* and *tacacs+*. The aaa authentication command includes the keywords **group radius** or **group tacacs+** to refer to these default groups. By default, all defined RADIUS servers end up in the radius group, and all defined TACACS+ servers end up in the tacacs+ group.

In some cases, particularly with larger-scale dial implementations, a design might call for the separation of different sets of RADIUS or TACACS+ servers. To do so, servers can be grouped by name. Example 9-6 shows an example configuration with two servers in a RADIUS group named fred, and shows how the **aaa authentication** command can refer to the group.

Example 9-6   *Configuring a RADIUS Server Group*

[handwritten left margin: When you have more than 1 radius groups]

```
! The next three commands create RADIUS group fred. Note that the servers are
! configured inside AAA group config mode, using the server subcommand. Note that
! IOS added the auth-port and acct-port parameters automatically.
R1(config)# aaa group server radius fred
R1(config-group)# server 10.1.1.3 auth-port 1645 acct-port 1646
R1(config-group)# server 10.1.1.4 auth-port 1645 acct-port 1646
! To use group fred instead of the default group, the aaa authentication
! commands need to refer to group fred, as shown next.
aaa new-model
aaa authentication enable default group fred local
aaa authentication login default group fred none
```

Overriding the Defaults for Login Security

The console, vty, and aux (routers only) lines can override the use of the default login authentication methods. To do so, in line configuration mode, the **login authentication** *name* command is used to point to a named set of configuration methods. Example 9-7 shows a named group of configuration methods called **for-console**, **for-vty**, and **for-aux**, with each applied to the related login method. Each of the named groups defines a different set of authentication methods. Example 9-7 shows an example that implements the following requirements:

- **console:** Try the RADIUS servers, and use the line password if no response.

- **vty:** Try the RADIUS servers, and use local usernames/passwords if no response.

- **aux:** Try the RADIUS servers, and do not authenticate if no response.

Example 9-7 *Overriding the Default Login Authentication Method*

```
! The configuration shown here has been added to the configuration from earlier
! examples.
aaa authentication login for-console group radius line
aaa authentication login for-vty group radius local
aaa authentication login for-aux group radius
! The methods are enabled below with the login authentication commands. Note that
! the local passwords still exist on the console and vtys; for the console,
! that password would be used (based on the line keyword in the aaa
! authentication command above) if the RADIUS servers are all nonresponsive.
! However, the vty password command would not be used by this configuration.
line con 0
 password 7 14141B180F0B
 login authentication for-console
line aux 0
 login authentication for-aux
line vty 0 4
 password 7 104D000A0618
 login authentication for-vty
```

you can set a diff AAA policy for all the different logon methods.

PPP Security

PPP provides the capability to use Password Authentication Protocol (PAP) and Challenge Handshake Authentication Protocol (CHAP) for authentication, which is particularly useful for dial applications. The default authentication method for CHAP/PAP is the reliance on a locally configured set of **username** *name* **password** *password* commands.

Cisco IOS supports the use of AAA authentication for PPP using the same general set of commands as used for login authentication. The configuration steps are as follows:

Key Topic

Step 1. Just as with login authentication, enable AAA authentication with the **aaa new-model** global command.

Step 2. Just as with login authentication, if used, configure RADIUS and/or TACACS+ servers, using the same commands and syntax as used for login and enable authentication.

Step 3. Similar to login authentication, define PPP to use a default set of authentication methods with the **aaa authentication ppp default** command. (The only difference is that the **ppp** keyword is used instead of **login**.)

Step 4. Similar to login authentication, use the **aaa authentication ppp** *list-name method1* [*method2...*] command to create a named group of methods that can be used instead of the default set.

Step 5. To use a named group of authentication methods instead of the default set, use the **ppp authentication** {*protocol1* [*protocol2*...]} *list-name* command. For example, the **ppp authentication chap fred** command references the authentication methods defined by the **aaa authentication ppp fred** command.

Layer 2 Security

The Cisco SAFE Blueprint document (available at www.cisco.com/go/safe) suggests a wide variety of best practices for switch security. In most cases, the recommendations depend on one of three general characterizations of the switch ports, as follows:

■ **Unused ports:** Switch ports that are not yet connected to any device—for example, switch ports that are pre-cabled to a faceplate in an empty cubicle

■ **User ports:** Ports cabled to end-user devices, or any cabling drop that sits in some physically unprotected area

■ **Trusted ports or trunk ports:** Ports connected to fully trusted devices, like other switches known to be located in an area with good physical security

The following list summarizes the best practices that apply to both unused and user ports. The common element between these types of ports is that a malicious person can gain access after getting inside the building, without having to gain further access behind the locked door to a wiring closet or data center.

■ Disable unneeded dynamic protocols like Cisco Discovery Protocol (CDP) and Dynamic Trunking Protocol (DTP).

■ Disable trunking by configuring these ports as access ports.

■ Enable BPDU Guard and Root Guard to prevent STP attacks and keep a stable STP topology.

■ Use either Dynamic ARP Inspection (DAI) or private VLANs to prevent frame sniffing.

■ Enable port security to at least limit the number of allowed MAC addresses, and possibly restrict the port to use only specific MAC addresses.

■ Use 802.1X user authentication.

■ Use DHCP snooping and IP Source Guard to prevent DHCP DoS and man-in-the-middle attacks.

Besides the preceding recommendations specifically for unused ports and user ports, the Cisco SAFE Blueprint makes the following additional recommendations:

■ For any port (including trusted ports), consider the general use of private VLANs to further protect the network from sniffing, including preventing routers or L3 switches from routing packets between devices in the private VLAN.

■ Configure VTP authentication globally on each switch to prevent DoS attacks.

- Disable unused switch ports and place them in an unused VLAN.

- Avoid using VLAN 1.

- For trunks, do not use the native VLAN.

The rest of this section's coverage of switch security addresses the points in these two lists of best practices, with the next subsection focusing on best practices for unused and user ports (based on the first list), and the following subsection focusing on the general best practices for unused and user ports (based on the second list).

Switch Security Best Practices for Unused and User Ports

The first three items in the list of best practices for unused and user ports are mostly covered in earlier chapters. For a brief review, Example 9-8 shows an example configuration on a Cisco 3560 switch, with each of these items configured and noted. In this example, fa0/1 is a currently unused port. CDP has been disabled on the interface, but it remains enabled globally, on the presumption that some ports still need CDP enabled. DTP has been disabled as well, and STP Root Guard and BPDU Guard are enabled.

Example 9-8   *Disabling CDP and DTP and Enabling Root Guard and BPDU Guard*

```
! The cdp run command keeps CDP enabled globally, but it has been disabled on
! fa0/1, the unused port.
cdp run
int fa0/0
 no cdp enable
! The switchport mode access interface subcommand prevents the port from trunking,
! and the switchport nonegotiate command prevents any DTP messages
! from being sent or processed.
 switchport mode access
 switchport nonegotiate
! The last two interface commands enable Root Guard and BPDU Guard, per interface,
! respectively. BPDU Guard can also be enabled for all ports with PortFast
! enabled by configuring the spanning-tree portfast bpduguard enable global
! command.
 spanning-tree guard root
 spanning-tree bpduguard enable
```
— interface commands, but

Port Security

Switch port security monitors a port to restrict the number of MAC addresses associated with that port in the Layer 2 switching table. It can also enforce a restriction for only certain MAC addresses to be reachable out the port.

To implement port security, the switch adds more logic to its normal process of examining incoming frames. Instead of automatically adding a Layer 2 switching table entry for the source MAC and port number, the switch considers the port security configuration and whether it allows that entry. By preventing MACs from being added to the switch table, port security can prevent the switch from forwarding frames to those MACs on a port.

Port security supports the following key features:

- Limiting the number of MACs that can be associated with the port

- Limiting the actual MAC addresses associated with the port, based on three methods:

  - Static configuration of the allowed MAC addresses

  - Dynamic learning of MAC addresses, up to the defined maximum, where dynamic entries are lost upon reload

  - Dynamic learning but with the switch saving those entries in the configuration (called *sticky learning*)

Port security protects against a couple of types of attacks. After a switch's forwarding table fills, the switch times out older entries. When the switch receives frames destined for those MACs that are no longer in the table, the switch floods the frames out all ports. An attacker could cause the switch to fill its switching table by sending lots of frames, each with a different source MAC, forcing the switch to time out the entries for most of or all the legitimate hosts. As a result, the switch floods legitimate frames because the destination MACs are no longer in the content-addressable memory (CAM), allowing the attacker to see all the frames.

An attacker could also claim to be the same MAC address as a legitimate user by simply sending a frame with that same MAC address. As a result, the switch would update its switching table and send frames to the attacker, as shown in Figure 9-2.

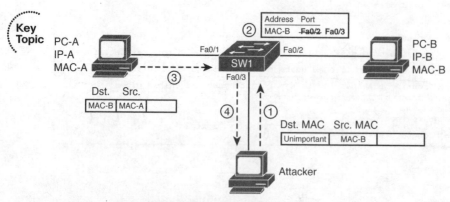

1. Attacker sources frame using PC-B's actual MAC.
2. SW1 updates its MAC address table.
3. Another frame is sent to destination MAC-B.
4. SW1 forwards frame to attacker.

Figure 9-2 *Claiming to Use Another Host's MAC Address*

Port security prevents both styles of these attacks by limiting the number of MAC addresses and by limiting MACs to particular ports. Port security configuration requires just a few configuration steps, all in interface mode. The commands are summarized in Table 9-4.

Table 9-4 *Port Security Configuration Commands*

Command	Purpose
switchport mode {access | trunk}	Port security requires that the port be statically set as either access or trunking
switchport port-security [maximum *value*]	Enables port security on an interface, and optionally defines the number of allowed MAC addresses on the port (default 1)
switchport port-security mac-address *mac-address* [vlan {*vlan-id* | {access | voice}}	Statically defines an allowed MAC address, for a particular VLAN (if trunking), and for either the access or voice VLAN
switchport port-security mac-address sticky	Tells the switch to remember the dynamically learned MAC addresses
switchport port-security [aging] [violation {protect | restrict | shutdown}]	Defines the Aging timer and actions taken when a violation occurs

Of the commands in Table 9-4, only the first two are required for port security. With just those two commands, a port allows the first-learned MAC address to be used, but no others. If that MAC address times out of the CAM, another MAC address can be learned on that port, but only one is allowed at a time.

The next two commands in the table allow for the definition of MAC addresses. The third command statically defines the permitted MAC addresses, and the fourth command allows for sticky learning. Sticky learning tells the switch to learn the MACs dynamically, but then add the MACs to the running configuration. This allows port security to be enabled and the existing MAC addresses to be learned, but then have them locked into the configuration as static entries simply by saving the running configuration. (Note that the **switchport port-security maximum** *x* command would be required to allow more than one MAC address, with *x* being the maximum number.)

The last command in the table tells the switch what to do when violations occur. The **protect** option simply tells the switch to perform port security. The **restrict** option tells it to also send Simple Network Management Protocol (SNMP) traps and issue log messages regarding the violation. Finally, the **shutdown** option puts the port in an err-disabled state, and requires a **shutdown/no shutdown** combination on the port to recover the port's forwarding state.

Example 9-9 shows a sample configuration, based on Figure 9-3. In the figure, Server 1 and Server 2 are the only devices that should ever be connected to interfaces Fast Ethernet 0/1 and 0/2, respectively. In this case, a rogue device has attempted to connect to fa0/1.

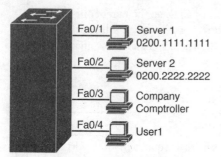

Figure 9-3   *Port Security Configuration Example*

Example 9-9   *Using Port Security to Define Correct MAC Addresses Connected to Particular Interfaces*

```
! FA0/1 has been configured to use a static MAC address, defaulting to allow
! only one MAC address.
interface FastEthernet0/1
 switchport mode access
 switchport port-security
 switchport port-security mac-address 0200.1111.1111
! FA0/2 has been configured to use a sticky-learned MAC address, defaulting to
! allow only one MAC address.
interface FastEthernet0/2
 switchport mode access
 switchport port-security
 switchport port-security mac-address sticky
! FA0/1 shows as err-disabled, as a device that was not 0200.1111.1111 tried to
! connect. The default violation mode is shutdown, as shown. It also lists the
! fact that a single MAC address is configured, that the maximum number of MAC
! addresses is 1, and that there are 0 sticky-learned MACs.
fred# show port-security interface fastEthernet 0/1
Port Security               : Enabled
Port Status                 : Err-Disabled
Violation Mode              : Shutdown
Aging Time                  : 0 mins
Aging Type                  : Absolute
SecureStatic Address Aging  : Disabled
Maximum MAC Addresses       : 1
Total MAC Addresses         : 1
Configured MAC Addresses    : 1
Sticky MAC Addresses        : 0
Last Source Address:Vlan    : f0f7.5538.f7a1:1
Security Violation Count    : 1
! FA0/2 shows as SecureUp, meaning that port security has not seen any violations
! on this port. Note also at the end of the stanza that the security violations
! count is 0. It lists the fact that one sticky MAC address has been learned.
```

this is not the MAC configured

```
fred# show port-security interface fastEthernet 0/2
Port Security            : Enabled
Port Status              : SecureUp
Violation Mode           : Shutdown
Aging Time               : 0 mins
Aging Type               : Absolute
SecureStatic Address Aging : Disabled
Maximum MAC Addresses    : 1
Total MAC Addresses      : 1
Configured MAC Addresses : 1
Sticky MAC Addresses     : 0
Last Source Address:Vlan : 0
Security Violation Count : 0
Security Violation count : 0
! Note the updated configuration in the switch. Due to the sticky option, the
! switch added the last shown configuration command.
fred# show running-config
(Lines omitted for brevity)
interface FastEthernet0/2
 switchport mode access
 switchport port-security
 switchport port-security mac-address sticky
 switchport port-security mac-address sticky 0200.2222.2222
```

Handwritten annotations: "no problem seen"; "first MAC learnt was added statically into the config"

Key Topic

The final part of the example shows that sticky learning updated the running configuration. The MAC address is stored in the running configuration, but it is stored in a command that also uses the **sticky** keyword, differentiating it from a truly statically configured MAC. Note that the switch does not automatically save the configuration in the startup config file.

Dynamic ARP Inspection

A switch can use DAI to prevent certain types of attacks that leverage the use of IP Address Resolution Protocol (ARP) messages. To appreciate just how those attacks work, you must keep in mind several detailed points about the contents of ARP messages. Figure 9-4 shows a simple example with the appropriate usage of ARP messages, with PC-A finding PC-B's MAC address.

The ARP message itself does not include an IP header. However, it does include four important addressing fields: the source MAC and IP address of the sender of the message, and the target MAC and IP address. For an ARP request, the target IP lists the IP address whose MAC needs to be found, and the target MAC Address field is empty, as that is the missing information. Note that the ARP reply (a LAN unicast) uses the source MAC field to imply the MAC address value. For example, PC-B sets the source MAC inside the ARP message to its own MAC address and the source IP to its own IP address.

Handwritten annotations: "request"; "ARP - target MAC is missing"

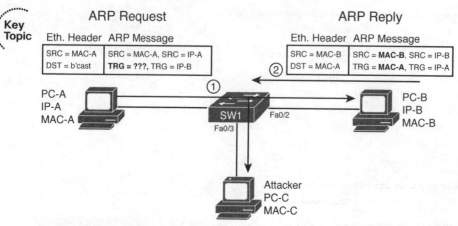

1. PC-A Sends ARP Broadcast Looking for
   IP-B's MAC Address (Target MAC)
2. PC-B Sends LAN Unicast ARP Reply

Figure 9-4   *Normal Use of ARP, Including Ethernet Addresses and ARP Fields*

An attacker can form a man-in-the-middle attack in a LAN by creative use of *gratuitous
ARPs*. A gratuitous ARP occurs when a host sends an ARP reply, without even seeing an
ARP request, and with a broadcast destination Ethernet address. The more typical ARP
reply in Figure 9-4 shows the ARP reply as a unicast, meaning that only the host that sent
the request will learn an ARP entry; by broadcasting the gratuitous ARP, all hosts on the
LAN will learn an ARP entry.

While gratuitous ARPs can be used to good effect, they can also be used by an attacker.
The attacker can send a gratuitous ARP, claiming to be an IP address of a legitimate
host. All the hosts in the subnet (including routers and switches) update their ARP tables,
pointing to the attacker's MAC address—and then later sending frames to the attacker
instead of to the true host. Figure 9-5 depicts the process.

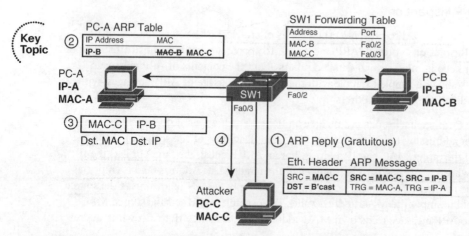

Figure 9-5   *Man-in-the-Middle Attack Using Gratuitous ARPs*

The steps shown in Figure 9-5 can be explained as follows:

1. The attacker broadcasts gratuitous ARP listing IP-B, but with MAC-C as the source IP and MAC.

2. PC-A updates its ARP table to list IP-B's associated address as MAC-C.

3. PC-A sends a frame to IP-B, but with destination MAC MAC-C.

4. SW1 forwards the frame to MAC-C, which is the attacker.

The attack results in other hosts, like PC-A, sending frames meant for IP-B to MAC address MAC-C—the attacker's PC. The attacker then simply forwards another copy of each frame to PC-B, becoming a man in the middle. As a result, the user can continue to work and the attacker can gain a much larger amount of data.

Switches use DAI to defeat ARP attacks by examining the ARP messages and then filtering inappropriate messages. DAI considers each switch port to be either untrusted (the default) or trusted, performing DAI messages only on untrusted ports. DAI examines each ARP request or reply (on untrusted ports) to decide whether it is inappropriate; if inappropriate, the switch filters the ARP message. DAI determines whether an ARP message is inappropriate by using the following logic:

Key Topic

Step 1. If an ARP reply lists a source IP address that was not DHCP-assigned to a device off that port, DAI filters the ARP reply.

Step 2. DAI uses additional logic like Step 1, but uses a list of statically defined IP/MAC address combinations for comparison.

Step 3. For a received ARP reply, DAI compares the source MAC address in the Ethernet header to the source MAC address in the ARP message. These MACs should be equal in normal ARP replies; if they are not, DAI filters the ARP message.

Step 4. Like Step 3, but DAI compares the destination Ethernet MAC and the target MAC listed in the ARP body.

Step 5. DAI checks for unexpected IP addresses listed in the ARP message, such as 0.0.0.0, 255.255.255.255, multicasts, and so on.

Table 9-5 lists the key Cisco 3560 switch commands used to enable DAI. DAI must first be enabled globally. At that point, all ports are considered to be untrusted by DAI. Some ports, particularly ports connected to devices in secure areas (ports connecting servers, other switches, and so on), need to be explicitly configured as trusted. Then, additional configuration is required to enable the different logic options. For example, DHCP snooping needs to be enabled before DAI can use the DHCP snooping binding database to perform the logic in Step 1 in the preceding list. Optionally, you can configure static IP addresses, or perform additional validation (per the last three points in the preceding list) using the **ip arp inspection validate** command.

[handwritten annotations in right margin:]
① *server/switch trunk ports need to be configured as trusted*
② *DHCP Snooping must be enabled*

[handwritten annotation in left margin:] 2

Table 9-5   *Cisco IOS Switch Dynamic ARP Inspection Commands*

Command	Purpose
ip arp inspection vlan *vlan-range*	Global command to enable DAI on this switch for the specified VLANs.
[no] ip arp inspection trust	Interface subcommand that enables (with the **no** option) or disables DAI on the interface. Defaults to enabled after the **ip arp inspection** global command has been configured.
ip arp inspection filter *arp-acl-name* vlan *vlan-range* [static]	Global command to refer to an ARP ACL that defines static IP/MAC addresses to be checked by DAI for that VLAN (Step 2 in the preceding list).
ip arp inspection validate {[src-mac] [dst-mac] [ip]}	Enables additional optional checking of ARP messages (per Steps 3–5 in the preceding list).
ip arp inspection limit {rate *pps* [burst interval *seconds*] | none}	Limits the ARP message rate to prevent DoS attacks carried out by sending a large number or ARPs.

Because DAI causes the switch to perform more work, an attacker could attempt a DoS attack on a switch by sending large numbers of ARP messages. DAI automatically sets a limit of 15 ARP messages per port per second to mitigate that risk; the settings can be changed using the **ip arp inspection limit** interface subcommand.

Max 15 ARP port/s by def.

DHCP Snooping

DHCP snooping prevents the damage inflicted by several attacks that use DHCP. DHCP snooping causes a switch to examine DHCP messages and filter those considered to be inappropriate. DHCP snooping also builds a table of IP address and port mappings, based on legitimate DHCP messages, called the *DHCP snooping binding table*. The DHCP snooping binding table can then be used by DAI and by the IP Source Guard feature.

DAI uses it too

Figure 9-6 shows a man-in-the-middle attack that leverages DHCP. The legitimate DHCP server sits at the main site, whereas the attacker sits on the local LAN, acting as a DHCP server.

The following steps explain how the attacker's PC can become a man in the middle in Figure 9-6:

Step 1.   PC-B requests an IP address using DHCP.

Step 2.   The attacker PC replies and assigns a good IP/mask, but using its own IP address as the default gateway.

Step 3.   PC-B sends data frames to the attacker, thinking that the attacker is the default gateway.

Step 4.   The attacker forwards copies of the packets, becoming a man in the middle.

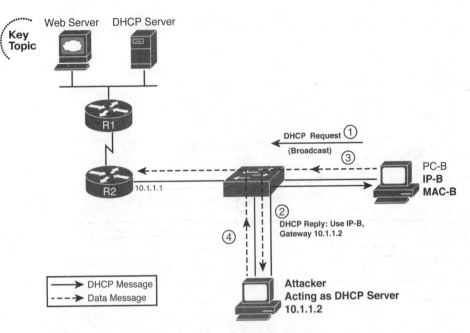

Figure 9-6 *Man-in-the-Middle Attack Using DHCP*

NOTE PC-B will use the first DHCP reply, so with the legitimate DHCP server only reachable over the WAN, the attacker's DHCP response should be the first response received by PC-B.

DHCP snooping defeats such attacks for ports that it considers to be untrusted. DHCP snooping allows all DHCP messages on trusted ports, but it filters DHCP messages on untrusted ports. It operates based on the premise that only DHCP clients should exist on untrusted ports; as a result, the switch filters incoming DHCP messages that are only sent by servers. So, from a design perspective, unused and unsecured user ports would be configured as untrusted to DHCP snooping.

DHCP snooping also needs to examine the DHCP client messages on untrusted ports, because other attacks can be made using DHCP client messages. DHCP servers identify clients based on their stated *client hardware address* as listed in the DHCP request. A single device could pose as multiple devices by sending repeated DHCP requests, each with a different DHCP client hardware address. The legitimate DHCP server, thinking that the requests are from different hosts, assigns an IP address for each request. The DHCP server will soon assign all IP addresses available for the subnet, preventing legitimate users from being assigned an address.

For untrusted ports, DHCP snooping uses the following general logic for filtering the packets:

Key Topic

1. It filters all messages sent exclusively by DHCP servers.

2. The switch checks DHCP *release* and *decline* messages against the DHCP snooping binding table. If the IP address in those messages is not listed with the port in the DHCP snooping binding table, the messages are filtered.

3. Optionally, it compares a DHCP request's client hardware address value with the source MAC address inside the Ethernet frame.

Of the three entries in this list, the first takes care of the fake DHCP server man-in-the-middle attack shown in Figure 9-6. The second item prevents an attacking host from releasing a legitimate host's DHCP lease, then attempting to request an address and be assigned the same IP address—thereby taking over any existing connections from the original host. Finally, the last item in the list prevents the DoS attack whereby a host attempts to allocate all the IP addresses that the DHCP server can assign in the subnet.

Table 9-6 lists the key configuration commands for configuring DHCP snooping on a Cisco 3560 switch.

Table 9-6 *Cisco IOS Switch Dynamic ARP Inspection Commands*

Command	Purpose
ip dhcp snooping vlan *vlan-range*	Global command to enable DHCP snooping for one or more VLANs
[no] ip dhcp snooping trust	Interface command to enable or disable a trust level on an interface; the **no** version (enabled) is the default
ip dhcp snooping binding *mac-address* **vlan** *vlan-id ip-address* **interface** *interface-id* **expiry** *seconds*	Global command to add static entries to the DHCP snooping binding database
ip dhcp snooping verify mac-address	Interface subcommand to add the optional check of the Ethernet source MAC address to be equal to a DHCP request's client ID
ip dhcp snooping limit rate *rate*	Sets the maximum number of DHCP messages per second to mitigate DoS attacks

IP Source Guard

The Cisco IOS switch IP Source Guard feature adds one more check to the DHCP snooping logic. When enabled along with DHCP snooping, IP Source Guard checks the source IP address of received packets against the DHCP snooping binding database. Alternatively, it checks both the source IP and source MAC addresses against that same database. If the entries do not match, the frame is filtered.

IP Source Guard is enabled using interface subcommands. To check just the source IP address, use the **ip verify source** interface subcommand; alternatively, the **ip verify source port-security** interface subcommand enables checking of both the source IP and MAC addresses. Optionally, you can use the **ip source binding** *mac-address* **vlan** *vlan-id ip-address* **interface** *interface-id* global command to create static entries that will be used in addition to the DHCP snooping binding database. *IE :*

To better appreciate this feature, consider the example DHCP snooping binding database shown in Example 9-10. DHCP snooping is enabled globally, and IP Source Guard is enabled on interface Fa0/1. Note that each of the database entries lists the MAC address and IP address, VLAN, and interface. These entries were gleaned from ports untrusted by DHCP snooping, with the DHCP snooping feature building these entries based on the source MAC address and source IP address of the DHCP requests.

Example 9-10   *Sample DHCP Snooping Binding Database*

Key Topic

```
SW1(config)# ip dhcp snooping
!
SW1(config)# interface FastEthernet0/1
SW1(config-if)# switchport access vlan 3
SW1(config-if)# ip verify source          — checks the IP address only
!
SW1# show ip dhcp snooping binding
Mac Address          Ip Address       Lease(sec)  Type            VLAN  Interface
-----------------    --------------   ----------  -------------   ----  ---------------
02:00:01:02:03:04    172.16.1.1       3412        dhcp-snooping   3     FastEthernet0/1
02:00:AA:BB:CC:DD    172.16.1.2       4916        dhcp-snooping   3     FastEthernet0/2
```

Because IP Source Guard was enabled using the **ip verify source** command under interface fa0/1, the only packets allowed coming into interface fa0/1 would be those with source IP address 172.16.1.1.

802.1X Authentication Using EAP

Switches can use IEEE 802.1X to perform user authentication, rather than the types of device authentication performed by many of the other features described in this section. User authentication requires the user to supply a username and password, verified by a RADIUS server, before the switch will enable the switch port for normal user traffic. Requiring a username and password prevents the attacker from simply using someone else's PC to attack the network without first breaking the 802.1X authentication username and password.

IEEE 802.1X defines some of the details of LAN user authentication, but it also uses the Extensible Authentication Protocol (EAP), an Internet standard (RFC 3748), as the underlying protocol used for authentication. EAP includes the protocol messages by which the user can be challenged to provide a password, as well as flows that create one-time passwords (OTP) per RFC 2289. Figure 9-7 shows the overall flow of LAN user authentication, without the details behind each message.

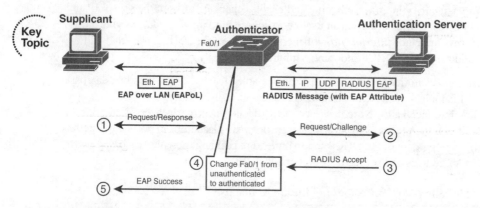

Figure 9-7   *802.1X for LAN User Authentication*

Figure 9-7 introduces a couple of general concepts plus several new terms. First, EAP messages are encapsulated directly inside an Ethernet frame when sent between the 802.1X *supplicant* (user device) and the 802.1X *authenticator* (switch). These frames are called *EAP over LAN (EAPoL)* frames. However, RADIUS expects the EAP message as a data structure called a *RADIUS attribute*, with these attributes sitting inside a normal RADIUS message. To support the two protocols, the switch translates between EAPoL and RADIUS for messages that need to flow between the supplicant and authentication server.

The rest of Figure 9-7 shows a simplistic view of the overall authentication flow. The switch and supplicant create an OTP using a temporary key, with the switch then forwarding the authentication request to the authentication server. The switch, as authenticator, must be aware of the results (Step 3), because the switch has a duty to enable the port after it is authenticated.

The 802.1X roles shown in Figure 9-7 are summarized as follows:

■ **Supplicant:** The 802.1X driver that supplies a username/password prompt to the user and sends/receives the EAPoL messages

■ **Authenticator:** Translates between EAPoL and RADIUS messages in both directions, and enables/disables ports based on the success/failure of authentication

■ **Authentication server:** Stores usernames/passwords and verifies that the correct values were submitted before authenticating the user

802.1X switch configuration resembles the AAA configuration covered in the section "Using a Default Set of Authentication Methods," earlier in this chapter. The switch configuration treats 802.1X user authentication as another option for AAA authentication, using the following steps:

Key Topic

Step 1. As with other AAA authentication methods, enable AAA with the **aaa new-model** global command.

Step 2. As with other configurations using RADIUS servers, define the RADIUS server(s) IP address(es) and encryption key(s) using the **radius-server host** and **radius-server key** commands.

Step 3. Similar to login authentication configuration, define the 802.1X authentication method (RADIUS only today) using the **aaa authentication dot1x default** command or, for multiple groups, the **aaa authentication dot1x group** *name* global command.

Step 4. Enable 802.1X globally using the **dot1x system-auth-control** global command.

Step 5. Set each interface to use one of three operational settings using the **authentication port-control {auto | force-authorized | force-unauthorized}** interface subcommand:

- Using 802.1X (**auto**)

- Not using 802.1X, but the interface is automatically authorized (**force-authorized**) (default)

- Not using 802.1X, but the interface is automatically unauthorized (**force-unauthorized**)

Example 9-11 shows a simple 802.1X configuration on a Cisco 3560 switch. The example shows a reasonable configuration based on Figure 9-3 earlier in the chapter, with servers off ports fa0/1 and fa0/2, and two users off ports fa0/3 and fa0/4. Also, consider fa0/5 as an unused port. Note that at the time of this writing, RADIUS is the only available authentication method for 802.1X in the Cisco 3560 switches.

Example 9-11 *Example Cisco 3560 802.1X Configuration*

```
! The first three commands enable AAA, define that 802.1x should use the RADIUS
! group comprised of all defined RADIUS servers, and enable 802.1X globally.
aaa new-model
aaa authentication dot1x default group radius
dot1x system-auth-control
continues
! Next, commands shown previously are used to define the default radius group.
! These commands are unchanged compared to earlier examples.
radius-server host 10.1.1.1 auth-port 1812 acct-port 1646
radius-server host 10.1.1.2 auth-port 1645 acct-port 1646
radius-server key cisco
! The server ports (fa0/1 and fa0/2), inside a secure datacenter, do not require
! 802.1x authentication.
```

```
int fa0/1
 authentication port-control force-authorized
int fa0/2
 authentication port-control force-authorized          - not checked
! The client ports (fa0/3 and fa0/4) require 802.1x authentication.
int fa0/3
 authentication port-control auto
int fa0/4
 authentication port-control auto          ← 802.1X
! The unused port (fa0/5) is configured to be in a permanently unauthorized
! state until the authentication port-control command is reconfigured for this
! port. As such, the port will only allow CDP, STP, and EAPoL frames.
int fa0/5
 authentication port-control force-unauthorized
```

Storm Control

Cisco IOS for Catalyst switches supports rate-limiting traffic at Layer 2 using the **storm-control** commands. Storm control can be configured to set rising and falling thresholds for each of the three types of port traffic: unicast, multicast, and broadcast. Each rate limit can be configured on a per-port basis.

You can configure storm control to operate on each traffic type based on either packet rate or a percentage of the interface bandwidth. You can also specify rising and falling thresholds for each traffic type. If you don't specify a falling threshold, or if the falling threshold is the same as the rising threshold, the switch port will forward all traffic up to the configured limit and will not wait for that traffic to pass a specified falling threshold before forwarding it again.

ACTIONS

When any of the configured thresholds is passed, the switch can take any of three additional actions, also on a per-port basis. The first, and the default, is that the switch can rate-limit by discarding excess traffic according to the configured command(s) and take no further action. The other two actions include performing the rate-limiting function and either shutting down the port or sending an SNMP trap.

Key Topic

Let's say that we have the following goals for a storm-control configuration:

- Limit broadcast traffic to 100 packets per second. When broadcast traffic drops back to 50 packets per second, begin forwarding broadcast traffic again.

- Limit multicast traffic to 0.5 percent of the 100-Mbps interface rate, or 500 kbps. When multicast traffic drops back to 400 kbps, begin forwarding multicast traffic again.

- Limit unicast traffic to 80 percent of the 100-Mbps interface rate, or 80 Mbps. Forward all unicast traffic up to this limit.

■ When any of these three conditions occurs and results in rate-limiting, send an SNMP trap.

The configuration that results is shown in Example 9-12.

[handwritten: stromcontrol (SC) kicks in]

Example 9-12   *Storm Control Configuration Example*

```
Cat3560(config)# interface FastEthernet0/10
Cat3560(config-if)# storm-control broadcast level pps 100 50
Cat3560(config-if)# storm-control multicast level 0.50 0.40
Cat3560(config-if)# storm-control unicast level 80.00
Cat3560(config-if)# storm-control action trap
Cat3560(config-if)# end
Cat3560# show storm-control fa0/10 unicast
Interface   Filter State   Upper        Lower        Current
---------   ------------   -----------  -----------  ----------
Fa0/10      Forwarding     80.00%       80.00%       0.00%
Cat3560# show storm-control fa0/10 broadcast
Interface   Filter State   Upper        Lower        Current
---------   ------------   -----------  -----------  ----------
Fa0/10      Forwarding     100 pps      50 pps       0 pps
Cat3560# show storm-control fa0/10 multicast
Interface   Filter State   Upper        Lower        Current
---------   ------------   -----------  -----------  ----------
Fa0/10      Forwarding     0.50%        0.40%        0.00%
Jun 10 14:24:47.595: %STORM_CONTROL-3-FILTERED: A Multicast storm detected on
    Fa0/10. A packet filter action has been applied on the interface.
! The preceding output indicates that the multicast storm threshold was
! exceeded and the switch took the action of sending
! an SNMP trap to indicate this condition.
```

[handwritten: SC stops]

[handwritten: 100M ×0.5 → kicks in   100M ×0.4 → stops]

Key Topic

One important caveat about storm control is that it supports only physical ports. The configuration commands are available on EtherChannel (port-channel) interfaces, but they have no effect.

[handwritten: ONLY PHYSICAL PORTS (iE: NO ETH. CHANNEL)]

General Layer 2 Security Recommendations

Recall that the beginning of the "Layer 2 Security" section, earlier in this chapter, outlined the Cisco SAFE Blueprint recommendations for user and unused ports and some general recommendations. The general recommendations include configuring VTP authentication globally on each switch, putting unused switch ports in an unused VLAN, and simply not using VLAN 1. The underlying configuration for each of these general recommendations is covered in Chapter 2, "BGP Routing Policies."

Additionally, Cisco recommends not using the native VLANs on trunks. The reason is that in some cases, an attacker on an access port might be able to hop from its access port VLAN to a trunk's native VLAN by sending frames that begin with multiple 802.1Q headers. This attack has been proven to be ineffective against Cisco switches. However, the attack takes advantage of unfortunate sequencing of programming logic in how a switch processes frames, so best practices call for not using native VLANs on trunks anyway. Simply put, by following this best practice of not using the native VLAN, even if an attacker managed to hop VLANs, if there are no devices inside that native VLAN, no damage could be inflicted. In fact, Cisco goes on to suggest using a different native VLAN for each trunk, to further restrict this type of attack.

The last general Layer 2 security recommendation covered in this chapter is to consider the use of private VLANs to further restrict traffic. As covered in Chapter 2, private VLANs restrict hosts on some ports from sending frames directly to each other. Figure 9-8 shows the allowed flows as dashed lines. The absence of a line between two devices means that private VLANs would prevent them from communicating. For example, PC1 and PC2 are not allowed to send frames to one another.

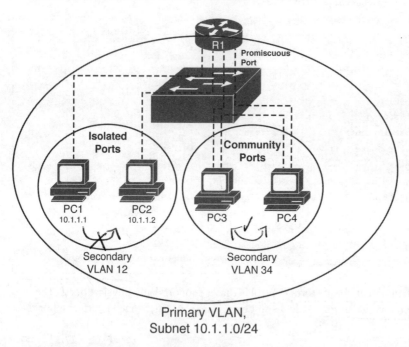

Figure 9-8 *Private VLAN Allowed Flows*

Private VLANs are created with some number of promiscuous ports in the primary VLAN, with other isolated and community ports in one or more secondary VLANs. Isolated ports can send frames only to promiscuous ports, whereas community ports can send frames to promiscuous ports and other community ports in the same secondary VLAN.

Private VLANs could be applied generally for better security by making user ports isolated, only allowing them access to promiscuous ports like routers, servers, or other network services. However, other, more recent additions to Cisco switches, such as DHCP snooping, DAI, and IP Source Guard, are typically better choices.

If private VLANs are used, Cisco also recommends additional protection against a trick by which an attacker can use the default gateway to overcome the protections provided by private VLANs. For example, in Figure 9-8, PC1 could send a frame with R1's destination MAC address but with PC2's destination IP address (10.1.1.2). The switch forwards the frame to R1 because R1's port is promiscuous. R1 then routes the packet to PC2, effectively getting around the private VLAN intent. To solve such a problem, the router simply needs an inbound access control list (ACL) on its LAN interface that denies traffic whose source and destination IP addresses are in the same local connected subnet. In this example, an **access-list 101 deny ip 10.1.1.0. 0.0.0.255 10.1.1.0 0.0.0.255** command would prevent this attack. (Of course, a few **permit** clauses would also be appropriate for the ACL.)

PVLAN attack

Workaround: ACL on the router interface

Layer 3 Security

The Cisco SAFE Blueprint also lists several best practices for Layer 3 security. The following list summarizes the key Layer 3 security recommendations from the SAFE Blueprint:

1. Enable secure Telnet access to a router user interface, and consider using Secure Shell (SSH) instead of Telnet.

2. Enable SNMP security, particularly adding SNMPv3 support.

3. Turn off all unnecessary services on the router platform.

4. Turn on logging to provide an audit trail.

5. Enable routing protocol authentication.

6. Enable the CEF forwarding path to avoid using flow-based paths like fast switching.

L3 sec. recommendations

Additionally, RFCs 2827 and 3704 outline other recommended best practices for protecting routers, Layer 3 forwarding (IP routing), and the Layer 3 control plane (routing protocols). RFC 2827 addresses issues with the use of the IP Source and Destination fields in the IP header to form some kind of attack. RFC 3704 details some issues related to how the tools of RFC 2827 can be best deployed over the Internet. Some of the details from those RFCs are as follows:

1. If a company has registered a particular IP prefix, packets with a source address inside that prefix should not be sent into that autonomous system from the Internet.

2. Packets should never have anything but a valid unicast source IP address, so packets with source IP addresses of loopback (127.0.0.1), 127.x.x.x, broadcast addresses, multicast addresses, and so on should be filtered.

3. Directed (subnet) broadcasts should not be allowed unless a specific need exists.

4. Packets for which no return route exists to the source IP address of the packet should be discarded (reverse-path-forwarding [RPF] check).

This section does not attempt to cover every portion of Layer 3 security, given the overall purpose of this book. The remainder of this chapter first provides some reference information regarding IP ACLs, which of course are often used to filter packets. This section ends with coverage of some of the more common Layer 3 attacks and how Layer 3 security can mitigate those attacks.

IP Access Control List Review

A relatively deep knowledge of IP ACL configuration and use is assumed to be prerequisite knowledge for readers of this book. In fact, many of the examples in the earlier sections of the book did not take the space required to explain the detailed logic of ACLs used in the examples. However, some reference information, as well as statements regarding some of the rules and practices regarding IP ACLs, is useful for general CCIE Routing and Switching exam study. Those details are presented in this section.

First, Table 9-7 lists the majority of the Cisco IOS commands related to IP ACLs.

Table 9-7   *IP ACL Command Reference*

Command	Configuration Mode and Description
access-list *access-list-number* {**deny** | **permit**} *source* [*source-wildcard*] [**log**]	Global command for standard numbered access lists.
access-list *access-list-number* [**dynamic** *dynamic-name* [**timeout** *minutes*]] {**deny** | **permit**} *protocol source source-wildcard destination destination-wildcard* [**precedence** *precedence*] [**tos** *tos*] [**log** | **log-input**] [**time-range** *time-range-name*] [**fragments**]	Generic syntax used with a wide variety of protocols. The options beginning with **precedence** are also included for TCP, UDP, and ICMP.
access-list *access-list-number* [**dynamic** *dynamic-name* [**timeout** *minutes*]] {**deny** | **permit**} **tcp** *source source-wildcard* [*operator* [*port*]] *destination destination-wildcard* [*operator* [*port*]] [**established**]	Version of **access-list** command with TCP-specific parameters; identical options exist for UDP, except for the **established** keyword.
access-list *access-list-number* {**deny** | **permit**} **icmp** *source source-wildcard destination destination-wildcard* [*icmp-type* [*icmp-code*] | *icmp-message*]	Version of **access-list** command to match ICMP packets.
access-list *access-list-number* **remark** *text*	Defines a remark.
ip access-list {**standard** | **extended**} *access-list-name*	Global command to create a named ACL.
[*sequence-number*] **permit** | **deny** *protocol source source-wildcard destination destination-wildcard* [**precedence** *precedence*] [**tos** *tos*] [**log** | **log-input**] [**time-range** *time-range-name*] [**fragments**]	Named ACL subcommand used to define an individual entry in the list; similar options for TCP, UDP, ICMP, and others.

Command	Configuration Mode and Description
ip access-group {*number* | *name* [**in** | **out**]}	Interface subcommand to enable access lists.
access-class *number* | *name* [**in** | **out**]	Line subcommand for standard or extended access lists.
ip access-list resequence *access-list-name* *starting-sequence-number increment*	Global command to redefine sequence numbers for a crowded ACL.
show ip interface [*type number*]	Includes a reference to the access lists enabled on the interface.
show access-lists [*access-list-number* | *access-list-name*]	Shows details of configured access lists for all protocols.
show ip access-list [*access-list-number* | *access-list-name*]	Shows IP access lists.

ACL Rule Summary

Cisco IOS processes the *Access Control Entries (ACE)* of an ACL sequentially, either permitting or denying a packet based on the first ACE matched by that packet in the ACL. For an individual ACE, all the configured values must match before the ACE is considered a match. Table 9-8 lists several examples of named IP ACL **permit** and **deny** commands that create an individual ACE, along with their meanings.

Key
Topic

Table 9-8   *Examples of ACL ACE Logic and Syntax*

Access List Statement	What It Matches
deny ip any host 10.1.1.1	IP packets with any source IP and destination IP = 10.1.1.1 only.
deny tcp any gt 1023 host 10.1.1.1 eq 23	IP packets with a TCP header, with any source IP, a source TCP port greater than (**gt**) 1023, plus a destination IP of 10.1.1.1 and a destination TCP port of 23.
deny tcp any host 10.1.1.1 eq 23	Same as previous example except that any source port matches, as that parameter was omitted.
deny tcp any host 10.1.1.1 eq telnet	Same results as the previous example; the syntax uses the **telnet** keyword instead of port 23.
deny udp 1.0.0.0 0.255.255.255 lt 1023 any	A packet with a source address in network 1.0.0.0/8, using UDP with a source port less than 1023, with any destination IP address.

The Port Number field is only matchable when the protocol type in an extended IP ACL ACE is UDP or TCP. In these cases, the port number is positional in that the source port matching parameter occurs right after the source IP address, and the destination port parameter occurs right after the destination IP address. Several examples were included in Table 9-8. Table 9-9 summarizes the matching logic used to match UDP and TCP ports.

Table 9-9 *IP ACE Port Matching*

Keyword	Meaning
gt	Greater than
lt	Less than
eq	Equals
ne	Not equal
range x-y	Range of port numbers, inclusive

ICMP does not use port numbers, but it does include different message types, and some of those even include a further message code. The IP ACL commands allow these to be matched using a rather long list of keywords, or with the numeric message type and message code. Note that these parameters are also positional, following the destination IP address. For example, the named ACL command **permit icmp any any echo-reply** is correct, but the command **permit icmp any echo-reply any** is syntactically incorrect and would be rejected.

Several other parameters can also be checked. For example, the IP precedence bits can be checked, as well as the entire ToS byte. The **established** parameter matches if the TCP header has the ACK flag set—indicative of any TCP segment except the first segment of a new connection setup. (The **established** keyword will be used in an example later in the chapter.) Also, the **log** and **log-input** keywords can be used to tell Cisco IOS to generate periodic log messages when the ACE is matched—one message on initial match and one every 5 minutes afterward. The **log-input** option includes more information than the **log** option, specifically information about the incoming interface of the packet that matched the ACE.

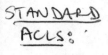

For ACL configuration, several facts need to be kept in mind. First, standard ACLs can only match the source IP address field. Numbered standard ACLs are identified with ACL numbers of either 1–99 or 1300–1999, inclusive. Extended numbered IP ACLs range from 100 to 199 and 2000 to 2699, again inclusive. Additionally, newly configured ACEs in numbered IP ACLs are always added at the end of the existing ACL, and ACEs in numbered IP ACLs cannot be deleted one at a time. As a result, to insert a line into the middle of a numbered ACL, the entire numbered ACL might need to be deleted (using the **no access-list** *number* global command) and then reconfigured. Named ACLs overcome that problem by using an implied or explicit sequence number, with Cisco IOS listing and processing the ACEs in an ACL in sequence number order.

Wildcard Masks

ACEs use *wildcard masks* (WC masks) to define the portion of the IP address that should be examined. WC masks represent a 32-bit number, with the mask's 0 bits telling Cisco IOS that those corresponding bits in the IP address must be compared when performing the matching logic. The binary 1s in the WC mask tell Cisco IOS that those bits do not need to be compared; as a result, these bits are often called "don't care" bits. Table 9-10 lists several example WC masks and the implied meanings.

Table 9-10 *Sample Access List Wildcard Masks*

Wildcard Mask	Description
0.0.0.0	The entire IP address must match.
0.0.0.255	Just the first 24 bits must match.
0.0.255.255	Just the first 16 bits must match.
0.255.255.255	Just the first 8 bits must match.
255.255.255.255	Automatically considered to match because all 32 bits are "don't care" bits.
0.0.15.255	Just the first 20 bits must match.
0.0.3.255	Just the first 22 bits must match.
17.44.97.33	A valid WC mask, it means match all bits except bits 4, 8, 11, 13, 14, 18, 19, 24, 27, and 32.

That last entry is unlikely to be useful in an actual production network, but unlike IP subnet masks, the WC mask does not have to list a single unbroken set of 0s and another unbroken string of 1s. A much more likely WC mask is one that matches a particular mask or prefix length. To find a WC mask to match hosts in a known prefix, use the following simple math: In decimal, subtract the subnet mask from 255.255.255.255. The result is the "right" WC mask to match that prefix length. For example, a subnet mask of 255.255.255.0, subtracted from 255.255.255.255, gives you 0.0.0.255 as a WC mask. This mask only checks the first 24 bits—which in this case is the network and subnet part of the address. Similarly, if the subnet mask is 255.255.240.0, subtracting from 255.255.255.255 gives you 0.0.15.255.

General Layer 3 Security Considerations

This section explains a few of the more common ways to avoid Layer 3 attacks.

Smurf Attacks, Directed Broadcasts, and RPF Checks

A smurf attack occurs when a host sends a large number of ICMP Echo Requests with some atypical IP addresses in the packet. The destination address is a *subnet broadcast*

[handwritten left margin: to affect all the IPs the broadcast reaches]

address, also known as a *directed broadcast address*. Routers forward these packets based on normal matching of the IP routing table, until the packet reaches a router connected to the destination subnet. This final router then forwards the packet onto the LAN as a LAN broadcast, sending a copy to every device. Figure 9-9 shows how the attack develops.

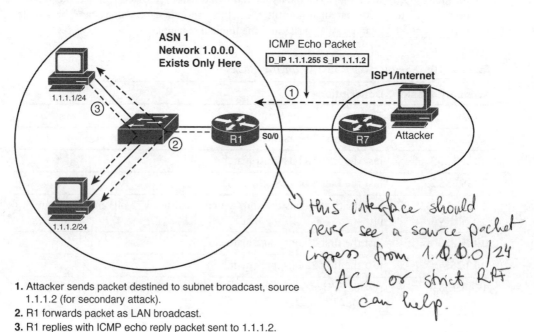

[handwritten note near figure: this interface should never see a source packet ingress from 1.0.0.0/24 ACL or strict RPF can help.]

1. Attacker sends packet destined to subnet broadcast, source 1.1.1.2 (for secondary attack).
2. R1 forwards packet as LAN broadcast.
3. R1 replies with ICMP echo reply packet sent to 1.1.1.2.

Figure 9-9   *Smurf Attack*

[handwritten left margin: to affect a target IP using a spoofed IP]

The other feature of a smurf attack is that the source IP address of the packet sent by the attacker is the IP address of the attacked host. For example, in Figure 9-9, many hosts can receive the ICMP Echo Request at Step 2. All those hosts then reply with an Echo Reply, sending it to 10.1.1.2—the address that was the source IP address of the original ICMP Echo at Step 1. Host 10.1.1.2 receives a potentially large number of packets.

[handwritten left margin: no directed broadcast]

Several solutions to this problem exist. First, as of Cisco IOS Software Release 12.0, IOS defaults each interface to use the **no ip directed-broadcast** command, which prevents the router from forwarding the broadcast onto the LAN (Step 2 in Figure 9-9). Also, a unicast Reverse-Path-Forwarding (uRPF) check could be enabled using the **ip verify unicast source reachable-via** {rx | any} [allow-default] [allow-self-ping] [*list*] interface subcommand. This command tells Cisco IOS to examine the source IP address of incoming packets on that interface. (Cisco Express Forwarding [CEF] must be enabled for uRPF to work.) Two styles of check can be made with this command:

Key Topic

- **Strict RPF:** Using the **rx** keyword, the router checks to see whether the matching route uses an outgoing interface that is the same interface on which the packet was received. If not, the packet is discarded. (An example scenario using Figure 9-9 will be explained shortly.)

■ **Loose RPF:** Using the **any** keyword, the router checks for any route that can be used to reach the source IP address.

The command can also ignore default routes when it performs the check (default) or use default routes when performing the check by including the **allow-default** keyword. Also, although not recommended, the command can trigger a ping to the source to verify connectivity. Finally, the addresses for which the RPF check is made can be limited by a referenced ACL. In the following example, both CEF and uRPF are enabled on R1 in Figure 9-9:

```
R1(config)# ip cef
R1(config)# int s 0/0
R1(config-if)# ip verify unicast source reachable-via rx allow-default
```

Now, because R1 in Figure 9-9 uses strict uRPF on s0/0, it would notice that its route to reach 1.1.1.2 (the source IP address of the packet at Step 1) did not refer to s0/0 as the outgoing interface—thereby discarding the packet. However, with loose RPF, R1 would have found a connected route that matched 1.1.1.2, so it would have allowed the packet through. Finally, given that AS1 should never receive packets with source addresses in network 1.0.0.0, as it owns that entire class A network, R1 could simply use an inbound ACL to discard any packets sourced from 1.0.0.0/8 as they enter s0/0 from the Internet.

Fraggle attacks use similar logic as smurf attacks, but instead of ICMP, fraggle attacks use the UDP Echo application. These attacks can be defeated using the same options as listed for smurf attacks.

Inappropriate IP Addresses

Besides smurf and fraggle attacks, other attacks involve the use of what can be generally termed inappropriate IP addresses, both for the source IP address and destination IP address. By using inappropriate IP addresses, the attacker can remain hidden and elicit cooperation of other hosts to create a distributed denial of service (DDoS) attack.

One of the Layer 3 security best practices is to use ACLs to filter packets whose IP addresses are not appropriate. For example, the smurf attack listed a valid source IP address of 1.1.1.2, but packets with that source address should never enter AS1 from the Internet. The Internet Assigned Numbers Authority (IANA) manages the assignment of IP prefix ranges. It lists the assigned ranges in a document found at www.iana.org/assignments/ipv4-address-space. A router can then be configured with ACLs that prevent packets based on known assigned ranges and on known unassigned ranges. For example, in Figure 9-9, an enterprise router should never need to forward a packet onto the Internet if that packet has a source IP address from another company's registered IP prefix. In the smurf attack case, such an ACL used at the attacker's ISP would have prevented the first packet from getting to AS1.

Routers should also filter packets that use IP addresses that should be considered bogus or inappropriate. For example, a packet should never have a broadcast or multicast source IP address in normal use. Also, an enterprise router should never receive a packet from an ISP with that packet's source IP address being a private network per RFC 1918. Additionally, that same router should not receive packets sourced from IP addresses in ranges currently unallocated by IANA. These types of IP addresses are frequently called *bogons*, which is a derivation of the word bogus.

Creating an ACL to match these bogon IP addresses is not particularly difficult, but it does require a lot of administrative effort, particularly to update it based on changes to IANA's assigned prefixes. You can use freeware called the Router Audit Tool (RAT) that makes recommendations for router security, including bogon ACLs. You can also use the Cisco IOS *AutoSecure* feature, which automatically configures ACLs to prevent the use of such bogus IP addresses.

[Handwritten margin note: Cisco AUTOSECURE]

TCP SYN Flood, the Established Bit, and TCP Intercept

A TCP SYN flood is an attack directed at servers by initiating large numbers of TCP connections, but not completing the connections. Essentially, the attacker initiates many TCP connections, each with only the TCP SYN flag set, as usual. The server then sends a reply (with TCP SYN and ACK flags set)—but then the attacker simply does not reply with the expected third message in the three-way TCP connection setup flow. The server consumes memory and resources while waiting on its timeouts to occur before clearing up the partially initialized connections. The server might also reject additional TCP connections, and load balancers in front of a server farm might unbalance the load of actual working connections as well.

Stateful firewalls can prevent TCP SYN attacks. Both the Cisco ASA Firewall and the Cisco IOS Firewall feature set (discussed in the next section) can be used to do this. The impact of TCP SYN attacks can be reduced or eliminated by using a few other tools in Cisco IOS.

One way to prevent SYN attacks is to simply filter packets whose TCP header shows only the SYN flag set—in other words, filter all packets that are the first packet in a new TCP connection. In many cases, a router should not allow TCP connections to be established by a client on one side to a server on the other, as shown in Figure 9-10. In these cases, filtering the initial TCP segment prevents the SYN attack.

[Handwritten margin note: One solution to use the ESTABLISHED keyword]

Cisco IOS ACLs cannot directly match the TCP SYN flag. However, an ACE can use the **established** keyword, which matches TCP segments that have the ACK flag set. The **established** keyword essentially matches all TCP segments except the very first TCP segment in a new connection. Example 9-13 shows the configuration that would be used on R1 to deny new connection requests from the Internet into the network on the left.

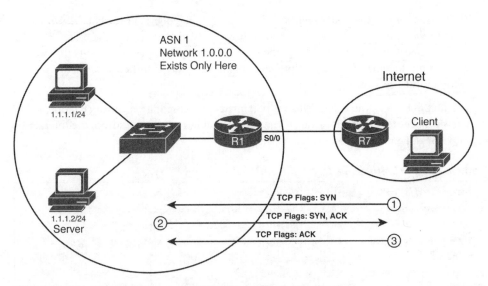

Figure 9-10 *Example Network: TCP Clients in the Internet*

Example 9-13 *Using an ACL with the* **established** *Keyword*

```
! The first ACE matches TCP segments that are not the first segment, and permits
! them. The second ACE matches all TCP segments between the same set of IP
! addresses, but because all non-initial segments have already been matched, the
! second ACE only matches the initial segments.
ip access-list extended prevent-syn
 permit tcp any 1.0.0.0 0.255.255.255 established
 deny tcp any 1.0.0.0 0.255.255.255
 permit (whatever)
!
interface s0/0
 ip access-group prevent-syn in
```

The ACL works well when clients outside a network are not allowed to make TCP connections into the network. However, in cases where some inbound TCP connections are allowed, this ACL cannot be used. Another Cisco IOS feature, called *TCP intercept*, provides an alternative that allows TCP connections into the network, but monitors those TCP connections for TCP SYN attacks.

TCP intercept operates in one of two different modes. In *watch mode*, it keeps state information about TCP connections that match a defined ACL. If a TCP connection does not complete the three-way handshake within a particular time period, TCP intercept sends a TCP reset to the server, cleaning up the connection. It also counts the number of new connections attempted over time, and if a large number occurs in 1 second ("large" defaulting to 1100), the router temporarily filters new TCP requests to prevent a perceived SYN attack.

— default [handwritten annotation above "Switching"]

PROXYING BTW THE SERVER & THE FW [handwritten annotation in left margin]

In *intercept mode,* the router replies to TCP connection requests instead of forwarding them to the actual server. Then, if the three-way handshake completes, the router creates a TCP connection between itself and the server. At that point, the router knits the two connections together. This takes more processing and effort, but it provides better protection for the servers.

Example 9-14 shows an example using TCP intercept configuration, in watch mode, plus a few changes to its default settings. The example allows connections from the Internet into AS1 in Figure 9-10.

Example 9-14 *Configuring TCP Intercept*

```
! The following command enables TCP intercept for packets matching ACL
! match-tcp-from-internet. Also, the mode is set to watch, rather than the
! default of intercept. Finally, the watch timeout has been reset from the
! default of 30 seconds; if the TCP connection remains incomplete as of the
! 20-second mark, TCP intercept resets the connection.
ip tcp intercept list match-tcp-from-internet
ip tcp intercept mode watch
ip tcp intercept watch-timeout 20
! The ACL matches packets sent into 1.0.0.0/8 that are TCP. It is referenced by
! the ip tcp intercept-list command listed above.
ip access-list extended match-tcp-from-internet
 permit tcp any 1.0.0.0 0.255.255.255
! Note below that the ACL is not enabled on any interfaces.
interface s0/0
! Note: there is no ACL enabled on the interface!
```

→ default is 30s [handwritten annotation beside "ip tcp intercept watch-timeout 20"]

Classic Cisco IOS Firewall

In some cases, access-list filtering might be enough to control and secure a router interface. However, as attackers have become more sophisticated, Cisco has developed better tools to deal with threats. The challenge, as always, is to make security features relatively transparent to network users while thwarting attackers. The Cisco IOS Firewall is one of those tools.

The classic IOS Firewall relies on *Context-Based Access Control (CBAC)*. CBAC is a function of the firewall feature set in Cisco IOS. It takes access-list filtering a step or two further by providing dynamic inspection of traffic that you specify as it traverses the router. It does this based on actual protocol commands, such as the FTP **get** command—not simply on Layer 4 port numbers. Based on where the traffic originates, CBAC decides what traffic should be permitted to cross the firewall. When it sees a session initiate on the trusted network for a particular protocol, which would normally be blocked inbound based on other filtering methods, CBAC creates temporary openings in the firewall to permit the corresponding inbound traffic to enter from the untrusted network. It permits only the desired traffic, rather than opening the firewall to all traffic for a particular protocol.

CBAC works on TCP and UDP traffic, and it supports protocols such as FTP that require multiple, simultaneous sessions or connections. You would typically use CBAC to protect your internal network from external threats by configuring it to inspect inbound traffic from the outside world for those protocols. With CBAC, you configure the following:

- Protocols to inspect

- Interfaces on which to perform the inspection

- Direction of the traffic to inspect, per interface

TCP Versus UDP with CBAC

TCP has clear-cut connections, so CBAC (and other stateful inspection and filtering methods) can handle it rather easily. However, CBAC works at a deeper level than simply protocols and port numbers. For example, with FTP traffic, CBAC recognizes and inspects the specific FTP control-channel commands to decide when to open and close the temporary firewall openings.

By comparison to TCP, UDP traffic is connectionless and therefore more difficult to handle. CBAC manages UDP by approximating based on factors such as whether the source and destination addresses and ports of UDP frames are the same as those that came recently, and their relative timing. You can configure a global idle timeout that CBAC uses to determine whether a segment arrived "close enough" in time to be considered part of the same flow. You can also configure other timeouts, including protocol-specific timeouts for TCP and UDP traffic.

Cisco IOS Firewall Protocol Support

When using CBAC, an IOS firewall can inspect a long list of protocols, and more are added over time. Common protocols that CBAC can inspect include the following:

- Any generic TCP session, regardless of application layer protocol

- All UDP "sessions"

- FTP

- SMTP

- TFTP

- H.323 (NetMeeting, ProShare, and so on)

- Java

- CU-SeeMe

- UNIX R commands (**rlogin, rexec, rsh**, and so on)

- RealAudio

- Sun RPC

- SQL*Net

- StreamWorks

- VDOLive

CBAC

Cisco IOS Firewall Caveats

As powerful as CBAC is for dynamic inspection and filtering, however, it has some limitations. You should be aware of a few restrictions and caveats about how CBAC works:

- CBAC comes after access-list filters are applied to an interface. If an access list blocks a particular type of traffic on an interface where you are using CBAC to inspect inbound traffic, that traffic will be denied before CBAC sees it.

- CBAC cannot protect against attacks that originate inside your network, where most attacks originate.

- CBAC works only on protocols that you specify it should inspect, leaving all other filtering to access lists and other filtering methods.

- To inspect traffic other than TCP- and UDP-transported traffic, you must configure a named inspection rule.

- CBAC does not inspect traffic destined to or originated from the firewall router itself, only traffic that traverses the firewall router.

- CBAC has restrictions on handling encrypted traffic. See the link in the "Further Reading" section, later in this chapter, for more details.

Cisco IOS Firewall Configuration Steps

Although configuring CBAC is not difficult, it does involve several steps, which are as follows:

Step 1. Choose an interface ("inside" or "outside").

Step 2. Configure an IP access list that denies all traffic to be inspected.

Step 3. Configure global timeouts and thresholds using the **ip inspect** commands.

Step 4. Define an inspection rule and an optional rule-specific timeout value using the **ip inspect name** *protocol* commands, for example, **ip inspect name actionjackson ftp timeout 3600**.

Step 5. Apply the inspection rule to an interface, for example, in interface configuration mode, **ip inspect actionjackson in**.

Step 6. Apply the access list to the same interface as the inspection rule, but in the opposite direction (inbound or outbound.)

Example 9-15 shows a router with one interface into the internal network and one interface into the external network. CBAC will be used on the external interface. This router has been configured to inspect all ICMP, TCP, and UDP traffic, using the inspection list CLASSIC_FW. TCP and UDP sessions will time out after 30 seconds, but ICMP sessions will time out after only 10 seconds. The access list IOS_FW permits routing traffic but denies all traffic that will be inspected by CBAC. The inspection rule is applied to the external interface, outbound. The access list is applied to that same interface, inbound. All TCP, UDP, and ICMP traffic bound out of the serial interface toward a host in the external network will be tracked. If an answering packet arrives, it will be allowed through via a dynamic entry in access list IOS_FW. Any external hosts that try to establish a session with an internal host will be blocked by access list IOS_FW, however.

The IOS firewall's operation is verified with the **show ip inspect sessions** command. Note that one Telnet session has been established.

Example 9-15 *Configuring Classic IOS Firewall with CBAC*

```
ip inspect name CLASSIC_FW icmp timeout 10
ip inspect name CLASSIC_FW tcp timeout 30
ip inspect name CLASSIC_FW udp timeout 30
!
ip access-list extended IOS_FW
 permit eigrp any any
 deny   tcp any any
 deny   udp any any
 deny   icmp any any
!
interface Serial0/0
 ip address 192.168.1.3 255.255.255.0
 ip access-group IOS_FW in          ← inbound
 ip inspect CLASSIC_FW out           opposite direction to the traffic
!
R2# show ip inspect sessions
Established Sessions
 Session 47699CFC (10.1.1.2:11003)=>(172.16.1.10:23) tcp SIS_OPEN
```

CBAC is a powerful IOS firewall feature set option that you should understand at the functional level before attempting the CCIE Routing and Switching qualifying exam. See the "Further Reading" section, later in this chapter, for a link to more information and configuration details on CBAC.

Cisco IOS Zone-Based Firewall

You can see from Example 9-15 that configuring even a simple classic IOS firewall can be complex. Also, classic IOS inspection policies apply to all traffic on the interface; you can't apply different policies to different groups of users.

Zone-based firewall (ZFW), available in IOS Release 12.4(6)T or later, changes that. The concept behind zone-based firewalls is similar to that used by appliance firewalls. Router interfaces are placed into security zones. Traffic can travel freely between interfaces in the same zone, but is blocked by default from traveling between zones. Traffic is also blocked between interfaces that have been assigned to a security zone and those that have not. You must explicitly apply a policy to allow traffic between zones. Zone policies are configured using the Class-Based Policy Language (CPL), which is similar to the Modular QoS Command-Line Interface (MQC) in its use of class maps and policy maps. Class maps let you configure highly granular policies if needed. A new class and policy map type, the *inspect* type, is introduced for use with zone-based firewalls.

NOTE   The MQC, class maps, and policy maps are explained in Chapter 3, "Classification and Marking."

ZFW enables the inspection and control of multiple protocols, including the following:

- HTTP and HTTPS

- SMTP, Extended SMTP (ESMTP), POP3, and IMAP

- Peer-to-peer applications, with the ability to use heuristics to track port hopping

- Instant-messaging applications (AOL, Yahoo!, and MSN as of this writing)

- Remote Procedure Calls (RPC)

Follow these steps to configure ZFW:

Step 1.   Decide the zones you will need, and create them on the router.

Step 2.   Decide how traffic should travel between the zones, and create zone-pairs on the router.

Step 3.   Create class maps to identify the interzone traffic that must be inspected by the firewall.

Step 4.   Assign policies to the traffic by creating policy maps and associating class maps with them.

Step 5.   Assign the policy maps to the appropriate zone-pair.

Step 6.   Assign interfaces to zones. An interface can be assigned to only one security zone.

To help you understand these steps, consider the network shown in Figure 9-11. Router Branch1 has two interfaces: a serial WAN interface and an Ethernet LAN interface. This is a simple example but one common in small branch offices where an IOS firewall might be used. The LAN interface will be placed in one zone, the LAN zone, and the WAN interface will be placed into the WAN zone.

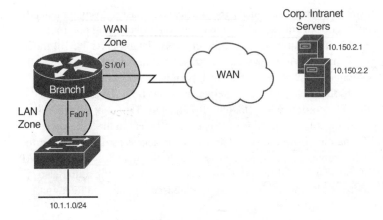

Figure 9-11 *Cisco IOS Zone-Based Firewall*

In this example, the network administrators have decided to apply the following policies to traffic from the LAN zone going through the WAN zone:

■ Only traffic from the LAN subnet is allowed.

■ HTTP traffic to corporate web-based intranet servers is allowed.

■ All other HTTP traffic is allowed but policed to 1 Mbps.

■ ICMP is blocked.

■ For all other traffic, the TCP and UDP timeouts must be lowered to 300 seconds.

For traffic initiated in the WAN zone and destined for the LAN zone, only SSH from the corporate management network is allowed.

So, you can see that you must configure two zones: LAN and WAN. The router automatically creates a zone for traffic to itself, called the *self zone*. By default, all traffic is allowed to and from this zone, but that can be configured. In this example, firewall policies will be applied to traffic from the LAN to the WAN zone, and also to traffic from the WAN to the LAN zone. Therefore, you need two zone pairs: LAN-to-WAN and WAN-to-LAN. To configure zones, use the global command **zone security** *name*. To configure zone pairs, use the global command **zone-pair security** *name* **source** *source-zone-name* **destination** *destination-zone-name*. Example 9-16 shows Steps 1 and 2: the zone and zone pair configuration.

Example 9-16 *Configuring ZFW Zones and Zone Pairs*

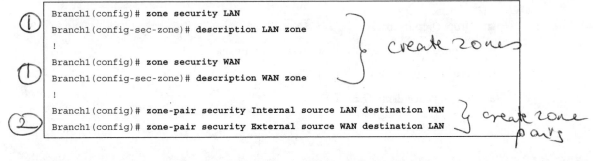

```
Branch1(config)# zone security LAN
Branch1(config-sec-zone)# description LAN zone
!
Branch1(config)# zone security WAN
Branch1(config-sec-zone)# description WAN zone
!
Branch1(config)# zone-pair security Internal source LAN destination WAN
Branch1(config)# zone-pair security External source WAN destination LAN
```

The next step is to create class maps to identify the traffic. Four class maps will be needed: three for the specific types of traffic that will have custom policies and one for all other traffic from the LAN. The router automatically creates a default class, but all traffic in this class is dropped. Example 9-17 shows access lists LAN_Subnet, which permits all traffic from the LAN subnet, and Web_Servers, which permits traffic to the corporate intranet web servers. Note that class map Corp_Servers matches both the access list Web_Servers and the HTTP protocol with a **match-all** statement. Thus, both the access list and the protocol type must be matched for the class map to have a hit. Likewise, class map Other_HTTP matches both the HTTP protocol and access list LAN_Subnet to permit only HTTP traffic from the local subnet. Class map ICMP matches only the ICMP protocol; because that traffic will be dropped, there is no need to have the router also check the source IP address. The router will use Network-Based Application Recognition (NBAR) to match HTTP and ICMP traffic.

Example 9-17 *Configuring ZFW Class Maps*

```
Branch1(config)# ip access-list extended LAN_Subnet
Branch1(config-ext-nacl)# permit ip 10.1.1.0 0.0.0.255 any
!
Branch1(config-ext-nacl)# ip access-list extended Web_Servers
Branch1(config-ext-nacl)# permit tcp 10.1.1.0 0.0.0.255 host 10.150.2.1
Branch1(config-ext-nacl)# permit tcp 10.1.1.0 0.0.0.255 host 10.150.2.2
!
Branch1(config-ext-nacl)# class-map type inspect match-all Corp_Servers
Branch1(config-cmap)# match access-group name Web_Servers
Branch1(config-cmap)# match protocol http
!
Branch1(config-cmap)# class-map type inspect Other_HTTP
Branch1(config-cmap)# match protocol http
Branch1(config-cmap)# match access-group name LAN_Subnet
!
Branch1(config-cmap)# class-map type inspect ICMP
Branch1(config-cmap)# match protocol icmp
!
Branch1(config-cmap)# class-map type inspect Other_Traffic
Branch1(config-cmap)# match access-group name LAN_Subnet
```

In Step 4, the previously created class maps are associated with policy maps. ZFW policy maps can take the following actions under each class:

- **Drop:** Drop the packet

- **Inspect:** Use Context-Based Access Control Engine

- **Pass:** Pass the packet

- **Police:** Police the traffic

- **Service-policy:** Use Deep Packet Inspection Engine

- **Urlfilter:** Use URL Filtering Engine

Recall that the TCP and UDP timers needed to be reduced to 300 seconds for the general network traffic. This is done through a parameter map. A parameter map modifies the traffic inspection behavior for a specific class in a policy map. In Example 9-18, the parameter map Timeouts sets the TCP and UDP idle timeouts to 300 seconds. Parameter maps can also set alerts and audit trails, and they control other session parameters such as number of half-open sessions. The policy map LAN2WAN associates all the class maps created so far, and applies the parameter map to the Other_Traffic class. It also polices Other_HTTP traffic to 1 Mbps with a burst rate of 8 KBps. Note that policy map configuration also uses the **type inspect** keywords.

Example 9-18 *Configuring ZFW Parameter Maps and Policy Maps*

```
Branch1(config)# parameter-map type inspect Timeouts
Branch1(config-profile)# tcp idle-time 300
Branch1(config-profile)# udp idle-time 300
!
Branch1(config-profile)# policy-map type inspect LAN2WAN
Branch1(config-pmap)# class type inspect Corp_Servers
Branch1(config-pmap-c)# inspect
!
Branch1(config-pmap-c)# class type inspect Other_HTTP
Branch1(config-pmap-c)# inspect
Branch1(config-pmap-c)# police rate 1000000 burst 8000
!
Branch1(config-pmap-c)# class type inspect ICMP
Branch1(config-pmap-c)# drop
!
Branch1(config-pmap-c)# class type inspect Other_Traffic
Branch1(config-pmap-c)# inspect Timeouts
%No specific protocol configured in class Other_Traffic for inspection. All
   protocols will be inspected
```

In Step 5, now that the policy is created, it must be assigned to a zone pair. This is analogous to assigning a service policy to an interface in the MQC. The command is **service-policy type inspect** *policy-map-name*, given under the zone pair configuration mode.

The final step, Step 6, is to assign the router interfaces to their appropriate zones. To do this, issue the command **zone-member security** *zone-name* in interface configuration mode. Looking back at Figure 9-11, you see that interface FastEthernet 0/1 connects to the LAN and interface Serial 1/0/1 connects to the WAN. Example 9-19 shows how the service policy is assigned to a zone pair, and the two interfaces are assigned to zones.

Example 9-19 *Assigning ZFW Service Policies and Zones*

```
Branch1(config)# zone-pair security Internal source LAN destination WAN
Branch1(config-sec-zone-pair)# service-policy type inspect LAN2WAN
Branch1(config-sec-zone-pair)# exit
!
Branch1(config)# interface fa 0/1
Branch1(config-if)# zone-member security LAN
!
Branch1(config-if)# interface s1/0/1
Branch1(config-if)# zone-member security WAN
!
!Verify the configuration
Branch1# show zone-pair security
Zone-pair name Internal
    Source-Zone LAN  Destination-Zone WAN
    service-policy LAN2WAN
Zone-pair name External
    Source-Zone WAN  Destination-Zone LAN
    service-policy not configured
```

[Handwritten annotations: "⑤ put the service-pol under the zonepair", "← assign the interface to the zones"]

So far you have seen some fairly complex firewall policies created and applied to traffic bound from the local LAN to the WAN. At this point, only responses can reach into the LAN. Another class map and service policy would need to be created to allow SSH sessions to be initiated from the WAN into the LAN. Then the policy map would be applied to the External zone pair. That configuration is not shown here, but would be a good exercise for you to do, to ensure that you understand the concepts behind ZFW.

Control-Plane Policing

[Handwritten annotation: "Zone-Based firewall"]

Firewalls and access lists affect traffic moving through the router, but what about traffic bound to the router itself? In the previous section, you saw that zone-based firewalls have a default "self-zone" that allows all traffic to it. You can apply an access list to the vty lines. But routers and switches must handle a variety of traffic, including BPDUs, routing updates, HSRP, CDP, CEF, process-switched packets, ARP, and management traffic such as SSH, SNMP, and RADIUS. All of these are processed by the router or switch's *control plane.* This raises the possibility that excessive traffic from any of these sources could overload the control plane and prevent the processing of other traffic. Whether that overload is caused by a malicious attacker or by accident, the result is still the same.

Control-plane policing (CoPP) addresses this problem by leveraging the MQC to rate-limit or drop control-plane traffic. Grouping types of traffic into class maps and then applying policies through a policy map allows you much greater control over the amounts and types of traffic processed by the control plane. As of this writing, CoPP is supported on most Cisco routers and multilayer switches.

NOTE   The MQC, class maps, and policy maps are explained in Chapter 3, "Classification and Marking."

Preparing for CoPP Implementation

Planning is the key to a successful CoPP implementation. You don't want to set the allowed rate for a class so low that important traffic is dropped, or so high that the processor is overworked. You also need to be careful in the way that you group traffic types to form classes. For example, perhaps you put all management traffic together in one class. Then an excess amount of one type of traffic could prevent you from using SSH to the router. On the other hand, placing each type of traffic into its own class would be unwieldy and very complex.

A typical procedure is to configure the class maps and then initially allow all traffic to be transmitted in the policy map. You would then monitor the traffic until you had a good idea of typical amounts for each class. It is important that you have an accurate picture of the expected router control-plane traffic. Otherwise you might, for example, configure CoPP on a Layer 3 switch, which then starts dropping BPDUs and creates a spanning-tree loop in the network.

As with a QoS implementation, you should carefully consider the number of classes, the types of traffic that will be grouped into each class, and the bandwidth allowed per class. Each network is different, but a typical grouping might be as follows:

- Malicious traffic, which is dropped. This is usually fragmented packets or packets using ports associated with known malicious programs.

- Routing protocols class, which is not limited.

- SSH and Telnet, limited to a small amount but enough to ensure connectivity when needed.

- Other management protocols such as SNMP, FTP, and TFTP.

- Network applications such as HSRP, DHCP, IGMP, and so on, if used.

- All other IP traffic.

- Default class, which would include Layer 2 protocols. The only Layer 2 protocol that can be explicitly assigned to a class in CoPP is ARP. All other Layer 2 protocols fall under the default class.

The only **match** options that can be used with CoPP class maps are IP precedence, DSCP, and access lists. You will likely configure a series of access lists to use in classifying traffic. Keep in mind that most routers only support policing of inbound traffic, so configure your access lists accordingly.

Implementing CoPP

After you have planned the classes to use and the initial amount of bandwidth to allow for each, use the following steps to implement CoPP:

Step 1. Create the access lists to classify traffic. A **permit** statement allows matching traffic to be placed into the class. A **deny** statement causes matching traffic to be evaluated by the next class map.

Step 2. Create the class maps and match the appropriate access lists, or either IP Precedence or DSCP values.

Step 3. Create a policy map and associate the class maps with it. Be aware that the class map statements in a policy map are evaluated from the top down. For this reason, you will likely place the malicious class at the top of the policy map to drop that traffic immediately.

Step 4. Under each class in the policy map, assign an allowed bandwidth amount and then specify a conform action and an exceed action. When you first implement CoPP, both of these actions will often be set to **transmit**. After monitoring for a period of time, the bandwidth amounts can be tuned and then the exceed action can be set to **drop** (except for the routing protocols.)

Step 5. Assign the policy map to the router or switch's control plane as a service policy.

Example 9-20 shows a CoPP implementation and a command to verify the actions of CoPP. In the interest of space, this is just a simple example showing three classes and simple access lists. Your implementation will likely be much more complex.

Example 9-20   *Implementing Control-Plane Policing*

```
!
!Access lists to classify the traffic
Extended IP access list BAD_STUFF
    10 permit tcp any any eq 5554 !Sasser worm port
    20 permit tcp any any eq 9996 !Sasser worm port
    30 permit ip any any fragments
!
Extended IP access list INTERACTIVE
    10 permit tcp 10.17.4.0 0.0.3.255 host 10.17.3.1 eq 22
    20 permit tcp 10.17.4.0 0.0.3.255 eq 22 host 10.17.3.1 established
!
Extended IP access list ROUTING
    10 permit tcp host 172.20.1.1 gt 1024 host 10.17.3.1 eq bgp
    20 permit tcp host 172.20.1.1 eq bgp host 10.17.3.1 gt 1024 established
    30 permit eigrp 10.17.4.0 0.0.3.255 host 10.17.3.1
!
!CoPP class maps
```

```
Class Map match-all CoPP_ROUTING (id 0)
   Match access-group name ROUTING

 Class Map match-all CoPP_BAD_STUFF (id 1)
   Match access-group name BAD_STUFF

 Class Map match-all CoPP_INTERACTIVE (id 2)
   Match access-group name INTERACTIVE
!
!CoPP policy map. Note that both the conform and the exceed actions
!are "transmit" for all classes except CoPP_BAD_STUFF. The class
!CoPP_ROUTING will continue to be "transmit" but after sufficient
!monitoring the CoPP_INTERACTIVE and default classess will be tuned
!and then "drop" will be configured as the exceed action
Policy Map CoPP
     Class CoPP_BAD_STUFF
       police cir 8000 bc 1500
         conform-action drop
         exceed-action drop
     Class CoPP_ROUTING
       police cir 200000 bc 6250
         conform-action transmit
         exceed-action transmit
     Class CoPP_INTERACTIVE
       police cir 10000 bc 1500
         conform-action transmit
         exceed-action transmit
     Class class-default
       police cir 10000 bc 1500
         conform-action transmit
         exceed-action transmit
   !
   !The CoPP policy applied to the device control plane
   control-plane
     service-policy input CoPP
   !
   !Verify the policy and its effects
R1# show policy-map control-plane
   Control Plane

     Service-policy input: CoPP

       Class-map: CoPP_BAD_STUFF (match-all)
continues
         14 packets, 832 bytes
         5 minute offered rate 0 bps, drop rate 0 bps
```

[Handwritten annotations: arrow pointing to "control-plane / service-policy input CoPP" — "this is how to add the service policy to the control plane"; arrow pointing to "show policy-map control-plane" — "Verification"]

```
      Match: access-group name BAD_STUFF
      police:
          cir 8000 bps, bc 1500 bytes
        conformed 14 packets, 832 bytes; actions:
          drop
        exceeded 0 packets, 0 bytes; actions:
          drop
        conformed 0 bps, exceed 0 bps

  Class-map: CoPP_ROUTING (match-all)
    0 packets, 0 bytes
    5 minute offered rate 0 bps, drop rate 0 bps
    Match: access-group name ROUTING
    police:
          cir 200000 bps, bc 6250 bytes
        conformed 0 packets, 0 bytes; actions:
          transmit
        exceeded 0 packets, 0 bytes; actions:
          transmit
        conformed 0 bps, exceed 0 bps

  Class-map: CoPP_INTERACTIVE (match-all)
    0 packets, 0 bytes
    5 minute offered rate 0 bps, drop rate 0 bps
    Match: access-group name INTERACTIVE
    police:
          cir 10000 bps, bc 1500 bytes
        conformed 0 packets, 0 bytes; actions:
          transmit
        exceeded 0 packets, 0 bytes; actions:
          transmit
        conformed 0 bps, exceed 0 bps

  Class-map: class-default (match-any)
    0 packets, 0 bytes
    5 minute offered rate 0 bps, drop rate 0 bps
    Match: any
    police:
          cir 10000 bps, bc 1500 bytes
        conformed 0 packets, 0 bytes; actions:
          transmit
        exceeded 0 packets, 0 bytes; actions:
          transmit
        conformed 0 bps, exceed 0 bps
```

Dynamic Multipoint VPN

IPsec is a commonly implemented method of forming secure tunnels from site to site or from remote users to a central site. However, it has limitations. In a site-to-site, hub-and-spoke environment, for example, all VPN traffic from spoke to spoke must traverse the hub site, where it must be unencrypted, routed, and then encrypted again. This is a lot of work for a VPN Concentrator, especially in a large environment with many spoke sites where a lot of traffic must flow between spokes. One result is additional network overhead and memory and CPU requirements at the central site. Another is significant configuration complexity at the hub router.

drawbacks of IPSec VPN

Dynamic Multipoint VPN (DMVPN) takes advantage of IPsec, GRE tunnels, and Next Hop Resolution Protocol (NHRP) to make IPsec scale better in a hub-and-spoke environment. DMVPN also supports traffic segmentation across VPNs and is VRF aware.

DMVPN better scaleable in this scenario

In a typical hub-and-spoke IPsec VPN environment, the hub router must have separate, statically configured crypto maps, crypto access lists, GRE tunnels, and **isakmp peer** statements for each spoke router. This is one of the limits of traditional hub-and-spoke VPN scalability that DMVPN eliminates. In a DMVPN environment, the spoke router connection information is not explicitly configured on the hub router. Instead, the hub router is configured for a single multipoint GRE (mGRE) tunnel interface and a set of profiles that apply to the spoke routers. Each spoke router points to one or more hubs, facilitating redundancy and load sharing. DMVPN additionally supports multicast traffic from hub to spoke routers.

The benefits of DMVPN compared to a traditional IPsec hub-and-spoke VPN environment include these:

Benefits of DMPVN

Key
Topic

- Simpler hub router configuration. A DMVPN hub router requires only one multipoint GRE tunnel interface, one IPsec profile, and no crypto access lists.

- Zero-touch at the hub router for provisioning spoke routers. The hub router does not require configuration when new spoke routers are brought online.

- Automatically initiated IPsec encryption, facilitated by NHRP.

- Dynamic addressing support for spoke routers. Instead of static configuration, the hub learns spoke router addresses when they register to the network.

- Dynamically created spoke-to-spoke tunnels. Spoke routers learn about each other using NHRP so that they can form tunnels between each other automatically instead of requiring spoke-to-spoke traffic to be encrypted, unencrypted, and routed at the hub router.

- VRF integration for MPLS environments.

A dynamic routing protocol (EIGRP, OSPF, BGP, RIP, or even ODR for small deployments) is required between the hub and the spokes. (Cisco recommends a distance vector protocol and therefore prefers EIGRP for large-scale deployments.) This is how spoke routers learn about the networks at other spoke routers. In a DMVPN environment, the next-hop IP address for a spoke network is the tunnel interface for that spoke.

Figure 9-12 shows a DMVPN network with one hub and three spoke routers. In this network, each spoke router has a permanent IPsec tunnel to the hub router. Each of the spokes, which are NHRP clients, registers with the NHRP server (the hub router). When a spoke router needs to send traffic to a private network on another spoke router, which it has learned about by using the dynamic routing protocol running between the hub and the spokes, that spoke router queries the NHRP server in the hub router for the outside IP address of the destination spoke router. When the NHRP server returns that information, the originating spoke router initiates a dynamic IPsec tunnel to the other spoke router over the mGRE tunnel. After the required traffic has passed and the connection has been idle for a preconfigured time, the dynamic IPsec tunnel is torn down to save router resources (IPsec security associations, or SAs).

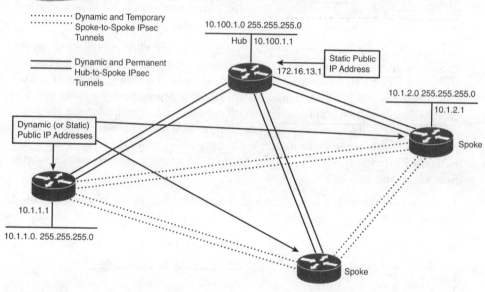

Figure 9-12 *Basic DMVPN Network*

Now that we have a working understanding of the concept behind DMVPNs, we need to explore the configuration necessary to deploy them. First, we must recognize that the configuration is broken up into a series of steps:

Step 1. Basic configuration of IP addresses.

Step 2. GRE Multipoint Tunnel configuration on all routers (for spoke-to-spoke connectivity).

Step 3. Configure IPsec to encrypt mGRE tunnels.

Step 4. DMVPN routing configuration.

Step 1: Basic Configuration of IP Addresses

As the configuration in Example 9-21 demonstrates, the IP addresses of the physical interfaces will be used to create the tunnels that are necessary to deploy a DMVPN.

Example 9-21 *DMVPN Configuration: Step 1*

```
R1(config)# interface fa 0/0
R1(config-if)# no shutdown
R1(config-if)# ip address 192.168.123.1 255.255.255.0
R1(config)# interface loopback 0
R1(config-if)# ip address 1.1.1.1 255.255.255.255
!!!!
R2(config)# interface fa 0/0
R2(config-if)# no shutdown
R2(config-if)# ip address 192.168.123.2 255.255.255.0
R2(config)# interface loopback 0
R2(config-if)# ip address 2.2.2.2 255.255.255.255
!!!!!
R3(config)# interface fa 0/0
R3(config-if)# no shutdown
R3(config-if)# ip address 192.168.123.3 255.255.255.0
R3(config)# interface loopback 0
R3(config-if)# ip address 3.3.3.3 255.255.255.255
```

Step 2: GRE Multipoint Tunnel Configuration on All Routers (for Spoke-to-Spoke Connectivity)

Now that Step 1 is complete, we will create the necessary tunnel interfaces, as illustrated in Example 9-22. Note that we configure an IP address on the tunnel 0 interface, but instead of defining a destination IP address, we will configure it as GRE multipoint. If we want to use a routing protocol like RIP, OSPF, or EIGRP, it will be necessary to define an **ip nhrp map multicast dynamic** command to allow multicast traffic to support those protocols. Additionally, for each DMVPN configured, we will require a unique network ID that is configured through the **ip nhrp network-id** command. If we choose to do so, we can specify a password for our NHRP process through the **ip nhrp authentication** command.

Example 9-22 *GRE Multipoint Tunnel Configuration*

```
!!!!!!!!!First we will start with the hub.
!!!!!!!!!!!!!!!!!!!!!!!!!!!!!!!!!!!!!!!!!!!!!
R1(config)# interface tunnel 0
R1(config-if)# ip address 172.16.123.1 255.255.255.0
R1(config-if)# tunnel mode gre multipoint
R1(config-if)# tunnel source fastEthernet 0/0
R1(config-if)# ip nhrp map multicast dynamic
R1(config-if)# ip nhrp network-id 1
R1(config-if)# ip nhrp authentication CISCO
!!!!!!!!!!!!!!!!!!!!
!!Now let's configure our spoke routers
!!!!!!!!!!!!!!!!!!!!!!
```

(handwritten note: } GRE tunnel info hub)

```
R2(config)# interface tunnel 0
R2(config-if)# ip address 172.16.123.2 255.255.255.0
R2(config-if)# tunnel mode gre multipoint
R2(config-if)# ip nhrp authentication CISCO
R2(config-if)# ip nhrp map multicast dynamic
R2(config-if)# ip nhrp map 172.16.123.1 192.168.123.1
R2(config-if)# ip nhrp map multicast 192.168.123.1
R2(config-if)# ip nhrp network-id 1
R2(config-if)# ip nhrp nhs 172.16.123.1
R2(config-if)# tunnel source fastEthernet 0/0
!!!!!!!!!!!!!!!!!!!!!!!!!!!!
R3(config)# interface tunnel 0
R3(config-if)# ip address 172.16.123.3 255.255.255.0
R3(config-if)# tunnel mode gre multipoint
R3(config-if)# ip nhrp authentication CISCO
R3(config-if)# ip nhrp map multicast dynamic
R3(config-if)# ip nhrp map 172.16.123.1 192.168.123.1
R3(config-if)# ip nhrp map multicast 192.168.123.1
R3(config-if)# ip nhrp network-id 1
R3(config-if)# ip nhrp nhs 172.16.123.1
R3(config-if)# tunnel source fastEthernet 0/0
```

(handwritten annotation: Spoke site config)

Observe that it was not necessary to apply many commands on the hub router. This means that the majority of the configuration will be assigned to the spokes where we use the **ip nhrp map** command to map the IP address of the Next Hop Server (NHS) to the outside IP address of the hub. In this particular deployment, 172.16.123.1 is the IP address on the tunnel interface of R1 and 192.168.123.1 is the outside IP address of R1. We need to use the **ip nhrp nhs** command to define exactly how to reach the IP address of the NHS.

The **ip nhrp map multicast** command configures the spoke router to send multicast traffic only to the hub router, not to other spoke routers.

As stated in Step 1, we are using the Fast Ethernet 0/0 interface as the source of the tunnels, and this is accomplished with the **tunnel source** command.

With this accomplished, we need to do some verification. The verification of our current DMVPN configuration is pretty straightforward, as demonstrated in Example 9-23.

Example 9-23 *Multipoint GRE Verification on the "Hub"*

(handwritten annotation: DMVPN VERIFI-CATION)

```
!!!!!!!!!!First we will start with the hub.
!!!!!!!!!!!!!!!!!!!!!!!!!!!!!!!!!!!!!!!!!!!!!!
R1# show dmvpn
Legend: Attrb --> S - Static, D - Dynamic, I - Incomplete
        N - NATed, L - Local, X - No Socket
        # Ent --> Number of NHRP entries with same NBMA peer
```

```
Tunnel0, Type:Hub, NHRP Peers:2,
 # Ent   Peer NBMA Addr Peer Tunnel Add State   UpDn Tm Attrb
 -----  --------------- --------------- ----- -------- -----
     1   192.168.123.2     172.16.123.2   UP     never D
     1   192.168.123.3     172.16.123.3   UP     never D
```

Example 9-23 shows us that R1 has two peers. There are a number of very useful fields in this output, as outlined in Table 9-11.

Table 9-11 *Useful Fields from the* **show dmvpn** *Command Output*

Header	Description
Ent	Represents the number of entries in the NHRP database for this spoke router.
Peer NBMA Addr	The IP address on the outside interface of the spoke router, in our example 192.168.123.2 and 192.168.123.3.
Peer Tunnel Add	The IP address on the tunnel interface of the spoke router.
State	Shows whether the tunnel is up or down.
UpDn Tm	Up or down time of the current state (up or down). Populated after the tunnels are in service.

We need to repeat this **show** command on the spokes and look at the output in Example 9-24.

Example 9-24 *Multipoint GRE Verification on the "Spokes"*

```
!!!!!!!!!!!!!!!!!!!!!!!!!!!!!!!!!!!!!!!!!!!!!!
R2# show dmvpn
Legend: Attrb --> S - Static, D - Dynamic, I - Incompletea
        N - NATed, L - Local, X - No Socket
        # Ent --> Number of NHRP entries with same NBMA peer


Tunnel0, Type:Spoke, NHRP Peers:1,
 # Ent   Peer NBMA Addr Peer Tunnel Add State   UpDn Tm Attrb
 -----  --------------- --------------- ----- -------- -----
     1   192.168.123.1    172.16.123.1   UP 00:43:44 S
!!!!!!!!!!!!!!!!!!!!!!!!!!!!!!!!!!!!!!!!!!!!!!!!!!!!!!!!!
R3# show dmvpn
Legend: Attrb --> S - Static, D - Dynamic, I - Incompletea
        N - NATed, L - Local, X - No Socket
        # Ent --> Number of NHRP entries with same NBMA peer


Tunnel0, Type:Spoke, NHRP Peers:1,
 # Ent   Peer NBMA Addr Peer Tunnel Add State   UpDn Tm Attrb
 -----  --------------- --------------- ----- -------- -----
     1   192.168.123.1    172.16.123.1   UP 00:46:58 S
```

At this juncture of our configuration, the spoke routers only have a tunnel that connects to the hub router. Now we need to test the "Dynamic" aspect of this configuration. We will do that by executing a series of ping tests. First, we will test reachability between the spokes and the hub and, finally, hub-to-hub reachability. This can all be seen in Example 9-25.

Example 9-25   *Testing the Dynamic Multipoint VPN Configuration Through* ping

```
!!!!!!!!!!!!!!!!!!!!!!!!!!!!!!!!!!!!!!!!!!!!
R2# ping 172.16.123.1

Type escape sequence to abort.
Sending 5, 100-byte ICMP Echos to 172.16.123.1, timeout is 2 seconds:
!!!!!
Success rate is 100 percent (5/5), round-trip min/avg/max = 4/4/8 ms
R3# ping 172.16.123.1

Type escape sequence to abort.
Sending 5, 100-byte ICMP Echos to 172.16.123.1, timeout is 2 seconds:
!!!!!
Success rate is 100 percent (5/5), round-trip min/avg/max = 4/4/8 ms
Both spoke routers are able to reach the hub. Now let's try to ping between the two
spoke routers:


R2# ping 172.16.123.3

Type escape sequence to abort.
Sending 5, 100-byte ICMP Echos to 172.16.123.3, timeout is 2 seconds:
!!!!!
Success rate is 100 percent (5/5), round-trip min/avg/max = 4/6/12 ms
!!!!!!!!!!!!!!!!!!!!!!!!!!!!!!!!!!!!!!!!!!!!!!!!!!!!!!!!!!!!!!!!!!!!!!!!!!!!!!!!!!!
!! The ping is working and this is the interesting part of multipoint GRE. The
!! spoke
!! routers will dynamically create a tunnel between each other as you can see below
!!!!!!!!!!!!!!!!!!!!!!!!!!!!!!!!!!!!!!!!!!!!!!!!!!!!!!!!!!!!!!!!!!!!!!!!!!!!!!!!!!!
!!
R2# show dmvpn
Legend: Attrb --> S - Static, D - Dynamic, I - Incompletea
        N - NATed, L - Local, X - No Socket
        # Ent --> Number of NHRP entries with same NBMA peer


Tunnel0, Type:Spoke, NHRP Peers:2,
 # Ent  Peer NBMA Addr Peer Tunnel Add State  UpDn Tm Attrb
 -----  --------------- --------------- ----- -------- -----
     1   192.168.123.1    172.16.123.1    UP 00:01:41 S
     1   192.168.123.3    172.16.123.3    UP    never D
R3# show dmvpn
```

```
Legend: Attrb --> S - Static, D - Dynamic, I - Incompletea
           N - NATed, L - Local, X - No Socket
           # Ent --> Number of NHRP entries with same NBMA peer


Tunnel0, Type:Spoke, NHRP Peers:2,
 # Ent  Peer NBMA Addr Peer Tunnel Add State  UpDn Tm Attrb
 ----- --------------- --------------- ----- -------- -----
     1   192.168.123.1     172.16.123.1   UP 00:01:42 S
     1   192.168.123.2     172.16.123.2   UP    never D S
```

Example 9-25 clearly illustrates that new tunnels have been dynamically established between R2 and R3. This means that the multipoint GRE is working.

However, this type of deployment would be very risky in a live environment because the default operation of DMVPN is to send traffic in clear text, and that is simply unacceptable.

Step 3: Configure IPsec to Encrypt mGRE Tunnels

To protect our deployment, we will apply IPsec to the DMVPN configuration. The process is illustrated in Example 9-26.

Example 9-26 *IPsec Configuration Through DMVPN*

```
!!!!!!!!!!!!!!!!!!!!!!!!!!!!!!!!!!!!!!!!!!!!
!!!!! All Devices in the DMVPN Configuration
!!!!!!!!!!!!!!!!!!!!!!!!!!!!!!!!!!!!!!!!!!!!
(config)# crypto isakmp policy 1
(config-isakmp)# encryption aes
(config-isakmp)# hash md5
(config-isakmp)# authentication pre-share
(config-isakmp)# group 2
(config-isakmp)# lifetime 86400
!
(config)# crypto isakmp key 0 NETWORKLESSONS address 0.0.0.0
(config)# crypto ipsec transform-set MYSET esp-aes esp-md5-hmac
!
(config)# crypto ipsec profile MGRE
(ipsec-profile)# set security-association lifetime seconds 86400
(ipsec-profile)# set transform-set MYSET
!
(config)# interface tunnel 0
(config-if)# tunnel protection ipsec profile MGRE
```

(Handwritten annotations:) ISAKMP Pol. — any source !!! — like a crypto map — assigning profile to the tun tunnel :).

Key Topic

If the DMVPN configuration relies on a dynamic IP address on the spoke routers, be sure to use IP address 0.0.0.0 when configuring the crypto isakmp key.

We need to verify whether our tunnels are now encrypted. Best practice at this point would be to shut and no shut our tunnel interfaces. This will ensure that the crypto configuration has been applied and that the tunnel interfaces come up as we hope. This process is described in Example 9-27.

Example 9-27 *Verification of IPsec-Encrypted Tunnels*

```
!!!!!!!!!!!!!!!!!!!!!!!!!!!!!!!!!!!!!!!!!!!
!!!!! All Devices in the DMVPN Configuration
!!!!!!!!!!!!!!!!!!!!!!!!!!!!!!!!!!!!!!!!!!!
(config)# interface tunnel 0
(config-if)# shutdown
(config-if)# no shutdown
!!!!!!!!!!!!!!!!!!!!!!!!!!
!!!! Next step is to check if IPSEC is active!!!!!!
!!!! From the HUB!!!!!!!!!
R1# show crypto session
Crypto session current status

Interface: Tunnel0
Session status: UP-ACTIVE
Peer: 192.168.123.2 port 500
  IKE SA: local 192.168.123.1/500 remote 192.168.123.2/500 Active
  IPSEC FLOW: permit 47 host 192.168.123.1 host 192.168.123.2
       Active SAs: 2, origin: crypto map

Interface: Tunnel0
Session status: UP-ACTIVE
Peer: 192.168.123.3 port 500
  IKE SA: local 192.168.123.1/500 remote 192.168.123.3/500 Active
  IPSEC FLOW: permit 47 host 192.168.123.1 host 192.168.123.3
       Active SAs: 2, origin: crypto map
!!!!!!!!!!!!!!!!!!!!!!!!!!!!!!!!!!!
!!! As you can see IPSEC is active for both peers. We will test rechability via
!!! sending some pings
!!!!!!!!!!!!!!!!!!!!!!!!!!!!!!!!!!!!!!!!!!!!!!!!!
R2# ping 172.16.123.1

Type escape sequence to abort.
Sending 5, 100-byte ICMP Echos to 172.16.123.1, timeout is 2 seconds:
!!!!!
Success rate is 100 percent (5/5), round-trip min/avg/max = 4/4/4 ms
R3# ping 172.16.123.1
```

```
Type escape sequence to abort.
Sending 5, 100-byte ICMP Echos to 172.16.123.1, timeout is 2 seconds:
!!!!!
Success rate is 100 percent (5/5), round-trip min/avg/max = 4/4/4 ms
!!!!!!!!!!!!!!!!!!!
!! Now we will verify that the packets are encrypted
!!!!!!!!!!!!!!!!!!!
R1# show crypto ipsec sa

interface: Tunnel0
    Crypto map tag: Tunnel0-head-0, local addr 192.168.123.1

   protected vrf: (none)
   local  ident (addr/mask/prot/port): (192.168.123.1/255.255.255.255/47/0)
   remote ident (addr/mask/prot/port): (192.168.123.2/255.255.255.255/47/0)
   current_peer 192.168.123.2 port 500
     PERMIT, flags={origin_is_acl,}
    #pkts encaps: 26, #pkts encrypt: 26, #pkts digest: 26
    #pkts decaps: 26, #pkts decrypt: 26, #pkts verify: 26
!!!!!!!!!!!!!!!!!!!!!!!
!!! Packets in the tunnel are encrypted.
!!!!!!!!!!!!!!!!!!!!!!
```

Step 4: DMVPN Routing Configuration

The tunnels are up and running and encrypted; however, there is no reachability between the loopbacks of any of the devices. To remedy this situation, we have two options. We could use static routing or one of our dynamic routing protocols.

In Example 9-28, we will illustrate how to run Open Shortest Path First (OSPF) across the mGRE tunnel interfaces.

Example 9-28 *OSPF Across MGRE Tunnel Interfaces*

```
!!!!!!!!!!!!!!!!!!!!!!!!!!!!!!!!!!!!!!!!!!!!!!!
!!!!! All Devices in the DMVPN Configuration
!!!!!!!!!!!!!!!!!!!!!!!!!!!!!!!!!!!!!!!!!!!!!!!
R1(config)# router ospf 1
R1(config-router)# network 1.1.1.1 0.0.0.0 area 0
R1(config-router)# network 172.16.123.0 0.0.0.255 area 0

R1(config)# interface tunnel 0
R1(config-if)# ip ospf network broadcast
R2(config)# router ospf 1
R2(config-router)# network 2.2.2.2 0.0.0.0 area 0
R2(config-router)# network 172.16.123.0 0.0.0.255 area 0
```

```
R2(config)# interface tunnel 0
R2(config-if)# ip ospf priority 0
R2(config-if)# ip ospf network broadcast
R3(config)# router ospf 1
R3(config-router)# network 3.3.3.3 0.0.0.0 area 0
R3(config-router)# network 172.16.123.0 0.0.0.255 area 0

R3(config)# interface tunnel 0
R3(config-if)# ip ospf priority 0
R3(config-if)# ip ospf network broadcast
!!!!!!!!!!!!!!!!!!!!!!!!!!
```

Key Topic

Previously we used the **ip nhrp map multicast** command on the spoke routers, which means that the spoke routers can only send OSPF hellos to the hub router. This means that we'll have an OSPF hub-and-spoke topology, and the spoke routers should never become the designated router (DR) or backup designated router (BDR).

As shown in Example 9-28, we used the OSPF broadcast network type so that the spoke routers will use each other's IP addresses as the next hop.

Now that this configuration is completed, we will do the verification necessary to check it all out. At this juncture, we are using OSPF verification commands, as illustrated in Example 9-29.

Example 9-29 *Verification of DMVPN Routing*

```
!!!!!!!!!!!!!!!!!!!!!!!!!!!!!!!!!!!!!!!!!!!!!!!
R1# show ip ospf neighbor

Neighbor ID     Pri    State          Dead Time    Address         Interface
2.2.2.2           0    FULL/DROTHER   00:00:33     172.16.123.2    Tunnel0
3.3.3.3           0    FULL/DROTHER   00:00:33     172.16.123.3    Tunnel0
R2# show ip ospf neighbor

Neighbor ID     Pri    State          Dead Time    Address         Interface
1.1.1.1           1    FULL/DR        00:00:31     172.16.123.1    Tunnel0
R3# show ip ospf neighbor

Neighbor ID     Pri    State          Dead Time    Address         Interface
1.1.1.1           1    FULL/DR        00:00:31     172.16.123.1    Tunnel0
The spoke routers have formed an OSPF neighbor adjacency with the hub router. Let's
check the routing tables:

R2# show ip route ospf
      1.0.0.0/32 is subnetted, 1 subnets
O        1.1.1.1 [110/11112] via 172.16.123.1, 00:04:16, Tunnel0
      3.0.0.0/32 is subnetted, 1 subnets
O        3.3.3.3 [110/11112] via 172.16.123.3, 00:04:16, Tunnel0
```

```
R3# show ip route ospf
      1.0.0.0/32 is subnetted, 1 subnets
O        1.1.1.1 [110/11112] via 172.16.123.1, 00:04:10, Tunnel0
      2.0.0.0/32 is subnetted, 1 subnets
O        2.2.2.2 [110/11112] via 172.16.123.2, 00:04:09, Tunnel0
!!!!!!!!!!!!!!!!!
!!!! R2 and R3 have learned about the other networks. Note that R2 and R3 are using
!!!! each other's IP address as the next hop for each other's networks.
!!!! Now to test via the ping utility
!!!!!!!!!!!!!!!!!

R2# ping 1.1.1.1 source loopback 0

Type escape sequence to abort.
Sending 5, 100-byte ICMP Echos to 1.1.1.1, timeout is 2 seconds:
Packet sent with a source address of 2.2.2.2
!!!!!
Success rate is 100 percent (5/5), round-trip min/avg/max = 4/4/4 ms
R2# ping 3.3.3.3 source loopback 0

Type escape sequence to abort.
Sending 5, 100-byte ICMP Echos to 3.3.3.3, timeout is 2 seconds:
Packet sent with a source address of 2.2.2.2
!!!!!
Success rate is 100 percent (5/5), round-trip min/avg/max = 4/4/4 ms
!!!!!!!!!!!!!!!!!!!!!!!!
!!!! R2 is able to reach the loopback interfaces of R1 and R3
!!!!!!!!!!!!!!!!!!!!!!!!!
```

IPv6 First Hop Security

In this section, we take a look at several common security threats on IPv6 campus access networks and explain the value of using first hop security (FHS) technology in mitigating these threats.

First Hop Security for IPv6

Anyone working in the network engineering market today has to recognize that there are a growing number of large-scale IPv6 deployments in enterprise, university, and government networks. To guarantee the success of each of these networks, we need to ensure that the IPv6 deployments are secure and are of a service quality that equals or exceeds that of the existing IPv4 infrastructure.

Network users must be comfortable that regardless of what type of network they are working on—IPv4 or IPv6—each shares the same levels of security and serviceability. From the network administrator's point of view, there also needs to be a similar assumption: that both IPv4 and IPv6 networks are secure environments with a high degree of traceability and quality assurance, thus allowing us to both avoid and trace any level of possible network incursion.

This situation is made somewhat more complicated in IPv6 environments as a direct result of the sheer size of these deployments as well as the advent of a number of new technology paradigms that were created to support the protocol. Thus it is a fair assumption that the majority of threats that impact an IPv6 enterprise are very much tied to the topology and nature of the given network itself. This means that security considerations for IPv6 environments are considerably different in that they have

- More end nodes allowed on individual links (up to 2^{64})

- Larger neighbor cache on end nodes

- Larger neighbor cache on the default router

Each of these elements actually serves to provide attackers with greater opportunities for denial of service (DoS) attacks. The security risks associated with IPv6 deployments, however, are not specifically limited to the topological aspects of the protocol. There are other threats associated with the protocols that might or might not be in use on that network. A few of these protocols include

- Neighbor Discovery Protocol (NDP) integrates all link operations in charge of determining address assignment, router discovery, and associated tasks like redirect.

- Dynamic Host Configuration Protocol (DHCP) has a smaller role in address assignment compared to IPv4.

- Noncentralized address assignment creates true challenges for controlling address misusage.

Thanks to an ever-increasing level of IPv6 deployments and the intrinsic differences between IPv4 and IPv6 outlined previously, it is very important to have both a secure IPv4 environment and a secure IPv6 environment. It will be useful to understand where IPv6 is used for the various aspects and how best to secure the IPv6 infrastructure when connecting systems and devices to a network link. This will involve taking a closer look at areas where opportunities might arise in the IPv6 topology. In this section, we will focus on the different links found in the network. Before we can discuss the method of securing these links, we first need to look at the fundamentals of link operations, because understanding the basic operation of links in an IPv6 deployment will better allow us to secure them.

Link Operations

When determining where we can secure link operations, we find that there are basically three different locations within the network where operations can be secured. These locations where security enforcement can take place are

- The end nodes

- The first hop within the network

- The last hop

Figure 9-13 illustrates these three locations by illustrating a very simple network.

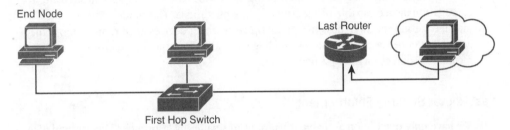

Figure 9-13 *Link Operation Security Enforcement*

We will look at each of the three locations more in depth now that we have identified where they are in a very small topology.

End Node Security Enforcement

This security model, a distributed model where the end nodes take care of themselves, does not provide any link operation with bottlenecks or single points of failure. This security model does not need central administration or operation as it is assumed that each node takes care of itself. To read more about this process of Secure Neighbor Discovery, consult RFC 3971. The ultimate level of security in this model is accomplished by what is referred to as a Secure Neighbor Discovery (SeND) deployment. We will discuss SeND in a later section because to understand how SeND helps us, we need to know a bit more about another protocol used for neighbor discovery. Suffice it to say that this model is especially good for threats coming directly from the link; however, it provides poor protection against threats from offlink devices. Another consideration for this model is that because of its distributed nature, a degree of complexity and heavy provisioning of end nodes is involved that spreads over the complete networking domain that is being secured. So this solution is good but has its limitations; plus based on our new understanding of its operation, we can easily see that it is not scalable. So now we need to look at the next security enforcement point in our topology.

First Hop Switch Security Enforcement

The first hop switch security model is based upon a centralized model. It is maintained and run by a centralized security administration and, as such, differs significantly from the end node method. In the end node method, we saw that the burden of security enforcement is pushed toward the first-hop device. Because the first hop switch security enforcement uses a centralized model, it has better scalability in that fewer devices are affected by the security tasks involved. This model makes the transition from a nonsecure link operation to a secure network easier as fewer components will have to be touched, monitored, and reconfigured.

Although this is a very convenient model for the network operator and the actual end user, it will be useful only in certain topologies in which all end users go through an aggregation device capable of securing the link operations. This model increases the intelligence and the awareness that first-hop networking devices need to have about the actual end nodes attached, thus also adding significantly to the required processing and memory resources on the first-hop switch.

Last Router Security Enforcement

We have only one option available if we want to secure the last router. This method, like the previous one, will be a centralized model, which is good for securing against threats coming from outside of the link that is being protected. A property of this model is that the attached link is protected as well as all the downstream network elements. This provides a significant enhancement over the previous security enforcement methods that we have discussed. But it is not an either/or scenario. The last router security enforcement model needs to combine with the first-hop switch model. Together these solutions can defeat threats that might originate from the inside the network. This is a necessity because it is possible that a device has been compromised and might be used by an assailant to affect the network infrastructure.

To operate effectively, this enforcement method requires the last-hop router to discover all the end nodes on the operational segment where the security process is being enforced. This is accomplished through the next protocol set that we have to discuss.

ICMPv6 and Neighbor Discovery Protocol

This section introduces the Internet Control Message Protocol version 6 (ICMPv6). In comparison with IPv4, IPv6 has an increased set of capabilities to simplify end-system autoconfiguration while at the same time running service detection by means of ICMP. Because of these new ICMP capabilities, the importance of ICMP for IPv6 is much higher than it ever was for IPv4.

One of the new functionalities within ICMPv6 is the Neighbor Discovery Protocol (NDP), which in its base specification is a nonauthenticated protocol. NDP is an application and operates on top of ICMPv6. NDP makes heavy usage of multicast packets for link efficiency.

The functional applications of NDP include

- Router discovery

- Autoconfiguration of addresses (stateless address autoconfiguration [SLAAC])

- IPv6 address resolution (replaces Address Resolution Protocol [ARP])

- Neighbor reachability (neighbor unreachability detection [NUD])

- Duplicate address detection (DAD)

- Redirection

Secure Neighbor Discovery (SeND)

We mentioned SeND in a previous section where we discussed end node security enforcement, but we deferred to mention exactly what the protocol was until now. In that we have a basic understanding of how ICMPv6 and NDP work, we need to also point out that their operation processes are not secure. It is SeND that adds security to the NDP and its operation; however, we will note later that this security enhancement has its limitations. So the best working definition of Secure Neighbor Discovery is a protocol that enhances NDP. It enhances the operation of NDP by providing three critical capabilities:

- Proof of address ownership
    - Makes stealing IPv6 addresses "impossible"
    - Used in router discovery, DAD, and address resolution
    - Based upon Cryptographically Generated Addresses (CGA)
    - Alternatively also provides non-CGAs with certificates
- Message protection
    - Message integrity protection
    - Replay protection
    - Request/response correlation
    - Used in all NDP messages
- Router authorization
    - Authorizes routers to act as default gateways
    - Specifies prefixes that routers are authorized to announce "on-link"

While SeND provides a significant security enhancement to the IPv6 neighbor discovery technology by introducing the enhancements we pointed out previously, it does not provide any end-to-end security and provides no actual packet confidentiality. Plus we need to recognize that that SeND is not a new protocol and still remains a protocol operating on the link. Secure Neighbor Discovery is just an "extension" to NDP and defines a set of new attributes by defining new network discovery options, new network discovery messages, and new attributes that describe the preferred behavior when a SeND node receives a message supported by SeND or not supported by SeND.

SeND technology works by having a pair of private and public keys for each IPv6 node in combination with new options like Cryptographically Generated Addresses (CGA) and RSA, which all work to provide a security shield against replay attacks.

Nodes that are using SeND cannot choose their own interface identifier because the interface identifier is cryptographically generated based upon the current IPv6 network prefix and the "public" key. However, the CGA interface identifier alone is not sufficient to guarantee that the CGA address is used by the appropriate node.

For this purpose, SeND messages are signed by using the RSA public and private key pair. For example, if node 1 wants to know the MAC address of node 2, it will tradition- ally send a neighbor solicitation request to the node 2 solicited node multicast address. Node 2 will respond with a corresponding neighbor advertisement containing the MAC address-to-IPv6 address mapping. In addition, node 2 will add the CGA parameters (which include among others the public key) and a private key signature of all neighbor advertisement fields. When node 1 receives this neighbor advertisement, it uses the public key to verify with the CGA address the private key signature of node 2. After this last step has been successfully completed, the binding on node 1 of the MAC address and CGA address of node 2 can be successfully finalized.

Note that this mechanism is simply an explanation to verify the correct relationship between a node MAC address and its CGA IPv6 address. SeND does not check any of the node's privileges to be allowed, or not allowed, on the network. If this is required, other means of infrastructure protection will be required, such as 802.1X (discussed ear- lier in this chapter).

Securing at the First Hop

The first hop for an end node is very often a Layer 2 switch. By implementing the right set of security features, this switch has the potential to solve many of the caveats attached to a SeND deployment and increase the link security model. The first-hop switch is strategically located to learn about all its neighbors, and hence the switch can easily either allow or deny certain types of traffic, end-node roles, and claims. In its central position, the first-hop switch can fulfill a number of functions. It will inspect the neighbor discovery (ND) traffic and provide information about Layer 2/Layer 3 binding and monitor the use of ND by host to spot potentially abnormal behaviors. Ultimately, the switch can block undesired traffic such as a rogue Router Advertisement (RA), rogue DHCP server advertisement, and data traffic coming from undesired IP addresses or pre- fixes.

Securing the IPv6 link is a cooperative effort, and all concerned parties or sites should be involved. Experience proves, however, that the first-hop switch is a key piece of this puz- zle and certainly plays a central role in link security, just like it did for IPv4. Compared to IPv4, IPv6 offers a number of technologies, such as SeND, that make security more flex- ible to deploy and more efficient at catching malicious behavior, paving the way for more secure deployments.

We can see the configuration of this feature in Example 9-30.

Example 9-30 *Securing the First Hop*

```
!!!!!!!!!!!!!!!!!!!!!!!!!!!!!!!!!!!!!!!!!!!
CAT2(config)# ipv6 access-list ACCESS_PORT
CAT2(config-ipv6-acl)# remark Block all traffic DHCP server -> client
CAT2(config-ipv6-acl)# deny udp any eq 547 any eq 546
CAT2(config-ipv6-acl)# remark Block Router Advertisements
CAT2(config-ipv6-acl)# deny icmp any any router-advertisement
CAT2(config-ipv6-acl)# permit any any
CAT2(config-ipv6-acl)# !
CAT2(config-ipv6-acl)# interface gigabitethernet 1/0/1
CAT2(config-if)# switchport
CAT2(config-if)# ipv6 traffic-filter ACCESS_PORT in
```

RA Guard

In typical IPv6 deployments, the majority of networks have a common attribute. That attribute is that their nodes are on a link layer bonded by some intermediary device. This device is typically a switch and describes a scenario where devices are not directly connected. This configuration makes it possible to use a mechanism called RA snooping. This concept of snooping has been present in computer networks for decades, in the form of features such as IGMP snooping or DHCP snooping. Furthermore, it is common knowledge that switches use only information provided by the link-layer header of received frames to forward those packets through the correct interface on a given device. The concept of snooping exceeds this behavior in that the switch will additionally inspect upper-layer information embedded in the packet. Based on that upper protocol layer information, the switch will take defined actions. These actions are either optimizing (IGMP) or security (DHCP, RA) in nature.

RA Guard is a mechanism designed against rogue RA attacks that uses an idea called RA Snooping as its foundation. The key condition that must be met prior to RA Guard deployment is that there must be some intermediary device in a network that all traffic will pass through. The switch in our analogy is where RA Guard is implemented. The core functionality of RA Guard is that it inspects Router Advertisements, and based on the information provided, it decides whether to drop or forward them. Note that RA Guard is not any particular protocol or strictly defined mechanism. It is an umbrella term describing a set of recommendations and a general description of prevention mechanisms that have been implemented by various vendors.

Example 9-31 outlines how RA Guard is implemented on a Catalyst switch.

Example 9-31 *RA Guard*

```
!!!!!!!!!!!!!!!!!!!!!!!!!!!!!!!!!!!!!!!!!!!!
Switch(config)# ipv6 nd raguard policy POLICY-NAME
! Defines the RA Guard policy name
```

```
Switch(config-ra-guard)# device-role {host | router}
!Specifies the role of the device attached to the port.
!!!!!!!!!!!!!!!!!!!!!!!!!!!!!!!!!!!!!!!!!
!The RA Guard policy can have several other optional options checking the hop limit,
!router preference etc. After the policy is configured, it has to be applied to
!appropriate interfaces.
!!!!!!!!!!!!!!!!!!!!!!!!!!!!!!!!!!!!!!!!!!
Switch(config)# interface INTERFACE
Switch(config-if)# ipv6 nd raguard attach-policy POLICY-NAME
! Applies the RA Guard policy
```

If a policy is configured with a device-role host, a switch will drop any RA messages received on an interface where the policy is applied, thus eliminating the RA attack. Interfaces toward a router should be configured with a policy where device-role is set to router.

DHCPv6 Guard

The DHCPv6 Guard feature blocks reply and advertisement messages that come from unauthorized DHCP servers and relay agents. This configuration is illustrated in Example 9-32.

Packets are classified into one of the three DHCP type messages. All client messages are always switched regardless of device role. DHCP server messages are only processed further if the device role is set to server. Further processing of server messages includes DHCP server advertisements (for source validation and server preference) and DHCP server replies (for permitted prefixes).

If the device is configured as a DHCP server, all the messages need to be switched, regardless of the device role configuration.

Example 9-32 *DHCPv6 Guard*

```
!!!!!!!!!!!!!!!!!!!!!!!!!!!!!!!!!!!!!!!!!!!!!!
CAT1# enable
CAT1# configure terminal
Enter configuration commands, one per line.  End with CNTL/Z.
CAT1(config)# ipv6 access-list acl1
CAT1(config-ipv6-acl)# permit host FE80::A8BB:CCFF:FE01:F700 any
CAT1(config-ipv6-acl)# ipv6 prefix-list abc permit 2001:0DB8::/64 le 128
CAT1(config-ipv6-acl)# ipv6 prefix-list abc permit 2001:0DB8::/64 le 128
CAT1(config)# ipv6 dhcp guard policy pol1
CAT1(config-dhcp-guard)# device-role server
CAT1(config-dhcp-guard)# match server access-list acl1
CAT1(config-dhcp-guard)# match reply prefix-list abc
CAT1(config-dhcp-guard)# preference min 0
CAT1(config-dhcp-guard)# preference max 255
```

```
CAT1(config-dhcp-guard)# trusted-port
CAT1(config-dhcp-guard)# interface GigabitEthernet 1/0/1
CAT1(config-if)# switchport
CAT1(config-if)# ipv6 dhcp guard attach-policy pol1 vlan add 1
!!!!!!!!!!!!!!!!!!!!!!!!!!
CAT1# show ipv6 dhcp guard policy pol1
Dhcp guard policy: pol1
        Trusted Port
        Target: Gi1/0/1


CAT1#
```

DHCPv6 Guard and the Binding Database

IPv6 Snooping is not a security feature in its own right. It builds a database table of IPv6 neighbors connected to the device created from information sources like DHCPv6, which we discussed in the previous section. This database, or binding table, is used by various IPv6 FHS features to validate the link-layer address (LLA), the IPv6 address, and the prefix binding of the neighbors to prevent spoofing and redirect attacks. This binding table will get automatically populated after IPv6 Snooping is enabled. The following output in Example 9-33 shows a sample content of an IPv6 binding table.

Example 9-33 *IPv6 Binding Table*

```
!!!!!!!!!!!!!!!!!!!!!!!!!!!!!!!!!!!!!!!!!!!!!!!!!
CAT1(config
Switch# show ipv6 neighbors binding
Binding Table has 4 entries, 4 dynamic
Codes: L - Local, S - Static, ND - Neighbor Discovery, DH - DHCP, PKT - Other
  Packet, API - API created
IPv6 address              Link-Layer addr Interface vlan prlvl  age    state
  Time left
ND  FE80::81E2:1562:E5A0:43EE  28D2.4448.E276  Gi1/15       1  0005    3mn REACHABLE
  94 s
ND  FE80::3AEA:A7FF:FE85:C926  38EA.A785.C926  Gi1/2        1  0005   26mn STALE
  86999 s
ND  FE80::10                   38EA.A785.C926  Gi1/2        1  0005   26mn STALE
  85533 s
ND  FE80::1                    E4C7.228B.F180  Gi1/7        1  0005    35s REACHABLE
  272 s
```

As we can see, the binding table has four entries beginning with "ND," which means that these associations were learned from snooping NDP packets. When a new entry is appended to the database, the following log message is generated on the switch (when "IPv6 snooping logging" is enabled).

```
%SISF-6-ENTRY_CREATED: Entry created A=2001:DB8:1:0:C04D:ABA:A783:2FBE V=1
  I=Gi1/15 P=0024 M=28D2.4448.E276
```

IPv6 Snooping is tightly integrated in the various IPv6 Guard features like DHCPv6 Guard and RA Guard. To allow those packets, you have to configure, for example, DHCPv6 Guard so that the switch knows that these DHCPv6 packets are legitimate and must not be filtered. The complete configuration for DHCPv6 Guard is done with the commands outlined in Example 9-34.

Example 9-34 *DHCPv6 Address Integrated with the IPv6 Binding Database*

```
!!!!!!!!!!!!!!!!!!!!!!!!!!!!!!!!!!!!!!!!!!!!!!!
CAT1(config)# ipv6 access-list dhcpv6_server
CAT1(config-ipv6-acl)# permit host FE80::1 any
CAT1(config-ipv6-acl)# $-list dhcpv6_prefix permit 2001:DB8:1::/64 le 128
CAT1(config)# ipv6 dhcp guard policy dhcpv6guard_pol
CAT1(config-dhcp-guard)# device-role server
CAT1(config-dhcp-guard)# match server access-list dhcpv6_server
CAT1(config-dhcp-guard)# match reply prefix-list dhcpv6_prefix
CAT1(config-dhcp-guard)# vlan configuration 1
CAT1(config-vlan-config)# ipv6 dhcp guard attach-policy dhcpv6guard_pol
CAT1(config-vlan-config)#
```

Essentially, Example 9-34 illustrates how we instruct the switch that DHCPv6 packets from FE80::1 (specified in the ACL) with a prefix of 2001:db8:1::/64 (specified in the prefix list) shall not be dropped. We combine these "elements" in a DHCPv6 Guard policy, which is then bound to VLAN 1. After the configuration is done, DHCPv6 is working again as intended and the DHCPv6 addresses are populated in the binding table indicated by the following log message:

```
%SISF-6-ENTRY_CREATED: Entry created A=2001:DB8:1:0:BCC1:41C0:D904:E1B9 V=1
   I=Gi1/15 P=0024 M=28D2.4448.E276
```

Looking into the binding table again, the IPv6 address now appears as shown in Example 9-35.

Example 9-35 *IPv6 Binding Database*

```
!!!!!!!!!!!!!!!!!!!!!!!!!!!!!!!!!!!!!!!!!!!!!!!
Switch# show ipv6 neighbors binding
Binding Table has 6 entries, 6 dynamic
Codes: L - Local, S - Static, ND - Neighbor Discovery, DH - DHCP, PKT - Other
   Packet, API - API created
Preflevel flags (prlvl):
0001:MAC and LLA match      0002:Orig trunk          0004:Orig access
0008:Orig trusted trunk     0010:Orig trusted access 0020:DHCP assigned
0040:Cga authenticated      0080:Cert authenticated  0100:Statically assigned
IPv6 address                Link-Layer addr Interface vlan prlvl  age    state
   Time left
ND  FE80::81E2:1562:E5A0:43EE      28D2.4448.E276  Gi1/15     1  0005   3mn
   REACHABLE   94 s
ND  FE80::3AEA:A7FF:FE85:C926      38EA.A785.C926  Gi1/2      1  0005   26mn
   STALE       86999 s
```

```
ND  FE80::10                         38EA.A785.C926  Gi1/2      1   0005    26mn
   STALE      85533
ND  FE80::1                          E4C7.228B.F180  Gi1/7      1   0005    35s
   REACHABLE  272 s
DH  2001:DB8:1:0:BCC1:41C0:D904:E1B9  28D2.4448.E276  Gi1/15     1   0024    3mn
   REACHABLE  87 s(166161s
```

Now we see an new entry starting with "DH," indicating that this binding was learned by snooping the DHCPv6 packet.

Now that DHCPv6 is working again, we have to configure an RA Guard policy to allow the router advertisements of our legitimate router. We will just configure the system so that the port (where our router is connected) is a "trusted port," which means that RAs are allowed regardless of the configuration in the policy. We will do this as illustrated in Example 9-36.

Example 9-36 *Trusting the Port*

```
!!!!!!!!!!!!!!!!!!!!!!!!!!!!!!!!!!!!!!!!!!!!!!
CAT1(config)# ipv6 nd raguard policy ra_pol
CAT1(config-nd-raguard)# device-role router
CAT1(config-nd-raguard)# trusted-port
CAT1(config-nd-raguard)# exit
CAT1(config)# int g1/0/1
CAT1(config-if)# ipv6 nd raguard attach-policy ra_pol
```

After the configuration is applied to g1/0/1, RAs will not be dropped by the switch.

IPv6 Device Tracking

The IPv6 device tracking feature provides IPv6 host tracking so that a neighbor table can be immediately updated when an IPv6 host disappears. The feature tracks the reachability of the neighbors connected through the Layer 2 switch on a regular basis to revoke network access privileges as they become inactive. We can see the configuration and verification of this feature in Example 9-37.

Example 9-37 *IPv6 Device Tracking*

```
!!!!!!!!!!!!!!!!!!!!!!!!!!!!!!!!!!!!!!!!!!!!!!
CAT1(config)# ipv6 neighbor binding vlan 100 interface Gi 1/0/1 reachable-lifetime
   100
CAT1(config)# ipv6 neighbor binding max-entries 100
CAT1(config)# ipv6 neighbor binding logging
!!!!!!!!!!!!!!!!!!!!!!!!!!!
!!!   Verification
!!!!!!!!!!!!!!!!!!!!!!!!!!!
CAT1# show ipv6 neighbor tracking
```

```
     IPv6 address            Link-Layer addr Interface vlan prlvl age    state
     Time left
ND  FE80::A8BB:CCFF:FE01:F500 AABB.CC01.F500 Et0/0    100 0002     0   REACHABLE
    8850
L   FE80::21D:71FF:FE99:4900  001D.7199.4900 Vl100    100 0080 7203    DOWN
    N/A
ND  2001:600::1               AABB.CC01.F500 Et0/0    100 0003     0   REACHABLE
    3181
ND  2001:300::1               AABB.CC01.F500 Et0/0    100 0007     0   REACHABLE
    9559
L   2001:400::1               001D.7199.4900 Vl100    100 0080 7188    DOWN
    N/A
```

IPv6 Neighbor Discovery Inspection

IPv6 ND inspection learns and secures bindings for stateless autoconfiguration addresses in L2 neighbor tables. IPv6 ND inspection analyzes neighbor discovery messages to build a trusted binding table database, and IPv6 neighbor discovery messages that do not conform are dropped. An ND message is considered trustworthy if its IPv6-to-Media Access Control (MAC) mapping is verifiable. Example 9-38 demonstrates the basic configuration of this feature.

Example 9-38 *IPv6 Device Tracking*

```
!!!!!!!!!!!!!!!!!!!!!!!!!!!!!!!!!!!!!!!!!!!!!!!
CAT1(config)# ipv6 nd inspection policy example_policy
CAT1(config-nd-inspection)# device-role switch
CAT1(config-nd-inspection)# drop-unsecure
CAT1(config-nd-inspection)# limit address-count 1000
CAT1(config-nd-inspection)# tracking disable stale-lifetime infinite
CAT1(config-nd-inspection)# trusted-port
CAT1(config-nd-inspection)# validate source-mac
CAT1(config-nd-inspection)# no validate source-mac
CAT1(config-nd-inspection)# default limit address-count
CAT1(config-nd-inspection)#
!!!!!!!!!!!!!!!!!!!!!!
!! Now to verify the configuration
!!!!!!!!!!!!!!!!!!!!!!
CAT1# show ipv6 nd inspection policy example_policy
Policy example_policy configuration:
  trusted-port
  device-role switch
  drop-unsecure
  tracking disable stale-lifetime infinite
Policy example_policy is applied on the following targets:
Target              Type  Policy              Feature       Target range
CAT1#
```

We see the policy but we do not see that it has been applied. The step is to ensure that we apply it to an interface, as shown in Example 9-39.

Example 9-39 *Applying IPv6 ND Inspection Policy*

```
!!!!!!!!!!!!!!!!!!!!!!!!!!!!!!!!!!!!!!!!!!!!!!!
CAT1(config)# int gi1/0/2
CAT1(config-if)# ipv6 nd inspection attach-policy example_policy
CAT1(config-if)# exit
CAT1(config)# exit
!!!!!!!!!!!
!!! Now to verify the configuration again
!!!!!!!!!!!
CAT1# show ipv6 nd inspection policy example_policy
*Mar  1 00:56:30.423: %SYS-5-CONFIG_I: Configured from console by console
Policy example_policy configuration:
  trusted-port
  device-role switch
  drop-unsecure
  tracking disable stale-lifetime infinite
Policy example_policy is applied on the following targets:
Target              Type  Policy          Feature         Target range
Gi1/0/2             PORT  example_policy  NDP inspection  vlan all
CAT1#
```

We can see now that the policy is applied to interface Gi1/0/2.

IPv6 Source Guard

IPv6 Source Guard is an interface feature between the populated binding table and data traffic filtering. This feature enables the device to deny traffic when it is originated from an address that is not stored in the binding table. IPv6 Source Guard does not inspect ND or DHCP packets; rather, it works in conjunction with IPv6 neighbor discovery (ND) inspection or IPv6 address glean, both of which detect existing addresses on the link and store them in the binding table. IPv6 Source Guard is an interface between the populated binding table and data traffic filtering, and the binding table must be populated with IPv6 prefixes for IPv6 Source Guard to work.

IPv6 Source Guard can deny traffic from unknown sources or unallocated addresses, such as traffic from sources not assigned by a DHCP server. When traffic is denied, the IPv6 address glean feature is notified so that it can try to recover the traffic by querying the DHCP server or by using IPv6 ND. The data-glean function prevents the device and end user from getting deadlocked, whereupon a valid address fails to be stored in the binding table, there is no recovery path, and the end user is unable to connect.

Figure 9-14 provides an overview of how IPv6 Source Guard works with IPv6 address glean.

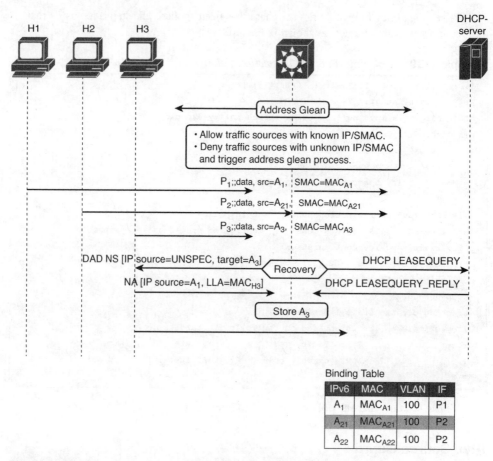

Figure 9-14 *IPv6 Source Guard and Address Glean*

Example 9-40 demonstrates how to configure IPv6 Source Guard and confirm the configuration.

Example 9-40 *IPv6 Source Guard Configuration and Verification*

```
!!!!!!!!!!!!!!!!!!!!!!!!!!!!!!!!!!!!!!!!!!!!
CAT2(config)# ipv6 access-list acl1
CAT2(config-ipv6-acl)# permit host FE80::A8BB:CCFF:FE01:F700 any
CAT2(config-ipv6-acl)# ipv6 prefix-list abc permit 2001:0DB8::/64 le 128
CAT2(config)# ipv6 dhcp guard policy pol1
CAT2(config-dhcp-guard)# device-role server
CAT2(config-dhcp-guard)# match server access-list acl1
CAT2(config-dhcp-guard)# match reply prefix-list abc
CAT2(config-dhcp-guard)# trusted-port
CAT2(config-dhcp-guard)# interface GigabitEthernet 1/0/1
CAT2(config-if)# switchport
CAT2(config-if)# ipv6 dhcp guard attach-policy pol1 vlan add 10
```

```
!!!!!!!!!!!!!!!
!!!! Now that the config is applied we will verify
!!!!!!!!!!!!!!
CAT2(config-if)# do show ipv6 dhcp guard policy pol1
Dhcp guard policy: pol1
        Trusted Port
        Target: Gi1/0/1

CAT2#
```

Port Access Control Lists (PACL)

Another method that can be used to protect devices is the Port Access Control List (PACL). This switching feature is very similar to the Router ACLs. These access lists are applied to switch ports and can be configured to operate in ingress or egress with regard to traffic flows. PACL should not be confused with VLAN Access Lists (VACL). In fact, if a PACL and a VACL are applied simultaneously, the PACL will be processed first by the switch IOS. In this situation, let's say that inbound traffic was permitted by the PACL; it will then be tested by the VACL. This process affords administrators more granular control over "interesting" traffic when it comes to transit devices like switches.

Example 9-41 illustrates both the basic configuration and the directional nature of these configuration tools.

Example 9-41 *PACL Configuration*

```
!!!!!!!!!!!!!!!!!!!!!!!!!!!!!!!!!!!!!!!!!!!!!!!!!!
CAT2(config)# int g1/0/1
CAT2(config-if)# ip access-group PACLIPList in
CAT2(config-if)# mac access-group PACLMACList in
CAT2(config-if)#
```

Foundation Summary

This section lists additional details and facts to round out the coverage of the topics in this chapter. Unlike most of the Cisco Press Exam Certification Guides, this "Foundation Summary" does not repeat information presented in the "Foundation Topics" section of the chapter. Please take the time to read and study the details in the "Foundation Topics" section of the chapter, as well as review items noted with a Key Topic icon.

Table 9-12 lists some of the key protocols covered in this chapter.

Table 9-12 *Protocols and Standards for Chapter 9*

Name	Standard
RADIUS	RFC 2865
Port-Based Network Access Control	IEEE 802.1X
EAP	RFC 3748
One-Time Password System	RFC 2289
Router Security	RFCs 2827 and 3704
Next Hop Resolution Protocol (NHRP)	RFC 2332
Secure Neighbor Discovery (SeND)	RFC 3971

Table 9-13 lists some of the most popular router IOS commands related to the topics in this chapter.

Table 9-13 *Router IOS Commands Related to Chapter 9*

Command	Description
service password-encryption	Global command to enable simple encryption of passwords
aaa group server radius | tacacs+ *group-name*	Global command to create the name of a group of AAA servers
aaa group server ldap	Defines the AAA server group with a group name and enters LDAP server group configuration mode
server *ip-address* [auth-port *port-number*] [acct-port *port-number*]	AAA group mode; defines a RADIUS server and ports used
radius-server host {*hostname* | *ip-address*} [auth-port *port-number*] [acct-port *port-number*] [timeout *seconds*] [retransmit *retries*] [key *string*] [alias{*hostname* | *ip-address*}]	Global mode; defines details regarding a single RADIUS server

Command	Description
radius-server key {**0** *string* | **7** *string* | *string*}	Global mode; defines the key used to encrypt RADIUS passwords
tacacs-server host {*host-name* | *host-ip-address*} [**key** *string*] [**nat**] [**port** [*integer*]] [**single-connection**] [**timeout** [*integer*]]	Global mode; defines details regarding a single TACACS+ server
tacacs-server key *key*	Global mode; defines the key used to encrypt the TACACS+ payload
aaa authentication enable default *method1* [*method2...*]	Global mode; defines the default authentication methods used by the **enable** command
aaa authentication login {**default** | *list-name*} *method1* [*method2...*]	Global mode; defines the default authentication methods used by console, vty, and aux logins
aaa authentication ppp {**default** | *list-name*} *method1* [*method2...*]	Global mode; defines the default authentication methods used by PPP
aaa new-model	Global mode; enables AAA globally in a router/switch
login authentication {**default** | *list-name*}	Line mode; defines the AAA group to use for authentication
ppp authentication {*protocol1* [*protocol2...*]} [**if-needed**] [*list-name* | **default**] [**callin**] [**one-time**] [**optional**]	Interface mode; defines the type of AAA authentication used by PPP
auto secure [**management** | **forwarding**] [**no-interact**]	Global mode; automatically configures IOS with the Cisco-recommended device security configuration
enable password [**level** *level*] {*password* | [*encryption-type*] *encrypted-password*}	Global mode; defines the enable password
enable secret [**level** *level*] {*password* | [*encryption-type*] *encrypted-password*}	Global mode; defines the enable password that is MD5 hashed
ip verify unicast reverse-path [*list*]	Interface subcommand; enables strict RPF
ip verify unicast source reachable-via {**rx** | **any**} [**allow-default**] [**allow-self-ping**] [*list*]	Interface subcommand; enables strict or loose RPF
username *name* {**nopassword** | **password** *password*}	Global mode; defines local usernames and passwords
username *name* **secret** {[**0**] *password* | **5** *encrypted-secret*}	Global mode; defines local usernames and MD5-hashed passwords
ip tcp intercept list *access-list-number*	Global mode; identifies an ACL to be used by TCP intercept

Command	Description
ip tcp intercept mode {intercept | watch}	Global mode; defines the mode used by TCP intercept
ip tcp intercept watch-timeout *seconds*	Global mode; defines the timeout used before acting to clean up an incomplete TCP connection
ip inspect name inspection-name protocol [timeout seconds]	Global mode; configures inspection rules for CBAC
ip inspect inspection-name {in | out}	Interface mode; applies a CBAC inspection rule to an interface
zone security *name*	Global mode; creates an IOS ZFW security zone
zone-pair security *name* **source** *source-zone-name* **destination** *destination-zone-name*	Global mode; creates IOS ZFW zone pairs
class-map type inspect *name*	Global mode; creates a ZFW class map
parameter-map type inspect *name*	Global mode; creates a ZFW parameter map
policy-map type inspect	Global mode; creates a ZFW service policy
service-policy type inspect *name*	Zone-pair configuration mode; assigns a policy map to a zone pair
zone-member security *zone-name*	Interface mode; associates an interface with a ZFW zone
show ip ips configuration	Displays detailed IOS IPS configuration information
crypto key pubkey-chain rsa	Global mode; creates an IOS IPS crypto key
ip ips signature-category	Global mode; load or make changes to an IPS signature package
ip ips *name*	Global mode; creates an IOS IPS signature rule
ip ips *name* **[outbound | inbound]**	Interface mode; assigns an IOS IPS rule to an interface
show ip ips configuration	Displays the IOS IPS configuration
ip nhrp authentication *password*	Configures password authentication for NHRP traffic
ip nhrp nhs *ip*	Identifies the IP address of the NHS server ("Hub")

Command	Description
ip nhrp map multicast	Identifies the IP address of the "Hub" such that multicast and broadcast traffic can be passed between DMVPN members. Additionally, this could be configured as dynamic rather than statically configured
ip nhrp map *nbma ip dmvpn ip*	Provides one-to-one mapping for reachability to the NBMA address of the hub
ip nhrp network-id *number*	Specifies the network number to be shared between devices participating in the same DMVPN cloud
ipv6 dhcp guard policy name	Defines the DHCPv6 Guard policy name and enters DHCP Guard configuration mode

Table 9-14 lists some of the Catalyst IOS switch commands used in this chapter.

Table 9-14   *Catalyst IOS Commands Related to Chapter 9*

Command	Description
spanning-tree guard root	Interface mode; enables Root Guard.
aaa authentication dot1x {default} *method1*	Global mode; defines the default authentication method for 802.1X. Only one method is available, because only RADIUS is supported.
arp access-list *acl-name*	Global mode; creates an ARP ACL with the stated name.
dot1x system-auth-control	Global mode; enables 802.1X.
dot1x port-control {auto | force-authorized | force-unauthorized}	Interface mode; defines 802.1X actions on the interface.
dot1x timeout {quiet-period *seconds* | reauth-period *seconds* | server-timeout *seconds* | supp-timeout *seconds* | tx-period *seconds*}	Global mode; sets 802.1X timers.
control plane	Global mode; accesses the router or switch control-plane configuration mode
service-policy input *name*	Control plane configuration mode; applies a policy map to the control plane
show policy-map control-plane	Displays the CoPP policy actions

Memory Builders

The CCIE Routing and Switching written exam, like all Cisco CCIE written exams, covers a fairly broad set of topics. This section provides some basic tools to help you exercise your memory about some of the broader topics covered in this chapter.

Fill In Key Tables from Memory

Appendix E, "Key Tables for CCIE Study," on the CD in the back of this book, contains empty sets of some of the key summary tables in each chapter. Print Appendix E, refer to this chapter's tables in it, and fill in the tables from memory. Refer to Appendix F, "Solutions for Key Tables for CCIE Study," on the CD, to check your answers.

Definitions

Next, take a few moments to write down the definitions for the following terms:

AAA, authentication method, RADIUS, TACACS+, MD5 hash, enable password, enable secret, ACS, SAFE Blueprint, DAI, port security, IEEE 802.1X, DHCP snooping, IP Source Guard, man-in-the-middle attack, sticky learning, fraggle attack, DHCP snooping binding database, EAP, EAPoL, OTP, supplicant, authenticator, authentication server, smurf attack, TCP SYN flood, TCP intercept, ACE, storm control, CBAC, classic IOS firewall, zone-based IOS firewall, IOS IPS, inspection rule, DMVPN, CoPP

Refer to the glossary to check your answers.

Further Reading

Network Security Principles and Practices, by Saadat Malik

Network Security Architectures, by Sean Convery

Router Security Strategies, by Gregg Schudel and David Smith

LAN Switch Security: What Hackers Know About Your Switches, by Eric Vyncke and Christopher Paggen

Cisco SAFE Blueprint Introduction: www.cisco.com/go/safe

Cisco IOS Security Configuration Guide: Securing the Data Plane, Release 12.4, www.cisco.com/en/US/docs/ios/sec_data_plane/configuration/guide/12_4/sec_data_plane_12_4_book.html

"IPv6 First Hop Security—Protecting Your IPv6 Access Network": www.cisco.com/c/en/us/products/collateral/ios-nx-os-software/enterprise-ipv6-solution/whitepaper_c11-602135.html

"Dynamic Multipoint VPN (DMVPN)," www.cisco.com/en/US/docs/ios/sec_secure_connectivity/configuration/guide/sec_DMVPN_ps6350_TSD_Products_Configuration_Guide_Chapter.html

Blueprint topics covered in this chapter:

This chapter covers the following subtopics from the Cisco CCIE Routing and Switching written exam blueprint. Refer to the full blueprint in Table I-1 in the Introduction for more details on the topics covered in each chapter and their context within the blueprint.

- Generic Routing Encapsulation (GRE) Tunnels

- Dynamic Multipoint VPN (DMVPN) Tunnels

- IPv6 Tunneling and Related Techniques

- Layer 2 VPNs

- IP Security (IPsec) with Preshared Keys

- Group Encrypted Transport VPNs (GET VPN)

Tunneling Technologies

Chapter 10 discusses the independent Virtual Private Network technologies that need to be mastered as part of the CCIE Routing and Switching exam. These technologies come in many forms and varieties, and mastering each of them will involve working with many different authentication or encryption features. This chapter will focus on all the necessary skills to implement each of the basic features that are part of the lab exam.

Note that our involvement with aspects of this technology that extend to more specific security studies will be kept to a minimum.

"Do I Know This Already?" Quiz

Table 10-1 outlines the major headings in this chapter and the corresponding "Do I Know This Already?" quiz questions.

Table 10-1 *"Do I Know This Already?" Foundation Topics Section-to-Question Mapping*

Foundation Topics Section	Questions Covered in This Section	Score
DMVPN	1–3	
IPv6 Tunnels	4	
Layer 2 VPNs	5–7	
GET VPNs	8, 9	
Total Score		

To best use this pre-chapter assessment, remember to score yourself strictly. You can find the answers in Appendix A, "Answers to the 'Do I Know This Already?' Quizzes."

1. The main benefit of DMVPN is that it allows the traditional hub-and-spoke network design to better support what feature?

   a. Packet transmission

   b. Scalability

   c. Quality of service

   d. Traffic shaping

2. Several protocols combine to support the idea of a DMVPN solution, but foundationally a stable working DMVPN environment relies heavily on a number of Cisco-enhanced technologies. Choose the correct technologies.

   a. Generic Routing Encapsulation (GRE) Protocol

   b. First-Hop Redundancy Protocol (FHRP)

   c. Next-Hop Resolution Protocol (NHRP)

   d. Dynamic Routing Protocol

   e. Secure DMVPN

   f. IPsec encryption protocols

3. What new message type is sent from the hub to the spoke to let the spoke know that there is a better path to the other spoke than through the hub?

   a. ICMP Redirect

   b. Proxy ARP

   c. NHRP Redirect

   d. Local Proxy ARP

4. In an ipv6ip auto-tunnel, the destination for an IPv4-compatible tunnel is automatically determined by what portion of the tunnel interface address?

   a. Upper-order 32 bits

   b. Lower-order 16 bits

   c. Upper-order 16 bits

   d. Lower-order 32 bits

5. L2VPN is the simplest solution available to allow clients to manage network features that include which of the following?

   a. Routing protocols

   b. Policing policies

   c. QoS mechanisms

   d. IOS management protocols

   e. IP management

6. The output of the following command indicates what status associated with the DMVPN configuration?

```
R2# show xconnect all

Legend: XC ST=Xconnect State, S1=Segment1 State, S2=Segment2 State
UP=Up, DN=Down, AD=Admin Down, IA=Inactive, NH=No Hardware
XC ST Segment 1 S1 Segment 2 S2
------+-------------------------------+--+--------------------------------
+--
DN ac Fa0/0(Ethernet) AD mpls 4.4.4.4:204 DN
```

   a. The pseudowire link is up.

   b. The pseudowire link is administratively down.

   c. The pseudowire link is down.

   d. The pseudowire link is operating normally.

7. What are the two primary segments used in an MPLS Layer 2 pseudowire?

   a. Segment 1

   b. Segment A

   c. Segment B

   d. Segment 1-2

   e. Segment 2

8. In any DMVPN solution, the most important function of the key server is the generation of encryption keys. What two keys are created as a result of this process?

   a. RSA

   b. TEK

   c. SHA1

   d. TLS

   e. KEK

9. When configuring DMVPN group members, the encryption policy is created through an IPsec profile. What tool is used to identify what packets require encryption?

   a. ip prefix-list

   b. PACL

   c. ACL

   d. VACL

Foundation Topics

GRE Tunnels

Generic Routing Encapsulation (GRE) defines a method of tunneling data from one router to another. To tunnel the traffic, the sending router encapsulates packets of one networking protocol, called the passenger protocol, inside packets of another protocol, called the transport protocol, transporting these packets to another router. The receiving router deencapsulates and forwards the original passenger protocol packets. This process allows the routers in the network to forward traffic that might not be natively supported by the intervening routers. For example, if some routers did not support IP multicast, the IP multicast traffic could be tunneled from one router to another using IP unicast packets.

GRE tunnels are useful for a variety of tasks. From the network standpoint, GRE tunnel traffic is considered GRE; that is, it's not IP unicast or multicast or IPsec or whatever else is being encapsulated. Therefore, you can use GRE to tunnel traffic that might not otherwise be able to traverse the network. An example of this is encapsulating multicast IP traffic within a GRE tunnel to allow it to pass across a network that does not support multicast.

GRE tunnels can also be used to encapsulate traffic so that the traffic inside the tunnel is unaware of the network topology. Regardless of the number of network hops between the source and destination, the traffic passing over the tunnel sees it as a single hop. Because tunnels hide the network topology, the actual traffic path across a network is also unimportant to the traffic inside the tunnel. If loopback addresses are used for source and destination addresses, the tunnel provides connectivity between the source and destination as long as there is any available route between the loopbacks. Even if the normal egress interface were to go down, traffic across the tunnel could continue to flow.

IPsec virtual tunnel interfaces (VTI) are routable interfaces used for terminating IPsec tunnels and are often an easy way to define protection between sites. VTIs simplify configuration of IPsec for protection of remote links, simplify network management, and support multicast. The IPsec VTI enables flexibility of sending and receiving both IP unicast and multicast encrypted traffic on any physical interface. For the purposes of the CCIE Exam, it's important to understand the benefits of virtual tunnel interfaces and how to configure a VTI using the various tunneling mechanisms including GRE, Layer 2 Virtual Private Networks (L2VPN), and Multiprotocol Label Switching (MPLS).

The router must be configured to pass the desired traffic across the tunnel. This is often accomplished using a static route to point traffic to the tunnel interface.

Example 10-1 shows a typical tunnel configuration on two routers. Both routers source traffic from a loopback interface and point to the corresponding loopback interface. IP addresses in a new subnet on these routers are assigned to the loopback interfaces.

Example 10-1   *GRE Tunnel Configuration*

```
R2# show run int lo0
interface Loopback0
 ip address 150.1.2.2 255.255.255.0
R2# show run int tun0
interface Tunnel0
  ip address 192.168.201.2 255.255.255.0
  tunnel source Loopback0
  tunnel destination 150.1.3.3
! Now on to R3:
R3# show run int lo0
interface Loopback0
 ip address 150.1.3.3 255.255.255.128
R3# show run int tun0
interface Tunnel0
 ip address 192.168.201.3 255.255.255.0
 tunnel source Loopback0
 tunnel destination 150.1.2.2
R3# show ip interface brief
Interface            IP-Address       OK? Method Status        Protocol
Serial0/2            144.254.254.3    YES TFTP   up            up
Serial0/3            unassigned       YES NVRAM  up            down
Virtual-Access1      unassigned       YES unset  up            up
Loopback0            150.1.3.3        YES NVRAM  up            up
Tunnel0              192.168.201.3    YES manual up            up
```

Dynamic Multipoint VPN Tunnels

There is no escaping the fact that VPN-based security architectures are proving their worth in modern distributed infrastructures. The ever-changing landscape of our networks demands that sensitive data be sent from point to point through different mediums, many of which, like the Internet, are insecure. So it should come as no surprise that tools to protect that data are also expanding and evolving.

Evolution is not the only external force acting on our network architectures. As network engineers, we find ourselves constantly looking at how things have been traditionally done, and asking ourselves whether those methods are going to be efficient and scalable for our individual organizational needs. Take the typical IPsec-based hub-and-spoke deployment model. This solution has been used for decades to provide interconnectivity for site-to-site networks, but looking at how our needs are constantly expanding, it becomes evident that what was traditional yesterday is rapidly become less and less adequate for larger or enterprise-size networks. These "enterprise" networks need a scalable and more dynamic solution that will provide secure transport of information across wide-area network topology through the application of dynamic features, like IPsec, that

[handwritten margin note: better scalability with DMVPN]

will optimize network performance by decreasing latency and maximizing bandwidth utilization.

Dynamic Multipoint VPN (DMVPN) technology is one such feature. DMVPN provides much-needed scalability to distributed infrastructures; scalability can help virtually any network expand simply and easily to its full potential.

DMVPN Operation

The main benefit of DMVPN is that it allows the tradition hub-and-spoke network design to better support scalability. This enhanced ability to service more capacity means reduced latency and optimized performance for traffic exchange between multiple sites. This one simple enhancement translates directly to a number of immediate benefits:

- Dynamic tunnels across hub-and-spoke topologies
- Increased network performance
- Reduced latency, which provides immediate optimization for "real-time" applications
- Reduced router configuration
- Ability to dynamically add more tunnels to new sites without modifying the hub router configuration ("zero-touch") *[handwritten margin note: add no config on the hub]*
- Dynamic IPsec encryption that eliminates packet loss
- Dynamic "spoke-to-spoke" tunnels between sites (intersite communication) that bypasses the hub
- Support for routing protocols over individual or all tunnels
- Support for multicast traffic
- Virtual Routing and Forwarding (VRF) awareness
- Supports MPLS
- Supports load balancing
- Automatically reroutes traffic during network outages

Geographic site isolation and the "slow" internetwork connections used to transport traffic between them have long plagued the distributed network deployment model, but keep in mind that other factors are also contributors, to include network availability and secure communications options. DMVPN is the perfect solution to the problem; it is secure, it is scalable, and it is self-healing.

DMVPN Components

Several protocols combine to support the idea of a DMVPN solution, but foundationally a stable working DMVPN environment relies heavily on a number of Cisco-enhanced technologies:

- Generic Routing Encapsulation (GRE) Protocol

- Next-Hop Resolution Protocol (NHRP)

- Dynamic routing protocols

- IPsec encryption protocols

DMVPN Operation

DMVPN primarily distills down to one clear-cut operation the creation of dynamic tunnel overlay networks. In this design, each spoke becomes a persistent IPsec tunnel to the hub. Keep in mind that spokes in this scenario will not build tunnels with other spokes. For this process to function reliably, the address of the hub must be known by all the spokes in the topology. Using this information, each spoke will register its actual address as a client to the NHRP server process running on the hub. It is this NHRP server that is responsible for maintaining a database of all the public interface addresses used by each spoke during its registration process. In situations where a spoke requires packets to be sent to a destination (in this case, a private address) on another spoke, it will solicit the NHRP server for the public (outside) address of the other spoke device so that it can create a direct tunnel. The reliance on the NHRP server eliminates the need for dynamic routing protocols to discover routes to spokes. We mentioned dynamic routing protocols in the previous list, but those protocols only create adjacencies between spoke devices and the hub.

After the spoke is informed of the peer address of the destination device (spoke), it will initiate a dynamic IPsec tunnel to that target, thus creating a dynamic spoke-to-spoke tunnel over the DMVPN topology. These tunnels are going to be established on demand, meaning whenever traffic is forwarded between spokes but after they have been created, packets can bypass the hub and use the tunnel directly.

To illustrate this process, we will pursue the implementation of the technology on the command line by taking an analytical look at the feature following the recommended three-phase implementation.

DMVPN Phase 1 introduces a simple hub-and-spoke topology where dynamic IP addresses on the spokes are used, as shown in Example 10-2.

Example 10-2 *Simple Hub-and-Spoke Topology with Dynamic IP Addresses*

```
!First we need ISAKMP Policy with pre-shared key configured. Note that in DMVPN we
!need to configure so-called "wildcard PSK" because there may be many peers. This
!is why a more common solution in DMVPN is to use certificates and PKI.


R1(config)# crypto isakmp policy 1
R1(config-isakmp)# encr 3des
R1(config-isakmp)# authentication pre-share
R1(config-isakmp)# group 2
```

```
R1(config-isakmp)# crypto isakmp key cisco123 address 0.0.0.0 0.0.0.0
R1(config)# crypto ipsec transform-set TSET esp-3des esp-sha-hmac
R1(cfg-crypto-trans)# mode transport
```

!The "mode transport" is used for decreasing IPSec packet size (an outer IP header
!which is present in tunnel mode is not added in the transport mode).

```
R1(cfg-crypto-trans)# crypto ipsec profile DMVPN
R1(ipsec-profile)# set transform-set TSET
R1(ipsec-profile)# exi
```

!There is only one interface Tunnel on every DMVPN router. This is because we use
!GRE \ multipoint type of the tunnel.

```
R1(config)# interface Tunnel0
R1(config-if)# ip address 172.16.145.1 255.255.255.0
R1(config-if)# ip mtu 1400
```

!Maximum Transmission Unit is decreased to ensure that DMVPN packet would not
!exceed IP MTU set on non-tunnel IP interfaces – usually a 1500 bytes (When
!"transport mode" isused then DMVPN packet consists of original IP Packet, GRE
!header, ESP header and outer IPSec IP header. If original IP packet size is close
!to the IP MTU set on real IP interface then adding GRE and IPSec headers may lead
!to exceeding that value)

```
R1(config-if)# ip nhrp authentication cisco123
R1(config-if)# ip nhrp map multicast dynamic
R1(config-if)# ip nhrp network-id 12345
```

!The Hub works as NHS (Next Hop Server). The NHRP configuration on the Hub is
!straight forward. First, we need NHRP network ID to identify the instance and
!authenticate key to secure NHRP registration. There is a need for NHRP static
!mapping on the Hub. The Hub must be able to send down all multicast traffic so
!that dynamic routing protocols can distribute routes between spokes. The line "ip
!nhrp map multicast dynamic" simply tells the NHRP server to replicate all multi
!cast traffic to all dynamic entries in the NHRP table (entries with flag
!"dynamic").

```
R1(config-if)# no ip split-horizon eigrp 145
```

```
!Since we use EIGRP between the Hub and the Spokes, we need to disable Split Horizon
!for that protocol to be able to send routes gathered from one Spoke to the other
!Spoke. The Split Horizon rule says: "information about the routing is never sent
!back in the direction from which it was received". This is basic rule for loop
!prevention.


R1(config-if)# tunnel source FastEthernet0/0
R1(config-if)# tunnel mode gre multipoint
R1(config-if)# tunnel key 12345
R1(config-if)# tunnel protection ipsec profile DMVPN


!A regular GRE tunnel usually needs source and destination of the tunnel to be
!specified. However in the GRE multipoint tunnel type, there is no need for a
!destination. This is because there may be many destinations, as many Spokes are
!out there. The actual tunnel destination is derived form NHRP database. The tunnel
!has a key for identification purposes, as there may be many tunnels on one
!router and the router must know what tunnel the packet is destined to.
```

DMVPN Phase 2 introduces a new feature, which is direct spoke-to-spoke communication through the DMVPN network. It is useful for companies that have communication between branches and want to reduce the hub's overhead. Example 10-3 describes DMVPN Phase 2 when Enhanced Interior Gateway Routing Protocol (EIGRP) is in use. This is important to understand the difference between routing protocols used in the DMVPN solution. They must be especially configured or tuned to work in the most scalable and efficient way. However, there are some disadvantages of using one protocol or another.

Example 10-3 *Hub-and-Spoke Topology with Spoke-to-Spoke Connection*

```
R1(config)# crypto isakmp policy 1
R1(config-isakmp)# encr 3des
R1(config-isakmp)# authentication pre-share
R1(config-isakmp)# group 2
R1(config-isakmp)# crypto isakmp key cisco123 address 0.0.0.0 0.0.0.0
R1(config)# crypto ipsec transform-set TSET esp-3des esp-sha-hmac
R1(cfg-crypto-trans)# mode transport
R1(cfg-crypto-trans)# crypto ipsec profile DMVPN
R1(ipsec-profile)# set transform-set TSET
R1(ipsec-profile)# exi
R1(config)# interface Tunnel0
R1(config-if)# ip address 172.16.145.1 255.255.255.0
R1(config-if)# ip mtu 1400
R1(config-if)# ip nhrp authentication cisco123
R1(config-if)# ip nhrp map multicast dynamic
R1(config-if)# ip nhrp network-id 12345
```

```
R1(config-if)# no ip split-horizon eigrp 145
R1(config-if)# no ip next-hop-self eigrp 145
```

(handwritten: } split horizone)

```
!The difference is in routing protocol behavior. The DMVPN Phase 2 allows for
!direct Spoke to Spoke communication. Hence, one spoke must send the traffic to the
!other spoke using its routing table information. In DMVPN Phase 1 the spoke sends
!all traffic up to the Hub and uses the Hub for Spoke to Spoke communication. How
!ever,in DMVPN Phase 2 a spoke must point to the other spoke directly.

!This is achieved by changing the routing protocol behavior. The EIGRP changes next
!hop in the routing update when sending it further so that, the Hub changes the
!next hop to itself when sending down the routing updates to the Spokes. This
!behavior can be changed by the command "no ip next-hop-self eigrp AS".

R1(config-if)# tunnel source FastEthernet0/0
R1(config-if)# tunnel mode gre multipoint

!Note that in DMVPN Phase 2 the Hub is in GRE Multipoint mode as it was in Phase 1.

R1(config-if)# tunnel key 12345
R1(config-if)# tunnel protection ipsec profile DMVPN
R1(config-if)# exi
%LINEPROTO-5-UPDOWN: Line protocol on Interface Tunnel0, changed state to up
%CRYPTO-6-ISAKMP_ON_OFF: ISAKMP is ON
R1(config)# router eigrp 145
R1(config-router)# network 172.16.145.0 0.0.0.255
R1(config-router)# network 192.168.1.0
R1(config-router)# no auto-summary
R1(config-router)# exi
```

After this procedure is completed, we can verify the configuration through a number of commands, a few of which can be seen in Example 10-4.

Example 10-4   *DMVPN Verification*

```
R1# sh crypto ipsec sa
interface: Tunnel0
Crypto map tag: Tunnel0-head-0, local addr 10.1.12.1
protected vrf: (none)
local  ident (addr/mask/prot/port): (10.1.12.1/255.255.255.255/47/0)
remote ident (addr/mask/prot/port): (10.1.24.4/255.255.255.255/47/0)
current_peer 10.1.24.4 port 500
PERMIT, flags={origin_is_acl,}
#pkts encaps: 19, #pkts encrypt: 19, #pkts digest: 19
#pkts decaps: 18, #pkts decrypt: 18, #pkts verify: 18
#pkts compressed: 0, #pkts decompressed: 0
```

```
#pkts not compressed: 0, #pkts compr. failed: 0
#pkts not decompressed: 0, #pkts decompress failed: 0
#send errors 0, #recv errors 0


!The traffic is going through the tunnel between the Hub and the Spoke. This traffic
!is an EIGRP updates as we have not initiated any traffic yet.


local crypto endpt.: 10.1.12.1, remote crypto endpt.: 10.1.24.4
path mtu 1500, ip mtu 1500, ip mtu idb FastEthernet0/0
current outbound spi: 0x49DC5EAF(1239178927)
inbound esp sas:
spi: 0xF483377E(4102240126)
transform: esp-3des esp-sha-hmac ,
in use settings ={Transport, }
conn id: 2003, flow_id: NETGX:3, crypto map: Tunnel0-head-0
sa timing: remaining key lifetime (k/sec): (4524624/3565)
IV size: 8 bytes
replay detection support: Y
Status: ACTIVE
inbound ah sas:
inbound pcp sas:
outbound esp sas:
spi: 0x49DC5EAF(1239178927)
transform: esp-3des esp-sha-hmac ,
in use settings ={Transport, }
conn id: 2004, flow_id: NETGX:4, crypto map: Tunnel0-head-0
sa timing: remaining key lifetime (k/sec): (4524622/3565)
IV size: 8 bytes
replay detection support: Y
Status: ACTIVE
outbound ah sas:
outbound pcp sas:
protected vrf: (none)
local  ident (addr/mask/prot/port): (10.1.12.1/255.255.255.255/47/0)
remote ident (addr/mask/prot/port): (10.1.25.5/255.255.255.255/47/0)
current_peer 10.1.25.5 port 500
PERMIT, flags={origin_is_acl,}
#pkts encaps: 17, #pkts encrypt: 17, #pkts digest: 17
#pkts decaps: 15, #pkts decrypt: 15, #pkts verify: 15
#pkts compressed: 0, #pkts decompressed: 0
#pkts not compressed: 0, #pkts compr. failed: 0
#pkts not decompressed: 0, #pkts decompress failed: 0
#send errors 0, #recv errors 0


!The traffic is going through the tunnel between the Hub and the Spoke. This traffic
```

```
!is an EIGRP update as we have not initiated any traffic yet.

local crypto endpt.: 10.1.12.1, remote crypto endpt.: 10.1.25.5
path mtu 1500, ip mtu 1500, ip mtu idb FastEthernet0/0
current outbound spi: 0x1FB68E8D(532057741)
inbound esp sas:
spi: 0xE487940A(3834090506)
transform: esp-3des esp-sha-hmac ,
in use settings ={Transport, }
conn id: 2001, flow_id: NETGX:1, crypto map: Tunnel0-head-0
sa timing: remaining key lifetime (k/sec): (4411380/3563)
IV size: 8 bytes
replay detection support: Y
Status: ACTIVE
inbound ah sas:
inbound pcp sas:
outbound esp sas:
spi: 0x1FB68E8D(532057741)
transform: esp-3des esp-sha-hmac ,
in use settings ={Transport, }
conn id: 2002, flow_id: NETGX:2, crypto map: Tunnel0-head-0
sa timing: remaining key lifetime (k/sec): (4411379/3563)
IV size: 8 bytes
replay detection support: Y
Status: ACTIVE
outbound ah sas:
outbound pcp sas:
```

DMVPN Phase 3 was introduced by Cisco to fix some disadvantages found in Phase 2. Specifically, these issues include scalability and performance issues. Example 10-5 illustrates how the DMVPN process is implemented:

- Phase 2 allows hub daisy-chaining, Open Shortest Path First (OSPF) single area, and a limited number of hubs because of OSPF DR/DBR election.

- Scalability: Phase 2 does not allow route summarization on the hub; all prefixes must be distributed to all spokes to be able to set up direct spoke-to-spoke tunnels.

- Performance: Phase 2 sends first packets through the hub using process switching (not Cisco Express Forwarding [CEF]), causing CPU spikes.

- DMVPN Phase 3 uses two NHRP enhancements to remedy the Phase 2 disadvantages outlined above:

  - **NHRP Redirect:** A new message is sent from the hub to the spoke to let the spoke know that there is a better path to the other spoke than through the hub.

  - **NHRP Shortcut:** A new way of changing (overwriting) CEF information on the spoke.

Example 10-5 *DMVPN Phase 3*

```
R2(config)# crypto isakmp policy 10
R2(config-isakmp)# encr 3des
R2(config-isakmp)# authentication pre-share
R2(config-isakmp)# group 2
R2(config-isakmp)# crypto isakmp key cisco123 address 0.0.0.0 0.0.0.0
R2(config)# crypto ipsec transform-set TSET esp-3des esp-sha-hmac
R2(cfg-crypto-trans)# mode transport
R2(cfg-crypto-trans)# crypto ipsec profile DMVPN
R2(ipsec-profile)# set transform-set TSET
R2(ipsec-profile)# exi
R2(config)# int Tunnel0
R2(config-if)# ip address 172.16.245.2 255.255.255.0
R2(config-if)# ip mtu 1400
R2(config-if)# ip nhrp authentication cisco123
R2(config-if)# ip nhrp map multicast dynamic
R2(config-if)# ip nhrp network-id 123
R2(config-if)# ip nhrp redirect

!NHRP Redirect is a special NHRP message sent by the Hub to the spoke to tell the
!spoke that there is a better path to the remote spoke than through the Hub. All
!it does is enforces the spoke to trigger an NHRP resolution request to IP
!destination. The "ip nhrp redirect" command should be configured on the Hub only.

R2(config-if)# tunnel source s0/1/0
R2(config-if)# tunnel mode gre multipoint
R2(config-if)# tunnel key 123
R2(config-if)# tunnel protection ipsec profile DMVPN
R2(config-if)# no ip split-horizon eigrp 245
Note that we do not need "no ip next-hop-self eigrp" command in the DMVPN Pahse 3.
R2(config-if)# exi
%CRYPTO-6-ISAKMP_ON_OFF: ISAKMP is ON
R2(config)# router eigrp 245
R2(config-router)# no auto
R2(config-router)# net 172.16.245.2 0.0.0.0
R2(config-router)# net 192.168.2.2 0.0.0.0
R2(config-router)# exi
```

IPv6 Tunneling and Related Techniques

When IPv6 development and initial deployment began in the 1990s, most of the world's networks were already built on an IPv4 infrastructure. As a result, several groups recognized that there was going to be a need for ways to transport IPv6 over IPv4 networks and, as some people anticipated, vice versa.

One of the key reasons for tunneling is that today's Internet is IPv4 based, yet at least two major academic and research networks use IPv6 natively, and it is desirable to provide mechanisms for hosts on those networks to reach each other over the IPv4 Internet. Tunneling is one of the ways to support that communication. *btw IPv 4&6.*

As you might gather, tunneling meets a number of needs in a mixed IPv4 and IPv6 world; as a result, several kinds of tunneling methods and techniques have emerged. This section looks at several of them and examines one in detail.

Tunneling Overview

Tunneling, in a general sense, is encapsulating traffic. More specifically, the term usually refers to the process of encapsulating traffic at a given layer of the OSI seven-layer model *within another protocol running at the same layer*. Therefore, encapsulating IPv6 packets within IPv4 packets and encapsulating IPv4 packets within IPv6 packets are both considered tunneling.

For the purposes of this book, which is to meet the CCIE Routing and Switching blueprint requirements, in this section, we are mostly interested in methods of carrying IPv6 over IPv4 networks, not the other way around. This chapter also does not explore methods of tunneling IPv6 inside IPv6. However, you should be aware that both of these types of tunneling exist, in addition to the ones covered here. With that in mind, consider some of the more common tunneling methods, starting with a summary shown in Table 10-2.

Table 10-2 *Summary of Tunneling Methods*

Tunnel Mode	Topology and Address Space	Applications
Automatic 6to4	Point-to-multipoint; 2002::/16 addresses	Connecting isolated IPv6 island networks.
Manually configured	Point-to-point; any address space; requires dual-stack support at both ends	Carries only IPv6 packets across IPv4 networks.
IPv6 over IPv4 GRE	Point-to-point; unicast addresses; requires dual-stack support at both ends	Carries IPv6, CLNS, and other traffic.
ISATAP	Point-to-multipoint; any multicast addresses	Intended for connecting IPv6 hosts within a single site.
Automatic IPv4-compatible	Point-to-multipoint; ::/96 address space; requires dual-stack support at both ends	Deprecated. Cisco recommends using Intra-Site Automatic Tunnel Addressing Protocol (ISATAP) tunnels instead. Coverage in this book is limited.

In case you are not familiar with implementing tunnels based on IPv4, take a moment to cover the basic steps involved: *How to implement an IPv4 tunnel:*

Step 1.   Ensure end-to-end IPv4 reachability between the tunnel endpoints.

Step 2.   Create the tunnel interface using the **interface tunnel** *n* command.

Step 3.   Select a tunnel source interface and configure it using the **tunnel source interface** {*interface-type-number* | *ip-address*} command.

Step 4.   For nonautomatic tunnel types, configure the tunnel destination using the **tunnel destination** {*ip-address* | *ipv6-address* | *hostname*} command. To use the **hostname** argument, Domain Name System (DNS) or local host name–to–IP address mapping is required.

Step 5.   Configure the tunnel IPv6 address (or prefix, depending on tunnel type).

Step 6.   Configure the tunnel mode using the **tunnel mode** *mode* command.

Table 10-3 shows the Cisco IOS tunnel modes and the destinations for the tunnel types covered in this section.

Table 10-3   *Cisco IOS Tunnel Modes and Destinations*

Tunnel Type	Tunnel Mode	Destination
Manual	**ipv6ip**	An IPv4 address
GRE over IPv4	**gre ip**	An IPv4 address
Automatic 6to4	**ipv6ip 6to4**	Automatically determined
ISATAP	**ipv6ip isatap**	Automatically determined
Automatic IPv4-compatible	**ipv6ip auto-tunnel**	Automatically determined

Let's take a closer look at the methods of carrying IPv6 traffic over an IPv4 network.

Manually Configured Tunnels

This tunnel type is point-to-point in nature. Cisco IOS requires statically configuring the destination addresses of these tunnels. Configuring a manual IPv6-over-IPv4 tunnel is almost identical to configuring an IPv4 GRE tunnel; the only difference is setting the tunnel mode. Example 10-6 and Figure 10-1 show a manually configured tunnel. IPv4 reachability has already been configured and verified, but is not shown.

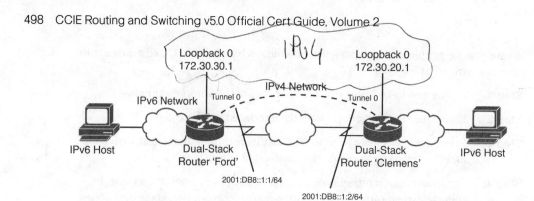

Figure 10-1 *Manually Configured Tunnel*

Example 10-6 *Manual Tunnel Configuration*

```
! In this example, Clemens and Ford are running IPv4 and OSPFv2 on their
! loopback 0 interfaces and the link that connects the two routers. This provides
! the IPv4 connectivity required for these tunnels to work.
!Configuration on the Ford router:
Ford# show run interface tunnel0
interface Tunnel0
 no ip address
 ipv6 address 2001:DB8::1:1/64
 tunnel source Loopback0
! In the tunnel destination, 172.30.20.1 is Clemens's Loopback0 interface:
 tunnel destination 172.30.20.1
 tunnel mode ipv6ip
Ford#
! Configuration on the Clemens router:
Clemens# show run interface tunnel0
interface Tunnel0
 no ip address
 ipv6 address 2001:DB8::1:2/64
 tunnel source Loopback0
! In the tunnel destination, 172.30.30.1 is Ford's Loopback0 interface:
 tunnel destination 172.30.30.1
 tunnel mode ipv6ip
! Demonstrating reachability across the tunnel:
Clemens# ping 2001:DB8::1:1
Type escape sequence to abort.
Sending 5, 100-byte ICMP Echos to 2001:DB8::1:1, timeout is 2 seconds:
!!!!!
Success rate is 100 percent (5/5), round-trip min/avg/max = 36/36/40 ms
Clemens#
```

Automatic IPv4-Compatible Tunnels

This type of tunnel uses IPv4-compatible IPv6 addresses for the tunnel interfaces. These addresses are taken from the ::/96 address space. That is, the first 96 bits of the tunnel interface addresses are all 0s, and the remaining 32 bits are derived from an IPv4 address. These addresses are written as 0:0:0:0:0:0:A.B.C.D, or ::A.B.C.D, where A.B.C.D represents the IPv4 address.

The tunnel destination for an IPv4-compatible tunnel is automatically determined from the low-order 32 bits of the tunnel interface address. To implement this tunnel type, use the **tunnel mode ipv6ip auto-tunnel** command in tunnel interface configuration mode.

IPv4-compatible IPv6 addressing is not widely deployed and does not conform to current global usage of the IPv6 address space. Furthermore, this tunneling method does not scale well. Therefore, Cisco recommends using ISATAP tunnels instead of this method, and for these reasons, this book does not explore this tunnel type further.

IPv6-over-IPv4 GRE Tunnels

GRE tunnels provide two options that the other tunnel types do not—namely, encapsulating traffic other than IPv6 and support for IPsec. Like the manually configured variety, GRE tunnels are designed for point-to-point operation. With IPv6 as the passenger protocol, typically these tunnels are deployed between edge routers to provide connectivity between two IPv6 "islands" across an IPv4 cloud.

Configuring GRE tunnels for transporting IPv6 packets over an IPv4 network is straightforward. The only difference between GRE and the manual tunneling example shown in Example 10-6 is the syntax of the **tunnel mode** command, which for GRE is **tunnel mode gre ipv6**.

Automatic 6to4 Tunnels

Unlike the previous two tunnel types that we have discussed, automatic 6to4 tunnels are inherently point-to-multipoint in nature. These tunnels treat the underlying IPv4 network as an NBMA cloud.

Key Topic

In automatic 6to4 tunnels, the tunnel operates on a per-packet basis to encapsulate traffic to the correct destination—thus its point-to-multipoint nature. These tunnels determine the appropriate destination address by combining the IPv6 prefix with the globally unique destination 6to4 border router's IPv4 address, beginning with the 2002::/16 prefix, in this format:

2002:*border-router-IPv4-address*::/48

This prefix-generation method leaves another 16 bits in the 64-bit prefix for numbering networks within a given site.

Cisco IOS supports configuring only one automatic 6to4 tunnel on a given router. Configuring these tunnels is similar to configuring the other tunnels previously discussed, except that the tunnel mode is configured using the **tunnel mode ipv6ip 6to4** command. Also, the tunnel destination is not explicitly configured for 6to4 tunnels because of the automatic nature of the per-packet destination prefix determination method that 6to4 uses.

In addition to the basic tunnel configuration, the extra step of providing for routing the desired packets over the tunnel is also required. This is usually done using a static route. For example, to route packets destined for prefix 2002::/16 over the tunnel0 6to4 tunnel interface, configure this static route:

```
ipv6 route 2002::/16 tunnel 0
```

Example 10-7 and Figure 10-2 show a sample of a 6to4 tunnel and the routers' other relevant interfaces to tie together the concepts of 6to4 tunneling. In the example, note that the Fast Ethernet interfaces and the tunnel interface get the bold portion of the prefix 2002:0a01:6401:: from the Ethernet 0 interface's IPv4 address, 10.1.100.1. For this type of tunnel to work, the tunnel source interface must be the connection to the outside world, in this case the Ethernet 2/0 interface. Furthermore, each Fast Ethernet interface where hosts connect is (and must be) a different IPv6 subnet with the 2002:0a01:6401 prefix.

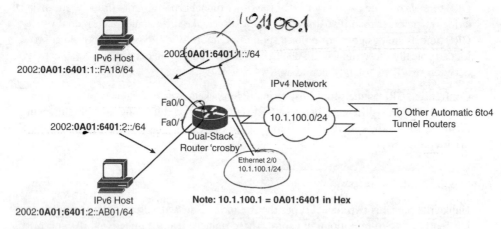

Figure 10-2 *Automatic 6to4 Tunnel Topology*

Example 10-7 *Automatic 6to4 Tunnel Configuration*

```
crosby# show running-config
! output omitted for brevity
interface FastEthernet0/0
 description IPv6 local host network interface 1 of 2
 ipv6 address 2002:0a01:6401:1::1/64
!
interface FastEthernet0/1
 description IPv6 local host network interface 2 of 2
 ipv6 address 2002:0a01:6401:2::1/64
!
interface Ethernet2/0
```

```
description Ethernet link to the outside world
ip address 10.1.100.1 255.255.255.0
!
interface Tunnel0
no ip address
ipv6 address 2002:0a01:6401::1/64
tunnel source Ethernet 2/0
tunnel mode ipv6ip 6to4
!
ipv6 route 2002::/16 tunnel 0
```

[handwritten annotations: "starts with 2002 prefix", "globally unique edge router IPv4 address", "external interface", "static route"]

ISATAP Tunnels

ISATAP, short for Intra-Site Automatic Tunnel Addressing Protocol, is defined in RFC 4214. Like 6to4, ISATAP tunnels treat the underlying IPv4 network as a nonbroadcast multiaccess (NBMA) cloud. Therefore, like 6to4, ISATAP tunnels support point-to-multipoint operation natively and determine destination on a per-packet basis. However, the method they use for determining the addressing for hosts and the tunnel interface differs from 6to4 tunnels. Otherwise, ISATAP and automatic 6to4 tunneling are similar.

ISATAP develops its addressing scheme using this format:

   [64-bit link-local or global unicast prefix]:0000:5EFE:[IPv4 address of the ISATAP link]

[handwritten: "+ IPv4", "64 bit LL or global"]

The ISATAP interface identifier is the middle part of the address, 0000:5EFE.

For example, let's say that the IPv6 prefix in use is 2001:0DB8:0ABC:0DEF::/64 and the IPv4 tunnel destination address is 172.20.20.1. The IPv4 address, converted to hex, is AC14:1401. Therefore the ISATAP address is

   2001:0DB8:0ABC:0DEF:0000:5EFE:AC14:1401

[handwritten: "64 bit", "32 bit", "32 bit", "172.20.20.1"]

Configuring an ISATAP tunnel on a router differs slightly from configuring the previous tunnel types in that it uses a different tunnel mode (**ipv6ip isatap**) and in that it must be configured to derive the IPv6 address using the EUI-64 method. EUI-64 addressing in a tunnel interface differs from EUI-64 on a nontunnel interface in that it derives the last 32 bits of the interface ID from the tunnel source interface's IPv4 address. This method is necessary for ISATAP tunnels to provide a mechanism for other tunnel routers to independently know how to reach this router.

One other key difference in ISATAP tunnels is important to know. By default, tunnel interfaces disable router advertisements (RA). However, RAs must be enabled on ISATAP tunnels to support client autoconfiguration. Enable RAs on an ISATAP tunnel using the **no ipv6 nd suppress-ra** command.

SLAAC and DHCPv6

Dynamic Host Configuration Protocol for IPv6, known as DHCPv6, is an upper-layer protocol that encompasses IPv6 address assignment dynamically. IPv6 is more complicated and provides more options than IPv4. DHCPv6 provides stateful DHCP services similarly to IPv6, but it also provides Stateless Address Autoconfiguration, or SLAAC. SLAAC is defined in RFC 4862, IPv6 Stateless Address Autoconfiguration. Stateless Address Autoconfiguration does not require the services of a DHCP server. In some cases, SLAAC only involves the router and the router advertisement messages, while in other cases, both the router advertisement (RA) message and other configuration parameters from a DHCP server are involved. SLAAC provides dynamic addressing without the services of DHCP.

NAT-PT

Although it is not technically a tunneling protocol, one of the methods of interconnecting IPv6 and IPv4 networks is a mechanism known as Network Address Translation–Protocol Translation (NAT-PT), defined in RFCs 2765 and 2766 (obsoleted by 4966). NAT-PT works by performing a sort of gateway function at the IPv4/IPv6 boundary. At that boundary, NAT-PT translates between IPv4 and IPv6. This method permits IPv4 hosts to communicate with IPv6 hosts and vice versa without the need for those hosts to run dual protocol stacks.

Much like NAT and PAT (NAT overloading) for IPv4, NAT-PT supports static and dynamic translations, as well as port translation.

NAT ALG

Network Address Translation–Protocol Translation is designed to communicate at the network layer, performing translation from IPv6 to IPv4 networks. Application Level Gateways (ALG) operate at the application layer of the OSI model while NAT-PT does not look at the payload. Thus an ALG allows communications at an application level from two disparate networks—one being IPv6 and another IPv4.

NAT64

Two advantages that network translation offers over tunneling include the following:

- Transparent services delivered to IPv6 Internet users by providers
- A seamless migration to IPv6

Network Address Translation IPv6 to IPv4, also known as NAT64, replaces NAT-PT as documented in RFC 6144 (Framework for IPv4/IPv6 Translation). NAT64 together with DNS64 was created to allow an IPv6-only client to initiate communications to an IPv4-only server. This can be done using manual or static bindings. NAT64 is also described in RFC 6146 (Stateful NAT64). Translation in NAT64 is performed using IP header translation and IP address translation between IPv6 and IPv4 using algorithms defined in RFC

6145 (IP/ICMP Translation Algorithm) and RFC 6052 (IPv6 Addressing of IPv4/IPv6 Translators). Three components to NAT64 include NAT64 prefix, NAT64 router, and DNS64 server.

Layer 2 VPNs

Market demand combined with modern high-bandwidth services and applications that use IP for transport necessitate that service providers modify the customary approach paradigm that they have used for years. One change that has been adopted in the service provider industry at large is the use of MPLS VPNs to satisfying bandwidth issues. However, note that service providers have two choices for VPN services: Layer 2 or Layer 3 VPNs. We will focus on Layer 2 VPNs in this section because it is the Layer 2 VPN that allows the service provider to simultaneously address high-bandwidth needs while providing "Layer 2" adjacency between physically isolated networks through the IP/MPLS-enabled service provider cloud. This particular service, L2VPN, is typically extended to customers who want to be responsible for their own networks. L2VPN is the simplest solution where a client wants to manage his own routing protocols, IP management, and QoS mechanisms; this means that the service provider only focuses on providing high-throughput Layer 2 connections. Many times these L2VPN connectivity solutions are described as "pseudowire" connections.

Specifically, Ethernet pseudowire (PW) allows Ethernet frames to traverse an operational MPLS cloud. Using this solution, the service provider extends Layer 2 adjacency between sites. This implies that spanning tree will run on the links, and devices connected through these connections will use the same subnet. This service has its own field name, Emulated Service, and operates over pseudowire. In addition to this, it is necessary to have an operational packet label switched network (MPLS network).

Ethernet pseudowire has two modes: raw mode and tagged mode.

Tagged Mode

The "tagged" in tagged mode makes reference to the 802.1Q tag. In the context of pseudowire, this has significance to the local and end-point devices. But we also need to point out that if the VLAN identifier is modified by the egress provider edge (PE), the Ethernet Spanning Tree Protocol might fail to work properly. This identifier is required to match on the attachment circuits at both ends of the connection. The identifier or the VLAN tag should match on each end of the link. The tagged mode of operation uses the pseudowire type 0x0004. Every frame sent on the PW must have a different VLAN for each customer; this is referred to as a "service-delimiting" VLAN tag. If a frame as received by a PE from the attachment circuit is missing a service-delimiting VLAN tag, the PE must prepend the frame with a dummy VLAN tag before sending the frame on the PW.

Raw Mode

If the pseudowire is operating in raw mode, the service-delimiting tag might or might not be added in the frame and has no significance to the end points. This mode uses pseudowire type 0x0005. If an Ethernet pseudowire is operating in raw mode, service-delimiting tags are never through the attachment circuit by the PE; it is mandatory that they are stripped from the frame before the frame is transmitted.

Layer 2 Tunneling Protocol (L2TPv3)

The Layer 2 Tunneling Protocol version 3 feature is an expansion of Layer 2 VPNs. As outlined in an IETF working group (RFC 3931 and RFC 4719), L2TPv3 provides several enhancements to L2TP to tunnel any Layer 2 payload over L2TP, by defining how the L2TP protocol tunnels Layer 2 payloads over an IP core network by using Layer 2 VPNs. L2TPv3 utilizes IP protocol ID 115. To configure L2TPv3 on a Cisco IOS device, two prerequisites are important to know. The first prerequisite is that the Cisco Express Forwarding (CEF) feature must be enabled using the **ip cef** or **ip cef distributed** command. The second prerequisite is that the loopback interface must have a valid IP address that is reachable from the remote PE device at the other end of an L2TPv3 control channel.

AToM (Any Transport over MPLS)

Example 10-8 illustrates how to configure a typical AToM configuration for the purpose of establishing Layer 2 adjacency between geographically isolated sites.

Example 10-8   *AToM Configuration*

```
!First we will create the xconnect configuration on routers.


R2(config)# int f0/0
R2(config-if)# xconnect 4.4.4.4 204 encapsulation mpls
R2(config-if-xconn)# end


!Now we do the matching configuration on the other device.


R4(config)# int f0/0
R4(config-if)# xconnect 2.2.2.2 204 encapsulation mpls
R4(config-if-xconn)# end
```

The **xconnect** command used on the F0/0 interface on both routers is used to create a bridged connection with the destination specified. The command is broken down with an **xconnect** keyword followed by the peering router address and the unique virtual circuit ID (VCID). The VCID must match on both ends of the connection. The encapsulation can be L2TPv2, L2TPv3, or MPLS. Never lose sight of the fact that there must be a unique address per router for each xconnect. Example 10-9 shows how to verify the pseudowire that we just created.

Example 10-9 *Pseudowire Verification*

```
R2# show xconnect all

Legend: XC ST=Xconnect State, S1=Segment1 State, S2=Segment2 State
UP=Up, DN=Down, AD=Admin Down, IA=Inactive, NH=No Hardware
XC ST Segment 1 S1 Segment 2 S2
------+-------------------------------+--+---------------------------
DN ac Fa0/0(Ethernet) AD mpls 4.4.4.4:204 DN
```

because physical if. down

An MPLS Layer 2 pseudowire has two segments. Segment 1 (S1) is for the customer-facing port. Segment 2 (S2) relates to the core configuration. The output of the **show** command reveals that Segment 1 of the connection is administratively shut down. We can correct this by bringing up each end of the remaining links, as illustrated in Example 10-10, and then repeat the verification.

Example 10-10 *Link Turn-Up and Verification*

```
!On all devices in the configuration bring up the interfaces on the media.

int f0/0
no shut

!Now we will verify the configuration.

R4# show xconnect peer 2.2.2.2 vcid 204

Legend: XC ST=Xconnect State, S1=Segment1 State, S2=Segment2 State
UP=Up, DN=Down, AD=Admin Down, IA=Inactive, NH=No Hardware
XC ST Segment 1 S1 Segment 2 S2
------+-------------------------------+--+---------------------------+--
UP ac Fa0/0(Ethernet) UP mpls 2.2.2.2:204 UP

!The S2 section has now been configured and verified to be working properly with
!state !(ST) of active(ac).
```

Virtual Private LAN Services (VPLS)

VPLS is a Layer 2 VPN service that enables geographically separate LAN segments to be interconnected as a single bridged domain over an MPLS network. VPLS over GRE enables VPLS across an IP network. The provider edge (PE) routers for VPLS over GRE must support VPLS and additional GRE encapsulation and decapsulation. An instance of VPLS must be configured on each PE router.

Overlay Transport Virtualization (OTV)

OTV looks like VPLS without the MPLS transport and multicast support similar to those used in Layer 3 VPNs. A technology typically deployed at the customer edge (CE), unlike VPLS, OTV is configured on each CE router or switch. OTV provides Layer 2 LAN extension over Layer 3-, Layer 2-, or MPLS-based networks. As of this publication, OTV is supported on Cisco IOS XE Software Release 3.5 or later and Cisco NX-OS Release 6.2(2) or later. One of the significant benefits or advantages of OTV is the fault-domain isolation feature; thus spanning-tree root does not change. With each CE having its own root, there is no intervention or planning required by the provider. OTV supports automatic detection of multihoming and ARP optimization.

GET VPN

Group Encrypted Transport (GET) VPN is a technology used to encrypt traffic going through unsecured networks. It leverages the IPsec protocol suite to enforce the integrity and confidentiality of data. Typical GET deployment consists of a router called Key Server (KS) and a couple of routers called Group Members (GM). The KS is used to create, maintain, and send a "policy" to GMs. The policy provides information as to what traffic should be encrypted by the GM and what encryption algorithms must be used. The most important function of KS is the generation of encryption keys. Two keys are used:

- **Transport Encryption Key (TEK):** Used by the GM to encrypt the data

- **Key Encryption Key (KEK):** Used to encrypt information between the KS and GM

A very important aspect of GET is that it does not set up any IPsec tunnels between GMs. It is not like DMVPN. Every GM has the policy (what to encrypt, what encryption algorithm to use, and what key is used by the encryption algorithm) and just encrypts every packet that conforms to its specific policy and sends it to the network using ESP (Encapsulated Security Payload). Note that it uses original IP addresses to route the packet out (this is called the IP Header Preservation mechanism); hence the packet can be routed toward every other router in the network as long as the routing table has such information.

Example 10-11 illustrates the initial stages used to create a functional GET VPN configuration. First we need Rivest, Shamir, and Adelman (RSA) keys to be used by our KS for the Rekey process. The KS must send out a new TEK (and KEK) before the TEK expires (default is 3600 seconds). It does this in a so-called Rekey phase. This phase is authenticated and secured by an ISAKMP SA, which is established between the KS and GM. This ISAKMP uses GDOI (Group Domain of Interpretation) messages (think of this as a mutation of Internet Key Exchange [IKE]) to build an SA and encrypt the GM registration. The GDOI uses UDP/848 instead of UDP/500, as IKE does.

The RSA keys are used to authenticate the KS to GM in the Rekey process.

Example 10-11 *GET VPN Basic Configuration*

```
!Remember that to generate new RSA keys you must have Hostname and Domain-name
!configured on the router.

R1(config)# ip domain-name cisco.com
R1(config)# crypto key generate rsa modulus 1024
The name for the keys will be: R1.cisco.com
% The key modulus size is 1024 bits
% Generating 1024 bit RSA keys, keys will be non-exportable...[OK]
R1(config)#
%SSH-5-ENABLED: SSH 1.99 has been enabled
Then we need ISAKMP paramaters, just like in regular IPSec configuration. Pre-shared
key must be specified on both KS and GM to be able to authenticate. This will be
used to establish ISAKMP SA to secure further GDOI messages.
R1(config)# crypto isakmp policy 10
R1(config-isakmp)# authentication pre-share
R1(config-isakmp)# exi
R1(config)# crypto isakmp key GETVPN-R5 address 10.1.25.5
R1(config)# crypto isakmp key GETVPN-R4 address 10.1.24.4

!The IPSec parameters must be configured on KS. These parameters are not used by KS
!itself. They are part of policy that will be sent down to the GMs. The IPSec
!profile tells the GM what encryption algorithm use.

R1(config)# crypto ipsec transform-set TSET esp-aes esp-sha-hmac
R1(cfg-crypto-trans)# crypto ipsec profile GETVPN-PROF
R1(ipsec-profile)# set transform-set TSET

!Now it's time to configure KS. To do that we need to specify The Group. One KS
!may have many groups and each group may have different security policy.

R1(ipsec-profile)# crypto gdoi group GETVPN
R1(config-gdoi-group)# identity number 1
R1(config-gdoi-group)# server local
%CRYPTO-6-GDOI_ON_OFF: GDOI is ON
```

Handwritten annotations: "RSA key uses domain name", "ISAKMP Pol.", "tset & IPSec profile", "Group Domain of Interpretation", "create a group"

Key Topic

Here we need to specify Rekey parameters. The Rekey phase can be performed in two ways:

■ **Unicast Rekey:** When we do not have multicast support in our infrastructure (might be the case when the ISP does not support multicast in its IP VPN cloud). The KS sends down a Rekey packet to every GM it knows of.

- **Multicast Rekey:** When we have a multicast-ready infrastructure, we can enable multicast Rekey and the KS generates only one packet and sends it down to all GMs at one time.

Example 10-12 demonstrates specifying the Rekey parameters.

Example 10-12 *Rekey Parameters*

```
R1(gdoi-local-server)# rekey authentication mypubkey rsa R1.cisco.com
R1(gdoi-local-server)# rekey retransmit 10 number 2
R1(gdoi-local-server)# rekey transport unicast


!By default every GM can register to KS as long as it has correct PSK configured (or
!valid Certificate in case of PKI). To authorize GMs to be able to register in this
!group on KS, you need to specify a standard ACL with GM's IP addresses. Our ACL is
!named GM-LIST.


R1(gdoi-local-server)# authorization address ipv4 GM-LIST
```
— GM's IP add.

Now it's time to configure a policy for our GMs. The encryption policy is created by the IPsec profile configured earlier. To tell the GMs what packets they should encrypt, we need another ACL (extended this time). Our ACL is named LAN-LIST. We can also specify a window size for time-based antireplay protection. The last important parameter is KS's IP address. This parameter must also be sent down to the GMs as the KS can be run on different IP addresses (such as loopback).

Example 10-13 demonstrates configuring a GET VPN policy.

Example 10-13 *GET VPN Policy*

```
R1(gdoi-local-server)# sa ipsec 1
R1(gdoi-sa-ipsec)# profile GETVPN-PROF
R1(gdoi-sa-ipsec)# match address ipv4 LAN-LIST      ← interesting traffic
R1(gdoi-sa-ipsec)# replay counter window-size 64
R1(gdoi-sa-ipsec)# address ipv4 10.1.12.1      → KS's IP
R1(gdoi-local-server)#
%GDOI-5-KS_REKEY_TRANS_2_UNI: Group GETVPN transitioned to Unicast Rekey.
R1(gdoi-local-server)# exi
R1(config-gdoi-group)# exi
R1(config)# ip access-list standard GM-LIST
R1(config-std-nacl)# permit 10.1.25.5
R1(config-std-nacl)# permit 10.1.24.4
R1(config-std-nacl)# exi


!Here's our "policy ACL". Note that we must exclude GDOI (UDP/848) from this policy
!as there is not much sense to encrypt something already encrypted.
```

```
R1(config)# ip access-list extended LAN-LIST
R1(config-ext-nacl)# deny udp any eq 848 any eq 848          ← GDOI excluded
R1(config-ext-nacl)# permit ip 192.168.0.0 0.0.255.255 192.168.0.0 0.0.255.255
R1(config-ext-nacl)# exi
```

Now we will configure the Group Members. The configuration in Example 10-14 would need to be performed on every Group Member.

Example 10-14 *GM Configuration*

```
R5(config)# crypto isakmp policy 10
R5(config-isakmp)# authentication pre-share
R5(config-isakmp)# exi
R5(config)# crypto isakmp key GETVPN-R5 address 10.1.12.1
R5(config)# crypto gdoi group GETVPN
R5(config-gdoi-group)# identity number 1
R5(config-gdoi-group)# server address ipv4 10.1.12.1
R5(config-gdoi-group)# exi

!This ACL is optional. In general we should configure our policy on KS only, but
!there are some situations when we need to exclude some flows from encryption. Like
!here, we were asked for excluding SSH traffic between 192.168.4.0/24 AND
!192.168.5.0/24 networks.

R5(config)# ip access-list extended DO-NOT-ENCRYPT
R5(config-ext-nacl)# deny tcp 192.168.4.0 0.0.0.255 eq 22 192.168.5.0 0.0.0.255
R5(config-ext-nacl)# deny tcp 192.168.5.0 0.0.0.255 192.168.4.0 0.0.0.255 eq 22
R5(config-ext-nacl)# deny tcp 192.168.4.0 0.0.0.255 192.168.5.0 0.0.0.255 eq 22
R5(config-ext-nacl)# deny tcp 192.168.5.0 0.0.0.255 eq 22 192.168.4.0 0.0.0.255
R5(config-ext-nacl)# exi
R5(config)# crypto map CMAP-GETVPN 10 gdoi
% NOTE: This new crypto map will remain disabled until a valid
group has been configured.
R5(config-crypto-map)# set group GETVPN
R5(config-crypto-map)# match address DO-NOT-ENCRYPT
R5(config-crypto-map)# exi
R5(config)# int s0/1/0.52
R5(config-subif)# crypto map CMAP-GETVPN
R5(config-subif)# exi
R5(config)#
%CRYPTO-5-GM_REGSTER: Start registration to KS 10.1.12.1 for group GETVPN using
  addr
10.1.25.5
R5(config)#
%CRYPTO-6-GDOI_ON_OFF: GDOI is ON
R5(config)#
```

```
%GDOI-5-GM_REKEY_TRANS_2_UNI: Group GETVPN transitioned to Unicast Rekey.
%GDOI-5-GM_REGS_COMPL: Registration to KS 10.1.12.1 complete for group GETVPN using
address 10.1.25.5


!See above SYSLOG messages. They indicate that GM has started registration process
!with KS and registered successfully.
```

Finally, we can verify the GET VPN configuration, as illustrated in Example 10-15.

Example 10-15 *Final GET VPN Verification*

```
R1# sh crypto gdoi group GETVPN
Group Name              : GETVPN (Unicast)
Group Identity          : 1
Group Members           : 2
IPSec SA Direction      : Both
Active Group Server     : Local
Group Rekey Lifetime    : 86400 secs
Group Rekey
Remaining Lifetime    : 86361 secs
Rekey Retransmit Period  : 10 secs
Rekey Retransmit Attempts: 2
Group Retransmit
Remaining Lifetime    : 0 secs
IPSec SA Number         : 1
IPSec SA Rekey Lifetime: 3600 secs
Profile Name            : GETVPN-PROF
Replay method           : Count Based
Replay Window Size      : 64
SA Rekey
Remaining Lifetime    : 3562 secs
ACL Configured          : access-list LAN-LIST
Group Server list       : Local


R1# sh crypto gdoi ks policy
Key Server Policy:
For group GETVPN (handle: 2147483650) server 10.1.12.1 (handle: 2147483650):
# of teks : 1  Seq num : 0
KEK POLICY (transport type : Unicast)
spi : 0x76749A6D99B3C0A3827FA26F1558ED63
management alg    : disabled  encrypt alg     : 3DES
crypto iv length  : 8          key size        : 24
orig life(sec): 86400       remaining life(sec): 86355
sig hash algorithm : enabled    sig key length   : 162
sig size          : 128
sig key name      : R1.micronicstraining.com
```

```
TEK POLICY (encaps : ENCAPS_TUNNEL)
spi                : 0xAF4FA6F8  access-list              : LAN-LIST
# of transforms    : 0  transform             : ESP_AES
hmac alg           : HMAC_AUTH_SHA
alg key size       : 16      sig key size        : 20
orig life(sec)     : 3600    remaining life(sec) : 3556
tek life(sec)      : 3600    elapsed time(sec)   : 44


R1# sh crypto gdoi ks acl
Group Name: GETVPN
Configured ACL:
access-list LAN-LIST deny udp any port = 848 any port = 848
access-list LAN-LIST permit ip 192.168.0.0 0.0.255.255 192.168.0.0 0.0.255.255


!Here's the ACL which tells the GMs what traffic they should encrypt.


R1# sh crypto gdoi ks members
Group Member Information :
Number of rekeys sent for group GETVPN : 1
Group Member ID    : 10.1.24.4
Group ID           : 1
Group Name         : GETVPN
Key Server ID      : 10.1.12.1
Rekeys sent        : 0
Rekeys retries     : 0
Rekey Acks Rcvd    : 0
Rekey Acks missed  : 0
Sent seq num :     0    0    0    0
Rcvd seq num :     0    0    0    0
Group Member ID    : 10.1.25.5
Group ID           : 1
Group Name         : GETVPN
Key Server ID      : 10.1.12.1
Rekeys sent        : 0
Rekeys retries     : 0
Rekey Acks Rcvd    : 0
Rekey Acks missed  : 0
Sent seq num :     0    0    0    0
Rcvd seq num :     0    0    0    0
```

Foundation Summary

This section lists additional details and facts to round out the coverage of the topics in this chapter. Unlike most of the Cisco Press Exam Certification Guides, this "Foundation Summary" does not repeat information presented in the "Foundation Topics" section of the chapter. Please take the time to read and study the details in the "Foundation Topics" section of the chapter, as well as review items noted with a Key Topic icon.

Table 10-4 lists the protocols mentioned in or pertinent to this chapter and their respective standards documents.

Table 10-4   *Protocols and Standards for Chapter 10*

Name	Standardized in
Generic Routing Encapsulation	RFC 2784
NHRP (Next-Hop Resolution Protocol)	RFC 2332
Basic Transition Mechanisms for IPv6 Hosts and Routers	RFC 4213
The Group Domain of Interpretation	RFC 3547
Layer 2 Virtual Private Network (L2VPN)	RFC 6136
Layer 2 Tunnel Protocol version 3	RFC 3931 and RFC 4719
IPv6 Stateless Address Autoconfiguration	RFC 4862
Stateful NAT64: Network Address and Protocol Translation	RFC 6146
Framework for IPv4/IPv6 Translation	RFC 6144

Memory Builders

The CCIE Routing and Switching written exam, like all Cisco CCIE written exams, covers a fairly broad set of topics. This section provides some basic tools to help you exercise your memory about some of the broader topics covered in this chapter.

Definitions

Next, take a few moments to write down the definitions for the following terms:

> GRE, ISATAP, 6to4, L2VPN, AToM, Tagged mode, Raw mode, DMVPN, GDOI, NHRP, Key Server, Group Members, IPsec profile, TEK, KEK, Unicast-Rekey, Multicast-Rekey

Refer to the glossary to check your answers.

Blueprint topics covered in this chapter:

This chapter covers the following subtopics from the Cisco CCIE Routing and Switching written exam blueprint. Refer to the full blueprint in Table I-1 in the Introduction for more details on the topics covered in each chapter and their context within the blueprint.

- Implement MPLS Layer 3 VPNs

- Implement Multiprotocol Label Switching (MPLS)

- Implement MPLS VPNs on PE, P, and CE routers

- Implement Virtual Routing and Forwarding (VRF)

- Implement Multi-VRF Customer Edge (VRF Lite)

CHAPTER 11

Multiprotocol Label Switching

Multiprotocol Label Switching (MPLS) remains a vitally important part of many service provider (SP) networks. MPLS is still growing in popularity in enterprise networks as well, particularly in larger enterprise internetworks. This chapter introduces the core concepts with MPLS, particularly its use for unicast IP forwarding and for MPLS VPNs.

"Do I Know This Already?" Quiz

Table 11-1 outlines the major headings in this chapter and the corresponding "Do I Know This Already?" quiz questions.

Table 11-1 *"Do I Know This Already?" Foundation Topics Section-to-Question Mapping*

Foundation Topics Section	Questions Covered in This Section	Score
MPLS Unicast IP Forwarding	1–4	
MPLS VPNs	5–9	
Other MPLS Applications	10	
VRF Lite	11	
Total Score		

To best use this pre-chapter assessment, remember to score yourself strictly. You can find the answers in Appendix A, "Answers to the 'Do I Know This Already?' Quizzes."

1. Imagine a frame-based MPLS network configured for simple unicast IP forwarding, with four routers, R1, R2, R3, and R4. The routers connect in a mesh of links so that they are all directly connected to the other routers. R1 uses LDP to advertise prefix 1.1.1.0/24, label 30, to the other three routers. What must be true for R2 to advertise a label for 1.1.1.0/24 to R1 using LDP?

   a. R2 must learn an IGP route to 1.1.1.0/24.

   b. R2 will not advertise a label to R1 because of Split Horizon rules.

   c. R2 can advertise a label back to R1 before learning an IGP route to 1.1.1.0/24.

   d. R2 must learn a route to 1.1.1.0/24 using MP-BGP before advertising a label.

2. In a frame-based MPLS network configured for unicast IP forwarding, LSR R1 receives a labeled packet, with a label value of 55. Which of the following could be true?

    a. R1 makes its forwarding decision by comparing the packet to the IPv4 prefixes found in the FIB.

    b. R1 makes its forwarding decision by comparing the packet to the IPv4 prefixes found in the LFIB.

    c. R1 makes its forwarding decision by comparing the packet to the MPLS labels found in the FIB.

    d. R1 makes its forwarding decision by comparing the packet to the MPLS labels found in the LFIB.

3. R1, R2, and R3 are all MPLS LSRs that use LDP and connect to the same LAN. None of the three LSRs advertise a transport IP address. Which of the following could be true regarding LDP operation?

    a. The LSRs discover the other two routers using LDP Hellos sent to IP address 224.0.0.20.

    b. Each pair of LSRs forms a TCP connection before advertising MPLS labels.

    c. The three LSRs must use their LAN interface IP addresses for any LDP TCP connections.

    d. The LDP Hellos use port 646, with the TCP connections using port 721.

4. In a frame-based MPLS network configured for simple unicast IP forwarding, MPLS TTL propagation has been enabled for all traffic. Which of the following could be true?

    a. A **traceroute** command issued from outside the MPLS network will list IP addresses of the LSRs inside the MPLS network.

    b. A **traceroute** command issued from outside the MPLS network will not list IP addresses of the LSRs inside the MPLS network.

    c. Any IP packet with a TCP header, entering the MPLS network from outside the MPLS network, would not have its IP TTL field copied into the MPLS TTL field.

5. An ICMP echo sent into the MPLS network from outside the MPLS network would have its IP TTL field copied into the MPLS TTL field. Which of the following is an extension to the BGP NLRI field?

    a. VRF

    b. Route Distinguisher

    c. Route Target

    d. BGP Extended Community

6. Which of the following controls into which VRFs a PE adds routes when receiving an IBGP update from another PE?

   a. Route Distinguisher

   b. Route Target

   c. IGP metric

   d. AS Path length

7. An ingress PE router in an internetwork configured for MPLS VPN receives an unlabeled packet. Which of the following is true?

   a. It injects a single MPLS header.

   b. It injects at least two MPLS headers.

   c. It injects (at least) a VPN label, which is used by any intermediate P routers.

   d. It uses both the FIB and LFIB to find all the required labels to inject before the IP header.

8. An internetwork configured to support MPLS VPNs uses PHP. An ingress PE receives an unlabeled packet and then injects the appropriate label(s) to the packet before sending the packet into the MPLS network. Which of the following is/are true about this packet?

   a. The number of MPLS labels in the packet will only change when the packet reaches the egress PE router, which extracts the entire MPLS header.

   b. The number of MPLS labels in the packet will change before the packet reaches the egress PE.

   c. The PHP feature will cause the egress PE to act differently than it would without PHP enabled.

   d. None of the other answers is correct.

9. Which of the following are true regarding a typical MPLS VPN PE BGP configuration, assuming that the PE-CE routing protocol is not BGP?

   a. It includes an **address-family vpnv4** command for each VRF.

   b. It includes an **address-family ipv4** command for each VRF.

   c. At least one BGP subcommand must list the value of the exported Route Target (RT) of each VRF.

   d. Peer connections to other PEs must be enabled with the **neighbor activate** command under the VPNv4 address family.

10. Which of the following answers help define which packets are in the same MPLS FEC when using MPLS VPNs?

   a. IPv4 prefix

   b. ToS byte

   c. The MPLS VRF

   d. The TE tunnel

11. Which of the following are true about the VRF Lite (Multi-VRF CE) feature?

   a. It provides logical separation at Layer 3.

   b. It requires the use of LDP or TDP.

   c. It uses VRFs, but requires static routing.

   d. It can be used on CE routers only when those routers have a link to a PE in MPLS VPN.

   e. It creates separate routing table instances on a router by creating multiple VRFs.

Foundation Topics

MPLS defines protocols that create a different paradigm for how routers forward packets. Instead of forwarding packets based on the packets' destination IP address, MPLS defines how routers can forward packets based on an MPLS label. By disassociating the forwarding decision from the destination IP address, MPLS allows forwarding decisions based on other factors, such as traffic engineering, QoS requirements, and the privacy requirements for multiple customers connected to the same MPLS network, while still considering the traditional information learned using routing protocols.

MPLS includes a wide variety of applications, with each application considering one or more of the possible factors that influence the MPLS forwarding decisions. For the purposes of the CCIE Routing and Switching written exam, this book covers two such applications in the first two major sections of this chapter:

- MPLS unicast IP

- MPLS VPNs

This chapter also includes a brief introduction to many of the other MPLS applications and to the VRF Lite (Multi-VRF CE) feature. Also, as usual, please take the time to check www.ciscopress.com/title/9781587144912 for the latest version of Appendix B, "CCIE Exam Updates," to find out whether you should read further about any of the MPLS topics.

Note   MPLS includes frame-mode MPLS and cell-mode MPLS, while this chapter only covers frame-mode MPLS. The generalized comments in this chapter might not apply to cell-mode MPLS.

MPLS Unicast IP Forwarding

MPLS can be used for simple unicast IP forwarding. With MPLS unicast IP forwarding, the MPLS forwarding logic forwards packets based on labels. However, when choosing the interfaces out which to forward the packets, MPLS considers only the routes in the unicast IP routing table, so the end result of using MPLS is that the packet flows over the same path as it would have if MPLS were not used, but all other factors were unchanged.

MPLS unicast IP forwarding does not provide any significant advantages by itself. However, many of the more helpful MPLS applications, such as MPLS Virtual Private Networks (VPN) and MPLS traffic engineering (TE), use MPLS unicast IP forwarding as one part of the MPLS network. So to understand MPLS as you would typically implement it, you need a solid understanding of MPLS in its most basic form: MPLS unicast IP forwarding.

MPLS requires the use of control plane protocols (for example, Open Shortest Path First [OSPF] and Label Distribution Protocol [LDP]) to learn labels, correlate those labels to particular destination prefixes, and build the correct forwarding tables. MPLS also requires a fundamental change to the data plane's core forwarding logic. This section begins by examining the data plane, which defines the packet-forwarding logic. Following that, this section examines the control plane protocols, particularly LDP, which MPLS routers use to exchange labels for unicast IP prefixes.

MPLS IP Forwarding: Data Plane

MPLS defines a completely different packet-forwarding paradigm. However, hosts do not and should not send and receive labeled packets, so at some point, some router will need to add a label to the packet and, later, another router will remove the label. The MPLS routers—the routers that inject (push), remove (pop), or forward packets based on their labels—use MPLS forwarding logic.

MPLS relies on the underlying structure and logic of Cisco Express Forwarding (CEF) while expanding the logic and data structures as well. First, a review of CEF is in order, followed by details about a new data structure called the MPLS *Label Forwarding Information Base (LFIB)*.

CEF Review

A router's unicast IP forwarding control plane uses routing protocols, static routes, and connected routes to create a *Routing Information Base (RIB)*. With CEF enabled, a router's control plane processing goes a step further, creating the CEF *Forwarding Information Base (FIB)*, adding a FIB entry for each destination IP prefix in the routing table. The FIB entry details the information needed for forwarding: the next-hop router and the outgoing interface. Additionally, the CEF *adjacency table* lists the new data-link header that the router will then copy in front of the packet before forwarding.

For the data plane, a CEF router compares the packet's destination IP address to the CEF FIB, ignoring the IP routing table. CEF optimizes the organization of the FIB so that the router spends very little time to find the correct FIB entry, resulting in a smaller forwarding delay and a higher volume of packets per second through a router. For each packet, the router finds the matching FIB entry, then finds the adjacency table entry referenced by the matching FIB entry, and forwards the packet. Figure 11-1 shows the overall process.

With this backdrop in mind, the text next looks at how MPLS changes the forwarding process using labels.

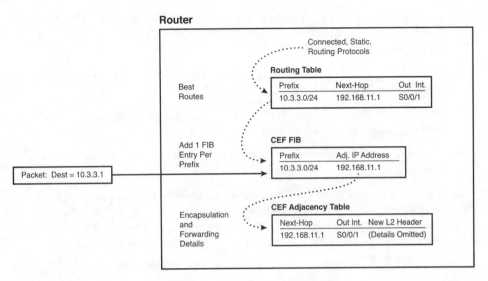

Figure 11-1 *IP Routing Table and CEF FIB—No MPLS*

Overview of MPLS Unicast IP Forwarding

Key Topic

The MPLS forwarding paradigm assumes that hosts generate packets without an MPLS label. Then, some router imposes an MPLS label, other routers forward the packet based on that label, and then other routers remove the label. The end result is that the host computers have no awareness of the existence of MPLS. To appreciate this overall forwarding process, Figure 11-2 shows an example, with steps showing how a packet is forwarded using MPLS.

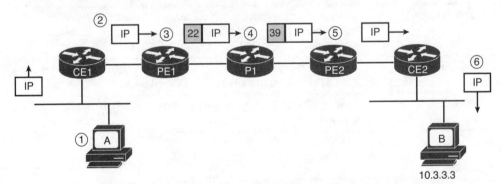

Figure 11-2 *MPLS Packet Forwarding—End to End*

The steps from the figure are explained as follows:

1. Host A generates and sends an unlabeled packet destined to host 10.3.3.3.

2. Router CE1, with no MPLS features configured, forwards the unlabeled packet based on the destination IP address, as normal, without any labels. (Router CE1 might or might not use CEF.)

3. MPLS Router PE1 receives the unlabeled packet and decides, as part of the MPLS forwarding process, to impose (push) a new label (value 22) into the packet and forwards the packet.

4. MPLS Router P1 receives the labeled packet. P1 swaps the label for a new label value (39) and then forwards the packet.

5. MPLS Router PE2 receives the labeled packet, removes (pops) the label, and forwards the packet toward CE2.

6. Non-MPLS Router CE2 forwards the unlabeled packet based on the destination IP address, as normal. (CE2 might or might not use CEF.)

The steps in Figure 11-2 show a relatively simple process and provide a great backdrop from which to introduce a few terms. The term *Label Switch Router (LSR)* refers to any router that has awareness of MPLS labels, for example, Routers PE1, P1, and PE2 in Figure 11-2. Table 11-2 lists the variations of the term LSR, and a few comments about the meaning of each term.

Key Topic

Table 11-2   *MPLS LSR Terminology Reference*

LSR Type	Actions Performed by This LSR Type
Label Switch Router (LSR)	Any router that pushes labels onto packets, pops labels from packets, or simply forwards labeled packets.
Edge LSR (E-LSR)	An LSR at the edge of the MPLS network, meaning that this router processes both labeled and unlabeled packets.
Ingress E-LSR	For a particular packet, the router that receives an unlabeled packet and then inserts a label stack in front of the IP header.
Egress E-LSR	For a particular packet, the router that receives a labeled packet and then removes all MPLS labels, forwarding an unlabeled packet.
ATM-LSR	An LSR that runs MPLS protocols in the control plane to set up ATM virtual circuits. Forwards labeled packets as ATM cells.
ATM E-LSR	An E-edge LSR that also performs the ATM Segmentation and Reassembly (SAR) function.

MPLS Forwarding Using the FIB and LFIB

To forward packets as shown in Figure 11-2, LSRs use both the CEF FIB and the MPLS LFIB when forwarding packets. Both the FIB and LFIB hold any necessary label information, as well as the outgoing interface and next-hop information.

The FIB and LFIB differ in that routers use one table to forward incoming unlabeled packets and the other to forward incoming labeled packets, as follows:

■ **FIB:** Used for incoming unlabeled packets. Cisco IOS matches the packet's destination IP address to the best prefix in the FIB and forwards the packet based on that entry.

■ **LFIB:** Used for incoming labeled packets. Cisco IOS compares the label in the incoming packet to the LFIB's list of labels and forwards the packet based on that LFIB entry.

Figure 11-3 shows how the three LSRs in Figure 11-2 use their respective FIBs and LFIB. Note that Figure 11-3 just shows the FIB on the LSR that forwards the packet using the FIB and the LFIB on the two LSRs that use the LFIB, although all LSRs have both a FIB and an LFIB.

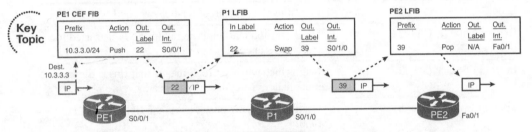

Figure 11-3 *Use of the CEF FIB and MPLS LFIB for Forwarding Packets*

The figure shows the use of the FIB and LFIB, as follows:

■ **PE1:** When the unlabeled packet arrives at PE1, PE1 uses the FIB. PE1 finds the FIB entry that matches the packet's destination address of 10.3.3.1—namely, the entry for 10.3.3.0/24 in this case. Among other things, the FIB entry includes the instructions to push the correct MPLS label in front of the packet.

■ **P1:** Because P1 receives a labeled packet, P1 uses its LFIB, finding the label value of 22 in the LFIB, with that entry stating that P1 should swap the label value to 39.

■ **PE2:** PE2 uses the LFIB as well, because PE2 receives a labeled packet. The matching LFIB entry lists a pop action, so PE2 removes the label, forwarding an unlabeled packet to CE2.

Note that P1 and PE2 in this example never examined the packet's destination IP address as part of the forwarding process. Because the forwarding process does not rely on the destination IP address, MPLS can then enable forwarding processes based on something other than the destination IP address, such as forwarding based on the VPN from which the packet originated, forwarding to balance traffic with traffic engineering, and forwarding over different links based on QoS goals.

The MPLS Header and Label

The MPLS header is a 4-byte header, located immediately before the IP header. Many people simply refer to the MPLS header as the MPLS label, but the label is actually a 20-bit field in the MPLS header. You might also see this header referenced as an MPLS *shim header*. Figure 11-4 shows the entire label, and Table 11-3 defines the fields.

Figure 11-4   *MPLS Header*

Table 11-3   *MPLS Header Fields*

Field	Length (Bits)	Purpose
Label	20	Identifies the portion of a label switched path (LSP).
Experimental (EXP)	3	Used for QoS marking; the field is no longer used for truly experimental purposes.
Bottom-of-Stack (S)	1	Flag, which when set to 1, means that this is the label immediately preceding the IP header.
Time-to-Live (TTL)	8	Used for the same purposes as the IP header's TTL field.

Of the four fields in the MPLS header, the first two, Label and EXP, should already be familiar. The 20-bit Label is usually listed as a decimal value in **show** commands. The MPLS EXP bits allow for QoS marking, which can be done using CB Marking, as covered in Chapter 3, "Classification and Marking." The S bit will make more sense after you examine how MPLS VPNs work, but in short, when packets hold multiple MPLS headers, this bit allows an LSR to recognize the last MPLS header before the IP header. Finally, the TTL field requires a little more examination, as covered in the next section.

The MPLS TTL Field and MPLS TTL Propagation

The IP header's TTL field supports two important features: a mechanism to identify looping packets and a method for the **traceroute** command to find the IP address of each router in a particular end-to-end route. The MPLS header's TTL field supplies the same features. In fact, using all defaults, the presence or absence of MPLS LSRs in a network has no impact on the end results of either of the TTL-related processes.

MPLS needs a TTL field so that LSRs can completely ignore the encapsulated IP header when forwarding IP packets. Essentially, the LSRs will decrement the MPLS TTL field, and not the IP TTL field, as the packet passes through the MPLS network. To make the entire process work, using all default settings, ingress E-LSRs, LSRs, and egress E-LSRs work as follows:

- **Ingress E-LSRs:** After an ingress E-LSR decrements the IP TTL field, it pushes a label into an unlabeled packet and then copies the packet's IP TTL field into the new MPLS header's TTL field.

- **LSRs:** When an LSR swaps a label, the router decrements the MPLS header's TTL field and always ignores the IP header's TTL field.

- **Egress E-LSRs:** After an egress E-LSR decrements the MPLS TTL field, it pops the final MPLS header and then copies the MPLS TTL field into the IP header TTL field.

Figure 11-5 shows an example in which a packet arrives at PE1, unlabeled, with IP TTL 4. The callouts in the figure list the main actions for the three roles of the LSRs as described in the previous list.

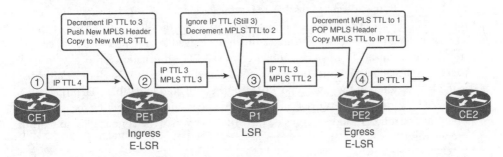

Figure 11-5 *Example of MPLS TTL Propagation*

The term *MPLS TTL propagation* refers to the combined logic as shown in the figure. In effect, the MPLS routers propagate the same TTL value across the MPLS network—the same TTL values that would have occurred if MPLS was not used at all. As you might expect, a truly looping packet would eventually decrement to TTL 0 and be discarded. Additionally, a **traceroute** command would receive ICMP Time Exceeded messages from each of the routers in the figure, including the LSRs.

However, many engineers do not want hosts outside the MPLS network to have visibility into the MPLS network with the **traceroute** command. SPs typically implement MPLS networks to create Layer 3 WAN services, and the SP's customers sit outside the MPLS network. If the SP's customers can find the IP addresses of the MPLS LSRs, it can annoy the customer who wants to see only customer routers, and it can create a security exposure for the SP.

Cisco routers can be configured to disable MPLS TTL propagation. When disabled, the ingress E-LSR sets the MPLS header's TTL field to 255, and the egress E-LSR leaves the original IP header's TTL field unchanged. As a result, the entire MPLS network appears to be a single router hop from a TTL perspective, and the routers inside the MPLS network are not seen from the customer's **traceroute** command. Figure 11-6 shows the same example as in Figure 11-5 but now with MPLS TTL propagation disabled.

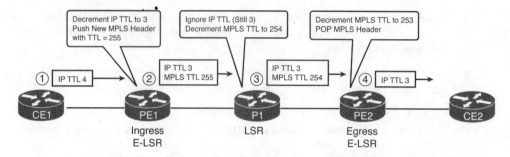

Figure 11-6 *Example with MPLS TTL Propagation Disabled*

Cisco supports the ability to disable MPLS TTL propagation for two classes of packets. Most MPLS SPs might want to disable TTL propagation for packets forwarded by customers, but allow TTL propagation for packets created by the SP's routers. Using Figure 11-5 again for an example, an SP engineer might be logged in to Router PE1 to issue a **traceroute** command. PE1 can be configured to use TTL propagation for locally created packets, which allows the **traceroute** command issued from PE1 to list all the routers in the MPLS cloud. At the same time, PE1 can be configured to disable TTL propagation for "forwarded" packets (packets received from customers), preventing the customer from learning router IP addresses inside the MPLS network. (The command is **no mpls ip propagate-ttl**.)

Note Although the PE1 router has TTL-Propagation disabled, *all* routers in the MPLS domain should also have TTL disabled for consistent output of the TTL propagation.

MPLS IP Forwarding: Control Plane

For pure IP routing to work using the FIB, routers must use control plane protocols, like routing protocols, to first populate the IP routing table and then populate the CEF FIB. Similarly, for MPLS forwarding to work, MPLS relies on control plane protocols to learn which MPLS labels to use to reach each IP prefix, and then populate both the FIB and the LFIB with the correct labels.

MPLS supports many different control plane protocols. However, an engineer's choice of which control plane protocol to use is mainly related to the MPLS application used, rather than any detailed comparison of the features of each control plane protocol. For example, MPLS VPNs use two control plane protocols: LDP and multiprotocol BGP (MP-BGP).

While multiple control plane protocols can be used for some MPLS applications, MPLS unicast IP forwarding uses an IGP and one MPLS-specific control plane protocol: LDP. This section, still focused on unicast IP forwarding, examines the details of label distribution using LDP.

Note   The earliest pre-standard version of LDP was called *Tag Distribution Protocol (TDP)*. The term *tag switching* was also often used instead of label switching.

MPLS LDP Basics

For unicast IP routing, LDP simply advertises labels for each prefix listed in the IP routing table. To do so, LSRs use LDP to send messages to their neighbors, with the messages listing an IP prefix and corresponding label. By advertising an IP prefix and label, the LSR is essentially saying, "If you want to send packets to this IP prefix, send them to me with the MPLS label listed in the LDP update."

The LDP advertisement is triggered by a new IP route appearing in the unicast IP routing table. Upon learning a new route, the LSR allocates a label called a *local label*. The local label is the label that, on this one LSR, is used to represent the IP prefix just added to the routing table. An example makes the concept much clearer. Figure 11-7 shows a slightly expanded version of the MPLS network shown earlier in this chapter. The figure shows the basic process of what occurs when an LSR (PE2) learns about a new route (10.3.3.0/24), triggering the process of advertising a new local label (39) using LDP.

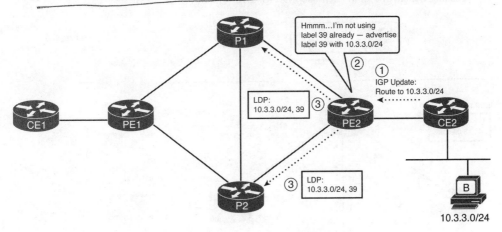

Figure 11-7   *LDP Process Triggered by New Unicast IP Route*

The figure shows the following simple three-step process on PE2:

1. PE2 learns a new unicast IP route, which appears in the IP routing table.

2. PE2 allocates a new *local label*, which is a label not currently advertised by that LSR.

3. PE2 uses LDP to advertise to neighbors the mapping between the IP prefix and label to all LDP neighbors.

Although the process itself is simple, it is important to note that PE2 must now be ready to process labeled packets that arrive with the new local label value in it. For example, in Figure 11-7, PE2 needs to be ready to forward packets received with label 39. PE2 will forward the packets with the same next-hop and outgoing interface information learned in the IGP Update at Step 1 in the figure.

Although interesting, the process shown in Figure 11-7 shows only the advertisement of one segment of the full label switched path (LSP). An MPLS LSP is the combined set of labels that can be used to forward the packets correctly to the destination. For example, Figures 11-2 and 11-3 show a short LSP with label values 22 and 39, over which packets to subnet 10.3.3.0/24 were sent. Figure 11-7 shows the advertisement of one part, or segment, of the LSP.

Note LSPs are unidirectional.

The routers in the MPLS cloud must use some IP routing protocol to learn IP routes to trigger the LDP process of advertising labels. Typically, for MPLS unicast IP routing, you would use an interior gateway protocol (IGP) to learn all the IP routes, triggering the process of advertising the corresponding labels. For example, Figure 11-8 picks up the process where Figure 11-7 ended, with PE2 advertising a route for 10.3.3.0/24 using EIGRP, causing other routers to then use LDP to advertise labels.

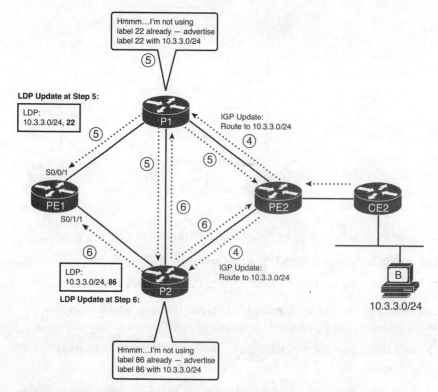

Figure 11-8 *Completed Process of Advertising an Entire LSP*

The steps in the figure are as follows, using numbers that continue the numbering from Figure 11-7:

4. PE2 uses EIGRP to advertise the route for 10.3.3.0/24 to both P1 and P2.

5. P1 reacts to the newly learned route by allocating a new local label (22) and using LDP to advertise the new prefix (10.3.3.0/24) to label (22) mapping. Note that P1 advertises this label to all its neighbors.

6. P2 also reacts to the newly learned route by allocating a new local label (86) and using LDP to advertise the new prefix (10.3.3.0/24) to label (86) mapping. P2 advertises this label to all its neighbors.

This same process occurs on each LSR, for each route in the LSR's routing table: Each time an LSR learns a new route, the LSR allocates a new local label and then advertises the label and prefix mapping to all its neighbors—even when it is obvious that advertising the label might not be useful. For example, in Figure 11-8, P2 advertises a label for 10.3.3.0/24 back to router PE2—not terribly useful, but it is how frame-mode MPLS LSRs work.

After the routers have all learned about a prefix using the IGP protocol, and LDP has advertised label/prefix mappings (bindings) to all other neighboring LSRs, each LSR has enough information with which to label-switch packets from ingress E-LSR to egress E-LSR. For example, the same data plane process shown in Figures 11-2 and 11-3 could occur when PE1 receives an unlabeled packet destined to an address in 10.3.3.0/24. In fact, the labels advertised in Figures 11-7 and 11-8 purposefully match the earlier MPLS data plane figures (11-2 and 11-3). However, to complete the full process, you need to understand a bit more about what occurs inside an individual router, in particular, a data structure called the MPLS Label Information Base (LIB).

The MPLS Label Information Base Feeding the FIB and LFIB

Key Topic

LSRs store labels and related information inside a data structure called LIB. The LIB essentially holds all the labels and associated information that could possibly be used to forward packets. However, each LSR must choose the best label and outgoing interface to actually use and then populate that information into the FIB and the LFIB. As a result, the FIB and LFIB contain labels only for the currently used best LSP segment, while the LIB contains all labels known to the LSR, whether the label is currently used for forwarding or not.

To make a decision about the best label to use, LSRs rely on the routing protocol's decision about the best route. By relying on the routing protocol, the LSRs can take advantage of the routing protocol's loop-prevention features and react to the routing protocol's choice for new routes when convergence occurs. In short, an LSR makes the following decision:

> For each route in the routing table, find the corresponding label information in the LIB, based on the outgoing interface and next-hop router listed in the route. Add the corresponding label information to the FIB and LFIB.

To better understand how an LSR adds information to the FIB and LFIB, this section continues the same example as used throughout the chapter so far. At this point, it is useful to examine the output of some **show** commands, but first, you need a little more detail about the sample network and the configuration. Figure 11-9 repeats the same sample network used in earlier figures in this chapter, with IP address and interface details included. The figure also notes on which interfaces MPLS has been enabled (dashed lines) and on which interfaces MPLS has not been enabled (solid lines).

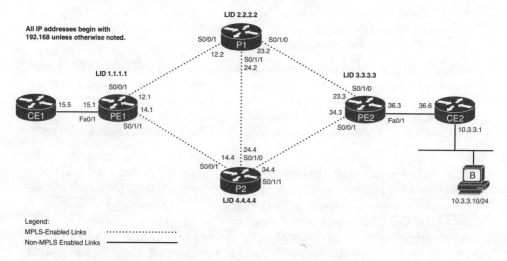

Figure 11-9 *Sample Network for Seeing the LIB, FIB, and LFIB*

The configuration of MPLS unicast IP routing is relatively simple. In this case, all six routers use EIGRP, advertising all subnets. The four LSRs enable MPLS globally and on the links noted with dashed lines in the figure. To enable MPLS for simple unicast IP forwarding, as has been described so far in this chapter, an LSR simply needs to enable CEF, globally enable MPLS, and enable MPLS on each desired interface. Also, IOS uses LDP by default. Example 11-1 shows a sample generic configuration.

Example 11-1 *MPLS Configuration on LSRs for Unicast IP Support*

```
! The first three commands enable CEF and MPLS globally, and
! use LDP instead of TDP
ip cef
! Repeat the next two lines for each MPLS-enabled interface
interface type x/y/z
 mpls ip
! Normal EIGRP configuration next - would be configured for all interfaces
router eigrp 1
 network ...
```

To see how LSRs populate the FIB and LFIB, consider subnet 10.3.3.0/24 again, and think about MPLS from Router PE1's perspective. PE1 has learned a route for 10.3.3.0/24 with EIGRP. PE1 has also learned (using LDP) about two labels that PE1 can use when forwarding packets destined for 10.3.3.0/24—one label learned from neighboring LSR P1 and the other from neighboring LSR P2. Example 11-2 highlights these details. Note that the labels do match the figures and examples used earlier in this chapter.

Example 11-2   *PE1's IP Routing Table and LIB*

```
PE1# show ip route 10.0.0.0
Routing entry for 10.0.0.0/24, 1 known subnets
  Redistributing via eigrp 1
D       10.3.3.0 [90/2812416] via 192.168.12.2, 00:44:16, Serial0/0/1
PE1# show mpls ldp bindings 10.3.3.0 24
  lib entry: 10.3.3.0/24, rev 2
        local binding:  label: imp-null
        remote binding: lsr: 2.2.2.2:0, tag: 22
        remote binding: lsr: 4.4.4.4:0, tag: 86
```

(handwritten annotation: to get to 2.2.2.2 → use tag 22 for this subnet)

Example 11-2 shows some mundane information and a few particularly interesting points. First, the **show ip route** command does not list any new or different information for MPLS, but it is useful to note that PE1's best route to 10.3.3.0/24 is through P1. The **show mpls ldp bindings 10.3.3.0 24** command lists the LIB entries from 10.3.3.0/24. Note that two remote bindings are listed—one from P1 (LDP ID 2.2.2.2) and one from P2 (LDP ID 4.4.4.4). This command also lists the local binding, which is the label that PE1 allocated and advertised to its neighbors.

> **Note**   The term *remote binding* refers to a label-prefix binding learned through LDP from some LDP neighbor.

From Example 11-2, you could anticipate that PE1 will use a label value of 22, and an outgoing interface of S0/0/1, when forwarding packets to 10.3.3.0/24. To see the details of how PE1 arrives at that conclusion, consider the linkages shown in Figure 11-10.

The figure shows the following steps:

1. The routing table entry to 10.3.3.0/24 lists a next-hop IP address of 192.168.12.2. PE1 compares that next-hop information to the list of interface IP addresses on each LDP peer and finds the LDP neighbor who has the IP address 192.168.12.2.

2. That same stanza of the **show mpls ldp neighbor** command output identifies the LDP ID (LID) of this peer, namely, 2.2.2.2.

3. PE1 notes that for that same prefix (10.3.3.0/24), the LIB contains one local label and two remote labels.

4. Among the known labels listed for prefix 10.3.3.0/24, one was learned from a neighbor whose LID is 2.2.2.2, with label (tag) value of 22.

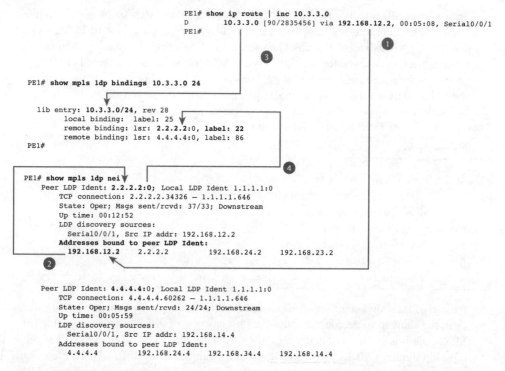

Figure 11-10 *PE1's Process to Determine the Outgoing Label*

As a result of these steps, PE1 knows it should use outgoing interface S0/0/1, with label 22, when forwarding packets to subnet 10.3.3.0/24.

Examples of FIB and LFIB Entries

As mentioned earlier in the chapter, the actual packet-forwarding process does not use the IP routing table (RIB) or the LIB. Instead, the FIB is used to forward packets that arrived unlabeled, and the LFIB is used to forward packets that arrived already labeled. This section correlates the information in **show** commands to the conceptual view of the FIB and LFIB data structures shown back in Figure 11-3.

First, again focusing on PE1, PE1 simply adds information to the FIB stating that PE1 should impose an MPLS header, with label value 22. PE1 also populates the LFIB, with an entry for 10.3.3.0/24, using that same label value of 22 and an outgoing interface of S0/0/1. Example 11-3 shows the contents of the two tables.

Example 11-3 *FIB and LFIB Entries for 10.3.3.0/24 on PE1*

```
! This next command shows the FIB entry, which includes the local tag (24), the
! tags (label) imposed, and outgoing interface.
R7# show ip cef 10.1.78.0 internal
10.1.78.0/32, epoch 0, flags receive, refcount 5, per-destination sharing
  sources: I/F
```

```
 subblocks:
  gsb Connected receive chain(0): 0x314E47F4
  Interface source: Serial0/0/0 flags: none
  Dependent covered prefix type cover need deagg, cover 10.1.78.0/24
 ifnums: (none)
 path 2C69F91C, path list 32278664, share 1/1, type receive, for IPv4
 receive for Serial0/0/0
 output chain: receive
! The next command lists the LFIB entry for 10.3.3.0/24, listing the same basic
! information-the local tag, the outgoing tag (label), and outgoing interface.
PE1# show mpls forwarding-table 10.3.3.0 24
Local   Outgoing      Prefix         Bytes tag   Outgoing    Next Hop
tag     tag or VC     or Tunnel Id   switched    interface
24      22            10.3.3.0/24    0           Se0/0/1     point2point
```

In the data plane example of Figure 11-3, PE1 received an unlabeled packet and forwarded the packet to P1, with label 22. The information in the top part of Example 11-3, showing the FIB, matches that same logic, stating that a tag (label) value of 22 will be imposed by PE1.

Next, examine the LFIB at P1, as shown in Example 11-4. As shown in Figure 11-3, P1 swaps the incoming label of 22 with outgoing label 39. For perspective, the example also includes the LIB entries for 10.3.3.0/24.

how it was adv. to me by someone on this if.

Example 11-4   *LFIB and LIB Entries for 10.3.3.0/24 on P1*

```
P1# show mpls forwarding-table 10.3.3.0 24
Local   Outgoing      Prefix         Bytes tag   Outgoing    Next Hop
tag     tag or VC     or Tunnel Id   switched    interface
22      39            10.3.3.0/24    0           Se0/1/0     point2point
P1# show mpls ldp bindings 10.3.3.0 24
  tib entry: 10.3.3.0/24, rev 30
        local binding:  tag: 22
        remote binding: tsr: 1.1.1.1:0, tag: 24
        remote binding: tsr: 4.4.4.4:0, tag: 86
        remote binding: tsr: 3.3.3.3:0, tag: 39
```

how I adv. it

these routers adv. this ntw. to me with these labels

The highlighted line in the output of the **show mpls forwarding-table** command lists the incoming label (22 in this case) and the outgoing label (39). Note that the incoming label is shown under the heading "local tag," meaning that label (tag) 22 was locally allocated by this router (P1) and advertised to other routers using LDP, as shown in Figure 11-8. P1 originally allocated and advertised label 22 to tell neighboring routers to forward packets destined to 10.3.3.0/24 to P1, with a label of 22. P1 knows that if it receives a packet with label 22, P1 should indeed swap the labels, forwarding the packet out S0/1/0 with a label of 39.

The LIB entries in Example 11-4 also reinforce the concept that (frame-mode) MPLS LSRs retain all learned labels in their LIBs, but only the currently used labels in the LFIB.

The LIB lists P1's local label (22) and the three remote labels learned from P1's three LDP neighbors. To create the LFIB entry, P1 used the same kind of logic shown in Figure 11-10 to correlate the information in the routing table and LIB and choose a label value of 39 and outgoing interface S0/1/0 to forward packets to 10.3.3.0/24.

To see an example of the pop action, consider the LFIB for PE2, as shown in Example 11-5. When PE2 receives a labeled packet from P1 (label 39), PE2 will try to use its LFIB to forward the packet. When populating the LFIB, PE2 can easily realize that PE2 should pop the label and forward an unlabeled packet out its Fa0/1 interface. Those reasons include the fact that PE2 did not enable MPLS on Fa0/1 and that PE2 has not learned any labels from CE2. Example 11-5 shows the outgoing tag as "pop label."

Example 11-5   *LFIB Entries for 10.3.3.0/24 on PE2*

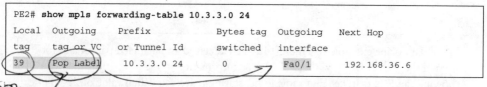

```
PE2# show mpls forwarding-table 10.3.3.0 24

Local   Outgoing    Prefix        Bytes tag  Outgoing    Next Hop
tag     tag or VC   or Tunnel Id  switched   interface
39      Pop Label   10.3.3.0 24   0          Fa0/1       192.168.36.6
```

Note that while the text in Example 11-5 only showed LFIB entries, every LSR builds the appropriate FIB and LFIB entries for each prefix, in anticipation of receiving both unlabeled and labeled packets.

Label Distribution Protocol Reference

Before wrapping up the coverage of basic MPLS unicast IP forwarding, you should know a few more details about LDP itself. So far, this chapter has shown what LDP does, but it has not provided much information about how LDP accomplishes its tasks. This section hits the main concepts and summarizes the rest.

LDP uses a Hello feature to discover LDP neighbors and to determine to what IP address the ensuing TCP connection should be made. LDP multicasts the Hellos to IP address 224.0.0.2, using UDP port number 646 for LDP (TDP uses UDP port 711). The Hellos list each LSR's LDP ID (LID), which consists of a 32-bit dotted-decimal number and a 2-byte label space number. (For frame-based MPLS, the label space number is 0.) An LSR can optionally list a *transport address* in the Hello message, which is the IP address that the LSR wants to use for any LDP TCP connections. If a router does not advertise a transport address, other routers will use the IP address that is the first 4 bytes of the LDP ID for the TCP connections.

After discovering neighbors through an LDP Hello message, LDP neighbors form a TCP connection to each neighbor, again using port 646 (TDP 711). Because the TCP connection uses unicast addresses—either the neighbor's advertised transport address or the address in the LID—these addresses must be reachable according to the IP routing table. After the TCP connection is up, each router advertises all its bindings of local labels and prefixes.

Cisco routers choose the IP address in the LDP ID just like the OSPF router ID. LDP chooses the IP address to use as part of its LID based on the exact same logic as OSPF, as summarized in Table 11-4, along with other details.

Table 11-4 *LDP Reference*

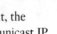

LDP   SUMMARY

LDP Feature	LDP Implementation
Transport protocols	UDP (Hellos), TCP (updates)
Port numbers	646 (LDP), 711 (TDP)
Hello destination address	224.0.0.2
Who initiates TCP connection	Highest LDP ID
TCP connection uses this address	Transport IP address (if configured), or LDP ID if no transport address is configured
LDP ID determined by these rules, in order of precedence	Configuration
	Highest IP address of an up/up loopback when LDP comes up
	Highest IP address of an up/up nonloopback when LDP comes up

This concludes the coverage of MPLS unicast IP forwarding for this chapter. Next, the chapter examines one of the more popular uses of MPLS, which happens to use unicast IP forwarding: MPLS VPNs.

MPLS VPNs

One of the most popular MPLS applications is called *MPLS Virtual Private Networks (VPN)*. MPLS VPNs allow a service provider, or even a large enterprise, to offer Layer 3 VPN services. In particular, SPs oftentimes replace older Layer 2 WAN services such as Frame Relay and ATM with an MPLS VPN service. MPLS VPN services enable the possibility for the SP to provide a wide variety of additional services to its customers because MPLS VPNs are aware of the Layer 3 addresses at the customer locations. Additionally, MPLS VPNs can still provide the privacy inherent in Layer 2 WAN services.

MPLS VPNs use MPLS unicast IP forwarding inside the SP's network, with additional MPLS-aware features at the edge between the provider and the customer. Additionally, MPLS VPNs use MP-BGP to overcome some of the challenges when connecting an IP network to a large number of customer IP internetworks—problems that include the issue of dealing with duplicate IP address spaces with many customers.

This section begins by examining some of the problems with providing Layer 3 services and then shows the core features of MPLS that solve those problems.

The Problem: Duplicate Customer Address Ranges

When an SP connects to a wide variety of customers using a Layer 2 WAN service such as Frame Relay or ATM, the SP does not care about the IP addressing and subnets used by those customers. However, to migrate those same customers to a Layer 3 WAN service, the SP must learn address ranges from the various customers and then advertise those routes into the SP's network. However, even if the SP wanted to know about all subnets from all its customers, many enterprises use the same address ranges—namely, the private IP network numbers, including the ever-popular network 10.0.0.0.

If you tried to support multiple customers using MPLS unicast IP routing alone, the routers would be confused by the overlapping prefixes, as shown in Figure 11-11. In this case, the network shows five of the SP's routers inside a cloud. Three customers (A, B, and C) are shown, with multiple customer routers connected to the SP's network. All three customers use network 10.0.0.0, with the three customer sites on the right all using subnet 10.3.3.0/24.

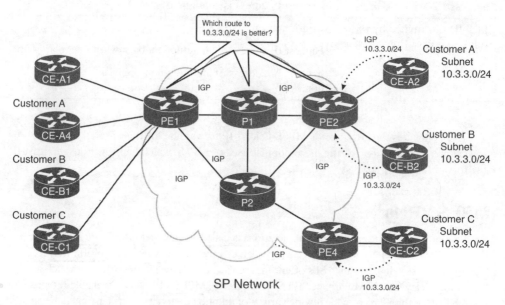

Figure 11-11 *Main Challenge with Supporting Layer 3 VPNs*

The first and most basic goal for a Layer 3 VPN service is to allow customer A sites to communicate with customer A sites—and only customer A sites. However, the network in Figure 11-11 fails to meet this goal for several reasons. Because of the overlapping address spaces, several routers would be faced with the dilemma of choosing one customer's route to 10.3.3.0/24 as the best route, and ignoring the route to 10.3.3.0/24 learned from another customer. For example, PE2 would learn about two different 10.3.3.0/24 prefixes. If PE2 chooses one of the two possible routes—for example, if PE2 picked the route to CE-A2 as best—PE2 could not forward packets to customer B's 10.3.3.0/24 off Router CE-B2. Also, a possibly worse effect is that hosts in one customer site might be able to send and receive packets with hosts in another customer's network. Following this same example, hosts in customer B and C sites could forward packets to subnet 10.3.3.0/24, and the routers might forward these packets to customer A's CE-A2 router.

The Solution: MPLS VPNs

The protocols and standards defined by MPLS VPNs solve the problems shown in Figure 11-11 and provide a much larger set of features. In particular, the MPLS VPN RFCs define the concept of using multiple routing tables, called *Virtual Routing and Forwarding (VRF) tables*, which separate customer routes to avoid the duplicate address range issue. This section defines some key terminology and introduces the basics of MPLS VPN mechanics.

MPLS uses three terms to describe the role of a router when building MPLS VPNs. Note that the names used for the routers in most of the figures in this chapter have followed the convention of identifying the type of router as CE, PE, or P, as listed here:

Key Topic

- **Customer edge (CE):** A router that has no knowledge of MPLS protocols and does not send any labeled packets but is directly connected to an LSR (PE) in the MPLS VPN.

- **Provider edge (PE):** An LSR that shares a link with at least one CE router, thereby providing a function particular to the edge of the MPLS VPN, including internal BGP (iBGP) and VRF tables.

- **Provider (P):** An LSR that does not have a direct link to a CE router, which allows the router to just forward labeled packets, and allows the LSR to ignore customer VPNs' routes.

The key to understanding the general idea of how MPLS VPNs work is to focus on the control plane distinctions between PE routers and P routers. Both P and PE routers run LDP and an IGP to support unicast IP routing—just as was described in the first half of this chapter. However, the IGP advertises routes only for subnets inside the MPLS network, with no customer routes included. As a result, the P and PE routers can together label-switch packets from the ingress PE to the egress PE.

Key Topic

PEs have several other duties as well, all geared toward the issue of learning customer routes and keeping track of which routes belong to which customers. PEs exchange routes with the connected CE routers from various customers, using either external BGP (eBGP), RIPv2, OSPF, or EIGRP, noting which routes are learned from which customers. To keep track of the possibly overlapping prefixes, PE routers do not put the routes in the normal IP routing table—instead, PEs store those routes in separate per-customer routing tables, called VRFs. Then the PEs use IBGP to exchange these customer routes with other PEs—never advertising the routes to the P routers. Figure 11-12 shows the control plane concepts.

Note The term *global routing table* is used to refer to the IP routing table normally used for forwarding packets, as compared with the VRF routing tables.

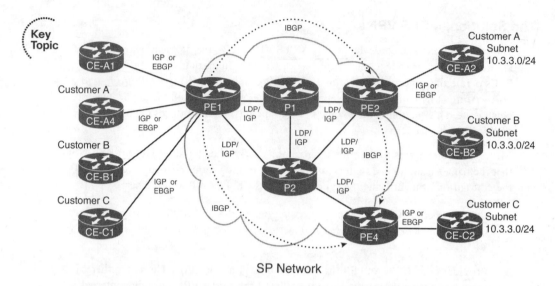

Figure 11-12 *Overview of the MPLS VPN Control Plane*

The MPLS VPN data plane also requires more work and thought by the PE routers. The PE routers do not have any additional work to do, with one small exception, as compared with simple unicast IP routing. The extra work for the PE relates to the fact that the MPLS VPN data plane causes the ingress PE to place two labels on the packet, as follows:

■   An outer MPLS header (S-bit = 0), with a label value that causes the packet to be label switched to the egress PE

■   An inner MPLS header (S-bit = 1), with a label that identifies the egress VRF on which to base the forwarding decision

Figure 11-13 shows a general conceptual view of the two labels and the forwarding process. The figure shows a subset of Figure 11-12, with parts removed to reduce clutter. In this case, a host in customer A on the left side of the figure sends a packet to host 10.3.3.3, located on the right side of the figure.

The figure shows the following steps:

1.   CE1 forwards an unlabeled packet to PE1.

2.   PE1, having received the packet in an interface assigned to VRF-A, compares the packet's destination (10.3.3.3) to the VRF-A CEF FIB, which is based on VRF-A's routing table. PE1 adds two labels based on the FIB and forwards the labeled packet.

3.   P1, acting just the same as with unicast IP routing, processes the received labeled packet using its LFIB, which simply causes a label swap. P1 forwards the packet to PE2.

4.   PE2's LFIB entry for label 2222 lists a pop action, causing PE2 to remove the outer label. PE2's LFIB entry for label 3333, populated based on the VRF for customer A's VPN, also lists a pop action and the outgoing interface. As a result, PE2 forwards the unlabeled packet to CE2.

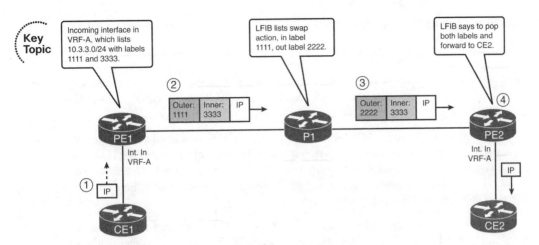

Figure 11-13   *Overview of the MPLS VPN Data Plane*

Note   In actual practice, Steps 3 and 4 differ slightly from the descriptions listed here, because of a feature called penultimate hop popping (PHP). This example is meant to show the core concepts. Figure 11-25, toward the end of this chapter, refines this logic when the router uses the PHP feature, which is on by default in MPLS VPNs.

The control plane and data plane processes described around Figures 11-12 and 11-13 outline the basics of how MPLS VPNs work. Next, the chapter takes the explanations a little deeper with a closer look at the new data structures and control plane processes that support MPLS VPNs.

MPLS VPN Control Plane

The MPLS VPN control plane defines protocols and mechanisms to overcome the problems created by overlapping customer IP address spaces, while adding mechanisms to add more functionality to an MPLS VPN, particularly as compared to traditional Layer 2 WAN services. To understand the mechanics, you need a good understanding of BGP, IGPs, and several new concepts created by both MP-BGP RFCs and MPLS RFCs. In particular, this section introduces and explains the concepts behind three new concepts created for MPLS VPNs:

■   VRFs

■   Route Distinguishers (RD)

■   Route Targets (RT)

The next several pages of text examine these topics in order. While reading the rest of the MPLS VPN coverage in this chapter, note that the text will keep expanding a single example. The example focuses on how the control plane learns about routes to the duplicate customer subnets 10.3.3.0/24 on the right side of Figure 11-12, puts the routes into the VRFs on PE2, and advertises the routes with RDs over to PE1 and then how RTs then dictate how PE1 adds the routes to its VRFs.

Virtual Routing and Forwarding Tables

To support multiple customers, MPLS VPN standards include the concept of a virtual router. This feature, called a VRF table, can be used to store routes separately for different customer VPNs. The use of separate tables solves part of the problems of preventing one customer's packets from leaking into another customer's network because of overlapping prefixes, while allowing all sites in the same customer VPN to communicate.

A VRF exists inside a single MPLS-aware router. Typically, routers need at least one VRF for each customer attached to that particular router. For example, in Figure 11-12, Router PE2 connects to CE routers in customers A and B but not in customer C, so PE2 would not need a VRF for customer C. However, PE1 connects to CE routers for three customers, so PE1 will need three different VRFs.

For more complex designs, a PE might need multiple VRFs to support a single customer. Using Figure 11-12 again as an example, PE1 connects to two CEs of customer A (CE-A1 and CE-A4). If hosts near CE-A1 were allowed to access a centralized shared service (not shown in the figure) and hosts near CE-A4 were not allowed access, PE1 would need two VRFs for customer A—one with routes for the shared service's subnets and one without those routes.

Each VRF has three main components, as follows:

- An IP routing table (RIB)

- A CEF FIB, populated based on that VRF's RIB

- A separate instance or process of the routing protocol used to exchange routes with the CEs that need to be supported by the VRF

For example, Figure 11-14 shows more detail about Router PE2 from Figure 11-12, now with MPLS VPNs implemented. In this case, PE2 will use RIP-2 as the IGP to both customer A (Router CE-A2) and customer B (Router CE-B2). (The choice of routing protocol used from PE-CE is unimportant to the depth of explanations shown here.)

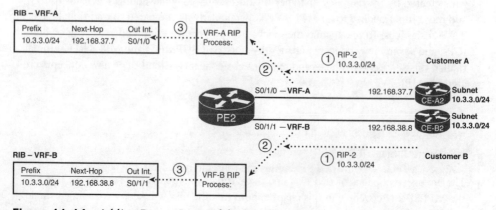

Figure 11-14 *Adding Routes Learned from a CE to VRFs on Router PE2*

The figure shows three parallel steps that occur with each of the two customers. Note that Step 1 for each customer does not occur at the same instant in time, nor does Step 2 or Step 3; the figure lists these steps with the same numbers because the same function occurs at each step. The explanation of the steps is as follows:

1. The CE router, which has no knowledge of MPLS, advertises a route for 10.3.3.0/24 as normal—in this case with RIP-2.

2. In the top instance of Step 2, the RIP-2 update arrives on PE2's S0/1/0, which has been assigned to customer A's VRF, VRF-A. PE2 uses a separate RIP process for each VRF, so PE2's VRF-A RIP process interprets the update. Similarly, the VRF-B RIP process analyzes the update received on S0/1/1 from CE-B2.

3. In the top instance of Step 3, the VRF-A RIP process adds an entry for 10.3.3.0/24 to the RIB for VRF-A. Similarly, the bottom instance of Step 3 shows the RIP process for VRF-B adding a route to prefix 10.3.3.0/24 to the VRF-B RIB.

> **Note**   Each VRF also has a FIB, which was not included in the figure. IOS would add an appropriate FIB entry for each RIB entry.

MP-BGP and Route Distinguishers

Now that PE2 has learned routes from both CE-A2 and CE-B2, PE2 needs to advertise those routes to the other PEs, in order for the other PEs to know how to forward packets to the newly learned subnets. MPLS VPN protocols define the use of IBGP to advertise the routes—all the routes, from all the different VRFs. However, the original BGP specifications did not provide a way to deal with the fact that different customers might use overlapping prefixes.

MPLS deals with the overlapping prefix problem by adding another number in front of the original BGP network layer reachability information (NLRI) (prefix). Each different number can represent a different customer, making the NLRI values unique. To do this, MPLS took advantage of a BGP RFC, called MP-BGP (RFC 4760), which allows for the redefinition of the NLRI field in BGP Updates. This redefinition allows for an additional variable-length number, called an *address family*, to be added in front of the prefix. MPLS RFC 4364, "BGP/MPLS IP Virtual Private Networks (VPNs)," defines a specific new address family to support IPv4 MPLS VPNs—namely, an MP-BGP address family called *Route Distinguishers (RD)*.

MP-BGP
address family
RD

Key Topic

RDs allow BGP to advertise and distinguish between duplicate IPv4 prefixes. The concept is simple: Advertise each NLRI (prefix) as the traditional IPv4 prefix, but add another number (the RD) that uniquely identifies the route. In particular, the new NLRI format, called VPN-V4, has the following two parts:

- A 64-bit RD
- A 32-bit IPv4 prefix

new NLRI format (pre-fix)

For example, Figure 11-15 continues the story from Figure 11-14, with Router PE2 using MP-BGP to advertise its two routes for IPv4 prefix 10.3.3.0/24 to PE1—one from VRF-A and one from VRF-B. The BGP Update shows the new VPN-V4 address family format for the NLRI information, using RD 1:111 to represent VPN-A and 2:222 to represent VPN-B.

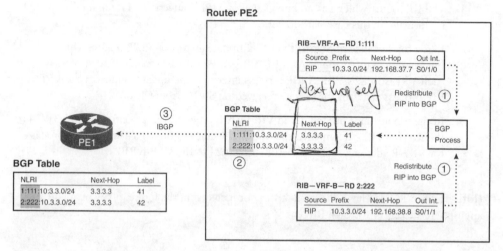

Figure 11-15 *Making Prefixes Unique Using an RD*

Note PE2 uses next-hop-self, and an update source of a loopback interface with IP address 3.3.3.3.

Without the RD as part of the VPN-V4 NLRI, PE1 would have learned about two identical BGP prefixes (10.3.3.0/24) and would have had to choose one of the two as the best route—giving PE1 reachability to only one of the two customer 10.3.3.0/24 subnets. With VPN-V4 NLRI, IBGP advertises two unique NLRI—a 1:111:10.3.3.0 (from VRF-A) and 2:222:10.3.3.0 (from VRF-B). As a result, PE1 keeps both NLRI in its BGP table. The specific steps shown in the figure are explained as follows:

1. PE2 redistributes from each of the respective per-VRF routing protocol instances (RIP-2 in this case) into BGP.

2. The redistribution process pulls the RD from each respective VRF and includes that RD with all routes redistributed from the VRF's routing table.

3. PE2 uses IBGP to advertise these routes to PE1, causing PE1 to know both routes for 10.3.3.0/24, each with the differing RD values.

Note Every VRF must be configured with an RD; the IOS **rd** VRF subcommand configures the value.

The RD itself is 8 bytes with some required formatting conventions. The first 2 bytes identify which of the three formats is followed. Incidentally, because IOS can tell which of the three formats is used based on the value, the IOS **rd** VRF subcommand only requires that you type the integer values for the last 6 bytes, with IOS inferring the first 2 bytes (the type) based on the value. The last 6 bytes, as typed in the **rd** command and seen in **show** commands, follow one of these formats:

- 2-byte-integer:4-byte-integer

- 4-byte-integer:2-byte-integer

- 4-byte-dotted-decimal:2-byte-integer

In all three cases, the first value (before the colon) should be either an Autonomous System Number (ASN) or an IPv4 address. The second value, after the colon, can be any value you want. For example, you might choose an RD that lists an LSR's BGP ID using the third format, like 3.3.3.3:100, or you can use the BGP ASN, for example, 432:1.

At this point in the ongoing example, PE1 has learned about the two routes for 10.3.3.0/24—one for VPN-A and one for VPN-B—and the routes are in the BGP table. The next section describes how PE1 then chooses the VRFs into which to add these routes, based on the concept of a Route Target.

Route Targets

One of the most perplexing concepts for engineers, when first learning about MPLS VPNs, is the concept of Route Targets (RT). Understanding the basic question of what RTs do is relatively easy, but understanding why MPLS needs RTs and how to best choose the actual values to use for RTs can be a topic for long conversation when building an MPLS VPN. In fact, MPLS RTs enable MPLS to support all sorts of complex VPN topologies—for example, allowing some sites to be reachable from multiple VPNs, a concept called overlapping VPNs.

PEs advertise RTs in BGP Updates as BGP Extended Community path attributes (PA). Generally speaking, BGP extended communities are 8 bytes in length, with the flexibility to be used for a wide variety of purposes. More specifically, MPLS defines the use of the BGP Extended Community PA to encode one or more RT values.

RT values follow the same basic format as the values of an RD. However, note that while a particular prefix can have only one RD, that same prefix can have one or more RTs assigned to it.

To best understand how MPLS uses RTs, first consider a more general definition of the purpose of RTs, followed by an example of the mechanics by which PEs use the RT:

> MPLS uses Route Targets to determine into which VRFs a PE places IBGP-learned routes.

Key Topic

Figure 11-16 shows a continuation of the same example in Figures 11-14 and 11-15, now focusing on how the PEs use the RTs to determine into which VRFs a route is added. In this case, the figure shows an *export RT*—a configuration setting in VRF configuration mode—with a different value configured for VRF-A and VRF-B, respectively. PE1 shows its import RT for each VRF—again, a configuration setting in VRF configuration mode—which allows PE1 to choose which BGP table entries it pulls into each VRF's RIB.

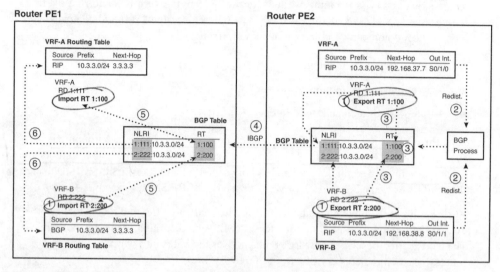

Figure 11-16   *Mechanics of the MPLS Route Target*

The figure has a lot of details, but the overall flow of concepts is not terribly difficult. Pay particular attention to the last two steps. Following the steps in the figure:

1. The two VRFs on PE2 are configured with an export RT value.

2. Redistribution out of the VRF into BGP occurs.

3. This step simply notes that the export process—the redistribution out of the VRF into BGP—sets the appropriate RT values in PE2's BGP table.

4. PE2 advertises the routes with IBGP.

5. PE1 examines the new BGP table entries and compares the RT values to the configured import RT values, which identifies which BGP table entries should go into which VRF.

6. PE1 redistributes routes into the respective VRFs, specifically the routes whose RTs match the import RT configured in the VRFs, respectively.

Note   It is sometimes helpful to think of the term *export* to mean "redistribute out of the VRF into BGP" and the term *import* to mean "redistribute into the VRF from BGP."

Each VRF needs to export and import at least one RT. The example in Figure 11-16 shows only one direction: exporting on the right (PE2) and importing on the left (PE1). However, PE2 needs to know the routes for the subnets connected to CE-A1 and CE-B1, so PE1 needs to learn those routes from the CEs, redistribute them into BGP with some exported RT value, and advertise them to PE2 using IBGP, with PE2 then importing the correct routes (based on PE2's import RTs) into PE2's VRFs.

In fact, for simple VPN implementations, in which each VPN consists of all sites for a single customer, most configurations simply use a single RT value, with each VRF for a customer both importing and exporting that RT value.

Note   The examples in this chapter show different numbers for the RD and RT values so that it is clear what each number represents. In practice, you can set a VRF's RD and one of its RTs to the same value.

Overlapping VPNs

MPLS can support overlapping VPNs by virtue of the RT concept. An overlapping VPN occurs when at least one CE site needs to be reachable by CEs in different VPNs.

Many variations of overlapping VPNs exist. An SP can provide services to many customers, so the SP actually implements CE sites that need to be reached by a subset of customers. Some SP customers might want connectivity to one of their partners through the MPLS network. For example, customer A might want some of its sites to be able to send packets to some of customer B's sites.

Regardless of the business goals, the RT concept allows an MPLS network to leak routes from multiple VPNs into a particular VRF. BGP supports the addition of multiple Extended Community PAs to each BGP table entry. By doing so, a single prefix can be exported with one RT that essentially means "make sure that all VRFs in VPN-A have this route," while assigning another RT value to that same prefix—an RT that means "leak this route into the VRFs of some overlapping VPN."

Figure 11-17 shows an example of the concepts behind overlapping MPLS VPNs, in particular, a design called a central services VPN. As usual, all customer A sites can send packets to all other customer A sites, and all customer B sites can send packets to all other customer B sites. Also, none of the customer A sites can communicate with the customer B sites. However, in addition to these usual conventions, CE-A1 and CE-B2 can communicate with CE-Serv, which connects to a set of centralized servers.

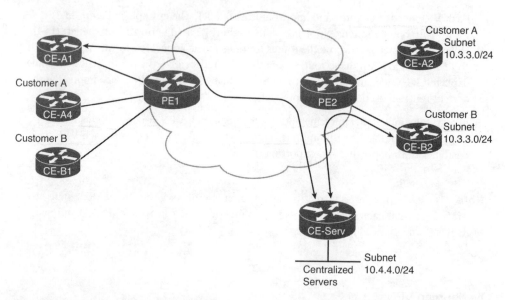

Figure 11-17 *Central Services VPN*

To accomplish these design goals, each PE needs several VRFs, with several VRFs exporting and importing multiple RTs. For example, PE1 needs two VRFs to support customer A—one VRF that just imports routes for customer A and a second VRF that imports customer A routes as well as routes to reach the central services VPN. Similarly, PE2 needs a VRF for the central services VPN, which needs to import some of the routes in VPN-A and VPN-B.

MPLS VPN Configuration

MPLS VPN configuration focuses primarily on control plane functions: creating the VRF and associated RDs and RTs, configuring MP-BGP, and redistributing between the IGP used with the customer and BGP used inside the MPLS cloud. Given this focus on control plane features, this section explains MPLS VPN configuration, leaving the data plane details for the later section "MPLS VPN Data Plane."

MPLS VPN configuration requires a fairly large number of commands. For the sake of learning the details of a straightforward MPLS VPN configuration, which still has a lot of commands, this section builds a sample configuration using the internetwork shown in Figure 11-18.

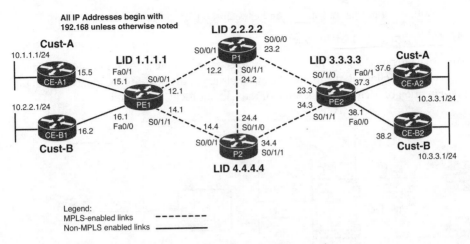

Figure 11-18 *Sample Internetwork for MPLS VPN Configuration*

The MPLS VPN design for this internetwork, whose configuration is demonstrated in the coming pages, uses the same RD and RT values seen throughout the earlier section "MPLS VPN Control Plane." Before moving into the configuration specific to MPLS VPNs, keep in mind that the internetwork of Figure 11-18 has already been configured with some commands, specifically the following:

■ All links between P and PE routers are configured with IP addresses, the IP address on the other end of each link is pingable, and these interfaces have been enabled for frame-mode MPLS with the **mpls ip** interface subcommand.

■ All P and PE routers use a common IGP (EIGRP with ASN 200 in this case), with all loopbacks and subnets between the P and PE routers being advertised. As a result, all P and PE routers can ping IP addresses of all interfaces on those routers, including the loopback interfaces on those routers.

■ Between each PE and CE, IP addresses have been configured, and the links work, but these subnets are not currently advertised by any routing protocol.

■ The PE router interfaces that connect to the CE routers do not have the **mpls ip** interface subcommand, because these interfaces do not need to be MPLS enabled. (The **mpls ip** command tells IOS that IP packets should be forwarded and received with an MPLS label.)

■ None of the features specific to MPLS VPNs have yet been configured.

MPLS VPN configuration requires many new commands and several instances of some of those commands. To help make sense of the various steps, the configuration in this section has been broken into the following four major areas:

1. Creating each VRF, RD, and RT, plus associating the customer-facing PE interfaces with the correct VRF

2. Configuring the IGP between PE and CE

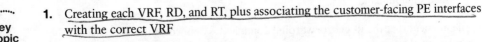

3.   Configuring mutual redistribution between the IGP and BGP

4.   Configuring MP-BGP between PEs

For visual reference, Figure 11-19 shows a diagram that outlines the four major configuration sections. Following the figure, the materials under the next four headings explain the configuration of each area, plus some of the relevant EXEC commands.

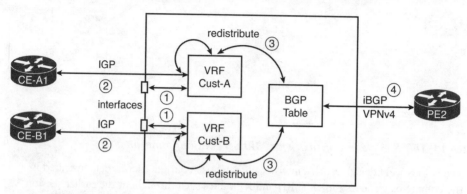

Figure 11-19   *Four Major Configuration Topics for MPLS VPNs*

Configuring the VRF and Associated Interfaces

After you understand the concept of a VRF, RD, and RT, as explained in the earlier section "MPLS VPN Control Plane," the configuration can be straightforward. Certainly, the simpler the design, like the basic nonoverlapping MPLS VPN design used in this section, the easier the configuration. To give you a taste of MPLS VPN configuration, this section uses the same RD and RT values as shown in Figure 11-15 and Figure 11-16, but with slightly different VRF names, as follows:

■   VRF Cust-A, RD 1:111, RT 1:100

■   VRF Cust-B, RD 2:222, RT 2:200

The configuration for each item occurs on the PE routers only. The customer router has no awareness of MPLS, and the P routers have no awareness of MPLS VPN features. The configuration uses these four commands:

Key
Topic

■   Configuring the VRF with the **ip vrf** *vrf-name* command

■   Configuring the RD with the **rd** *rd-value* VRF subcommand

■   Configuring the RT with the **route-target** {**import**|**export**} *rt-value* VRF subcommand

■   Associating an interface with the VRF using the **ip vrf forwarding** *vrf-name* interface subcommand

The moment that the **ip vrf forwarding** command is applied to the interface, the IP address of the interface will be removed, necessitating its reapplication.

Example 11-6 shows the configuration, with additional comments following the example.

Example 11-6   *VRF Configuration on PE1 and PE2*

```
! Configuration on PE1
! The next command creates the VRF with its case-sensitive name, followed by
! the definition of the RD for this VRF, and both the import (from MP-BGP)
! and export (to MP-BGP) route targets.
ip vrf Cust-A
 rd 1:111
 route-target import 1:100
 route-target export 1:100

ip vrf Cust-B
 rd 2:222
 route-target import 2:200
 route-target export 2:200


! The next highlighted command associates the interface (Fa0/1) with a VRF
! (Cust-A)
interface fastethernet0/1
 ip vrf forwarding Cust-A
 ip address 192.168.15.1 255.255.255.0

! The next highlighted command associates the interface (Fa0/0) with a VRF
! (Cust-B)
interface fastethernet0/0
 ip vrf forwarding Cust-B
 ip address 192.168.16.1 255.255.255.0
```

Configure VRF & import/export RTs (handwritten annotation)

assign the VRF to an interface (handwritten annotation)

```
! Configuration on PE2
ip vrf Cust-A
 rd 1:111
 route-target import 1:100
 route-target export 1:100

ip vrf Cust-B
 rd 2:222
 route-target import 2:200
 route-target export 2:200

interface fastethernet0/1
 ip vrf forwarding Cust-A
 ip address 192.168.37.3 255.255.255.0

interface fastethernet0/0
 ip vrf forwarding Cust-B
 ip address 192.168.38.3 255.255.255.0
```

The configuration on both PE1 and PE2 shows two VRFs, one for each customer. Each VRF has the required RD, and at least one import and export route tag. The planning process must match the exported RT on one PE router to the imported RT on the remote PE, and vice versa, for the two routers to exchange routes with MP-BGP. In this case, because no overlapping VPN sites are expected, the engineer planned a consistent single RT value per customer, configured on every PE, to avoid confusion.

In addition to the obvious parts of the configuration, Example 11-6 unfortunately hides a couple of small items. First, the **route-target both** command could be used when using the same value as both an import and export RT. IOS then splits this single command into a **route-target import** and **route-target export** command, as shown. In addition, the **ip vrf forwarding** interface subcommand actually removes the IP address from the interface and displays an informational message to that effect. To complete the configuration, Example 11-6 shows the reconfiguration of the same IP address on each interface, expecting that the address was automatically removed.

[handwritten margin notes: route-target both! ; IP removal from the if.]

Configuring the IGP Between PE and CE

The second major configuration step requires adding the configuration of a routing protocol between the PE and CE. This routing protocol allows the PE router to learn the customer routes, and the customer routers to learn customer routes learned by the PE from other PEs in the MPLS cloud.

Any IGP, or even BGP, can be used as the routing protocol. Often, the customer continues to use its favorite IGP, and the MPLS provider accommodates that choice. In other cases, the provider might require a specific routing protocol, often BGP in that case. The example in this section makes use of EIGRP as the PE-CE routing protocol.

Regardless of the routing protocol used between the PE and CE, the new and interesting configuration resides on the PE router. The engineer configures the CE router so that it becomes a peer with the PE router, using the same familiar IGP or BGP commands (nothing new there). The PE, however, must be VRF-aware, so the PE must be told the VRF name and what interfaces to consider when discovering neighbors inside that VRF context.

Note   The rest of this section refers generally to the PE-CE routing protocol as an IGP, because EIGRP is used in these examples. However, remember that BGP is also allowed.

The configuration for EIGRP as the PE-CE routing protocol requires these steps:

■ Configuring the EIGRP process, with an ASN that does not need to match the CE router, using the **router eigrp** *asn* global command.

■ Identifying the VRF for which additional commands apply, using the **address-family ipv4 vrf** *vrf-name* **autonomous-system** *asn* router subcommand.

- From VRF configuration submode (reached with the **address-family ipv4 vrf** command), we can still configure the ASN to match the CE router's **router eigrp** *asn* global command. This is accomplished through the **autonomous-system** *asn* command. Note that this command is being deprecated.

- From VRF configuration submode, configure the **network** command. This command only matches interfaces that include an **ip vrf forwarding** *vrf-name* interface subcommand, with a VRF name that matches the **address-family ipv4 vrf** command.

- From VRF configuration submode, configure any other traditional IGP router subcommands (for example, **no auto-summary** and **redistribute**).

Continuing the same example, both Customer A and Customer B use EIGRP, and both use EIGRP ASN 1 on the **router eigrp** command. PE1 will become EIGRP neighbors with both CE-A1 and CE-B1, but only in the context of the corresponding VRFs Cust-A and Cust-B. Example 11-7 shows the configuration on these three routers.

Example 11-7   *EIGRP Configuration: CE-A1, CE-B1, and PE1*

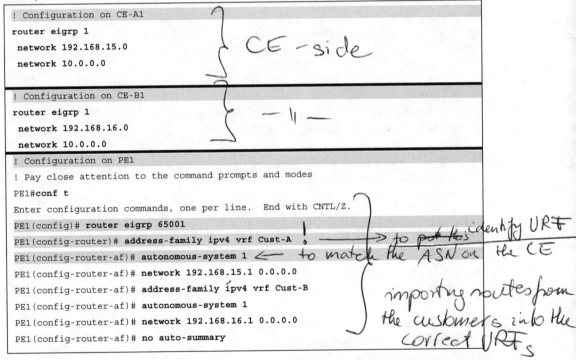

```
! Configuration on CE-A1
router eigrp 1
 network 192.168.15.0
 network 10.0.0.0
```

```
! Configuration on CE-B1
router eigrp 1
 network 192.168.16.0
 network 10.0.0.0
```

```
! Configuration on PE1
! Pay close attention to the command prompts and modes
PE1#conf t
Enter configuration commands, one per line.  End with CNTL/Z.
PE1(config)# router eigrp 65001
PE1(config-router)# address-family ipv4 vrf Cust-A
PE1(config-router-af)# autonomous-system 1
PE1(config-router-af)# network 192.168.15.1 0.0.0.0
PE1(config-router-af)# address-family ipv4 vrf Cust-B
PE1(config-router-af)# autonomous-system 1
PE1(config-router-af)# network 192.168.16.1 0.0.0.0
PE1(config-router-af)# no auto-summary
```

The configuration in Example 11-7 has two potential surprises. The first is that the **router eigrp 65001** command's ASN (65,001) does not need to match the CE routers' ASN values. Instead, the ASN listed on the **autonomous-system** subcommand inside the address family submode must match (keep in mind that this command is hidden inside context-sensitive help). In this case, both Customer A and B use the same EIGRP ASN (1), just to show that the values do not have to be unique.

The second potential surprise is that the commands that follow the **address-family ipv4 vrf Cust-A** command apply to only the Cust-A VRF and interfaces. For example, the **network 192.168.15.1 0.0.0.0** command tells IOS to search only interfaces assigned to VRF Cust-A—namely, Fa0/1 in this case—and only attempt to match those interfaces using this **network** command.

Note that similar configuration is required between PE2 and the two CE routers on the right side of Figure 11-19, but that configuration is not listed in Example 11-7.

At this point in the configuration, the VRFs exist on each PE, the PE-CE interfaces are assigned to the VRFs, and the PE routers should have learned some routes from the CE routers. As a result, the PE should have EIGRP neighborships with the CE routers, and the PE should have learned some customer routes in each VRF. Example 11-8 lists a few **show** commands for PE1's Cust-A VRF that demonstrate the per-VRF nature of the PEs.

Example 11-8 *show Commands on PE1 Related to VRF Cust-A*

```
! The next command shows the EIGRP topology table, just for VRF Cust-A
PE1# show ip eigrp vrf Cust-A topology


IP-EIGRP Topology Table for AS(1)/ID(192.168.15.1) Routing Table: Cust-A
Codes: P - Passive, A - Active, U - Update, Q - Query, R - Reply,
       r - reply Status, s - sia Status

P 10.1.1.0/24, 1 successors, FD is 156160
        via 192.168.15.5 (156160/128256), FastEthernet0/1
P 192.168.15.0/24, 1 successors, FD is 28160
        via Connected, FastEthernet0/1
! The next command shows EIGRP neighbors, just for VRF Cust-A. Note that PE1
! actually has 4 EIGRP neighbors: 1 for VRF Cust-A, 1 for VRF Cust-B, and two for
! the EIGRP instance used to exchange routes inside the MPLS cloud.


PE1# show ip eigrp vrf Cust-A neighbors
IP-EIGRP neighbors for process 1
H   Address              Interface       Hold Uptime   SRTT   RTO  Q   Seq
                                         (sec)         (ms)        Cnt Num
0   192.168.15.5         Fa0/1            12 00:21:40    1    200  0   3

! the next command lists IP routes for VRF Cust-A
PE1# show ip route vrf Cust-A


! lines omitted for brevity


C    192.168.15.0/24 is directly connected, FastEthernet0/1
     10.0.0.0/24 is subnetted, 1 subnets
D       10.1.1.0 [90/156160] via 192.168.15.5, 00:21:56, FastEthernet0/1
PE1#
```

```
! Finally, the last command shows that the normal routing table does not have
! any routes for customer route 10.1.1.0/24, nor for the connected subnet
! between PE1 and CE-A1 (192.168.15.0/24).
PE1# show ip route | include 10.1.1
PE1#
PE1# show ip route | include 192.168.15
PE1#
```

Most of the output from the **show** commands in Example 11-8 should look familiar, but the commands themselves differ. These commands mostly list a parameter that identifies the VRF by name.

For those completely new to VRFs and MPLS VPNs, pay close attention to the output of the **show ip route vrf Cust-A** and **show ip route** commands. The first of these commands lists the connected route on PE1's Fa0/1 (192.168.15.0/24) and one EIGRP-learned route (10.1.1.0/24, learned from CE-A1). However, the final two **show ip route** commands, which display routes from the normal IP routing table, do not contain either route seen in the Cust-A VRF, because interface Fa0/1 and the EIGRP configuration associates those routes with VRF Cust-A.

Configuring Redistribution Between PE-CE IGP and MP-BGP

After the completion of configuration Steps 1 and 2 (per Figure 11-19), the PE routers have IGP-learned customer routes in each VRF, but they have no ability to advertise these routes across the MPLS VPN cloud. The next step takes those IGP-learned routes and injects them into the BGP table using redistribution. At the same time, the PE routers also need to use redistribution to pull the BGP-learned routes into the IGP, for the appropriate VRFs.

For BGP to advertise routes between the PE routers, IP prefixes must first be injected into a router's BGP table. As discussed back in Chapter 1, "Fundamentals of BGP Operations," the two most common methods to inject new routes into the BGP table are redistribution and the BGP **network** command. The BGP **network** command works well when injecting a small number of predictable prefixes (for example, when injecting the public IP address prefix used by a company). The redistribution process works best when the prefixes are not predictable, there might be many, and when the routes are not destined for the Internet core routers' routing tables (all true when using MP-BGP for MPLS). So, MPLS VPN BGP configurations typically use redistribution.

The mechanics of the MPLS VPN mutual redistribution configuration requires that both the IGP and BGP be told the specific VRF for which redistribution occurs. Redistribution takes routes from the IP routing table. When configured specific to a particular VRF, that redistribution acts on the VRF IP routing table.

Key Topic

The configuration of the **redistribute** command, under both the BGP and IGP process, uses the **address-family ipv4 vrf** *vrf-name* command to set the VRF context as shown in Example 11-7. The **redistribute** command then acts on that VRF. Other than this new detail, the redistribution configuration is no different than before we introduced the concept of VRFs. Example 11-9 shows the redistribution configuration on Router PE1.

Example 11-9 *PE1 EIGRP and BGP Mutual Redistribution Configuration*

```
PE1# conf t
Enter configuration commands, one per line.  End with CNTL/Z.

! The next command moves the user to BGP config mode. The following
! command identifies the VRF, and the third command in sequence tells
! IOS to take EIGRP routes from the VRF routing table.

PE1(config)# router bgp 65001
PE1(config-router)# address-family ipv4 vrf Cust-A
PE1(config-router-af)# redistribute eigrp 1

! Next, the same concept is configured for VRF Cust-B.
PE1(config-router-af)# address-family ipv4 vrf Cust-B
PE1(config-router-af)# redistribute eigrp 1

! Next, EIGRP is configured, with the redistribute command being issued
! inside the context of the respective VRFs due to the address-family commands.

PE1(config-router-af)# router eigrp 65001
PE1(config-router)# address-family ipv4 vrf Cust-A
PE1(config-router-af)# redistribute bgp 65001 metric 10000 1000 255 1 1500

! next, the same concept is configured, this time for VRF Cust-B.

PE1(config-router-af)# address-family ipv4 vrf Cust-B
PE1(config-router-af)# redistribute bgp 65001 metric 5000 500 255 1 1500
```

[handwritten annotation: redist. from eigrp]

[handwritten annotation: red. BGP into EIGRP]

The metrics used at redistribution can be set with the **redistribute** command, the **default-metric** command, or a **route-map**. In Example 11-9, the **redistribute bgp** command sets the EIGRP metric components because EIGRP does not have an inherent default metric when redistributing into EIGRP. However, BGP uses a default metric (BGP MED) of using the integer metric to the redistributed route, so the **redistribute eigrp** command did not require a default metric setting.

Note The metric values are required, but the values chosen have no particular significance.

Assuming a similar (if not identical) configuration on the other PE routers, the PE routers should all now have customer routes in their BGP tables, as shown in Example 11-10.

Example 11-10   *PE1 BGP Table with Prefixes of Customers A and B*

```
! The BGP table for all VRFs, in succession, are listed next. Note that only
! locally injected routes are listed, but no routes for the prefixes on the
! other side of the MPLS cloud.

PE1# show ip bgp vpnv4 all
BGP table version is 21, local router ID is 1.1.1.1
Status codes: s suppressed, d damped, h history, * valid, > best, i - internal,
              r RIB-failure, S Stale
Origin codes: i - IGP, e - EGP, ? - incomplete
   Network          Next Hop          Metric LocPrf Weight Path
Route Distinguisher: 1:111 (default for vrf Cust-A)
*> 10.1.1.0/24      192.168.15.5      156160        32768 ?
*> 192.168.15.0     0.0.0.0                0        32768 ?
Route Distinguisher: 2:222 (default for vrf Cust-B)
*> 10.2.2.0/24      192.168.16.2      156160        32768 ?
*> 192.168.16.0     0.0.0.0                0        32768 ?

! Next, note that show ip bgp does not list the BGP table entries for
! either VRF.

PE1# show ip bgp
PE1#

! Next, an example of how to display BGP table entries per VRF.

PE1# show ip bgp vpnv4 rd 1:111
BGP table version is 21, local router ID is 1.1.1.1
Status codes: s suppressed, d damped, h history, * valid, > best, i - internal,
              r RIB-failure, S Stale
Origin codes: i - IGP, e - EGP, ? - incomplete

   Network          Next Hop          Metric LocPrf Weight Path
Route Distinguisher: 1:111 (default for vrf Cust-A)
*> 10.1.1.0/24      192.168.15.5      156160        32768 ?
*> 192.168.15.0     0.0.0.0                0        32768 ?
```

Configuring MP-BGP Between PEs

The fourth and final configuration step in this section defines the MP-BGP connections between PEs. After being configured, PEs can exchange prefixes in VPNv4 (VPN for IPv4) format. In other words, BGP prepends the RD in front of the IPv4 prefix to make each prefix unique.

To configure each peer, some commands appear as normal with BGP in non-MPLS configurations, and others occur inside a new VPNv4 address family context. Comparing this MPLS VPN BGP configuration to traditional BGP configuration:

Key Topic

- The PE neighbors are defined under the main BGP process, not for a particular address family.

- Commonly, MPLS VPN designs use a loopback as update source on the PE routers; in such cases, the **neighbor update-source** command is also under the main BGP process.

- The PE neighbors are then activated, using the **neighbor activate** command, under the VPNv4 address family (**address-family vpnv4**).

- BGP must be told to send the community PA (**neighbor send-community** command, under the **address-family vpnv4** command).

- The VPNv4 address family does not refer to any particular VRF.

- Only one iBGP neighbor relationship is needed to each remote PE; there is no need for a neighbor per VRF on each remote PE.

Example 11-11 shows the configuration for Step 4 on both PE1 and PE2.

Example 11-11   *BGP Configuration on PE Routers PE1 and PE2*

```
!PE1 - BGP config for VPNv4
! note the new configuration sub-mode for the address family, with the
! suffix of "-af" at the end of the command prompt.


PE1# conf t
Enter configuration commands, one per line.  End with CNTL/Z.
PE1(config)# router bgp 65001
PE1(config-router)# neighbor 3.3.3.3 remote-as 65001
PE1(config-router)# neighbor 3.3.3.3 update-source loop0
PE1(config-router)# address-family vpnv4
PE1(config-router-af)# neighbor 3.3.3.3 activate
PE1(config-router-af)# neighbor 3.3.3.3 send-community

!PE2 - BGP config for VPNv4
PE2(config)#router bgp 65001
PE2(config-router)# neighbor 1.1.1.1 remote-as 65001
PE2(config-router)# neighbor 1.1.1.1 update-source loop0
PE2(config-router)#
PE2(config-router)#address-family vpnv4
PE2(config-router-af)# neighbor 1.1.1.1 activate
PE2(config-router-af)# neighbor 1.1.1.1 send-community
```

At this point, the BGP neighbor relationships can form, and the configuration process is complete, at least for this example. However, although this sample configuration uses many configuration commands—roughly 35 commands just for the PE1 MPLS configuration for the example in this section—many additional configuration options exist, and a wide variety of **show** and **debug** options, too. Example 11-12 lists some **show** command output that confirms the current state of the control plane.

Example 11-12 *Current BGP Status After the Completed Configuration*

```
! The next command confirms that the MP-BGP prefixes are not displayed by
! the show ip bgp command.
PE1# show ip bgp

PE1#

! The next command shows the per-RD BGP table. The highlighted lines shows the
! overlapping 10.3.3.0/24 part of the two customers' address spaces.

PE1# show ip bgp vpnv4 all
BGP table version is 33, local router ID is 1.1.1.1
Status codes: s suppressed, d damped, h history, * valid, > best, i - internal,
              r RIB-failure, S Stale
Origin codes: i - IGP, e - EGP, ? - incomplete


   Network          Next Hop        Metric LocPrf Weight Path
Route Distinguisher: 1:111 (default for vrf Cust-A)
*> 10.1.1.0/24      192.168.15.5     156160         32768 ?
*>i10.3.3.0/24      3.3.3.3          156160    100      0 ?
*> 192.168.15.0     0.0.0.0               0         32768 ?
*>i192.168.37.0     3.3.3.3               0    100      0 ?
Route Distinguisher: 2:222 (default for vrf Cust-B)
*> 10.2.2.0/24      192.168.16.2     156160         32768 ?
*>i10.3.3.0/24      3.3.3.3          156160    100      0 ?
*> 192.168.16.0     0.0.0.0               0         32768 ?
*>i192.168.38.0     3.3.3.3               0    100      0 ?


! The next command lists the per-VRF routing table for Cust-A.

PE1# show ip route vrf Cust-A
! lines omitted for brevity
C    192.168.15.0/24 is directly connected, FastEthernet0/1
     10.0.0.0/24 is subnetted, 2 subnets
B       10.3.3.0 [200/156160] via 3.3.3.3, 01:33:49
D       10.1.1.0 [90/156160] via 192.168.15.5, 02:02:31, FastEthernet0/1
B    192.168.37.0/24 [200/0] via 3.3.3.3, 01:33:49

! Now on router CE-A1
! The next command confirms that the customer router (CE-A1) has learned
```

```
! the route for 10.3.3.0/24, as advertised by CE-A2.

CE-A1# show ip route
! lines omitted for brevity
C    192.168.15.0/24 is directly connected, Vlan111
     10.0.0.0/24 is subnetted, 2 subnets
D       10.3.3.0 [90/156416] via 192.168.15.1, 01:34:12, Vlan111
C       10.1.1.0 is directly connected, Loopback1
D    192.168.37.0/24 [90/28416] via 192.168.15.1, 01:34:12, Vlan111
```

MPLS VPN Data Plane

The explanations of the VRF, RD, and RT features explain most of the details of the MPLS VPN control plane. VRFs allow PEs to store routes learned from various CEs, even if the prefixes overlap. The RD allows PEs to advertise routes as unique prefixes, even if the IPv4 prefixes happen to overlap. Finally, the RT tells the PEs which routes should be added to each VRF, which provides greater control and the ability to allow sites to be reachable from multiple VPNs.

At the end of the process, however, to support the forwarding of packets, ingress PEs need appropriate FIB entries, with Ps and PEs needing appropriate LFIB entries. This section focuses on explaining how LSRs fill the FIB and LFIB when using MPLS VPNs.

As usual for this chapter, this section focuses on how to forward packets to subnet 10.3.3.0/24 in the customer A VPN. To begin this examination of the MPLS VPN data plane, consider Figure 11-20. This figure repeats the same forwarding example shown in Figure 11-13 but now shows a few details about the FIB in the ingress PE and the LFIB entries in the P and egress PE routers.

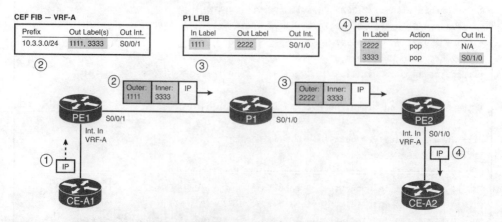

Figure 11-20 *Ingress PE FIB and Other Routers' LFIBs*

The numbered steps in the figure are as follows:

1. An unlabeled packet arrives on an interface assigned to VRF-A, which will cause ingress PE1 to use VRF-A's FIB to make a forwarding decision.

2. Ingress PE1's VRF-A FIB entry for 10.3.3.0/24 lists an outgoing interface of S0/0/1 and a label stack with two labels—an inner label of 3333 and an outer label of 1111. So PE1 forwards the packet with these two labels pushed in front of the IP header.

3. P1 uses the LFIB entry for incoming (local) label 1111, swapping this outer label value to 2222.

4. PE2 does two LFIB lookups. PE2 finds label 2222 in the table and pops that label, leaving the inner label. Then PE2 looks up the inner label 3333 in the LFIB, noting the pop action as well, along with the outgoing interface. So PE2 forwards the unlabeled packet out interface S0/1/0.

Note As was the case with the example shown in Figure 11-13, the details at Steps 3 and 4 will differ slightly in practice, as a result of the PHP feature, which is explained around Figure 11-25 at the end of this chapter.

The example shows the mechanics of what happens in the data plane after the correct FIB and LFIB entries have been added. The rest of this topic about the MPLS VPN data plane examines how MPLS VPN LSRs build these correct entries. While you read this section, it is helpful to keep in mind a couple of details about the purpose of the inner and outer label used for MPLS VPNs:

Key Topic

- The outer label identifies the segments of the LSP between the ingress PE and the egress PE, but it does not identify how the egress PE should forward the packet.

- The inner label identifies the egress PE's forwarding details, in particular the outgoing interface for the unlabeled packet.

Key Topic

Building the (Inner) VPN Label

The inner label identifies the outgoing interface out which the egress PE should forward the unlabeled packet. This inner label, called the *VPN label*, must be allocated for each route added to each customer VRF. More specifically, a customer CE will advertise routes to the PE, with the PE storing those routes in that customer's VRF. To prepare to forward packets to those customer subnets, the PE needs to allocate a new local label, associate the label with the prefix (and the route's next-hop IP address and outgoing interface), and store that information in the LFIB.

Figure 11-21 shows PE2's routes for 10.3.3.0/24 in both VRF-A and VRF-B and the resulting LFIB entries. The figure shows the results of PE2's process of allocating a local label for each of the two routes and then also advertising those labels using BGP. (Note that the LFIB is not a per-VRF table; the LFIB is the one and only LFIB for PE2.)

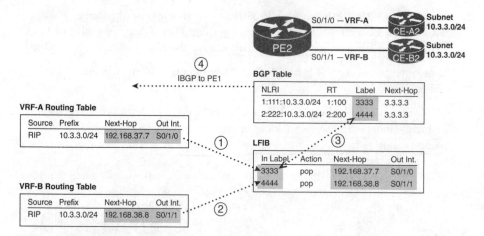

Figure 11-21 *Creating the VPN Label LFIB Entry on the Egress PE*

The steps shown in the figure are as follows:

1. After adding a route for 10.3.3.0/24 to VRF-A, PE2 allocates a local label (3333) to associate with the route. PE2 then stores the local label and corresponding next hop and outgoing interface from VRF-A's route for 10.3.3.0/24 into the LIB (not shown) and LFIB.

2. PE2 repeats the logic in Step 1 for each route in each VRF, including the route in VRF-B shown at Step 2. After learning a route for 10.3.3.0/24 in VRF-B, PE2 allocates a different label value (4444), associates that route's next-hop IP address and outgoing interface with the new label, and adds the information to a new LFIB entry.

3. PE2 adds the local labels to the BGP table entry for the routes, respectively, when redistributing routes into BGP.

4. PE2 uses IBGP to advertise the routes to PE1, with the BGP Update including the VPN label.

As a result of the first two steps in the figure, if PE2 receives a labeled packet and analyzes a label value of 3333, PE2 would be able to forward the packet correctly to CE-A2. Similarly, PE2 could correctly forward a received labeled packet with label 4444 to CE-B2.

Note   Steps 3 and 4 in Figure 11-21 do nothing to aid PE2 to forward packets; these steps were included to be referenced at an upcoming step later in this section.

Creating LFIB Entries to Forward Packets to the Egress PE

The outer label defines the LSP from the ingress PE to the egress PE. More specifically, it defines an LSP used to forward packets to the BGP next-hop address as advertised in BGP Updates. In concept, the ingress PE adds the outer label to make a request of the core of the MPLS network to "deliver this packet to the egress PE—which advertised this particular BGP next-hop address."

MPLS VPNs use an IGP and LDP to learn routes and labels, specifically to learn the label values to use in the outer label. To link the concepts together, it can be helpful to think of the full control plane process related to the LSP used for the outer label, particularly Step 4 onward:

1. A PE, which will be an egress PE for this particular route, learns routes from some CE.

2. The egress PE uses IBGP to advertise the routes to an ingress PE.

3. The learned IBGP routes list some next-hop IP address.

4. For MPLS VPNs to work, the PE and P routers must have advertised a route to reach the BGP next-hop addresses.

5. Likewise, for MPLS VPNs to work, the PE and P routers must have advertised labels with LDP for the routes to reach the BGP next-hop addresses.

6. Each P and PE router adds its part of the full end-to-end LSP into its LFIB, supporting the ingress PE's ability to send a packet to the egress PE.

For example, Figure 11-21 shows PE2 advertising two routes to PE1, both with BGP next-hop IP address 3.3.3.3. For MPLS to work, the collective PE and P routers need to advertise an IGP route to reach 3.3.3.3, with LDP advertising the labels, so that packets can be label-switched toward the egress PE. Figure 11-22 shows the basic process. However, note that this part of the process works exactly like the simple IGP and LDP process shown for unicast IP forwarding in the first half of this chapter.

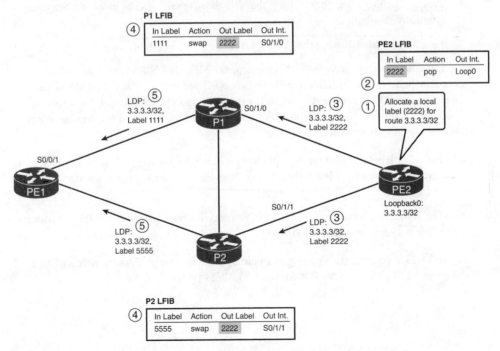

Figure 11-22 *Creating the LFIB Entries to Reach the Egress PE's BGP Next Hop*

The steps in the figure focus on the LFIB entries for prefix 3.3.3.3/32, which matches PE2's BGP next-hop IP address, as follows. Note that the figure does not show all LDP advertisements but only those that are particularly interesting to the example.

1. PE2, upon learning a route for prefix 3.3.3.3/32, allocates a local label of 2222.

2. PE2 updates its LFIB for the local label, listing a pop action.

3. As normal, PE2 advertises to its LDP neighbors the label binding of prefix 3.3.3.3/32 with label 2222.

4. P1 and P2 both independently learn about prefix 3.3.3.3/32 with the IGP, allocate a local label (1111 on P1 and 5555 on P2), and update their LFIBs.

5. P1 and P2 advertise the binding of 3.3.3.3/32, along with their respective local labels, to their peers.

Figure 11-20 showed the FIB and LFIB entries required for forwarding a packet from CE-A1 to CE-A2, specifically into subnet 10.3.3.0/24. Figures 11-21 and 11-22, and their associated text, explained how all the LFIB entries were created. Next, the focus turns to the FIB entry required on PE1.

Creating VRF FIB Entries for the Ingress PE

The last part of the data plane analysis focuses on the ingress PE. In particular, the ingress PE uses the following logic when processing an incoming unlabeled packet:

1. Process the incoming packet using the VRF associated with the incoming interface (statically configured).

2. Forward the packet using that VRF's FIB.

The FIB entry needs to have two labels to support MPLS VPNs: an outer label that identifies the LSP with which to reach the egress PE and an inner label that identifies the egress PE's LFIB entry that includes the correct outgoing interface on the egress PE. Although it might be obvious by now, for completeness, the ingress PE learns the outer and inner label values as follows:

■ The outer label is based on the LIB entry, specifically for the LIB entry for the prefix that matches the BGP-learned next-hop IP address—not the packet's destination IP address.

■ The inner label is based on the BGP table entry for the route in the VRF that matches the packet's destination address.

Figure 11-23 completes the ongoing example by showing the process by which PE1 adds the correct FIB entry into VRF-A for the 10.3.3.0/24 prefix.

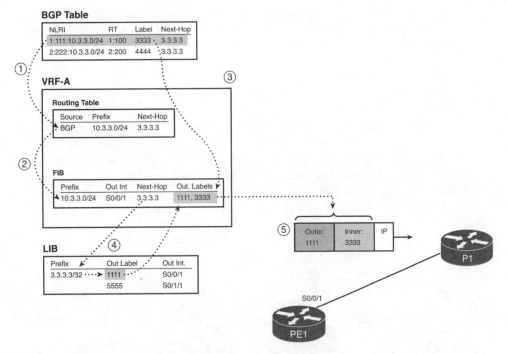

Figure 11-23 *Creating the Ingress PE (PE1) FIB Entry for VRF-A*

The figure picks up the story at the point at which PE1 has learned all required BGP and LDP information, and it is ready to populate the VRF routing table and FIB.

PE1's BGP table holds the VPN label (3333), while PE1's LIB holds the two labels learned from PE1's two LDP neighbors (P1 and P2, labels 1111 and 5555, respectively). In this case, PE1's best route that matches BGP next-hop 3.3.3.3 happens to point to P1 instead of P2, so this example uses label 1111, learned from P1.

The steps in the figure are explained as follows:

1. PE1 redistributes the route from BGP into the VRF-A routing table (based on the import RT).

2. PE1 builds a VRF-A FIB entry for the route just added to the VRF-A routing table.

3. This new FIB entry needs to include the VPN-label, which PE1 finds in the associated BGP table entry.

4. This new FIB entry also needs to include the outer label, the one used to reach the BGP next-hop IP address (3.3.3.3), so PE1 looks in the LIB for the best LIB entry that matches 3.3.3.3 and extracts the label (1111).

5. Ingress PE1 inserts the MPLS header, including the two-label label stack.

At this point, when PE1 receives a packet in an interface assigned to VRF-A, PE1 will look in the VRF-A FIB. If the packet is destined for an address in prefix 10.3.3.0/24, PE1 will match the entry shown in the figure, and PE1 will forward the packet out S0/0/1, with labels 1111 and 3333.

Penultimate Hop Popping

The operation of the MPLS VPN data plane works well, but the process on the egress PE can be a bit inefficient. The inefficiency relates to the fact that the egress PE must do two lookups in the LFIB after receiving the packet with two labels in the label stack. For example, the data plane forwarding example used throughout this chapter has been repeated in Figure 11-24, with a summary description of the processing logic on each router. Note that the egress PE (PE2) must consider two entries in its LFIB.

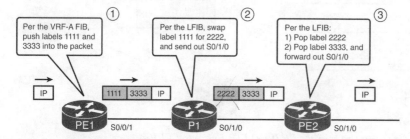

Figure 11-24   *Two LFIB Lookups Required on the Egress PE*

To avoid this extra work on the very last (ultimate) LSR, MPLS uses a feature called *penultimate hop popping (PHP)*. (*Penultimate* simply means "1 less than the ultimate.") So the penultimate hop is not the very last LSR to process a labeled packet, but the second-to-last LSR to process a labeled packet. PHP causes the penultimate-hop LSR to pop the outer label, so that the last LSR—the ultimate hop if you will—receives a packet that only has the VPN label in it. With only this single label, the egress PE needs to look up only one entry in the LFIB. Figure 11-25 shows the revised data plane flow with PHP enabled.

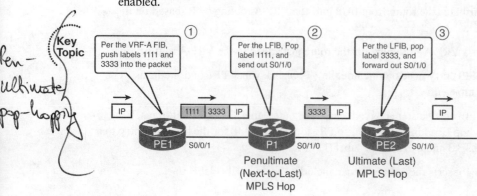

Figure 11-25   *Single LFIB Lookup on Egress PE Because of PHP*

Other MPLS Applications

This last relatively short section of the chapter introduces the general idea about the protocols used by several other MPLS applications. To that end, this section introduces and explains the concept of a *Forwarding Equivalence Class (FEC)* and summarizes the concept of an FEC as used by various MPLS applications.

Key Topic

Frankly, this chapter has already covered all the concepts surrounding the term FEC. However, it is helpful to know the term and the FEC concept as an end to itself, because it helps when comparing various MPLS applications.

Generally speaking, an FEC is a set of packets that receives the same forwarding treatment by a single LSR. For simple MPLS unicast IP forwarding, each IPv4 prefix is an FEC. For MPLS VPNs, each prefix in each VRF is an FEC—making the prefix 10.3.3.0/24 in VRF-A a different FEC from the 10.3.3.0/24 prefix in VRF-B. Alternately, with QoS implemented, one FEC might be the set of packets in VRF-A, destined to 10.3.3.0/24, with DSCP EF in the packet, and another FEC might be packets in the same VPN, to the same subnet, but with a different DSCP value.

For each FEC, each LSR needs a label, or label stack, to use when forwarding packets in that FEC. By using a unique label or set of labels for each FEC, a router has the ability to assign different forwarding details (outgoing interface and next-hop router.)

Each of the MPLS applications can be compared by focusing on the information used to determine an FEC. For example, MPLS traffic engineering (TE) allows MPLS networks to choose to send some packets over one LSP and other packets over another LSP, based on traffic loading—even though the true end destination might be in the same location. By doing so, SPs can manage the flow of data over their high-speed core networks and prevent the problem of overloading the best route as determined by a routing protocol, while barely using alternate routes. To achieve this function, MPLS TE bases the FEC concept in part on the definition of an MPLS TE tunnel.

You can also compare different MPLS applications by listing the control plane protocols used to learn label information. For example, this chapter explained how MPLS VPN uses both LDP and MP-BGP to exchange label information, whereas other MPLS applications use LDP and something else—or do not even use LDP. Table 11-5 lists many of the common MPLS applications, the information that determines an FEC, and the control plane protocol that is used to advertise FEC-to-label bindings.

Key Topic

Table 11-5 *Control Protocols Used in Various MPLS Applications*

Application	FEC	Control Protocol Used to Exchange FEC-to-Label Binding
Unicast IP routing	Unicast IP routes in the global IP routing table	Tag Distribution Protocol (TDP) or Label Distribution Protocol (LDP)
Multicast IP routing	Multicast routes in the global multicast IP routing table	PIM version 2 extensions

Application	FEC	Control Protocol Used to Exchange FEC-to-Label Binding
VPN	Unicast IP routes in the per-VRF routing table	MP-BGP
Traffic engineering	MPLS TE tunnels (configured)	RSVP or CR-LDP
MPLS QoS	IP routing table and the ToS byte	Extensions to TDP and LDP

Implement Multi-VRF Customer Edge (VRF Lite)

VRF Lite, also known as Multi-VRF CE, provides multiple instances of IP routing tables in a single router. By associating each interface/subinterface with one of the several VRF instances, a router can create Layer 3 separation, much like Layer 2 VLANs separate a Layer 2 LAN domain. With VRF Lite, engineers can create internetworks that allow overlapping IP address spaces without requiring Network Address Translation (NAT), enforce better security by preventing packets from crossing into other VRFs, and provide some convenient features to extend the MPLS VPN concept to the CE router.

VRF Lite uses the same configuration commands already covered earlier in the section "MPLS VPN Configuration." The rest of this short section introduces VRF Lite, first by explaining how it can be configured as an end to itself (without MPLS). Following that, the use of VRF Lite to extend MPLS VPN services to the CE is explained.

VRF Lite, Without MPLS

As an end to itself, VRF Lite allows the engineer to separate IP internetworks into different domains or groupings without requiring separate routers and without requiring separate physical connections. Normally, to provide separation of Layer 3 domains, several tools might be used: ACLs to filter packets, route filters to filter routes, NAT to deal with overlapping IP address spaces, and separate physical links between sites. With only a single IP routing table in a router, some problems present a bigger challenge that might have been best solved using a separate router.

The mechanics of VRF Lite configuration match the configuration listed as Steps 1 and 2 from the "MPLS VPN Configuration" section, earlier in this chapter. The router configuration begins with multiple VRFs. Then, the interfaces are associated with a single VRF, so the router will choose the VRF to use when forwarding packets based on the VRF association of the incoming interface. Finally, any routing protocols operate on specific VRFs.

For example, consider Figure 11-26, which shows a simple design of a small portion of an internetwork. In this case, two companies merged. They had offices in the same pair of cities, so they migrated the users to one building in each city. To keep the users separate, the users from each former company sit inside a company-specific VLAN.

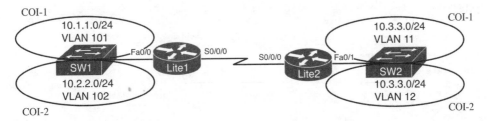

Figure 11-26   *Design Used for VRF Lite*

The design shows the overlapping subnets on the right side of Figure 11-26 (10.3.3.0/24). The engineers could have such reassigned IP addresses in one of the subnets and ignored VRF Lite. However, because of other security considerations, the design also calls for preventing packets from hosts in one former company from flowing into subnets of the other former company. One solution then is to create two VRFs per router.

Beyond the configuration already shown for MPLS VPNs, as Steps 1 and 2 from the "MPLS VPN Configuration" section, the only other new configuration step is to ensure that the routers use subinterfaces on links that support traffic for multiple VRFs. VRF Lite requires that each interface or subinterface be associated with one VRF, so to share a physical link among VRFs, the configuration must include subinterfaces. For example, a design might use Ethernet, with trunking, and the associated subinterface configuration.

In the case of a leased line, however, the typical High-Level Data Link Control (HDLC) and PPP configuration does not allow for subinterfaces. In such cases, most configurations use Frame Relay encapsulation, which does allow for subinterfaces. However, an actual Frame Relay network is not necessary; instead, the engineer chooses a Data-Link Connection Identifier (DLCI) to use for each VC—the same DLCI on each end—and configures a point-to-point subinterface for each such DLCI.

Example 11-13 shows the complete configuration for VRF Lite for the design shown in Figure 11-26, including the Frame Relay configuration on the serial link.

Example 11-13   *VRF Lite Configuration on Router Lite-1*

```
! CEF is required. The VRF configuration still requires both an RD and
! an import/export RT. Without MPLS however, the values remain local.
ip cef

ip vrf COI-1
 rd 11:11
 route-target both 11:11

ip vrf COI-2
 rd 22:22
 route-target both 22:22

! Next, the user chose DLCI 101 and 102 for the two Frame Relay subinterfaces.
! Note that the other router must match these DLCI values. Also, note that each
```

```
! Frame Relay subinterface is associated with a different VRF.

int s0/0/0
 encapsulation frame-relay
 clock rate 1536000
 no shut
 description to Lite-2

int s0/0/0.101 point-to-point
 frame-relay interface-dlci 101
 ip address 192.168.4.1 255.255.255.252
 no shutdown
 ip vrf forwarding COI-1

int s0/0/0.102 point-to-point
 frame-relay interface-dlci 102
 ip address 192.168.4.5 255.255.255.252
 no shutdown
 ip vrf forwarding COI-2

! Next, the usual 802.1Q router config is listed, matching the VLANs
! shown in Figure 11-26. Note that each subinterface is also associated
! with one VRF.

int fa0/0
 no ip address
 no shut
 description to C-1
int fa0/0.1
 encapsulation dot1q 101
 ip vrf forwarding COI-1
 ip addr 10.1.1.100 255.255.255.0

int fa0/0.2
 encapsulation dot1q 102
 ip vrf forwarding COI-2
 ip addr 10.2.2.100 255.255.255.0

! Finally, the EIGRP configuration, per VRF - nothing new here compared
! to the MPLS VPN configuration. Note that router Lite-2 would also need
! to configure the same autonomous-system 1 commands, but the router
! eigrp asn command would not need to match.

router eigrp 65001
 address-family ipv4 vrf COI-1
  autonomous-system 1
```

```
network 10.0.0.0
no auto-summary
address-family ipv4 vrf COI-2
  autonomous-system 1
  network 10.0.0.0
  no auto-summary
```

VRF Lite with MPLS

The other name for VRF Lite, *Multi-VRF CE*, practically defines its use with MPLS VPNs. From a technical perspective, this feature allows a CE router to have VRF awareness, but it remains in the role of CE. As such, a CE using Multi-VRF CE can use multiple VRFs, but it does not have the burden of implementing LDP, pushing/popping labels, or acting as an LSR.

From a design perspective, the Multi-VRF CE feature gives the provider better choices about platforms and where to put the relatively large workload required by a PE. A multi-tenant unit (MTU) design is a classic example, where the SP puts a single Layer 3 device in a building with multiple customers. The SP engineers could just make the CPE device act as PE. However, by making the CPE router act as CE, but with using Multi-VRF CE, the SP can easily separate customers at Layer 3, while avoiding the investment in a more powerful Layer 3 CPE platform to support full PE functionality. Figure 11-27 shows such a case.

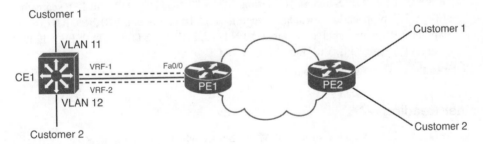

Figure 11-27   *Design Used for VRF Lite*

Foundation Summary

Please take the time to read and study the details in the "Foundation Topics" section of the chapter, as well as review the items noted with a Key Topic icon.

Memory Builders

The CCIE Routing and Switching written exam, like all Cisco CCIE written exams, covers a fairly broad set of topics. This section provides some basic tools to help you exercise your memory about some of the broader topics covered in this chapter.

Fill In Key Tables from Memory

Appendix E, "Key Tables for CCIE Study," on the CD in the back of this book, contains empty sets of some of the key summary tables in each chapter. Print Appendix E, refer to this chapter's tables in it, and fill in the tables from memory. Refer to Appendix F, "Solutions for Key Tables for CCIE Study," on the CD, to check your answers.

Definitions

Next, take a few moments to write down the definitions for the following terms:

FIB, LIB, LFIB, MPLS unicast IP routing, MPLS VPNs, LDP, TDP, LSP, LSP segment, MPLS TTL propagation, local label, remote label, label binding, VRF, RD, RT, overlapping VPN, inner label, outer label, VPN label, PHP, FEC, LSR, E-LSR, PE, CE, P, ingress PE, egress PE, VRF Lite, Multi-VRF CE

Refer to the glossary to check your answers.

Further Reading

Cisco Press publishes a wide variety of MPLS books, which can be found at www.ciscopress.com. Additionally, you can see a variety of MPLS pages from www.cisco.com/go/mpls.

CHAPTER 12

Final Preparation

The first 11 chapters of this book cover the portion of technologies, protocols, and considerations required to be prepared to pass the 400-101 CCIE Routing and Switching written exam. While these chapters supply the detailed information, most people need more preparation than simply reading the first 11 chapters of this book. This chapter details a set of tools and a study plan to help you complete your preparation for the exams.

This short chapter has two main sections. The first section lists the exam preparation tools useful at this point in the study process. The second section lists a suggested study plan now that you have completed all the earlier chapters in this book.

> **Note** Note that Appendixes E and F exist as soft-copy appendices on the CD included in the back of this book.

Tools for Final Preparation

This section lists some information about the available tools and how to access the tools.

Pearson Cert Practice Test Engine and Questions on the CD

The CD in the back of the book includes the Pearson Cert Practice Test engine—software that displays and grades a set of exam-realistic multiple-choice questions. Using the Pearson Cert Practice Test engine, you can either study by going through the questions in Study Mode or take a simulated (timed) CCNA Security exam.

The installation process requires two major steps. The CD in the back of this book has a recent copy of the Pearson Cert Practice Test engine. The practice exam—the database of CCIE Routing and Switching exam questions—is not on the CD.

> **Note** The cardboard CD case in the back of this book includes the CD and a piece of paper. The paper lists the activation key for the practice exam associated with this book. *Do not lose the activation key.*

Install the Software from the CD

The software installation process is pretty routine as compared with other software installation processes. To be complete, the following steps outline the installation process:

Step 1. Insert the CD into your PC.

Step 2. The software that automatically runs is the Cisco Press software to access and use all CD-based features, including the exam engine and the CD-only appendices. From the main menu, click the option to **Install the Exam Engine**.

Step 3. Respond to Windows prompts as with any typical software installation process.

The installation process will give you the option to activate your exam with the activation code supplied on the paper in the CD sleeve. This process requires that you establish a Pearson website login. You will need this login to activate the exam, so please register when prompted. If you already have a Pearson website login, there is no need to register again. Just use your existing login.

Activate and Download the Practice Exam

After the exam engine is installed, you should then activate the exam associated with this book (if you did not do so during the installation process) as follows:

Step 1. Start the Pearson Cert Practice Test (PCPT) software from the Windows **Start** menu or from your desktop shortcut icon.

Step 2. To activate and download the exam associated with this book, from the **My Products** or **Tools** tab, click the **Activate** button.

Step 3. At the next screen, enter the activation key from the paper inside the cardboard CD holder in the back of the book. After it is entered, click the **Activate** button.

Step 4. The activation process will download the practice exam. Click **Next**, and then click **Finish**.

When the activation process is completed, the **My Products** tab should list your new exam. If you do not see the exam, make sure that you have selected the **My Products** tab on the menu. At this point, the software and practice exam are ready to use. Simply select the exam and click the **Use** button.

To update a particular exam that you have already activated and downloaded, simply select the **Tools** tab and click the **Update Products** button. Updating your exams will ensure that you have the latest changes and updates to the exam data.

If you want to check for updates to the Pearson Cert Practice Test exam engine software, simply select the **Tools** tab and click the **Update Application** button. This will ensure that you are running the latest version of the software engine.

Activating Other Exams

The exam software installation process, and the registration process, only has to happen once. Then, for each new exam, only a few steps are required. For example, if you buy another new Cisco Press Official Cert Guide or Pearson IT Certification Cert Guide, extract the activation code from the CD sleeve in the back of that book; you don't even need the CD at this point. From there, all you have to do is start the exam engine (if it is not still up and running) and perform Steps 2 through 4 from the previous list.

Premium Edition

In addition to the free practice exam provided on the CD-ROM, you can purchase additional exams with expanded functionality directly from Pearson IT Certification. The Premium Edition of this title contains an additional two full practice exams as well as an eBook (in both PDF and ePub format). In addition, the Premium Edition title also has remediation for each question to the specific part of the eBook that relates to that question.

Because you have purchased the print version of this title, you can purchase the Premium Edition at a deep discount. There is a coupon code in the CD sleeve that contains a one-time-use code as well as instructions for where you can purchase the Premium Edition.

To view the Premium Edition product page, go to www.informit.com/title/9780133591057.

The Cisco Learning Network

Cisco provides a wide variety of CCIE Routing and Switching preparation tools at a Cisco Systems website called the Cisco Learning Network. This site includes a large variety of exam preparation tools, including sample questions, forums on each Cisco exam, learning video games, and information about each exam.

To reach the Cisco Learning Network, go to www.cisco.com/go/learningnetwork or just search for "Cisco Learning Network." You will need to use the login you created at www.cisco.com. If you don't have such a login, you can register for free. To register, simply go to www.cisco.com, click **Register** at the top of the page, and supply the requested information.

Memory Tables

Like most Official Cert Guides from Cisco Press, this book purposefully organizes information into tables and lists for easier study and review. Rereading these tables can be very useful before the exam. However, it is easy to skim over the tables without paying attention to every detail, especially when you remember having seen the table's contents when reading the chapter.

Instead of simply reading the tables in the various chapters, this book's Appendices E and F give you another review tool. Appendix E lists partially completed versions of many of the tables from the book. You can open Appendix F (a PDF file on the CD that comes with this book) and print the appendix. For review, you can attempt to complete the tables. This exercise can help you focus on the review. It also exercises the memory connectors in your brain; plus it makes you think about the information without as much information, which forces a little more contemplation about the facts.

Appendix F, also a PDF file located on the CD, lists the completed tables to check your work. You can also just refer to the tables as printed in the book.

Chapter-Ending Review Tools

Chapters 1–11 have several features in the Exam Preparation Tasks sections at the end of the chapter. You might have already worked through these in each chapter. It can also be useful to use these tools again as you make your final preparations for the exam.

Suggested Plan for Final Review/Study

This section lists a suggested study plan until you take the 400-101 CCIE Routing and Switching written exam. Certainly, you can ignore this plan, use it as is, or just take suggestions from it.

The plan uses three steps:

Step 1. **Review Key Topics and DIKTA Questions:** You can use the table that lists the key topics in each chapter, or just flip the pages looking for key topics. Also, reviewing the "Do I Know This Already" (DIKTA) questions from the beginning of the chapter can be helpful for review.

Step 2. **Complete Memory Tables:** Open Appendix E on the CD, and print the entire appendix, or print the tables by major part. Then complete the tables.

Step 3. **Use the Pearson Cert Practice Test Engine to Practice:** The Pearson Cert Practice Test engine on the CD can be used to study using a bank of unique exam-realistic questions available only with this book.

Using the Exam Engine

The Pearson Cert Practice Test engine on the CD includes a database of questions created specifically for this book. The Pearson Cert Practice Test engine can be used either in study mode or practice exam mode, as follows:

- **Study mode:** Study mode is most useful when you want to use the questions for learning and practicing. In study mode, you can select options like randomizing the order of the questions and answers, automatically viewing answers to the questions as you go, testing on specific topics, and many other options.

- **Practice Exam mode:** This mode presents questions in a timed environment, providing you with a more exam-realistic experience. It also restricts your ability to see your score as you progress through the exam and view answers to questions as you are taking the exam. These timed exams not only allow you to study for the actual 400-101 CCIE Routing and Switching written exam, but they also help you simulate the time pressure that can occur on the actual exam.

When doing your final preparation, you can use study mode, practice exam mode, or both. However, after you have seen each question a couple of times, you will likely start to remember the questions, and the usefulness of the exam database might go down. So, consider the following options when using the exam engine:

- Use this question database for review. Use study mode to study the questions by chapter, just as with the other final review steps listed in this chapter. Plan on getting another exam (possibly from the Premium Edition) if you want to take additional simulated exams.

- Save the question database, not using it during your review of each book part. Save it until the end, so you will not have seen the questions before. Then, use practice exam mode to simulate the exam.

Picking the correct mode from the exam engine's user interface is pretty obvious. The following steps show how to move to the screen from which to select study or practice exam mode:

Step 1. Click the **My Products** tab if you are not already in that screen.

Step 2. Select the exam that you want to use from the list of available exams.

Step 3. Click the **Use** button.

When you take these actions, the engine should display a window from which you can choose **Study Mode** or **Practice Exam Mode**. When in study mode, you can further choose the book chapters, limiting the questions to those explained in the specified chapters of the book.

Summary

The tools and suggestions listed in this chapter have been designed with one goal in mind: to help you develop the skills required to pass the 400-101 CCIE Routing and Switching written exam. This book has been developed from the beginning to not just tell you the facts but also to help you learn how to apply the facts. No matter what your experience level is leading up to taking the exams, it is our hope that the broad range of preparation tools, and even the structure of the book, will help you pass the exam with ease. We hope you do well on the exam.

Answers to the "Do I Know This Already?" Quizzes

Chapter 1

1. D
2. C
3. A and D
4. D
5. A and B
6. C
7. A and C
8. A, D, and E
9. D
10. A and B
11. A, C, and E
12. C

Chapter 2

1. B and D
2. C
3. A
4. A and B
5. B
6. A and C
7. B and C
8. A
9. E
10. A
11. C

12. D
13. A and D
14. C

Chapter 3

1. C
2. A and D
3. A, B, and E
4. B and D
5. A
6. A and B
7. D
8. B and E
9. A
10. A and B
11. C and D

Chapter 4

1. C
2. A and B
3. E
4. B
5. A and B
6. A
7. C
8. D
9. A

Chapter 5

1. C
2. C
3. B, C, and D
4. A
5. B
6. C
7. A and C
8. A

Chapter 6

1. B
2. D
3. C and D
4. B
5. C
6. D

Chapter 7

1. B, C, and D
2. C
3. A and D
4. D
5. D
6. D
7. E

Chapter 8

1. C
2. D
3. D

4. C and E
5. A and C
6. C and D
7. B
8. C and D
9. A, C, and D
10. C

Chapter 9

1. D
2. A
3. C
4. A, B, and E
5. D
6. B
7. D
8. A and B
9. B

Chapter 10

1. B
2. A, C, D, and F
3. C
4. D
5. A, C, and E
6. C
7. A and E
8. B and E
9. C

Chapter 11

1. A

2. D

3. B

4. A

5. A

6. B

7. B

8. B and C

9. B and D

10. A and C

11. A and E

CCIE Exam Updates

Over time, reader feedback allows Cisco Press to gauge which topics give our readers the most problems when taking the exams. Additionally, Cisco might make small changes in the breadth of exam topics or in the emphasis of certain topics. To assist readers with those topics, the authors create new materials clarifying and expanding upon those troublesome exam topics.

The document you are viewing is Version 1.0 of this appendix and there are no updates. You can check for an updated version at www.ciscopress.com/title/9781587144912.

Index

Numerics

802.1X authentication, 423-426

A

AAA (authentication, authorization, and accounting), 406-410

enabling, 407

RADIUS server groups, configuring, 410

accessing CLI via Telnet, 405

ACE (access control entry) logic, 431-432

ACLs, 430-433

ACE logic, 431-432

command reference, 430

PACLs, 475

rules, 431-432

VACLs, 475

wildcard masks, 433

ACS (Cisco Access Control Server), 407

activating the practice exam, 574

active state (BGP), 16

adaptive shaping, 222

address families, 58

adjacencies (PIM-DM), forming, 329-330

administrative scoping, 328-329

administrative weight, BGP decision process, 101-104

advertising BGP routes, 31-40

best route selection, 33-34

rules, 40

AF (Assured Forwarding) PHB, 141-142

converting values to decimal, 142

aggregate-address command, 25-29

route filtering, 81-82

AGGREGATOR PA, 94

Anycast RP with MSDP, 365-367

AS (autonomous systems)

BGP sync, disabling, 46-47

confederations, 47-52

configuring, 49-52

routing loops, preventing, 47

eBGP neighbors, configuring, 13-14

iBGP neighbors, 9-12

configuring, 11-12

neighbor relationships, requirements for, 14-15

AS_CONFED_SEQ segment, 82

AS_PATH PA, 8, 94

prepend feature, 109-112

private ASNs, removing, 108-109

route filtering, 82-93

examples, 87-91

C

D

E

M

N

O

S

T

V

W

X-Y-Z

Check out the NEW learning materials for v5.0 exam release!

Increase learning, comprehension, and certification readiness with these Cisco Press products!

Cisco CCIE Routing
and Switching v5.0
Configuration Practice Labs
9780133786316

Cisco CCIE Routing and
Switching v5.0 Troubleshooting
Practice Labs
9780133786330

Cisco CCIE Routing and
Switching v5.0 Configuration
and Troubleshooting
Practice Labs Bundle
9780133786323

Cisco CCIE Routing and
Switching v5.0 Official
Cert Guide, Volume 1
9781587143960

New Resource
Cisco CCIE
Routing and Switching
v5.0 Official Cert Guide,
Volume 1 Premium Edition
eBook/Practice Test
9780133481648

Cisco CCIE
Routing
and Switching v5.0
Official Cert Guide,
Volume 2
9781587144912

New Resource
Cisco CCIE Routing and
Switching v5.0 Official
Cert Guide, Volume 2
Premium Edition
eBook/Practice Test
9780133591057

Cisco CCIE Routing and
Switching v5.0 Official
Cert Guide Library
9781587144929

New Resource
CCIE Routing and Switching
v5.0 Exam Roundup
LiveLessons (Networking Talks)
9780789754035

SAVE ON ALL NEW
CCIE R&S v5.0 Products
www.CiscoPress.com/CCIE